New Jersey
Environmental Law
Handbook

New Jersey Environmental Law Handbook

Ninth Edition

Edited/Co-authored by
Albert I. Telsey

Lanham • Boulder • New York • London

Published by Bernan Press
An imprint of The Rowman & Littlefield Publishing Group, Inc.
4501 Forbes Boulevard, Suite 200, Lanham, Maryland 20706
www.rowman.com
800-462-6420

6 Tinworth Street, London, E11 5AL, United Kingdom

ISBN: 978-1-64143-344-0
E-ISBN: 978-1-64143-345-7

∞™ The paper used in this publication meets the minimum requirements of American National Standard for Information Sciences—Permanence of Paper for Printed Library Materials, ANSI/NISO Z39.48-1992.

Praise for *New Jersey Environmental Law Handbook, Ninth Edition*

THIS BOOK was written by more than 50 of New Jersey's top environmental lawyers and consultants. It was completely revamped in 2014 and updated in 2019.

THIS BOOK covers buying, selling, remediating, funding, and developing contaminated property; litigating disputes; and obtaining permits for special lands and activities impacting air, water, hazardous waste, solid waste, health and safety, and renewable energy.

THIS BOOK is beautifully organized and designed to be a frequently consulted reference so the reader can access information quickly and move on with the tasks at hand.

—Jerry Fitzgerald English, Esq.

Jerry English is a former NJDEP Commissioner, NJ State Senator, and Counsel to the Governor. She is currently a member of the NJ Justice Stewart G. Pollack Environmental Inns of Court and a partner at Lindabury, McCormick, Estabrook & Cooper, P.C. located in Westfield, New Jersey, where she practices environmental law.

Summary of Contents

Contents

Acknowledgments

The editors and contributing authors would like to thank the following for their contributions in the production of *New Jersey Environmental Law Handbook*, Ninth Edition:

Shaw Smith Williams, Esq., Seton Hall University School of Law 2013
Stephanie Rogacki, NJIT
Lauren Patterson, Meyner and Landis LLP
Liz Duguay, Meyner and Landis LLP
Ajay Satwik Vadlaputi, NJIT
Ria Navneet Patel, NJIT
Jeffrey Reaves, NJIT

Introduction

Albert I. Telsey, Esq.

Knowing what environmental laws and regulations say is one thing; but understanding what they mean is another. This book provides the reader with a busload of New Jersey's most experienced environmental law practitioners who have distilled the meaning of the state's environmental laws and regulations into understandable bite-sized chunks, which they present in clearly written chapters with useful practice tips as a bonus.

Chapters 1 and 2 address the land and how to buy and sell it when it is contaminated. This is a big concern in New Jersey given the state's long industrial history because contamination can negatively impact land use, land value, tax obligations, wildlife and human health, safety and welfare. These chapters describe how negotiating parties deal with Pandora's box, which contains the contamination and the strict cleanup liability associated with it; how this liability is addressed by negotiating parties using escrows, insurance, and other techniques; how the contamination is actually cleaned up in a practical sense using an environmental consultant and a Licensed Site Remediation Professional; and the tax consequences associated with cleanup costs.

Chapter 3 drills deeper into the business mechanics of buying and selling contaminated property by describing how public and private financing is used to purchase and clean up contaminated property. Money may not buy happiness but it can help you clean up and purchase contaminated property. Lenders often finance contaminated property and they enjoy statutory environmental liability protection, which is also described in this chapter.

Chapter 4 addresses how litigation is used to resolve environmental liability and natural resource damage disputes that are unable to be resolved amicably. Sections in this chapter include how environmental liabilities are litigated under the New Jersey Spill Compensation and Control Act (Spill Act); how environmental class-action and mass torts are addressed in New Jersey; how litigation is waged against insurance carriers who have provided old comprehensive general liability policies that, to the surprise of many, still provide coverage; how environmental issues are addressed when local government designates underutilized and/or contaminated areas as areas in need of redevelopment or rehabilitation; and how environmental liability is addressed in bankruptcy, property tax appeals, administrative and civil penalty actions, criminal enforcement, and environmental justice.

Chapter 5 describes how New Jersey has legislated and regulated specific types of lands in New Jersey including coastlands, wetlands, flood hazard areas, riparian lands, highlands, pinelands, meadowlands, farmlands, Green Acres, and historic preservation lands.

Chapters 6 to 10 address the big regulatory programs associated with air, water quality/water supply, sewerage/wastewater treatment, solid waste, and hazardous waste.

Chapter 11 addresses human health and safety concerns, chapter 12 addresses wildlife protection, chapter 13 addresses chemical regulations, and chapter 14 addresses renewable energy.

This book is called a "Handbook" because it lets the reader hold a 1,000-book library in one hand. I want to thank the editor, Melissa Clarke, Esq., the authors, and student assistants whose talents made this book a one-handed reality. I also want to thank Bernan Press for publishing this *Handbook* and making it accessible to so many.

Albert I. Telsey, Esq., coauthor/editor
Meyner and Landis, LLP, Newark, New Jersey

DISCLAIMER: This book does not provide legal advice for any particular matter. The author's opinions are their own and do not represent the position of NJDEP or any other state agency.

Chapter 1

Buying and Selling Contaminated Property

Albert I. Telsey, Esq.

Most real estate deals in New Jersey come with a Pandora's box. Inside the box is one of three things: (1) a huge environmental problem impacting soil, groundwater, surface water, and/or indoor air quality; (2) something less dramatic; or (3) nothing. How do you figure out what is inside your box? How do you figure out your liability for cleanup? How do you protect yourself from environmental liability or limit its financial impact? How do you decide if going ahead with your deal makes financial sense? How do you clean up the box if you decide to move forward? This section addresses those questions.

The key to drafting environmental provisions in sale, lease, and loan documents is that the drafter, preferably an environmental attorney, knows at the outset of contract negotiations the entire life cycle of the cleanup process because he may have to address a number of unique issues associated with the cleanup as it moves to completion over the next few years. For example, how does a seller let a buyer investigate the property for contamination during the due diligence period? If the buyer agrees to buy the property, should the cleanup be done pre-closing or post-closing? Should the buyer or seller do the cleanup? How do the parties deal with a previous owner or operator already undertaking cleanup work? How and when, if at all, should the seller be released and/or indemnified from his obligation to provide a buyer with clean property? If contamination is going to be left onsite under controlled circumstances, such as with a Deed Notice in the case of contaminated soil or a Classification Exception Area (CEA) in the case of contaminated groundwater, who monitors, samples, submits reports, pays fees, and posts financial assurance for these long-term environmental legacy issues? Who pays for natural resource damages (NRD) if they are assessed?

STRICT LIABILITY

Pandora's box creates stress in real estate transactions because most environmental laws in New Jersey make current and past owners and operators who discharged hazardous substances strictly, jointly and severally liable for remediation costs without regard to fault. These laws include the Spill Compensation and Control Act, N.J.S.A. 58:10-23.11 (Spill Act), Industrial Site Recovery Act, N.J.S.A. 13: 1K-6 et seq. (ISRA), and Underground Storage Tank Act, N.J.S.A. 58:10A-21 et seq. In addition, the Site Remediation Reform Act, N.J.S.A. 58:10C-1 et seq., and the Administrative Requirements for the Remediation of Contaminated Sites, N.J.A.C 7:26C et seq., create an affirmative obligation for liable parties to actually undertake cleanup within prescribed time periods.

Under these laws, newly minted current owners of contaminated property become responsible for all past environmental sins, whether they had anything to do with the discharges or knew anything about them. The new owners may have causes of action for contribution against prior responsible parties, but few buyers want to buy a lawsuit. They want to buy property. Therefore, the mantra to remember is that buying, selling, leasing, mortgaging, foreclosing, or accepting contaminated property as a gift leaves the current owner responsible for all environmental sins of the past. Mix strict liability with an unopened Pandora's box, and the parties have a recipe for anxiety and tension.

DEFENSES TO LIABILITY

There are some statutory defenses to liability but most do not provide practical protection. Practical protection is usually provided in contracts by parties negotiating at arm's length with the assistance of an attorney knowledgeable about environmental matters. The Spill Act and ISRA, for example, provide that a current owner is not responsible for preexisting contamination under the following circumstances:

   a. **Act of war, act of God, or sabotage**. These causes of contamination are rare and of little protection.
   b. **Innocent purchaser defense**. A purchaser or beneficiary who acquires property after undertaking all appropriate inquiry prior to acquisition is not liable for preexisting contamination. All appropriate inquiry means the purchaser had a consultant investigate the property in accordance with the Technical Requirements for Site Remediation, N.J.A.C. 7:26E et seq., and that the preliminary assessment report (Phase 1 report) and site investigation report (Phase 2 report) (as may be necessary) confirmed the presence or absence of contamination.

   There is a common misperception that the innocent purchaser statute protects the buyer from liability for everything the investigation discovers. That is incorrect. The innocent purchaser protection statute protects the buyer from liability for everything a properly conducted investigation did *not* uncover. That is usually very little or nothing. However, because the due diligence inspection does an effective job identifying all areas of environmental concern at the property, it becomes the foundation for addressing the risks and obligation associated with transacting a contaminated property.

c. **NFA or NJDEP-approved Remedial Action Workplan**. If a buyer acquires property with a No Further Action (NFA) letter issued by NJDEP or a Response Action Outcome (RAO) issued by a Licensed Site Remediation Profession (LSRP), the buyer will not be liable under the Spill Act and common law for contamination existing before the issuance of the NFA or RAO, as long as the purchaser acquired the property after the discharge occurred; did not cause the discharge, is not responsible for the discharge, and is not a corporate successor to the discharger; notifies the NJDEP if historic contamination is later discovered on the property and maintains all conditions to a previously issued NFA or RAO.

However, the NFA or RAO must be issued for the entire site if the purchaser is to be protected from not having to do further work at the site. If the NFA was issued for only a specific area of concern, such as a certain leaking underground storage tank and nothing else, the previously issued NFA or RAO does not protect the buyer from having to address newly discovered preexisting areas of concern, such as a contaminated former septic system. In addition, the NFA or RAO does not protect the buyer from discharges that occurred after issuance of the NFA or RAO. That is why a due diligence inspection is still recommended even if the property has an NFA or RAO, especially if it was not recently issued.

If the purchaser acquires the property with a preexisting NJDEP-approved Remedial Action Workplan, the purchaser must complete the work required by the workplan to obtain statutory protection.[1] The workplan merely provides the recommended plan for addressing the delineated areas of concern. It still has to be cleaned up.

d. **Government liability protection**. A governmental entity that acquires ownership of real property through bankruptcy, tax delinquency, abandonment, escheat, eminent domain, condemnation, or any circumstance in which the governmental entity involuntarily acquires title by virtue of its function as sovereign, or where the governmental entity acquires the property by any means for the purpose of promoting the redevelopment of that property is exempt from liability under the Spill Act or common law. This exemption was provided to encourage governmental entities to deal with contaminated property in the normal course of government business. This is a good liability exemption for governmental entities, but it does not apply to private entities.

e. **Lender liability defense**. Lenders often refused to lend on contaminated property for fear that foreclosing on the property after default might make the lender a current owner and therefore strictly liable for cleanup. The Spill Act has safe harbor provisions that permit lenders to foreclose without assuming liability. However, the liability protection is not as absolute as it is for governmental entities. See chapter 3 section 3 Lender Liability Safe Harbors.

f. **NRD defense**. NRD is a penalty assessed by NJDEP for the loss of use of the natural resource while it is contaminated. It is in addition to the cost of remediation. For example, during the period of time groundwater is contaminated and is being cleaned up it is not usable for its intended potable purpose. NJDEP can assess an NRD penalty for the time period the groundwater remains contaminated and unusable for potable purposes. NRD penalties can also be assessed for damage to surface waters, wetlands, and other governmentally owned resources.

NJDEP has often been unpredictable in its assessment of NRD penalties, which created uncertainty between a buyer and seller of contaminated property. A buyer might require a seller to approach NJDEP, settle the NRD penalty, and pay it. A seller might not want to do that claiming NJDEP might never assess an NRD penalty. As a consolation seller might agree to indemnify buyer against NRD. A buyer might reject the indemnity on the grounds that it may be useless in the future if seller no longer exists or is financially unable to meet its indemnification obligation.

In order to provide a solution to this tension the Spill Act was amended to provide that, as long as a buyer does not agree to assume NRD by contract, NJDEP will not assess NRD against a buyer.[2] This liability protection is one of the better ones because its trigger is simple and clear.

g. **ISRA liability protection**. The Industrial Site Recovery Act (ISRA) is a unique New Jersey law that requires an owner or operator of an industrial establishment, usually a manufacturing facility, to clean up the property before ceasing operations or transferring the business, property, or corporate ownership to another. The idea behind the law was that industrial establishments often discharged contamination, so it makes sense to require cleanup as a condition to sale or transfer because that is when money is on the table. The parties can also enter into a Remediation Certification with NJDEP promising to remediate the property after closing and to post a remediation funding source as security for the promise. Failure to comply with ISRA permits the purchaser to rescind the sale transaction and recover damages.[3]

These environmental liability protection statutes usually have limited application in the real world. Even when they do apply they do not practically solve the contamination problem. Not being liable for cleanup does not mean a cleanup is not necessary. Often, a buyer must clean up contamination even if he is not liable because otherwise he may not be able to use, lease, or sell the property if it remains contaminated. Transacting parties have to address real contamination, not theoretical liability in their contracts.

POINTS OF VIEW IN A REAL ESTATE TRANSACTION

Primary stakeholders in a real estate transaction include the seller, buyer, lender, municipality, NJDEP, and LSRP. Each stakeholder often has a different point of view about whether a Pandora's box exists on the property, who is going to open it, how it will be opened, who is going to pay to open it, who is going to pay to remediate what is inside the box, and how remediation will actually be undertaken.

Sellers tend to be less interested in knowing what is inside the box because as current owners they often have to pay cleanup costs. Buyers tend to be more interested in knowing what is inside the box because they do not want to be stuck with contaminated property. The role of NJDEP and the LSRP is to make sure the cleanup gets done in accordance with established procedures regardless of whether a seller or buyer does it. Municipalities tend to be hands-off remediation details, except when a municipality can dictate remediation terms in the context of redevelopment.

SUMMARY OR REMEDIATION LIFE CYCLE

The better an attorney understands the details associated with the remediation process from beginning to end, the better the contract will be written for all parties. The remediation life cycle has five remediation steps: Step 1. Preliminary assessment—this is often referred to as a phase 1 or due diligence inspection where the site is inspected, knowledgeable people are interviewed, and records are reviewed. Step 2. Site investigation—this involves sampling to confirm the presence of contamination in areas identified in the preliminary assessment report as suspicious. Once contamination is confirmed, notice to NJDEP is required. Step 3. Remedial investigation—this involves delineating the full extent of the known contamination in all media; that is, figuring out the horizontal and vertical dimensions of Pandora's box. Step 4. Remedial action—this is when the remediation work gets done—excavation, disposal, treatment in place, engineering, and institutional controls such as a Deed Notice or CEA, and so on. Step 5. Completion. This is the "Holy Grail" when the LSRP issues the RAO confirming that the site is protective of human health, safety, and the environment. Sometimes the RAO has conditions, such as Remedial Action Permits, which regulate Deed Notices and CEAs and which require long-term sampling, monitoring, reporting, payment of fees, and other work associated with the selected protective remedy. See chapter 2 section 1 The Environmental Remediation Process.

PURCHASE/SALE AGREEMENT

An environmental attorney resolves the tension that may occur between buyer and seller during the life cycle of remediation by writing the rules of remediation into the contract. The rules of remediation reduce surprises and hard feelings later, which in turn reduce the risk of litigation. The following are rules of remediation often found in the contract.

Access/Due Diligence

From a seller's point of view, due diligence is an invitation to a stranger (the buyer) to look around and try to find contamination. The rules for access and due diligence usually include the following provisions: term of access (commonly thirty to ninety days); notice (reasonable advanced notice to seller before entry); scope of work (usually standard phase 1 work; sometimes phase 2 work); performance of work (buyer's consultant to pay all costs, comply with applicable laws and standards, repair damage); stop work (seller can tell buyer to stop if work is beyond agreed-upon scope or for violation of other conditions); and indemnity and insurance (buyer to indemnify seller against claims and damages caused by the due diligence contractors; and buyer or buyer's consultant to provide seller with general liability, workers' compensation, auto and consultant errors, and omission insurance). Prior to the end of the due diligence period, a buyer can often walk away for any reason or no reason, regardless of what the investigation reveals.

The environmental due diligence section of the contract may also address the following topics:

Seller's Representations and Warranties

A seller may tell a buyer he knows nothing about the environmental condition of the property; he knows only what are in certain reports; or he knows the property is not contaminated. A seller is rarely a guarantor or insurer as to the environmental integrity of the property even if he makes encouraging representations and warranties. Such statements are only useful for a claim of misrepresentation if they are later proven to be false. To win such a claim usually requires some proof of intent to mislead.

Reliance on Seller's Environmental Reports

Sometimes a seller can provide a fairly detailed trove of reports that describe the environmental condition of the property. These are helpful to a buyer but may not usually be relied upon as the buyer's sole source of due diligence information. For example, the reports may be old, leaving a buyer to wonder what has transpired at the property since the reports were written. Even if the reports are current and show the property is clean, a buyer has no privity of contract with the consultant who was paid by someone else to write the report. In other words, a buyer cannot legally rely on the report. A buyer could contact the consultant who wrote the report and ask for a third-party reliance letter. That letter states that even though the report was written only for someone else the consultant will allow the buyer as a third party to rely on the report, usually in exchange for money. The buyer still has to be sure he bought a report that complies with recognized standards of due diligence investigation and that the consultant is competent. In addition, if the report is stale, six months old or older, there may still be the need to get a fresh report prepared.

Use of an LSRP

It is common for sellers to prohibit an LSRP from doing a buyer's due diligence inspection, requiring instead that a non-LSRP environmental consultant do it. Regardless of contractual confidentiality provisions, LSRPs are bound by law to report to NJDEP the discovery of immediate environmental concerns; that is, concerns that may imminently impact human health, safety, or the environment. Sellers are loath to lose control of this kind of sensitive information. Non-LSRPs, however, are not obligated to report this kind of information to NJDEP.

Phase 2 Testing

Letting a buyer sample soil and/or groundwater heightens a seller's concern because now a buyer is literally drilling deeper to find seller's problems. If phase 2 testing is going to be permitted, the contract may have to be written to lock in the buyer so he does not walk away and leave the seller with harmful information about the environmental condition of the property or to require that the buyer keep the information to himself and not disclose it to the seller or others if the buyer is going to walk away.

If phase 2 testing is permitted then additional issues will have to be addressed as part of the access section of the contract including the scope of work (details associated with the sampling plan will have to be provided and approved in advance); cost of work (should usually be buyer's cost); utility mark outs (make sure buyer is responsible for properly marking utilities before drilling); split sampling (does the seller want samples to analyze to keep the buyer honest); storage of equipment, materials, and waste (where, how, and for how long can these materials be stored); disposal of waste (all drill cuttings must be removed from the property with buyer identified as the generator, not seller, in order to avoid labeling seller as a responsible party in a paper trail); and written reports. (Does buyer provide them to seller, keep confidential, or disclose to others?)

Pre-closing Remediation

Old school tactics often made the seller complete the entire cleanup pre-closing, using seller's money without the buyer contributing any money. This usually satisfied a buyer and a buyer's lender because they knew the property would be clean at closing. The other popular old school scenario was having the buyer do the entire cleanup with buyer's money in exchange for a deep discount to purchase price or walking away during due diligence if the cost of remediation was too high. These are all or nothing scenarios with little coordination or cooperation among the parties.

Seller doing it all is common in ISRA transactions where the seller by law must do the entire cleanup prior to closing title. Buyer doing it all may work if the seller is under enough financial distress to offer the property at a significantly discounted price, and the buyer is shrewd enough to take a gamble based on limited information that the cleanup cost is manageable. The distressed sale option is common with a financially desperate seller as well as a lender, condemning agency, municipality or trustee that is selling or auctioning a foreclosed or condemned property. The distressed sale option is often accompanied by contract terms that prohibit due diligence all together or that prohibit contract cancellation no matter what due diligence discloses.

In the all or nothing scenarios it is common for the contract to permit the buyer to walk away before the end of due diligence without giving reasons to seller. It is also common for a buyer to keep its due diligence report to himself and not provide it to seller because seller often does not want to be in possession of information about contamination that might force him to notify NJDEP and take action if he is not inclined to do so. If the buyer walks away silently then the seller may suspect the buyer found contamination but will not know for sure. Since the seller presumably has no independent knowledge of contamination, seller is usually under no obligation to confirm contamination and undertake cleanup, despite the suspicion created by buyer's walk away.

The all or nothing approach has drawbacks for both parties. For example, (i) if the seller agrees to pay for all the cleanup pre-closing, seller could be at the mercy of remediating whatever contamination buyer's due diligence uncovered using seller's money regardless of cost; (ii) it could take years for seller to complete the cleanup pre-closing and close the transaction, thereby delaying buyer's use of the property and frustrating the business goals of the buyer and his partners; and (iii) having seller do the cleanup pre-closing puts both parties at the mercy of seller's available funds and seller's motivation to complete the cleanup.

In addition, if everyone just walks away after due diligence uncovers contamination, this do-nothing decision avoids the contamination, which is the single most important issue that requires attention. The next time the seller tries to sell the property it is likely the subsequent buyer will find the same problems and also walk away. The risk of a buyer walking away is high because the all-or-nothing scenario provides few opportunities for cooperation. Therefore, the all or nothing scenarios can make the parties spend professional fees for a transaction that is likely to take a long time to close or to ultimately fail. This does not make sense and is the reason why contracting parties now work on contract solutions that encourage cooperation instead of entrenchment. They find that a cooperative approach to the problem of Pandora's box can be mutually beneficial to getting a transaction to close and to close quickly.

Post-closing Remediation

When opening up Pandora's box a seller is fearful that the cost of cleanup will be more than he can bear or even more than the purchase price. A buyer is fearful that if he assumes the cost of cleanup it may make his planned business venture unprofitable. To figure out the best solution requires that the parties design in advance each plank that takes them to the Holy Grail (an RAO issued by the LSRP).

It is common now for parties to develop contract rules of remediation that advance the mutual goal of closing. These contract rules address remediation by, for example, (i) determining in advance the standard of cleanup acceptable to the parties (e.g., commercial, residential, etc.) and whether the parties will permit the use of soil or groundwater Remedial Action Permits (RAPs) as a cost-savings solution, (ii) sharing the costs associated with investigation and remediation using negotiated milestones and an escrow, and (iii) using third-party fixed fee cleanup and liability assumption contractors to lock in the cost of cleanup with an indemnification and insurance policy backstop. This last option is discussed in section 3.2. The upshot of all this pre-planning is that the parties are often more willing to close and do remediation post-closing because the potential unknowns have been worked out fairly well in advance.

Environmental Escrow

Common contract planks are cost milestones for the anticipated costs of opening up Pandora's box and dealing with what is inside. For example, the old school playbook would require the buyer to pay all its due diligence costs and seller to pay all costs of remediation without knowing how much remediation was going to cost. To protect seller's slide into the unknown depths of remediation costs the parties could set money milestones at the outset of the contract. For example, the parties could agree that seller pays all costs up to the purchase price and the buyer pays all costs in excess of the purchase price; or buyer pays $50,000 in excess of the purchase price and seller pays the balance; or seller pays $50,000 over the purchase price and buyer pays the balance; or buyer pays the first $50,000 over purchase price, seller pays the next $50,000, buyer the next $50,000, and so on The milestones and cost-sharing formulas can be developed in a variety of ways depending upon negotiating strength of the parties, details of the transaction, and other factors. The advantage to this approach is that it provides risk management that can be factored into a business plan for seller and buyer.

At the early stage of contract negotiation, before the cost of cleanup is known, money milestones are often based on instinct, intuition, experience, hubris, business goals, and other factors. But at this early stage of the process the cost-sharing decision is missing the most important element—a reasonable estimate as to the ultimate cost of cleanup. Developing good rules of remediation includes doing enough sampling at the property during due diligence to get to a reasonably defensible cleanup estimate. That way, the money sharing milestones can be overlaid on top of a reasonable estimate to give seller and buyer a reasonable expectation of what their cleanup cost share will be.

Getting the reasonably defensible cleanup estimate pre-closing lets the seller know if the cleanup will cost less than the purchase price. If the cleanup costs more than the purchase price, seller may not want to undertake cleanup now but prefer to terminate the transaction and continue using the property. Getting the reasonably defensible cleanup estimate also lets buyer know how much he may have to contribute to make the seller willing to sell, which is a number buyer needs to factor into his business pro forma to confirm his proposed project will still be profitable if he has to factor in cleanup costs he otherwise did not plan to pay.

A common technique for cost sharing is for the buyer's due diligence consultant to delineate the vertical and horizontal extent of Pandora's box so the consultant can reasonably estimate the cleanup costs. The parties then decide if 100 percent, 150 percent, or some other percentage of that amount is placed into an environmental escrow. This environmental escrow is usually funded from the purchase price. Seller can have his own consultant truth-test the estimate. Seller can hold the escrow. Buyer can hold the escrow. Seller can do the work. Buyer can do the work. Under this escrow scenario the seller or buyer uses the money to obtain an RAO from an LSRP. When the RAO is issued, the balance of the escrow is released to seller. This type of escrow is common.

Three-Year NJDEP Audit

Often a buyer may require that the escrow remain in place for three years after the date the RAO is issued. That is because the NJDEP has the power to audit 10 percent of the RAOs issued by any LSRP. In the event the RAO is audited and rescinded by NJDEP due to LSRP error or some other reason, the parties at least have the balance of the escrow to use to correct the error.

Environmental Legacy Issues

Years ago all contamination had to be removed from soil and groundwater. This was costly, unnecessary, and a handicap to putting contaminated property back to productive use. Often contaminated properties were mothballed. Over the years, studies proved that contaminated soil could be left in place with an engineering control, such as an asphalt cap, and an institutional control, such as a recorded deed notice notifying the world that soil contamination remains on site as reflected on an attached map. Studies also proved that contaminated groundwater could be left unaddressed because, as long as the source area of contamination was removed, dissolved contamination in groundwater often attenuated over time to regulatory standards due to natural chemical and biological degradation. NJDEP regulates natural degradation of groundwater by way of a CEA. NJDEP has classified most groundwater in the state as potable. By demarcating a certain area of groundwater as contaminated but subject to natural degradation, NJDEP is recognizing that the defined area of groundwater contamination is a limited exception to the general classification that the groundwater in the area is potable.

A deed notice and CEA are regulated by NJDEP through a RAP. A deed notice RAP can last thirty years or longer. A CEA RAP can last from a few years to thirty years or longer.

These permits are considered legacy environmental issues that a responsible party must maintain. The responsible parties are usually the person doing the cleanup (often a seller) and the property owner (often a buyer). Together they are identified as co-permittees on the RAP.

It is important for contract drafters to be aware of these legacy remedies because the financial assurance costs associated with maintaining an RAP must be addressed as part of the contract remediation rules. For example, the financial assurance component for a deed notice RAP can be $25,000 to $50,000 or more; the financial assurance component for a CEA RAP can be tens or hundreds of thousands of dollars. The yearly fee for the permit and the costs to prepare biennial certification over thirty years are also significant. Determining who pays how much of these costs and how they will be escrowed and used is an important consideration.

Buyer or Seller to Do Cleanup

A seller is concerned that a buyer-controlled cleanup will result in an expensive and conservative cleanup plan being paid with seller's escrow money leaving little escrow for the seller and perhaps even costing more than the escrow. A buyer is concerned that a seller-controlled cleanup will cut corners to save money, interfere with the buyer's use and development of the property, and be undertaken with little enthusiasm since the seller no longer owns the property. Both of these concerns are somewhat muted now that cleanup is controlled by an independent LSRP who acts as a pseudo-NJDEP case manager. The LSRP can make all decisions as to remedial strategy, cost, and time of implementation.

Some sellers are willing to let the buyer do the cleanup by giving the buyer a credit on the purchase price in the amount of the expected cleanup in exchange for a release or release/indemnity from buyer at closing. This often provides the quickest way for seller to get closure and walk away with finality. Sometimes a seller wants cleanup control post-closing because he believes he can manage the escrow better than buyer, thereby preserving an escrow balance that will be released to seller after issuance of the RAO. Sometimes a buyer wants a seller to be in control of the cleanup post-closing because seller is supposed to do the work anyway, and the buyer is neither in need of a fast remedy nor inclined to do the work as long as the money is in escrow for seller to do it.

Coordinating Remediation with Redevelopment

In those instances where the parties want the seller to do cleanup post-closing, the parties must provide access to seller and his LSRP. There are a few unique issues to address with regard to post-closing remediation access by a seller as opposed to pre-closing due diligence access by a buyer.

Often the buyer's planned use or redevelopment of the property (e.g., new building or parking lot) can be used as a cap to cover contaminated soil that will be left on site by seller with a deed notice. The parties need to address in advance how the seller can use the buyer's redevelopment plans for the seller's remediation obligations.

For example, a buyer may intend to excavate a foundation or basement for a new building in an area where the seller intended to leave contaminated soils in place with a deed notice. Excavation can be considered a remediation expense, a redevelopment cost, or both. The cost of excavating and disposing contaminated soil is more expensive than the cost of excavating and disposing clean soil. Some parties provide that buyer must pay all excavation and disposal costs of the contaminated soil since seller was entitled to leave it in place as an appropriate remedy using a deed notice. Sometime the parties agree to split the cost of disposal. For example, if the cost to dispose of clean soil is $20/ton, and the cost to dispose of contaminated soil is $80/ton, the parties might agree that seller will pay the difference of $60/ton, since that cost is related to the contamination.

A dispute may also arise when the parties have not agreed in advance on what costs are "remediation costs" versus "redevelopment costs." For example, a 6-inch asphalt cap covering an area of contaminated soil is just as protective a barrier as covering the area with a building or gold bricks. If the parties have not identified in advance how much of the escrow can be used as a cap and what form the cap can take, a buyer might try to use the environmental escrow to pay for some of his redevelopment costs disguised as remediation costs.

Dispute Resolution

If one party does not like what the other party is doing with regard to the scope of cleanup or the costs associated with certain tasks, the parties need a dispute resolution provision. The first recourse is to try to work things out amicably. If that fails it is common to include a provision that compels the parties to pursue mediation, arbitration or litigation. These options can be costly and time consuming. An alternative is to go to a pre-selected independent LSRP who is given authority by both sides to decide disputes with finality. Costs of the independent LSRP are split 50/50. Sometimes the parties may be unable or unwilling to select an independent LSRP. In that instance, each party can select its own LSRP who together will select the independent LSRP. This option can be less costly and time consuming than mediation, arbitration, or litigation.

Indemnification and Release

At closing a seller often gives an indemnity to buyer promising to remediate all preexisting contamination. This promise goes hand-in-hand with the money in the environmental escrow. Once the seller delivers the RAO post-closing, the seller may then want to terminate his indemnity since his promise has been met. The attorney for a seller believes a buyer should be weaned from the protection of seller's indemnity once the RAO is issued because the RAO provides a covenant not to sue from NJDEP, which may be considered a replacement to seller's indemnity to buyer, even though the covenant not to sue does not cover third-party claims. Buyer may agree to retire seller's indemnity but only after the third anniversary of the RAO to avoid the three-year NJDEP audit period and possible RAO reopener.

At closing a seller may want a release and indemnity from buyer for any new discharges occurring after closing, since the seller does not want to be responsible for anything new the buyer might discharge. The parties often use the buyer's due diligence inspection report as the baseline establishing the preexisting environmental conditions at the property.

In addition, at closing the seller may also want the buyer to provide seller with an indemnity and release for all past and future environmental conditions at the property no matter who is responsible for them. If provided, this indemnity and release will only be activated upon issuance of the RAO or three years thereafter as the parties may negotiate.

This approach represents a changing of the guard. Seller lived up to his obligation to provide an RAO. Seller waited three additional years for a NJDEP audit. If nothing happened during that three-year period, seller gets his release and indemnity and is free to go.

At this point, buyer has had the comfort of an unaudited RAO that includes a covenant not to sue by NJDEP and possession of excess environmental escrow money in the event the RAO was audited. In addition, the buyer should be in possession of enough financial assurance posted by seller in support of a deed notice RAP and CEA RAP, if they were used as remedies, to cover these legacy environmental costs. Therefore, the buyer was protected by three pots of money—the environmental escrow, the deed notice RAP financial assurance, and the CEA RAP financial assurance. By releasing the seller and returning the balance of the environmental escrow, buyer will still possess the RAP financial assurances. This is often a balanced and fair outcome.

There are a couple of issues not addressed by this tidy wrap-up. The first is the threat of NJDEP reopening the RAO after the three-year audit period. This can be addressed two ways. A buyer can purchase a pollution legal liability (PLL) insurance policy to cover that risk, or a buyer can negotiate an indemnity with the LSRP in charge of the cleanup to cover damages incurred in the event the RAO is reopened due to his negligence; otherwise, the LSRP does not get the LSRP job at the outset of the cleanup. The PLL insurance policy has its limitations by way of exclusions and premium costs as compared to risk. The LSRP indemnity has its limitations because newly discovered environmental issues may be unrelated to LSRP negligence. In addition, an LSRP may not give an indemnity.

LSRP AGREEMENT

Remediating parties must now hire an LSRP to oversee the remediation process. The LSRP contract should address the following issues:

- Scope of work (task-by-task, entire site cleanup, etc.).
- The form of RAO (site-wide RAO that provides statutory liability protection against unknowns discovered later or an area-specific RAO that does not provide statutory protection for unknowns discovered later).
- Indemnification (for LSRP negligence; damages originating from use, storage, and disposal of hazardous substances; costs incurred as a result of an NJDEP audit, NJDEP takeover, or the LSRP Oversight Board taking action against the LSRP for his work performed at the property; inadequate work done by a prior LSRP which the contracted LSRP certified as reliable; failure to comply with applicable laws and regulations; revocation of the RAO; failure to meet regulatory and mandatory deadlines; also, indemnification should not be limited to the cost of the contract fees since damages might be more than that amount).
- Insurance (make sure it includes pollution and errors and omission coverage; and client is provided a certificate of insurance confirming the client is covered as an additional insured referencing the LSRP contract just executed).
- Confidentiality/record keeping (all documents are to be kept confidential and submitted to NJDEP only when required by NJDEP regulations).
- Code of conduct (LSRP must adhere to statutory LSRP code of conduct).
- LSRP's assumptions, limitations, and qualifications to the work (these often include no guarantee; no payment of NJDEP fees or fines; no responsibility for maintaining RAO conditions; no presumption that prior work approved by NJDEP or a prior LSRP is satisfactory; no responsibility for damages caused by the client's failure to disclose information; no third-party reliance; no responsibility for the consequences of hindered access; no responsibility for reporting a claim to the client's insurance company; no responsibility for asbestos, radon, or lead paint; and no responsibility for laboratory error).

NOTES

1. N.J.S.A. 58:10-23.11g.d(2).
2. N.J.S.A. 58:10-23.11f22.
3. N.J.S.A. 13:1k-13.

Chapter 2

Remediating Contaminated Property

Section 1

The Environmental Remediation Process

Glenn P. Brukardt

The environmental remediation process can be broken down into a series of incremental steps. Information from the earlier step is used to determine the design of the next step until all contamination is identified, delineated, and remediated sufficiently for the property to be protective of human health, safety, and the environment. When that occurs, a Licensed Site Remediation Professional (LSRP) can issue the Holy Grail—a Response Action Outcome (RAO).

The investigation and remediation process generally described herein is used regardless of the size of the cleanup. The purpose of this section is to briefly explain the investigation, delineation, and remediation steps, and how an environmental consultant working with an LSRP uses the tools in the consultant's toolbox to provide cost-efficient and effective service to the client. There are exceptions to the information presented here, but the following provides the basic process superstructure.

STAKEHOLDERS

Different stakeholders involved with a site and environmental remedial project will likely have different goals and points of view.

For example, a buyer may want to know about *all* the contamination on a site, because he becomes strictly liable for preexisting contamination; a seller may be less inclined to know about anything he is not legally obligated to know about, since he is looking to leave the site; a tenant may want to know the baseline of contamination so the landlord will become responsible for preexisting contamination pursuant to the lease; a lender needs to protect itself in the event of default, foreclosure, and sale; a broker needs to know the extent of contamination in order to properly counsel a prospective buyer; an insurer needs to know to properly underwrite the risk, coverage, and exclusions; a neighbor needs to know to determine if he is in harm's way; and a governmental entity needs to know to determine if enforcement should be undertaken for noncompliance or if a property tax appeal might be successful. As you can see, there are many players, with sometimes divergent and contradictory agendas.

In addition to the multiple players, each with their own end-goal, each stakeholder may also need to know different things about the contamination depending upon the goal of the stakeholder for the specific project at hand. For example, a lender may want to know materially different things about the property depending upon whether the bank is assessing a new loan for a new client, assessing a new loan for an existing important client with strong financials and payment history, pursuing a foreclosure on the property, undertaking the fiduciary management or liquidation of an estate portfolio, acquiring the portfolio of another bank, or purchasing a new branch or headquarters location.

When there are different stakeholders involved in a transaction with potentially competing goals, which is commonly the case, it is important for all stakeholders to understand why the investigation and remediation are going to occur and what the blended goal of the work will be. To help achieve that goal, it is important to gather the necessary professional team, which normally includes an environmental real estate attorney, environmental consultant, LSRP, and lender.

1. **Real Estate/Environmental Counsel**: A stakeholder will likely need an attorney versed in the discipline at hand (e.g., real estate, litigation, corporate, estate planning, etc.) and environmental matters. This can be one individual or two. Many times, the lead counsel will bring in environmental cocounsel, as needed.

2. **Environmental Consultant and/or LSRP**: A stakeholder will likely require the services of an LSRP and a non-LSRP. As of November 3, 2009, the New Jersey Department of Environmental Protection (NJDEP) transferred a majority of the remediation program oversight duties to private contractor LSRPs, which have replaced the former NJDEP Case Managers. The switch from Case Managers to LSRPs was legislated in the Site Remediation Reform Act of 2009. This change was implemented for both economic and practical purposes, as thousands of NJDEP case files were sitting open and unresolved for years, hampering the return of contaminated properties to productive and/or highest and best use.

   There are over 500 LSRPs in New Jersey and about seven times that number of non-LSRP environmental consultants working in the State. LSRPs are essentially deputized NJDEP Case Managers who must be licensed, adhere to a strict code of ethics, and put the interest of the State of New Jersey (i.e., protection of human health, safety, welfare, and the environment) ahead of the interests of the LSRPs clients (that pay the LSRP) and/or the consulting firm (that employs the LSRP) if the objectives of the LSRP conflict with those of the client or employer. The LSRPs are subject to significant civil and criminal penalties if they act contrary to the obligations inherent in their license and must wear their license and the associated responsibilities at all times; the LSRP badge cannot be set aside at the LSRP's discretion.

   To counterbalance the State-leaning focus of the LSRP, environmental projects are often designed, approved, and implemented by a joint non-LSRP/LSRP team. Sometimes the same firm employs both individuals; sometimes they work for separate firms. Recently, it has become common for LSRPs to set up a solo, or small firm, practice to review third-party non-LSRP consultant work, foregoing their own projects. The LSRP/non-LSRP team retains the traditional NJDEP balance of responsibility. That is, a non-LSRP designs and implements investigation and remediation work, and the LSRP reviews, approves, or modifies the workplans and results, much like an NJDEP Case Manager of old system.

This new process results in faster and more cost-effective cleanups because the LSRP is hired and fired directly by the client and meets project milestones/completion dates largely dictated by the client. This is superior to the former NJDEP model that assigned an often overworked Case Manager, who literally might not be able to review a particular submission for years, not necessarily due to lack of dedication but simply because there were too few NJDEP Case Managers for the large numbers of open cases. The New LSRP model has been successfully closing remedial projects that have languished for years under the old NJDEP Case Manager system.

3. **Financial Institution**: There are many financial institutions in New Jersey that are environmentally savvy and routinely lend on environmentally impaired property. The key tools these banks use are third-party environmental consultants to review (with the bank's interest paramount) a borrower-generated remedial plan and the establishment of post-closing environmental escrow accounts to make remedial payments in accordance with a pre-designed plan of action and budget (similar to draws from a construction loan). Often these bank-required escrows are funded with a contingency clause, which can range from 10 percent to 100 percent+ of the proposed budget, once the budget is vetted, to account for future remedial uncertainties. The escrow may also have a replenisher clause, which requires replenishment of the escrow by the borrower or another if the escrow balance dips below a preset floor dollar figure before the remedial work is fully completed, or if the project percent-complete does not match the project budget-spent.

4. **NJDEP**: Although the NJDEP has transferred the lion's share of oversight in the site remediation arena to the LSRPs, they still retain ultimate oversight of the site remediation program, issue certain permits associated with the remedial process (outside the purview of the LSRP), review a myriad of new forms that must be submitted by the LSRPs, and retain the right to ultimately override an LSRP's technical decisions and rescind a final RAO if they feel the same was issued in error (they typically have a thirty-six-month timeframe, post-RAO, to review and rescind a RAO, called a *reopener* period).

5. **Environmental Insurer**: In larger deals that require greater certainty as to the risk even at the expense of additional cost, an environmental insurer in addition to, or in lieu of, an escrow, can be employed. See chapter 3, section 2.

MEDIA TO BE REMEDIATED

Most remedial projects involve one or more contaminated media, primarily the following: soil, groundwater, soil vapor/gas, and indoor air, building materials, and surface water/sediment.

Soil and groundwater contamination comprise the bulk of most cleanup projects and will be the focus of this subsection. However, soil vapor and indoor air have become hot-button issues in New Jersey over the past several years due to the migration of potentially harmful vapors into habitable spaces. As such, air assessments and associated corrective action have become more prevalent components in the overall remedial program. Building material impacts are usually associated with industrial buildings (e.g., contaminants staining or impregnating the floors and/or walls in shop or production areas). Surface water and sediment impacts are less common because fewer sites have surface water and/or sediment features. However, impacts to surface water and sediments tend to be more costly to address, not only due to strict ecological-based cleanup standards, but due to the fact that remediation in sensitive surface water ecosystems usually involves securing additional environmental permits from other regulatory departments in the NJDEP, including, but not limited to, wetlands, flood hazard areas, riparian areas, coastal zones, and stream corridors. In addition, sampling and dredging sediment, if required, is expensive.

PRIMARY REMEDIAL MEASURES EMPLOYED

Practically speaking, there is no *de minimus* amount of hazardous material that can be spilled or discharged into New Jersey's environment that does not have to be reported to the NJDEP. However, a spill that needs to be reported does not always equate to a spill that needs to be remediated at all or in its entirety.

To determine whether the contaminant levels exceed NJDEP standards, there are numerical remedial cleanup levels for hundreds of hazardous compounds for each of the media noted earlier. If a hazardous compound is detected/reported via testing/ observation above a standard in one or more media, a party responsible for remediation undertakes some sort of corrective action. The standards differ for each media. For example, the cleanup standard for benzene differs for soil, groundwater, soil vapor, indoor air, surface water, and sediment. Multiply this combination by hundreds of hazardous compounds, and there are literally thousands of remedial cleanup standards that can apply to a single site.

Reduced to its simplest expression, remediation is action taken to reduce the concentration of a hazardous compound in all media to below its NJDEP cleanup standard or to otherwise leave the contaminant in place in a manner that will be protective of human health and the environment. The following is a description of some of the common remedial tools used in the industry for different media.

SOIL REMEDIATIONS

Just because a person has identified and reported to NJDEP the spill of a hazardous compound, for example, a fuel oil leak into the soil around a heating oil underground storage tank (UST), that does not mean that the spill has to be remediated. If the levels of petroleum hydrocarbons in the soil are below the most stringent NJDEP soil remediation standard, a person can close the incident *without* conducting any remedial work. There still will be costs associated with the investigation of the spill, because money will be expended collecting and analyzing soil samples, completing technical forms and submitting documentation to NJDEP. However, the *remedial* component can be avoided, which is a huge time and cost saver.

With benzene, a common contaminant in gasoline and fuel oil spills, there is a different NJDEP remediation standard depending upon the media impacted, such as soil or groundwater, as well as specific soil cleanup standards for benzene, including a benzene residential soil standard, benzene nonresidential soil standard (for industrial/commercial sites), benzene impact to groundwater standard, and various benzene ecological standards. Therefore, four or more benzene standards exist for soil alone. A person responsible for remediation has to be sure to use the proper standards when designing a remedial plan. This holds true for hundreds of other hazardous compounds regulated by the NJDEP.

Gasoline, for example, is not a single contaminant but rather a blend of hazardous compounds. Therefore, in a gasoline spill, all the hazardous compounds that constitute gasoline must be assessed. These include benzene, toluene, ethyl benzene, xylene, and many other volatile organic compounds. Fuel oil is also made up of a blend of hazardous compounds different from gasoline in many respects, which requires a sampling protocol that captures the assessment of all of its component compounds.

These two examples alone show that determining whether a spill must be remediated involves checking multiple soil samples against multiple hazardous constituent standards. For that reason, most sampling data is presented in spreadsheet format to allow for easy data tracking against NJDEP compliance standards.

The data comparison effort is further complicated by the sometimes nonintrusive differences in the NJDEP standards. For example, it would seem intuitive that the residential standard for hazardous compounds would be lower than the nonresidential standard for that compound. It would also seem intuitive that a person responsible for remediating a nonresidential discharge would have to clean it up to nonresidential standards. But that is not always the case. For example, with regard to the heavy metal chromium, NJDEP is most concerned with soil dust inhalation hazards and has set the industrial cleanup standard significantly lower than the residential standard. The Department is concerned that truck traffic may stir up dust at a business site, which is something less likely to occur at a residential property. Therefore, for each remedial design, all the soil standards should be carefully reviewed to select the appropriate standard to apply to the project at hand.

The following are typical options available for remediating contaminated soil:

1. **Deed Notice**: Leave the contaminated soil in-place and record a notice with the county clerk to notify future owners, lenders, and others that there is contaminated soil remaining onsite. The Deed Notice is usually associated with an engineering control, such as the placement of a building or parking lot over the affected area or the placement of a fence around the area.
2. **Excavation**: Excavate the contaminated soils and remove them from the site. This is often referred to as *dig and dump*.
3. **In-situ Treatment**: Treat the soil in-place. There are many in-situ treatment options on the market today. Most of the innovative remedial technologies fall into this category.

4. **Ex-situ Treatment**: Dig out the soil, treat it someplace else, return it to its place of origin, and put it back in the ground. This remedy is not nearly as common as in-situ treatment.

Before a party responsible for conducting the remediation can choose a remedial option, he or she must delineate the horizontal and vertical extent of the soil contamination. That work typically occurs in phases, usually starting with a site investigation (SI), followed by a remedial investigation (RI). Generally speaking, an SI involves soil sampling with a drill rig, a backhoe and/or with hand tools to confirm if soil contamination exists above NJDEP standards. This is the first step in determining whether remediation is necessary. An RI involves more soil sampling (both in a horizontal and vertical direction) to determine the size of the contaminated area.

By the way of example, if a person spilled a gallon of oil onto the ground once a day every day for a period of time and let it seep into the soil over months or years, that oil would travel down and out like a stain soaking into a sponge. The RI phase essentially pokes holes in the ground deeper and further out from the stain source to determine the physical dimensions of the stain, or "plume," in remedial parlance. Capturing the outer dimensions of the plume may take one, two or more sampling efforts. Once the plume is fully delineated and the types of hazardous compounds are identified (heavy metal, solvent, fuel oil, pesticide, and so on), the person responsible for conducting the remediation can determine which remediation method makes the most sense from an economic and timing standpoint.

Deed Notice

A Deed Notice allows the person to leave contamination onsite that is above the most stringent NJDEP cleanup standard, as long as it is capped or otherwise isolated so as to be protective of human health and the environment. The NJDEP permits this option because remediating all the contaminated soil in New Jersey, especially within established urban areas, by digging it out or treating it in-situ or ex-situ is impractical and economically infeasible. For example, a person would literally have to excavate the majority of the historic contaminated fill in the Ironbound Section of Newark and truck it someplace else if a Deed Notice was not a permissible remedy.

For a Deed Notice with a cap or fencing to be approvable, a person responsible for conducting the remediation must demonstrate that the physical limits of the contamination have been delineated and that any contaminated soil above NJDEP standards that remains in place will not act as a continuing source or potential source of groundwater contamination. Therefore, if contaminated soil is continuing to release contamination into groundwater, like an oil-soaked sponge, the groundwater will not be able to recover from the constant assault. In that situation, NJDEP will not allow the person to employ a Deed Notice without first addressing the soil contamination using one of the proactive remedial methods. Contaminated historic fill, discussed here, is an exception.

If the contaminated soil extends off the subject property, use of Deed Notice gets a bit more complicated, since a neighboring property owner does not have to allow a Deed Notice on his or her property related to some else's contamination. Therefore, bifurcation of the remediation may be necessary—namely, use of a Deed Notice on the onsite portion with the offsite portion addressed through other remedial means. An exception exists for contamination that extends onto public rights-of-way such as roads. In that situation, the person responsible for conducting the remediation can file a Notice in Lieu of Deed Notice, which allows the Deed Notice to exist in the roadway as long as appropriate governmental agencies and utility companies who use the roadway are notified about the details of the contamination.

Capping the area of concern usually occurs in one or more of the following ways: asphalt pavement (e.g., parking lots, ingress/egress roads, etc.); building foundations; clean soil caps (usually six to twenty-four inches in thickness, with or without geo-textile membranes and ultimately covered in landscaping, lawn, rip-rap, etc.); and/or fencing with warning signage (for either permanent use in wooded or remote areas or temporary use).

The Deed Notice must be filed with the NJDEP and recorded with the county clerk. The documentation notifies the NJDEP of contaminated soil left in place, which is then logged into the Department's database. Anyone searching the database online (e.g., a neighbor, buyer, bank, litigant, etc.) can find the Deed Notice details. A caretaker must also be identified to ensure the cap is properly maintained over time. There is also a financial assurance required (a letter of credit, a line of credit, bond, insurance policy, etc.) to demonstrate to NJDEP that funds are in place to both care for the cap and to file biennial paperwork for a thirty-year period. The average amount is approximately $25,000, although it can be higher. Some small businesses, governmental agencies, and other uses are exempt from the financial assurance requirement.

Historic Fill

Some properties in urban areas of New Jersey, especially former low-lying areas, have been historically filled with imported nonnative soil or slag derived from unknown sites, often other construction sites or nearby manufacturing facilities. Much of this filling occurred in the late nineteenth century and continued into the 1960s and later, before environmental regulations came into effect. This historic fill commonly contains low levels of hazardous compounds above NJDEP cleanup standards, usually heavy metals such as arsenic, lead, and zinc, and semi-volatile organic compounds typically found in asphalt. The result is that many urban areas are contaminated with historic fill, even though current and historic use has been benign (such as office, retail, or residential). Deed Notices are commonly used as the preferred remedy at these locations since these sites cannot realistically be *dug up*.

Excavation Option

If the amount of contaminated soil at a site is manageable—that is, if the volume of soil is relatively small and the depth of contamination is not too deep—it may make financial sense to simply excavate the contaminated soil and dispose of it offsite. This avoids the Deed Notice option and the legacy obligations associated with it. To undertake an excavation remedy, post-remedial excavation soil samples are required to ensure full removal of all the suspect impacted soils, or if a RI was previously completed that fully delineated the area of concern with clean soil borings, the excavation could be extended to the clean borings. Waste classification soil samples are usually collected during the excavation process to confirm the material meets the chosen disposal facility material acceptance criteria.

Excavated soils may be disposed of in an in-state or out-of-state landfill licensed to accept contaminated soil; other disposal facilities may treat the soil or recycle it for landfill cover or other uses. Recycling is commonly a preferred option, to avoid the potential for long-term liability at a landfill facility that may, in the future, be run poorly and become a site for enforcement activity.

The excavation option does not work as well where the contamination is deep (usually 20 feet or deeper), which may require expensive sheeting or shoring to prevent the excavation from collapsing; where the contaminated soil extends into the water table, which means the excavation must be dewatered and the excavated saturated soil dried prior to transportation; and/or the contamination extends up to, or under, buildings or utility lines, which will have logistical and/or structural concerns if the supporting soils are removed. These drawbacks can be overcome but usually not without considerable added expense.

In-Situ Option

In-situ soil remediation options are numerous and varied. Most involve the use of biological agents—that is, the injection of microbes into the ground that use the contaminant as a source of food or energy—or chemical agents—that is, the injection of chemicals into the ground, which chemically react with the contaminants and result in reducing them to benign end products such as water, carbon dioxide, salts and other compounds. This process is called in-situ chemical oxidation (ISCO). There are many different biological and chemical products on the market; some have been used for decades. New products periodically enter the market place claiming good results on certain types of contaminants. This section will provide a general outline as to how the in-situ process works regardless of the specific product injected.

To inject any product into the ground requires preapproval from NJDEP through a Permit-By-Rule (PBR). A PBR application explains to NJDEP what product will be injected into the ground and/or groundwater (a biological or ISCO agent); its effectiveness (whether it has been used and/or approved by the NJDEP previously, and if so, the PBR approval process will be much faster); how the product will be injected (typically the product is injected into temporary or permanent injection points, such as 2-inch diameter soil borings or plastic/stainless steel slotted points); the number and layout of the injection points (typically in a grid or geometric pattern biased toward hot spot contamination locations); the product loading rate (how much product will be injected into each point); how many injection rounds are anticipated (typically two to four weeks apart with two to four injection rounds in all); and how the process will be monitored to demonstrate if the in-situ injection process is working (typically this involves establishing pre-injection, post-injection, and interim injection sampling to demonstrate product success).

Injection projects tend to be more expensive and time-consuming than most simple direct excavation projects; however, they are a good remedy for large volumes of contamination or deep contamination that is too expensive or impractical to dig out and for contamination near or under building, underground utilities and/or active yard areas, such as parking, ingress/egress and production areas, where excavation would disrupt building use or site operations.

Ex-Situ Option

Ex-situ remediation typically involves excavating soils, temporarily staging it, treating the contaminants and reintroducing the contamination into the ground. This option is not used often unless there is ample room to stage and treat the soil, the excavation can remain open or inaccessible for a period of time, and the treatment process can be sufficiently quickened or improved by the excavation and manipulation of the soil aboveground. The same general techniques used for in-situ treatment are used for ex-situ treatment.

GROUNDWATER REMEDIATION

Although groundwater can sometimes intersect with surface water, such as streams, groundwater is not surface water. "Groundwater" is a term that captures the large reservoirs of water that exist below the ground and is synonymous with the term "aquifer." Groundwater in New Jersey varies in depth—some places as little as inches below grade and other places as much as 75 feet or deeper. However, as a general guide, groundwater in New Jersey is typically within 5 to 25 feet below ground.

Groundwater fills the space between the soil particles in the ground (which is called an overburden aquifer), or it fills the fissures and cracks in bedrock (which is called a bedrock aquifer). There can be multiple aquifers or separate and distinct layers of water below the ground separated by dry layers, like layers in a cake. These aquifer layers can be several feet thick or several hundred feet thick. Some aquifers can be contaminated while others above or below it can be clean.

The uppermost aquifer is usually the object of remediation because it is closest to the ground surface. This makes sense since sources of contamination commonly emanate from leaking tanks, septic systems, drywells, leaking drums, and so on which are usually at the ground surface or close to it, and contamination from these sources seeps downward, hitting the shallowest groundwater first. This is a typical scenario but not the only one.

Groundwater flows like a stream or river; however, groundwater flow is *much* slower than surface water, sometimes on the order of feet or even as little as inches per year. But, even though it can be very slow, it *will* move and commonly carry the contaminants along with it. In coastal areas, the movement of groundwater can also be influenced by the tides, reversing direction much like surface water.

Contamination in groundwater can take two forms: dissolved product—that is, the contaminants mix into the water (like sugar mixes and dissolves in a glass of tea)—or free product—that is, the contaminant floats to top of the aquifer (like most petroleum compounds) or sinks to the bottom (like most solvents).

Groundwater remediation of dissolved and free product in New Jersey falls into two broad categories: monitored natural attenuation (MNA) and active remediation. These two remedial options are vastly different in terms of scope, cost, and timeframes.

Like soils, groundwater can be impacted by hazardous dissolved components but not require remediation. There are groundwater cleanup standards set by NJDEP for hundreds of hazardous compounds. If a hazardous compound dissolved in groundwater is reported in laboratory data *below* the cleanup standard for that compound, then groundwater remediation is not required.

The NJDEP classifies groundwater into three categories—potable, pristine, and brackish. The pristine areas are essentially the aquifers underlying the Pinelands in central/southern New Jersey where no hazardous compounds can be above natural background levels. The balance of the State, except for brackish coastline areas, is considered potable, where NJDEP's dissolved-phase standards apply. Groundwater is considered potable even in areas where it has been contaminated for decades from historic industrial activity such as in areas of Newark, Paterson, Camden, Elizabeth, and other manufacturing communities. NJDEP still requires that groundwater in these areas be remediated to potable standards. The theory is that these areas may have a potable use at some future date, and NJDEP does not want to *write off* the natural resources of the State, such as groundwater.

To determine groundwater quality, an SI and RI study must be implemented similar to the studies for soil remediation earlier. However, instead of soil borings, the installation of wells, or slotted pipes, into the ground is required, which intersect with the groundwater (like sticking a straw into the ground). These plastic pipes can be a temporary well point or a permanent monitoring well. Each option has pros and cons.

A temporary well point is a temporary slotted pipe (usually plastic), drilled directly in the ground, with a groundwater sample collected immediately after installation. The well point is then physically removed. These types of sampling points are relatively quick and easy to install and cost less than a conventional monitoring well. However, the significant drawback to a well point is that the resultant water sample pulled from this hastily installed point is often turbid, which means there is a significant amount of tiny suspended soil particles floating in the water (such as silt, clay and sand particles). When a groundwater sample from a well point is delivered to a laboratory to be analyzed, the liquid is supposed to be clear. If the laboratory groundwater sample is cloudy with sediment, some of those very small particles of soil can get into the testing machinery and commonly result in false-positive groundwater contaminant results. Essentially, the laboratory equipment is not sampling the water but the tiny bits of soil floating *in* the water. This can create havoc when determining whether the groundwater is really contaminated. Once false-positive groundwater data is generated, dismissing that data can be difficult without installing and sampling a properly constructed monitoring well.

Regardless of this drawback, a temporary well point may still be a preferable option to a groundwater monitoring well for the following reasons: a monitoring well requires a NJDEP well permit and a week or more to secure (and many due diligence timeframes do not allow for such delays); each monitoring well requires more time, care, and cost to install when compared to a well point because wells are often bigger than a well point; monitoring wells typically cannot be sampled until they settle for a two-week period after installation (another time delay); and monitoring wells eventually have to be properly sealed and paperwork filed with the NJDEP confirming proper closure, at further added costs.

On the other hand, the advantage to a monitoring well is that most wells are installed with a designed gravel or sand filter around the slotted pipe, which screens and filters out most of the fine soils from the surrounding geologic formation, eliminating or significantly reducing turbid samples. Hence the groundwater data from monitoring wells tend to be cleaner and more accurate. This is really important, because NJDEP groundwater cleanup standards are very low, and a proper well with a non-turbid sample is the best shot at meeting the NJDEP groundwater criteria.

Once the groundwater data is determined to be accurate and found to be above NJDEP standards, the person conducting remediation must determine how to best undertake the remediation. Typically, if the person has encountered floating or sinking free product, active remediation or removal of this product will be required. The remediation of sinking free product is one of the hardest remedial processes to undertake, because the contamination can be very deep below the ground and may be trapped in cracks within a bedrock aquifer, making it extremely difficult and costly to recover and/or remediate.

If dissolved-phase contaminated groundwater is encountered, the NJDEP will require a minimum of two consecutive rounds of groundwater data below cleanup standards before considering the groundwater remediated. This will require sampling of one or more wells multiple times.

Sampling at the upgradient or upstream edge of the groundwater flowing onto the subject property is often recommended because a person is *not* responsible for remediating contamination in groundwater that is flowing onto the site from an offsite, upgradient source. This is helpful in two circumstances. First, if a source of groundwater contamination is not found onsite but found to be migrating onsite from an offsite source, then the onsite party has no obligation to remediate the contamination migrating onsite. Instead, the offsite responsible party must complete the remediation. Second, if the source of contamination is from both an onsite and offsite source, the onsite party only has to remediate to the upgradient contamination level, not the NJDEP standard, since the upgradient contamination level would be considered the *background* cleanup level for the site, instead of the NJDEP cleanup standard. This exception can save *considerable* cleanup expenses.

Assuming the hazardous compounds do not fall below regulatory standards after two consecutive rounds, the implementation of a groundwater remedial plan will be required. This section will discuss MNA and active remediation.

MNA Groundwater Option

For MNA, the NJDEP will allow the contaminated groundwater to remain in place as long as there is no free product, no one is drinking or using the water, and the contaminants are not impacting an ecosystem (such as a nearby stream, wetland, and the like). The theory is that natural forces, such as biological and/or natural chemical degradation and dissolution and/or dispersion, will break down the dissolved-phase contaminants to below NJDEP standards over time. But there is an important caveat. An engineering model must be created using NJDEP-approved engineering calculations for the compounds in question that confirms the compounds will break down before they reach any person or sensitive ecosystem. The model and the timeframe calculated from it (usually a period of years) is called a Classification Exception Area (CEA).

The CEA is an institutional control that allows the groundwater to remediate on its own. From a practical standpoint, most NJDEP-approved CEA durations fall into the three to thirty-year range. During this natural degradation period, the person responsible for monitoring the CEA must sample the groundwater periodically to ensure the contaminants are breaking down as the engineering model has predicted. This sampling can take place monthly, quarterly, yearly, or even longer, depending upon circumstances. The sampling protocol will be set forth in the approved CEA document.

The expectation is that each sampling round should show lower contaminant levels, to prove the dissolved-phase compounds are degrading over time. However, expectations may not pan out. The predictive CEA model may not accurately predict onsite conditions and contaminant levels may not go down over time. If that occurs, the CEA model may have to be recalculated using more accurate onsite conditions data, and a new CEA model and timeframe may have to be developed.

Sometimes, however, a party undertaking cleanup may not be able to simply recalculate a failed CEA. For example, this may be the case if the CEA timeframe goes out to long, say beyond fifty to seventy-five years; the groundwater contaminant plume physically extends to a point that a person's drinking well or a surface ecosystem like a stream or wetland is impacted; the contaminant levels are actually increasing over time; and/or material free product appears in groundwater. If any of these events occur, NJDEP may not allow the MNA to continue. In that case, groundwater would have to be actively treated. Active groundwater remediation is usually the most expensive component of environmental remediation, which is why a MNA alternative is often first-pursued.

Active Groundwater Treatment Option

If MNA cannot be used, the least expensive active remedial method to employ involves a process called enhanced fluid recovery (EFR). EFR refers to using a vacuum truck, similar to a septic system pump-truck, to pump groundwater from one or more monitoring wells or from larger wells, called recovery wells (usually six inches or more in diameter). EFR essentially uses the monitoring wells or recovery wells as straws to suck out the contaminated groundwater at the source for disposal offsite. For low levels of free product and/or dissolved-phase contamination in localized spots, EFR is a relatively low cost, proven and successful remedial tool. But it is not a panacea and will not address wide-scale groundwater remediation.

For larger groundwater problems, in-situ procedures similar to those described for soils earlier (i.e., biological and/or chemical injections) are commonly used. There are also more sophisticated remedial processes using forced air, heat, cold (soil freezing) and granular activated carbon, among others. These systems, called air sparging, soil vapor extraction, or pump and treat, tend to be expensive, long-term solutions that have to operate for years. Often, these active systems are operated until the gross contamination is removed, and then the balance of the groundwater remedy is addressed with an MNA CEA.

Many times, especially in more developed/urban areas, groundwater contamination flows under neighboring downstream parcels. To delineate the extent of groundwater contamination to fashion an appropriate remedy, access to the neighboring property may be required to install soil borings, monitoring wells or both. The person undertaking remediation must get consent to access the neighboring property; usually through the execution of a former Access Agreement. If consent is denied, the remediation party can get a court order compelling the neighbor to provide access.

OTHER MEDIA

In addition to the soil and groundwater impacts noted earlier, a site can concurrently experience impacts on soil vapor/gas and indoor air, building materials, surface water, and sediment. Each of these additional media is briefly discussed here.

Soil Vapor/Gas and Indoor Air

If groundwater is contaminated with certain types of volatile hazardous compounds (e.g., compounds found in gasoline, fuel oil and solvents, such as dry cleaning fluids and other chemicals that readily vaporize), and these spills occurred close to, or under, occupied buildings at concentrations above certain NJDEP thresholds, the NJDEP requires an assessment of the hazardous vapors in the soil below the occupied buildings (i.e., below the slabs). If these sub-slab air samples exceed certain other threshold levels, then indoor air must be sampled for these same compounds, and active indoor air remedial systems must be installed to abate the compounds if they exist above indoor air threshold levels.

The vapor intrusion assessment radius drawn around contaminated monitoring wells may extend beyond property lines. Therefore, checking vapors and air in neighboring buildings is commonly required, again, usually employing formal Access Agreements. If there are elevated vapor levels in these offsite buildings raising health concerns, imagined or real, this issue may lead to litigation, especially at or near residential areas, schools, daycare facilities, nursing homes, and so on. Soil vapor remedial systems typically include installing sub-slab vapor collection and venting systems, similar in design and layout to common radon remedial systems.

Building Materials

The most important issue to remember in this media category is that concrete floors and walls, if stained or impacted by manufacturing operations and slated for demolition, will need to be sampled prior to demolition and offsite disposal. Sometimes a consultant may collect a chip sample of the heaviest stained concrete areas and assume that all the demolished concrete from walls and floors is contaminated to a similar degree. This can result in concrete disposal and/or reuse costs that are artificially high because it can capture large volumes of less contaminated or noncontaminated concrete and treat it as heavily contaminated concrete for disposal purposes. The better option is to sample the concrete in a partially crushed condition similar to the way the concrete would be disposed of or reused onsite.

Surface Water

Many sites, especially in urban locations, do not have a water feature on or bordering the property, so surface water is not commonly encountered. However, if a water feature is present at the property, it does not have to be automatically sampled. Sampling would only be required if there is evidence that it has been contaminated by onsite operations or has the potential for being impacted. Also, similar to sampling the groundwater at an upgradient location, many times the most important sampling to undertake in a surface water study is at the upstream location. If contamination is flowing past or onto the property from upstream, the property owner is not responsible for remediating it, since it is originating from an offsite source. In urban areas, it is common to have surface waters impacted by hazardous compounds at low levels, so this offsite-source issue is critical to confirm.

Sediment

NJDEP ecological-based soil/sediment standards are stricter than residential soil standards, sometimes by a factor of ten or more. These standards apply to sediment in streams, swales, wetland areas, and other environmentally sensitive locations. Even in urban areas, there are commonly small pockets of wetlands and/or drainage swales that may be subject to these extremely strict cleanup standards.

The best way to avoid remediating to these standards is to simply avoid sampling in sensitive ecosystems, unless there is a regulatory or contractual obligation or incentive to undertake such sampling. Once sampling is performed and data is generated, the results cannot be ignored. Remediation options for sediments are similar to soils, except for the stricter cleanup standards, which usually equates to more time and money spent on the remedial process.

RAO or NFA

The goal at the end of remediation process is to secure a RAO from the LSRP or a No Further Action (NFA) letter from the NJDEP if they have retained jurisdiction over the cleanup. Not all RAOs and NFAs are created equal.

The most comprehensive RAO to obtain at the end of the remediation process is a site-wide unconditional RAO. *Sitewide* means the RAO covers the *entire* site and not just for a portion of the site. The term *unconditional* is important as well. It means there is no Deed Notice or CEA associated with the site. It also means there is no soil or groundwater contamination remaining at the site, and the site meets all NJDEP standards. A conditional RAO means the site has a Deed Notice and/or a CEA, which comes with post-RAO monitoring requirements (i.e., the environmental remediation process will still have long-term legacy issues and costs).

An Area-of-Concern (AOC)-specific RAO simply covers the AOC(s) referenced in the RAO and nothing else. Again, it can be conditional or unconditional.

The date the RAO was issued is also important to note. If the RAO is dated years, or even just months, prior to the current date, and the site remained active, there *may* have been spills or discharges that occurred *after* the RAO was issued that are *not* covered by the RAO. This is an important point to consider, which may ultimately require an additional inspection of the property to ensure no new environmental AOCs exist.

Also, all RAOs have a three-year reopener period. This thirty-six-month post-RAO timeframe allows the NJDEP to audit any RAO issued by any LSRP; if the NJDEP feels the RAO issuance was technically unjustified, they can force the LSRP to rescind the same. This three-year reopener concept and timeframe have important transactional implications and should be addressed to the satisfaction of all parties in any purchase and sales contract, as well as in any loan documentation.

Even though LSRPs have replaced NJDEP Case Managers for most projects, NJDEP has retained control of certain remedial programs, including the remediation of residential heating USTs. Also, for recalcitrant responsible parties who have failed to hire an LSRP, the NJDEP may take over the remediation via a Direct Oversight program. In Direct Oversight, the NJDEP will decide *unilaterally* the remedial approach to be taken, regardless of cost, and charge the responsible party accordingly. NJDEP Direct Oversight is not a program one wants to find themselves in.

Similar to a RAO, a NFA can be issued as conditional or unconditional, sitewide or AOC-specific. The NFA does not have a reopener, but it can be rescinded if it was based upon false, inaccurate, or incomplete information submitted to the NJDEP. Rescission of a NJDEP-issued NFA by the NJDEP at a later date is uncommon, but it can happen if material information was withheld from the NJDEP.

Section 2

Managing Environmental Risk with Insurance

Gordon C. Duus, Esq.

Environmental insurance can be used to manage environmental risk, so that the insurer assumes the risks that the insured would prefer to avoid. In real estate and commercial transactions, and in litigation settlements, this may allow the parties to overcome issues concerning the allocation of environmental liability that are sometimes significant obstacles to closing a transaction or settling litigation.

NEGOTIATED POLICIES

Unlike most insurance policies, which are contracts of adhesion, environmental insurance policies are routinely negotiated with the insurer. To obtain coverage that best meets the needs of the insured, a knowledgeable environmental attorney who is familiar with the transaction or litigation, the environmental condition of the insured property, and the language of environmental insurance policies must negotiate the language of endorsements to the policy in an effort to ensure that the policy will cover the risks that need to be managed.

INSURANCE BROKER

To seek environmental insurance, one needs an insurance broker, as insurance companies typically will not communicate with a potential insured unless it has a broker. The selection of a broker with significant environmental insurance experience can save time and money. Experienced brokers may be found at Sterling Environmental Services, AON, Willis, and Marsh.[1]

An experienced broker can help select the companies from which to pursue coverage proposals (i.e., the least risk averse), choose the right coverage for the matter at hand, review the proposals to decide which appear to provide the best coverage as a starting point for negotiations, and preliminarily negotiate the language of the policy in an attempt to obtain the coverage sought by the insured. While the broker works for, and represents the interests of, the insured, as compensation they receive a percentage of the premium from the insurance company when the policy is bound and the premium paid. Brokers that have experience with environmental insurance can save the insured substantial legal fees by performing some of the tasks that would otherwise need to be performed by the insured's attorney.

POLLUTION LEGAL LIABILITY COVERAGE

Pollution legal liability (PLL) policies are the policies most often used to manage transactional environmental risks and can provide coverage for certain cleanup costs, third-party claims, and other environmental risks, discussed here. Although for years AIG (now Chartis) was the carrier most willing to provide the PLL policy coverage sought by insureds, recently ACE, XL, and Zurich have been the least risk-averse insurers that are best able to address transactional issues. Other companies now issuing PLL coverage include Beazley, Chubb, Berkley, C. V. Starr, Ironshore, and Great American. An experienced broker can help select the insurers from which coverage proposals should be sought in a particular situation. The broker can help review the proposals to decide which appear to provide the best coverage as a starting point for negotiations.

Coverage for Cleanup Costs

PLL policies provide two types of cleanup coverage for pollution occurring at the insured property: coverage for new discoveries of preexisting conditions and coverage for new conditions.

New Discoveries of Preexisting Conditions

PLL policies may cover the cost to clean up preexisting pollution conditions discovered after policy inception but not known to the insured prior to the inception of the policy period. The cost to clean up preexisting pollution conditions known to the insured prior to the inception of the policy period is typically excluded from coverage under a PLL policy but may be covered by cost-cap coverage, as discussed here. Sometimes it is possible to negotiate preexisting pollution coverage for conditions known to exist on the site that either have been the subject of regulatory closure (e.g., written confirmation from the appropriate state environmental agency that they have been cleaned up) or that the insurer concludes have little risk of giving rise to a cleanup obligation exceeding the deductible. If those pollution conditions later require further cleanup (e.g., the issue resolved by regulatory closure is reopened for some reason), then those costs would be covered. Further, some policies provide that known pollution conditions that are excluded from coverage at policy inception will be covered after both regulatory closure during the policy period and insurer approval if those issues are later reopened and further remediation is required.

An insured is required to disclose all known contamination as part of underwriting and in a signed application. There is ordinarily an exclusion in the policy for any discharges of pollution that were known to the insured but not disclosed to the insurance company prior to policy inception. In the exclusion, the insurer generally has the right to cancel the policy (and retain some or all of the premium) if the insured failed to make the required disclosure. For that reason, it is advisable to negotiate an endorsement to the policy that lists all of the documents in the insured's possession that were disclosed to the insurer documenting the presence of contamination at, or migrating from, the insured property. That way, when the insurance company expressly excludes from coverage certain discharges of pollution described in the documents listed on the endorsement, all other discharges of pollution described in the disclosed documents would ordinarily not be excluded from coverage. Further, it minimizes the risk that the policy would be canceled for failure to make full disclosure to the insurer by documenting what was disclosed.

New Conditions

New-conditions coverage is for the cost to clean up pollution first arising during the policy period. Typically, this is coverage for the risk that current operations on the insured property may cause pollution conditions. The insurer will ordinarily prepare a policy endorsement describing the types of operations for which there will be coverage, which may exclude coverage if the operations change. Even if the main transactional concern is the risk of discovering preexisting pollution conditions, by purchasing new-conditions coverage the insured can avoid future disputes with the insurer over the timing of the discharge of pollution for which coverage is sought.

Third-Party Claims for Bodily Injury or Property Damage

PLL policies ordinarily provide coverage for property damage and bodily injury to third parties arising from pollution conditions on, or migrating from, the insured property.

Property Damage

Property damage includes the "tangible" property of a third party, including real and personal property, as well as diminution of property value, stigma damages, loss of use, and natural resource damages. Cleanup costs are not included in the definition of third-party property damage because they are insured, if at all, under the cleanup coverage discussed earlier. Property damage coverage excludes damage to the insured property.

Bodily Injury

Bodily injury often includes disease, mental injury, or death resulting from a pollution condition. Third parties are often defined to exclude the employees of any named insured. While the employees of a named insured would ordinarily be covered by workers' compensation, the exclusion may result in one named insured having no insurance for claims by the employees of another named insured (which would *not* be covered by the workers' compensation policy of the insured who is not their

employer). Care must be taken during policy negotiation to avoid or minimize coverage gaps.

Claims from Any Pollution Condition

Although the cleanup of pollution conditions known to exist at policy inception are
often excluded from coverage under a PLL policy, ordinarily coverage can be negotiated for third-party claims for property damage and bodily injury arising from all
types of pollution conditions, including those that are known to the insured at the
inception of the policy.

Coverage for Legal Costs

PLL policies cover legal costs to defend claims covered by the policy. For example,
the policy would provide coverage for the legal fees incurred (i) overseeing the
remediation of pollution conditions on, or migrating from, the insured property; or
(ii) defending third-party claims for property damage or bodily injury. Generally, the
insurer has the right and obligation to defend the claim, usually with counsel chosen
by the insured where permitted by law. Even where no such law applies, some insurers
will consent to using the insured's counsel if they accept the legal fee rates ordinarily
paid by the insurer in that locale.

Other PLL Coverage

PLL coverage is also available for business interruption or loss of rent at the insured
property that arises from pollution conditions. To obtain this coverage, the insurer
often requires substantial information concerning the covered businesses. Uncertainty
about the nature of operations at the site or the tenants that will conduct them, or the
presence of significant known pollution conditions at the property, may make underwriting of coverage for business interruption or loss of rent difficult and premiums
uneconomical.

   PLL coverage can be obtained for claims arising from hazardous waste disposal at
locations not owned by the insured and for pollution conditions arising from transporting the hazardous waste to those locations.

COST-CAP COVERAGE

Cost-cap policies are sometimes used in contaminated property transactions to cover
the risk that the cost to clean up the contamination known to exist at the inception
of the policy will exceed the remedial cost estimates prepared prior to the inception
of the policy. Coverage is not provided until such remedial costs exceed the self-
insured retention ("SIR," similar to a deductible), and any coinsurance layer above
the SIR that must be paid before coverage attaches. Generally, the SIR is based
upon the price under a guaranteed cleanup cost contract (sometimes referred to as a
fixed price contract) entered into between an environmental consultant and the party

responsible for paying the cost of the cleanup, pursuant to which the environmental consultant agrees to pay all remedial costs in excess of the guaranteed cleanup cost or the amount of the fixed price contract. The party responsible for paying the cost of the cleanup pays the consultant all of the cleanup costs that constitute the SIR (i.e., up to the guaranteed cleanup cost or the amount of the fixed-price contract). The consultant under the guaranteed cleanup cost contract or fixed-price contract usually agrees to pay all costs in excess of the SIR, which would include any coinsurance layer under the cost-cap policy.

Several years ago, some insurers issued cost-cap coverage for certain consultants without either an approved cleanup plan or any coinsurance layer, usually for those consultants with a good claims history under cost-cap policies. Today, approved cleanup plans and a coinsurance layer are routinely required to obtain cost-cap coverage.

From 2008 to at least 2013, few insurers were willing to provide cost-cap coverage, as excessive claims made cost-cap coverage an unprofitable product for them. Recently, insurers' engineering and underwriting for cost-cap coverage have become problematic, the coinsurance layers have gotten larger (sometimes equal to the amount of the cleanup cost or SIR), the coverage limits are capped (e.g., not exceeding the amount of the cleanup cost or SIR), and the premiums have gotten significantly larger. The few insurers issuing cost-cap coverage have come to view it as catastrophic coverage. For these reasons, many of those involved with environmental insurance have concluded that, for most intents and purposes, cost-cap coverage is no longer available except from certain insurers under limited circumstances.

CONCLUSION

Practitioners whose clients are involved in real estate or commercial transactions or litigation where environmental pollution is, or could become, an issue should advise those clients how environmental insurance may be used to allocate environmental risks and increase the likelihood of closing the transaction or settling the case.

NOTE

1. The opinions of the author are not endorsed by the publisher or editors. The reader is advised to consult knowledgeable counsel for guidance.

Section 3

Taxation of Common Environmental Transactions

Franklin W. Boenning, Esq.
(9th Ed. Revisions), Alan Rubin, Esq.,
and Michael W. Cole, EA, Esq. (8th Ed.)

This section provides New Jersey practitioners with an overview of two common tax issues that arise in the course of environmental representation: (i) the appropriate tax accounting for remediation expenditures and (ii) determining the deductibility of a fine or penalty.[1] Expenses for remediation must undergo an analysis to determine whether they may be immediately deducted against gross income as an expense, or must be capitalized and depreciated over time. Fines and penalties are generally not deductible, unless payments are categorized as restitution or remediation, in which case certain requirements must be met to deduct the expense. In general New Jersey follows the federal rules and guidelines for the calculation of New Jersey taxable income.[2] Accordingly, a separate discussion is not provided when federal and state tax rules are substantially aligned.

REMEDIATION COSTS: CAPITALIZATION VERSUS DEDUCTIBILITY

In general, Section 162 of the Internal Revenue Code allows "expenses paid or incurred . . . in carrying on any trade or business" to be deducted from gross income.[3] Often, expenditures related to environmental investigation or remediation may be taken as an immediate deduction against income, but at times certain costs must be capitalized and recovered over time.[4] Determining if an expenditure qualifies as an immediate expense (and deducted) or capitalized (and depreciated over time) is often difficult because "[t]he distinction between capital expenditures and ordinary and necessary business expenses evades easy description."[5] Section 162(a) allows for necessary expenditures arising in the ordinary course of business to be deducted against income in the year incurred.[6] "An expenditure which returns the property to the state it was in before [] and which does not make the relevant property more valuable, more useful, or longer-lived, is usually deemed a deductible repair."[7] On the other hand,

§ 263 requires expenditures that "materially enhances the value, use, life expectancy, strength, or capacity" of an asset to be capitalized and recovered over time through amortization or depreciation.[8] "If an expense were to fall under the language of section 263(a), that section would 'trump' the deductibility provision of section 162(a) and the expense would have to be capitalized."[9]

Deductibility—Ordinary and Necessary Expenses under § 162(a)

Deductions are available for remediation costs that arise from "amounts paid for repairs and maintenance" in the ordinary course of business.[10] Remediation expenses may increase the value of an asset and require the application of the capitalization rules found in § 263. However, courts have created a carve-out from the capitalization rules by allowing a deduction for the remediation of assets contaminated by the taxpayer in the regular and ordinary course of business.[11] The expenses need not to occur on a regular schedule but may merely arise out of an ordinary transaction of the business, and therefore, even a one-time expense may qualify under these rules.[12] A deduction for the cost of remediation of real property may be available if:

1. The taxpayer contaminated the property in the ordinary course of business;
2. The remediation activities only restored property to pre-contamination status;
3. The remediation did not allow for a new use of the property;[13] and
4. The expenditure does not relate to a general plan of improvement.[14]

A break in the ownership of the contaminated land prior to remediation will often not restrict deductibility so long as the contamination occurred solely from the operations of the entity conducting the remediation.[15] When expenditures for remediation do not qualify as repair expenses the taxpayer should apply § 263(a) and capitalize the expenses.[16]

Capital Expenditures—Permanent Improvements under § 263(a)

Section 263(a) requires the capitalization of remediation costs for "permanent improvements or betterments made to increase the value of any property."[17] Expenditures that create a new asset,[18] make the property available for a new use,[19] relate to an overall plan for improvement,[20] remove a defect from prior use or user,[21] or increase the value of the property[22] will be capitalized by either assigning basis to a new asset or increasing the basis of one already in existence.[23] Capitalization is less beneficial to a taxpayer because it removes the immediate deduction available to repairs expenses and further makes all subsequent disposals subject to recapture rules.[24]

Land does not have a useful life as it cannot be exhausted, absent mining or other event, and is therefore not subject to cost recovery of § 167.[25] Thus, expenses that are capitalized to land will increase the taxpayer's tax basis in the land and will be recovered at the time of disposal.[26] Structural improvements or fixtures, such as a water treatment plant, constructed on real property during remediation are new assets and should be capitalized for depreciation.[27] Prior to 2012, § 198 allowed an election to deduct otherwise capital expenditures of remediation costs from ordinary income.[28]

The previously allowed deductions under § 198 are treated as depreciation for gain/loss calculations.[29] Section 198 has expired, and as such, the election to deduct capital expenditures related to environmental remediation is no longer available.[30]

Taxpayers That Produce Inventory Subject to § 263A

Section 263A requires certain taxpayers to capitalize on direct and indirect expenditures related to the production of inventory.[31] Section 263A will apply to remediation expenditures including an expenditure that would otherwise qualify as a deduction under § 162(a).[32] The Treasury Regulations to § 263A provide for the available methods to calculate the expenses "capitalized" in a given year.[33] Remediation expenses already capitalized under § 263 may still be impacted by § 263A. The annual cost recovery allowance may be treated as an indirect expense and thus included in the inventory value.[34] The application of § 263A on New Jersey tax returns should generally be identical because it is a "method of accounting."[35]

FINES FOR THE VIOLATIONS OF FEDERAL LAWS

Fines and penalties are generally not allowed as deductions in the calculation of taxable income. Only the "ordinary and necessary expenses paid or incurred . . . in carrying on any trade or business" are allowed as a deduction against income during the taxable year.[36] Since fines and penalties are not "ordinary and necessary" business expenses, they are generally not deductible. Code Section 162(f) states that "[n]o deduction . . . shall be allowed for any amount paid or incurred to, or at the direction of, a government [] entity in relation to the violation of any law" or for a government investigation into a potential violation of the law.[37]

Step One—Payments to the Government or Its Agents

A payment that originates from a liability to a government[38] will be nondeductible if it arose from the failure to comply with a substantive or procedural rule or regulation. The Treasury Regulations provide four examples of a fine or similar penalty which will be nondeductible, including amounts:

1. paid pursuant to a conviction, guilty plea, or plea of *nolo contendere* for a felony or misdemeanor crime;
2. paid as a civil penalty imposed by federal, state, or local law;
3. paid in settlement of actual or potential liability for a fine or penalty; or
4. forfeited as collateral posted in a proceeding which could result in the imposition of such a fine or penalty.[39]

A fine or penalty not arising from a governmental source (e.g., pursuant to a private contract) will generally be deductible as an ordinary and necessary business expense under § 162(a) since it is not imposed by a government (foreign or domestic) or an entity serving as an agency or instrumentality of a government.[40] Accordingly, a fine or penalty issued by the EPA or NJDEP is usually nondeductible because such agencies are covered under the awning of "government" for both federal and state tax calculations.[41]

It should be noted that the government need not "pocket" the funds from the violation;[42] instead, the government must only exercise control of the payment. Consequently, payments to a nongovernmental entity as a result of a settlement with a governmental entity will be considered fines or penalties if the payment to the nongovernmental entity is in lieu of a payment to satisfy a governmental obligation.[43] Courts have thus focused on the quid pro quo nature of the transaction in applying § 162(f) in settlement agreements.[44]

Step Two—Differentiating between Punitive and Remedial Natures

Of course, it is easy to determine when payments of fines or penalties are made to a government. For that reason, the bulk of most court decisions appear to focus on the "remedial or punitive nature review" of fine and penalty expenditures.[45] Courts have historically considered fines to be related to criminal actions or "imposed for the purposes of enforcing the law and as punishment for a violation thereof" and therefore nondeductible.[46] Similarly, courts will find that expenditures related to punitive damages are instituted to "punish or deter."[47] And thus, punitive damages have been held to be nondeductible under § 162(f) as violations of public policy.[48] Public policy, in contrast, has not been violated by the payment of compensatory, remedial, and administrative compliance-driven damages.[49] Thus, payment of restitution, compensation, or remediation or to promote administrative compliance with regulations can be deductible as "ordinary and necessary" business expenses. Each law requires courts to look at the legislative intent to establish the purpose the payment "ultimately serves."[50]

Violations of environment-related rules are often punitive in nature, seeking to punish violators and deter future noncompliance.[51] For example, penalties under the Clean Air Act[52] are designed to punish violators of the law and therefore payments of these assessments are nondeductible.[53] Payments related to the timing of compliance are generally allowable as ordinary business expenses.[54] For instance, late filing fees for submission forms are designed to promote compliance and is, therefore, a deduction allowable under § 162(a).[55] In the event that payment could serve both punitive and remedial goals, the ultimate purposes of the payment are considered.[56] As a consequence, a singular payment may allocate specific amounts as deductible and others as nondeductible as required. [57]

The enactment of Section 13306(a) of the Tax Cuts and Jobs Act in 2017 amended Section 162(f), leaving the "punitive versus remedial" test set forth above but adding an additional hurdle to maintain the deductibility of the payment. The new section retains the old language that fines or penalties are generally nondeductible (except to the extent the taxpayer can establish what portion of the payment constitutes restitution for damage or is paid to come into compliance with law) but adds the requirement that such payment must be *identified in the court order or settlement agreement as restitution or an amount paid to come into compliance*. Thus, the revised Section 162(f)(2)(A) sets forth three criteria to overcome the disallowance, and thus allow a deduction, for payments made to the government. First, the taxpayer must establish that the amount paid or incurred constitutes restitution (including remediation of property) for damage or harm caused by violation (or potential violation) of any law or paid to come into compliance with any law which was violated.[58] Second, amounts paid must be identified as restitution or an amount paid to come into compliance in the settlement agreement or court order.[59] Third, in the case of restitution for failure to pay any tax, the payment is deductible to the extent the tax payment would have been deductible.[60] The final sentence of this section concludes that the mere identification in the settlement agreement alone (requirement 2) *shall not be sufficient* to conclusively establish that the first criteria is met. Therefore, practitioners are advised to ensure that sufficient findings of restitution or compliance are included in such settlement agreements.

The Tax Cuts and Jobs Act also added a new section, 6050X, to the Internal Revenue Code which requires government agencies to report each settlement amount greater than $600 that is deductible to the IRS and the relevant taxpayer on a form akin to Form 1099. Such form is required to set forth (1) the amount to which Section 162(f)(1) applies (i.e., not deductible); (2) the amount that constitutes restitution or remediation of property (i.e., deductible); and (3) any amount required to be paid for the purpose of coming into compliance with any law or involved in the investigation or inquiry (i.e., deductible). The findings and identification requirement set forth in 162(f)(2)(A) and subsequent reporting by the agency responsible for the settlement or court order should eliminate many disputes over the questions of deductibility since the parties will have carefully considered the facts and language long before the payments are made and tax returns filed.

Fines and Penalties for Violations of Environmental Laws under New Jersey Statute

New Jersey generally follows the federal law on the deductibility of fines and penalties for environmental violations. N.J.S.A. 54:10A-4(k)(2)(G)(i) disallows the deduction of any civil, administrative, or criminal fine or penalty related to environmental law violations[61] or treble damages for failure to comply with a Spill Act Directive to remove or arrange for removal of an unauthorized discharge.[62] After calculating federal taxable income these amounts, to the extent deducted for federal purposes, must be added back to determine New Jersey taxable income.[63]

Expenses Related to the Defense of a Position

Legal fees and expenses related to defending a criminal or civil matter are generally deductible under § 162(a) as ordinary and necessary business expenses when arising from a trade or business.[64] Public policy is not offended when a person or corporation pays counsel for its defense, as it would frustrate public policy of the adversary system of criminal justice not to allow persons charged with a crime or violation to have counsel to represent them.[65] Consequently, legal fees and expenses related to the defense of a governmental claim against a trade or business are not penalties under § 162(f).[66] Also, legal expenses related to compliance with a settlement or judgment are deductible because such actions are "part in parcel" of a proceeding.[67]

NOTES

1. *IRS Circular 230 Disclosure*: This chapter is designed to present general rules and is not intended to constitute legal advice or tax advice applicable to any particular situation. Any tax advice contained in this document is not intended or written to be used, and cannot be used, for the purpose of (i) avoiding penalties under the Internal Revenue Code or (ii) promoting, marketing, or recommending to another party any transaction or matter that is contained in this document. Any use of the words could, should, would, and so on are for discussion purposes only and does not constitute advice that should be relied upon nor indicate required actions that IRS or the recipient must or shall take. A tax expert should be consulted to ascertain the proper application of these continuously fluctuating laws to your particular situation.

2. N.J.S.A. 54:10A-4(k); see also *Koch v. Dir., Div. of Taxation*, 722 A.2d 918 (1999).

3. *Comm'r v. Tellier*, 383 U.S. 687, 694 (1966).

4. *INDOPCO, Inc. v. Comm'r*, 503 U.S. 79, 83-84 (1992).

5. *Dominion Res., Inc. v. United States*, 219 F.3d 359, 370 (4th Cir. 2000).

6. I.R.C. § 162(a).

7. *Plainfield—Union Water Co. v. Comm'r*, 39 T.C. 333, 337 (1962).

8. *Plainfield—Union Water Co. v. Comm'r*, 39 T.C. 333, 338 (1962).

9. *PNC Bancorp, Inc. v. Comm'r*, 212 F.3d 822, 827 (3rd Cir. 2000).

10. Treas. Reg. § 1.162-4T(a).

11. *United Dairy Farmers, Inc. v. United States*, 267 F.3d 510, 519 (6th Cir. 2001).

12. *INDOPCO, Inc. v. Comm'r*, 503 U.S. 79, 85-86 (1992).

13. *United Dairy Farmers, Inc. v. United States*, 267 F.3d 510, 519 (6th Cir. 2001) (summarizing relevant administrative guidance and case precedence); see also Dominion Res., Inc. v. United States, 219 F.3d 359, 370 (4th Cir. 2000).

14. *Norwest Corp. & Subsidiaries v. Comm'r*, 108 T.C. 265, 280 (1997).

15. I.R.S. Tech. Adv. Mem. 9627002 (July 5, 1996); *United Dairy Farmers, Inc. v. United States*, 267 F.3d 510, 519 (6th Cir. 2001).

16. *PNC Bancorp, Inc. v. Comm'r*, 212 F.3d 822, 827 (3rd Cir. 2000).

17. I.R.C. § 263(a); see also Letter Ruling 200108029 (full discussion of repairs and maintenance compared against capital expenditures is beyond scope of this discussion); *and further* I.R.S. Tech. Adv. Mem. 9315004 (for additional discussion as it relates to environmental cleanup).

18. *Comm'r v. Lincoln Savings & Load Ass'n*, 403 U.S. 345, 354 (1971).

19. *United Dairy Farmers, Inc. v. United States*, 267 F.3d 510, 519 (6th Cir. 2001) (summarizing relevant administrative guidance and case precedence); *see also Dominion Res., Inc. v. United States*, 219 F.3d 359, 370 (4th Cir. 2000).

20. *Norwest Corp. & Subsidiaries v. Comm'r*, 108 T.C. 265, 280 (1997).

21. *United Dairy Farmers, Inc. v. United States*, 267 F.3d 510, 519 (6th Cir. 2001) ("[W]hen a taxpayer improves property defects that were present when the taxpayer acquired the property, the remediation of those defects are capital in nature.") *Id.* at 518.

22. *Cinergy Corp. v. United States*, 55 Fed. Cl. 489, 517 (2003).

23. I.R.C. § 263(a) and Let. Rul. 200108029.

24. See generally I.R.C. § 263A(e), 1245, and 1250.

25. Treas. Reg. § 1.167(a); see also I.R.C. § 167.

26. I.R.C. § 1001.

27. I.R.C. § 167 and § 168(c).

28. I.R.C. § 198.

29. I.R.C. § 198(e).

30. I.R.C. § 198(h)

31. I.R.C. § 263A(a)(1)(A); see also Treas. Reg. § 1.263A-1(c)(3) and § 1.263A-1(e)(3).

32. Rev. Rul. 2004-18.

33. Rev. Rul. 2004-18.

34. *Author's Note*: The expansive nature of § 263A and the multiple allocation and calculation methods are beyond the scope of this article. Consult with a tax professional for proper application.

35. *Sitar v. Dir., Div. of Tax.*, 2009 WL 2365983, at *7 (N.J. Super. Ct. App. Div. Aug. 4, 2009 Unpublished).

36. 26 U.S.C. 162(a).

37. 26 U.S. C. 162(f).

38. *Taley Indus., Inc. v. Comm'r*, 116 F.3d 382, 385-86 (9th Cir. 1997); see also TAM 118420-05 (Mar. 31, 2006).

39. Treas. Reg. § 1.162-21(b)(1)(i) et seq.

40. Payments that do not qualify as a fine or penalty arising from the government should be reviewed under the applicable law for proper treatment.

41. Treas. Reg. § 1.162-21(a); see also *Colt Indus., Inc. v. United States*, 11 Cl. Ct. 140 (1986), *aff'd*, 880 F.2d 1311 (10th Cir. 1989).

42. *Waldman*, at 1389.

43. *Waldman*, at 1389.

44. *Allied-Signal, Inc. v. Comm'r*, T.C. Memo 1992-204, 95-1 USTC ¶ 50,151 (*unpublished*).

45. *True v. United States*, 894 F.2 1197, 1204 (10th Cir. 1990).

46. *Bailey v. Comm'r*, 756 F.2d 44, 47 (6th Cir. 1985).

47. *Mid. Atl. Distributions Inc. v. Comm'r*, 72 T.C. 1136, 1143 (1979).

48. *Mid. Atl. Distributions Inc. v. Comm'r*, 72 T.C. 1136, 1143 (1979).

49. *S. Pac. Trans. Co. v. Comm'r*, 75 T.C. 497, 652 (1980); see also Treas. Reg. 1.162-21(b)(2).

50. I.R.S. Tech. Adv. Mem. 2006-29-030 (Mar. 31, 2006) (citing *Taley Indus., Inc. v. Comm'r*, 116 F.3d 382, 385-86 (9th Cir. 1997), and *Mason Dixon Lines, Inc. v. United States*, 708 F.2d 1043,147 (6th Cir. 1983).

Author's Note: The reference to a Technical Advice Memorandum occurs because it is the most complete review of the Service's position on fines and penalties as they related to environmental remediation. Please be aware that citation is to a nonbinding authority for both the Taxpayer and the Service and therefore it may not be relied upon by anyone other than the taxpayer for whom it was composed. The unsettled nature of these transactions requires a thorough review of precedence and facts to establish the appropriate tax treatment. Based upon the limited case precedence, courts appear to be inclined to first apply the Origin and Character of the Claim test followed by a separate determination to establish if the fine or penalty is punitive or remedial in nature. *Inds., Inc. v. Comm'r*, 116 F.3d 382, 385-86 (9th Cir. 1997). The limited scope and space of this publication does not facilitate a full discussion of this method nor its slightly altered use as it applies to environmental remediation expenditures.

51. See generally I.R.S. Tech. Adv. Mem. 2006-29-030 (Mar. 31, 2006); see also *Colt Indus., Inc. v. United States*, 11 Cl. Ct. 140 (1986), *aff'd*, 880 F.2d 1311 (10th Cir. 1989) (Discussion of punitive nature of the Clean Water Act and Clean Air Act.), *True v. United States*, 894 F.2d 1197 1206 (10th Cir. 1990) (Clean Water Act had a punitive purpose as per the legislative intent.), *S & B Restaurant Inc. v. Comm'r*, 73 T.C. 1226, 1232 (1980) (The application of Pennsylvania laws and regulations of environmental penalties requires the same review as federal laws. While not punitive in this case there were other parts of the Clean Streams Law that would constitute nondeductible punitive fines.).

52. Clean Air Act 42 U.S.C. § 7401 (1970 as amended).

53. *Colt Indus, Inc. v. United States*, 11 Cl. Ct. 140 (1986), *aff'd*, 880 F.2d 1311 (10th Cir. 1989).

54. *True v. United States*, 894 F.2 1197, 1204 (10th Cir. 1990).

55. *Allied Signal Inc. v. Comm'r*, T.C.M. 1992-204 (1992), 95-1 USTC ¶ 50,151 (unpublished) (citing *Waldman v. Comm'r*, 88 T.C. 1384, 1387 (1987)).

56. *Taley Indus., Inc. v. Comm'r*, 116 F.3d 382, 385-86 (9th Cir. 1997); see also *S & B Restaurant, Inc. v. Comm'r*, 73 T.C. 1226, 1232 (1980).

57. *True v. United States*, 603 F. Supp. 1370, 1374 (D. Wyo. 1985), *reversed on other grounds*, 894 F.2d 1197 1206 (10th Cir. 1990) (citing *United States v. Texas Pipeline Co.*, 611 F.2d 345, 347 (10th Cir. 1979).

58. 26 U.S.C. 162(f)(2)(A)(i).

59. 26 U.S.C. 162(f)(2)(A)(ii).

60. 26 U.S.C. 162(f)(2)(A)(iii).

61. N.J.S.A. 54:10A-4(k)(2)(G)(i) (This exception does not apply, and fines or penalties may be deducted, if issued for violations that occurred due to Acts of God beyond the reasonable control of the violator [e.g., fire, riot, sabotage, flood, storm event, or natural cause]).

62. N.J.S.A. 54:10A-4(k)(2)(G)(ii).

63. N.J.S.A. 54:10A-4(k)(2)(G)(i).

64. *Allied Signal Inc. v. Comm'r*, T.C.M. 1992-204 (1992), 95-1 USTC ¶ 50,151 (unpublished).

65. *Comm'r v. Tellier*, 383 U.S. 687, 694 (1966).

66. Treas. Reg. 1.162-21(b)(2).

67. *Allied Signal Inc. v. Comm'r*, T.C.M. 1992-204 (1992), 95-1 USTC ¶ 50,151 (unpublished).

Chapter 3

Funding/Financing/Incentives

Section 1

Public Financing

Robert Beinfeld, Esq., and David B. Thompson

This chapter focuses on the financing of infrastructure and environmental capital projects. Infrastructure and environmental capital projects can be financed in several different ways some of which depend upon the nature of the owner of the facilities to be financed. Funding sources include owner equity, borrowed monies, government grant, and incentive programs. This chapter describes procedures and alternatives relating to borrowed monies.

The nature of the owner of the infrastructure or environmental capital project is important in determining the potential lenders, the processes and procedures for obtaining monies, and the cost of such monies. Certain types of owners can borrow funds on a tax-exempt basis (i.e., under federal tax laws, the lender does not have to pay income tax on the received interest income). Since a tax-exempt loan is financially better for the lender than a taxable loan, the lender will offer a lower interest rate and the owner will realize a cheaper source of capital. In general, governmental entities and certain nongovernmental entities providing public services, such as hospitals, universities, not-for-profit corporations, regulated public utility companies, and redevelopers, can benefit from tax-exempt loans.

GOVERNMENTAL ENTITIES

Governmental entities in New Jersey that are authorized to borrow money for infrastructure and environmental capital projects are primarily counties, municipalities, municipal sewerage authorities, municipal and county utility authorities, county improvement authorities, municipal redevelopment agencies, and various State authorities and agencies. These governmental entities can be divided into two broad categories: governmental entities with taxing power (i.e., counties and municipalities) and governmental entities without taxing power (i.e., sewerage authorities, utility authorities, improvement authorities, redevelopment agencies, and State authorities and agencies).

Governmental entities with taxing power are authorized to borrow money for infrastructure and environmental capital projects under and pursuant to the provisions of the Local Bond Law.[1] The governing body of the county or municipality would authorize borrowing by passing on first reading a bond ordinance that, among other things, describes the capital project and authorizes an amount of debt to be incurred for the project. The governing body at a subsequent meeting would hold a public hearing on the bond ordinance after advertised notice and would pass the bond ordinance on second reading. The bond ordinance would become effective twenty days after a notice of adoption is published.

Governmental entities without taxing power are authorized to borrow money for infrastructure and environmental capital projects under and pursuant to the provisions of their respective enabling acts including the Sewerage Authorities Law,[2] the Municipal and County Utilities Authorities Law,[3] the County Improvement Authorities Law,[4] the Local Redevelopment and Housing Law,[5] and applicable State authority and agency statutes. The governing body of the authority or agency would authorize borrowing by adopting a bond resolution that, among other things, describes the capital project and authorizes an amount of debt to be incurred for the project. If the governmental entity is not a State authority or agency (i.e., if the governmental entity is a "local" authority or agency), the bond resolution and borrowing plan in most cases must be submitted for review by the New Jersey Local Finance Board within the Division of Local Government Services in the Department of Community Affairs.[6] The Local Finance Board would hold a hearing on the proposed borrowing and issue written findings which may contain recommendations. The findings and recommendations, if any, must then be reviewed by the members of the governing body of the local authority or agency. The bond resolution would become effective after adoption by the governing body of the entity and usually, in the case of a State authority or agency, the approval of the Governor.

After the bond ordinance or bond resolution is effective, the governmental entity can borrow money on either a temporary, short-term basis or a permanent, long-term basis. In general, the process for borrowing on a short-term basis is less involved than the process for borrowing on a long-term basis, and governmental entities with taxing power can secure loans more easily than governmental entities without taxing power. A short-term borrowing for a governmental entity is accomplished by the issuance of bond anticipation notes or similar obligations. In the case of counties and municipalities, bond anticipation notes must mature within one year. The source of payment for bond anticipation notes is either long-term bonds, which would be paid over the course of several years, or other similar "renewal" bond anticipation notes. Bond anticipation notes may also be paid in part or in whole through an appropriation in the annual budget. In general, bond anticipation notes of a county or a municipality may be renewed for a period not exceeding ten years. The principal amount of the bond anticipation notes must be reduced, in an amount calculated in accordance with the provisions of the Local Bond Law, on the third and each subsequent renewal anniversary of the initial borrowing. For governmental entities with taxing power, the borrowing process for short-term bond anticipation notes is often less involved than the borrowing process for long-term bonds as certain notice, credit rating, public bidding, and disclosure requirements may not be applicable. Various factors relating to the particular circumstances of the borrowing, such as the credit position and history of the governmental entity, the size of the borrowing, market conditions, and investor preferences, should be taken into account in choosing the bond anticipation note borrowing process that is likely to produce the lowest interest rate.

The lender (i.e., the commercial bank or investment bank) to a county or municipality in connection with a long-term borrowing is required to be determined pursuant to a competitive "best interest rate" bidding process. The lender to a county or municipality in connection with a short-term borrowing or to an authority or agency in connection with a short-term or long-term borrowing is not required to be determined pursuant to a competitive interest rate bidding process and may be selected at the discretion of the governmental entity. The governmental entity will typically evaluate several factors when deciding whether or not to negotiate an interest rate directly with a lender of its choosing or to utilize a competitive interest rate bidding process to select a lender and an interest rate. The governmental entity usually engages specialized financial professionals, such as a bond counsel and a financial advisor, to assist it with this decision as well as several other aspects of the borrowing process including the preparation and submission of materials to credit rating agencies and the preparation of a disclosure document, known as an official statement, meeting the requirements of federal securities laws for distribution to potential investors.

Short-term bond anticipation notes and long-term bonds sold by a county or a municipality are, in almost all instances, full faith and credit obligations and the county or the municipality is obligated to levy ad valorem taxes upon all the taxable property within its jurisdiction for the payment of the principal of and interest on its bond anticipation notes and bonds without limitation as to rate or amount (i.e., amounts necessary to pay such principal and interest are required to be appropriated each year in the annual budget and are a specific exclusion from the tax levy cap). Short-term bond anticipation notes and long-term bonds sold by an authority or agency are not secured by the power to levy taxes but are instead often secured by the revenues produced by the financed assets (i.e., user fees and charges) or by the physical assets themselves. In order to provide additional security to investors and thus reduce the interest rate associated with such "revenue" notes and bonds, a local authority or agency without taxing power may enter into an agreement with a county or municipality that requires such entity with taxing power to make payments sufficient to pay the notes and bonds in certain circumstances. This type of agreement must be expressly authorized by the enabling statute of the particular local authority or agency and, depending on the circumstances, may be referred to as a service agreement, a deficiency agreement, a guaranty agreement, or a subsidy agreement.

As described earlier, the interest on bond anticipation notes and bonds of all governmental entities is usually exempt from federal income taxation.

OTHER ENTITIES

Various nongovernmental entities that provide public services, such as hospitals, universities, not-for-profit corporations, regulated public utility companies, and redevelopers, are eligible under federal tax law to benefit from tax-exempt financing for infrastructure and environmental capital projects. Unlike governmental entities that can borrow money directly, nongovernmental entities must borrow money "through" a governmental entity in order to receive the tax-exemption benefit. In New Jersey, municipalities and counties generally are prohibited from borrowing money on behalf of nongovernmental entities. Nongovernmental entities, therefore, must identify a different governmental entity to act as an on behalf of borrower or "conduit issuer." The primary conduit issuers in New Jersey are the New Jersey Health Care Facilities Financing Authority, the New Jersey Educational Facilities Authority, the New Jersey Economic Development Authority, the New Jersey Infrastructure Bank (formerly, the New Jersey Environmental Infrastructure Trust), various county improvement authorities, and various local redevelopment and housing agencies. The rules and regulations of each governmental conduit issuer describe in detail the types of entities and capital projects that such conduit issuer is authorized to finance.

In general, the New Jersey Health Care Facilities Financing Agency undertakes borrowings on behalf of not-for-profit hospitals,[7] the New Jersey Educational Facilities Authority undertakes borrowings on behalf of State universities and other not-for-profit institutions of higher education,[8] the New Jersey Economic Development Authority undertakes borrowings on behalf of entities whose projects increase employment and provide economic growth,[9] various county improvement authorities undertake borrowings on behalf of certain not-for-profit entities,[10] and local redevelopment and housing agencies undertake borrowings on behalf of certain qualified redevelopers.[11] In addition, the State has established a conduit issuer known as the New Jersey Infrastructure Bank (formerly, the New Jersey Environmental Infrastructure Trust) specifically for funding infrastructure and environmental capital projects.[12] The I-Bank provides the borrower an interest rate that is typically at least one-half or three-quarters less than the interest rate available from other lenders due to certain State subsidies and programmatic features. Borrowers from the I-Bank include all types of governmental entities and nongovernmental entities. The rules, regulations, and policies of the I-Bank describe the eligible borrowers, the eligible projects, the minimum borrower credit requirements, and the somewhat unique borrowing process.

The borrowing process for nongovernmental entities borrowing through one of the aforementioned conduit issuers, other than the I-Bank, is similar to the borrowing process for governmental issuers without taxing power described earlier. The advantage of borrowing through a governmental conduit issuer is that the nongovernmental entity will realize interest rate savings as a result of the tax exemption. Possible disadvantages of borrowing through a governmental conduit issuer include schedule inflexibility, political and policy concerns, additional review and procedural compliance requirements, additional fees and the applicability of various State bidding, employment, reporting, and other laws.

TYPE OF LOAN

In general, and in connection with any short-term or long-term borrowing by any governmental or nongovernmental entity, the loan can be characterized as either a direct purchase or a public offering. A direct purchase often involves one sophisticated, institutional lender such as a commercial bank. This type of loan is exempt from the disclosure requirements of federal securities laws. A public offering involves the sale of securities (i.e., bonds or bond anticipation notes) to many investors through a broker-dealer acting as an underwriter and is subject to the rules and regulations of various federal and state regulatory bodies including the Securities and Exchange Commission. As a result of these regulatory requirements, a public offering typically requires more documentation and professional involvement than a direct purchase. In most cases, borrowings for governmental entities, with or without taxing power, are undertaken by means of a public offering either because of a requirement in New Jersey law or because under the circumstances it tends to provide the lowest interest rate. Nongovernmental entities that borrow through conduit issuers usually have fewer statutory constraints and may have financial and credit considerations that make a direct purchase borrowing more suitable.

PUBLIC OFFERING

As described earlier, most borrowings for infrastructure and environmental capital projects in New Jersey are undertaken by means of a public offering of municipal securities. Over time, the public offering process has become more complex and complicated.

One reason for the increased complexity is the changed nature of the public offering marketplace itself. The changed nature of the marketplace has made it increasingly challenging for many governmental entities and nongovernmental entities to access capital by means of a public offering. The event that precipitated this change was the credit crisis of 2008 and the collapse of the real estate market. This event irrevocably damaged the credit and bankrupted almost all of the independent bond insurance companies whose "AAA"-rated guarantees were ubiquitous in the municipal securities marketplace and highly relied upon by investors. The guarantees were purchased by governmental and nongovernmental entities and, in effect, transformed their municipal securities into the highest quality of investment-grade debt. When the bond insurers went bankrupt, which was caused by guarantees on defaulting real estate debt as opposed to guarantees on tax-exempt municipal debt, the bond insurance policies became worthless and the municipal securities were no longer assigned a "AAA" credit rating. As a result, investors in the municipal public offering marketplace have changed the focus of their credit analysis. Investors now focus more on the debt-paying ability of the actual obligor as opposed to the debt-paying ability of the bond insurer. The credit rating of the governmental entity (or, in the case of a conduit issuer, the nongovernmental entity underlying obligor) has, therefore, become a more crucial factor in the determination of the interest rate. Consequently, in addition to preparing an official statement (i.e., a public disclosure document that sets forth all material information concerning the governmental entity or the nongovernmental entity underlying obligor and the infrastructure or environmental capital project being financed), it is often advisable to make a detailed, personalized presentation to the municipal bond rating agency or agencies that will assign a credit rating. This detailed and personalized rating agency presentation allows the governmental entity or the nongovernmental entity underlying obligor to go beyond the objective information that is included in the official statement and to describe in more subjective terms its financial information and managerial capabilities.

A second reason for the increased complexity of public offerings is the changed nature of the federal securities law regulatory environment. There has been a significant increase in the last several years of federal regulation, activity, and enforcement in the municipal securities area. Securities regulators such as the Securities and Exchange Commission and the Municipal Securities Regulatory Board generally have limited power to directly regulate the issuance of municipal securities. These agencies, however, indirectly regulate the issuance of municipal securities through their power to regulate broker-dealers that underwrite and trade municipal securities. Recently, these agencies have used their indirect power to influence and cause a change in the public offering process for municipal securities. For example, the Securities and Exchange Commission has adopted a rule that holds a broker-dealer responsible for determining that the official statement includes the material information necessary for the ultimate investor to make an informed decision concerning its purchase of the municipal security. In addition, by rule of the Securities and Exchange Commission many broker-dealers are required to confirm that the governmental entity or the nongovernmental entity underlying obligor has agreed to, and in fact does, provide certain financial information and notice of certain events in the form of continuing disclosure to the public marketplace by using a specially designated website maintained by the Municipal Securities Rulemaking Board. Even though these and other rules apply to the broker-dealer community, they effectively increase the requirements applicable to governmental entities and nongovernmental entity underlying obligors in public offerings. The governmental entity or the nongovernmental entity underlying obligor must undertake the necessary action, work, and document preparation so that the broker-dealer will be able to satisfy the applicable federal regulatory requirements. Failure on the part of a governmental entity or a nongovernmental entity underlying obligor to undertake such steps may result in its inability to borrow monies by means of a public offering.

In addition, there can be a significant liability to a governmental entity or nongovernmental entity underlying obligor in connection with a public offering of municipal securities for disseminating misleading initial or continuing disclosure information. In recent years, the Securities and Exchange Commission has expanded its monitoring and examination of public offerings of municipal securities to assure compliance with the antifraud provisions of the federal securities laws. Governmental entities and nongovernmental entity underlying obligors have, therefore, become increasingly diligent and attentive to their initial and continuing disclosure obligations.

A third reason for the increased complexity of public offerings and direct purchases, as well, is the changed nature of the federal tax law regulatory environment. There has been heightened attention in the last several years from the section of the Internal Revenue Service charged with monitoring compliance with the tax-exempt debt provisions of the Internal Revenue Code. The cases, statutes, rulings, regulations, proposed regulations, private letter rulings, guidance releases, and other materials governing initial issuance and post-issuance federal tax law requirements are highly detailed, technical, and specialized.

Furthermore, recent negotiations on federal budget matters involving the Senate, the House of Representatives, the President, and various committees have resulted in several different budgetary proposals all of which would affect in one way or another the tax exemption of municipal securities. Governmental entities and nongovernmental entity underlying obligors must evaluate and assess the current and future effects of these proposals prior to undertaking a public offering, or direct purchase, of municipal securities.

In summary, the tax-exempt financing of infrastructure and environmental capital projects provides a low-cost opportunity to many types of governmental entities and nongovernmental entity underlying obligors. These tax-exempt financings can be undertaken in a number of different ways that involve various degrees of complexity, documentation, responsibility, and liability. It is, therefore, important for governmental entities and nongovernmental entity underlying obligors to consult with their financial professionals and advisors when considering the method of financing an infrastructure or environmental capital project.

NOTES

1. N.J.S.A. 40A:2-1 *et seq.*
2. N.J.S.A. 40:14A-1 *et seq.*
3. N.J.S.A. 40:14B-1 *et seq.*
4. N.J.S.A. 40:37A-44 *et seq.*
5. N.J.S.A. 40:12A-1 *et seq.*
6. N.J.S.A. 40A:5A-1 *et seq.*
7. N.J.S.A. 26:2I-1 *et seq.*
8. N.J.S.A. 18A:72A-1 *et seq.*
9. N.J.S.A. 34:1B:1 *et seq.*
10. N.J.S.A. 40:37A-44 *et seq.*
11. N.J.S.A. 40:12A-1 *et seq.*
12. N.J.S.A. 58:11B 1 *et seq.*

Section 2

Real Estate Development Financing

George T. Vallone

This chapter will cover the fundamentals of real estate development finance from the perspective of the developer. The role of the developer is to locate development opportunities where land, with or without existing buildings on it, can be purchased and improved by building ground-up new buildings or renovating existing buildings, to a use that will have a finished value sufficiently in excess of the cost to meet the yield expectations of the equity capital plus a profit for the developer.

A key to structuring real estate deals that will attract equity capital from investors and debt capital from lenders is understanding the influence of risk on the cost of capital. This chapter will begin with an understanding of the risk management process wherein cost and revenue risk is classified, identified, quantified, and then reduced or eliminated with the goal being to increase the availability and reduce the cost of capital. Financing real estate development using a model called the capital stack, and understanding the purpose of the different layers in the stack, will be explained as well as the influence of risk on the cost associated with each layer of the stack. Negotiation strategies with capital providers, alternative financing strategies, and structured seller-financed transactions will be explained, in conjunction with the principles of financial metrics and the effect of leverage on yield.

REAL ESTATE INVESTING

Real estate investing is the process of (a) purchasing vacant or underutilized land and maximizing its value by constructing improvements, or (b) purchasing income-producing property and improving its value by increasing revenues and or decreasing expenses. This chapter will focus mainly on financing ground-up real estate development. The first objective in order to redevelop real estate (including any of the income-producing segments) is to gain control of the property.

CONTROL OF PROPERTY

For most developers, control of property is preferred over ownership, especially in the early stages of the development process where there are significant unknown risks. Controlling a development site gives the developer the right to reduce or eliminate those risks without necessarily incurring the costs of ownership. Control of property can be accomplished by using various types of agreements: Memorandums of Agreement, Memorandums of Understanding, Purchase Contracts, and Options. A purchase contract that provides a substantial amount of time to fulfill zoning and environmental contingencies has a very high value to a developer. Having control of the property allows for the various risk management processes to proceed, lowering risk and increasing value. Obtaining necessary zoning and environmental approvals enhance the value of the property because, by vesting those entitlements, the risk is reduced. This predictability renders the property attractive to investors and more profitable to the developer. As the development risks are reduced, the cost of capital is lowered for the developer and execution risk is lowered for the seller. The downside of a purchase contract is that, once all the contingencies are satisfied, the buyer must close or be exposed to a lawsuit from the seller (a claim called "Specific Performance") which can force the developer to close or face financial consequences.

Another way to control property is through options. An option gives the buyer the right to purchase the property without the obligation to do so. The option price is usually around 5 percent of the purchase price, and it is usually not refundable. The advantage of having an option to purchase a development site is that it frees the buyer from the obligation to close but still allows for all of the developer's risk management contingencies to be satisfied. Options, like Purchase Contracts, can also provide for a phased takedown if the site is large enough to be subdivided into separate parcels.

MANAGING THE MAJOR RISKS IN
REAL ESTATE DEVELOPMENT

The Major Risks

The major risks[1] in real estate development are entitlement risk, environmental risk, construction risk, market risk, and financial risk. The cost of capital is directly related to the degree of risk of the investment. Developers reduce the cost of capital via a risk management process. A discussion of each risk category and how developers manage, reduce, or eliminate risk in order to obtain a cheaper cost of capital follows.

Developers manage risk in order to increase the probability of success and to reduce the cost of capital. Just the perception of risk in real estate development will affect whether or not capital providers decide to invest. The cost of capital increases with the perception of risk at all layers of the capital stack. The capital stack is the total cost of a redevelopment project and is made up of hard costs, soft costs, and land cost. Within the debt layers (bank construction loans, permanent mortgages, or Mezzanine debt) and within the equity layers (sponsor's and investor's equity capital), the cost of capital always reflects the risk.

Certainty and time are the key factors that influence risk perception. Certainty depends on the developer's ability to predict the strength and nature of the market at the time of the project's completion. Time influences certainty. The farther into the future one must predict important market factors, the more risk that will be associated with the prediction.

Entitlement Risk

The permitted use for which a piece of property is zoned is referred to as its entitlement. If a property is zoned to build 100 residential apartments over a single level parking deck, this would be referred to as its "entitlement" or the "as-of-right" zoning. In order to determine the as-of-right for a piece of property, local knowledge or research is required.

In New Jersey, zoning is a municipal function. Therefore, the as-of-right of any given piece of property can be determined by looking at two documents, the Municipality's Zoning Map and the Zoning Ordinance. The Zoning Map shows every block and lot in a municipality and the zone that the property lies within. If it happens to be located in a redevelopment area, then the Redevelopment Area Ordinance will be applied. The Zoning Ordinance shows the permitted use in each zone, and what the standards are for that permitted use.

If a property to be developed has an as-of-right or is "entitled" for the desired use, then all that is required is a Preliminary and Final Site Plan Approval from the municipality's Planning Board. Notwithstanding that a project is as-of-right, the Municipal Land Use Law still requires a public hearing during which objectors may try to dissuade the Planning Board from granting the approval for the project. If a subject development site is not entitled for the intended use, then a use change must be obtained in order for it to be developed. Use changes are the purview of the Zoning Board of Adjustment, not the Planning Board which only reviews as-of-right applications.

If the political winds in a municipality are generally pro-development, then having the City Council amend the zoning ordinance to make a development site permitted for the developer's intended use is generally a much less risky way to gain entitlements than going through a use variance application in front of the Zoning Board of Adjustment (ZBA). Although a City Council rezoning process may add three to six months to the approval process, the certainty of then applying for an as-of-right Site Plan Approval before the Planning Board as opposed to a use change and, or substantial variances from what is currently permitted before the ZBA can be well worth the delay. The reason for this lies in called appeal risk and the nuances of the zoning appeal process. In New Jersey (NJ), an objector to a zoning approval granted by either the Planning Board or the ZBA may file suit within the statutory time limit allowed to file an appeal. In NJ that time limit is forty-five days from publication of the Board's memorializing resolution in the local newspaper. In an appeal to a Planning Board vote to approve an as-of-right application, the Planning Board is presumed to be correct and the plaintiff's legal team has the burden to prove the Board acted improperly. On the other hand, in an appeal of a ZBA vote to approve an application for a change of use (with or without variances) the ZBA's attorney and the applicants team has the burden to defend the approval and prove that the Board acted properly in granting the relief the applicant sought—a much higher (and therefore riskier) bar to clear.

Environmental Risk

In the redevelopment arena, environmental risk is often a part of the risk management process. The New Jersey State Planning Act has encouraged redevelopment of NJ's thirteen urban cores and their surrounding suburbs. Many areas in the urban and suburban development tiers were historically industrial in nature, and contamination is often found in buildings, soil, and groundwater beneath these properties. This contamination must be remediated in order to redevelop these sites.

There is a risk reduction process that can insulate the buyer of a potentially contaminated property from unlimited liability regarding the cost of environmental remediation. Prior to the purchase of a potentially contaminated piece of property, the developer must pay attention to the Innocent Purchaser Defense protocols outlined by the Federal Comprehensive Environmental Response Compensation and Liability Act ("CERCLA" or "Superfund") and state-specific protocols like the New Jersey Spill Compensation and Control Act ("Spill Act"). Following these protocols may afford the developer liability protections commonly referred to as the "Innocent Purchaser," "Bona Fide Purchaser," and/or "Contiguous Property Owner" defenses.

In order to establish the legal grounds for these defenses, before the buyer takes title to the site the buyer must conduct a Phase 1 Environmental Site Assessment (ESA) study (in New Jersey, it is called a Preliminary Assessment or PA) of the property. This assessment process is essentially a history search to see if prior historical uses of the property could have resulted in contamination. It also includes a database study to determine if there were recorded spills or any enforcement actions against the prior owner(s) who caused the contamination (i.e., the "Responsible Party" or "RP"). Based on the results of this assessment, further investigation may, or may not be suggested. If the results of the Phase 1 ESA (or PA) identify known or suspected areas of concern, then a Phase 2 Site Investigation (SI) is undertaken. The SI is an invasive process involving testing potential contaminants in buildings, soil, and groundwater that identifies, delineates, and quantifies the Areas Of Concern (AOCs). The extent to which a developer expedites the SI sampling protocols (which increase the cost of lab testing) depends on the burn rate of the developer's capital. The burn rate is the daily cost of the capital invested in the project.

With the information developed during the SI, a Remedial Action Work Plan (RAWP) is prepared which details what cleanup work must be done to remediate the known AOCs. The next step is to take the RAWP and create a detailed written scope of work (SOW) required to implement the RAWP. Utilizing the SOW, the developer then bids out the work to several remediation contractors so a Guaranteed Maximum Price (GMP) contract can be signed. This process quantifies the cost of dealing with the known environmental risk. One risk reduction tool available to the developer at this stage is to purchase an insurance policy that protects against the potential cost of unknown contamination that was inadvertently missed during the PA or SI phase and is discovered during the remediation. That insurance is referred to as a Pollution Legal Liability (PLL) policy. A PLL policy will pay for the cost of remediating unknown AOCs that are discovered during the implementation of the RAWP. If the developer did not purchase a PLL insurance policy but had established the Innocent Purchaser Defense before taking title to the property and, once he begins the remediation work, he discovers previously unknown contamination and if the cost of cleaning up this unknown contamination renders the redevelopment not economically feasible, the developer has some options. First, the developer has the option to abandon the site in which case the environmental liability reverts to the former owner—the RP. The RP now has knowledge of the contamination and, in most instances would then have an obligation to remediate those AOCs, a situation the seller probably does not want. That situation could lead to another option for the developer. He could renegotiate the purchase price by disclosing all the facts and persuading the seller to reduce the purchase price to the point where the redevelopment once again becomes economically feasible.

A GMP contract protects against the known environmental risks at a development site, and a PLL insurance policy protects against unknown environmental contamination that may be discovered during the cleanup.

In order to clean up a contaminated property to protect public health and the environment at the least cost possible, knowledge of the ultimate use for the property and the type of construction required is critical. A Restricted Use Cleanup is usually the most cost-effective way to redevelop a Brownfield site. A restricted use cleanup means that certain types and concentration levels are left on-site but exposure pathways are blocked by the use of engineering controls (i.e., "Capping the Site"), and the public is noticed by the use of institutional controls (i.e., Deed Notices or information notices filed with the appropriate environmental authority). Other considerations a developer undertakes when pursuing a restricted use cleanup include who will be performing and paying for the Operating and Maintenance (O&M) function. A RAWP may be designed to have a lower initial cost but a higher O&M cost or vice versa. Another consideration is whether programs like New Jersey's Brownfield Reimbursement program, Hazardous Discharge Site Remediation Fund, or other forms of low-interest loans and grants, which can reduce the cost of remediation are available. Finally, the developer must gauge the market perception of the risk associated with a restricted use cleanup may have in terms of economic consequences that affect the value of the property in the future when the property is put into service or resold.

Construction Risk

Making certain that a project can be built for the budgeted cost of construction is the goal of construction risk management. The most impactful time to conduct construction risk management is during the design phase but it must continue through every step of the design process which is creating the detailed construction documents (CDs). A complete set of CDs includes three elements: construction plans, scopes of work, and specifications.

The design team is composed of architects and engineers, typically experts in disciplines like civil, environmental, geotechnical, structural, mechanical, HVAC, electrical, plumbing, traffic, landscape design, and a construction manager (CM). It is critically important that a CM be a part of the design team to assure that, as the CDs evolve, the improvements can be built within the hard (construction) cost budget for the project.

The more complete (i.e., detailed) the CDs are, the more certainty there will be when the developer bids out the work. The risk that the developer will not get the job he wants and at the price he budgeted is greatly reduced. Asking a general contractor (GC) to propose a GMP contract is the best way to fix construction costs. A GMP coupled with a scheduled Completion Guarantee assures that the GC can be held responsible for bringing the project in on budget and on time. Missing or inaccurate information in the CDs will be justification for GC to incur extra costs and back-charge the developer. Back-charges increase the overall cost of construction and can impact completion deadlines. The thoroughness and completeness of the CDs directly correlate to the certainty that the GMP will meet the developer's budget and schedule.

There are two primary ways to manage the construction of a development project, using a GC or a CM. GCs can provide GMP and Completion Guarantees as part of their responsibility. This is an advantage for the developer who wishes to be assured of the project cost. The disadvantage is that if the job gets built under budget, then it is usually the GC who keeps the money saved. Using a GC instead of a CM, therefore, has the potential to misalign the goals of the parties. Depending on the quality of the CDs, the developer may expect the work done to one standard but the GC may build to another.

A CM, on the other hand, acts as the owner's representative. Budget guarantees and completion guarantees can still be obtained by incorporating them into the writing of the contract, (for example using part of the CM's Fee as a cost overrun contingency) but more commonly, these guarantees occur only at the subcontractor level. In the CM model, there is no single general entity that wraps all of the subcontractor responsibilities under one hat, as is the case with a GC model. The advantage of using a CM is that any cost savings usually go to the developer's bottom line, increasing the project profit. A CM can charge either a fixed monthly fee or a percentage of hard cost fee as the method of payment. The greatest advantage to using a CM versus a GC, however, is in the way the GC must estimate and price uncertainty. When a project being built by a GC goes into construction, not all of the GC's subcontractors' bids have been obtained. Since the subcontractor bids are not certain, the GC must build in his best guess, which means building in a contingency. Under the CM model, work can commence sooner even though all costs are not finalized until each contract is bought out. This method is called "Fast-Track Construction," and. there is no need to build in a contingency to cover the uncertainty of the subcontracts whose work will begin later in the process. Particularly on large projects, where it is more likely that the complete SOW is not finalized in advance on all trades, using a CM allows the developer to manage construction risk at the actual individual subcontractor level.

Market Risk

Managing market risk involves the collection of information that will drive the marketing decision-making process. The objective of the marketing decision-making process is to optimize decisions regarding pricing, product, promotion, and place. The quality of the information collected during the market risk management process greatly influences the reliability of the revenue projections made by the developer and thereby the perception of market risk by the capital providers.

The two major market risks that must be dealt with in the redevelopment process are analyzing and predicting market-rate pricing and absorption rates. Market-rate pricing is the price a finished product will sell or rent for in the open market. The most difficult part of the analysis involves predicting future pricing and operating cost increases over a five- or ten-year period. The process of applying annual increases to sale prices or rents is called "trending."

The absorption rate is the speed at which product either sells or rents (i.e., how fast the market demand "absorbs" the inventory). It is typically measured on a monthly basis, either per residential unit (rental or condo) or per commercial square foot (office, retail, or industrial space). The pace at which inventory is absorbed is critical in cash flow analysis as it directly influences yield and typically informs when the exit strategy can be implemented.

The best sources of market information are market studies and appraisals, which provide the developer with current market data, known as comparable market statistics or "comps," and demographic trend analysis which is used to project future market conditions. The best indicator of what your product will sell or rent for, and how quickly the market will absorb it, is to study the results of comparable projects in the same competitive market area. Historical data from comparable projects combined with demographics is also critical in establishing trending rates.

Knowing the demographic breakdown of your market helps to determine the depth and breadth of potential market demand, the optimal pricing level to make it affordable to that market and informs decisions about the marketing and promotion of your offering.

The other side of the market analysis is the careful analysis of every other comparable project in your market area. This is referred to as the supply-side analysis, and it will determine the size and mix of residential units on the market, amenities being offered, pricing, and also helps forecast future supply within the relevant time period of your development. Research at the Zoning or Planning Departments of the municipality you are working in will provide information on all projects that have recently received approvals in your market area, called "pipeline inventory," in order to determine whether or not these offerings will be coming to the market at the same time as your offering.

There are two very important reasons to analyze and define what the competitive market area is for a given new development. The first reason is to determine the size of the market. The second is to determine how to reach the market in terms of media selection for advertising, promotion, and public relations activities.

Appraisals are another tool used to lower financial risk. The research involved in producing an appraisal is similar to the work done for a market study. Conclusions in appraisals incorporate the conclusions of a market study (most-likely-pricing, absorption rate, etc.); however, the objective of the appraisal is to determine value. The results of the appraisal are expressed in financial terms which can vary based on the specific appraisal assignment.[2] Since an appraiser is typically familiar with the revenue and hard and soft cost budgets, he can use this information to predict residual land values, that is, what the developer should pay for the land. Market risk can be substantially reduced when a project can be built in phases. Measuring the results of the initial phase of a development project can inform the developer whether adjustments need to be made to the product mix, pricing, design, or marketing strategy in subsequent phases, thereby making predictions of what the results should be in those phases more accurate. Having the ability to "Pre-Sell" or "Pre-Lease" a project reduces market risk because the investment in the construction of the asset does not begin until after the market demand for it has been demonstrated.[3]

UNDERWRITING FINANCIAL RISK: "THE CAPITAL STACK"

The total amount of capital required to build out a project (i.e., the project capitalization) is often referred to as the "capital stack." The capital stack consists of land cost, hard costs, and soft costs and it is made up of debt and equity layers where each layer represents a different level of risk and therefore carries a commensurately different level of pricing. Graphically, the capital stack can be shown on a bar chart where, for example, the top 1 percent is the sponsor's (aka the developer's equity) layer, the next 9 percent down the bar is the investor's equity, the next 20 percent is the Mezzanine debt layer, and the bottom 70 percent is bank debt layer.

The debt layers at the bottom of the capital stack can have multiple sub-layers. A construction loan usually requires a first mortgage on the subject property and is therefore referred to as the "senior loan." Secondary financing may be permitted by the senior lender. Since secondary financing's lien position is subordinated to the senior lender, it is referred to as the junior loan. A junior loan is most often the result of seller financing. It can also occur if the senior lender agrees to fund cost overruns with an additional tranche of financing.

The equity portion of the capital stack typically has two components: the investor's capital and the sponsor's (i.e., the developer's) capital. On large capital stacks, a sponsor may employ an intermediate layer between debt and equity which is referred to as a Mezzanine layer or Mezzanine debt; both are often simply referred to as Mezz.

Beginning at the bottom of the capital stack are the debt layers. Construction loan debt is typically in the range of up to 60 percent to 75 percent of the capital stack. It typically costs one to three points (one point represents 1 percent of the loan amount) payable at the loan closing, and a monthly interest rate usually in the range of 1 percent to 5 percent over the bank's benchmark rate. Examples of typical benchmark rates are the prime rate, LIBOR, or the treasury bill rate.

On larger projects' capital stacks, a developer may employ a Mezzanine layer which can go from the construction loan layer up to as high on the stack as 90 percent.

The top layer of the capital stack is the equity layer. If you are using Mezzanine financing, the equity layer will typically go from 90 percent to 100 percent of project capitalization. The equity layer typically has an investor component and a sponsor component. The ratio of investor to sponsor equity varies in real estate development but can be skewed as high as 90 percent investor and 10 percent sponsor. The pricing of equity layers has several components. The first component is the preferred rate of return, often referred to as the "Pref." The Pref is like an interest rate on the investor capital, but it accrues and accumulates to the back-end of the deal and is only payable after the debt layers (senior, junior, and Mezzanine) have been repaid in full. Profit share is the second component of equity repayment. It is the percentage of the profits allocated between the investor and the sponsor once the initial investment and the Pref have been repaid. The final consideration is the hierarchy of repayment between the investor and the sponsor. It is either sequential or pari passu. Sequential means the investor is repaid the principal portion of their investment plus the Pref first, and then the developer gets his principal and Pref. Then the remaining profit is split. Pari passu means the investor and sponsor get repaid their principal, interest, and profit distribution, at the same time and in proportion to their investment.

MANAGING FINANCIAL RISK FOR THE EQUITY INVESTOR

Managing entitlement, environmental, construction, and market risks all lower financial risk which is reflected in the cost of capital at every layer of the capital stack. Moreover, lower risk perception increases the likelihood that an investor or lender will provide capital for a development project. Once the decision to go forward has been made by investors, the financial risk of the investment itself must be addressed for the same reason—to lower the cost of capital. The developer uses a toolbox of methods to reduce risk and to convince the investors to lower his capital costs.

The track record of the developer is of critical importance to the investor. The developer must be able to demonstrate a successful track record of returning investment capital with appropriate and anticipated returns. The best way to demonstrate a track record is to show completed projects and to give references of the investors who have had a satisfactory experience with the developer.

Leverage is the term used to describe the magnification of the return on an equity investment by minimizing high-cost equity and maximizing lower cost Mezzanine and low-cost conventional debt. Just as a large amount of weight can be lifted by using a lever and fulcrum, using the maximum amount of debt (which requires only the payment of points and interest) while using the minimum amount of equity (which requires preferred returns and equity participation) magnifies or "leverages" the return on the equity.

The age-old expression that the three most important characteristics for successful real estate development are "Location, Location, Location" is as true today as it has ever been. Developing property in a great location reduces risk because it will earn the highest rent or sale price in a strong market and is less affected by negative external events (such as an economic recession) than property in inferior locations.

Sequential payback with preferred returns on an investor's capital is the best way to reduce risk for the investor because it prioritizes the distribution of cash 100 percent to the investor until all of his initial investment and the preferred return has been paid. Much in the way an auto insurance policy carries a "deductible amount" which provides for coverage above the deductible amount, the preferred return is the developer's "profit deductible" limit. Until the developer earns enough to pay back the investor plus the investor's Pref, he earns nothing.

Once the investment capital and preferred return have been paid on both the investor equity and the sponsor equity, it is then time for profit distributions.

Typically, profits are split between the investor and the developer/sponsor in one of two ways. The first approach is referred to as a "Straight Split." In this arrangement, the percent of the profit paid to the investor and the percent of the profit paid to the developer are in the same ratio whether or not the actual profit on the project is below, equal to, or above what the developer projected it would be. A Straight Split profit distribution model tends to penalize the investor when actual profits turn out to be lower than projected, and it does not reward the developer/sponsor when the profits turn out to be significantly higher than the projected profits. The other way of sharing profit between a developer and his investors is called the "Waterfall" method. The Waterfall method offers downside protection for the investor by shifting more of the profit toward the investor at lower profit levels. Conversely, it rewards the developer/sponsor by shifting more of the profits to the developer when the profits turn out to be higher than projected. It accomplishes this by using hurdle rates and promotes.

Once a Waterfall system of profit distribution is agreed to between the investor and the developer, the details of the agreed-to Waterfall are usually listed on a spreadsheet which includes three columns: the hurdle rate, the investor share of profits, and the developer share of profits. The hurdle rate column lays out in increasing increments the Internal Rate of Return (IRR) that will become hurdles for the developer to achieve. The second and third columns (the investor's share and the developer's share of profit) are the ratio of splits of the profit that occurs as the investor's IRR is achieved. Each time a higher hurdle rate is achieved, the developer's share of the profit is increased (or "promoted") to a higher share of the profits.

By setting up the table so that at lower IRR rates the investor gets more of the profit and, as the IRR for the investor increases, the developer's share of the profits is promoted to a larger and larger share. This lowers financial risk for the equity investor due to the fact that it distributes a larger share of profit distributions to the investor at the lower IRR rates, giving the investor downside protection while it increases ("promotes)" the developer's share of the profits as a reward for the developer producing *above-pro forma* results as the investor achieves higher and higher IRR rates.

Equity Financing

"Equity financing" is the term used to describe investment capital at the top of the capital stack. It is made up of the sponsor equity, which is the equity capital provided by the developer, and investor equity, which can be provided by high net worth individuals or investment funds.

Private equity is the term used to describe investor equity capital. By definition, it is usually unsecured and nonrecourse to the developer/sponsor. Since private equity lies at the top of the capital stack, it carries the highest risk/reward profile. It is usually provided by individuals with high net worth or privately or publicly owned investment funds, like investment partnerships, advisory funds, hedge funds, and institutional or pension funds. Most small and some medium-size developers use private equity sources to fill the top layer of their capital stack. Large private and publicly traded developers use retained earnings and sell commercial paper to raise capital for use as equity.

Sponsor equity is at the highest level of the capital stack. It is also typically the smallest layer in the stack as most sponsor/developers want to minimize the use of their own money and maximize the use of other people's money, thereby allowing them to develop more deals. Most investors require a sponsor to put up some of their own money. The term they usually use is "skin in the game," meaning a financial stake in the success of the project. If the project underperforms and cannot produce enough return to repay the equity layers in the capital stack, then the developer may lose all of his money before the investor loses any. Conversely, this can be the most profitable layer of the capital stack if the project turns out to produce positive returns and the developer benefits from the promoted profits interest from a Waterfall.

Mezzanine Financing

Mezzanine financing fills the layers of the capital stack generally between the senior lender and the equity investors (typically between 70 percent and 90 percent). Because of its higher position in the capital stack, it carries a higher risk exposure level and is priced accordingly. Mezz debt costs vary with overall interest rate fluctuations but are generally in the 8 percent to 20 percent interest rate range plus three to five points plus the customary fees and expenses associated with conventional debt. Mezz debt is a hybrid financing tool because it has some characteristics of equity and some characteristics of debt.

Mezz debt is like equity financing because it is usually nonrecourse (requires no personal guarantee of repayment), it is usually unsecured (requires no mortgage on the property being financed as collateral), and its repayment is subordinated to the senior (construction or permanent) mortgage lender. Due to these characteristics, construction lenders typically allow Mezzanine financing and equity to complete the capital stack. Mezzanine financing is like debt because it is a loan, it is evidenced by a note, it has a fixed interest rate, and it has a fixed term for repayment. Most importantly, there is usually no profit participation with the Mezz lender.

Mezzanine financing is usually used to reduce the amount of equity financing in the capital stack. This has the effect of adding leverage to the developer/sponsor's and investor's share of the profits. Since Mezzanine financing is a "fixed cost," the developer will want to use more Mezzanine financing when he believes there is a significant upside potential to project earnings thereby magnifying his and the investor's potential share of that upside. Conversely, if the developer feels the upside is relatively fixed and wants to protect his position against downside risk, he will use little or no Mezzanine financing and instead use more equity.

Debt Financing

The largest portion of the capital stack, and also the least risky layer, is the debt financing portion referred to as senior and junior debt. It generally covers from zero up to 70 percent of the capital stack. It is the least expensive layer, generally costing just 1 percent to 3 percent above the bank's benchmark rate plus 1 to 3 points, often called commitment fees, plus expenses like appraisals, legal, environmental, and construction review. There are a variety of sources for senior debt financing. Commercial banks and savings banks are the most common lending sources for the senior debt portion of the capital stack. Their loan limits vary based on the size of the bank, and they are typically comfortable with construction lending and permanent mortgage financing.[4]

There are four primary uses for debt financing: acquisition, development, construction, and permanent loan financing. Acquisition debt is used for the purchase of an asset. Development debt is used to prepare a site for either renovations or ground-up development. It includes costs for zoning and environmental approvals as well as construction documentation required for building permits. Construction debt is for the renovation or ground-up construction costs and typically begins upon the obtaining of all required building permits and lasts until completion of construction, as evidenced by the issuance of a Certificate of Occupancy. Permanent loan financing is provided as the takeout, meaning the replacement, for construction loan financing. It is usually for the long-term amortization (the payoff of principal along with current interest) of A, D, and C financing.

Some lenders will provide acquisition, development, construction, and permanent (A, D, C, and P) loans as a package. The cost of debt at the senior level of the capital stack (up to generally 70 percent) is very low relative to the higher layer costs of Mezzanine and equity capital. Generally, the cost of debt includes one or more points, with each point being equal to 1 percent of the loan amount, transaction costs such as commitment fees, appraisal and legal costs, and interest which is usually fixed as a spread over the bank's benchmark rate. Benchmark rates usually reflect the lender's cost of capital. The most commonly utilized commercial benchmark lending rate is the prime rate.

The term of the loan depends upon the purpose of the loan. In the development world, there are generally three relevant terms related to the length of the loan. Construction, when thought of in terms of the length of the loan, usually includes the acquisition and development timeframe if the loan is an A, D, and C facility. Generally, construction loans are in the three to five-year range.

The mini-perm loan is usually a short-term loan that can be negotiated in a construction loan commitment for an income-producing asset. The mini-perm is used to repay a construction loan and act as a "bridge" to a long-term permanent loan when the permanent loan has the requirement for asset stabilization. Stabilization is a term used to describe the point where a new rental building reaches a predetermined occupancy level and net operating income (NOI) level. If, for example, a construction loan on a rental property was for three years then the developer might negotiate a mini-perm to pay off the construction loan upon issuance of the Certificate of Occupancy. The mini-perm loan might be for an additional three years which would allow the developer to reach the stabilized NOI. Once an income-producing asset reaches stabilization, it is perceived by lenders as having minimal risk and is a very desirable long-term full amortization loan. This means the costs and interest rates can be negotiated very competitively with the long-term permanent mortgage lender.

A full amortization loan usually has a fifteen- to thirty-year term that allows for monthly payments that include a portion of the loan principal and the interest for the total loan amount outstanding for the given month. A different version of a full amortization loan is a loan that carries a balloon payment. If a thirty-year loan carries a ten-year "balloon" payment, then for ten years the mortgage will amortize based on a thirty-year term loan but at the end of year ten, the entire remaining loan amount balloons, meaning it will have to be paid off or refinanced.

YIELD MEASUREMENT

Yield measurement refers to the metrics involved in analyzing real estate development returns using mathematical equations. As in all mathematical models, the veracity of the assumptions, which become the input factors to the equation, is critical to the veracity of the result. The primary objective of risk management in real estate development in terms of yield measurement is to make the input assumptions as accurate as possible so that the output of the equations can be relied upon.

Yield measurement in a For-Sale business model is a more predictable and, in some ways, easier process. That is because the asset being developed is going to be sold upon completion, upon occupancy, or upon stabilization. Since the time frame being measured is short, the risk of making assumptions is lower. The risk of predicting the asset's future sale price or of predicting interest rate changes in the next three years carries with it much less uncertainty then attempting to predict these factors ten years or more in the future.

Yield measurement in a For-Rent business model is less predictable and more difficult to do accurately. A For-Rent business model usually projects a minimum of ten years of cash flow and assumes a liquidity event (either a sale or refinancing of the asset) at the end of the cash flow period. The developer constructing the For-Rent model must predict the rental rate and expense increases over time, a process called "Trending." He must also make assumptions on interest rate fluctuations over time (even though he will typically factor in straight permanent loan financing) because of the significant impact interest rate fluctuations in the future would have on the critically important assumption called the "capitalization rate."

The following yield metric (equations) are some of the commonly used measurement tools in real estate finance.

- **Capitalization ratio (cap rate) also referred to as yield on cost** is the penultimate yield measurement because it measures the return on invested dollars. It is useful in measuring any type of financial asset but is particularly useful in the measurement of real estate assets. In real estate development, the cap rate is used to analyze the spread between the capitalization rates of a comparable existing income-producing assets versus the projected (i.e., to-be-built) investment's cap rate. The spread represents the risk premium that justifies the investment itself. The formula is: NOI / Total Investment
- **Cash return on investment (CROI)**—This metric is also known as the "Cash on Cash ROI." This metric measures the return on the remaining cash after debt service and invested capital, by excluding all noncash items, such as depreciation expense, and the portion of loan payments that are made to reduce the principal loan balances. More information on cap rates appears in section 13.4 below. The formula is: Cash ROI = Remaining Cash After Debt Service / Total Investment

- **Total return on investment (TROI)**—This metric differs from CROI in that it accounts for that portion of the CROI that is not accounted by any reduction in the principal amount within the total of all loan payments made during the relevant period. It measures the ratio between remaining cash after debt service plus principal payments and invested capital. The formula is: Total Return on Investment = Remaining Cash—(Debt Service + Principal Reduction) / Total Investment
- **Net Operating Income (NOI)**—This metric measures the income that remains after all operating expenses (including vacancy and collection losses) have been paid. Note that NOI is also the numerator in the quotient used to calculate the capitalization rate value. The formula is: NOI = Gross Income—Total Operating Expenses
- **Debt Service Coverage Ratio (DSCR)**—The DSCR yield metric is especially important to lenders as it measures the ratio of available cash, after all operating expenses have been paid, and the cash required to make debt service (a.k.a.—the mortgage payment). A DSCR of 1.2 is typical for a lender to require for an income-producing property as it ensures that there will be 20 percent more cash available then is required to cover the debt service payment. The formula is: DSCR = NOI / Debt Service (where debt service = required principal +interest payment due to the lender over relevant measurement period—usually at the end of year 1)

Capitalization Rates ("Cap Rates")

The present value of an income-producing asset is related to its current and future NOI. Capitalizing an asset is the process of converting a cash flow stream into a single value known as a capitalization or "cap rate." Capitalizing an existing income-producing asset is a relatively straightforward process where you take the NOI and divide it by the cost of the asset. For example, a building that cost $1,000,000 and had a NOI of $60,000 per year would have a 6 percent cap rate value. Capitalizing an asset to be built in the future is a much more difficult process. As was discussed above, uncertainty creates risk and risk increases cost. This concept is highly relevant to the establishment of a cap rate that will be used to value an asset that will be built in the future.

The difficulty with cash flow modeling in a redevelopment scenario resides in the uncertainty associated with making future assumptions regarding income and expense. Assumptions regarding NOI involve rental rates, absorption rates, vacancy, and collection loss assumptions. Assumptions regarding operating expenses involve operating costs, utility costs, property taxes, and other customary expenses which usually increase over time (trending assumptions) but at different and often unpredictable rates. The uncertainty of making these future assumptions causes a capital provider to want to build in a risk premium. The risk premium compensates the capital provider for the additional uncertainty of future projections. The risk premium is generally in the range of 150 to 300 basis points (where 100 basis points equal a 1 percent increase) over the actual capitalization rate that would be derived if the asset was completed and the income was stabilized today. Compared to the existing income-producing asset example above, if an investor was being asked to finance a building that is projected to cost $1,000,000 and to begin producing income in three years, he would want to see the developer's assumptions lead to a realistic conclusion that the building could produce $80,000 per year of NOI (an 8 percent cap rate). The 2 percent (or 200 basis points) risk premium is a safety margin that compensates the investor for taking on the uncertainty of the developer's future assumptions regarding the construction cost and NOI of an asset that does not yet exist.

NEGOTIATING REAL ESTATE JOINT VENTURES WITH INVESTORS

Negotiating a real estate joint venture is a complicated process. Of paramount importance in the ultimate success of these negotiations is the establishment of trust between the investor and the developer. Trust is established primarily through reputation and credibility. Reputation is a result of the track record and references from satisfied partners that each side can provide to the other. Credibility is established by the demonstration of knowledge regarding the primary areas of the risk and the process of risk management utilized to minimize or eliminate risk that has been gained through practical experience.

Once trust has been established between the investor and the developer, the specific investment opportunity is then underwritten using the various yield measurement and analytical tools described earlier in this chapter. After the efficacy of the specific investment opportunity has been established and the investor desires to provide equity capital to the developer then the specifics of the joint venture are negotiated. Negotiating a real estate joint venture involves consideration, discussion, and negotiation between the developer and equity investor of many different terms and factors. The following is a list of six of the primary terms and factors between a developer and his investors that need to be negotiated and agreed upon in order to form a successful joint venture.

- **Equity Participation Ratio** is the ratio of investor to sponsor equity needed to fill the equity layer at the top of the capital stack. It usually ranges from 90/10 to 50/50. Typically, the more equity a sponsor can put into a joint venture, the greater his percentage of ownership will be.
- **Preferred Return** is the minimum return on investment required by the equity investor before he or she begins to split profits with his or her developer partner. In most cases, the preferred return negotiated by the investor and developer accrues on both the investor's and the developer/sponsor's equity investment at the same rate.
- **Priority of Capital Return** is usually the next item to be negotiated. This deal term refers to the sequence of the return of equity capital. It is usually sequenced in one of two ways; Prioritized or pari passu. Prioritized capital return usually means that the developer agrees to repay the equity investor's principal and preferred return before the developer's equity plus the preferred return is repaid. When equity capital is returned on a pari passu basis, it means that at the time the equity capital returns begin, the equity investor and developer receive their investment back at the same time and in equal proportion to the equity participation ratio.

- **Profit Distributions** are probably the most important term in the joint venture negotiation between an equity investor and a developer/sponsor. The tension over the negotiation of this term results from the investor's viewpoint that he is entitled to own at least the same percentage of the venture as his equity capital represents as a percentage of total equity capital versus the developer/sponsor's viewpoint that he should be entitled to own a disproportionately larger share of the venture (i.e., larger than the percentage of his equity capital contribution represents as a percentage of total equity capital) to compensate him for the intangible but real value of identifying the opportunity, gaining control over it, conceptualizing the value proposition, reducing risk, and then offering it to the investor. Of the two methods commonly used for profit distributions, Straight Splits versus Waterfalls, it is the Waterfall method that usually brings this issue into balance by satisfying these opposing viewpoints.
- **Developer Fees** are often paid to the developer to manage the operational aspects of the project. Much as the preferred returns compensate the equity capital providers for the time value of their capital, the developer fee compensates the developer for the time value of his commitment to managing the project. Developer fees are usually expressed as a percentage of project cost and vary depending upon the size of the project. In a small project, the developer fee could be 5 percent of the total project cost while in a large project it could be as low as 2 percent of hard cost only. Typically, the fee is payable in equal monthly installments based on the total number of months the developer projects to reach an agreed-upon milestone like project completion, sellout, or stabilization.
- **Developer Overhead Reimbursement**—A developer, when acting as a project manager, will often utilize some or all of their office facilities and staff (the developer's "overhead") to manage the project. It is not uncommon for the developer to seek reimbursement for that overhead. This reimbursement can be based on actual charges incurred, or more typically, it is a fixed monthly amount that is agreed upon and referred to as the "administration expense" on the developer's pro forma under soft costs.

NEGOTIATING JOINT VENTURES WITH LANDOWNERS

Negotiating real estate development joint ventures with a landowner is similar to negotiating joint ventures with private equity sources. As discussed above, establishing trust between the developer and the landowner is of paramount importance. The level of sophistication of the average landowner with respect to investing in real estate can vary greatly. It is therefore very important that the developer makes sure that the land owner understands real estate development risks, how developers finance projects by constructing his capital stack, and the different risk/reward layers in the developer's capital stack.

The property owner who has a high-risk tolerance and wishes to maximize the value of his land can participate at the equity investor level by contributing his property to the joint venture free and clear (i.e., with no debt) as his equity capital contribution. The landowner with less risk tolerance could participate by financing some or all of the land price as a junior (second mortgage loan) or Mezzanine loan. The landowner with the least risk tolerance could provide a senior (first mortgage loan often called purchase money mortgage) to a developer which would allow the developer to own the property and obtain all of the entitlements and permits needed to construct the improvements without having to pay the entire purchase price up front. At that point, the landowner could convert the loan to equity, subordinate to a junior or Mezzanine position or, having functioned as a bridge loan lender for the developer to reduce risk, simply obtain repayment of the purchase money mortgage once the developer puts his capital stack in place and exit the transaction.

The valuation of land to be contributed to a joint venture as equity is generally handled in one of two ways. If the landowner is in the process of selling his property when approached by a developer who wants to contribute to a joint venture, then the selling price of the property might be the value for purposes of the landowner's equity contribution. This approach may create inequity between the parties as ultimately the seller may have underpriced his property, or the developer may have paid more than fair market value.

A better way to value land that is contributed to a joint venture is to use a formula-based pricing model. Under this valuation method, the landowner and developer establish a market-based valuation standard that is applied to the use of approval granted by the governing zoning authority for the intended development. Typical market-based valuation standards are an agreed-upon price per square foot of commercial space or an agreed-upon price per unit of a residential building. A formula-based pricing model can help assure the seller that the value of his land contribution that will ultimately be credited to his capital account as equity is fairly calculated based on its real value to the joint venture.

Once the valuation of the landowner's contribution of his property as equity capital is determined, the remaining deal terms that need to be negotiated closely mirror those that would typically be negotiated between the developer and an equity capital provider. There are, however, some important nuances to be noted.

One of the nuances of joint venturing with a landowner is the application of some type of appreciation rate to the capital account where the land value was contributed. In much the same way that equity capital earns a preferred return as compensation for the time value of the investment, a capital contribution consisting of land can be similarly compensated for time value. This negotiation must consider such factors as the location of the land and whether or not it would have appreciated in the absence of the development joint venture, the likelihood that the property would have sold at the asking price if the landowner had not opted for the development joint venture, the time it was anticipated to take to consummate a sale of the property, and the valuation ultimately agreed-upon for the capital contribution.

Professional tax planning is critical to the financial results achieved for a landowner in a development joint venture. The characterization of income as ordinary income versus capital gain, and the resulting difference in potential tax liability when land is "contributed" to a development entity as equity capital can be enormous. The IRS considers a land developer who intends to build and sell homes or condominiums, for example, to be a "dealer," and profit derived from the development of land is normally characterized as ordinary income and carries with it a maximum federal income tax rate of 37 percent. Conversely, when land is "sold" to a development entity and subordinated to construction and permanent financing, the "land profit" can be characterized as capital gains which carries a federal rate of just 20 percent.

If a landowner is unwilling or unable to contribute his land as equity capital to a joint venture with the developer, there are several ways to structure the land purchase transaction that can result in the owner realizing a higher sale price, and the developer realizing a higher profit then would be achieved with an "all cash-as is" sale. The overall objective in a structured seller-financed land purchase is to balance the land-owner's risk tolerance with his desire to earn more than he would realize by simply selling the property outright. Again, it is important to stress that the developer must establish trust, credibility, and must make sure that the landowner has a thorough understanding of the capital stack, and how the various layers of the stack each carry a different risk/reward profile. Equally important in persuading a seller to provide financing to a developer is making sure that the seller recognizes the developer's familiarity with development risk and the risk management process. When the land-owner understands the risk/reward spectrum in the capital stack, he can determine where he wants to place his seller financing.

If a landowner (Seller) decides to finance the sale of his property with a first mortgage, he is in a very low-risk position at the bottom of the capital stack. If the developer is unable to pay off the mortgage, the seller can foreclose and take back the property keeping whatever cash the developer put down at the closing. Addition-ally, any of the soft cost improvements, like zoning or environmental approvals that the developer obtained becomes the property of the landowner, thus reducing risks and adding value in a subsequent sale to another developer. There are ways to further lower the risk of the seller financing the sale to the developer that could be part of the negotiation like allowing the seller to hold the deed to the property in escrow and sign a Confession of Judgment in the event of a default.

If a landowner (seller) decides to finance the sale of his property with a second mortgage, he is now in a higher risk position as he has stepped up the capital stack into the layer between senior debt and equity. However, the landowner can lower his risk position by initially financing the sale of the property with the first mortgage and requiring the developer, as a condition to the seller's subordination to a second mortgage position, to perform all of the predevelopment activities necessary (entitle-ment, environmental, construction permits, and market research) to close on first mortgage construction financing. The landowner now has the further benefit of the senior construction lender's underwriting team performing the due diligence required for construction financing which further lowers the landowner's risk of subordination. The landowner's risk, even though he has a secured position with the second mort-gage on the property is, that in the event of a default, the only way he can protect his position is to pay off the first mortgage.

Some senior debt lenders view this as positive because if there is a developer default then there is another interested party (the second mortgage holder) that has an interest in paying off the senior lender to preserve their position and security in the asset. Other senior construction lenders view this as a negative and require that no secondary financing be placed on the property they are financing as they want to be in a position of having the first and only mortgage. Often times, the senior lender can be convinced to allow secondary financing on a development site by negotiating exactly what will occur in the event of a borrower default. This agreement is referred to as an inter-creditor agreement. The benefit to the developer is obvious as he can now place a senior debt (first mortgage loan) for construction financing on the property with the land loan being subordinated to the senior lender thus greatly reducing the need for higher-priced Mezz or equity financing to complete the land acquisition.

If a landowner (Seller) is comfortable with providing financing in the form of a Mezzanine loan on his property, then there is likely to be no issue with the senior construction lender because Mezz financing is usually unsecured by any lien on the property. Additionally, senior construction lenders are comfortable with Mezzanine financing because it is also usually nonrecourse to the borrower and therefore does not create a contingent liability which could impair the developer's credit profile to the senior lender's underwriter. Finally, some of the complications with closing Mezz financing on a development project (like inter-creditor agreements) can be simplified and expedited when dealing with a landowner who typically would not have the same institutionally imposed legal requirements.

CONCLUSION

In conclusion, having an understanding of the capital stack, the layers that compose it, and their associated costs and risks allows for the real estate professional to advise his landowner/client on the use of redevelopment as a viable exit strategy. Furthermore, understanding what the risks are in redevelopment, and how a professional developer manages those risks, can lead to the conclusion that teaming up with a trustworthy, experienced, and credible redeveloper can make redevelopment not just a viable exit strategy but a highly profitable one.

NOTES

1. "Risk" is the product of the probability or likelihood of an undesired event occurring and the consequences that may result from that event. "Risk informed" means having adequate knowledge of associated risk to be able to make appropriate decisions relative to the risk. "Risk reduction" includes taking measures to minimize the probability or likelihood and/or consequences of risk. Risk Management is the process of identifying, quantifying, and reducing or eliminating risk.

2. For example, the value of a for-sale asset, like a condominium project, is usually based on projected profit which is determined by estimating net sales minus total project cost (Land Cost + Hard Cost + Soft Costs). The value in a for-rent project is determined by estimating net operating income of the finished product and dividing it by total cost. The result is referred to as the "Build-To Yield."

3. In residential development, Pre-Sales are fairly common in larger scale developments. Homebuyers are typically willing to commit to purchase one or two years in advance of a delivery date, particularly if they feel they are getting a Pre-Construction discount or that they are purchasing at the beginning of a large-scale development that will have high demand. In either instance, the belief that prices will escalate after the presale promotion is over or as the

subsequent phases of the project are completed drives consumers to buy. Pre-leasing is not typically used in residential rental development, as renters normally begin looking for a new apartment three months before they need it. In commercial development, pre-leasing is typically called "build to suit."

4. Institutional lenders are those who have large corporate clients with large pension funds to invest or large groups of individual investors who pool their assets and manage their investments. They are usually looking for larger loans with long-terms and low risk. These type of lenders typically do not want to finance construction projects as they are generally short-term loans and will only participate if there is an opportunity to also provide long-term take out permanent financing.

Lender Liability Safe Harbors

Gordon C. Duus, Esq.

In New Jersey, the liability of a lender for hazardous substance contamination affecting the collateral for loans is determined by reference to both state law, principally the Spill Compensation and Control Act, N.J.S.A. 58:10-23.11 et seq. ("Spill Act"), and federal law, principally the Comprehensive Environmental Response, Compensation and Liability Act, 42 U.S.C. Section 9601 et seq. Those laws were amended in an attempt to provide clear protections for lenders, referred to as a "safe harbor." Prior to amendment, it was unclear what actions lenders could take and still avoid liability for hazardous substances on property that served as collateral for a loan. That uncertainty made it difficult for lenders to decide how best to protect their interests in the context of existing loans and made lenders more reluctant to accept properties that either had or were likely to have hazardous substance contamination issues as collateral for a new loan. The amendments were designed to allow lenders to make business decisions with a clearer understanding of what activities could be undertaken to protect their interests while still avoiding New Jersey and federal liability for the hazardous substances.

NEW JERSEY SAFE HARBOR FOR LENDERS

The Spill Act provides that "any person who has discharged a hazardous substance, or is in any way responsible for any hazardous substance, shall be strictly liable, jointly and severally, without regard to fault, for all cleanup and removal costs no matter by whom incurred."[1] Before the Spill Act safe harbor amendment was enacted, the statute provided no clear guidance to a lender regarding what actions it could take to protect its interests without being "in any way responsible" under the Spill Act, leaving that matter for judicial interpretation. In 1993, New Jersey amended the Spill Act to provide a safe harbor for lenders from Spill Act liability.[2] In particular, the amendment provides that a person who maintains indicia of ownership of a vessel, facility, or underground storage tank facility (collectively, "Facility") and who does not participate in the management of the Facility is not deemed to be an owner or operator of the Facility, shall not be deemed the discharger or responsible party for a discharge from the Facility, and shall not be liable for cleanup costs or damages resulting from discharges from the Facility pursuant to the Spill Act or the Underground Storage of Hazardous Substances Act (USHSA),[3] except to the limited extent that liability may still apply after foreclosure under the Spill Act safe harbor amendment,[4] as discussed below.

Indicia of Ownership

The amendment defines "indicia of ownership," the holding of which is protected from Spill Act liability, as evidence of a security interest,[5] evidence of interest in a security interest, or evidence of an interest in real or personal property acquired incident to foreclosure and its equivalents[6] (collectively, "Foreclosure").[7] Evidence of such interests include mortgages, deeds of trust, liens, surety bonds, and guarantees of obligations, title held pursuant to a lease financing transaction in which the lessor does not initially select the leased property, and legal or equitable title obtained pursuant to Foreclosure. Evidence of such interests also includes assignments, pledges, or other rights to or forms of encumbrance against property that are primarily to protect a security interest. A person is not required to hold title or a security interest in order to maintain indicia of ownership.

Lender as Holder

A lender who maintains indicia of ownership primarily to protect a security interest is defined by the amendment as a "holder."[8] A holder includes the initial holder (such as a loan originator), any subsequent holder (such as a successor-in interest or subsequent purchaser of the security interest on the secondary market), a guarantor of an obligation, surety, or any other person who holds ownership indicia primarily to protect a security interest, or a receiver or other person who acts on behalf or for the benefit of a holder.

Primarily to Protect a Security Interest

In order to qualify for the Spill Act safe harbor, the holder's indicia of ownership must be held primarily for the purpose of securing payment or performance of an obligation but does not include indicia of ownership held primarily for investment purposes or ownership indicia held primarily for purposes other than as a protection for a security interest.[9] A holder may have other, secondary reasons for maintaining indicia of ownership, but the primary reasons why any ownership indicia are held shall be as protection for a security interest.

Spill Act Lender Liability Generally

Under the safe harbor amendment, a holder who does not participate in the management of the Facility is not deemed to be an owner or operator of the Facility, shall not be deemed the discharger or responsible party for a discharge from the Facility and shall not be liable for cleanup costs or damages resulting from discharges from the Facility except to the extent that liability may apply to holders after Foreclosure, as discussed below.[10]

Participation in the Management

To describe when the lender loses the safe harbor protections, the amendment defines "active participation in the management" or "participation in the management" as "actual participation in the management or operational affairs by the holder of the security interest and shall not include the mere capacity, or ability to influence, or the unexercised right to control" the Facility.[11]

A holder of a security interest is considered to be in active participation in the management, while the borrower is still in possession, and is therefore exposed to Spill Act liability, only if the holder either:

a. exercises decision-making control over the borrower's environmental compliance, such that the holder has undertaken responsibility for the borrower's waste disposal or hazardous substance handling practices; or
b. exercises control at a level comparable to that of a manager of the borrower's enterprise, such that the holder has assumed or manifested responsibility for the overall management of the enterprise encompassing the day-to-day decision-making of the enterprise with respect to:
   1. environmental compliance; or
   2. all, or substantially all, of the operational[12] (as opposed to financial or administrative)[13] aspects of the enterprise other than environmental compliance.[14]

Spill Act Safe Harbor

The Spill Act safe harbor amendment describes what activities lenders may undertake and still avoid Spill Act liability. Aside from the general rule protecting lenders involved in response actions and cleanups, those permitted activities depend upon whether they take place before the lender holds indicia of ownership, after the lender holds indicia of ownership but before Foreclosure, and after the lender acquires the collateral property through Foreclosure. The federal district court has indicated that the Spill Act safe harbor amendment is to be applied retroactively.[15]

Further, the amendment provides that it should not be construed to require a holder of a security interest to conduct or require an environmental inspection and that the liability of the holder of the security interest under the Spill Act is not based on or affected by a failure to conduct an environmental inspection.[16] Also, the amendment indicates that a holder of an interest in an underground storage tank is not obligated to comply with the provisions of the Underground Storage of Hazardous Substances Act, N.J.S.A. 58:10A-21 et seq., unless the holder loses the Spill Act safe harbor exemption.[17]

Response Actions and Cleanups

A holder does not participate in the management of a Facility by making any response or performing any response action or undertaking any cleanup or removal or similar action under federal or New Jersey environmental law.[18]

Acts Prior to Holding Indicia of Ownership

"No act or omission prior to the time that indicia of ownership are held primarily to protect a security interest constitutes evidence of participation in management."[19] So, before acquiring title, the lender may (1) undertake or require an environmental inspection of the Facility in which indicia of ownership are to be held; (2) require a prospective borrower to clean up a Facility; or (3) comply or come into compliance (whether before or after the time that indicia of ownership are held primarily to protect a security interest) with any applicable law or regulation, and such action will not be considered participation in the management of the Facility. However, a holder is not required to conduct or require an inspection to qualify for the protection provided by the safe harbor amendment, and the liability of a holder is not based on or affected by the holder not conducting or not requiring an inspection.

Acts after Holding Indicia of Ownership but Prior to Foreclosure

Actions that are consistent with holding indicia of ownership primarily to protect a security interest do not constitute participation in management for purposes of the Spill Act safe harbor provisions.[20] The authority for the holder to make such actions may, but need not, be contained in contractual or other documents specifying requirements for financial, environmental and other warranties, covenants, conditions, representations or promises from the borrower. Loan policing and workout activities cover and include all activities up to Foreclosure.

Policing Activities Prior to Foreclosure. A holder who engages in policing activities prior to Foreclosure will remain within the Spill Act safe harbor provided that the holder does not by such actions participate in the management of the Facility.[21] Such actions include requiring the borrower to clean up the Facility during the term of the security interest; requiring the borrower to comply or come into compliance with applicable laws, rules and regulations during the term of the security interest; securing or exercising authority to monitor or inspect the Facility in which indicia of ownership are maintained, or the borrower's business or financial conditions during the term of the security interest; or taking other actions to adequately police the loan or security interest (such as requiring the borrower to comply with any warranties, covenants, conditions, representations, or promises from the borrower).

Workout Activities Prior to Foreclosure. A holder who engages in workout activities prior to Foreclosure will remain within the Spill Act safe harbor provided that the holder does not by such action participate in the management of the Facility.[22] "Workout" refers to those actions by which a holder, at any time prior to Foreclosure, seeks to prevent, cure, or mitigate a default by the borrower or obligor, or preserve or prevent the diminution of the value of the security. Workout activities include restructuring or renegotiating the terms of the security interest; requiring payment of additional rent or interest; exercising forbearance; requiring or exercising rights pursuant to an assignment of accounts or other accounts owing to an obligor; providing specific or general financial or other advice, suggestions, counseling, or guidance; and exercising any right or remedy the holder is entitled to by law or under any warranties, covenants, conditions, representations, or promises from the borrower.

Acts after Foreclosure

The indicia of ownership, held after Foreclosure, continue to be maintained primarily as a protection for a security interest provided that the holder did not participate in the management prior to Foreclosure and that the holder undertakes to sell, re-lease property held pursuant to a lease financing transaction (whether by a new lease financing transaction or substitution of the lessee), or otherwise divest itself of the Facility in a reasonable expeditious manner in accordance with the means and procedures specified in the Spill Act safe harbor amendments.[23] Such a holder may liquidate, maintain business operations, undertake environmental response actions pursuant to New Jersey and federal law, and take measures to preserve, protect, or prepare the secured asset prior to sale or other disposition, without losing status as a person who maintains indicia of ownership primarily to protect a security interest.

Establishing Holder's Intent. For purposes of establishing that a holder is seeking to sell or re-lease property held pursuant to a new lease financing transaction (whether by a new lease financing transaction or substitution of the lessee) or to divest a Facility in a reasonably expeditious manner, the holder may use whatever commercially reasonable means are relevant or appropriate with respect to the Facility or may employ the means specified in the law.[24]

Offers of Fair Consideration. A holder that outbids, rejects, or fails to act upon a written, bona fide firm offer[25] of fair consideration[26] within ninety days of receipt of the offer, which offer is received at any time after six months following the date of Foreclosure,[27] shall not be deemed to be using a commercially reasonable means for the purpose of the Spill Act safe harbor.[28] The six-month period begins to run from the time that the holder acquires a marketable title, provided that the holder, after the expiration of any redemption or other waiting period provided by law, was acting diligently to acquire marketable title. A holder that outbids, rejects, or fails to act upon an offer of fair consideration for the Facility within the ninety-day period establishes that the ownership indicia in the secured property are not held primarily to protect the security interest, unless the holder is required, in order to avoid liability under federal or New Jersey law, to make a higher bid, to obtain a higher offer, or to seek or obtain an offer in a different manner.[29]

Listing the Facility. A holder is proceeding in a commercially reasonable manner after Foreclosure by, within twelve months following Foreclosure, listing the Facility with a broker, dealer, or agent who deals with the type of property in question or by advertising the Facility as being for sale or disposition on at least a monthly basis in either a real estate publication or a trade or other publication suitable for the Facility in question, or a newspaper of general circulation[30] covering the area where the property is located.[31] The twelve-month period begins to run from the time that the holder acquires marketable title, provided that the holder, after the expiration of any redemption or other waiting period provided by law, was acting diligently to acquire marketable title.

Five-year Time Limit. A holder must sell or re-lease the property held pursuant to a new lease financing transaction or otherwise divest such Facility in a reasonably expeditious manner not later than five years after the date of foreclosure, except that a holder may continue to hold the property for longer than five years without losing status as a person who maintains indicia of ownership primarily to protect a security interest if the holder has made a good faith effort to sell, re-lease, or otherwise divest itself of the property using commercially reasonable means or other procedures pre-scribed by the Spill Act; the holder has obtained any approvals required pursuant to applicable federal or New Jersey banking or other lending laws to continue in posses-sion of the property; and the holder has exercised reasonable custodial care to prevent or mitigate any new discharges of hazardous substances from the Facility that could substantially diminish the market value of the property.[32]

No Protection against Liability for New Discharges. The liability exemption granted to holders after Foreclosure does not apply to liability for any new discharge[33] of hazardous substances from the Facility occurring after the date of Foreclosure that is caused by acts or omissions of the holder which can be shown to have been negligent.[34]

No Protection for Arranging for Off-site Disposal or Treatment. The safe harbor exemption for liability granted to holders of indicia of ownership to protect a security interest does not apply to liability pursuant to applicable law or regulation for arranging for the off-site disposal or treatment of a hazardous substance or by accept-ing for transportation and disposal of a hazardous substance at an off-site facility selected by the holder.[35]

Underground Storage Tank Facilities. A holder who acquires an underground storage (UST) facility continues to hold the exemption from liability for the UST facility granted by the Spill Act safe harbor if there is an operator of the UST facility, other than the holder, who is in control of the UST facility or has responsibility for compliance with applicable federal and New Jersey requirements.[36] If an operator does not exist, the law specifies what actions a holder must perform to continue to maintain the safe harbor exemption from liability for the UST facility.[37] An UST facility may be temporarily closed until a subsequent purchaser has acquired marketable title to the UST facility, at which point the purchaser must either operate the UST facility in accordance with applicable federal and New Jersey law or permanently close or remove the UST facility.[38]

Required Post-Foreclosure Notices to the NJDEP

Pre-Foreclosure Discharges. If a holder forecloses on a Facility at which it has actual knowledge a discharge of hazardous substances occurred or began prior to the date of Foreclosure, the holder shall, within thirty days of the date of Foreclosure, notify the NJDEP that Foreclosure has occurred or shall be subject to a civil penalty not to exceed $25,000.[39]

Post-Foreclosure Discharges. The holder shall immediately notify the NJDEP of any new discharge of hazardous substances of which it has actual knowledge, occur-ring after the date of Foreclosure from a Facility, or shall be subject to a civil penalty not to exceed $10,000 per day for each violation.[40]

No Loss of Status. The failure to give the required notices of pre-Foreclosure or post-Foreclosure discharges will not cause the holder to lose its status as a person who maintains indicia of ownership primarily to protect a security interest.[41]

NJDEP's Rights Retained

The Spill Act safe harbor amendment[42] provides that nothing in it shall be deemed to prohibit or limit the rights of the NJDEP to clean up a property or, pursuant to N.J.S.A. 58:10-23.11f of the Spill Act, to obtain a lien on the property of a discharger or holder in order to recover cleanup costs[43] or to direct the holder to take any emergency response actions, including closure of the Facility necessary to prevent, contain, or mitigate a continuing or new discharge of hazardous substances that poses an immediate threat to the environment or to the public health, safety, or welfare.[44] Any recovery of cleanup costs from a holder pursuant to a lien obtained by the NJDEP is limited to the actual financial benefit conferred on such holder by a cleanup or removal action, and shall not exceed the amount realized by the holder on the sale or other disposition of the property.[45]

NOTES

1. N.J.S.A. 58:10-23.11g(c)(1).
2. P.L. 1993, c.112; N.J.S.A. 58:10-23.11g4 through 23.11g8.
3. N.J.S.A. 58:10A-21 *et seq.*
4. N.J.S.A. 58:10-23.11g5.
5. N.J.S.A. 58:10-23.11g4.
6. "Foreclosure" and "Foreclosure and its equivalents" mean purchase at foreclosure sale, acquisition or assignment of title in lieu of foreclosure; termination of a lease of other repossession; acquisition of a right to title or possession; an agreement in satisfaction of the obligation; or any other formal or informal manner (whether pursuant to law or under warranties, covenants, conditions, representations or promises from the borrower) by which the holder acquires title to or possession of the secured property. N.J.S.A. 58:20-23.11g4.
7. N.J.S.A. 58:10-23.11g4.
8. *Id.*
9. N.J.S.A. 58:10-23.11g4.
10. N.J.S.A. 58:10-23.11g5.
11. N.J.S.A. 58:10-23.11g4.
12. Operational aspects of the enterprise that lead to liability include functions such as that of facility manager, underground storage tank facility manager, plant manager, operations manager, chief operating officer, or chief executive officer. N.J.S.A. 58:10-23.11g4.
13. Financial or administrative aspects that do not lead to liability include functions such as that of credit manager, accounts payable or receivable manager, personnel manager, controller, chief financial officer, or similar functions. N.J.S.A. 58:10-23.11g4.
14. N.J.S.A. 58:10-23.11g4.
15. *Kemp Industries, Inc. v. Safety Light Corp.*, 857 F.Supp. 373, 396-97 (D.N.J. 1994).
16. N.J.S.A. 58:10-23.11g8.
17. N.J.S.A. 58:10-23.11g8a.
18. N.J.S.A. 58:10-23.11g4.
19. *Id.*
20. *Id.*
21. *Id.*
22. *Id.*
23. N.J.S.A. 58:10-23.11g6.

24. N.J.S.A. 58:10-23.11g6(a).

25. A "written, bona fide offer" means a legally enforceable, commercially reasonable, cash offer solely for the foreclosed Facility, including all material terms of the transaction, from a ready, willing, and able purchaser who demonstrates to the holder's satisfaction the ability to perform. N.J.S.A. 58:10-23.11g6(b)(1).

26. "Fair consideration" is the subject of a detailed definition in the law. N.J.S.A. 58:10-23.11g4.

27. "Date of foreclosure" means the date on which the holder obtains legal or equitable title to the Facility pursuant to or incident to foreclosure. N.J.S.A. 58:10-23.11g4.

28. N.J.S.A. 58:10-23.11g6(b)(1).

29. N.J.S.A. 58:10-23.11g6(b)(2).

30. "General circulation" is defined as "one with a circulation over 10,000, or one suitable under any applicable federal, New Jersey or local rules of court for publication required by court order or rules of civil procedure." N.J.S.A. 58:10-23.11g6(c).

31. N.J.S.A. 58:10-23.11g6(c).

32. N.J.S.A. 58:10-23.11g6(d).

33. Nothing in subsection N.J.S.A. 58:10-23.11g6(e) shall be deemed to impose liability for a new discharge from the Facility that is authorized pursuant to a federal or New Jersey permit or cleanup procedure. N.J.S.A. 58:10-23.11g6(e)(2).

34. N.J.S.A. 58:10-23.11g6(e)(1).

35. N.J.S.A. 58:10-23.11g6(e)(3).

36. N.J.S.A. 58:10-23.11g6(f)(1).

37. N.J.S.A. 58:10-23.11g6(f)(2).

38. N.J.S.A. 58:10-23.11g6(g).

39. N.J.S.A. 58:10-23.11g7(c)(1).

40. N.J.S.A. 58:10-23.11g7(c)(2).

41. N.J.S.A. 58:10-23.11g7(c)(3).

42. N.J.S.A. 58:10-23.11g4 through 23.11g8.

43. N.J.S.A. 58:10-23.11g7(a).

44. N.J.S.A. 58:10-23.11g7(b).

45. N.J.S.A. 58:10-23.11g7(a).

Chapter 4

New Jersey Environmental Litigation

Section 1

Environmental Litigation Overview

Mark L. Manewitz, Esq.

Justice Pollack, in his now-famous *Ventron* decision, stated, "Those who poison the land must pay for its cure."[1] New Jersey litigation founded on this principle is the subject of this chapter.

THE SPILL ACT

The State of New Jersey and municipal corporations aggrieved by the discharge of hazardous substances can seek compensation under several theories of law including nuisance, ultra-hazardous activities in violation of the common law, trespass, and, most importantly, the Spill Compensation and Control Act (Spill Act), N.J.S.A. 58:10-23.11 et seq.[2]

The Spill Act was enacted to provide funds to abate toxic nuisances.[3] The key factor necessary to bring litigation under the Act is a discharge of hazardous substances. Hazardous substances are defined under the Spill Act in a manner broader than that of the federal counterpart, the Comprehensive Environmental Response Compensation and Liability Act (CERCLA or Superfund), 42 U.S.C. §§ 9601-9675, as New Jersey's definition includes petroleum, as well as other hazardous substances.[4]

The Spill Act is the successor statute to historical common law concepts of nuisance and ultra-hazardous activities. Justice Pollack in *Ventron* analyzed the imposition of strict liability in the early English decision of *Rylands v. Fletcher*.[5] The concept articulated in *Rylands*, and affirmed by Justice Pollack in *Ventron*, arises out of imposing strict liability on a landowner for undertaking ultra-hazardous activity. In the modern litigation context, plaintiffs, whether public entities or private individuals, follow in the traditions set down by the English common law and confirmed in *Ventron*.

In the case of the discharge of a hazardous substance, the NJDEP is authorized to undertake a publicly funded cleanup of the discharge, should a private party refuse or not be available.[6] In those instances, the attorney general is empowered to seek reimbursement for the State's cleanup expenditures. The Spill Act has been amended to enable private plaintiffs to seek reimbursement for costs expended in the cleanup of a hazardous substance on their property caused by a third party.

Potentially Responsible Parties (PRP)

The Spill Act provides that

> any person who has discharged a hazardous substance, or is in any way responsible for any hazardous substance, shall be strictly liable, jointly and severally, without regard to fault, for all cleanup and removal costs no matter by whom incurred. Such person shall also be strictly liable, jointly and severally, without regard to fault, for all cleanup and removal costs incurred.[7]

The phrase "in any way responsible" gives the Spill Act retroactive applicability to anyone who owned the site at the time of the discharge or who is aware of the discharge and failed to take appropriate action and clean it up.

Plaintiffs

Aside from the governmental and public agencies which are charged with the responsibility for public health and safety, buyers and owners of property which became aware of or discover contamination of their property may seek compensation for costs expended on cleanup of said property from discharge. Former operators and owners of property as well as adjacent neighbors who added a substance that may have contaminated the property can also be plaintiffs. The question a plaintiff must answer in order to establish a claim under the Spill Act is whether it can prove the time of discharge and match that time of ownership to the defendant.[8]

Defendants

Defendants include all former owners, operators, or neighbors who are active dischargers of hazardous substances which have impacted the property (by way of groundwater or soil). Such defendants include former tenants or operators of property or the adjacent property, former owners, and, obviously, current dischargers.

Recent case law has modified the Spill Act to clarify the problem of former owners in the chain of title of contaminated property who did not own the property at the time of discharge.[9] Retroactive liability is not unlimited, according to *N.J. Department of Environmental Protection v. Dimant*.[10] In *Dimant*, the court found that while there had been a discharge, liability depended upon the nexus between that discharge and the damages suffered. Absent such a nexus, the defendant could not be considered liable.[11] Under the Spill Act, the discharge must be connected to the specific environmental damage "in some real, not hypothetical, way . . . it is not enough . . . to 'ask the trier of fact to supply the link.'"[12]

Multiple Dischargers/Defendants

Since liability under the Spill Act is joint and several, the implication is that multiple dischargers are jointly and severally liable:

> Any person who has discharged a hazardous substance, or is in any way responsible for any hazardous substance, shall be strictly liable, jointly and severally, without regard to fault, for all cleanup and removal costs no matter by whom incurred.[13]

The provision for joint and several liability is also referenced in the Spill Act's contribution section.[14]

Multiple defendants raise an interesting and perhaps difficult question of proof for both public and private defendants. Under *Dimant*, the plaintiff must prove that a discharge took place during the ownership or operation of the property; failure to prove the discharge caused damage during that period of time is not enough to prove liability. Moreover, passive migration of a prior spill is not enough to constitute a "discharge."[15] Of course, however, "ownership or control of the property at the time of discharge" will suffice to establish liability as a person "in any way responsible" for a discharge.[16] Federal and state courts alike have considered joint and several liability under the Spill Act where there are multiple defendants (either multiple dischargers or multiple owners at the time of discharge) and have held that liability is joint and several, as opposed to several or divisible.[17]

Contribution under the Spill Act

As discussed earlier, defendants are jointly and severally responsible for all cleanup costs under the Spill Act.[18] Yet, as evidenced by several New Jersey environmental and general tort cases, a defendant facing potential liability may request the court apportion fault to other defendants; however, it is defendants who bear the burden of proof in establishing that joint and several liability should be foregone and that the harm at issue is capable of apportionment.[19] Likewise, defendants in a Spill Act case may seek to avoid the brunt of liability by initiating a separate contribution action against other liable parties and thus become "contribution plaintiffs."[20]

Contribution plaintiffs face a similar burden of proof as other plaintiffs under the Spill Act. These parties need not establish the extent to which individual contribution defendants are liable; rather, contribution plaintiffs need only prove that contribution defendants qualify as liable under the general provisions of the Spill Act.[21] The court may apportion damages according to equitable factors as it deems appropriate.[22]

Defenses and Marcantuone

Defenses to liability under the Spill Act include acts or omissions solely caused by war, sabotage, or God (or a combination thereof).[23] The Spill Act also provides limited liability for the beneficiaries of an estate which contains contaminated property, fiduciaries which hold the property to protect a security interest, and trustees administering an estate or trust which contains contaminated property.[24] In each instance, plaintiffs must evaluate the scope of the defense. Defendants carry the burden to show that they meet the elements of the defense or liability limitation.

There is an innocent purchaser defense available to one who acquired the property after the discharge and did not know or have reason to know of the hazardous discharge.[25] The legislature established this innocent purchase defense for those who acquired contaminated property prior to September 14, 1993. The defense has four elements:

1. The defendant acquired the property after the discharge;
2. At the time of the purchase or acquisition defendant did not know or have any reason to know that hazardous substances (as defined under the Spill Act) have been discharged on or from the property;
3. The defendant did not discharge the hazardous substance; and
4. The person gave notice to the NJDEP upon actual discovery of the discharge.[26]

However, a recent case has cast doubt on the innocent purchaser defense. In *New Jersey Schools Dev. Auth. v. Marcantuone*,[27] the Appellate Division held that liability existed under the Spill Act for a property owner who failed to conduct due diligence in regards to possible environmental contamination. The landowner in *Marcantuone* had purchased property before the amendment to the 1993 Spill Act that created an "innocent purchaser" defense for those buying property after the amendment's effective date. Following the reasoning of cases stretching back to the initial adoption of the Spill Act in 1977, the trial court found that the property owner was not liable for the cleanup of the contamination at the site, which had been caused by discharges of a dry-cleaning chemical prior to the time the current owner took title in 1985. The trial court found that the owner had not discharged the chemical so was not liable as a "discharger" under the Spill Act and was not "in any way responsible" for the discharged chemicals, as this owner had not owned or operated the site when the discharges occurred and had not owned or controlled the discharged chemicals.

The Appellate Division reversed the trial court decision in light of a 2001 amendment to the Spill Act which had created a defense to Spill Act liability for pre-1993 purchasers of already contaminated land if they could demonstrate that they had undertaken "all appropriate inquiry on the previous ownership and uses of the property based upon generally accepted good and customary standards" at the time of purchase. Although prior case law had stated that pre-1993 purchasers of already contaminated land had no liability under the Spill Act, the Appellate Division found that the 2001 amendment created liability for such pre-1993 purchasers unless the buyer could demonstrate it had undertaken "all appropriate inquiry." The court reasoned that the 2001 amendment to the Spill Act reversed the prior case law, which had long been relied upon by the real estate industry. The Appellate Division conceded that "although it may seem counterintuitive to infer liability from legislation establishing an affirmative defense, logic dictates that this is the case."[28]

In the wake of *Marcantuone*, trial courts "must first determine what the generally accepted good and customary standards were at the time defendants acquired title to the property. Defendants can then present evidence as to what pre-purchase efforts and investigation they undertook. Liability will depend upon whether defendants satisfied the prevailing standard as found by the court."[29] Thus it would appear from *Marcantuone* that a defendant will face liability under the Spill Act if he or she did not conduct due diligence at the time of purchase, even prior to September 14, 1993, but the scope of this liability is not yet clear since there are no cases interpreting this additional requirement.[30]

ENVIRONMENTAL LITIGATION BEYOND THE SPILL ACT

In addition to the Spill Act, a plaintiff can assert the equitable factors which justify a complaint under the common law, as articulated by the Court in *T&E Industries, Inc. v. Safety Light Corp.*[31]

In *T&E Industries*, defendants placed hazardous wastes in the form of radium ore[32] on the property. The plaintiff sued on the basis of nuisance, negligence, misrepresentation, fraud, and strict liability for an abnormally dangerous activity.

The elements of the abnormally dangerous-activity doctrine, which is premised on the principle that "one who carries on an abnormally dangerous activity is subject to liability for harm to the person, land or chattels of another resulting from the activity, although he has exercised the utmost care to prevent the harm," are:

(a) existence of a high degree of risk of some harm to the person, land or chattels of others;
(b) likelihood that the harm that results from it will be great;
(c) inability to eliminate the risk by the exercise of reasonable care;
(d) extent to which the activity is not a matter of common usage;
(e) inappropriateness of the activity to the place where it is carried on; and
(f) extent to which its value to the community is outweighed by its dangerous attributes.

A plaintiff who seeks recovery of costs incurred and damages from the contamination of property where the seller has either deliberately or inadvertently hidden the actual condition of the property may rely on modern concepts of justice and fair dealing with respect to the sale of real property, including rescission of the contract and damages.[33] The question remains, however, whether a purchaser's duty to perform appropriate due diligence vitiates a cause of action for concealment or deliberate silence concerning property contamination.

For a negligence claim, a plaintiff must establish that a duty existed between the defendant and plaintiff with respect to contamination of the property. This duty can be inferred from contractual obligations (which are most often merged into the sale and no longer applicable after closing). The proof necessary to show negligence is a higher standard than that of the strict liability standard of the Spill Act. If the proofs are available under the circumstances of a particular case, the consequential damages available to a plaintiff can go beyond the cost of cleanup and renovating. If there are personal injuries arising out of the contamination of the property, the plaintiff must consider a negligence cause of action.

The elements of negligent misrepresentation include (1) an incorrect statement by the seller; (2) the representation or statement is negligently made; (3) the plaintiff justifiably lied upon the negligent statement of the defendant; and (4) there has been a resulting injury.[34] Again, the plaintiff must be concerned in a contamination case that the source of the damages or injury could not reasonably have been revealed by appropriate due diligence which met the standard of the time at which the purchase was made.

There are five elements necessary to prove fraud: (1) a material misrepresentation of a past or present fact, (2) knowledge by the defendant that the material misrepresentation is false, (3) defendant's intent that the plaintiff rely upon the false material misrepresentation, (4) reasonable reliance by the buyer/plaintiff, and (5) damages resulting from the transaction.

Traditional Defenses

Liability between owners and subsequent owners can arise out of a number of traditional liability causes of action.[35] The New Jersey statute of limitation for contracts for sale of property[36] provides for a six-year statute of limitation on contracts not involving the sale of goods. Note that the accrual date is the date when the right to begin a lawsuit first arises. The same six-year statute applies to the breach of fiduciary duty which may also arise out of a contract.

Another cause of action asserted in environmental matters includes fraud and fraudulent concealment. The statute of limitation for a claim of fraud is six years.[37] The accrual date is generally from when the defrauded party knew or should have known of the act or omission giving rise to the claim of fraud. Fraudulent concealment has a two-year statute of limitation since it is a tort; however, the cause of action does not accrue until the plaintiff discovers the element alleged to be the basis of the claim of fraudulent concealment. Sometimes this occurs when a buyer is made aware of an environmental contamination which impacts neighboring properties. Under that circumstance, the property owner would have two years from the notice by an injured party or the State of New Jersey of its responsibility for contamination to bring a claim of fraudulent concealment.

In addition, a plaintiff may also make a claim for negligent handling of environmental injury, and the limitation period is two years for personal injury and six years for damage to property.[38]

NOTES

1. *State Department of Environmental Protection v. The Ventron* Corp., et al., 94 N.J. 473, 493 (1983).

2. The Spill Act provides that its remedies are *in addition to* existing common law or statutory remedies. For example, in *Ventron*, the parties were liable under common law principles for failure to abate a nuisance (i.e., the discharge of mercury) and the damage arising out of that nuisance.

3. *Id.* at 482.

4. N.J.S.A. 58:10-23.11b.

5. L.R. 1EX 265 (1866), aff'd. L.R. 3L 330 (1868).

6. For example, where the property is abandoned and the former owners are bankrupt.

7. N.J.S.A. 58:10-23.11g.

8. Under *Dimant*, a plaintiff also has the burden of proof to establish a nexus between the discharge and damage in order to establish claim under the Spill Act.

9. See *N.J. Sch. Dev. Auth. v. Marcantuone* and *Dimant, infra.*

10. 212 N.J. 153 (2012).

11. *Id.*

12. *Id.* at 182, quoting *N.J. Tpke. Auth. v. PPG Indus.*, 197 F.3d 96, 105 n.9 (3d Cir. 1999).

13. N.J.S.A. 58:10-23.11g.c.(1).

14. N.J.S.A. 58:10-23.11f.a.(2)(a).

15. *Atlantic Cty. Mun. Util. Auth. v. Hunt*, 210 N.J. Super. 76, 96-100 (App. Div. 1986).

16. *Ventron, supra*, at 502.

17. *See U.S. v. Rohm and Haas Co., et al*, 939 F. Supp. 1142, 1156 (D.N.J. 1996); *New Jersey Dep't. of Envt'l. Prot. v. Dimant*, 212 N.J. 153, 178 (2012); *Handy &Harman v. Borough of Park Ridge*, 302 N. J. Super. 558, 565 (App. Div. 1997); *New Jersey Dep't of Envt'l Prot. v. Exxon Mobil Corp.*, 393 N.J. Super. 388, 401 (App. Div. 2007).

18. N.J.S.A. 58:10-23.11g.c(1)("Except as provided in section 2 of P.O. 2005, c.43 (C.58:10-23.11g.12), any person who has discharged a hazardous substance, or is in any way responsible for any hazardous substance, shall be strictly liable, jointly and severally, without regard to fault, for all cleanup and removal costs no matter by whom incurred.").

19. See generally *Dafler v. Raymark Industries, Inc.*, 259 N.J. Super. 17, 29 (App. Div. 1992), *aff'd*, 132 N.J. 96 (1993*); Sullivan v. Combustion Engineering*, 248 N.J. Super. 135 (App. Div.) *certif. den.* 126 N.J. 341 (1991); *Fosgate v. Corona*, 66 N.J. 268 (1974).

20. See N.J.S.A. 58:10-23.11.f.a(2)(a).

21. N.J.S.A. 58:10-23.11f.a(2)(a)("Whenever one or more dischargers or persons cleans up and removes a discharge of a hazardous substance, those dischargers and persons shall have a right of contribution against all other dischargers and persons in any way responsible for a discharged hazardous substance or other persons who are liable for the cost of the cleanup and removal of that discharge of a hazardous substance. . . . In an action for contribution, the contribution plaintiffs need prove only that a discharge occurred for which the contribution defendant or defendants are liable pursuant to the provision of subsection c. of section 8 of P.L. 1976, c. 141 (C.58:10-23.11g), and the contribution defendant shall have only the defenses to liability available to parties pursuant to subsection d. of section 8 of P.L. 1976, c. 141 (C.58:10-23.11g).").

22. *Id.* See, for example, *Hatco Corp. v. W.R. Grace & Co. Conn.*, 849 F. Supp. 931, 972-73 (D.N.J. 1994) (noting that activities taking place during defendant's ownership were driving force behind cleanup warranted increased percentage of liability).

23. N.J.S.A. 58:10-23.10; see also *Lansco, Inc. v. Dep't of Envtl. Prot.*, 145 N.J. Super. 433 (App. Div. 1976).

24. N.J.S.A. 58:10-23.11g 9. The liability of trustees and fiduciaries is limited to the value of the property or assets derived from the contaminated property. The contaminated property is part of a trust or decedent's estate "only the assets of the trust or estate, or assets of any discharger other than the fiduciary of such trust or estate, shall be subject to the obligation to pay for the cleanup of the discharge." *Id.*

25. N.J.S.A. 58:10-23.11.g.d.(2).

26. There are specific parameters required for the timeliness of notice of a discharge to the NJDEP which may be subject to discovery in litigation where a defendant seeks to prove the four elements of the innocent purchaser defense.

27. 428 N.J. Super. 546 (App. Div. 2012), *certif. denied*, 2013 N.J. Lexis. 509 (2013).

28. *Id.* at 549. This analysis is a study in the concept of unintended consequences. The Spill Act amendment was intended by the Legislature to create a defense against liability similar in scope to the all appropriate inquiry defense of innocent purchasers under CERCLA. However, that standard did not apply to pre-September 14, 1993 owners until the Appellate Division pointed out the implications of the Spill Act Amendment.

29. *Id.* at 560-61.

30. The Appellate Division in *Marcantuone* essentially backs away from its prior decision recognizing the standard for pre-September 14, 1993, purchasers in *White Oak Funding, Inc. v. Winning*, 341 N.J. Super. 294 (App. Div.), *certif. denied*, 170 N.J. 209 (2001). Unresolved issues which plaintiffs must take into account until the courts or legislature give us definitive decisions to include pre-1993 purchasers of contaminated property under ambit of liability under the Spill Act include: can pre-1993 purchasers rely on the superseded holding in *White Oak Funding*? Will the courts allow old cases to be reopened and new defendants to be found in previously decided cases? At a minimum, the *Marcantuone* case will require a demonstration of due diligence appropriate to the time to meet this new standard of innocent purchaser defense.

31. 123 N.J. 371 (1991).

32. Radium is not only a hazardous substance but "an abnormally dangerous substance".

33. See *Weintraub v. Krobatsch*, 64 N.J. 445 (1974). In *Weintraub*, the seller was merely silent as to the condition of the property which was infested with roaches, and the infestation was not visible during a daylight inspection. Deliberate concealment or nondisclosure of a contamination not observed by inspectors justified rescission of the contract and damages.

34. See *H. Rosenblum, Inc. v. Adler*, 93 N.J. 324 (1983).

35. For example, where the environmental clause under the contract of sale survives closing (as a matter of negotiation) and is not merged into the deed.

36. N.J.S.A. 2A:14-1.

37. N.J.S.A. 2A:14-1.

38. N.J.S.A. 2A:14-1.

Section 2

Mass Tort and Class Actions in New Jersey

Martin P. Schrama, Esq., Stefanie Colella-Walsh, Esq., and H. Matthew Taylor, Esq. (8th Ed. only)

This chapter seeks to provide a better understanding of the most common complex litigation models used to resolve New Jersey environmental tort claims, the class action, and the mass tort. The former is a long-standing product of both federal and state law and is often used to resolve diverse disputes across the country. The latter is a more recently devised mechanism also initially developed under federal procedure, devised to efficiently resolve large, complex tort actions. The history, use, and application of each respective model will be considered in the context of both federal and state court proceedings involving environmental torts.

WHAT IS AN ENVIRONMENTAL TORT?

The complexity, drama, and, in many cases, the sheer magnitude of environmental tort cases have captured the imagination and attention of the public in recent decades. This can be seen in the popularity of the film *A Civil Action*, starring John Travolta, which chronicles the contamination of neighborhood drinking wells throughout Woburn, Massachusetts.[1] Similarly, the movie *Erin Brockovich*, starring Julia Roberts, depicts the litigation over widespread groundwater contamination in and around Hinkley, California.[2] The relatively recent surge in the popularity and frequency of this type of litigation has emerged at the intersection of related areas of law.

An environmental tort action presents a combination of environmental law and tort law. It can be difficult to neatly define environmental law. The term is understood to mean the universe of statutes, regulations, and actions at common law impacting environmental interests.[3] Separate from exclusively administrative or regulatory functions, a tort system's fundamental purpose is corrective justice intended to provide a peaceful means to restore injured parties to their original condition for harm caused by another's wrongful conduct. It is a fault-based compensation system for vindicating individual rights, but the tort system is also guided by a notion of deterrence directed at preventing future harms.[4] The specific issues sought to be addressed through the legal hybrid of environmental torts include both harm to individuals from hazardous

97

substances introduced into an environment, as well as harm to property or natural habitat. Such tort claims may include nuisance, trespass, negligence, battery, strict liability, restitution, and waste. There is also a broad range of potential categories of damages to property (such as diminution of value, stigma, and loss of use and enjoyment), bodily injury damages (such as pain and suffering, risk of future injury, emotional distress, and medical surveillance/monitoring), and equitable or enhanced damages (such as injunctive relief and punitive damages).[5]

CLASS ACTION VERSUS MASS TORT: WHAT'S THE DIFFERENCE?

Generally, in a class action, a complaint is filed on behalf of a small number of named parties alleging an injury on behalf of themselves and other similarly situated individuals whose identities are yet unknown. In a mass tort, by contrast, individual complaints are brought by separate parties, and though those cases are consolidated before a single judge, they maintain their individual case status.

Class Action Model

"Class action" is a term used to describe a group of individuals, designated as a class that has common interests in the outcome of litigation. The class action is a procedural device created under *Federal Rule of Civil Procedure* 23 (and later under its New Jersey state court analog *Rule* 4:32-1), which allows for global resolution of common claims. Through the prosecution of claims on behalf of an entire certified class, the class action mechanism provides a representative model of resolution.

Federal Class Actions under Federal Rule of Civil Procedure 23

In 1938, Congress approved the first *Federal Rules of Civil Procedure*, including *Rule* 23, which provided for class actions. In 1966, Congress approved changes to *Rule* 23 that created a three-part classification system with requirements specific to each of the three types of traditional class action classifications. These three types are defined in *Federal Rule of Civil Procedure* 23(b) and consist of (1) actions where prosecuting separate actions by or against individual class members would create a risk of inconsistent or varied adjudications with respect to individual class members that would establish incompatible standards for the party opposing the class or adjudications that, as a practical matter, would substantially impair nonclass members' ability to protect their interests; (2) actions where the party seeks final injunctive or declaratory relief with respect to the class as a whole; or (3) actions where the court finds that questions of law or fact common to class members predominate over any questions affecting only individual members and that a class action is superior to other available methods for fairly and efficiently adjudicating the controversy.

The current *Federal Rule of Civil Procedure* 23 prescribes a number of conditions and prerequisites for class certification. At the outset, an individual or group of individuals can seek class status only if (1) the class is so numerous that joinder of all members is impracticable, (2) there are questions of law or fact common to the class, (3) the claims or defenses of the representative parties are typical of the claims or defenses of the class, and (4) the representative parties will fairly and adequately protect the interests of the class.[6] Once these prerequisites have been established, a party seeking class certification under *Fed.R.Civ.P.* 23(b)(3) must then also show that (1) common questions of law or fact predominate, and (2) a class action is the superior way to adjudicate the controversy.[7]

New Jersey Class Actions under New Jersey Court Rule 4:32-1

New Jersey's state class action model shares a similar history with its federal counterpart and the current New Jersey state class action rule models *Federal Rule of Civil Procedure* 23 in wording and structure.[8] Thus, in order to maintain a class action under the New Jersey state standard, an individual or group of individuals must also satisfy the numerosity, commonality, typicality, and adequacy of representation showings also required under *Federal Rule of Civil Procedure* 23.

As most foreign defendants are aware, New Jersey law governing class certification is not coextensive with federal law. Despite the similarities in construction, the New Jersey class certification standard is interpreted more liberally than its federal counterpart. Indeed, not only are the factors required to certify a class all weighed with a presumption in favor of certification, but New Jersey courts have also endorsed the view that the state class action lawsuit is the appropriate vehicle to aggregate claims for individuals with small or nominal damages that otherwise could not seek redress. Further, unlike their federal counterparts, New Jersey courts have a general aversion to analyzing the merits of the plaintiffs' underlying claims in class certification determinations.[9] Moreover, the New Jersey state courts' more liberal interpretation of class action standards is not the only consideration for would-be class action defendants. The basic premise of the theory of federal diversity jurisdiction is founded on the interests of protecting nonresident litigants from local bias in the courtroom.[10] Therefore, not surprisingly, foreign defendants routinely seek to remove class actions to federal court whenever possible and recent legal trends have facilitated this preference.

The Class Action Fairness Act

Primary among these legal trends is the *Class Action Fairness Act of 2005* (CAFA), which introduced additional avenues of removal by altering the management and practice of class action litigation in federal and state courts. Concern that state courts would be hearing "nationwide class actions" that were more properly resolved in federal court led Congress to expand the federal subject matter jurisdiction over class actions, essentially making all class actions federal court cases.[11] CAFA created federal subject matter jurisdiction where (1) the proposed class has over 100 members; (2) the aggregated claims of class members exceed $5,000,000, exclusive of costs and interest; and (3) any members of the class of plaintiffs is a citizen of a different state from any defendant. In addition, Congress also expanded a class action defendant's removal opportunity through the creation of a new removal statute. This statute, 28 *U.S.C.* §1453 prevents plaintiffs from including claims against in-state defendants for the sole purpose of avoiding removal and now allows removal of a class action without regard to whether any defendant is a citizen of the state in which the action is brought. The new removal statute allows removal "without the consent of all defendants," which prevents plaintiffs from "joining a defendant who might be willing to break with other defendants as to removal or negotiating favorably with a defendant who would oppose removal." Finally, the statute eliminates the prohibition on removal of a diversity class action to federal court more than one year after the action commenced.

Despite the clear push to move class action litigation into federal court, CAFA contains several notable exceptions. First is the "home state exception," which allows state courts to decide issues between local parties in which "local interests . . . presumably would predominate." To satisfy this exception, more than two-thirds of the proposed class members and all the "primary defendants" must be citizens of the state in which the class action was originally filed. Second, CAFA also contains a "local controversy exception," which forces the federal court to decline jurisdiction under similar circumstances. This carve-out allows state courts to adjudicate many local controversies that would otherwise fall under the "home state exception," but contain at least one out-of-state defendant. The proposed class action must fulfill four requirements to fall within this exception: (1) greater than two-thirds of the class members are citizens of the state in which the action was originally brought, (2) at least one defendant from which "significant relief is sought" and "whose alleged conduct forms a significant basis" for the asserted claims is a citizen of the state in which the action was brought, (3) the "principal injuries resulting from the alleged conduct or any related conduct of each defendant" occurred in the forum state, and (4) no other class action involving similar factual allegations was filed against any of the same defendants in the past three years.[12] Manifested in this exception to the CAFA strictures is the clear indication that the class action model, whether in federal or state court, is a disfavored method of handling complex environmental tort causes of action, for various reasons set forth here.

The Class Action Model and Environmental Torts

The 1980s saw a sudden increase in environmental tort suits, at times resulting in thousands of lawsuits being filed within the same jurisdiction with nearly identical fact patterns of exposure. Initially, the class action model seemed like a good fit to resolve these voluminous filings and to decrease judicial docket backlogs. However, courts noted that the nature of these environmental tort claims did not fit very well into a class action framework, because the claims often lacked a discrete set of facts to prove liability and because proximate causation differed in degree among potential class members. Thus, early on, there was a general hesitance to grant class certification of environmental tort claims, since they were thought to lack commonality on questions of damages and exposure. Notwithstanding these concerns, some courts saw class action treatment as an essential or the only viable, tool to provide plaintiffs access to redress. Still, courts continued to note the inherent difficulties of the class action model to adequately handle the mass environmental claims.[13]

Further, while the onerous requirements of *Federal Rule of Civil Procedure* 23 have traditionally been exceedingly difficult to establish in environmental tort cases, the U.S. Supreme Court made it even more difficult to vault the standards for class certification in *Wal-Mart Stores, Inc. v. Dukes*, 131 *S. Ct.* 2541 (2011). In that case, the U.S. Supreme Court heightened the standards for class certification in most applicable circumstances, giving rise to an increasing expanse of like-minded decisions. Plaintiffs must now show "significant proof" to satisfy the commonality requirement for class certification. The burden is on the district judge to conduct a rigorous analysis, at times overlapping with the merits of the plaintiffs' underlying claims, to determine whether to grant class certification. In the wake of *Dukes* and its growing progeny, federal courts have been especially reluctant to certify classes given this new heightened commonality requirement.

New Jersey state courts have also found that class actions are not well suited to handle environmental tort litigations. New Jersey courts have expressly held, with some exceptions, that the class action model was not superior to other available methods where the court believed it would need to make substantial findings of fact in relation to individual members of the proposed class.[14] Thus, the class action model remains a poor fit for the adjudication of environmental torts, and the preferred method of handling complex environmental tort litigation is through the more recently developed mass tort model.

The Mass Tort Model

Environmental torts involving a relatively small number of individual claimants are frequently filed as multi-plaintiff lawsuits or multiple lawsuits consolidated before a single judge. However, cases involving more than a few plaintiffs, along with complex emissions and exposure issues, are much more appropriately subject to complex litigation treatment through establishment of a mass tort.[15] The term "mass tort" is generally used to connote a consolidation of related mass personal injury and property damage lawsuits, involving claims by numerous plaintiffs against a limited number of defendants. Mass torts are consolidated for certain purposes that permit the court system to manage a large volume of similar but discrete claims. Many times, it is the varying liability, damages and procedural issues across individual, or categories of, mass tort cases that render those cases much less amenable to class action treatment, and more suited to mass action consolidation.

Federal Multidistrict Litigation

Similar to class actions, the federal mass tort standards developed first, followed by the New Jersey state analog. Congress established the judicial panel on multidistrict litigation (JPML) in April 1968 and granted it authority to transfer pretrial proceedings for civil cases involving common questions of fact to a single judicial district. The JPML is empowered to transfer virtually any type of civil case filed in the federal district courts into multidistrict litigation (MDL).

The chief justice of the United States appoints the members of the JPML, which is composed of seven district or appellate court judges, each of whom must be from a different judicial circuit. The transfer of an action may be initiated by the JPML itself or upon a motion filed with the JPML by a party desiring the transfer. Congress authorized the JPML to approve the consolidation and coordination of pretrial proceedings with the goal of achieving a balance between efficiency and fairness. The aim is consolidation in order to avoid conflicting contemporaneous pretrial rulings, and the JPML has discretion regarding which judge will preside over the MDL proceedings. The JPML can assign the consolidated MDL case to a district judge to whom the cases are transferred, or it may assign the proceedings to an experienced judge from a district that does not have any of the consolidated cases. The JPML can also request that a judge from another district or circuit be assigned temporarily by the chief justice or the chief judge of the circuit. The JPML also has authority to remand the consolidated action back to the originating, transferor court. In keeping with the overall purpose of judicial economy, a remand is appropriate where it will "best serve the expeditious disposition of the litigation."[16]

The benefits of an MDL include uniform pleadings, discovery and motion practice before a judge that has the experience and resources to effectively manage complex litigation. The MDL structure also allows for the conservation of court system resources and permits the plaintiffs' attorneys to pool and maximize their resources. In this manner, MDL's are effective in avoiding conflicting rulings and employing specialized case management mechanisms (such as the preparation and use of "bellwether cases"). However, by its express purpose and application, the MDL proceeding consolidates lawsuits from federal district courts across the country into one localized federal court. For this reason, MDL consolidation is not frequently used for environmental tort cases, which tend to involve localized and geographically isolated incidents of toxic exposure. [17]

Furthermore, in the instance where all of the defendants reside and have their principal place of business located outside of New Jersey, this can give rise to diversity for federal jurisdiction purposes.[18] Thus, despite the CAFA carve-out provisions and the obvious benefits of having local environmental tort matters handled through the state's established complex litigation structure, removal of environmental tort litigation to federal court by diverse defendants can have the unfortunate effect of circumventing the structures put in place specifically for addressing this type of complex litigation. In such a case, the litigation would likely be consolidated in federal court but without the numerous benefits of federal MDL or state multicounty litigation (MCL) treatment. Accordingly, jurisdictional considerations permitting, an MCL is, in the majority of circumstances, the most appropriate and effective model for managing complex local New Jersey environmental tort claims.

Multicounty Litigation

Again, New Jersey's state mass tort model is patterned upon its federal counterpart. In 2003, the New Jersey Supreme Court announced a process that would allow mass tort filings to be coordinated and managed in unified statewide proceedings.[19] *New Jersey Court Rule* 4:38A was promulgated to help clarify the process of mass tort designation. An officially approved mass tort is designated as an MCL.[20] A party that seeks MCL status must make an application to the Assignment Judge of any vicinage or directly apply to the Supreme Court, through the administrative director of the courts, to have the case(s) classified as an MCL. A notice and comment period follows the MCL designation application. The New Jersey Supreme Court then decides whether MCL status is warranted and assigns the case to one of the three judges, currently sitting in Bergen, Middlesex, or Atlantic counties. In deciding whether MCL status is appropriate, the court is guided by various factors, including whether the proposed cases (1) involve a large number of parties; (2) involve many claims with common, recurrent issues of law and fact associated with a single complex environmental or toxic tort; (3) involve geographical dispersion of the parties; and (4) exhibit a high degree of commonality of injury or damages. In addition to these concerns, the court will consider whether centralization will expedite or delay the litigation and whether any party is unfairly prejudiced by MCL status.[21] Environmental and toxic tort claims are one of the three main variants of MCL designation:

> The definition of an MCL in New Jersey derives from an identification of certain common case characteristics. Each group of cases designated as an MCL do exhibit many, if not all, of these characteristics. Thus far, there have been three general classes of cases determined to be MCLs. These include:
>
> * large numbers of claims associated with a single product—for example, diet drugs or other large products liability cases such as tobacco, Norplant, breast implant, Propulsid, Rezulin, PPA, and latex litigation.
> * mass disasters: these cases are characterized by common technical and legal issues. The Durham Woods pipeline explosion litigation is a good example of this type of case.
> * *complex environmental cases and toxic torts: these cases are characterized by a large number of parties with claims arising from a common event. An example of this type of case is the Ciba-Geigy litigation, alleging air, water, and soil pollution.*[22]

Thus, a common theme in most of these large, complex litigations is long-term emissions of toxic substances, to which plaintiffs were allegedly exposed through air, soil, and/or water pathways. One such example is the *Bristol-Myers Squibb* environmental contamination litigation, involving property damage and bodily injury claims in the community surrounding a century-old drug manufacturing complex in New Brunswick, New Jersey.[23] There is also the *Pompton Lakes* environmental contamination litigation, involving similar claims concerning a chemical plant in Pompton Lakes, New Jersey.[24] Before that, corresponding claims were brought in the *Ciba-Geigy* environmental contamination litigation, involving a chemical plant in Toms River, New Jersey.[25]

Much like the MDL structure, the virtues of achieving MCL status are readily apparent. Generally, the cases are consolidated before a single judge that has the experience and resources to effectively manage complex litigation, utilizing established procedures such as standardized and technologically augmented forms of pleadings, discovery, motion practice, and orders. These procedures are certainly used as a matter of necessity in large, complex litigation, but are invariably instrumental in efficiently managing and resolving the claims. Specifically, with regard to New Jersey environmental torts, the MCL framework permits consolidation of related claims of plaintiffs that might have relocated to other counties, states, or countries, permitting those claims to be litigated, together, in or around the county where the environmental torts took place.

CONCLUSION

New Jersey federal and state courts continue to evolve in their methods of meeting the considerable demands of complex environmental tort litigation. The clear trend is movement away from the class action model toward the many benefits afforded through the mass tort model. Within the mass tort model, when jurisdictional considerations permit, an MCL is, in the majority of circumstances, the most appropriate and effective model for managing complex local New Jersey environmental tort claims.

NOTES

1. See *Anderson v. WR Grace & Co.*, 628 *F. Supp.* 1219 (D. Mass. 1986); see also Jonathan Harr, *A Civil Action*, Random House, 1995.

2. See *Anderson v. Pacific Gas & Electric Co.*, No. BCV-00822 (San Bernadino County Super. Ct., settlement July 2, 1996).

3. See, e.g., *Black's Law Dictionary* (10th ed. 2014); 2 *Environmental Law Practice Guide* § 11B.02 (2018) (Environmental law is a collective body of rules and regulations, orders and statutes, constraints and allowances that are all concerned with the maintenance and protection of the natural environment of a country); see also 1 *Toxic Torts Guide* § 1.02 (2018).

4. The New Jersey statutory definition of an environmental tort is "a civil action seeking damages for personal injuries or death where the cause of the damages is the negligent manufacture, use, disposal, handling, storage or treatment of hazardous or toxic substances." *N.J.S.A.* § 2A:15-5.3(f)(1).

5. Thus, the broader term "toxic tort," encompassing claims based upon virtually any exposure to harmful substances, is frequently viewed as synonymous with the term environmental tort, in describing a personal injury case that involves exposure of people or property to a toxic substance. Though amenable to complex litigation treatment, workplace or lifestyle related toxic tort claims (most notably asbestos exposure or tobacco use), are not encompassed within the generally accepted definition of environmental torts. 5 *Law of Hazardous Waste* § 17.01 (2018); 5 *Law of Hazardous Waste* § 17.04 (2018); *see, also, Comment: You Can Teach an Old Dog New Tricks: The Application of Common Law in Present-Day Environmental Disputes*, 11 *Vill. Envtl. L.J.* 59 (2000).

6. These factors are set forth in detail in the corresponding *Federal Rules of Civil Procedure*:

  Fed.R.Civ.P. 23(a)(1)—Numerosity; *Fed.R.Civ.P.* 23(a)(2)—Commonality; and *Fed.R.Civ.P.* 23(a)(3)—Typicality; *Fed.R.Civ.P.* 23(a)(4) - Adequacy of Representation.

7. The different forms of class actions are also set forth in detail in the corresponding *Federal Rules of Civil Procedure*: *Fed.R.Civ.P.* 23(b)(1) - Risk of Inconsistent or Dispositive Adjudications; *Fed.R.Civ.P.* 23(b)(2) - Declaratory or Injunctive Relief; and *Fed.R.Civ.P.* 23(b)(3) - Predominance and Superiority. Class certification under *Fed.R.Civ.P.* 23(b)(3) was traditionally the most commonly sought in environmental tort litigation, as it specifically contemplates monetary damages and permits potential class members to opt-out of the class.

8. These factors are set forth in detail in the parallel *New Jersey Court Rules*: *N.J. Ct. R.* 4:32-1(a)(1)—Numerosity; *N.J. Ct. R.* 4:32-1(a)(2)—Commonality; *N.J. Ct. R.* 4:32-1(a)(3)—Typicality; *N.J. Ct. R.* 4:32-1(a)(4) - Adequacy of Representation; *N.J. Ct. R.* 4:32-1(b)

(1) - Risk Of Inconsistent Or Dispositive Adjudications; *N.J. Ct. R.* 4:32-1(b)(2) - Declaratory Or Injunctive Relief; and *N.J. Ct. R.* 4:32-1(b)(3) - Predominance And Superiority.

9. See, generally, *Leveling the Playing Field in the Garden State: A Guide to New Jersey Class Action Case Law*, 37 *Rutgers L. J.* 399.

10. See Christopher Pinahs, *Note, Diversity Jurisdiction and Injunctive Relief: Using a 'Moving-Party Approach' to Value the Amount in Controversy*, 95 *MINN. L. REV.* 1930, Fn. 27 (2011) (citing *Bank of the U.S. v. Deveaux*, 9 *U.S.* (5 Cranch) 61, 86 (1809), *overruled in part by Louisville C. & C.R. Co. v. Letson*, 43 *U.S.* (2 How.) 497 (1844); *Guar. Trust Co. v. York*, 326 *U.S.* 99, 111 (1945) ("Diversity jurisdiction is founded on assurance to non-resident litigants of courts free from susceptibility to potential local bias."); *Erie R.R. Co. v. Tompkins*, 304 *U.S.* 64, 74 (1938) (Stating that "[d]iversity of citizenship jurisdiction" prevents "discrimination in state courts against those not citizens of the State")).

11. Note, also, that the United States Supreme Court's decisions in *Daimler AG v. Bauman*, 571 *U.S.* 117 (2014); and *Bristol-Myers Squibb Co. v. Superior Court*, 137 *S. Ct.* 1773 (2017), though addressing product liability claims, essentially hold that a plaintiff may only properly bring a lawsuit in the plaintiff's home state - subject to removal by a foreign defendant, or in the defendant's home state—thereby not subject to removal.

12. See, generally, *Construction and Application of Class Action Fairness Act of 2005*, Pub. L. 109-2, 119 Stat. 4 (2005), 18 *A.L.R. Fed.* 2d 223; 5 *Moore's Federal Practice - Civil* § 23.63A, *State Class Actions May Be Removed to Federal Court* (2018).

13. See, generally, *Propriety, Under Rules 23(a) and 23(b) of Federal Rules of Civil Procedure, as Amended in 1966, of Class Action Seeking Relief Against Pollution of Environment*, 19 *A.L.R. Fed.* 2d 303.

14. See 1 *LexisNexis Practice Guide NJ Personal Injury* § 6.20 (2019): "[T]he majority of mass torts are not well suited for class action treatment, and courts have historically refused to certify classes in the toxic tort setting. *See Lafferty v. Sherwin-Williams Co.*, 2018 *U.S. Dist. LEXIS 141549* at *15 (D.N.J. Aug. 21, 2018) (alleged contamination resulting from manufacture of paint, varnish, and related products; class was wholly unascertainable without individualized investigation and fact-finding); *Goasdone v. American Cyanamid Corp.*, 354 *N.J. Super.* 519, 533–37 (Law Div. 2002) (denying certification of medical-monitoring class of workers exposed to dyes, noting that individual issues such as significance and length of exposure as well as individual health effects and histories make it difficult to satisfy element of commonality). *See also Ortiz v. Fibreboard Corp.*, 527 *U.S.* 815, 845 n.20 (1994) (stating that mass accident resulting in injuries to numerous persons is ordinarily not appropriate for class action because of likelihood that significant questions of damages, liability, and defenses would affect individuals in different ways); *Rowe v. E.I. Dupont De Nemours & Co.*, 2008 *U.S. Dist. LEXIS* 103528, at *60 (D.N.J. Dec. 23, 2008) (alleged contamination of drinking supply caused by defendant's release of certain perfluorinated materials; although some elements of medical monitoring relief may be subject to common proof, elements of significant exposure, increased risk of disease, and necessity of medical monitoring posed numerous individualized issues that could not be proved on class-wide basis)."

15. See, generally, *Manual for Complex Litigation* (4th ed., 2004); *N.J. Judiciary, Mass Tort (Non-Asbestos) Resource Book* (4th ed. 2014).

16. http://www.jpml.uscourts.gov/overview-panel-0.

17. In fact, some environmental torts are so extensive in potentially affected plaintiffs, geographical area and damages that an MDL is the only appropriate procedural vehicle. Such was the case in *In Re: Oil Spill by the Oil Rig Deepwater Horizon*, MDL No. 2179.

18. Note that the *Class Action Fairness Act of 2005* may apply to mass torts, as well as class actions, in certain circumstances. *But see Abraham v. St. Croix Renaissance Grp., L.L.L.P.*, 719

F.3d 270 (3d Cir. 2012) (Local-controversy and home-state exceptions can render environmental torts immune to CAFA removal).

19. New Jersey had traditionally been a jurisdiction of choice for mass tort filings. As many large pharmaceutical companies are headquartered in New Jersey, plaintiffs in defective drug cases could file in New Jersey Superior Court without the fear of being removed to federal court. In addition, New Jersey has traditionally hosted the operations of extremely waste intensive commercial operations throughout the state. One of the other primary advantages to filing suit in New Jersey was not having to contend with the strictures of the federal standard on expert opinion, set forth in *Daubert v. Merrell Dow Pharmaceuticals, Inc.*, 509 *U.S.* 579 (1993). This less stringent evidentiary standard was held especially applicable in environmental torts. *See Rubanick v. Witco Chem. Corp.*, 125 *N.J.* 421, 433 (1991); *Landrigan v. Celotex Corp.*, 127 *N.J.* 404, 413–14 (1992) (Holding that consideration should be given to the fact that the plaintiffs' proofs in an environmental tort case are much more onerous than in other tort claims). This trend seems to have abated somewhat in recent years for various reasons. For example, though beyond the scope of this chapter, New Jersey has recently adopted at least a large portion of *Daubert* in its still evolving opinion in *In re Accutane Litig.*, 234 *N.J.* 340 (2018); see also https://www.natlawreview.com/article/new-jersey-s-evolving-expert-opinion-standard-and-its-effect-multicounty-mass-tort.

20. *Rule* 4:38A. Centralized Management of Multicounty Litigation

The Supreme Court may designate a case or category of cases as Multicounty Litigation to receive centralized management in accordance with criteria and procedures promulgated by the Administrative Director of the Courts upon approval by the Court. Promulgation of the criteria and procedures will include posting in the Multicounty Litigation Information Center on the Judiciary's internet website (judiciary.state.nj.us).

21. https://njcourts.gov/attorneys/mcl/mclfaq.html.

22. See *N.J. Judiciary, Mass Tort (Non-Asbestos) Resource Book* (4th ed. 2014), at pp. 1–4 (emphasis added).

23. https://www.njcourts.gov/attorneys/mcl/atlantic/bms.html.

24. https://www.njcourts.gov/attorneys/mcl/misc/archives/pomptonlakes.html.

25. https://www.njcourts.gov/attorneys/mcl/misc/archives/cibageigy.html.See *N.J. Judiciary, Mass Tort (Non-Asbestos) Resource Book* (4th ed. 2014), at pp. 1–4 (emphasis added).

Section 3

Insurance Coverage for Environmental Liabilities

Henry R. Booth, Eric E. Tomaszewski, Esq., and Alexander D. Lehrer, Esq.

As part of any initial client consultation regarding an incidence of environmental contamination to property, practitioners should elicit as much information as possible about available insurance that may potentially cover any losses related to that contamination. Coverage may ultimately be found under several different types of policies and in a variety of factual circumstances. Conversely, to be considered viable, a claim for coverage related to environmental contamination must arguably be able to withstand various factual and legal defenses to coverage available to carriers. Accordingly, the factual circumstances related to the release of any hazardous substance should be carefully analyzed against the backdrop of whatever coverage may have been purchased by the client.

Any effort to determine what insurance may be available to potentially cover losses related to environmental contamination usually begins with the comprehensive general liability (CGL) policy. A typical CGL policy provides that:

> The Company will pay on behalf of the insured all sums which the insured shall become legally obligated to pay as damages because of
>
> (a) bodily injury, or
> (b) property damage
>
> to which this insurance applies caused by an occurrence . . .

Over time, carriers and policyholders have fought vigorously over how these and other terms and conditions of CGL policies govern property damage and bodily injury claims for environmental contamination. As explained in greater detail in this chapter, New Jersey is generally considered a favorable jurisdiction for insureds pursuing insurance coverage for environmental claims under CGL policies. New Jersey courts have rendered numerous decisions interpreting CGL policy terms and exclusions in a more advantageous manner for policyholders than courts in other states. New Jersey's favorable treatment of coverage claims for environmental contamination makes choice-of-forum/choice-of-law issues particularly important. Practitioners would be well-advised to consider what other states could potentially exercise jurisdiction over a particular coverage dispute as part of any early client consultation to guard against a possible "race to the courthouse" scenario where an insurer could first file suit in a more insurer-favorable state.

Applying the multifactored analysis provided by the Restatement (Second) of Conflicts of Laws, the New Jersey Supreme Court has held that New Jersey substantive law applies to sites located in New Jersey.[1] In addition, the Third Circuit has used that same test to find that New Jersey substantive law applied to a Pennsylvania waste site "because the insured is a New Jersey corporation with its main plant and headquarters in New Jersey and the relevant insurance policy was negotiated and paid for in New Jersey."[2] By comparison, when a non-New Jersey insured files suit in New Jersey over a contaminated site located in another state, the New Jersey Supreme Court has applied the substantive law of that state where the site is located in making coverage determinations.[3]

PROOF OF COVERAGE

Obviously, obtaining actual insurance policies from the client is the best way to determine and prove what insurance coverage may be available to cover claims for environmental contamination to property. If the policies are not available, however, there are other ways to identify and establish convincing proof that CGL insurance coverage was purchased and affords coverage through secondary evidence.

Naturally, the carriers must first be identified. Many types of documents other than the actual policy will identify insurers including, but not limited to, certificates of insurance, cover notes, broker's slips (London Market Insurance only), schedules of insurance, and various broker-generated documents (e.g., premium invoices, accounting records, canceled checks, correspondence, etc.). These documents are also likely to include policy numbers, which can be used to obtain copies of policies from the carrier who generally has a duty to research its files and provide copies of any policies.

It is well settled in New Jersey that the insured has the burden of proving that the policy, under which it seeks coverage, existed.[4] That burden includes evidence of the policy's terms and conditions, which can be proven by a preponderance of evidence absent any claim of fraud.[5] Although insurance certificates, cover notes, broker records, and accounting material do not typically provide policy terms and conditions, New Jersey courts have taken into account such secondary evidence in considering whether the insured's burden of establishing the existence and terms of coverage has been met. For example, in *Newport Assoc. Phase I Developers Ltd P'ship v. Travelers Cas. & Sure. Co.*, the Court held that certificates of insurance do not create or bind coverage.[6] A standard certificate of insurance only evidences the existence of policies to which it refers; it does not alter the terms of an indemnity agreement or the parties' contract, nor does it alter or amend the terms of the policies to which it refers.[7] Nevertheless, the *Newport* Court held that the insurance certificates were "admissible at trial on the issue of whether the parties intended plaintiffs to be covered under the policies."[8]

In the case where "a policy is lost or mislaid, it is proper to introduce another policy coupled with evidence that it is the same in form as the policy sued on."[9] New Jersey courts have considered proof of premium payments and the method of computation or amount paid when faced with proving the existence and provisions of an insurance policy.[10] Courts also look to the standard-form language used by the Insurance Services Office to aid in the construction of coverage afforded by a missing policy. Most CGL policy numbers have a prefix, which may be used as a marker identifying the type of cover being written—an obvious example is "CLP"—Comprehensive Liability Policy. Accordingly, if you know the policy number you can often find a corresponding exemplary form. In making this connection it is important to know the era in which the coverage was written or the policy period. In addition, policies of an excess insurer will invariably show the carrier and limits of underlying primary insurance.

In *Borough of Sayreville v. Bellefonte Ins. Co.*[11] the insured brought an action to recover under lost or missing CGL insurance policies from the time period 1970 to 1974. There was no dispute, however, that the insurer had issued the insured primary policies from 1975 to 1977 or regarding the terms of those later policies. The Appellate Division found that there was nothing in the record to suggest that the insurer had used a form of CGL policy between 1970 to 1974 that was any different from the form used between 1975 and 1977.[12] The insured also presented copies of schedules for the underlying insurance from 1970 to 1974 that listed the policies by number, type, applicable limits, and dates of coverage. Accordingly, the court "conclude[d] that sufficient evidence exist[ed] to suggest a chance that plaintiff's burden by a preponderance as to [the] existence of the policies can be shouldered."[13]

It is vital to understand what type of evidence is necessary to prosecute a productive insurance recovery action, whether or not the claim may ultimately be litigated. Engaging an insurance archaeology consultant with experience in uncovering sufficient evidence of the existence and terms of coverage can often prove valuable both for productive settlement negotiations or supporting a claim for litigation. That process, however, will still usually require some initial information from which to begin a search.

DUTY TO INDEMNIFY FOR "DAMAGES" AND DUTY TO DEFEND

Insurers have two basic obligations under standard-form CGL policies: (1) the duty to indemnify the insured for "all sums which the insured shall become legally obligated to pay as damages because of bodily injury or property damage" and (2) "the duty to defend any suit against the insured seeking damages."[14] These two related obligations carry particular significance in the context of property damage claims related to environmental contamination because of the procedural posture in which such claims can arise, and, in certain jurisdictions, they can be interpreted to preclude coverage because of those procedural circumstances. For example, in California, the duty to defend requires a formal lawsuit be filed and the duty to indemnify is limited to money ordered to be paid by a court.[15] In that jurisdiction, an insured who remediates contamination in response to an administrative order or does so voluntarily to comply with existing environmental laws may be unable to obtain coverage for the costs related to such efforts.

New Jersey courts do not apply such a restrictive interpretation of these obligations. As an initial matter, the New Jersey Supreme Court has held that the plain, nontechnical meaning of "damages" is not limited to reimbursement of money damages to a third-party but encompasses response costs imposed upon an insured required to remediate environmental damage.[16] In addition, damages are not necessarily limited to costs of remediating contamination but can include efforts to abate further contamination.[17] Moreover, the insurer's duty to indemnify does not require a formal lawsuit.[18] Additionally, the New Jersey Supreme Court in *Flomerfelt v. Cardiello* held that the duty to defend is governed by "separate principles" from the duty to indemnify the insured such that when a complaint is filed against an insured that might be covered by the policy language, evaluating the duty to defend requires a "comparison between the allegations set forth in the [complaint] and the language of the insurance policy."[19] New Jersey has further held that the duty to defend is specific to each claim made against the insured "irrespective of the claim's actual merit."[20]

Where the discharge of hazardous substances makes an insured strictly liable for the costs of remediating contamination caused by that discharge, such as under the Spill Compensation and Control Act,[21] the insurer must indemnify the loss even where no administrative order has been issued or lawsuit commenced.[22] New Jersey courts have previously found a strong public policy basis for these decisions to avoid punishing policyholders who voluntarily meet their legal obligation to remediate contamination by delaying or depriving them of coverage.[23] With the passage of the Site Remediation Reform Act,[24] which provides an affirmative remediation obligation, mandatory deadlines for conducting such remediation, and decreased government involvement, any residual concern over not being covered for "voluntary" remedial efforts may disappear completely. Many carriers, however, continue to refer to the "lawsuit defense" in their reservation of rights letters in response to such claims.

New Jersey courts have also held that sums incurred in remediating a site as required by the Industrial Site Recovery Act[25] (f/k/a the Environmental Cleanup Responsibility Act) constitute covered damages under CGL policies.[26] In addition, the New Jersey Supreme Court has held that expenses incurred to investigate the nature and extent of contamination present, which, in some instances, may exceed the actual costs of remediation, qualify as defense costs when incurred after a claim is tendered to the carrier.[27] Civil fines or penalties assessed by a regulatory agency, however, do not constitute "damages" under standard CGL policies.[28]

With respect to anti-assignment clauses in an occurrence policy, the New Jersey Supreme Court recently held that once an insured's loss has occurred, an anti-assignment clause in an occurrence policy may not provide a basis for an insurer's declination of coverage based on the insured's assignment of the right to invoke policy coverage for that loss.[29]

OWNED PROPERTY EXCLUSION

Standard CGL policies usually include exclusionary language providing that the insurance does not apply to (a) property owned or occupied by or rented to the insured; (b) property used by the insured; or (c) property in the care, custody, or control of the insured. Insurers frequently cite this language, referred to as the "owned-property exclusion," when responding to coverage claims related to the remediation of contaminated soil on an insured's own property. While New Jersey courts have routinely found this exclusion to bar CGL coverage for damage to such "first-party" property,[30] its application to environmental claims often requires additional considerations, including (a) distinguishing between damage to groundwater and soil; (b) allocating costs of remediation between first and third-party property; and (c) determining whether the exclusion applies when costs are incurred to prevent damage to third-party property. Policyholders should consider these fact-sensitive issues and the scope of the owned-property exclusion when evaluating the scope of potential CGL coverage for environmental claims.

New Jersey courts have consistently held that groundwater is a natural resource owned by the State and represents third-party property for purposes of the owned-property exclusion.[31] The exclusion does not bar coverage for damage to groundwater, even if that groundwater is located directly beneath the insured's property.[32] Costs arising from specific efforts to remedy groundwater contamination, such as the installation of wells or in-situ treatment, may represent covered damages under CGL policies, even if undertaken on the policyholder's property.[33]

To avoid having a claim barred by the owned-property exclusion, a policyholder *must* be able to demonstrate damage to third-party property. Without evidence of any past or present injury to third-party property, the exclusion bars coverage for remedial actions intended to prevent future injury, even if the threat to groundwater or off-site property appears to be imminent or immediate.[34] Even where the removal of contaminated soil may be a step in the process of groundwater remediation, soil removal will not be covered if the groundwater is not contaminated.[35] These subsurface distinctions between first and third-party property often require courts to allocate response costs based on the nature of the remedial action in order to determine what is owed to the policyholder.[36]

EXPECTED OR INTENDED

Prior to 1966, standard-form CGL policies provided coverage for property damage caused by "accident," which was usually an undefined term within the policy.[37] In 1966, insurers began to revise such policies to provide coverage based on an "occurrence," which was generally defined as "an accident, including injurious exposure to conditions, which results, during the policy period, in bodily injury or property damage that was *neither expected nor intended* from the standpoint of the insured."[38] Predicating CGL coverage on property damage being unexpected or unintended has sparked a great deal of litigation between insureds and insurers over time, particularly in the context of claims for environmental contamination. Although not expressly an exclusion provision, insurers bear the burden to prove that the damage was expected or intended and usually engage in extensive discovery regarding an insured's historic operations to try to meet that burden.

When analyzing an insured's historic operations for purposes of the "expected or intended" issue, New Jersey courts initially apply a subjective standard wherein CGL coverage will only be excluded if a policyholder's intentional action is accompanied by the intent to cause actual damage.[39] In exceptional circumstances, however, courts can establish an insured's intent to cause environmental damage through an objective approach that "focuses on the likelihood that an injury will result from an actor's behavior rather than the wrongdoer's subjective state of mind."[40] The New Jersey Supreme Court provided for an objective standard in exceptional circumstances in recognition of the fact that "proof of subjective intent to cause environmental harm will rarely be available."[41] In this inherently fact-sensitive analysis, courts examine the following circumstances: "[T]he duration of the discharges, whether the discharges occurred intentionally, negligently, or innocently, the quality of the insured's knowledge concerning the harmful propensities of the pollutants, whether regulatory authorities attempted to discourage or prevent the insured's conduct, and the existence of subjective knowledge concerning the possibility or likelihood of harm."[42]

In practice, analyzing whether such exceptional circumstances exist often places the court in the difficult position of considering conduct or actions dating back to the 1950s without the hindsight of today's environmental standards.[43] Beyond documentary evidence and the testimony of former employees, this issue often inspires the retention of expert witnesses with the requisite experience to testify with respect to what the policyholder "should have known" about the potential for environmental damage at the time the acts were committed.

POLLUTION EXCLUSIONS: QUALIFIED AND ABSOLUTE

In or around 1973, insurers began adding a broad policy exclusion to standard CGL policies that excluded bodily injury or property damage arising out of the discharge, dispersal, release, or escape of smoke, vapor, soot, fumes, acids, alkalis, toxic chemicals, waste materials, irritants, or other contaminants. This exclusion, however, included a qualification that it does not apply where the discharge, dispersal, release, or escape was "sudden and accidental." Ever since its introduction, the applicability of this "qualified pollution exclusion," in particular the meaning of "sudden and accidental," has been the subject of numerous disputes between insurers and policyholders and division among courts around the country.

Disputes over the meaning of "sudden and accidental" often revolve around whether the term "sudden" requires a temporal element. In New Jersey's seminal case on the issue, *Morton Int'l, Inc. v. Gen. Accident Ins. Co. of Am.*, the Supreme Court initially concluded that the term "sudden" included a temporal element, generally connoting an event that begins abruptly or without prior notice.[44] Based on a review of the regulatory and drafting history related to the exclusion, however, the Court found that, when seeking permission to use the provision, the insurance industry explained to the New Jersey Department of Banking and Insurance and other regulators that the exclusion was not intended to alter coverage by "exclud[ing] any risk which was not excluded in the original policies."[45] Accordingly, the Court limited the scope of the exclusion to the reasonable expectation of regulators based on that explanation and did not add any temporal element.[46] Courts in many other jurisdictions, however, do include such a temporal element when analyzing this exclusion.[47]

Notwithstanding that New Jersey courts have not given any effect to the term "sudden," the discharge must still be "accidental." The qualified pollution exclusion will bar coverage where "the insured intentionally discharges a known pollutant, *irrespective* of whether the resulting property damage was intended or expected."[48] The qualified pollution exclusion narrows coverage further than the conditions imposed only by the "occurrence" definition, by eschewing the issue of intent or expectation when the discharge is intentional.[49] Similar to the "occurrence" definition, however, New Jersey courts apply a subjective analysis in applying the qualified pollution exclusion by requiring a demonstration that the insured actually knew the discharge contained a pollutant.[50]

In 1986, insurers amended the pollution exclusion to more broadly bar CGL coverage for contamination without the "sudden and accidental" qualification. This "absolute pollution exclusion clause" generally prohibits coverage for traditional environmental claims under most factual circumstances.[51] The development and prevalence of the "absolute pollution exclusion" have given rise to a number of different "environmental insurance policies" that specifically insure against risks that are now excluded under standard CGL policies. Several examples of these "environmental insurance policies" are discussed in chapter 3, section 2.

TRIGGER ISSUES

Coverage under a CGL policy is "triggered" if the date the injury or damage takes place falls within the term of the policy. Although a relatively simple concept, in the context of complex environmental claims, where contamination occurs over a protracted period of time, it is often difficult to determine when the discharge occurred and what particular policies are triggered. Four principal triggers of coverage theories have been adopted by courts around the country: (1) *exposure*, where each policy on the risk when contaminants are released into the environment is triggered; (2) *manifestation*, where each policy on the risk when the contamination is discovered is triggered; (3) *injury-in-fact*, where each policy on the risk when the covered damage actually occurs is triggered; and (4) *continuous trigger*, where all policies on the risk from the initial release of contaminants through the discovery of contamination are triggered.

New Jersey courts analyze insurance claims for environmental damage using the continuous trigger theory.[52] Under the continuous trigger theory, courts consider environmental contamination a "progressive indivisible injury or damage result[ing] from exposure to injurious conditions,"[53] which may be the case where contaminants migrate from soil to groundwater and further into previously uncontaminated areas. The continuous trigger, while advantageous to the policyholder, still requires the insured to demonstrate when the release of contamination first occurred and that it was continuous, which can sometimes be a difficult burden to overcome. In certain circumstances, however, the analysis may be relatively straightforward. For example, in *Quincy Mut. Fire Ins. Co. v. Borough of Bellmawr*, the New Jersey Supreme Court held that with respect to claims related to landfill dumping: "The natural and unavoidable progression of the original dumping, which must be deemed the 'exposure' [ ] is the starting point of an 'occurrence' that triggers coverage. . . . The property, that is, the landfill, was contaminated as soon as the toxic material was dumped, for that is when the toxins began their damaging journey through the ground."[54]

In *Franklin Mut. Ins. Co. v. Metro. Prop. & Cas. Ins. Co.*, the court held that the continuous trigger theory is applicable as a method of "allocate[ing] damages between insurers" "if the date of the occurrence of the injury cannot be pinpointed."[55] The Court in *Franklin* recognized that the continuous trigger theory was appropriate because the

> difficulty with environmental contamination claims is that the damage that triggers insurance liability does not occur as a result of a single event, but usually is attributable to events that begin, develop and intensify over a sustained period of time and therefore, the damages have occurred or been triggered along a continuous timeline during which several successive policies issued to the insured were in effect.[56]

In *Benjamin v. State Farm Ins. Co.*, an unpublished opinion, the insurer interpreted the decision in *Franklin* to mean that courts use the continuous trigger theory only when the "date of the occurrence of the injury cannot be pinpointed" and is thus inapplicable when the "evidence is indisputable" that an oil release began and ended before a particular date.[57] The N.J. Federal District Court explained that the insurer had misinterpreted the decision in *Franklin* and stated that if the date for the damage and not the date of the act cannot be pinpointed, courts will use the continuous trigger theory.[58]

ALLOCATION OF ENVIRONMENTAL DAMAGES

Assuming there are no applicable exclusions to bar a claim for environmental damage, and if that damage triggers policies over multiple policy periods, a court must then decide how that loss will be allocated (i.e., apportioned or divided) between the triggered policies and, in certain circumstances, the insured itself. Several different issues may arise as part of this process, but courts usually focus first on the manner in which triggered policies respond to the loss. Most jurisdictions across the country apply either a "pro rata"[59] or "all sums"[60] approach to allocating environmental damage.

The New Jersey Supreme Court, however, took a somewhat different track for allocating losses among triggered policies in *Owens-Illinois, Inc. v. United Ins. Co.*[61] The Court rejected both the "all sums" method and a purely per year *pro-rata* method instead adopting a *pro-rata* allocation formula "related both to time on the risk and the degree of risk assumed."[62] Under the *Owens-Illinois* method, if an insured had $100,000 in coverage in one year and $900,000 in coverage the second year, and claimed environmental damage amounting to $100,000 suffered over both years, the court would allocate $10,000 of loss to the first policy year and $90,000 to the second. A few years later, in *Carter-Wallace, Inc. v. Admiral Ins. Co.*,[63] the Court refined its approach by finding that the "degree of risk assumed" included any excess level insurance held by the policyholder, not simply the primary policies.[64] Under *Owens-Illinois* and *Carter-Wallace*, whichever years provide a policyholder the most overall coverage (primary and excess) will bear the largest percentage of the loss. In some instances, an excess policy in one year could be triggered before reaching the policy limits of the primary coverage in another year.

There have been several additional complexities added to the *Owens-Illinois* methodology since *Carter-Wallace* as well. In *Champion Dyeing & Finishing Co. Inc. v. Centennial Ins. Co.*, the Appellate Division clarified that, given that the advent of the absolute pollution exclusion in 1986 rendered CGL coverage for environmental claims commercially unavailable, the allocation cutoff date occurs when coverage for environmental risks could no longer be purchased.[65] This decision has significant implications in relation to the continuous trigger where, in some instances, the environmental damage is not discovered until after 1985. In *Universal-Rundle Corp. v. Commercial Union Ins. Co.*, the Appellate Division held that, where a policyholder settles with one of its carriers, the settlement represents that insurer's full allocated share and precludes any further recovery of any additional losses that might otherwise be attributable to that insurer's coverage period from any other insurer.[66]

In 2004, the New Jersey Supreme Court held in *Benjamin Moore Co. v. Aetna CAs & Sur. Co.*, that in a long-tail environmental exposure case of liability coverage under multiple policies, the insured was required to satisfy the full deductible for each triggered policy before it was entitled to indemnity from the insurer and was not entitled to pro-rata allocation of the deductibles to the aggregated loss.[67]

Most recently, the New Jersey Supreme Court issued another decidedly pro-insured opinion in *Farmers Mut. Fire Ins. Co. of Sale v. N.J. Property-Liability Ins. Guaranty Assoc.*[68] Therein, one carrier argued that the *Owens-Illinois* allocation methodology required the New Jersey Property-Liability Insurance Guaranty Association[69] to assume the liability allocated to another insolvent insurer.[70] The Court held that the New Jersey Legislature's 2004 amendment of the Guaranty Association's enabling statute mandated that the limits of all other coverages, primary and excess, be exhausted before the Guaranty Association is obligated to pay benefits.[71] Importantly, the Court also rejected an argument that the policyholder is required to "bear the loss for the carrier's insolvency before the insured received any statutory benefits" from the Guaranty Association.[72]

Generally speaking, New Jersey's continuous trigger and *Owens-Illinois* allocation methodology are advantageous to policyholders with environmental claims because they enable viable claims against multiple insurers, including excess carriers above the primary layer in some instances. Where claims are asserted against multiple insurers and the potential liabilities of any particular insurer are diminished by allocation, settlement(s) may often be achieved on a cost-benefit basis.

NOTES

1. See *Gilbert Spruance Co. v. Pa. Mfr. Ass'n Ins. Co.*, 134 N.J. 96, 98 (1993).

2. *Gen. Ceramics Inc. v. Firemen's Fund Ins. Cos.*, 66 F.3d 647, 657 (3d Cir. 1995).

3. See *HM Holdings, Inc. v. Aetna Cas. & Sur. Co.*, 154 N.J. 208, 214-15 (1998); see also *Unisys Corp. v. Ins. Co. of N. Am.*, 154 N.J. 217, 223 (1998); *Pfizer. Inc. v. Emp'r Ins.*, 154 N.J. 187, 205 (1998).

4. See *Borough of Sayreville v. Bellefonte Ins. Co.*, 320 N.J. Super. 598, 602 (App. Div. 1998) (citing 21 APPLEMAN ON INSURANCE §12094, at 22 (1980)).

5. *Id.* at 604.

6. See *Newport Assoc. Phase I Developers Ltd. P'ship v. Travelers Cas. & Sur. Co.*, 2013 WL 10090299, 12 (App. Div. 2015) (unpublished)

7. *Id.*

8. *Id.* at *12

9. *Id.* at 602(citing 21 APPLEMAN §12354 at 470-71.

10. See *McNeilab, Inc. v. North River Ins. Co.*, 645 F.Supp. 525, 540 (D.N.J. 1986), *aff'd*, 831 F.2d 287 (3d Cir. 1987) (citing *Prather v. Am. Motorists Ins. Co.*, 2 N.J. 496 (1949)) ("the premium can be used in establishing the extent of coverage when the extent of coverage is in doubt").

11. *Borough of Sayreville*, 320 N.J. Super. 598.

12. *Id.* at 605.

13. *Id.* (considering, in face of missing auto insurance policies, "the specimen copy of the insurance issued by the [carrier] . . . at the time of the accident as the next best evidence") (citing *Del. v. Nat'l Auto. Ins. Co.*, 290 A.2d 675, 677 (Del. Ch. 1972))).

14. See, e.g., *CPS Chem. Co., Inc. v. Cont'l Ins. Co.*, 222 N.J. Super. 175, 181-82 (App. Div. 1988); *Broadwell Realty Servs., Inc. v. Fidelity & Cas. Co. of N.Y.*, 218 N.J. Super. 516, 521 (App. Div. 1987), *overruled, in part, by Morton Int'l, Inc. v. Gen. Accident Ins. Co.*, 134 N.J. 1 (1993).

15. See *Certain Underwriters at Lloyd's of London v. Superior Court*, 24 Cal. 4th 945, 961 (Cal. 2001).

16. See *Morton*, 134 N.J. at 22-28.

17. See *CPS Chem.l*, 222 N.J. Super. at 182-83.

18. See, e.g., *Metex Corp. v. Federal Ins. Co.*, 290 N.J. Super. 95, 103-07 (App. Div. 1996) (insured voluntarily conducted remediation prior to formal agency directive); *Summit Assocs. Inc. v. Liberty Mut. Fire Ins. Co.*, 229 N.J. Super. 56, 60, 62 (App. Div. 1988) (insured received verbal direction from township health officer); *Broadwell Realty*, 218 N.J. Super at 525 (insured received "directive letter" from NJDEP); *Lansco, Inc. v. Dep't of Envtl. Prot.*, 138 N.J. Super. 275, 279 (Ch. Div. 1975), *aff'd* 145 N.J. Super. 433 (App. Div. 1976) (insured given only verbal notice of liability for cleanup from NJDEP inspector).

19. *Flomerfelt v. Cardiello*, 202 N.J. 432, 444 (2010)

20. *Voorhees v. Preferred Mut. Ins. Co.*, 128 N.J. 165, 173 (1992).

21. *N.J.S.A.* 58:10-23.11 *et seq.*

22. See *Metex Corp.*, 290 N.J. Super. at 104-05.

23. *Id.* at 115-16.

24. *N.J.S.A.* 58:10C-1 *et seq.*

25. *N.J.S.A.* 13K-1 *et seq.*

26. See *Fed. Ins. Co. v. Purex Indus., Inc.*, 972 F. Supp. 872, 885 (D.N.J. 1997); *Crest-Foam Corp. v. Aetna Ins. Co.*, 320 N.J. Super. 509, 520-21 (App. Div. 1999); *Strnad v. N. River Ins. Co.*, 292 N.J. Super. 476, 482 (App. Div. 1996).

27. See *Gen. Accident Ins. Co. of Am. v. Dep't of Envtl. Prot.*, 143 N.J. 462, 478-79 (1996).

28. See *Twp. of Gloucester v. Md. Cas. Co.*, 668 F. Supp. 394, 401-02 (D.N.J. 1987).

29. *Givaudan Fragrances Corp. v. Aetna Cas. & Surety Co.*, 227 N.J. 322, 328 (2017). (successor's assignment of its right to coverage under CGL policies for the occurrence of environmental contamination to corporation was post-loss assignment, and thus, consent-to-assignment condition, or anti-assignment provisions, in the policies were void as to the assignment.)

30. See *Broadwell Realty*, 218 N.J. Super. at 528-29; *see also Summit Assocs.*, 229 N.J. Super. at 64.

31. See *State v. Signo Trading Int'l, Inc.*, 130 N.J. 51, 65-67 (1992); *Ohaus v. Cont'l Cas. Ins. Co.*, 292 N.J. Super. 501, 508-09 (App. Div. 1996); *Reliance Ins. Co. v. Armstrong World Indus., Inc.*, 292 N.J. Super. 365, 377-80 (App. Div. 1996); *Kentopp v. Franklin Mut. Ins. Co.*, 293 N.J. Super. 66, 76-78 (App. Div. 1996).

32. See *Sagendorf v. Selective Ins. Co. of Am.*, 293 N.J. Super. 81, 97 (App. Div. 1996); *Ohaus*, 292 N.J. Super. at 508; *Morrone v. Harleysville Mut. Ins. Co.*, 283 N.J. Super. 411, 419-20 (App. Div. 1995).

33. See *Sagendorf*, 293 N.J. Super. at 86, 97-98.

34. See *Signo Trading*, 130 N.J. at 63-64.

35. See *Muralo Co., Inc. v. Emp'r Ins.*, 334 N.J. Super. 282, 290-91 (App. Div. 2000), *certif. denied* 167 N.J. 632 (2001).

36. See *Universal-Rundle Corp. v. Commercial Union Ins. Co.*, 319 N.J. Super. 223, 241 (App. Div. 1999).

37. See *Morton*, 134 N.J. at 31.

38. *Id.* at 32 (internal citation omitted) (emphasis added).

39. See *Morton*, 134 N.J. at 83-85; *see also Voorhees* 128 N.J. at 184-85.

40. *Morton*, 134 N.J. at 83-84 (internal citation omitted).

41. *Morton*, 134 N.J. at 85-86.

42. *Id.* at 86-87.

43. See *CPC Int'l. Inc. v. Hartford Accident & Indem. Co.*, 316 N.J. Super. 351, 376 (App. Div. 1998).

44. *Morton*, 134 N.J. at 72.

45. *Id.* at 36-44, 69.

46. *Id.* at 73-78.

47. See *Northville Indus. Corp. v. Nat'l Union Fire Ins. Co. of Pittsburg*, 679 N.E. 2d 1044, 1046-47 (N.Y. 1997); *Redevelopment Auth. of the City of Philadelphia v. Ins. Co. of N. Am.*, 675 A.2d 1256, 1259 (Pa. Super. Ct. 1996).

48. *Morton*, 134 N.J. at 78 (emphasis added).

49. See *Universal-Rundle*, 319 N.J. Super. at 234-35.

50. *Id.* at 235-36.

51. See *Nav-Its, Inc. v. Selective Ins. Co. of Am.*, 183 N.J. 110, 123-24 (2005)(defined "traditional environmental pollution as "environmental catastrophe related to intentional industrial pollution); see also *Castoro & Co., Inc. v. Hartford Acc. And Indemnity Co., Inc.*, 2016 WL 5660438, *7 (D.N.J.) (Court held that because of *Nav-Its* "intent to pollute" requirement, any CGL policy provision that tries to circumvent this test is invalid and ineffectual.")

52. See *Owens-Illinois, Inc. v. United Ins. Co.*, 138 N.J. 437, 455-56 (1994); *Carter-Wallace, Inc. v. Admiral Ins. Co.*, 154 N.J. 312, 321-23 (1998); *see also Astro Pak Corp. v. Fireman's Fund. Ins. Co.*, 284 N.J. Super. 491, 499-500 (App. Div. 1995); *Morrone*, 283 N.J. Super. at 415-16.

53. *Carter-Wallace*, 154 N.J. at 321 (internal citation omitted).

54. *Quincy Mut. Fire. Ins. Co. v. Borough of Bellmawr*, 172 N.J. 409, 431 (2002) (internal citation omitted).

55. *Franklin Mut. Ins. Co. v. Metro. Prop. & Cas. Ins. Co.*, 406 N.J. Super. 586, 592 (App. Div. 2009)

56. *Id.* at 591.

57. *Benjamin v. State Farm Ins. Co.*, 2017 WL 3535023, 23 (D.N.J. 2017) (Unpublished)

58. *Id.*

59. In "pro rata" jurisdictions, triggered policies provide coverage in proportion to the amount of damage that takes place during the overall period of the loss. This method, which is often referred to as "time on the risk," depends on certain policy language limiting coverage to

damage occurring "during the policy period." For example, a two-year policy included within a ten-year period of triggered coverage will assume twenty percent of the loss. "Pro rata" jurisdictions often require the insured to bear a proportionate portion of the loss if it was self-insured or there was a gap in coverage during the period of triggered coverage.

60. In "all sums" jurisdictions, the policyholder may select one or more policies within the triggered coverage period, which, in turn, must respond in full, subject to the coverage limits of the policy. This method is often referred to as the "joint and several," "vertical exhaustion," or "vertical spike" method. Although most "all sums" jurisdictions allow insurers selected by the policyholder to subsequently seek contribution from other insurers within the triggered coverage period, the policyholder is usually not required to participate in the reallocation process unless it assumed a self-insured risk.

61. 138 N.J. 437 (1994).

62. *Id.* at 475-76.

63. 154 N.J. 312 (1998).

64. *Id.* at 326-27.

65. See 355 N.J. Super. 262, 276-77 (App. Div. 2002).

66. See *Universal-Rundle*, 319 N.J. Super. at 245-46.

67. *Benjamin Moore & Co. v. Aetna Cas. & Sur. Co.*, 179 N.J. 87, 102 (2004)

68. 2013 WL 5311272 (September 24, 2013).

69. The New Jersey Legislature passed the New Jersey Property-Liability Insurance Guaranty Association Act, *N.J.S.A.* 17:30A-1 *et seq.*, to "mitigate the financial distress to insureds and claimants caused by an insurance company's insolvency" by standing in the place of insolvent carriers up to policy limits with a maximum limit of $300,000. *Id.* at *8-9 (citing Senate Bill Statement, S. 1004, c. 17 (April 11, 1974).

70. *Id.* at *4.

71. *Id.* at *9-10.

72. *Id.* at 11.

Section 4

Redevelopment

Joseph Maraziti Jr., Esq., Joanne Vos, Esq.,
Aileen Brennan, Esq., Fred Heyer, P.P., A.I.C.P.,
and Susan Gruel, P.P.

This section presents an introduction to the use of the Local Redevelopment and Housing Law (LRHL), N.J.S.A. 40A:12A-1 et seq., by New Jersey municipalities to revitalize brownfields or otherwise "blighted" areas. The effective and prompt redevelopment of cities and towns is critical to the economic vitality and community life of New Jersey, the reason being that in the last decade, hundreds of thousands of acres of the landscape of the State have been designated for limited or no new development.[1]

REZONING, REHABILITATION, REDEVELOPMENT, AND NON-CONDEMNATION REDEVELOPMENT

If a municipality is considering the potential use of statutory redevelopment pursuant to the LRHL, consideration should first be given to the potential effectiveness of alternative tools. Given the controversy associated with the use of eminent domain, in many cases, a redevelopment designation should be considered after alternative options have been exhausted. Rezoning, rehabilitation, and non-condemnation redevelopment, in accordance with recent amendments to the LRHL, are such options. The following table compares those options, including the level of municipal authority and impact, and illustrates the limited control that a municipality has in the rezoning context. This section assumes that the rezoning option is not chosen and discusses the processes associated with redevelopment, rehabilitation, and non-condemnation redevelopment.

119

	Rezoning	Rehabilitation	Redevelopment	Non-condemnation Redevelopment
Active Municipal Role		x	x	x
Passive Municipal Role	x			
Must Satisfy Designation Criteria (Area Study)		x	x	x
Redevelopment Plan		x	x	x
Municipality Selects Redeveloper		x	x	x
Build as of Right	x			
Maximum Municipal Control		x	x	x
Condemnation Option			x	x
Improvements Limited to "Rational Nexus"	x			
Negotiate Community Amenities		x	x	x
Long-term Tax Exemption Option			x	x
Short-term Tax Exemption Option		x	x	x

REDEVELOPMENT

The first step in the redevelopment process is the adoption of a resolution by the governing body to request that the Planning Board undertake the preparation of a Redevelopment Study to determine whether the area is in need of redevelopment according to the criteria in the LRHL. The resolution must state whether the process is intended to result in "condemnation redevelopment."

An Area in Need of Redevelopment Study

The Redevelopment Study involves the preparation of a map of the study area and a professional evaluation of the study area to determine whether it meets one or more of the following criteria which are detailed in the LRHL, N.J.S.A. 40A:12A-5:

a. Substandard, unsafe, unsanitary, dilapidated, or obsolescent building conditions;
b. Discontinuance or abandonment of commercial, manufacturing, or industrial buildings;
c. Public vacant land that has remained so for ten years and is unlikely to be developed;
d. Deleterious use, design, or layout with a detrimental impact on the community;
e. Growing or total lack of proper utilization due to the condition of title or diversity of ownership;
f. Natural disasters causing material depreciation;
g. "Enterprise Zone" designation; or
h. Consistency with Smart Growth Policies per law or regulation.

The statutory redevelopment process and philosophy in New Jersey have changed significantly in recent years. These changes are due to a national strengthening of concern about individual property rights combined with recent New Jersey case law. Most importantly, the heavy reliance on criterion (e) as a "catchall" category has been curtailed as a result of the New Jersey Supreme Court's decision in *Gallenthin Realty Development, Inc. v. Paulsboro*[2] to limit the "lack of utilization" to narrow title issues, rather than to the examination of "other conditions." The court reiterated that Redevelopment Studies must contain conclusions grounded in substantial evidence, utilizing information from many sources to document redevelopment-worthy conditions.[3]

The New Jersey Supreme Court provided further clarity in interpreting the redevelopment criteria in *62–64 Main Street, LLC and 59–61 Moore St, LLC v. Mayor and Council of the City of Hackensack, et al.*[4] In *Main Street*, the plaintiff property owners challenged the City's designation of its properties as "in need of redevelopment," alleging that *Gallenthin* required that, in order to satisfy the criteria the properties must suffer "deterioration or stagnation that negatively affects surrounding areas." The Court denied the owners' challenge, holding that *Gallenthin* only applied to properties designated under subsection (e).

The Redevelopment Study is traditionally prepared by the in-house planning staff or a planning consultant. Due to the adversarial environment associated with addressing the substantial evidence standard, there may be a need to bring in other experts, such as police, fire, construction officials, architects/engineers, and real estate, traffic, and environmental professionals.

An Area in Need of Redevelopment Process

Strict adherence to the procedural requirements of the LRHL is absolutely essential to prevent judicial invalidation of the redevelopment designation. The process begins with the governing body authorizing the Planning Board to undertake a preliminary investigation as to whether the proposed area is an area in need of redevelopment. This can be accomplished either by listing the lots and blocks and/or referencing a map which graphically shows the study area boundaries. It is important to note that the governing body establishes the physical boundary of the area to be studied. If the governing body does not authorize the study of a specific area, the Planning Board does not have the authorization to hold a public hearing on those areas. The governing body can modify or supplement its initial authorizing resolution to expand or modify the area of the Planning Board's investigation.

Once the Redevelopment Study and map are prepared, the Planning Board is required to hold a public hearing. A copy of the notice must be published in a newspaper of general circulation in the municipality once per week for two consecutive weeks, and the last publication shall be not less than ten days prior to the date for the hearing.[5] In addition, a copy of the notice must be mailed at least ten days prior to the date of the hearing to the last owner of each parcel *within the area* using the assessment records of the municipality.[6] Further, notice must be sent to all persons as noted on the assessment records as claimants of interest in any of the affected properties.[7] The public hearing is intended to permit the Planning Board to hear all persons who are interested in or would be affected by the redevelopment area designation. Strict adherence to the procedural requirements of the redevelopment law is critical to sustaining any challenges which may be filed against the designation.

It is important to note that in this process, the Planning Board operates under the procedures of the LRHL and not the Municipal Land Use Law. For example, unlike the notice requirements of the Municipal Land Use Law, the notice is not sent to property owners within 200 feet of the area under review; rather, it is directed at the owners within the study area. The Planning Board then conducts a public hearing, at which witnesses are sworn and subject to cross-examination. If the Planning Board concludes that some or all of the area satisfies one or more of the statutory criteria, it adopts a resolution recommending that the governing body designate the area as one in need of redevelopment. Thereafter, the governing body may designate some or all of the area as a redevelopment area by the adoption of a resolution. There is no statutory requirement that the governing body provides an opportunity for a public hearing on the resolution, but in practice, many do so.

Ten days after the Condemnation Redevelopment Area determination, notice must be provided to the property owners and objectors stating that the power of eminent domain is available and advising that the recipient must bring a legal challenge within forty-five days after receipt of the notice or be precluded from challenging the designation thereafter.[8]

NON-CONDEMNATION REDEVELOPMENT

The LRHL was recently amended to include non-condemnation redevelopment as yet another method of redevelopment. This method of redevelopment does not allow for the exercise of eminent domain powers but does retain all the other features and powers of a redevelopment designation. The process is identical to that required for condemnation redevelopment. In those instances, the redevelopment determination by the municipality would include a "non-condemnation redevelopment area" designation. If the municipality is ultimately unable to acquire any such property that is designated as a "non-condemnation redevelopment area," it may initiate the process to determine whether the said property is a "condemnation area property."[9] The entire process must be initiated as if the initial redevelopment determination had not been made. Any such determination must be based upon the conditions existing at the time of the new investigation and not at the time of the "non-condemnation redevelopment area" designation.[10]

REHABILITATION

In many situations, a rehabilitation designation under N.J.S.A. 40A:12A-14 may be an appropriate alternative tool. Rehabilitation areas are treated just like redevelopment areas with two important exceptions: there is no eminent domain and tax abatement is limited to short-term abatement. There have been changes in the LRHL which have significantly increased the applicability of a rehabilitation designation.

Area in Need of Rehabilitation Study

Pursuant to N.J.S.A. 40:12A-14a, the following conditions must exist to designate an area in need of rehabilitation:

1.) A significant portion of structures therein are in a deteriorated or substandard condition;
2.) More than half of the housing stock in the delineated area is at least fifty years old;
3.) There is a pattern of vacancy, abandonment, or underutilization of properties in the area;
4.) There is a persistent arrearage of property tax payments on the properties in the area;
5.) Environmental contamination is discouraging improvements and investment in properties in the area; or
6.) A majority of the water and sewer infrastructure in the delineated area is at least fifty years old and is in need of repair or substantial maintenance.

Area in Need of Rehabilitation Process

In short, the process for an area in need of rehabilitation designation is a simpler process than a redevelopment designation in that there is no formal investigation or public hearing required by the Planning Board, and the designation criteria are primarily based on objective facts. The role of subjective judgment is very narrow. The process is initiated by the adoption of a resolution by the governing body forwarding a Rehabilitation Study to the Planning Board, together with a proposed resolution to establish the rehabilitation designation. The Planning Board has a forty-five-day period to provide its review and comments to the governing body. Once the Planning Board provides its comments or after the passage of forty-five days after submittal of the report by the governing body, the governing body may designate the area—which may include the entire municipality—as an area in need of rehabilitation. No public hearing need be provided by the governing body, although it is good practice to do so.

The rehabilitation designation does not trigger the condemnation powers, nor does it allow a long-term payment in lieu of taxes but rather permits a five-year phased tax abatement.

THE REDEVELOPMENT PLAN

Once an area is designated, the next step in the redevelopment process is the preparation of a redevelopment plan. The plan may be prepared by the municipality, or the municipality may request that it be prepared by the Planning Board. If it is prepared by the municipality, it must be forwarded to the Planning Board for its review and comment. The Planning Board is provided a forty-five-day review period, during which time it may conduct a public hearing but is not required by statute to do so. After the Planning Board provides its comments or forty-five days have passed since the proposed plan was provided to it, the governing body may adopt the redevelopment plan.

The redevelopment plan must be adopted by the passage of an ordinance after notice and a public hearing.

The redevelopment plan can be considered to be a hybrid between a municipal master plan and a zoning ordinance. A redevelopment plan shall include an outline for the planning, development, redevelopment, or rehabilitation of the project area sufficient to indicate the following:

a. Its relationship to definitive local objectives as to appropriate land uses, the density of population and improved traffic and public transportation, public utilities, recreational and community facilities, and other public improvements.
b. Proposed land uses and building requirements in the project area.
c. Adequate provision for the temporary and permanent relocation, as necessary for residents in the project area, including an estimate of the extent to which decent, safe, and sanitary dwelling units affordable to displaced residents will be available to them in the existing local housing market.
d. An identification of any property within the redevelopment area which is proposed to be acquired in accordance with the redevelopment plan.
e. Any significant relationship between the redevelopment plan and (i) the master plan of contiguous municipalities; (ii) the master plan of the county in which the municipality is located; and (iii) the State Development and Redevelopment Plan adopted pursuant to the State Planning Act.
f. As of the date of the adoption of the resolution finding the area to be in need of redevelopment, an inventory of all housing units affordable to low and moderate income households, as defined pursuant to N.J.S.A. 52:27D-304, that are to be removed as a result of implementation of the redevelopment plan, whether as a result of subsidies or market conditions listed by affordability level, number of bedrooms, and tenure.
g. A plan for the provision, through new construction or substantial rehabilitation of one comparable, affordable replacement housing unit for each affordable housing unit that has been occupied at any time within the last eighteen months, that is subject to affordability controls, and that is identified as to be removed as a result of implementation of the redevelopment plan.

The municipality has an option as to how the redevelopment plan relates to the municipal development regulations. The plan may supersede the applicable provisions of the municipal development regulations or may constitute an overlay zoning district within the redevelopment area. If the municipality chooses to have the redevelopment plan supersede the zoning ordinance, there must be explicit language in the redevelopment plan that amends the zoning map. Further, the zoning map must indicate the redevelopment area to which the redevelopment plan applies.

IMPLEMENTATION OF THE REDEVELOPMENT PLAN

Upon adoption of a redevelopment plan, the municipality or redevelopment entity which is designated by the governing body may proceed with the redevelopment of the area; only thereafter may negotiations with a proposed redeveloper proceed. The powers of the municipality or designated redevelopment entity are extremely broad and can include acquiring property by condemnation, if necessary, clearing any area owned or acquired and installing, constructing, or reconstructing public infrastructure essential to the preparation of sites for use in accordance with the redevelopment plan, contracting for professional services, contracting with public agencies or redevelopers for the undertaking of any project or redevelopment work, negotiating and collecting revenues from a redeveloper to defray the costs of the redevelopment entity, making loans to redevelopers to finance any redevelopment work, leasing or conveying property or improvements to any other party without public bidding, requesting that the Planning Board recommend and the governing body designate a particular area as being in need of redevelopment, and studying the recommendations of the Planning Board or governing body for the redevelopment of any area. Once adopted, the redevelopment plan can be amended from time to time by following all the procedures necessary for the initial adoption.

CONDEMNATION OF CONTAMINATED PROPERTY

Typically, when environmentally contaminated land is condemned, the property is valued as if remediated, and the funds are then paid into court. The condemner may later pursue these funds in cost recovery for reimbursement of the cleanup costs. This methodology was established in 2003 by the New Jersey Supreme Court in *New Brunswick v. Suydam Investors, LLC.*[11] The recent Appellate Division opinion in *Borough of Paulsboro v. Essex Chemical Corp.*[12] indicates that this methodology need not be applied when the condemned property consists of or is part of a landfill that has been closed with the approval of the New Jersey Department of Environmental Protection. However, the reach of this decision is likely beyond landfills, and the takeaway is that if a condemned property has no realistic liability to conduct remedial activities, an escrow will not be required for the cleanup costs, and any such remedial activities conducted at the site would be at the condemner's cost.

THE REDEVELOPMENT AGREEMENT

Each Redevelopment Agreement should include the following key provisions:

1. **Project Description**: It is essential that there be as precise as possible a description of exactly what will be constructed in the redevelopment area so that the vision of the community is achieved.
2. **Project Schedule**: The LRHL requires that the commencement date be included, and good practice calls for milestone dates and a completion date to guard against "land banking" and delay.
3. **Project Escrows**: Escrows to pay the staff and professional fees for the municipality are commonly provided for.

4. **Community Amenities**: Under the LRHL, the municipality may negotiate for amenities; the "rational nexus" rule of the MLUL does not apply.
5. **Infrastructure Improvements**: A description of all the on-site and off-site infrastructure required for the project should be included.
6. **Remediation Responsibility**: With few exceptions, the redeveloper assumes the cost and responsibility for all remediation.
7. **Tax Exemption Option (Payments in Lieu of Taxes)**: The LRHL authorizes but does not require the municipality to agree to a financial agreement to adjust ratable taxes for up to thirty years.
8. **Affordable Housing**: The obligation to provide some or all of the affordable housing units generated by the project is often assumed by the redeveloper.
9. **Termination**: Provisions regarding termination rights prevent weak projects from languishing and contributing to or worsening the distress in the area.

CONCLUSION

Considering the significance of the recent amendments to the LRHL, there is the expectation that new vitality will be injected into the effort to redevelop New Jersey's cities and towns in order to stimulate improvements to the economy, the environment, and quality of life. Municipalities have various options available to them to promote such redevelopment, and each potential redevelopment area must be considered on a case-by-case basis, taking all of the factors discussed herein into account.

NOTES

1. Examples include lands impacted by the adoption of the Highlands Act, the approval of a referendum to borrow $1 billion to preserve 1 million acres of open space and farmland, and county and municipal open space trust funds.
2. 191 N.J. 344 (2007). The issue in this case was whether the terms "not fully productive" and "stagnant" are interchangeable and fall under the definition of "blighted" as originally intended by the New Jersey Constitution. The Supreme Court decided that the Legislature did not intend for N.J.S.A. 40A:12A 5(e) to incorporate the term "not fully productive" in the "Blighted Areas" clause of the Constitution. (N.J. Const., art. VIII, §3, ¶1). The Court reasoned that the original definition of "blighted" in the Constitution was intended to rehabilitate cities, specifically, certain urban areas. The recent amendments to the LRHL discussed in this section incorporate the *Gallenthin* holding that property may not be condemned based upon underutilization alone.
3. Such sources include, but are not limited to, applications for building permits, code violations, variance applications, variances granted, police records, extent of private real estate transactions, economic activity and productivity, occupancy rates, environmental conditions, maps detailing blighting factors and tax delinquencies, usage of public transportation to determine underutilization of parking lots, lot-by-lot and block-by-block findings, physical inspection of structures, and photographs. *Id.*
4. 221 N.J. 129 (2015)
5. N.J.S.A. 40A:12A-6b3(d).

6. *Id.*

7. *Id.*

8. In *Harrison Redevelopment Agency v. DeRose*, 398 N.J.Super. 361, 942 (App. Div. 2008), the court considered (1) what information is required in a written notice to a property owner regarding impending redevelopment; (2) what constitutes a fair and adequate individual written notice; and (3) if adequate notice is not provided, whether a property owner has the right to challenge the redevelopment plan after forty-five days. The Appellate Division held that the city was required to provide property owners with individual notice of blight designation, and further, that any property receiving such a notice has a right to challenge the redevelopment designation after 45 days if adequate and individual written notice was not provided in a timely manner. The recent amendments to the LRHL discussed in this article address the due process issues in DeRose by requiring municipalities to advise property owners within the proposed redevelopment area of the municipality's intention to either exercise or not exercise its eminent domain powers.

9. N.J.S.A. 40A:12A-6b5(g).

10. *Id.*

11. 77 N.J. 2 (2003).

12. A-5248-10T4 (2012).

Section 5

Bankruptcy and Environmental Claims

Susanne Peticolas, Esq.

The guiding principle of New Jersey environmental law, the "polluter pays,"[1] is designed to extract retribution and protect the taxpayer from paying for the activities of others. This stands in stark contrast to the second chance, "fresh start" principles of bankruptcy law,[2] under which a debtor is given a fresh start through a discharge of most debts either via liquidation of assets under Chapter 7 or via a reorganization plan under Chapter 11 or Chapter 13. When the debtor seeking the fresh start is an alleged polluter, these policies come into direct conflict.[3] Serious and extensive environmental liabilities can defeat a successful reorganization and dilute and delay recoveries.[4] Moreover, depending on the circumstances, other potentially responsible parties, sometimes with less culpability, may end up shouldering the bulk of the cleanup costs.[5] On the other hand, when a major corporation undergoes a reorganization under Chapter 11 and emerges without crushing environmental liabilities, there is the potential for general societal benefit in the form of continued employment, participation in the economy, and tax revenues.[6]

THE AUTOMATIC STAY

When a debtor files a petition for bankruptcy protection, a stay of actions against the debtor to collect pre-petition claims goes into effect by operation of law under section 362 of the Bankruptcy Code.[7] The purpose of the stay is to preserve the debtor's estate.[8] Actions taken in violation of the automatic stay are void ab initio.[9] The stay does not apply to actions commenced by the debtor. Nor does the automatic stay apply to actions taken by governmental agencies in the exercise of police or regulatory power.[10] Under this police power exception, the government is also permitted to enforce "nonmonetary" judgments against a debtor's estate.[11] Thus the City of New York was permitted to continue its suit against the debtor for reimbursement of pre-petition costs and a mandatory injunction in *City of New York v. Exxon Corp.*[12] The court noted that "Congress meant to except damage actions for completed violations of environmental laws from the action of the stay."[13] In *Penn Terra Ltd. v. Department*

129

of Envtl. Resources,[14] the Third Circuit found that the Department of Environmental Resources' action to enforce the Commonwealth Court's injunction to rectify harmful environmental hazards fell squarely within the state's police and regulatory powers and thus was not subject to the automatic stay. Moreover, although enforcement of the injunction would require the debtor to expend monies to implement the remediation plan at issue, the court determined that such monetary expenditures did not transform the injunction into a money judgment, because it was not intended to provide compensation for past injuries nor was it reducible to a sum certain.[15] Similarly, the court in *W.R. Grace & Co. v. State of New Jersey Department of Envtl. Prot.* held that government action to fix a penalty for violation of environmental laws was an appropriate exercise of police and regulatory power because "[s]tatutory penalties provide the 'teeth' to New Jersey's environmental laws."[16] In *U.S. v. Nicolet, Inc.*, the court noted that section 362(b)(4) permits proceedings to fix penalties even up to entry of a money judgment.[17] It is the collection of the money judgment that is subject to the automatic stay.

ABANDONMENT OF CONTAMINATED PROPERTY

A trustee has the power to abandon property that is burdensome to the estate under section 554 of the Bankruptcy Code.[18] However, this power is not unlimited. In 1986, in its landmark *Midlantic* decision, the U.S. Supreme Court held that "a trustee in bankruptcy may not abandon property in contravention of a state statute or regulation that is reasonably designed to protect the public health or safety from identified hazards."[19] The properties at issue in *Midlantic* were highly contaminated—at one site with oil-polluted subsoil and at the other with 470,000 gallons of toxic and carcinogenic waste oil in deteriorating containers. The Court found a narrow exception to section 554 of the Bankruptcy Code, stating,

> Congress did not intend for § 554(a) to pre-empt all state and local laws. The Bankruptcy Court does not have the power to authorize an abandonment without formulating conditions that will adequately protect the public's health and safety. Accordingly, without reaching the question whether certain state laws imposing conditions on abandonment may be so onerous as to interfere with the bankruptcy adjudication itself, we hold that a trustee may not abandon property in contravention of a state statute or regulation that is reasonably designed to protect the public health or safety from identified hazards.[20]

In a footnote, the Court cautioned that this exception to the trustee's abandonment power is a "narrow one."[21] Thus, presumably a trustee may abandon contaminated property if the property does not present an imminent danger to the public safety and health. The U.S. District Court for the District of New Jersey analyzed this narrow exception in *In re St. Lawrence Corp.*, where a Chapter 7 trustee moved to abandon property as burdensome or of inconsequential value and benefit to estate.[22] The district court held that once the trustee has demonstrated that the property is burdensome or of inconsequential value, the burden switches to the party opposing the abandonment, in this case, the New Jersey Department of Environmental Protection ("NJDEP").

In *St. Lawrence*, NJDEP took the position that funds in the estate must be used to determine whether there was contamination, and if so, used to clean it up. In view of the fact that NJDEP did not even know if the property was contaminated, let alone presenting imminent danger, the court found that the trustee was justified in abandoning the property.

"CLAIM" UNDER BANKRUPTCY LAW

Central to the bankruptcy proceeding is the concept of a "claim." A claim must be asserted within the filing deadline and, if an objection to the claim is filed, allowed by the bankruptcy court in order for a creditor to receive any share of the estate proceeds. In addition, most pre-petition claims are generally subject to discharge either by the confirmation of a plan in a Chapter 11 case or, but only as to individual debtors, a discharge of debtor issued in a Chapter 7 case.[23]

"Claim" is defined broadly as a:

(A) right to payment, whether or not such right is reduced to judgment, liquidated, unliquidated, fixed, contingent, matured, unmatured, disputed, undisputed, legal, equitable, secured, or unsecured; or (B) right to an equitable remedy for breach of performance if such breach gives rise to a right to payment, whether or not such right to an equitable remedy is reduced to judgment, fixed, contingent, matured, unmatured, disputed, undisputed, secured, or unsecured.[24]

This broad definition sweeps in unliquidated, contingent, future environmental claims, when there is little information available on their potential size.[25] Complex environmental sites can require years of study to analyze the problem and determine an appropriate remediation path. A bankruptcy proceeding does not provide the luxury of lengthy environmental studies spanning decades.[26] As a result, the parties must engage in a sophisticated form of environmental estimation satisfactory to the bankruptcy court, the environmental creditors, the debtor, and in some cases, the public.[27] Given that the bankruptcy estates of most debtors are insufficient to satisfy all creditors, claims are categorized and accorded priority based on the categorization. In order of priority, they are secured claims, post-petition administrative expenses, pre-petition priority claims, unsecured claims, and equity interests.[28] As a practical matter, claimants seek to have their claims categorized as secured claims or administrative expenses in order to enjoy the benefit of priority.

Secured Claims

Environmental claims enjoy no special priority under the bankruptcy laws, but both CERCLA[29] and the Spill Act[30] provide for liens against the property of a party that may face liability under the statute, often referred to as a potentially responsible party (PRP). The CERCLA lien arises by operation of law at the time the cleanup and removal costs are incurred by the United States, or when the PRP is provided with notice by certified or registered mail, whichever is later.[31] The lien is perfected when notice is filed with the appropriate State office and can be enforced through an action in rem.[32] In an action pending in the district court, a debtor asserted that the government's claims under section 107(a) of CERCLA against the individual debtor defendants, together with an in rem action against debtor's property, were subject to the automatic stay because the combination would have the effect of converting the United States into a secured creditor.[33] In response, the United States noted that the lien had been perfected prior to the bankruptcy filing, and that although the in rem claims would be subject to the automatic stay, the in personam section 107(a) claims were not.[34] Relying on the Third Circuit decision in *United States v. Nicolet*[35], the district court held that the in personam claims as an exercise of police power were not subject to the automatic stay, a decision affirmed by the Third Circuit on appeal.[36]

Under the Spill Act, any expenditure by the state pursuant to the Spill Act constitutes a lien on all property owned by the discharger when a notice of the lien is filed with the clerk of the Superior Court describing the costs incurred and the property subject to the cleanup. The lien created on the subject property, described as a "super lien," takes priority over earlier-filed liens[37] and has retroactive effect.[38] The lien on all other property of the discharger is effective as of the date of filing the notice of the lien.

Administrative Expenses

Under the Bankruptcy Code, "actual, necessary costs and expenses of preserving the estate" are accorded priority as administrative expenses.[39] In *Chateaugay*, the Second Circuit upheld the determination that all cleanup costs assessed post-petition with respect to sites currently owned by the debtor for pre-petition releases or threatened releases of hazardous substances were entitled to administrative priority. The debtor and unsecured creditors objected arguing that EPA was simply attempting to convert pre-petition contingent claims into priority claims by incurring response costs. The Second Circuit noted that "EPA is doing more than fixing the amount of its claims; it is acting, during administration of the estate, to remedy the ongoing effects of a release of hazardous substances." It concurred with the district court that since a trustee could not abandon property in contravention of state and local laws intended to protect health and safety, expenses incurred in removing the environmental threat were necessary to preserve the estate.[40] In another case, claims for post-petition remediation costs of property no longer owned by the debtor based on a contract were not recognized as administrative expenses.[41]

In *In re GI-Holdings*, the bankruptcy court determined that post-petition claims for remediation pursuant to a remediation agreement in connection with an EPA Administrative Order on Consent were not entitled to priority as administrative expenses because the costs being sought were not "actually and necessarily incurred in preserving the estate for the benefit of its creditors."[42] Furthermore, the costs did not qualify for the imminent harm exception to the general rule that environmental compliance costs to remedy pre-petition conduct are treated as general unsecured claims. That exception permits the use of funds to address environmental harms that pose an identifiable and imminent harm arising from pre-petition conduct. In such cases, the expenditure is treated as an administrative expense entitled to priority. The court distinguished *In re Conroy*, where post-petition remediation expenses were accorded priority as administrative expenses on the grounds that the expenses in *Conroy* were incurred by the state environmental agency.[43] On appeal, the district court affirmed this determination, noting that "remediation of the Site is being achieved through other means: the Novak Group continues to clean up the hazardous waste under the EPA's Administrative Order. Because G-I is not needed to complete the cleanup, it should be afforded the fresh start promised by bankruptcy."[44]

Claims of Governmental Authorities

The seminal case on the issue is *In re Chateaugay Corporation*. In *Chateaugay*, the Second Circuit determined that EPA claims for pre-petition releases and threatened releases were dischargeable claims, while certain injunctive remedies were non-dischargeable, and cleanup costs were entitled to administrative priority. The court held that unincurred CERCLA response costs for pre-petition releases were properly defined as "claims" because EPA would have a right to payment.[45] The court also determined that response costs for a pre-petition release or threatened release of hazardous substances was a claim even when it had not yet been discovered by EPA or anyone else.[46] While EPA argued that it would be forced to litigate and fix claims in the bankruptcy court for post-confirmation response costs, the Court held that such costs were merely "contingent" claims subject to estimation.[47] As the court noted, "nothing prevents the speedy and rough estimation of CERCLA claims for the purposes of determining EPA's voice in the Chapter 11 proceedings, with ultimate liquidation of the claims to await the outcome of normal CERCLA enforcement proceedings in which EPA will be entitled to collect its allowable share (full or pro rata, depending on the reorganization plan) of incurred response costs."[48] Such allowed claims are treated as unsecured and generally recoup less than the amount of the claim.

The court acknowledged that EPA "obviously prefers in this case to keep its CERCLA claim outside of bankruptcy so that it may present it, without reduction, against the reorganized company it anticipates will emerge from bankruptcy, one may well speculate whether, if unincurred CERCLA response costs are not claims, some corporations facing substantial environmental claims will be able to reorganize at all."[49] Because *Chateaugay* could be read to include costs to remedy completely unknown contamination within the definition of "claim" provided it related to pre-petition conduct, the court in *In re National Gypsum*, expressly carved out such unknown potential claims. The district court, in *In re National Gypsum*, limited the scope of claims for future response costs and future natural resource damages to those based on pre-petition conduct resulting in release or threatened release that were fairly within the contemplation of the parties.[50]

PRP Claims

The law is more troublesome when the claimant is a PRP and the claim is for contribution. Under section 502(e)(1)(B) of the Bankruptcy Code, contingent claims for contribution or reimbursement asserted by claimants who are co-liable with the debtor are disallowed.[51] The purpose is understandable: to avoid duplicate claims against the debtor.[52] In the context of environmental claims, it presents problems for PRPs engaged in lengthy cleanups. In many cases, there has not been a determination of liability or an allocation of responsibility. Many PRP groups undertake significant remedial activity under consent orders with the agency and/or pursuant to private PRP agreements setting out interim allocations. The PRP agreements are usually confidential. In instances where both the PRP group and the agency assert claims for the same site, they may not have the same interests. In the *Marcal* bankruptcy, both the Cooperating Parties Group (CPG) and EPA asserted claims for remediation of the Passaic River.[53] Initially, EPA filed a proof of claim on behalf of EPA and several other agencies for $946,000,000.[54] The CPG asserted claims for $816,100.[55] When EPA reached an agreement with the debtor for $3 million, both the CPG and two of its members, Maxus Energy Corporation and Tierra Solutions, Inc. filed objections.[56] Their concerns boiled down to a concern that the amounts to be recovered by EPA and potentially credited against their own liability were too low in view of the likely remediation costs for the river, at that time estimated at nearly $1 billion. Indeed, estimates at the time were that EPA would recover about 50 percent of the allowed claim and only the recovered amount would be credited to other PRPs under CERCLA.[57] Ultimately, the settlement between EPA and the debtor was approved by the bankruptcy court and the claims of the CPG and Maxus/Tierra were withdrawn.[58]

In contrast to the outcome in *Marcal*, in the *Chemtura* case a proof of claim for contribution for past and future remediation costs filed by the DS&G Remedial Trust was not disallowed.[59] What distinguished the DS&G Remedial Trust claim from a number of other disallowed PRP claims in the same bankruptcy matter was the trust itself. Since the entity filing the proof of claim was the trust, not the PRP grantors, a key factor, co-liability on the debt, was absent. Accordingly, the claim was allowed.[60]

In *In re Allegheny International, Inc.*, the purchaser of debtor's steel plants was allowed to assert claims for cleanup costs where the purchaser had incurred the costs directly and was asserting section 107 CERCLA claims.[61] The court noted, "Section 502(e)(1)(B) is not a means of immunizing debtors from contingent liability but instead protects debtors from multiple liability on contingent debts."[62] In this case, the response costs involved were not owed to or incurred by EPA or any other third party.[63]

Claims for Injunctive Relief

The question arises whether a creditor's right to injunctive relief constitutes a claim for bankruptcy purposes. Both NJDEP and PRPs can seek injunctive relief under a variety of environmental statutes. Where the claim for injunctive relief can be converted into a money judgment and thus constitute a right to payment, the U.S. Supreme Court, in *Ohio v. Kovacs*,[64] held that it is a "claim" that must be brought in a timely manner and is subject to discharge at the end of the case. Some courts have held that if compliance with the injunction requires the debtor to pay a third party to perform, the obligation is one for the payment of money and constitutes a claim.[65] Other courts have held that such a test is too broad since compliance with most orders will require the expenditure of money.[66] In one case where the order was for cleanup pursuant to the Resource Conservation and Recovery Act, the government was not entitled to demand payment in lieu of action, and therefore the claim was not dischargeable in bankruptcy.[67] Where the environmental order is to stop an ongoing and continuing threat, it is not a "repackaged claim for damages" even where the debtor no longer owns the property.[68]

In *AM Int'l v. Datacard Corp.*,[69] the Seventh Circuit affirmed the district court ruling that allowed Datacard Corp., a subsequent purchaser of the debtor's property, to assert both section 107 CERCLA claims and RCRA claims for injunctive relief against the debtor after confirmation of the plan of reorganization which took place in 1984.[70] The property had not been purchased until 1986, a time when not even the debtor realized that it faced CERCLA liability for the contamination.[71] Thus, clearly the purchaser did not have sufficient information to tie the debtor to the contamination prior to confirmation. The district court's determination that the RCRA claim was not discharged in bankruptcy was upheld because RCRA only provides injunctive relief, not money damages.[72] In contrast, the court in *Route 21 Associates* determined that a right to specific performance under a contract for remedial work could be monetized and therefore could be discharged.[73]

Statute of Limitations

Although environmental liability and remediation both have long timelines, the applicable statutes of limitation for environmental claims under CERCLA are comparatively short. For a cost recovery claims under CERCLA § 107, the statute of limitations is six years from initiation of physical on-site construction of the remedial action.[74] For a removal action, the statute runs within three years of completion of the removal.[75] Contribution claims under § 113 must be brought within three years of the date of judgment for recovery of CERCLA costs, the date of a CERCLA administrative order, or a judicially approved settlement.[76] In contrast, the New Jersey Spill Act does not have a limitation on contribution claims.[77]

It is not always easy to determine when a statute of limitations has run, particularly in CERCLA cases. But as a precautionary measure, claimants are safer asserting a possibly barred claim, because it is well established that statute of limitations is an affirmative defense in bankruptcy court.[78]

In *Maxus Liquidating Trust v. YPF Inc., et al.*,[79] although the underlying claims involve massive environmental liability, the statute of limitations addressed by the court related to a claim of fraudulent conveyance implemented through complex corporate transactions. Denying a motion to dismiss, the court held that because the actions were one step in a multiyear multistep fraudulent activity, the statute of limitations had not run. The judge ruled that the allegations tracked the scenario described in *Tronox*,[80] namely a scheme in which

> a shrewd and unscrupulous enterprise . . . divests itself of 'substantially all of its assets' . . . continue to satisfy environmental liabilities from the cash flow of the combined entity until the statute of limitations period had run and the divestiture was ready for completion, and then split the good assets from the bad. If the architects of such a scheme could claim the statute of limitations had already run by virtue of the first step in the scheme, they would have free reign to hinder and delay creditors so long as they could do it in two steps several years apart.[81]

Successor Liability

Under both state law and federal law, successor liability can attach to an entity that acquires only assets. The question arises as to whether a party that purchases assets in a bankruptcy context where claims are discharged is insulated from future environmental costs. Such bankruptcy sales are frequently ordered "free and clear of any such interests in such property" under § 363(f) of the Bankruptcy Code. The general corporate rule that a purchase of assets is not a purchase of liabilities has been undermined in the CERCLA context.[82] The Court in *Allis Chalmers* applied a "substantial continuity" test for successorship.[83] It further noted that even though a predecessor allegedly still existed, the key was whether the predecessor could provide a remedy, a determination that had to await discovery.[84] The court held that merely because the sale of assets took place in a bankruptcy proceeding under § 363(f) did not determine whether there was liability. The issue turned on whether the environmental claim existed at the time of the bankruptcy proceedings such that the bankruptcy court had the jurisdiction to discharge the claim.[85] While there are no cases squarely on point in New Jersey, prospective asset purchasers should take warning from the *Allis Chalmers* case.[86]

CONCLUSION

In its 2004 report, "Cleaning Up The Nations Waste Sites: Markets And Technology Trends," EPA estimated that as many as 350,000 contaminated sites would require remediation over the next 30 years at a projected cost of $250 billion.[87] This turns out to be, unfortunately, a conservative estimate in light of contaminated sediment mega-sites, such as the Lower Passaic River, carrying remediation estimates of over a billion dollars.[88] In the 2004 report, EPA admitted that most of this expenditure would be borne by the owners of the properties and those potentially responsible for the contamination.[89] The enormity of the costs makes it inevitable that government agencies and PRPs will find themselves navigating the conflicting goals of bankruptcy law and environmental law.

NOTES

1. *In re Kimber Petroleum Corp.*, 110 N.J. 69, 90 (1988)(Wilentz, C.J., dissenting).
2. *Local Loan Co. v. Hunt*, 292 US 234, 244 (1934).
3. *In re Combustion Equipment Associates, Inc.*, 838 F.2d 35, 37 (2d Cir. 1988)
4. In the Marcal Paper Mills Inc. chapter 11 proceeding, the U.S. Environmental Protection Agency filed a claim for $946 million dollars. The debtor claimed that EPA's demands were holding up the reorganization plan. "EPA wants paper company in bankruptcy to pay nearly $1B to clean up New Jersey river," U.S. Water News Online, July 2007, http://www.uswaterne ws.com/archives/arcquality/7epaxwant7.html.
5. *In re GI-Holdings, Inc.*, 2005 U.S. Dist. LEXIS 48056, at 49

6. See Corporate Press Release, GM 363 Asset Sale Approved by U.S. Bankruptcy Court, 07-06-2007, media.gm.com/media/us/en/gm/news.detail.html/content/Pages/news/us/en/2009/Jul/0706_AssetSale.html.

7. 11 U.S.C. § 362.

8. *Midlantic National Bank v. New Jersey Dept. of Envtl. Prot.*, 474 U.S. 494, 503 (1986).

9. *Constitution Bank v. Tubbs,* 68 F.3d 685, 691 (3d Cir. 1995).

10. 11 U.S.C. § 362(b)(4); *In re Madison Indus., Inc.*, 161 B.R. 363, 366-67 (D.N.J. 1993) (DEP's action seeking injunctive relief against the debtor for violations of RCRA was exercise of State's police power and exempt from automatic stay). See also, *United States v. Alsol Corporation, et al.*, No. 14-3253, Opinion of Third Circuit (August 7, 2015) (*In personam* claims as an exercise of police power not subject to automatic stay).

11. 11 U.S.C. § 362(b)(5).

12. *City of New York v. Exxon Corp.*, 932 F.2d 1020 (2d 1991)

13. *Id.* at 1024.

14. 733 F.2d 267, 278 (3d Cir. 1984).

15. *Id.*

16. 412 B.R. 657, 664 (D. Del. 2009). Although the District Court held that NJDEP's suit was not barred by the automatic stay provision, it upheld the validity of the bankruptcy court's injunction barring the suit. *Id.* at 657.

17. 857 F.2d 202, 209 (3d Cir. 1988) (court must determine whether the government proceeding relates principally to the protection of the government's pecuniary interest in the property or in the public policy of safety and welfare in determining if the automatic stay applies); *U.S. v. LTV Steel Co.*, 269 B.R. 576 (W.D. Pa. 2001) (seeking penalties for past violations of the Clean Air Act is exempt from the automatic stay).

18. Section 554 of the Bankruptcy Code states:

(a)   After notice and a hearing, the trustee may abandon any property of the estate that is burdensome to the estate or that is of inconsequential value and benefit to the estate.

(b)   On request of a party in interest and after notice and a hearing, the court may order the trustee to abandon any property of the estate that is burdensome to the estate or that is of inconsequential value and benefit to the estate.

(c)   Unless the court orders otherwise, any property scheduled under section 521(a)(1) of this title not otherwise administered at the time of the closing of a case is abandoned to the debtor and administered for purposes of section 350 of this title.

(d)   Unless the court orders otherwise, property of the estate that is not abandoned under this section and that is not administered in the case remains property of the estate.

11 U.S.C.A. § 554.

19. *Midlantic Nat. Bank v. New Jersey Dept. of Envtl. Prot.*, 474 U.S. 494, 507 (1986).

20. *Id.* at 506-07 (1986).

21. *Id.* at 507 n.9. ("This exception to the abandonment power vested in the trustee by § 554 is a narrow one. It does not encompass a speculative or indeterminate future violation of such laws that may stem from abandonment. The abandonment power is not to be fettered by laws or regulations not reasonably calculated to protect the public health or safety from imminent and identifiable harm.").

22. *In re St. Lawrence Corp.*, 239 B.R. 720 (Bankr. D.N.J. 1999), *aff'd*, 248 B.R. 734 (D.N.J. 2000).

23. 11 U.S.C. § 727(b); *United States v. Whizco*, 841, F.2d 147, 148 (6th Cir.1988) ("a discharge in bankruptcy discharges the debtor from all debts that arose before bankruptcy").

24. 11 U.S.C. § 101(5).

25. *In re National Gypsum Company,* 139 B.R. 397, 401 (N.D. Tex. 1992) (significant portion of EPA claims were unliquidated, relating to future response costs and future natural resource damages).

26. The contamination in the sediment of the Passaic River has been subjected to study pursuant to several Administrative Orders on Consent, for nearly 20 years. See EPA Fact Sheet Diamond Alkali Co., New Jersey, EPA Region 2, http://www.epa.gov/region02/superfund/np l/0200613c.pdf, at 2.

27. See, e.g., Redwine, McMurtry, Berz, "The GM Bankruptcy - The Environmental Story," The Metropolitan Corporate Counsel, September 2012, at 44.

28. *In re Torwico Elecs., Inc.,* 131 B.R. 561, 564-565 (Bankr. D.N.J. 1991), *rev'd and vacated sub nom. Torwico Elecs., Inc. v. N.J. Dep't of Envtl. Prot. & Energy,* 153 B.R. 24 (D.N.J. 1992), *aff'd sub nom. In re Torwico Elecs., Inc.,* 8 F.3d 146 (3d Cir. 1993).

29. 42 U.S.C. § 9607(l).

30. N.J.S.A. 58:10-23.11f(f). There is an exception to the superlien for properties comprising of six or fewer units used exclusively for residential purposes. In such situations, the lien does not take priority over previously and properly filed liens. *Id.*

31. 42 U.S.C. § 9607(l)(2).

32. 42 U.S.C. § 9607(l)(4)

33. *United States of America v. Alsol Corp., et al.,* Civ. A. No. 2:13-cv-00380-KSH-CLW, Defendants' Memorandum of Law in Opposition to the United States' Motion for an Order declaring that the United States' *In Personam* action Against Debtor Defendants is not Subject to the Bankruptcy Code's Automatic Stay, July 1, 2013, at 7.

34. *Id.,* Reply Brief of the United States in Support of Its Motion for an Order Declaring that the United States' *In Personam* Action Against Debtor Defendants Is Not Subject to the Bankruptcy Code's Automatic Stay, July 8, 2013, at 4.

35. *United States v. Nicolet, Inc.,* 857 F.2d 202 (3d Cir. 1988).

36. *United States v. Alsol Corporation, et al.,* No. 14-3253, Opinion of the Third Circuit (August 7, 2015)

37. *Kessler v. Tarrats,* 194 N.J. Super 136, 147 (App. Div. 1984).

38. *Simon v. Oldmans Township,* 203 N.J. Super. 265, 373 (Ch. 1985)

39. 11 U.S.C. § 503(b)(1)(A) (1988).

40. *In re Chateaugay,* 944 F.2d 997, 1010 (2d Cir. 1991); see also *In re National Gypsum Company,* 139 B.R. 397, 401, 413 (N.D. Tex. 1992) (post-petition response costs incurred in connection with the debtor's presently owned property held to be "administrative expenses" provided they were necessitated by conditions posing an imminent and identifiable harm to the environment); *Dept of Envtl. Resources v. Conroy,* 24 F.3d 568 (3d Cir. 1994) (remediation costs incurred by state agency to remove hazardous substances from debtor's property entitled to treatment as administrative expense; court reasoned that property could not be abandoned and remediation was required to prevent imminent harm and preserve bankruptcy asset.).

41. *Route 21 Associates of Belleville, Inc. v. MHC, Inc.* 486 B.R. 75, 91 (S.D.N.Y. 2012); *In re Mahoney-Troast Constr. Co.,* 189 B.R. 57 (Bankr. D.N.J. 1995) (Where there was no imminent threat to public health, former landlord's cleanup costs incurred post-petition not administrative expenses).

42. 308 B.R. 196, 212 (Bankr. D.N.J. 2004) (quoting *In re Molnar Bros.,* 200 B.R. 555, 558 (Bankr. D.N.J. 2001)). Significantly, the PRP group did not file a proof of claim in the bankruptcy. *Id.* at 201. Rather, the group sought reimbursement of the debtor's share as an administrative expense. *Id.* at 202. The bankruptcy court also determined that the PRP group's claims for reimbursement of remediation expenses were not contingent, since the PRP group had already expended the funds and they were not claims owed to a common debtor since the funds were owed to the PRP group, as opposed to a governmental entity. *Id.* at 212. However,

on appeal, the district court reversed, holding that such a determination was premature. 2005 U.S. Dist. LEXIS 48056, at 45 (D.N.J. 2005)

43. 24 F.3d 568 (3d Cir. 1994).

44. 2005 U.S. Dist. LEXIS 48056, at 49

45. *In re Chateaugay*, 944 F.2d 997, 1004 (2d Cir. 1991). *Cf. DMJ Assoc., L.L.C. v. Capasso*, 565 B.R. 27 (E.D.N.Y. 2016) (summary judgment denied where environmental claims at issue, contribution under § 113(f) or a PRP cost recovery claim under § 107, did not exist at the time the bankruptcy petition was filed in 1982. Since no cognizable claims existed at the time of the bankruptcy petition, they were not discharged by the bankruptcy, even though the conduct giving rise to liability took place pre-petition).

46. *In re Chateaugay*, 944 F.2d at 1004.

47. *Id.* at 1005.

48. *Id.* at 1005-06

49. *Id.* at 1005.

50. 139 B.R. 397, 407 (N.D. Tex. 1992). *Cf. Shieldalloy Metaluorgical Corp. v. State Dep't of Envtl. Prot.*, 743 F. Supp. 2d 429, 443 (D.N.J. 2010) (Court rejects reorganized debtor's claim of breach of settlement agreement approved by bankruptcy court where dispute could not arise until 2009 when NJDEP acquired licensing authority from NRC, well after confirmation of the plan).

51. Section 502(e)(1)(B) of the Bankruptcy Code provides:

> The court shall disallow any claim for reimbursement or contribution of an entity that is liable with the debtor on or has secured the claim of a creditor, to the extent that such claim for reimbursement or contribution is contingent as of the time of allowance or disallowance of such claim for reimbursement or contribution.

52. One way of avoiding the duplicate claims issue is to enter into a stipulation with the environmental agency and the debtor and approved by the court that the common claims, if allowed will be treated as one claim, with the apportionment determined separately and among themselves. See, e.g., *Route 21 Associates of Belleville, Inc. v. MHC, Inc.* 486 B.R. at 80.

53. *In re Marcal Paper Mills, Inc.*, Case No. 06-20886 (MS), Lower Passaic River Study Area Site Cooperating Parties, Proof of Claim, May 22, 2007; United States of America, Proof of Claim, June 14, 2007.

54. *Id.* United States of America, Proof of Claim, June 14, 2007.

55. *Id.* Lower Passaic River Study Area Site Cooperating Parties Proof of Claim, May 22, 2007.

56. *Id.* Doc. No. 1066 and 1067, Aug. 10, 2007.

57. In *In re Marcal*, EPA filed a proof of claim for nearly a billion dollars for anticipated cleanup costs and natural resource damages associated with contamination in the Passaic River. The claim was settled for $3 million, with an expectation that the ultimate payout would be 52 percent or so. Doc. No. 1264-3, p.5. Theoretically, other PRP's were entitled to a dollar for dollar credit, but only of amounts actually received by EPA. EPA Settlement Agreement, Doc. No. 1264-2, p. 3-4. Since EPA contends that PRPs are jointly and severally liable, they could be stuck with the shortfall on the allowed claim as an "orphan" share.

58. *In re Marcal Paper Mills, Inc.*, 7/18/2003 Minute of Hearing on Motion to Enter Settlement filed by Creditor United States; see also, "Under Deal, Judge Tosses $946M Marcal Claim," http://www.law360.com/articles/63372.

59. Okoye and Songonuga, "At the Intersection of Environmental and Bankruptcy Laws," New Jersey Law Journal, Vol. 213 - No. 3, July 15, 2013.

60. *Id.*

61. *In re Allegheny International, Inc.*, 126 B.R. 919, 922 (W.D. PA 1991).

62. *Id.* at 923.

63. *Id.* at 923-24.

64. 469 U.S. 274, 282-83 (1985). Significantly, the state of Ohio had secured the appointment of a receiver to take possession of debtor Kovacs' nonexempt assets and assets of the corporate defendants and to comply with the injunction to clean up hazardous waste on his property rather than to prosecute Kovacs under the environmental laws. When Kovacs filed for bankruptcy, the state conceded that the only performance they were seeking from Kovacs was payment of money. *Id.*

65. *United States v. Whizco Inc.*, 841 F.2d 147, 148 (6th Cir. 1988). In a case involving an injunction under the Surface Mining Control and Reclamation Act of 1977, 30 U.S.C. § 1201 *et seq.*, the Sixth Circuit affirmed the District Court in holding that the debtor "could not perform the reclamation work ordered 'other that by payment of money,' and therefore the injunction was a debt dischargeable in bankruptcy." The payment of money referred to payment to a third party to perform the reclamation work.

66. *U.S. v. Apex Oil Co.*, 579 F.3d 734, 737 (7th Cir. 2009) (RCRA order does not provide for damages in lieu of compliance).

67. *Id.*

68. *In Re Torwico Electronics*, 8 F.3d 146, 150-52 (3d Cir. 1993) (debtor had access to the site, state had not performed any cleanup on its own, order was issued under statutory sections which do not allow state to perform cleanup and sue for reimbursement).

69. 106 F.3d 1342, 1348 (7th Cir. 1997).

70. Although the court determined that the claims were not barred by the 1984 bankruptcy confirmation, in 1993 the debtor AMI was once again in financial trouble and had filed for bankruptcy again. The automatic stay was lifted on these proceedings in order to liquidate Datacard's claims. Thus Datacard's claims still faced scrutiny in the second bankruptcy.

71. *Id.*

72. *Id.* Although the court relied on the *Torwico* case and *Meghrig v. KFC W.*, Inc., 116 S. Ct. 1251 (1996) to conclude that the RCRA claim was not discharged, the same analysis the court used for the CERCLA claim would have saved the RCRA claims as well.

73. *Route 21 Associates of Belleville, Inc. v. MHC, Inc.*, 486 B.R. at 89.

74. 42 U. S. C. § 9613 (g) (2)(B).

75. 42 U. S. C. § 9613 (g) (2)(A).

76. 42 U. S. C. § 9613 (g) (3)(A)-(B).

77. *Morristown Associates v. Grant Oil Co.*, N. J. (2015).

78. *Cf. Midland Funding, LLC v. Johnson*, 137 S. Ct. 1407 (2017). (U.S. Supreme Court held that filing obviously time-barred proof of claim in a bankruptcy proceeding not a "false, deceptive, misleading, unfair or unconscionable debt collection practice" within the meaning of the Fair Debt Collection Practices Act because statute of limitations is affirmative defense.)

79. *Maxus Liquidating Trust v. YPF S.A., et al.*, Case No.:18-50489 (Bankr., D.Del. February 15, 2019). The court also held that a claim for alter ego can constitute an independent claim when coupled with allegations of another wrong, such as a breach of fiduciary duty or a fraudulent conveyance.

80. *Tronox Inc. v. Kerr McGee Corp. (In re Tronox Inc.)*, 503 B.R. 239, 271 (Bankr. S.D.N.Y. 2013)

81. *Id.*

82. *United States v. Gen. Battery Corp*, 423 F.3d 294, 305 (3d Cir 2005).

83. *Ninth Avenue Remedial Group v. Allis-Chalmers Corp*, 195 B.R. 716, 726 (N.D. Ind. 1996).

84. *Id.*

85. *Id.* at 731. *Cf. DMJ Assoc., L.L.C. v. Capasso*, 565 B.R. at 35 (no discharge of environmental claims that did not exist prior to bankruptcy petition).

86. In *Thomas G. Betts Corp. v. Myers Power Products, Inc.*, 2006 U.S. Dist. LEXIS 3492, *25 (D.N.J. 2006) the court held that a 363(f) asset purchaser took the assets free and clear of product liability claims, relying on the expansive interpretation of "interest in such property" outlined in the Third Circuit decision, *In re Transworld Airlines*, 322 F.3d 283 (3d Cir. 2003). The court did not reach the *Allis-Chalmers* issue limiting the scope of 363(f) to interests existing prior to the sale of assets because the injury at issue had predated the sale. *Id.* at *24, n. 4.

87. http://epa.gov/superfund/accomp/news/30years.htm.

88. https://community.njsba.com/blogs/njsba-staff/2019/01/25/status-of-lower-passaic-river-and-berrys-creek-stu.

89. http://epa.gov/superfund/accomp/news/30years.htm

Section 6

Natural Resource Damages

David J. Mairo, Esq., Katherine E. Suell, Esq., and Matthew R. Conley, Esq.

New Jersey defines natural resources as "all land, fish, shellfish, wildlife, biota, air, waters and other such resources owned, managed, held in trust or otherwise controlled by the State."[1] As enunciated in the Spill Compensation and Control Act (Spill Act), the Legislature has declared that the State "is the trustee, for the benefit of its citizens, of all natural resources within its jurisdiction."[2] The Spill Act creates a comprehensive legislative scheme that renders persons "in any way responsible" for a discharge 'strictly liable, jointly, and severally, without regard to fault' for all cleanup and removal costs."[3]

The Spill Act defines a "discharge" as "any intentional or unintentional action or omission resulting in the releasing, spilling, leaking, pumping, pouring, emitting, emptying or dumping of hazardous substances into the waters or onto the lands of the State, or into waters outside the jurisdiction of the State when damage may result to the lands, waters or natural resources within the jurisdiction of the State." "Cleanup and removal costs" mean all direct and indirect costs associated with a discharge,[4] and with the State prescribed as the designated trustee of all natural resources within its jurisdiction, the court has found that definition "sufficiently broad to encompass the [New Jersey Department of Environmental Protection's] power to assess damages caused to natural resources and to require compensation for their loss of use."[5]

PUBLIC TRUST DOCTRINE

The public trust doctrine, which is deeply ingrained in New Jersey's common law,[6] embodies the principle that certain natural resources (e.g., navigable water, wildlife, tidally flowed land, etc.) are common property held in trust by the State to be preserved and maintained for the benefit of the people.[7] The doctrine ensures that no entity unreasonably interferes with the public's ability to use, access, and enjoy the State's natural resources.

The doctrine has seen its clearest expression when used to defend the public's right to use and enjoy the State's extensive beaches. The doctrine has been successfully employed to defend navigation, fishing, bathing, swimming, and other shore-related activities taking place on the tidal lands seaward of the mean high watermark.[8] The doctrine applies only to damages to natural resources and cannot be used to recover for damages to man-made improvements to those resources.[9]

The doctrine is the bedrock of the State's power to seek reparations for damages to natural resources. In conjunction with a 2003 policy directive, the New Jersey Department of Environmental Protection (NJDEP or Department), which is the designated trustee for natural resources within the State, uses powers derived from the common law public trust doctrine and statutory authority, including the State's Spill Compensation and Control Act, N.J.S.A. 58:10-23.11 et seq., to pursue natural resource damages.

ROLE OF THE NEW JERSEY DEPARTMENT OF ENVIRONMENTAL PROTECTION

The commissioner of the NJDEP is the designated trustee charged with administering and protecting the State's natural resources.[10] To date, contrary to the federal government, the NJDEP has declined to create a regulatory apparatus that would, subject to public notice and comment, govern natural resource damages in New Jersey. The NJDEP has instead elected to pursue natural resource damages through litigation by the Office of the Attorney General. Within the NJDEP is an Office of Natural Resource Restoration, which was established in the mid-1990s and is tasked with administering the State's Natural Resource Restoration programs.

The Office of Natural Resource Restoration serves a few functions: it generally ensures that damages to natural resources are properly characterized; it coordinates with responsible parties to implement an appropriate restoration project; and it acts as the liaison between the responsible party implementing the project and other NJDEP programs. The Office of Natural Resource Restoration is also responsible for providing litigation support to the Attorney General's office.

In 2003, the NJDEP issued a policy directive regarding natural resource damages.[11] The directive is a regulatory document which outlines the State's methodology for pursuing natural resource damage claims. Though casting a broad net, the directive set forth three categories of sites that would be excluded on the basis that the cost of recovery or restoration would be less than the cost of pursuing the claim. Those three categories of sites are sites where "the responsible parties are residential homeowners residing at the site at which the claim arises; . . . the only responsible parties are small businesses with a limited ability to pay; . . . sites that meet the qualifying criteria for DEP's 'Cleanup Star' Program."[12]

The NJDEP's stated preference when it comes to resolving natural resource damages is restoration projects: "For all claims, the Department's preference is for the performance of restoration work and resource protection in lieu of money damages, provided that reasonable allowance is made for monitoring and oversight to ensure accountability."[13] Examples of restoration could include projects which result in the purification of air and water near the site of the impact, acquisition, and preservation of analogous resources, facilitation of the pollination of crops and natural vegetation, or abatement of nonpoint source pollution.

Restoration projects are required to bear some relation or nexus to the impacted resources. The responsible party or person implementing the restoration should be prepared to articulate the connection between the injury as characterized by the Office of Natural Resource Restoration and the proposed restoration. In this way, the Department's Natural Resource Restoration program is quite similar to the hierarchy set up under the Freshwater Wetlands Protection Act which articulates first a preference for on-site mitigation followed by a monetary exchange for credits at various wetland mitigation banks at an increasing distance from the site of impact.[14] The Department's desire for restoration at or close to the site of the impact is uniform throughout its programs. The NJDEP may also "recover compensatory restoration damages for the ecological services and values lost as a result of the discharge."[15] Such "[c]ompensatory restoration damages include damages for the loss of use of a natural resource."[16]

NATURAL RESOURCE DAMAGE LITIGATION

Following the 2003 directive, which was viewed as a clear message communicating the NJDEP's desire to invigorate a powerful enforcement tool, the NJDEP initiated more than 120 lawsuits seeking natural resource damages, the vast majority of which settled quickly. However, several lawsuits continued through discovery, motion practice, and trial. With the election of Governor Chris Christie in 2010, the State's Natural Resource Damages program became largely dormant. However, in August 2018, the NJDEP behind newly elected governor Philip Murphy simultaneously filed three new lawsuits seeking natural resource damages, in what was largely considered a public statement that the NJDEP is reinvigorating its enforcement role.[17] Contrary to NJDEP's prior practice, each of the recent lawsuits for natural resource damages demanded a jury.

At this time, it is generally well settled that the NJDEP's power to assess damages to natural resources is essentially as expansive as the scope of damages recoverable.[18] Consequently, natural resource damage litigation has largely focused on the methodologies employed in valuing the natural resource and calculating the resultant damage caused by the contamination of them.

As previously described, recoverable damages fall into three categories: the NJDEP's costs in assessing the damage; physical restoration of the damaged resource to its pre-discharge condition (a/k/a "primary restoration damages"); and compensatory damages for the lost use and services caused by contamination of the natural resource (aka "compensatory restoration damages" or "lost use damages").[19] While the scope and breadth of the NJDEP's power and authority are substantial, it still must prove by a preponderance of credible evidence that physical restoration of the resource is appropriate, necessary, and cost-effective, especially when presented with an alternate restoration plan.[20] Likewise, with respect to compensatory damages couched in economic factors, the basis for the calculation should "reflect or be equivalent to the loss."[21] In other words, the damage for which compensation is sought must be derived from an actual loss resulting from the injury.

New Jersey's Supreme Court has also underscored what many have thought should have been a bright-line element all along; namely, the NJDEP must prove that the party being held responsible for a discharge indeed caused the alleged natural resource damage. In *New Jersey Department of Environmental Protection v. Dimant*, 212 N.J. 153 (2012), the Court held that to obtain any damages under the Spill Act, the Department must prove by a preponderance of the evidence that a reasonable connection or nexus exists between the discharge, the discharger, and the contamination (or injury). Absent that nexus, the Department can neither recover nor assess cleanup costs or natural resource damages.

The *Dimant* Court explained that a

> nexus . . . must be demonstrated to exist between the discharge for which one is responsible . . . and the contaminated site for which cleanup and other related authorized costs are incurred. . . .[22] [I]t is not enough for a plaintiff to simply prove that a defendant produced a hazardous substance and that the substance was found at the contaminated site[.][23]

To date, however, the NJDEP has not formally promulgated regulations adopting the methodologies utilized to calculate natural resource damages for restoration. Therefore, even if a nexus exists, the absence of such regulations has proven problematic to the NJDEP's pursuit of natural resource damages and left such damages vulnerable to challenges to expert opinions that employ questionable methodologies to quantify and monetize natural resource injuries.[24]

ALLOCATION OF MONEY RECOVERED FOR NRD

How the NJDEP is permitted to administer or allocate the recovered primary and compensatory restoration damages was the subject of a 2017 amendment to New Jersey's Constitution. The 2017 amendment to Paragraph 9 of Section II of Article VIII of the New Jersey Constitution stipulates how the NJDEP may utilize the natural resource damages collected from responsible parties and expressly provides that the Office of Natural Resource Restoration may apply these monies to pay for "costs incurred by the State to repair, restore, or replace damaged or lost natural resource of the State, or permanently protect the natural resources of the State, or for paying the legal or other costs incurred by the State to pursue settlements and judicial and administrative awards relating to natural resource damages."

Additionally, the 2017 amendment established a system by which the NJDEP must prioritize the use of these monies. The first priority is the immediate area in which the natural resource damage occurred and if no reasonable project is available or there is money left over after satisfying the first priority, the second priority is the same water region in which the natural resource damage occurred. If money is still left over or no reasonable first or second priority projects are available, then the geographic constraints are lifted and the NJDEP may use the funds to either permanently protect natural resources of the State; or repair, restore, or replace damaged or lost natural resources of the State.[25]

LIMITATIONS PERIOD FOR THE STATE TO BRING
A NATURAL RESOURCE DAMAGES CLAIM

The statute of limitations period within which the State may bring a claim for natural resource damages is governed by what is known as the "extension statute" found at N.J.S.A. 58:10B-17.1. Subsection b(1) of the extension statute provides that

> [e]xcept where a limitations provision expressly and specifically applies to actions commenced by the State or where a longer limitations period would otherwise apply, and subject to any statutory provisions or common law rules extending limitations periods, any civil action concerning the payment of compensation for damage to, or loss of, natural resources due to the discharge of a hazardous substance, commenced by the State pursuant to the State's environmental laws, shall be commenced within five years and six months next after the cause of action shall have accrued.[26]

The following subsection then addresses when a cause of action accrues. "For purposes of determining whether a civil action subject to the limitations periods specified in paragraph (1) of this subsection has been commenced within time, no cause of action shall be deemed to have accrued prior to January 1, 2002 or until the completion of the remedial action for the entire contaminated site . . . , whichever is later."[27] In *New Jersey Department of Environmental Protection v. Exxon Mobil Corp.*, the court held that the extension statute applied to both statutory and common law claims.[28] Courts have not yet interpreted the term "remedial action" in this context but the NJDEP is likely to maintain that the remedial action is ongoing until issuance of an Unrestricted Use Remedial Action Outcome.

STATUTORY EXEMPTIONS AND DEFENSES
FROM NATURAL RESOURCE DAMAGES

Statutory exemptions from Spill Act liability for cleanup and removal costs are found at N.J.S.A. 58:10-23.11f22. This section of the Spill Act was enacted to encourage the redevelopment of brownfields by allaying redevelopers' concerns that by acquiring contaminated property they were also inheriting its environmental liabilities.

Defenses to natural resource damages are found at N.J.S.A. 58:10-23.11g.d. In addition to the force majeure types of defenses which assert that an unavoidable circumstance beyond the control of the parties prevents performance, this section is particularly significant because it outlines the steps that either must be taken or must have been taken prior to acquisition of real property in order to assert what is known as the "innocent purchaser defense."

PRACTICAL ADVICE

In practice, while there are sites where natural resource damage assessments can reach into the millions or even billions of dollars, most assessments are in the thousands of dollars. The NJDEP formula for determining the cost associated with injuries to groundwater had been readily available on the Department's website to use.[29] Unfortunately, at this time it has inexplicably been removed from the NJDEP website. However, the formula was relatively straightforward and was as follows:

> The area of contamination (measured in square feet) is calculated and multiplied by the annual recharge rate. The resultant figure is then multiplied by the number of years the contamination is expected to persist. That volume is considered to the total number of gallons of impacted groundwater. Damages are determined by multiplying the number of gallons by the highest local rate for potable water to arrive at a dollar figure.

Although the NJDEP continues to face obstacles with respect to how natural resource damages are calculated, there is no question that protection of natural resources remains a priority for the Department. The NJDEP has stated publicly that the most recent round of natural resource damage lawsuits is the start of a larger initiative centered on natural resource damages and environmental justice. The State has encouraged responsible parties to voluntarily approach the Department to resolve natural resource damage liability. A defendant or responsible party who offers to engage in some Natural Resource Restoration project will very likely earn the goodwill of the Department.

The simpler Natural Resource Restoration projects should be kept in mind during negotiations with the NJDEP. Items such as an acquisition of land for aquifer recharge, rehabilitation of impacted wetlands, restoration of appropriate habitats for injured species, and enhancement of public access to shorelines and other natural resources are all opportunities for responsible parties to enhance their position in a settlement. A defendant who can identify other damages to natural resources for which they may not be responsible and demonstrate a willingness to aid the repair or replacement for those resources or resource services will likely be offering unexpected, but welcome, benefits to the Department.

In litigating the issue of natural resource damages against the Department, the most recent opinions emphasize the burdens of proof that must be met by the NJDEP for each category of damages. And where Spill Act liability for a discharge (and the resulting contamination) is not necessarily in dispute, the regulated community should make full use of the guidance offered by the Court's opinion in *Dimant* by focusing on the distinction between the discharge and the damage caused therefrom as a potential starting point of developing a defense.

In those lawsuits, the contested issues largely turn on the scope of the alleged injury, expert proofs and the practicability of a restoration remedy. Assessing natural resource damages, particularly compensatory restoration damages, typically requires a multifaceted and detailed scientific assessment of whether, and the extent to which, the contamination has caused an injury—that is, a detrimental impact to the resource's ecological and human services and even its intrinsic "value" to the public. Needless to say, the imprecise nature of natural resource "value" and "uses" provides natural resource trustees with ample opportunity to influence and control a natural resource damage assessment—particularly given the dearth of regulation or guidance.

For the foreseeable future, it appears that NJDEP will continue to set natural resource damages policy by litigating specific sites on a case-by-case basis while encouraging the regulated community to approach it voluntarily to resolve potential natural resource damage liability. For those parties that find themselves in litigation, there are many discrete but important legal issues that will likely need to be assessed, including, inter alia, the State's right to a jury, retroactivity of natural resource damages liability, third-party liability, viability of certain common law claims, and alleged injury to natural resources caused by land improvements such as fill material and road construction.

NOTES

1. N.J.S.A. 58:10-23.11b.
2. N.J.S.A. 58:10-23.11a.
3. N.J.S.A. 58:10-23.11g.c(1).
4. N.J.S.A. 58:10-23.11b.
5. *N.J. Dep't of Envtl. Prot. v. Exxon Mobil Corp.*, 393 N.J. Super. 388, 403 (App. Div. 2007); see also, *E.I. du Pont de Nemours & Co. v. N.J. Dep't of Envtl. Prot.*, 283 N.J. Super. 331, 341 (App. Div. 1995); N.J.S.A. 58:10-23g(2).
6. *Van Ness v. Borough of Deal*, 78 N.J. 174, 179 (1978); *Arnold v. Mundy*, 6 N.J.L. 1 (1821).
7. *Matthews v. Bay Head Imp. Ass'n*, 95 N.J. 306 (1984).
8. *Matthews v. Bay Head Imp. Ass'n*, 95 N.J. 306 (1984); *Slocum v. Borough of Belmar*, 238 N.J. Super. 179 (1989).
9. *Hyland v. Borough of Allenhurst*, 148 N.J. Super. 437 (App. Div. 1977).
10. Executive Order No. 192, September 14, 1988, available at: http://njlegallib.rutgers.edu/eo/docs/kean/order192-/index.pdf
11. Policy Directive 2003-07, available at: http://www.nj.gov/dep/commissioner/policy/pdir2003-07.htm.
12. Policy Directive 2003-07, available at: http://www.nj.gov/dep/commissioner/policy/pdir2003-07.htm.
13. Policy Directive 2003-07, available at: http://www.nj.gov/dep/commissioner/policy/pdir2003-07.htm.
14. N.J.S.A. 13:9B-1 et seq.; N.J.A.C. 7:7A.
15. *N.J. Dep't of Envtl. Prot. v. Essex Chemical Corp*, 2012 N.J. Super. Unpub. LEXIS 593, *15 (N.J. Super. Ct. App. Div. Mar. 20, 2012) (citing *Exxon Mobil, supra*, 393 N.J. Super. at 406)
16. *Exxon Mobil*, 393 N.J. Super. at 410.
17. *NJDEP v. Pechiney Plastics; NJDEP v. Deull Fuel Co.; NJDEP v. Hess Corp.* A short time later, NJDEP filed a fourth NRD lawsuit, *NJDEP v. SL Industries*.
18. *In re Kimber Petroleum Corp.*, 110 N.J. 69 (1988); *N.J. Dep't of Envtl. Prot. v. Ventron Corp.*, 94 N.J. 473, 502, 468 A.2d 150 (1983); *N.J. Dep't of Envtl. Prot. v. Exxon Mobil Corp.*, 393 N.J. Super. 388 (App. Div. 2007).
19. *Exxon Mobil*, 393 N.J. Super. at 406, 410; *Essex Chemical Corp*, 2012 N.J. Super. Unpub. LEXIS 593, *15; *New Jersey Site Remediation Industry Network v. New Jersey Department of Environmental Protection*, Docket No. A-5272-97T3 slip op. at 21 (App. Div., April 17, 2000) (*per curiam*) *cert. den.* 165 N.J. 528 (2000).

20. *Essex Chemical Corp,* 2012 N.J. Super. Unpub. LEXIS 593, *23-24.

21. *Id.*

22. *Dimant,* 212 N.J. at 177.

23. *Id.* at 182.

24. *NJDEP v. Exxon,* Mer-L-2933-02 (Law Div. August 24, 2007) (rejecting the NJDEP's formula for calculating restoration damages for injury to groundwater)

25. NJDEP Office of Natural Resource Restoration, "Constitutional Amendment." Available at: https://www.state.nj.us/dep/nrr/amendment.htm

26. N.J.S.A. 58:10B-17.1b(1).

27. N.J.S.A. 58:10B-17.1b(2).

28. 420 N.J. Super. 395, 410-11 (App. Div. 2011).

29. Calculations for determining injuries to groundwater formerly available at: http://www.nj.gov/dep/nrr/nri/nri_gw.htm.

Section 7

Real Property Tax Appeals

Thomas M. Olson, Esq., and Allan C. Zhang, Esq.

All real property in the State of New Jersey is assessed at its fair market value as of October 1 of the pretax year.[1] Fair market value has been defined as "the price which would be agreed upon for the property in an arm's length transaction between a knowledgeable buyer and a knowledgeable seller, neither being under compulsion to act."[2] There are many different factors which can affect the value of real property for property tax purposes, including the existence of environmental contamination on the property and the obligation of the property owner to remediate that contamination. The courts in New Jersey have wrestled for the past thirty years with how to deal with the effect of environmental contamination on the value of real property for property tax purposes. The courts have in most instances based their decisions on whether the applicable environmental statutes mandate a cleanup of the property, as well as whether the properties are still in use by the party responsible for the contamination.

THE *INMAR* DECISION

The seminal property tax case in New Jersey is *Inmar Associates v. Borough of Carlstadt*, 112 N.J. 593 (1988). That case involved challenges to property tax assessments by two separate owners of environmentally contaminated land. One of the owners, GAF Corp., operated an asphalt siding plant on the property that was still in use during the tax year under appeal. The other property, owned by Inmar Associates, consisted of a 5.9-acre tract of land in the Hackensack Meadowlands on which sixty-seven abandoned chemical storage tanks were located. The Inmar property had been placed on the federal Superfund list. With respect to the GAF property, the court affirmed the tax court's ruling which found that it was unable to quantify the effect that compliance with the Environmental Cleanup Responsibility Act (ECRA)[3] would have had on the market value of the property as of the assessing date due to insufficient proofs. While GAF had estimated cleanup costs of $450,000, no sampling study had taken place, no cleanup plan had been approved by DEP, and the property was still in use.

With respect to the Inmar property, the Court found that the property owner had presented sufficient proofs regarding projected cleanup costs. The Court recognized that environmental contamination may have an impact upon the fair market value of real property and that it should be taken into account when valuing property for real property tax purposes.[4] The Court recognized that governmental environmental restrictions and requirements will have an unavoidable economic impact on the true value of contaminated properties, and that impact should be considered when valuing such properties. As a result, properties that are the subject of environmental contamination and which are subject to governmentally imposed environmental remediation requirements must reflect the impact of that contamination on market value.[5]

The *Inmar* Court, however, struggled with the exact methodology to be utilized when considering the impact of this contamination upon the true value of contaminated property. The Court noted that the three classic approaches to value used in the appraisal of real estate—the cost, market data, and income approaches—all have severe limitations when applied to contaminated properties due to the absence of adequate market data. After discussing several possible methodologies, such as treating the cost to cure the contaminated property as a capital improvement, which can be depreciated over the beneficial life of the property, as well as treating contaminated property as "special purpose" property, the Court indicated that it would leave the determination of the appropriate valuation methodology to the competency of the appraisal community and the judges of the tax court. Indeed, the Court noted that it had recently reaffirmed the unique capability and responsibility of the tax court to exercise its power and expertise in determining the value of the property. The Court, however, did emphasize that it did not consider a dollar for dollar deduction of the costs to cure the contamination from the true value of the property to be an appropriate methodology.[6] Thus the case was remanded to the tax court for valuation of the property taking into account the environmental contamination.[7]

POST-*INMAR* DECISIONS

In *University Plaza Realty Corp. v. Hackensack*,[8] the court dealt with a situation involving the impact of asbestos contamination on the true value of an office building. The court began by distinguishing the *Inmar* decision, noting that the *Inmar* decision involved a situation where there was a governmental prohibition on the sale of property contaminated with toxic waste and an obligation on the property owner to remediate that contamination. No such restrictions applied to an asbestos-contaminated property, and there were no governmental restrictions on the sale of property contaminated by asbestos. The court found that buyers and sellers of the property would require this remediation as part of any transfer of the property. As a result, the court found a value for the subject property and then deducted dollar for dollar from that value the cost of the asbestos abatement on the property. The Appellate Division affirmed, adding that the tax court's opinion was a "case specific analysis" and not a holding that a dollar for dollar deduction from the true value of a property was a proper valuation methodology in every non-mandated remediation case.[9]

Badische Corp. (BASF) v. Town of Kearney[10] involved a closed and contaminated industrial plant. The owner had closed operations on the property, thereby triggering a statutory cleanup operation. The owner had also submitted a site evaluation and sampling plan to the NJDEP, had begun sampling and had received test results prior to the valuation date, although no actual cleanup plan had been submitted, nor had the NJDEP placed any restrictions on the use of the buildings. The owner had created a $10 million reserve to cover the estimated costs of cleanup.

The Appellate Division found that contamination was present and that the proposed cleanup costs clearly had an impact on value and must be addressed, reversed the tax court's decision that the owner had not met its burden of proof regarding cleanup costs, and remanded for reconsideration consistent with the principals in *Inmar*. The Appellate Division also provided the following principles for assessing the value of unused, contaminated property subject to mandatory cleanup at owner's expense:

(a) Market value is impacted by contamination and that impact cannot be ignored;
(b) Costs cannot reduce the value of the property on a dollar for dollar basis;
(c) Nonclassical, flexible approaches to valuing such property are required; and
(d) Treating the costs of cleanup as a depreciable capital improvement "contains the seeds of useful doctrine."[11]

Metuchen I, LLC v. Borough of Metuchen[12] involved the former Oakite Realty facility which was utilized as a manufacturing plant from 1960 to 1990, during which time the properties became contaminated with industrial pollutants. At the time of the appeal, the industrial operations at the property had been shut down and the property sold. The parties agreed that the fair market value of the properties as of the relevant valuation dates was $1,800,000.00. The only issue for determination by the court was how that value should be reduced to take into account the contamination present at the property.

The plaintiff introduced evidence that the cleanup costs net of demolition totaled $1,460,177.00. The plaintiff also attempted to take a 10 percent deduction from the value of the property for the stigma associated with the contamination. The plaintiff further indicated that the $1,460,177.00 cleanup cost would be incurred over a two-year period. The defendant municipality conceded that the remediation costs for the cleanup were $1,460,177.00 but contended that cleanup on the property would take significantly longer than two years, and an appropriate discounting should be employed by the court to reflect this fact. The defendant also disagreed with the plaintiff's 10 percent stigma adjustment. The *Metuchen I* court first found that the valuation should not be diminished by any stigma value. The court noted that while *Inmar* recognized the potential for the impact of stigma on the valuation of environmentally contaminated property, plaintiff's expert had failed to introduce satisfactory evidence to establish the 10 percent deduction for the alleged stigma.[13] The court did, however, agree that a deduction should be made for the anticipated cleanup costs of $1,460,177.00 but found that the appropriate cleanup period was five years rather than two. The court thus discounted the projected cleanup costs over a five-year period[14] and deducted these costs from the agreed-upon value of the subject property of $1,800,000.00.[15]

RECENT DECISIONS

In *Pan Chemical Corp. v. Borough of Hawthorne*,[16] the taxpayer had occupied the subject property for fifty-five years and had manufactured industrial coding, color dispersions, inks and polish on the property. In 1999, the owner moved its manufacturing operations and most of its employees to another location. It left only three employees on the polluted property and continued to utilize only two of the seven buildings located on the property. The owner testified that the reason it did not shut down operations completely on the site was to avoid triggering its legal obligation to clean up the property under ISRA, N.J.S.A. 13:1K-6 to 14.[17]

The plaintiff property owner appealed the property tax assessment, arguing that the contaminated condition of the property mandated a reduction in the assessed value of the subject property. The tax court concluded it would not be appropriate to make an adjustment for environmental contamination under *Inmar* when a property was still in use but determined that the *Pan Chemical* property should be treated as closed, in light of the fact that the majority of the property owner's operations and employees had been moved to another parcel, and reduced the assessments accordingly to account for the environmental contamination.

On appeal, the Appellate Division reversed, reasoning:

> It, therefore, appears that Pan Chem[ical] would have it both ways. It wanted the property to be deemed "in use" during the years on appeal for the sole purpose of avoiding the costly cleanup mandated by ISRA. Now, Pan Chem[ical] wants the property to be deemed "not in use" over the same period of time in order to claim a reduced tax liability.[18]

The court then held that if the property is not to be treated as closed for statutory cleanup purposes then it is not unfair to treat the property as not closed for tax assessment purposes. Otherwise, there could be a "windfall tax benefit to the very persons responsible for the toxic condition, even though no clean-up costs are incurred."[19] The court further held that the degree to which a property is "in use" or "closed down" cannot be left to subjective standards and that ISRA provides a rational, objective standard by which to determine whether a property is "in use" for tax purposes.

In *Orient Way Corp. v. Lyndhurst*,[20] the subject property consisted of 8.88 acres improved with obsolete industrial improvements.[21] It was undisputed that the property was polluted with dangerous compounds as the result of the industrial activities carried out prior to the time the plaintiffs took the title.[22] The court emphasized that neither party suggested that the plaintiff contributed to the contamination on the property. The plaintiff did, however, agree to assume full responsibility for remediation of the contamination as part of plaintiff's plan to redevelop the parcel.

Plaintiff's predecessor in title ceased all operations on the property in 2003, triggering a statutory obligation to remediate the environmental contamination under ISRA.[23] Because plaintiff's predecessor had already begun an investigation of the property's contamination and had expressed an interest in conducting a voluntary cleanup of the property, NJDEP did not proceed under ISRA to compel remediation. Environmental studies prepared with respect to the property by the prior owner, Benedict Miller, Inc.

(BMI) determined that the estimated cleanup costs of the property were somewhere between $2,400,000.00 and $3,000,000.00.

Plaintiff subsequently purchased the property from an affiliate of BMI "as is" for $2,500,000.00. There was evidence that the parties were aware of the contamination at the time of the purchase, the statutory obligation to remediate if voluntary action was not taken, and the existing estimate of cleanup costs. There was also evidence that the sale was an arm's length transaction. Prior to closing, Plaintiff took steps to have reports prepared by environmental experts which detailed the contamination and set forth a proposed cleanup plan. Following the closing, Plaintiff tried to engage the DEP to facilitate the approval of its remediation plan. While waiting for DEP approval of its cleanup plan, an unrelated construction company, also owned by plaintiff's principal, began using the subject property for outdoor storage of contracting materials, stone crushing, the storage and repair of its equipment and trucks, and for interior office use. A small amount of the materials stored on the property was sold to third parties, but plaintiff also intended to use a portion of the stone crushed on the property as a cap to cover the polluted areas, pursuant to its remediation plan.

The court found, utilizing the *Pan Chemical* analysis, that the plaintiff was not precluded from securing the benefit of an adjustment of the assessed value of its property based on the environmental contamination on the property. There was no effort made by the plaintiff to avoid remediation of the property. In fact, the plaintiff's intention in purchasing the property was to remediate the contamination, as evidenced by the plaintiff's voluntary assumption of the cleanup at the time of its purchase of the property. The court emphasized that there was no evidence in the record that any activity on the property during the plaintiff's ownership contributed to the contamination. The use of the property by the plaintiff's construction company, while it awaited approval of its remediation plan, did not change the court's conclusion.

The court further noted that *Inmar* and *Pan Chemical* do not require a total abandonment of a parcel before the effect of environmental contamination can be considered for local property tax assessment purposes. If the property owner is not responsible for the pollution, is not related to the party or parties who polluted the property, has voluntarily assumed responsibility for cleaning up the property, and is actively pursuing approval of a remediation plan, then the property owner should not be burdened by a requirement that it abandon the property in order to benefit from a reduction in the tax assessment to reflect the existence of contamination. Indeed, a contrary holding would discourage remediation of the property.

The court found that the nonpolluting owner's use of the property during the remediation approval process would be an important factor in the calculation of the assessment. If the use of the property is extensive, income-generating, and unhindered by the pending remediation, then the property's income-generating potential may meet or exceed any reduction attributable to the contamination. If, however, the use of the property is incidental and generates no substantial income, while the owner in good faith attempts to advance the cleanup, then the use of the property will have little if any impact on its assessed value.

The court then arrived at the taxable value of the subject property by utilizing the recent sale of the subject property. It did so despite the fact that the parties had stipulated to a higher value for the property as if "clean and unencumbered" leaving the issue of the appropriate deduction, if any, for environmental contamination for the court to decide. The court declined to adopt this approach, finding that the record in this case was different from *Inmar, Badische,* and *Metuchen I,* where the courts were faced with finding the true market value of the contaminated property without evidence of market sales. Here, there was no need to resort to the discounting of estimated remediation costs or similar measures to determine the effect of the subject property's contamination on value, since there had been an arm's length sale of the subject property which actually took into account the effect of the contamination on the property's true value.

Methode Electronics v. Willingboro[24] involved a small industrial facility which manufactured printed circuit boards and automotive airbag parts. The property became heavily contaminated. In 1988, volatile organic compounds were discovered in the groundwater which had traveled to neighboring properties. There was also the threat of toxic vapors seeping into the air and structures located on the subject property as well as on nearby parcels.

All manufacturing operations closed on the property in 1999. Methode demolished the manufacturing building located on the site but kept the concrete slab that previously served as the floor of the manufacturing facility to serve as a cap to prevent toxic vapors from escaping into the air. An extensive monitoring well and vapor extraction system was put in place across the entire property. No business activities had taken place on the property since 1999.

Methode appealed its 2010 and 2011 property tax assessments claiming the extensive contamination on the property and the ongoing remediation rendered the property unmarketable and valueless. Methode produced the testimony of an environmental specialist who was the manager of the remediation project at the property. Methode also produced a real estate appraiser who indicated that the property could not be developed in any meaningful fashion in its present state, had no realistic possibility of being fully remediated at any identifiable future date, and posed the threat of liability to any potential purchaser due to its continued capacity to produce toxic vapors.

The court found that this matter differed from the *Inmar, Pan Chemical, Orient Way* and other decisions which have considered the effect of environmental contamination on the valuation of property for tax assessment purposes. The underlying assumption in those cases was that the subject properties in those matters could be remediated to the point that they could be used or developed, thereby giving them some market value. It was not reasonably likely that the Methode property could be used or developed at any point in the foreseeable future due to (1) the relatively small nature of the property and most of the property was burdened with a remediation well, monitoring well, and the concrete vapor cap; (2) the regulating authority, the DEP, had determined that the remediation and monitoring wells, along with the concrete cap, must remain in place, functioning and accessible, for an indeterminate period of years and possibly decades; (3) the expert testimony established that the property could not be developed in a meaningful fashion; and (4) the property continued to emit toxic vapors onto the subject property as well as neighboring properties.

Given these factors, along with the fact that there was no evidence in the record as to how long the remediation would take to complete, as well as the extensive placement of remediation wells across the property and the concrete cap, the Court agreed with plaintiff's position that the subject property should only be assessed at a nominal value and entered a judgment assessing the property at a value of $2,000.

In *ACP Partnership v. Garwood Borough*,[25] the plaintiff argued that environmental contamination and the costs associated with remediation of the property had to be considered when determining the true market value of the property. The Borough, however, argued that the property possessed a distinct "in use" value due to plaintiff's continued operations on the property, and thus, as held in *Inmar*, the application of "normal assessment techniques" in valuing the property was appropriate. Given the upcoming trial date in the case, the tax court's ruling on this issue would be critical to the expert appraisers for both parties.

The facts were undisputed. After decades of industrial activity on the subject property, the property had become contaminated. The plaintiff acquired title to the property in 1991 and had voluntarily taken measures to investigate the environmental condition of the property. After years of sampling results from the soil and groundwater, it was revealed that the soil on the subject property was contaminated with high levels of volatile chemicals and solvents. As a result, the subject property was placed on the NJDEP's Known Contaminated Sites List. Plaintiff had provided a remedial action work plan to NJDEP and applied for and received a 50 percent innocent party grant from the Hazardous Discharge Site Remediation Fund as plaintiff was not the party responsible for the discharge of hazardous substances or wastes on the property. In 2013, it was further discovered that potential contamination may extend down to the bedrock beneath the subject property which would dramatically increase the estimated contaminant mass size from earlier studies.

Notwithstanding the contamination, the property continued to be operated as a multi-tenanted and multi-structure industrial and warehouse complex. The improvements contained approximately 230,000 sq. ft. and the plaintiff leased the property to tenants utilizing it for various warehouse and industrial uses. Plaintiff also occupied a small portion of the building for self-storage.

The court recognized that the facts presented an anomaly from those in prior precedents. First, the plaintiff acquired title to the subject property prior to the statutory changes which required the former owner of the contaminated property to be obligated to clean up the property. The contamination of the subject property occurred prior to plaintiff's acquisition of the property and plaintiff had neither caused nor exacerbated the situation, as evidenced by plaintiff's successful application in receiving the 50 percent innocent party grant. Second, the plaintiff voluntarily sought to investigate and contribute to remediation efforts on the property. Based on these facts, the court applied the holding in *Inmar*, whereby the court was required to take into consideration the environmental condition of the subject property. Furthermore, the current "in use" status of the subject property could not be ignored and thus the use of "normal assessment techniques" had to be utilized. However, the court noted that "such techniques must be tempered by the costs encountered by the taxpayer in addressing the environmental condition of the property." Although the court did not offer a methodology to account for the effect the contamination had on the value of the property, the court left the issue of making any adjustments as to the contamination to the "competence of the appraisal community."

CONCLUSION

As set forth above, recent court decisions in New Jersey have recognized that environmental contamination may have an impact on the value of real property for property tax purposes. However, the courts have struggled with the appropriate methodology to be employed when determining how that contamination should be considered as it relates to a property's true value. The general theme of the decisions appears to be that environmental contamination may be considered, provided that the subject property is no longer in use by the polluting party and that the applicable provisions of ISRA and other environmental statutes will determine whether the property is still "in use" for tax assessment purposes. In addition, while the courts have exercised flexibility and discretion in considering how environmental contamination detracts from the true value of property, it is also clear that a methodology which merely deducts the cost of environmental remediation dollar for dollar from the value of the property is not appropriate. As evidenced by recent court decisions, this continues to be a fluid and evolving area of the law.[26]

NOTES

1. N.J.S.A. 54:4-23.

2. See *West Deptford Twp. v. Gloucester County Bd. Of Taxation,* 6 N.J. Tax 79, 87 (Tax Ct. 1983); *Brockway Glass v. Twp. of Freehold,* 10 N.J. Tax 356, 371 (Tax Ct. 1989), *aff'd,* 12 N.J. Tax 263 (App. Div. 1991), *remanded on other grounds,* 130 N.J. 3 (1992).

3. N.J.S.A. 13:1K-6 to 14. ECRA was re-designated the Industrial Site Remediation Act ("ISRA") in 1993.

4. *Inmar,* 112 N.J. at 606.

5. *Id.*

6. *Id.* at 606–09

7. *Id.* at 609.

8. 12 N.J. Tax 354 (Tax Ct. 1992), *aff'd,* 264 N.J. Super. 353 (App. Div. 1993), *certif. denied,* 134 N.J. 481 (1993).

9. 264 N.J. Super. at 358-359.

10. 288 N.J. Super. 171 (App. Div. 1996).

11. 288 N.J. Super. at 182–83.

12. 21 N.J. Tax 283 (Tax Ct. 2004).

13. *In re Custom Distribution Services,* 216 B.R. 136 (Bankr. D.N.J. 1997), *aff'd in part, rev'd in part on other grounds* 224 F. 3d 235 (3rd Cir. 2000), contains an excellent discussion of stigma, as well as environmental and valuation issues in general. See also, *CIBA Specialty Chemicals Corp. v. Twp. of Dover,* N.J. Tax Court Unpub. opinion (Tax Ct. 2013), where the court held that the impact of contamination upon the value of an entire 200-acre parcel must be considered, even though only a portion of the site was contaminated. See also, *Jaylin Holdings, LLC v. Manchester Twp.*, N.J. Tax Unpub. opinion (Tax Ct. 2014), which rejected plaintiff's expert's opinion that the existence of a pine snake habitat on a portion of the property prevented virtually all development on the property, as the evidence showed that a portion of the property could be commercially developed.

14. The evidence in the record established that the owner contemplated completion of the remediation process over a period of five years. The court found that that discounting the

remaining cleanup costs over five years rather than deducting all of the costs in every year once the cleanup had begun was more appropriate, as the property is worth more as the cleanup progresses.

15. 21 N.J. Tax at 295.

16. 404 N.J. Super. 401 (App. Div. 2009), *certif. denied*, 198 N.J. 472 (2009).

17. Indeed, the property owner indicated that a statutory cleanup obligation would be triggered if 90 percent of operations on the property ceased, and therefore, intentionally continued 15 percent of its operations on the property in order to avoid this statutory trigger. The owner also conceded that it had made no efforts to improve or maintain the property, other than to remove several leaking storage tanks.

18. 404 N.J. Super. at 411.

19. 404 N.J. Super. at 413–14 quoting *Univ. Plaza Realty Corp. v. City of Hackensack*, 264 N.J. Super. 353, 357 (App. Div. 1993).

20. 27 N.J. Tax 361 (Tax Ct. 2013); *aff'd* 28 N.J. Tax 272 (App. Div. 2014).

21. The site was formally the Delaware Lackawanna and Weston Railroad Locomotive Facility, initially developed in 1906 to manufacture and repair locomotives and railcars.

22. Plaintiff intended to remediate the property prior to redevelopment under the Brownfield and Contaminated Site Remediation Act ("Brownfield Act"), N.J.S.A. 58:106-1 *et seq.*

23. N.J.S.A. 13:1K-6 to 14.

24. 28 N.J. Tax 289 (Tax Ct. 2015).

25. 29 N.J. Tax 102 (Tax Ct. 2016).

26. It is interesting to note that in the eminent domain context, the impact of environmental contamination is dealt with differently. In an eminent domain action the condemned property is valued as if remediated, with an appropriate escrow held by the condemner for the costs of remediation pending a separate cost recovery action. See *Housing Authority of the City of New Brunswick v. Suydam Investors, LLC*, 177 N.J. 2 (2003). See also, *Borough of Paulsboro v. Essex Chemical Corp.*, 427 N.J. Super. 123 (App. Div. 2012), *certif. denied*, 212 N.J. 459 (2012), where the Court held that the *Suydam* principle did not apply where the condemned property contained a closed sanitation landfill which required no feasible remediation.

Section 8

Administrative/Civil Enforcement

Lanny S. Kurzweil, Esq.,[1] Amanda Dumville, Esq., and Keith E. Lynott, Esq. (8th Ed.)

The New Jersey Legislature has armed the New Jersey Department of Environmental Protection (NJDEP or the Department) with a panoply of cumulative and nonexclusive remedies to enforce the State's environmental laws. Within each major statutory program, the NJDEP is authorized to pursue a variety of judicial or administrative actions to compel compliance with the substantive mandates, standards, emission and discharge limitations, permit conditions, and other requirements imposed by statute, administrative rule, or agency-issued permit or directive. New Jersey courts have, for the most part, liberally construed the NJDEP's enforcement powers, concluding that robust enforcement is necessary to enable the agency to fulfill its mission of protecting human health and the environment. Employing its broad enforcement powers, the NJDEP annually initiates thousands of enforcement actions, including 6,784 such actions in fiscal year 2017 and 6,901 in fiscal year 2018.[2]

THE NJDEP'S ENFORCEMENT ORGANIZATION

The NJDEP maintains a separate Division for Compliance and Enforcement, led by an assistant commissioner. The section is currently divided into Divisions of Water and Land Use Enforcement, Air and Hazardous Materials Enforcement, and Licensing Operations, Solid Waste, and Pesticide Enforcement. The section also operates a Facilitated Settlement Program unit, which seeks to effect the negotiable resolution of enforcement matters. The NJDEP's Site Remediation Program maintains its own Investigations and Enforcement unit. The Office of the Attorney General represents the NJDEP in enforcement proceedings before the Office of Administrative Law (OAL) and the New Jersey courts.

New Jersey's environmental laws and regulations confer broad powers on the NJDEP to enter the premises of a regulated party to assess compliance with statutory and regulatory requirements and permit conditions and/or to determine whether a violation has occurred. The Department's authorizing legislation provides that it has the power to "[e]nter and inspect any property, facility, building, premises, site or place for the purpose of investigating an actual or suspected source of pollution of the environment and conducting inspections, collecting samples, copying or photocopying documents or records, and for otherwise ascertaining compliance or noncompliance with any laws, permits, orders, codes, rules and regulations of the department."[3] The Water Pollution Control Act[4] grants the Department and local agencies—such as sewer authorities—"right of entry to all premises in which a discharge source is or might be located or in which monitoring equipment or records required by a permit are kept, for purposes of inspection, sampling, copying or photographing." The Air Pollution Control Act and Solid Waste Management Act contain similar provisions.[5]

Permits issued by the Department pursuant to its various programs may explicitly require the permittee to consent to entry to the permittee's facility for purposes of performing compliance inspections.

New Jersey courts have upheld the authority of the NJDEP to conduct warrantless searches of premises of parties subject to the Department's major environmental programs. Thus, in *In re Dep't of Environmental Protection*,[6] the Court upheld a permit condition, contained in an approval for the construction and operation of a wastewater treatment facility, which condition expressly authorized a right of entry consistent with the WPCA.[7] The court held that it chose "to view [the permittee's] activity . . . as being integrally related to the issue of water pollution and conservation of resources, which is an activity extensively regulated in this State."[8] As a result, the court concluded the warrantless search was authorized under the "pervasive government regulation" exception to the prohibition on unreasonable searches mandated by the Fourth Amendment to the United States Constitution.[9]

Permits authorizing wastewater discharges, air emission sources, or hazardous waste storage and handling activities also typically provide for periodic monitoring, measurement or testing of discharges or emissions, extensive recordkeeping, and reporting of violations. Such requirements enable the Department to adduce evidence of violations of standards, discharge, or emission limits or to permit other conditions from a regulated party's own records.

GENERAL ENFORCEMENT REMEDIES AND PROCEDURES

To effect compliance with statutory or regulatory requirements established by its various programs dealing with discharges of hazardous substances, contaminated site remediation, water pollution, and solid and hazardous waste management, the NJDEP is typically empowered to commence actions in the New Jersey courts seeking injunctive relief, including mandatory injunctive relief, prohibiting violations and compelling corrective action. Indeed, the NJDEP is permitted to seek injunctive relief compelling a responsible party to correct violations or perform remediation of environmental conditions even if it has not first conducted administrative proceedings to determine whether the actions sought are necessary or appropriate.

Thus, in *Dep't of Envtl. Prot. v. Kafil*,[10] the Appellate Division reversed a trial court's denial of an injunction sought by NJDEP to require a party to perform remediation. The Court concluded that, even though the NJDEP has regulatory powers to determine whether such remediation is warranted, the existence of such an alternative "cannot be seen to bar DEP from availing itself, at its reasonable election, of another remedy clearly established in [the statute], a direct civil action seeking injunctive relief."[11] To hold otherwise and restrict the NJDEP's authority to seek an injunction "is to deprive the Department of the broad remedial sweep so evidently contemplated by the Legislature[.]"[12]

The NJDEP may also pursue civil actions in the courts seeking judicial imposition of civil monetary penalties. Most statutory programs provide for very substantial monetary penalties for violations and ordinarily provide that, in respect of continuing violations, each day during which the violation continues is deemed to result in a separate and distinct violation, warranting a separate monetary penalty. The Department is typically empowered to seek such penalties in a summary proceeding under the Penalty Enforcement Law of 1999.[13] Rules 4:70 and 4:67 of the New Jersey Rules of Court, in turn, provide for such summary proceedings to "enforce a civil penalty imposed by any statute or ordinance."[14]

The NJDEP may recover such civil penalties authorized under its various statutory programs without a showing of intention to violate the particular statute or rule at issue. Thus, in *Dep't of Envtl. Prot. v. Lewis*,[15] a matter involving alleged violations of the Solid Waste Management Act,[16] the Water Pollution Control Act,[17] and the Pinelands Protection Act,[18] the Court concluded that

> [t]he cited statutes giving rise to imposition of civil penalties and remedies neither refer to nor require a finding of intent to violate the act before their remedies may be invoked. In that regard they are clearly akin to 'strict liability' statutes, . . . the violation of which can result in civil penal sanctions regardless of moral culpability or the need for a finding of *mens rea* such as is often the case under the criminal law.[19]

In addition to authorizing enforcement via a civil action in a court, whether for injunctive relief, penalties, or both, most statutory programs also authorize the Department to issue administrative orders requiring compliance, suspending or revoking permits, and/or assessing civil monetary penalties. To pursue enforcement via such administrative means, the NJDEP must first provide notice to the alleged violator of the specific violation and the amount of the penalty assessed—typically through an Administrative Order and Notice of Civil Penalty Assessment—and must afford the respondent an opportunity for an adjudicatory hearing. Most statutory programs require the recipient of an administrative order to request such an adjudicatory hearing within twenty calendar days of receipt of the notice.

Courts have held that the prescribed statutory period for requesting an adjudicatory hearing to challenge an administrative enforcement action initiated by the NJDEP is a jurisdictional requirement and may not be waived, excused, or enlarged. Thus, in *N.J. Dep't of Envtl. Prot. v. Mazza and Sons, Inc.*,[20] the Court held that a "statutory time limit for requesting an administrative hearing . . . is mandatory and jurisdictional." However, in (limited) circumstances involving "substantial compliance" with such a statutory requirement, courts have held a party's right to a hearing is preserved even if a request for hearing is not received by the Department within the required time period.[21]

An administrative hearing to challenge an administrative order and civil penalty assessment imposed by the NJDEP is ordinarily conducted as a "contested case" within the OAL and is subject to the Administrative Procedure Act[22] and the procedures established for such "contested case" proceedings in the OAL.[23] Although the NJDEP has discretion to deny a requesting party such an adjudicatory hearing, it is highly unlikely to do so in circumstances involving a timely request for such a hearing to challenge an administrative enforcement action.

A request for an adjudicatory hearing must usually specify the defenses to each of the Department's findings of fact as set forth in the order or notice commencing the administrative proceeding.[24] Denials of such findings must "fairly meet the substance of the findings denied."[25] General denials are not permitted; instead, the alleged violator must state the facts as such party "believes it or them to be."[26] The respondent must also supply information supporting the request and "specific reference" to, or copies of, other written documents relied upon.[27]

Following a hearing before the OAL, the administrative law judge (ALJ) must file recommended findings of fact and conclusions of law with the Commissioner of the NJDEP ("Commissioner").[28] The Commissioner must permit each party to submit written exceptions, objections and replies thereto, and to present argument.[29] The Commissioner must adopt, reject, or modify the ALJ's recommended decision within forty-five days of receipt (or, in the absence of such action, the decision of the ALJ becomes final).[30] The Commissioner may not reject or modify findings of fact as to issues of credibility of lay witness testimony, unless he or she determines from a review of the record that such findings are arbitrary, capricious, or unreasonable or are not supported by sufficient, competent, and credible evidence in the record.[31] The Commissioner must state "with particularity" reasons for rejecting any findings of fact and must make new or modified findings supported by sufficient, competent, and credible evidence in the record.[32]

A party may seek judicial review of a final determination of the NJDEP as to an administrative order and penalty assessment by taking an appeal to the Appellate Division of the Superior Court. The Appellate Division conducts a de novo review of the proceeding, based on the administrative record. A party seeking such review in the Appellate Division must file a notice within forty-five days of the day in which the administrative order becomes final.[33] However, the NJDEP may also seek to enforce final administrative orders by initiating an action in the Superior Court to convert the order into a docketed judgment.

As discussed in the previous section, many statutory programs also authorize the NJDEP to petition the attorney general to seek criminal sanctions, including fines and terms of imprisonment, for violation of the statutory or regulatory requirements.

STATUTORY OR REGULATORY PROGRAMS TO MITIGATE CIVIL PENALTIES

In recognition of the harsh consequences that can result from strict enforcement of New Jersey's myriad environmental laws and regulations, the Legislature and the

NJDEP itself have adopted various means by which a party can obtain some relief, albeit highly limited, from the enforcement consequences that would otherwise result from a violation. Of particular interest are the Grace Period Law,[34] the NJDEP's Self-Disclosure policy, and its policy on Supplemental Environmental Programs.

Grace Period Law

The Legislature adopted the Grace Period Law in 1995, declaring that "[e]xpanding the use of grace (compliance) periods will promote compliance," "[e]stablishing a policy for the consistent application of grace (compliance) periods for minor violations is a proper exercise of the [NJDEP's] enforcement discretion," and "[e]stablishing and employing grace (compliance) periods for minor violations will ensure the administration of an effective consistent, sensible and fair enforcement program."[35] The statute applies to virtually all of the environmental laws enacted by the Legislature, including the Spill Act, ISRA, WPCA, APCA, and the SWMA.[36]

The Grace Period Law instructs the NJDEP (or local governmental agency), upon identification of a violation which the NJDEP has designated as "minor," to issue an order, notice of violation, or other enforcement document that "notifies the person responsible for the violation that a penalty may be imposed unless the activity or condition constituting the minor violation is corrected and compliance is achieved within the period of time specified" in such order, notice, or other enforcement document.[37] The order, notice, or other enforcement document must then specify a period for correction of the minor violation, which period must generally be no less than thirty days and no more than ninety days.[38] The cure period may be extended for up to ninety days in the NJDEP's discretion and the period may be tolled "due to a lack of required action by the [NJDEP] or local government agency[.]"[39]

If a person responsible for a "minor violation" corrects the same within the specified period, the NJDEP may not impose a penalty for the violation.[40] In addition, a person that "voluntarily discloses" to the NJDEP the existence of such a "minor violation," together with all relevant circumstances relating to the violation, within thirty days of discovery of the same, and that thereafter remedies the violation within the required time period, is not subject to a monetary penalty.[41]

The Department may require the person that has committed the violation to verify that compliance has been achieved by appropriate certification or other documentation.[42] Although a penalty is not imposed for a "minor violation," the Grace Period Law does not limit the authority of the NJDEP to seek injunctive or other relief that may be available in the circumstances.[43]

If a person fails to correct the violation within the prescribed period, the NJDEP may proceed to assess a penalty.[44] Such penalty can be retroactive to the date on which the enforcement document was first issued.[45]

The Grace Period Law directs the NJDEP to promulgate regulations "designating specific types or categories of violations within each regulatory and enforcement program of each environmental law as minor and non-minor violations."[46] The statute establishes the criteria for designating violations as "minor," which criteria relate both to the nature of the violation and the putative violator, as follows:

- The violation is not the result of "purposeful, knowing, reckless or criminally negligent conduct";
- The violation poses "minimal risk" to the public health, safety, and natural resources;
- The violation does not "materially and substantially undermine or impair the goals of the regulatory program";
- The activity or condition has existed for less than twelve months prior to discovery;
- The person committing the violation has not been "identified in a previous enforcement action" as responsible for the same or similar violation at the same facility or site in the preceding twelve-month period;
- The person responsible for the violation "has not been identified" as responsible for the same or similar violations "that reasonably indicate a pattern of illegal conduct and not isolated incidents"; and
- The violation is capable of correction within the specified time period.[47]

Pursuant to the Grace Period Law, the NJDEP has, within its various rules establishing policies and procedures for civil penalty assessment, identified certain violations as "minor" and established a time period for correction for each such violation. For example, in the ARRRCS, the NJDEP has identified numerous violations as "minor" (e.g., failure to submit a copy of a remedial action workplan, status report, or site health and safety plan to the clerk of the municipality, county health department, or local health agency) and periods for correction (e.g., thirty days).[48]

Self-Disclosure Policy

The NJDEP has adopted a policy that permits a person to obtain a 75 to 100 percent reduction of a penalty in certain circumstances in which the person independently discovers, discloses, and corrects the violation.[49]

The Self-Disclosure policy applies to certain violations that a person "voluntarily discovers."[50] A violation is "voluntarily discovered" even if there is a legal requirement to report it but is not "voluntarily discovered" if it is revealed through a "legally mandated monitoring or sampling requirement."[51]

In order to be eligible for penalty reduction, a party must "fully disclose" the violation to NJDEP within twenty-one days of discovery.[52] The date of such discovery is the date that an "officer, director, employee or agent" of the regulated party "has an objectively reasonable basis for believing that a violation has, or may have, occurred."[53]

The party must also discover or disclose the violation "independent of any regulatory agency or third-party complainant."[54] A violation is discovered independently if it occurs prior to discovery by a state or federal agency or certified local health agency or local government agency, prior to an inspection or "notification of a scheduled inspection" by the NJDEP, or U.S. Environmental Protection Agency, other governmental authority, prior to the commencement of an enforcement action, and prior to the filing of a citizen suit or complaint by third party or the reporting of the violation by a "whistleblower" employee.[55]

Upon discovery of the violation, the party must "promptly correct it" within the timeframe specified in a settlement document to be entered with the NJDEP, or in the absence of such a settlement document, within 60 or 180 days (for small businesses).[56]

The self-disclosed violation may not be a "repeat violation," as defined in the Proposed Self-Disclosure Rule, which provides that "repeat violations" are those identical or substantially similar violations committed and identified in the previous twelve- or, in some cases, thirty-six-month period.[57] The party must also agree, in a settlement document, to take "appropriate action" to prevent recurrence of the violation and to "implement measures acceptable" to the NJDEP to mitigate any harm caused by the violation.[58] The violation cannot be the result of past failure to take "reasonable and appropriate" action to prevent recurrence following earlier discovery of the same or similar violation.[59]

Finally, the violation cannot have "caused serious actual harm to human health or the environment" or imminent risk of such harm."[60] Nor can it be the result of "purposeful, knowing, reckless or criminally negligent conduct."[61]

The Proposed Self-Disclosure Policy requires the disclosing party to submit a completed Self-Disclosure form to the NJDEP.[62] If the violation is eligible for penalty reduction under the policy, the NJDEP and the disclosing party must then enter into a "settlement document" identifying the violation(s), establishing the timeframe for correction, and providing for the amount of penalty reduction.[63]

If a party satisfies all the requirements for penalty reduction, the NJDEP "shall reduce" the amount of the penalty "that it would otherwise seek or assess" for the violation by 75 percent for certain violations, 100 percent for others, and 100 percent for all eligible violations committed by small business.[64] At the same time, however, the NJDEP "retains full discretion" to recover any economic benefit secured as a result of any violation."[65] Moreover, the Self-Disclosure policy cannot be invoked to reduce a mandatory minimum penalty required under the WPCA, or to modify the express limitations on the NJDEP's settlement authority under that statute.[66]

In the event a self-disclosed violation is not eligible for penalty reduction under the Proposed Self-Disclosure Policy, the NJDEP is free to pursue "any other enforcement remedy it deems appropriate."[67] As a result, a party submitting such a Self-Disclosure notification is taking a chance the NJDEP will reject the request for penalty reduction under one or more of the (subjective) criteria noted above and proceed to assess the maximum penalty. Self-Disclosure Reports submitted to the NJDEP are subject to public access under the Open Public Records Act.[68]

Supplemental Environmental Project Policy

The NJDEP has published a guidance document that encourages the Division of Compliance and Enforcement to include "Supplemental Environmental Projects" or "SEPs" in settlement agreements that resolve enforcement actions.[69] A SEP is "an environmentally beneficial project that a respondent voluntarily agrees to perform as a condition of settling an enforcement action."[70] It is an action a party is not otherwise required to perform and as to which the public or the environment is the primary beneficiary.[71]

A responsible party may submit a proposal to perform a SEP in partial mitigation of a civil penalty assessment.[72] If the SEP proposal is accepted, incorporated into the settlement agreement, and satisfactorily implemented, the amount of a penalty can be reduced by the cost of a SEP.[73] For each dollar spent implementing a SEP, one dollar can be deducted from the settlement amount up to 75 percent of the total penalty amount provided for in a settlement agreement.[74] For violations of the WPCA, a SEP cannot offset the penalty by more than 50 percent.[75]

A SEP, typically a pollution reduction project of some type (e.g., planting of trees in a public park, electrification projects, solar panel installations, stormwater basin improvements), must normally have a "direct relationship" to the underlying violation.[76] Such a "direct relationship" means that the SEP is performed "near the site of the violation" and reduces the adverse impact to public health and the environment to which the violation contributes, reduces the likelihood of similar violations in the future, or reduces the overall risk to public health or the environment affected by the violation.[77] The NJDEP may accept a SEP with an "indirect relationship" to the violation if it "advances the Department's mission or a Department priority" and directly benefits public health and/or the environment.[78]

Acceptance of a SEP proposal is within the NJDEP's discretion.[79] In evaluating a proposal, the NJDEP considers a number of factors, including the capacity of the respondent to perform it, the availability of NJDEP resources to negotiate and draft the SEP provision of a settlement document and to verify that the SEP has been completed, the compliance history of the violator, the suitability of the SEP itself, whether the SEP reduces "environmental burdens in an overburdened community," and consultation with and support from residents in the community.[80]

A SEP must "include concrete and measurable environmental benefits" and may not merely involve a monetary donation, a program of general education, or a project that has no environmental benefit.[81] A SEP may also not include a project that the respondent has "previously planned, initiated, implemented, budgeted for, or completed," or that is required by law or necessary to return to compliance.[82]

If a SEP proposal is accepted, the project is then incorporated into a settlement agreement.[83] The agreement must provide for start and end dates and project deliverables and must specify the consequences if the SEP is not completed.[84] The respondent must agree in the settlement document to provide periodic progress reports on implementing a SEP and other evidence of performance (e.g., photos or invoices detailing purchases).[85] The respondent must also verify final completion of a SEP.[86]

Although a SEP is, by definition, a project that a party is not otherwise required by law to perform, it becomes a legal requirement once incorporated into a settlement document.[87] A party that fails to perform a SEP can be subject to penalties.[88]

By performing a SEP, a responsible party may satisfy its obligations to pay a monetary penalty by performing a beneficial project rather than simply writing a check to the State Treasury. Nevertheless, the cost of a SEP represents a civil penalty and the respondent may not represent otherwise to any taxing authority or other governmental agency.[89] Publicity relating to a SEP must make clear the SEP was completed in settlement of an enforcement action.[90]

CITIZEN ENFORCEMENT OF ENVIRONMENTAL LAWS

New Jersey law also permits private citizens in certain circumstances to enforce environmental law and rules. The Environmental Rights Act[91] is the principal vehicle for such citizen enforcement.

The ERA establishes a cause of action to private individuals or groups or to a municipality or governmental body (other than the NJDEP) against another party: (i) to enforce a specific environmental statute, regulation, or ordinance;[92] or (ii) where there is no specific standard set forth in a statute, regulation, or ordinance, "for the protection of the environment, or the interest of the public therein, from pollution, impairment or destruction."[93] The ERA authorizes a court to impose declaratory and equitable relief and to assess civil monetary fines for a violation of law.[94]

Pursuant to the ERA, a court can also award attorneys' fees to the "prevailing party" that "achieved reasonable success on the merits."[95] In order to proceed with an action under the ERA, a putative plaintiff must give thirty days' notice of intent to sue to the prospective defendant and to the attorney general of New Jersey.[96]

Courts generally describe the ERA as creating a private right of action to enforce *other* New Jersey environmental statutes. Thus,

> [t]he ERA does not itself confer any substantive rights. Rather, it grants private plain-tiffs standing to enforce other New Jersey environmental statutes "as an alternative to inaction by the government which retains primary prosecutorial responsibility." The government is "entrusted initially with the right to determine the primary course of action to be taken." However, where the government has "failed or neglected to act in the best interest of the citizenry or has arbitrarily, capriciously or unreasonably acted," a private plaintiff can bring an action under the ERA. Thus, the primary goal of the ERA is to limit lawsuits by private litigants to those instances where the government has not acted.

Mayor and Council of the Borough of Rockaway v. Klockner & Klockner.[97] As a result, under *Klockner & Klockner* and other cases, a putative plaintiff under the ERA must demonstrate both that a defendant is violating an applicable environmental law or standard and that the NJDEP has "failed or neglected to act" or has "arbitrarily, capriciously or unreasonably" acted.

Cases applying the ERA make clear that the right to pursue a claim under the stat-ute is highly dependent on the particular facts as determined by the trial court. As the Court in *Township of Howell v. Waste Disposal, Inc.*[98] stated:

> [T]here is no *per se* rule which will serve as an appropriate solution to all situations which may be posited [in ERA actions]. Rather the solution lies within the framework of the individual set of facts in each case.

In *Player v. Motiva Enterprises LLC*,[99] the U.S. District Court for the District of New Jersey dismissed an ERA claim. In doing so, it characterized the NJDEP's action with respect to the cleanup of groundwater contamination as "consistent and pervasive":

> Here the record indicates consistent and pervasive NJDEP oversight of the remediation process, requiring Defendant to regularly test Plaintiffs' wells and institute interim and permanent groundwater recovery systems. Plaintiffs have not claimed that the NJDEP failed to act or acted unreasonably, and there are no grounds for finding NJDEP inaction sufficient to permit a private ERA suit.[100]

In contrast, in *Township of Howell*,[101] the lower court dismissed the ERA claim of the Township of Howell and its Board of Health against Waste Disposal, Inc. (WDI), which was responsible for the cleanup and closure of a sanitary landfill. WDI had entered into several administrative consent orders with the State, and agreed to, among other things, install a cap, a slurry wall, a well point-pump collection system, and a leachate collection system.

The plaintiffs brought the ERA action after the NJDEP conducted a compliance review and determined that WDI failed to meet the compliance dates set forth in the administrative consent orders. The NJDEP intervened as plaintiff (and alleged claims against WDI). Thereafter, NJDEP and WDI entered into a partial settlement. Following the partial settlement, the trial court dismissed the Township's and the Board of Health's claims under the ERA.

The Appellate Division overturned the dismissal and remanded for a factual determination with respect to the NJDEP's actions, stating:

[S]hould the trial court determine that DEP has adequately, fairly and fully enforced the statutory requirements against WDI including the various reliefs authorized thereby, with due regard for the special local interests of the Township and the Board of Health, the court may determine to reenter its judgments of dismissal. On the other hand, the court may conclude that the DEP has not exhausted all reliefs and remedies which should be made available to either one or both plaintiffs and that the goals of that legislation would be served better by allowing them to continue with some portion of the suit. *Or it may determine that DEP has not fairly and adequately considered and protected the rights and peculiar interests of the Board of Health or the Township in their representative capacities in its settlement with WDI. In such case it may fashion an order allowing them to proceed on a limited basis.* In sum, the trial court must first ascertain the extent of the violations alleged and the adequacy and reasonableness of remedial action being pursued and contemplated by DEP before it may compel these plaintiffs to forego their right to sue.[102]

NOTES

1. With credit and much gratitude to my former McCarter & English, LLP partner, Keith E. Lynott, Esq., whose previous work on this chapter was extensive.

2. NJDEP Enforcement Actions for Fiscal year 2017 and 2018: https://www13.state.nj.us/DataMiner

3. N.J.S.A. 13:1D-9(d).

4. N.J.S.A. 58:10A-6(g).

5. N.J.S.A. 26:2C-9(b)(4); N.J.S.A. 13:1E-9.

6. 177 N.J. Super. 304 (App. Div. 1981), distinguished on other grounds by *State v. Heine*, 424 N.J. Super. 48 (App. Div. 2012)

7. *Id.* at 314 (citing N.J.S.A. 58:10A-6(g)).

8. *Id.* at 313.

9. *Id.* at 315; see also *State v. Bonaccurso*, 227 N.J. Super. 159, 167 (Law Div. 1988) (Water Pollution Control Act's statutory framework authorizing of warrantless entry is "constitutionally sufficient").

10. 395 N.J. Super. 597 (App. Div. 2007).

11. *Id.* at 601.

12. *Id.* at 603.

13. N.J.S.A. 2A:58-10, *et seq.*

14. Rules Governing the Courts of the State of New Jersey, N.J.R. 4:70 and 4-67.

15. 215 N.J. Super. 564 (App. Div. 1987).

16. N.J.S.A. 13:1E-1 *et seq.*

17. N.J.S.A. 58:10A-1, *et seq.*

18. N.J.S.A. 13:18A-1, *et seq.*

19. 215 N.J. Super. at 572-73 (citations omitted).

20. 406 N.J. Super. 13, 26 (App. Div. 2009) (internal quotation marks omitted); see also *Schaible Oil Co., Inc. v. N.J. Dep't of Envtl. Prot.*, 246 N.J. Super. 29 (App. Div. 1991), *certif. denied*, 126 N.J. 387 (1991); *Midland Glass Co. v. N.J. Dep't Envtl. Prot.*, 136 N.J. Super. 194 (App. Div. 1975).

21. *D.R. Horton, Inc.-New Jersey v. N.J. Dep't Envtl. Prot.*, 383 N.J. Super. 405 (App. Div. 2006) (request for administrative hearing was mailed four days before expiration of twenty day period but not received until two days after the period).

22. N.J.S.A. 52:14B-1, *et seq.*

23. N.J.A.C. 1:1, *et seq.*

24. See, for example, N.J.A.C. 7:26C-9.10; N.J.A.C. 7:26-5.3; N.J.A.C. 7:27A-3.4; N.J.A.C. 7:14-8.4.

25. *Id.*

26. *Id.*

27. *Id.*

28. N.J.S.A. 52:14B-10(c); N.J.A.C. 1:1-18:6.

29. *Id.*; N.J.A.C. 1:1-18.4.

30. *Id.*; N.J.A.C. 1:1-18.6.

31. *Id.*

32. *Id.*

33. N.J.R. 2:4-1(b).

34. N.J.S.A. 13:1D-125, *et seq.*

35. N.J.S.A. 13:1D-125.

36. N.J.S.A. 13:1-126 (definitions).

37. N.J.S.A. 13:1D-127(a).

38. N.J.S.A. 13:1D-127(b).

39. *Id.*

40. N.J.S.A. 13:1D-127(c).

41. N.J.S.A. 13:1D-130.

42. N.J.S.A. 13:1D-127(c).

43. N.J.S.A. 13:1D-127(d).

44. N.J.S.A. 13:1D-128.

45. *Id.*

46. N.J.S.A. 13:1D-129(a). The NJDEP did not actually promulgate such rules for a decade.

47. N.J.S.A. 13:1D-129(b).

48. N.J.A.C. 7:26C-9.5.

49. Proposed rule 7:33, published in the New Jersey Register, August 18, 2003 (referred to herein as "Proposed Self-Disclosure Rule"). The NJDEP proposed administrative regulations to implement this policy in August 2003, with the stated objective of providing "an incentive to companies to comprehensively review their operations, and report and correct violations." Summary of Proposed Self-Disclosure Rule published in the New Jersey Register, August 18,

2003. However, the NJDEP never promulgated the proposed rules. Instead, it is implementing the policy, as reflected in the proposed (but not adopted) rule, as a matter of the exercise of its enforcement discretion.

50. Proposed Self-Disclosure Rule, 7:33-3.1(a)(1).

51. *Id.*

52. Proposed Self-Disclosure Rule, 7:33-3.1(a)(2).

53. *Id.*

54. Proposed Self-Disclosure Rule, 7:33-3.1(a)(3).

55. *Id.*

56. Proposed Self-Disclosure Rule, 7:33-3.1(a)(4).

57. Proposed Self-Disclosure Rule, 7:33-3.1(a)(5).

58. Proposed Self-Disclosure Rule, 7:33-3.1(a)(6) and (7).

59. Proposed Self-Disclosure Rule, 7:33-3.1(a)(8).

60. Proposed Self-Disclosure Rule, 7:33-3.1(a)(9).

61. *Id.*

62. Proposed Self-Disclosure Rule, 7:33-2.1.

63. Proposed Self-Disclosure Rule, 7:33-2.1(d)(3)(i).

64. Proposed Self-Disclosure Rule, 7:33-3.1(b).

65. Proposed Self-Disclosure Rule, 7:33-3.1(c).

66. Proposed Self-Disclosure Rule, 7:33-1.2(c).

67. Proposed Self-Disclosure Rule, 7:33-2.1(d)(3)(ii).

68. Proposed Self-Disclosure Rule, 7:33-4.1(a).

69. NJDEP, Standard Operating Procedures For Incorporating Supplemental Environmental Projects Into Settlement Agreements, December 5, 2011 ("SEP Policy").

70. SEP Policy at 1.

71. *Id.*

72. SEP Policy at 3.

73. *Id.*

74. *Id.*

75. SEP Policy at 3-4.

76. SEP Policy at 3.

77. *Id.*

78. *Id.*

79. SEP Policy at 5.

80. *Id.*

81. SEP Policy at 4.

82. *Id.*

83. SEP Policy at 5.

84. *Id.*

85. SEP Policy at 5-6.

86. *Id.*

87. SEP Policy at 2.

88. *Id.*

89. SEP Policy at 3.

90. *Id.*

91. N.J.S.A. 2A:35A-1, *et seq.* (the "ERA").

92. N.J.S.A. 2A:35A-4(a).

93. N.J.S.A. 2A:35A-4(b).

94. N.J.S.A. 2A:35A-4(a).

95. N.J.S.A. 2A:35A-10a.

96. N.J.S.A. 2A:35A-11.

97. 811 F.Supp. 1039, 1054 (D.N.J. 1993) (internal citations omitted; emphasis added).

98. 207 N.J. Super. 80, 95 (App. Div. 1986).

99. 2006 WL 166452 (D.N.J. 2006).

100. *Id.* at *13. The District Court's dismissal of the ERA action was affirmed by the Third Circuit but solely on the basis that plaintiff did not comply with the notice requirements of the ERA.

101. *Township of Howell*, 207 N.J. Super. 80.

102. *Id.* at 95-98 (emphasis added).

Section 9

Criminal Enforcement

Edward R. Bonanno, Esq.

WHAT MAKES AN ENVIRONMENTAL VIOLATION A CRIME?

In New Jersey, and in other jurisdictions, most environmental enforcement actions are handled through civil or administrative proceedings. Criminal enforcement is generally reserved for the most egregious environmental violations in which the offenders knowingly, persistently, or flagrantly disregard their environmental responsibilities.[1] In determining whether a criminal action is warranted in a particular matter, prosecutors will consider the following factors when reviewing the case: (1) mental state of the offender, (2) nature of the offense, (3) motive, (4) impact on regulatory program, and (5) traditional crimes.[2]

For the first factor, prosecutors will assess whether the violator acted purposely or intentionally, or whether the conduct was accidental. Prosecutors will also consider whether the violator has been a repeat offender which would make it more likely that the violator possessed some type of criminal intent. It would also be more important for a prosecutor to pursue a case against a persistent violator to protect the integrity of the environmental regulatory program. For the second factor, prosecutors will evaluate the actual or potential damage to human health and the environment that resulted from the violator's conduct. If a party discharges a highly toxic material, such as cyanide, a prosecutor will view the conduct more seriously than if a person discharges an inert material. For the third factor, motive, prosecutors will consider whether the violator acted out of simple greed or whether the violator did not have the financial ability to comply. If a company has no assets, but its owners do, prosecutors will not be very sympathetic to a claim that the company did not have the ability to live up to its environmental responsibilities. With respect to the fourth factor, prosecutors will look unfavorably upon a violator who has taken actions such as concealing information from the New Jersey Department of Environmental Protection (NJDEP). For factor five, if prosecutors find that the violator has engaged in other traditional crimes, such as theft, fraud, forgery, or racketeering, they will be more apt to bring a criminal enforcement action against that violator.

NEW JERSEY'S CRIMINAL ENVIRONMENTAL
ENFORCEMENT AGENCIES

In New Jersey, the lead agency for environmental crimes investigations and prosecutions is the New Jersey Attorney General's Office, Division of Criminal Justice (DCJ) Environmental Crimes Unit within DCJ's Specialized Crime Bureau. Almost forty years ago, New Jersey established one of the first units in the nation dedicated to the investigation and prosecution of any crimes relating to the environment. Since that time, the DCJ, through the Environmental Crimes Bureau (ECB) and now through the Environmental Crimes Unit (ECU), has investigated and prosecuted violations of all of New Jersey's environmental crimes statutes as well as traditional crimes, such as fraud, theft, and racketeering that have an impact on State environmental regulatory programs and on public health and safety. The ECB receives the cases that it investigates and prosecutes from the NJ DEP, county and local health departments, county and local law enforcement, environmental groups, and private citizens. With decreasing State budgets over the last decade, the ECB/ECU has less staff than it had during its first thirty years and handles fewer cases, but it still has been able to prosecute some significant cases involving the environment and public health and safety.

On occasion, a few of the County Prosecutors' Offices will handle a smaller environmental crimes case. Moreover, if there is a large multi-jurisdictional event, such as an oil spill from a cargo ship in the port of New York or Philadelphia, federal agencies, including U.S. EPA, the Coast Guard, the U.S. Attorney's Office, and U.S. Department of Justice Environmental Crimes Section, may be involved in the investigation and prosecution. With the decrease in the number of cases that DCJ ECU is now able to handle, the U.S. Department of Justice Environmental Crimes Section, with the U.S. Attorney for New Jersey, has played a larger role in prosecuting environmental crime in New Jersey.[3]

The type of cases prosecuted by the DCJ ECB/ECU, as well as by the U.S. Department of Justice Environmental Crimes Section, has also changed over the past forty years. In the early years of criminal enforcement, prosecutors used then-recently enacted criminal statutes to deal with blatant criminal conduct, such as the midnight dumping of drums of toxic waste and direct discharges of chemical wastes into rivers and streams.[4] As a result of effective civil and criminal enforcement, better industry compliance programs, and changes in the types of industry in the State, the cases that State and Federal prosecutors investigate and prosecute today are generally more discrete and less blatant but no less important. Federal and State prosecutors now often deal with fraudulent submissions to the DEP and other regulatory agencies and with the unlawful handling of toxic materials such as asbestos and lead.[5]

In recent years, DCJ ECB/ECU has prosecuted a number of cases involving the submission of fraudulent water quality sampling data for the DEP Safe Drinking Water program and false data for the New Jersey Pollution Discharge Elimination System (NJPDES) permit program.[6] In *State v. William Muzzio*, Indictment No. 12-08-000139-S, the DCJ ECU obtained a five-year State prison sentence against defendant Muzzio for releasing asbestos dust and debris while performing unlicensed asbestos work at a daycare center. In *State v. Frank Rizzo and Michael Kouvaras*, Indictment No. 12-06-000126-S, in 2015, the DCJ ECU obtained a three-year State prison sentence against Rizzo, the owner of a demolition company, and a one-year county jail sentence against codefendant Kouvaras, for unlawfully removing asbestos from a demolition site and using workers who were neither trained nor equipped to perform the work safely and in compliance with the law. In *State v. Edward O'Rourke*, Accusation No. 15-12-593-A, in 2015, DCJ ECU secured a three-year State prison sentence against O'Rourke, the licensed operator of the New Brunswick and Milltown public drinking water system for failing to conduct required drinking water tests and then submitting false data to the DEP.

ENVIRONMENTAL CRIMINAL STATUTES

Water Pollution

New Jersey's water pollution crimes closely track those found in the federal Clean Water Act (CWA).[7] Under New Jersey's Water Pollution Control Act, a person can be guilty of a crime if they unlawfully discharge a pollutant, as that term is broadly defined, into waters of the State, which would include surface water, groundwater, and sewer systems. An unlawful discharge would be one that occurs without a permit or in violation of a permit. If the unlawful discharge causes a significant adverse environmental effect or if it places another person in imminent danger of death or serious bodily injury, the potential fines and terms of imprisonment are significantly higher.[8]

Hazardous Waste/Hazardous Substances/Toxic Pollutants

New Jersey prosecutors will use crimes from the Criminal Code, specifically N.J.S.A. 2C:17-2a(2), and from the Solid Waste Management Act, specifically N.J.S.A. 13:1E-9g, h and i, to prosecute cases involving the unlawful handling and disposal of hazardous waste, hazardous substances, and toxic pollutants. The criminal provisions in the Solid Waste Management Act closely track those in the Resource Conservation Recovery Act.[9]

One of the challenges that prosecutors face when handling these types of cases is establishing that the material in question is, in fact, a hazardous waste or substance or a toxic pollutant. As set forth in the Solid Waste Management Act and its underlying regulations, a hazardous waste must be a solid waste that meets certain specific hazardous waste criteria, such as the characteristics of ignitability, corrosivity, reactivity, or toxicity (40 CFR sec. 261.20), or contains a listed waste (40 CFR sec. 261.30). The material must be a waste; it cannot be a product. If the chemical material is not a waste, a person who stores the material haphazardly cannot be prosecuted for a hazardous waste crime unless the material leaks out onto the ground.

A toxic pollutant must be a compound that is listed under DEP or EPA regulations. These lists contain many different compounds, including PCBs, cyanides, dioxins, and asbestos. For a prosecution for the unlawful release or discharge of a toxic pollutant, while there is no specific threshold level required beyond the detection limit, courts will in some situations refer to the DEP regulations that set the Residential and Non-Residential Direct Contact Soil Clean-Up Criteria.[10] Under the Spill Act and its underlying regulations, a "hazardous substance" includes various listed chemical compounds as well as petroleum products. With certain specific limited exceptions, virtually all discharges of hazardous substances must be reported to the DEP.[11]

New Jersey prosecutors have used both the Criminal Code and the Asbestos Control and Licensing Act, specifically N.J.S.A. 34:5A-41, to prosecute those who improperly handle asbestos, a listed toxic pollutant. Generally, when New Jersey prosecutors bring an action against a contractor who improperly handles asbestos, they will charge the contractor with removing asbestos without having a Department of Labor license to do so, contrary to the Asbestos Control and Licensing Act and with unlawfully releasing a listed toxic pollutant, contrary to N.J.S.A. 2C:17-2a(2).[12]

New Jersey has also established crimes for the unlawful handling of regulated medical waste. In 1989, in response to the public outcry over the washing up of floatable debris, including syringes, onto New Jersey's beaches, the Legislature enacted the Regulated Medical Waste Act[13] which contains criminal provisions for the unlawful handling and disposal of regulated medical waste[14] One the ECB's more notable recent prosecutions under this statute involved a dentist who dumped 260 dental-type needles and other medical type debris into the Townsend Inlet in Avalon. Within a short period of time, that debris washed up on Avalon's beaches forcing their closure on a summer weekend.[15]

Solid Waste

In 2003, in response to an increase in the unlawful dumping of truckloads of debris in urban areas, the New Jersey Legislature enacted the Solid Waste Crimes Law to provide prosecutors with better legal tools for addressing this growing problem. Under N.J.S.A. 13:1E-9.6, a person who knowingly disposes of or causes the disposal of or transports at least 1,000 cubic yards of solid waste to a place not authorized to receive it by NJDEP commits a second-degree crime. One thousand cubic yards would equal fifty 20-cubic-yard containers. The Solid Waste Crimes law has third and fourth crimes for unlawful disposal and transportation activities based for different amounts under 1,000 cubic yards and the mens rea involved. Unlike the Solid Waste Utility Control Act's fourth-degree solid waste crimes that require that the person be engaged in the business of solid waste collection or disposal, the Solid Waste Crimes law's provisions apply whether or not the person is a licensed hauler charging customers for solid waste services.[16]

Within a short time of the enactment of the Solid Waste Crimes Law, the ECB prosecuted a number of individuals for unlawfully disposing of truckloads of construction/demolition debris and old used tires in open areas in Jersey City, Newark, and Paterson.[17] The successful prosecution of these cases, which in several instances resulted in the defendants receiving prison sentences, led to a substantial reduction in unlawful dumping in these cities.[18]

Within the Solid Waste Management Act, there is also a disorderly persons offense for unlawful dumping. This provision has been used by the ECB, County Prosecutors, and local police to prosecute solid waste dumpers. Under N.J.S.A. 13:1E-9.3 to 4, it is a disorderly persons offense, but not a crime, to transport, collect, or dispose of solid waste in excess of 0.148 cubic yards of solids (roughly the size of an outdoor trash bag) or 30 gallons of liquids at a place not authorized by NJDEP to accept it. Under N.J.S.A. 13:1E-9.4, for a violation of this disorderly persons provision, the conveyances used to transport or dispose of the solid waste may be subject to forfeiture.

Public Safety

The Criminal Code also contains provisions that address situations in which the mishandling of hazardous materials creates a public safety risk. Under N.J.S.A. 2C:17-2c, if a person recklessly creates the risk of widespread injury or damage through the handling or storage of hazardous materials, they commit a third-degree crime. If the conduct violated any law, rule, or regulation intended to protect public health and safety, the crime becomes one of the second degree. Under N.J.S.A. 2C:17-2e, a widespread injury is defined as serious bodily injury to five or more people or five or more habitations or to a building that would normally have contained twenty-five or more people. Prosecutors have used this criminal provision to pursue cases against those who have improperly and unsafely handled hazardous materials which do not fall within the purview of New Jersey's hazardous waste laws.

Land Use

While there have been relatively few State prosecutions for violations of the environmental land use statutes and regulations that is likely to change with the increasing growth and development pressures in the State. Under the Freshwater Wetlands Protection Act, a person who purposely, knowingly or recklessly violates the Act or any underlying rule or regulation, or order issued thereto, or makes a false statement in a document filed with NJDEP or that must be maintained under the Act is guilty of a third-degree crime.[19] In 2007, the Legislature added criminal provisions to the Coastal Area Facility Review Act, Flood Hazard Area Control Act, and the Waterfront Development Act. In each of these Acts, a person who purposely, knowingly, or recklessly violates that Act or any underlying rule or regulation, or order issued thereto, or makes a false statement in a document filed with NJDEP or that must be maintained under that Act is guilty of a third-degree crime.[20]

Statute of Limitations

New Jersey has no statute of limitations for many environmental crimes. Under N.J.S.A. 2C:1-6a(2), a prosecution for a crime contained in the Solid Waste Management Act, Regulated Medical Waste Act, Air Pollution Control Act, Asbestos Control and Licensing Act, and the Water Pollution Control Act may be commenced at any time.

CRIMINAL CULPABILITY

With a few limited exceptions, environmental crimes require some type of criminal intent. Most require purposeful, knowing, or reckless conduct and a few provide for a negligent mental state. Each of these mental states is defined in N.J.S.A. 2C:2-2 of the Criminal Code. For negligence, the Code definition requires criminal negligence, not ordinary negligence as some Federal Courts have allowed for federal prosecutions under the Clean Water Act.[21]

A number of Federal Courts have found that when knowledge is an element of the environmental offense, the knowledge element is satisfied upon a showing that the defendant was aware that he was performing the proscribed acts. In those cases, the Courts have held that the prosecution does not have to establish that the defendant knew that his conduct was illegal. However, under the reasoning of this line of cases, the prosecution may still need to show that the defendant had knowledge of the status of a permit and the permit requirements if the defendant is charged with violating that permit.[22] A number of Federal Courts have held that the prosecution does not need to prove that the defendant knew the chemical nature of the hazardous waste or pollutant.[23] However, in *United States v. Ahmad*, the Court ruled that for a Clean Water Act violation, the prosecution had to establish that the defendant had knowledge of the nature of the substance, otherwise, someone who honestly and reasonably believed that he was discharging water may find himself guilty of a felony if the substance turns out to be something else.[24]

SEARCH AND SEIZURE ISSUES

Regulatory Agencies

NJDEP has broad powers to inspect regulated facilities and to enter and inspect any property or building to investigate an actual or suspected source of pollution.[25] Under the permits it issues, NJDEP also possesses broad authority to conduct compliance inspections. However, if the owner of the facility refuses to allow for a regulatory inspection, or if the inspection would constitute a search beyond the scope of the regulatory agency's statutory authority, the agency may be required to obtain an administrative warrant or court order to enter the premises at issue.[26]

Law Enforcement Agencies

Unless one of the warrant exceptions applies, law enforcement will need to obtain a search warrant to search and seize evidence from the premises in question. One of the warrant exceptions that arise in the context of an environmental crimes case is the Community Caretaker doctrine. Under this doctrine, when there is an environmental incident, such as a chemical spill or leak, law enforcement is entitled to and will need to respond to assess what the danger is, determine what assistance is needed, and secure the area to protect the public. Under the Community Caretaker doctrine, while a law enforcement official may have a right to be on the premises immediately after the incident, that does not entitle police to stay there and gather evidence without a warrant.[27] However, if police are properly at the site under the Community Caretaker doctrine, anything that they observe in plain view would be admissible evidence.

Another exception to the warrant requirement that may arise in the context of an environmental case is the Open Fields doctrine. Under federal law, and it would appear under state law as well, law enforcement may enter an open fields area without a warrant. An "open field" would be an undeveloped and unoccupied area away from a home or other structure.[28] While law enforcement may enter an open field area, they may be well advised to obtain a warrant if they wish to return to the area to obtain evidence.

Law enforcement would not need to obtain a warrant to search and seize abandoned property. For example, if drums are abandoned in a public area, such as a roadside, police do not need to get a warrant to open them and obtain samples.[29] However, if the drums are disposed of on someone's property, they may need to obtain a warrant to secure samples of the contents.[30]

PARALLEL PROCEEDINGS ISSUES

Investigative Issues

Parallel proceedings are simultaneous or concurrent criminal, civil, or administrative enforcement actions against the same parties for the same type of violation. When there are parallel investigations or proceedings, NJDEP or any other regulatory agency can share with law enforcement information gathered through civil or administrative discovery or inspections provided that there is a good faith basis for initiating the civil or administrative action.[31] Civil regulators who conduct statutorily authorized inspections or execute administrative search warrants may subsequently share the information that they obtain with law enforcement as long as they were conducting the inspection or search for a legitimate civil/administrative purpose, and not to gather evidence for prosecutors at their direction or anticipated direction.[32] However, the government may not deliberately manipulate a civil proceeding in order to obtain evidence against a criminal defendant.[33]

Law enforcement may share information that they obtain through their criminal investigation, including evidence from interviews, surveillance and search warrants. However, they cannot disclose grand jury materials, which would include grand jury transcripts, documents, and books and records obtained through a grand jury subpoena.[34] Unless a Court finds that those seeking the grand jury materials from the prosecutor have made a strong showing of a particularized need that outweighs the need for grand jury secrecy, the prosecutor may not disclose the grand jury materials, other than as required under the criminal discovery rules.[35] Prosecutors may also not be able to disclose information to civil litigants because of the New Jersey Wiretap and Electronic Surveillance Act disclosure restrictions or to avoid compromising an ongoing investigation.[36]

Sentencing Issues

Since the Supreme Court's ruling in *Hudson v. United States*, 522 U.S. 93, 99 (1997), which has been followed by New Jersey's courts, the law is well established that the Double Jeopardy Clause of the U.S. Constitution does not bar the imposition of criminal sanctions and civil penalties in parallel enforcement actions.[37] Unless a Court finds that the civil sanction is so punitive in purpose or effect to transform it into a criminal sanction, it would not trigger the Double Jeopardy Clause.[38]

NOTES

1. Ed Neafsey and Edward Bonanno, *Environmental Crimes: Considerations in Prosecutions*, New Jersey Lawyer, No. 159, February/March 1994 at 37.

2. Ed Neafsey, Edward Bonanno, Robert Lytle, John Kennedy and Bruce Kmosko, *Environmental Prosecutions: Investigation to Sentencing*, National Association of Attorneys General (1996) at 63-64.

3. *United States v. Toy*, U.S. Department of Justice Office of Public Affairs January 25, 2018 (prosecution for Resource Conservation Recovery Act "RCRA" violations); *United States v. Malek Jalal*, U.S. Department of Justice Office of Public Affairs April 7, 2017 (prosecution for biofuel fraud).

4. Edward Bonanno, *Evolution of Criminal Environmental Enforcement*, Environmental Law Reporter, Vol. 39, No. 5 (May 2009) at 10352.

5. Edward Bonanno, *Evolution of Criminal Environmental Enforcement*, Environmental Law Reporter, at 10352.

6. *State v. Edward O'Rourke*, Accusation No. 15-12-593-A (N.J. Sup. 2016); *State v. Cardolite Corporation*, Accusation No. 17-7-165-A (N.J. Sup. 2017); *State v. Mansmann and Mowell*, Indictment No. 13-02-00039-S(N.J. Sup. (2013); *State v. Accurate Analytical Laboratories*, Accusation No. 08-12-00535 (N.J.Sup. 2008).

7. Water Pollution Control Act, *N.J.S.A.* 58:10A-10f. Clean Water Act, 33 U.S.C.A. sec. 1319(c).

8. See *N.J.S.A.* 58:10A-10f (1) and (4).

9. 42 U.S.C.A. sec. 6928(d).

10. See N.J.A.C. 7:26D.

11. *N.J.S.A.* 58:10-23.11b; N.J.A.C. 7:1e-5.3.

12. *State v. Muzzio*, Indictment No. 12-08-00139-S (N.J. Sup. Court 2012); *State v Maple*, Accusation No. 08-070679 (N.J. Sup. Court 2008).

13. *N.J.S.A.* 13:1E-48.20.1 et seq.

14. Under the Act's regulations, regulated medical waste includes the following types of materials: cultures and stocks; pathological wastes; human blood and blood products; sharps (used and unused); animal waste, e.g., carcasses of body parts and isolation wastes. N.J.A.C. 7:26-3A.6.

15. *State v. McFarland*, Indictment No. 08-11-00260-S (N.J. Sup. Court. 2008).

16. See N.J.S.A. 48:13A-6; N.J.S.A. 13:1E-9.6.

17. Edward Bonanno, *Evolution of Criminal Environmental Enforcement*, Environmental Law Reporter, at 10353.

18. Edward Bonanno, *Evolution of Criminal Environmental Enforcement*, Environmental Law Reporter, at 10353.

19. *N.J.S.A.* 13:9B-21(f)

20. *N.J.S.A.* 13:19-18(f); *N.J.S.A.* 58:16A-63(f); *N.J.S.A.* 12:5-6(g).

21. See *United States v. Hanousek*, 176 F. 3d 116 (9 Cir. 1999); *United States v. Ortiz*, 427 F. 3d 1278, 1283 (10 Cir. 2005); *United States v. Pruett*, 681 F.3d 232, 242-243 (5 Cir. 2012).

22. See *United States v. Snook*, 366 F. 3d 439, 443 (7 Cir. 2004) (CWA); *United States v. Ho*, 311 F. 3d 589, 605 (5 Cir. 2002)(Clean Air Act "CAA"), cert. den. 539 U.S. 914 (2003);

United States v. Overholt, 307 F. 3d 1231, 1251 (10 Cir. 2002) (RCRA); *United States v. Wilson*, 133 F. 3d 251 (4 Cir 1997) (CWA); *United States v. Sinskey*, 119 F. 3d. 712 (8 Cir. 1997); *United States v. Hopkins*, 53 F. 3d 533 (2d Cir 1995) (CWA); *United States v. Weitzenhoff*, 35 F. 3d 1275 (9 Cir. 1994), cert. den. 513 U.S. 1128 (1995) (CWA); *United States v. Laughlin*, 10 F. 3d 961, 966 (2 Cir. 1993), cert. den. 114 S. Ct. 1649 (1994) (RCRA); Cf. *United States v. Atlantic States*, 2007 U.S. Dist. LEXIS 56562 (2007).

23. See *United States v. Kelly Tech. Coatings*, 157 F. 3d 432, 440 (6 Cir. 1998) (RCRA); *United States v. Goldsmith*, 978 F. 2d 643, 645 (11 Cir. 1992))(for a RCRA violation, the government needed to prove that the defendant knew that the chemical waste had the potential to be harmful to others and the environment, or in other words that it was not an innocuous substance like water).

24. *United States v. Ahmad*, 101 F. 3d 386, 391 (5 Cir. 1996).

25. See *N.J.S.A.* 13D-9d; *N.J.S.A.* 59:10A-6g; Matter of Department of Environmental Protection, 177 N.J. Super. 304, 307-315 (App. Div. 1981).

26. *New Jersey Department of Environmental Protection v. Huber*, 213 N.J. 338 (2013).

27. See *State v. Bogan*, 200 N.J. 61, 73 (2009).

28. See *United States v. Dunn*, 480 U.S. 294 (1987); *State v. Bonacurso*, 227 N.J. Super. 159 (Law Div. 1988).

29. See *State v. Aziz Sunzar*, 331 N.J. Super. 248 (Law Div. 1999).

30. See *State v. Hempele*, 120 N.J. 182 (1990).

31. See *U.S. v. Kordel*, 397 U.S. 1, 6 (1970); Edward R. Bonanno, *Parallel Proceedings Issues for Criminal and Civil Enforcement*, New Jersey Lawyer, February 2005 at 17.

32. See Edward Bonanno, *Parallel Proceedings for Criminal and Civil Enforcement*, at 18; United States Department of Justice, Land and Natural Resources Division, Directive 5-87, Guidelines for Civil and Criminal Parallel Proceedings (1987).

33. *State v. Kobrin Securities*, 111 N.J. 307, 317 (1988); *United States v. Kordel*, supra, 397 U.S. at 11.

34. R. 3:6-6; R. 3:6-7; In re Grand Jury Proceedings, 851 F.2d 860, 866-867 (6 Cir. 1988).

35. See *State v. Doliner*, 96 N.J. 236, 246 (1985); R. 3:13-3.

36. See *N.J.S.A.* 2A:156-17.

37. See *State v. Black*, 153 N.J. 438, 443 (1998).

38. See *State v. Black*, supra, 153 N.J. at 443.

Section 10

Environmental Justice

The New Jersey Approach

Vanessa Day, Esq., New Jersey Department
of Environmental Protection

In some communities across the United States, there is a fight for environmental justice. The United States Environmental Protection Agency (USEPA) defines environmental justice as "the fair treatment and meaningful involvement of all people regardless of race, color, national origin, or income with respect to the development, implementation and enforcement of environmental laws, regulations and policies."[1]

The environmental justice movement is an outgrowth of the civil rights movement, in that it started when communities organized to seek environmental protection and equity. Dr. Robert Bullard, known as the father of environmental justice, is a leader and advocate on environmental justice matters. Dr. Bullard served as a member of the National Environmental Justice Advisory Council which advised President Clinton. Dr. Bullard, highlighting how environmental injustice develops in many communities, has stated, "whether by conscious design or institutional neglect, communities of color in urban ghettos, in rural 'poverty pockets', or on economically impoverished Native-American reservations face some of the worst environmental devastation in the nation."[2]

In 1994, President Clinton, in one of the earliest federal efforts to address environmental justice concerns, signed Executive Order 12898 directing federal agencies to take actions to address environmental justice issues in minority and low-income populations. This federal action sparked the development of environmental justice policy action on the state level—including State of New Jersey which has been working on its own environmental justice policy for many years. Under Governor Phil Murphy, the State has redoubled its efforts to address environmental justice by making a strong commitment to *"building a stronger, fairer New Jersey economy requires taking an innovative approach to community revitalization that acknowledges economic prosperity and environmental sustainability are not competing goals but mutually reinforcing ideals."*[3] This chapter outlines New Jersey's past, present, and future efforts and goals to achieve environmental justice.

THE HISTORICAL EVOLUTION OF ENVIRONMENTAL JUSTICE POLICY IN NEW JERSEY

Absent any statute or associated regulations mandating the consideration of environmental justice in State decisions, New Jersey addresses environmental justice by executive and administrative orders, guidance, and policy.

In 1998, Commissioner Robert Shinn created the Environmental Equity Task Force to create "state policies and guidance documents to develop a pollution permit process, which allowed early, expanded public participation for environmental justice communities." These policies were implemented by Commissioner Shinn with an administrative order and screening procedures to determine if a community is overburdened with pollution. Commissioner Shinn, also, proposed environmental justice regulations (34 N.J.R. 665(a)) which ultimately proved unwieldy and were withdrawn by Shinn's successor, Bradley Campbell, and replaced by an executive order signed by then-governor McGreevey.[4]

Executive Order 96 (February 18, 2004)

In Executive Order 96, Governor McGreevey assured the citizens of New Jersey equal environmental protection under the law. EO 96 authorized the Department of Environmental Protection (DEP) commissioner to reconstitute the existing Environmental Justice Advisory Council (EJAC). The composition of the fifteen-member EJAC was diverse with one-third from grassroots or faith-based community organizations with the remainder from various academic, public health, environmental, local governments, labor, and business organizations. EJAC task was to make recommendations to the DEP commissioner and the Environmental Justice Task Force.

Additionally, the order directed the commissioners of DEP and Department of Health and Senior Services (DHSS) to convene a multiagency task force called the Environmental Justice Task Force. "The Task Force shall be an advisory body, the purpose of which is to make recommendations to State Agency heads regarding actions to be taken to address environmental justice issues consistent with agencies' existing statutory and regulatory authority."[5] The Task Force was empowered to review petitions filed by communities and create action plans to reduce or avoid additional environmental burdens.

The executive order recognized the serious health implications of exposure to fine particulate emissions, such as premature death and asthma, especially in urban communities. EO 96 directed DEP and the Department of Transportation (DOT) to work together to reduce fine particulate pollution from stationary and mobile diesel emissions sources. EO 96 also recognized the need for DEP and DHSS to provide public health and environmental information in Spanish and English and acknowledged the poor and minority communities are more reliant on subsistence fishing. To address these concerns, the executive order directed DEP, DHSS, and the Department of Agriculture to collaborate, develop, and issue protective fish consumption advisories and provide educational material to the public.

Executive Order 131 (February 5, 2009)

Building on Governor McGreevey's efforts, Governor Corzine signed Executive Order 131 stating that all residents of State of New Jersey deserve to live in communities free from the effects of pollution and are entitled to participate in decision-making that affects their environment regardless of race, ethnicity, color, national origin, or income. EO 131 acknowledged the cumulative exposure and disproportional impact on predominantly low-income persons and persons of color from multiple polluting sources and directed the executive branch to promote and review programs to ensure the programs met the needs of the communities served and to address disproportionate exposures to environmental hazards these communities face. EO 131 required all executive branch agencies involved in decisions affecting environmental quality and public health to provide opportunities for the public to participate in the decision-making. In addition, EO 131 extended the life of the EJAC until December 31, 2013.

Executive Order 60 (April 20, 2011)

In Executive Order 60, signed on April 20, 2011, Governor Christie echoed his predecessors and acknowledged the cumulative exposure to pollution and other hazards from multiple sources in urban communities create a disproportionate impact on the health, well-being, and quality of life of persons living in those communities, and those impacts are exacerbated by exposure to diesel exhaust in urban settings.

EO 60 authorized a three-year pilot program conducted by DEP and DOT to reduce emissions from non-road diesel-powered equipment used in selected publicly funded state construction contracts. The program required diesel-powered equipment used in one or more projects in urban areas and DEP provided funding to reimburse the cost of diesel emission retrofit technology installed under the pilot program.

Administrative Order No. 2016-08 (September 12, 2016)

Building on Governor Christie's executive order, DEP commissioner Robert Martin issued Administrative Order No. 2016-08 to address environmental justice concerns and restore the EJAC which was not authorized to operate from December 31, 2013, to September 12, 2016. EJAC was now tasked to advise the commissioner on environmental justice and public health issues through the DEP's Office of Environmental Justice and focus on a community-based approach with measurable goals and outcomes. EJAC was authorized to operate under this order until December 31, 2018.

Executive Order 23 (April 20, 2018)

In Executive Order 23, Governor Murphy expressed a strong commitment to leading an administration that ensures all New Jersey residents equal protection under the law including environmental protection. The governor acknowledged that historically low-income communities and communities of color have been exposed to disproportionately high and unacceptably dangerous levels of air, water, and soil pollution, with the accompanying potential for increased public health impacts. Furthermore, EO 23 recognized that in addition to environmental degradation, these communities often face other serious problems such as health risks and housing challenges. EO 23 directs DEP, in consultation with the Department of Law and Public Safety and other relevant departments, to take the lead in developing guidance for all state departments and agencies for the consideration of environmental justice in carrying out their responsibilities. After the publication of the final guidance document, all state departments and agencies must consider the issue of environmental justice and make evaluations and assessments in accordance with the guidance to the extent not inconsistent with law. EJAC was continued by EO 23.

Executive Order No. 63 (April 2, 2019)

On April 2, 2019, Governor Murphy signed Executive Order 63. This EO, among other things, requires as part of the distributed impacts analysis and where data is available, state entities should give due consideration to "Environmental Justice," meaning that in conceiving and fashioning proposed regulations, state entities should identify and address, as appropriate and practicable, disproportionately high and adverse human health or environmental effects of the program, policy, or activity on minority and low-income populations. In addition, EO 63 directs state entities to consider the cumulative impacts of their regulations.

PRACTICAL APPLICATION OF ENVIRONMENTAL JUSTICE IN NEW JERSEY

South Camden Citizens Struggle for Environmental Justice

This line of litigation began when NJDEP issued permits to St. Lawrence Cement Company (SLC). SLC started construction at risk in a low-income and pollution-burdened community. "On March 8, 1999, SLC entered into a lease with South Jersey Port Corporation, to lease 11.7 acres of land at Broadway Terminal, 2500 Broadway, Camden, NJ 08104, located within the Waterfront South neighborhood."[6] SLC proposed and built a GBFS (Granulated Blast Furnace Slag) grinding facility. GBFS is an additive to Portland cement. The air emissions from the facility were particulate matter (dust), mercury, lead, manganese, nitrogen oxides, carbon monoxide, sulfur oxides, and volatile organic compounds.[7] The community's citizens were in opposition to this facility. The South Camden community consisted of many children, elderly, and people with chronic health conditions such as asthma. The citizens complained of particulate emissions and increased truck traffic in their neighborhood.

Initially, the plaintiffs alleged that NJDEP's permit evaluation and approval process violated Title VI of the Civil Rights Act of 1964. Federal District Court judge Orlofsky vacated the permits issued by NJDEP enjoined SLC from operating until further order of the Court and remanded the case to NJDEP to evaluate the permit consistent with his ruling.[8] "Five days after the ruling, on April 24, 2001, however, the US Supreme Court decided the case of *Alexander v. Sandoval*, 532 U.S. 275,121 S. Ct. 1511, 149 L. Ed. 2d 517 (2001), which effectively overruled Judge Orlofsky's decision."[9] The Supreme Court held that Title VI "extends no further than the Four-teenth Amendment" and prohibits only intentional discrimination."[10] Therefore, the plaintiffs needed to prove discriminatory intent to show a violation of Title VI of the Civil Rights Act of 1964.

The line of litigation was terminated with *S. Camden Citizens in action v. N.J. Dep't of Envtl. Prot.*, Civil Action No. 01-702(FWL), 2006 U.S. Dist. Lexis 45765 (D.N.J. Mar 31, 2006). This case was decided on motions for summary judgment filed by SLC and NJDEP. In their Second Amended Complaint, the Plaintiffs asserted a private nuisance claim against SLC, alleging that "dust, soot, vapors and fumes, as well as noise and vibrations" from the Facility and diesel truck traffic associated with the Facility have "unreasonably interfered with the plaintiffs' use and enjoyment of their property [*sic*]."[11]

The Court analyzed two claims: the private nuisances against SLC and the dis-crimination claim against DEP. First, the Court analyzed the private nuisances against SLC. The Court noted plaintiffs entered a Stipulation and Consent Order with SLC. The plaintiffs did not succeed with the claim against SLC because they were unable to prove SLC was the proximate cause of their injury. The Court wrote, "Plaintiffs have produced no credible proofs of the harm or nuisance they suffered as a result of SLC's operations and they have failed to prove the causation element of their claim [as] they have made no effort to single out the nuisance at their properties allegedly caused by SLC as opposed to other area industries."[12]

Second, the Court analyzed the intentional discrimination claim against DEP. "To prove intentional discrimination by facial neutral conduct, a plaintiff must show that the relevant decisionmaker (e.g., a state legislature) adopted the policy at issue 'because of', not merely 'in spite of', its adverse effects upon an identifiable group."[13] The Supreme Court has more directly stated that the "important starting point" for assessing discriminatory purpose is the "impact of the official action" and "whether it bears more heavily on one race than another."[14] To assess discriminatory purpose the court will consider the following factors: the impact of an official action, the his-torical background of the decision, the specific sequence of events leading up to the challenged decision, departures from the normal procedural sequence, the legislative or administrative history especially any contemporary statements by members of the decision-making body, and the foreseeability of any disparate impact of the action.[15] In its opinion the Court quoted the Penick Court, which stated, "disparate impact and foreseeable consequences, without more, do not establish a constitutional violation."[16] The Court's grant of summary judgment in favor of DEP highlights how difficult proving specific intent to discriminate against an environmental justice community can be.

Compliance Assistance and Enforcement
Sweeps in Environmental Justice Areas

In 2002, when serving as assistant commissioner, Lisa Jackson conducted compliance assistance and enforcement sweeps in environmental justice areas as a two-phase program. The first phase was compliance assistance and community outreach to help individuals, business, and government operations to come into compliance. The second phase was enforcement inspections of sources in the environmental justice area. "For example, in October 2002, NJDEP's compliance and enforcement program conducted its first ever, week-long, multimedia enforcement sweep in Camden. Working with county officials, the State Police, and the USEPA, the department mobilized more than seventy inspectors and conducted 764 investigations. Inspectors found noncompliance with laws that regulated water quality, solid and hazardous waste, air pollution, and land use activities."[17] A compliance assistance and enforcement sweep was also conducted in Patterson, NJ, in 2003.

ENVIRONMENTAL JUSTICE IN NEW JERSEY: CURRENT INITIATIVES AND THE FUTURE

Community Collaborative Initiative (CCI)

DEP's CCI seeks to work directly with community organizations, businesses, local governments, and other interested stakeholders to solve challenging environmental issues and revitalize communities across the State. The core mission of the CCI is community involvement, revitalization, technical and administrative assistance, leveraging resources, and creating projects.[18]

Camden Collaborative Initiative is one example of a CCI that has creatively and successfully resolved some complex environmental issues. Launched on January 24, 2013, the Camden Collaborative Initiative involves the City of Camden, with the support of Cooper's Ferry Partnership, Camden County Municipal Utilities Authority, New Jersey DEP, and the USEPA and has completed successful projects like the Kroc Community Center on the former Harrison Ave Landfill.[19] This former landfill is now a flourishing community center with an aquatic center with an eight-lane competition pool and water park; fitness center including fitness equipment and free weights; gymnasium; library lounge; and computer lab. This center provides fitness and aquatic classes and other community education classes for the community.[20] The project was possible through a collaboration of private donations, and state and federal funds; 160 jobs were created.[21,22]

On March 13, 2019, New Jersey Economic Development Authority (NJEDA) and DEP announced a partnership to expand CCI to new municipalities around the state. *"The Community Collaborative Initiative exemplifies Governor Murphy's commitment to revitalizing New Jersey's communities in a way that puts environmental sustainability front and center and remains true to residents' priorities,"* said DEP commissioner Catherine R. McCabe, *"the program has already been a tremendous success, with significant benefits for New Jersey's most vulnerable populations. We are excited to collaborate with NJEDA to replicate this success around the state."*[23]

Currently, there are CCIs in Trenton, Perth Amboy, and Bayonne. As of this writing, the list of additional cities has not been finalized. However, the expansion of CCI intends to include Newark and Paterson with NJEDA providing funding to allow DEP to dedicate additional resources to the endeavor.[24] For more information on Community Collaboratives Initiatives or starting one in your community contact:

Franklin B. McLaughlin
New Jersey Department of Environmental Protection

Office of Brownfield Reuse
Community Collaborative Initiative
401 E. State Street, 5th Floor
Trenton, NJ 08625-0420
609-633-8227
Frank.mclaughlin@dep.nj.gov

Administrative Consent Orders (ACO) and Supplement Environmental Projects

A Supplemental Environmental Project (SEP) is an environmentally beneficial project that a respondent voluntarily agrees to perform as a condition of settling an enforcement action. A SEP is an activity that the violator would not otherwise have been required to perform, and in which the public or the environment is the primary beneficiary.

SEPs can be an opportunity for environmental justice communities to benefit and reduce the pollution burden they suffer. According to the current SEP policy dated December 5, 2011, a SEP may have a direct or indirect relationship with the underlying violation, statute, and geographic area impacted in order to bring about meaningful environmental improvement. Acceptance of a SEP as part of a settlement agreement is at the discretion of the DEP. After the final penalty settlement amount has been determined, the penalty is then adjusted to account for the cost of the SEP. "For each dollar spent on the SEP, one dollar can be deducted from the penalty amount, up to 75% of the total penalty agreed to in the settlement. However, 50% is the maximum offset allowed for violations of the Water Pollution Control Act."[25]

Groundwork Elizabeth is a 501(c) (3) nonprofit in Elizabeth, NJ. This nonprofit works with NJDEP, county and local government, private partners, and the community to complete various projects to improve access to healthy foods, strategies to build sustainable agricultural systems, develop green-focused career opportunities, and provide quality of life in socially and economically challenged areas of the City of Elizabeth, Union Township, and other urban sections of Union County. "DEP's Office of Environmental Justice is coordinating the P.E.A.S. program's oversight with Groundwork Elizabeth. Overall, the DEP has provided $250,000 toward the $403,125 initiative to improve community sustainability within the City of Elizabeth and neighboring Union Township in Union County."[26]

SEPs have benefited communities throughout the state. Examples of some of the more noteworthy SEPs are the Waterfront South Rain Gardens in Camden, Hawk Rise Sanctuary in Linden, and Solar Panels at Red Bank School. For more detail information on these SEPs and other SEP examples, please visit www.nj.gov/dep/enforcement/seps. To propose your own SEP or get more information about the SEP process, contact your compliance and enforcement inspector or send an email to SEP@dep.nj.gov.

Environmental Rights Act

Environmental Justice Practitioners may consider using the Environmental Rights Act to achieve environmental justice. In 1974, the Legislature passed the Environmental

Rights Act. The Legislature recognized the need to enable citizens to bring lawsuits to protect the environment. "The Legislature finds and determines that the integrity of the State's environment is continually threatened by pollution, impairment and destruction, that every person has a substantial interest in minimizing this condition, and that it is therefore in the public interest to enable ready access to the courts for the remedy of such abuses."[27] The Environmental Rights Act is found at NJSA §§2A:35A-1—2A:35A-14.

In *Township of Howell v. Waste Disposal, Inc.*, 207 N.J. Super. 80 (1986), 504 A.2d 19, the appellate court outlined the circumstances and requirements necessary for a citizen to bring a lawsuit under the Environmental Rights Act. The key question in the case was "who and under what circumstances can persons other than the State Department of Environmental Protection sue to enforce diverse environmental protection legislation enacted in New Jersey."[28]

The defendant Waste Disposal, Inc. (WDI) entered an administrative consent order pursuant to the Solid Waste Act to resolve alleged violations of groundwater and sediment contamination from toxic volatile organics and metal from defendant's landfill. Subsequently, WDI failed to comply with the ACO. DEP reserved the right to enforce the ACO in Superior Court if WDI breached the ACO agreement.

While DEP was trying to obtain compliance with ACO from WDI, the Township of Howell (Township) and its Board of Health filed a complaint in Superior Court, Chancery Division requesting injunctive relief and statutory penalties against WDI for the alleged violations of the Solid Waste Act. "WDI sought a dismissal of the complaint on the grounds that plaintiffs lacked standing, had failed to exhaust their administrative remedies and that the court lacked subject matter jurisdiction."[29] The Court dismissed the complaint and the plaintiffs appealed.

While the appeal was pending, WDI entered a second ACO with DEP for compliance of the alleged violations. The Township was a signatory to the second agreement. When the compliance check was conducted, DEP found that WDI failed to timely comply with terms of the second ACO. The Township unilaterally filed to obtain injunctive relief, damages, cleanup costs and penalties for the alleged violations. The Township sued under the Solid Waste Act, the Environmental Rights Act, the Spill Compensation and Control Act (Spill Act), Water Pollution Act, strict liability, and common law negligence. WDI answered the complaint and among the defenses was the Township didn't have standing and the complaint was barred by the doctrine of preemption and the DEP was vested with exclusive authority to enforce the administrative consent order.[30]

The Court recognized DEP is the primary enforcement authority of environmental legislation but there may be circumstances when a citizen needs the ability to enforce environmental law and the Court will oversee the process to harmonize interests. In cases where the state agency has failed or neglected to act in the best interest of the citizenry or has arbitrarily, capriciously or unreasonably acted, then a court should permit interested persons to continue with enforcement under the Environmental Rights Act. Cf. *Student Public Interest Research Group v. Fritzsche, Dodge & Olcott*, 579 F. Supp. 1528 (D.N.J. 1984), aff'd 759 F.2d 1131 (3rd Cir. 1985). In enacting the Environmental Rights Act the Legislature has recognized that the DEP may fail to act to correct a particular problem or not take proper and necessary action where conflicting interests appear. Further, in a given situation DEP may seek less than full relief available under relevant legislation. In such a case, there is a clear right granted to other "persons" to seek such relief under the Environmental Rights Act. No court should enforce grudgingly that right simply because of supervisory difficulties which may be encountered."[31] The Court held "by recognizing the DEP role of primary enforcement of environmental legislation, absent bad faith, negligence or inaction indicating abdication of its responsibilities, a court will be in a position to protect and harmonize all interests protected by the complex maze of environmental legislation and maintain an orderly progression of litigation arising therefrom."[32] The case was remanded to the trial court for reconsideration consistent with the opinion. The Environmental Rights Acts can be a useful tool in appropriate circumstances to achieve environmental justice.

Volkswagen Settlement to Help Overburdened Communities

On October 25, 2016, and May 17, 2017, two Partial Consent Decrees were approved between the United States, California, and Volkswagen to, among other things, offset excess NOx emissions. The Partial Consent Decrees established a $2.93 billion Environmental Mitigation Trust to provide funds to all fifty states, the District of Columbia, Puerto Rico, and federally recognized tribes and to implement actions to counter the air-quality impacts of excess NOx emissions resulting from the use of the defeat devices. The trustee for the Mitigation Trust approved New Jersey's beneficiary status on January 29, 2018. The DEP is designated as the lead agency to administer the funds. The initial allocation to New Jersey is $72.2 million, based on the estimate that 17,000 registered vehicles in the State were equipped with these defeat devices. EPA structured the Trust to ensure that a portion of the mitigation funds would go to projects to reduce diesel exhaust and ozone pollution in communities that have historically borne a disproportionate share of the adverse impacts of such emissions. The Trust structure is consistent with DEP's priorities to revitalize New Jersey's communities and protect public health, especially vulnerable populations.

"Our goal is to use New Jersey's share of the national Volkswagen settlement to develop programs that are consistent with Governor Murphy's commitment to reduce smog as well as greenhouse gas emissions, advance environmental justice goals in urban areas and expand the use of electric vehicles," said DEP commissioner R. McCabe.[33] New Jersey was allocated $72 million of the $2.9 billion federal settlement. The Department conducted public outreach and solicited ideas for projects for use of the settlement funds. The DEP press release dated February 28, 2019, listed one focus of the funds will be on environmental justice communities which are disproportionately impacted by pollution and resulting health impacts.[34]

"Through this settlement, we have the opportunity to make investments to clean up our air, righting a wrong for disproportionately impacted communities and setting New Jersey on a path to a clean energy and transportation future," said Governor Phil Murphy.[35] The Murphy administration is making these goals a reality in New Jersey. On February 28, 2019, Commissioner Catherine R. McCabe announced moving forward on the State's commitment to clean transportation, the DEP is transmitting to the Volkswagen Environmental Mitigation Trust for an allocation of $11.2 million from

New Jersey's share of the federal Volkswagen settlement for hundreds of electric-vehicle charging outlets across the state and new electric NJ TRANSIT buses in the City of Camden.[36] Eight million dollars is proposed to the Volkswagen Mitigation Trust for allocation to purchase eight new electric transit buses to be operated in the City of Camden according the DEP press release dated February 28, 2019. For more information, please visit the NJDEP website at www.nj.gov/dep/vw.

Pending Legislation

S1700 (Introduced February 5, 2018)—Concerns environmental permits in over-burdened communities. On February 5, 2018, Sponsors Senator Loretta Weinberg and Senator Troy Singleton introduced Senate Bill S1700 to address permitting concerns in burdened communities.[37] As introduced, S1700 allowed anyone in a community to petition the DEP for a "burdened community" designation. The bill charged the DEP with the task of reviewing the petitions for approval or denial within sixty days. Also, S1700 gave the authority to designate an area as burdened on the DEP's own initiative. Paragraph 2 (a) of the Bill outlines an application process for the petitioners. Paragraph 2(b) proscribed criteria for the DEP to use to designate a community or area as burdened. Paragraph 2 (c) requires the DEP to notify the municipality where the burdened community is located and the petitioner if applicable, so the DEP can designate a representative for the burdened community. Paragraph (3) states requirements that the Department must fulfill before granting a permit in an overburdened community. Some of the requirements included preparing a report evaluating the cumulative, environmental and public impacts to the burdened community and public hearings. S1700 gives the Department authority to deny a permit regardless of any other provision of law if the issuance of the permit together with cumulative adverse health and environmental impacts will pose an unreasonable risk to the health of the residents or the environment of the burdened community. Notable is the prohibition of the DEP issuing a permit in burdened community unless the municipality where the community is located passes an ordinance approving the project.

    S1700 (Amended January 24, 2019) and Assembly Bill No. 5094 (Introduced February 25, 2019)[38] modifies S1700 (Introduced February 5, 2018) as follows:

(1) Defined "Burdened community" as any census tract, as delineated in the most recent federal decennial census, that is ranked in the bottom 33 percent of census tracts in the State for median annual household income. This is race-neutral and removes the task from the Department of evaluating the petitions for the designation of burdened communities.
(2) Limited the applicability of the bill to eight types of facilities. Some of the facility types have capacity specifications.
(3) Clarified the law is applicable to new and expansion of existing facilities.
(4) Shifted the preparation of the required report from the Department to the applicant.
(5) Gave the Department the discretion to hold more than one public hearing due to the permit complexity.
(6) DEP is required to adopt and update a list of burdened communities.

(7) This bill removed the mandate for the municipalities to approve ordinances approving the project before DEP could issue the permit. This bill requires DEP to consider the support or lack thereof from the community and municipal ordinances regarding the project in the decision to grant or deny the permit.

Environmental Opportunity Zone Act—NJSA 54:4-3.150 et seq.

The Environmental Opportunity Zone Act can be used to revitalize environmental justice communities by providing a tax exemption to help clean up contaminated properties. The Legislature created this exemption to promote revitalization and remediation of contaminated underutilized or abandoned properties. In addition, the Legislature found that a disproportionate percentage of these properties are located in older urban municipalities. The revitalization of these properties will bring tax rateables back to the municipalities and other local governments, create job opportunities, and foster urban development. The Legislature's intent is to return these abandoned or underutilized contaminated properties to productive purposes (commercial, residential, or other productive purpose) after remediation.[39]

According to N.J.S.A. §54:4-3.153, "the governing body of a municipality may, by ordinance, designate one or more qualified real properties in that municipality as an environmental opportunity zone."[40] The items that the governing body must include are listed in N.J.S.A. §54:4-3.154.[41] The property tax exemption term is ten years except that a tax exemption may be extended up to fifteen years, at the municipality's option. To receive the tax exemption, the property owner is required to remediate the environmental opportunity zone property in compliance with the remediation regulation adopted by DEP pursuant to P.L. 1993, c.139 (C.58:10B-1 et. al.). Also, the property owner will enter an administrative consent order with the Department to perform the remediation pursuant to the order. Once the remediation is complete, the EOZ property should be returned to a commercial, industrial, residential, or other productive purpose during the time period of the tax exemption.

Before the exemption is granted NJSA §54:4-3.155 requires a written application filed with the tax assessor of the taxing district where the EOZ is located and approval of the application by the governing body by resolution or ordinance, as required by enabling ordinance.[42] The application is a form prescribed by the Director of the Division of Taxation, in the Department of Treasury, and should be available for claimants from the municipality constituting the taxing district. The exemption that is granted shall take effect upon the approval by the governing body and it shall be recorded on the permanent official tax records in the taxing district with the termination date.

In accordance with N.J.S.A. § 54:4-3.156, each approved exemption must be evidenced by a financial agreement between municipality and the applicant. The agreement will outline the amount in lieu of real property taxes computed according to N.J.S.A. §54:4-3.156 (b).[43] There are three very beneficial provisions for anyone interested in revitalizing an EOZ:

(1) NJSA §54:4-3.156 (c), the amount of "taxes otherwise due" shall be determined by using the assessed valuation of the EOZ at the time of approval by the assessor

of the exemption, regardless of any improvement made to the EOZ thereafter and as if the designation of the EOZ had not occurred.[44]

(2) NJSA §54:4-3.156(b), provides for a ten-year tax exemption with no payment in lieu of taxes otherwise due the first year following the administrative consent order.[45]

(3) NJSA § 54:4-3.158 (b) and (c), owner or operator of property within an EOZ, who undertakes a remediation of the property, shall be exempt from the requirement to establish a remediation funding source pursuant to section 25 of P.L. 1993, c. 139 (c.58:10B-3).[46] This exemption from the requirement to establish a remediation fund is applicable even if the owner or operator of an EOZ property does not apply for a property tax exemption.

Redevelopment can be beneficial in environmental justice communities if implemented in a proper manner. Care must be used to ensure that the development in environmental justice communities actually benefit the communities rather than harm the poor and low-income residents by pushing them out of the area. Developers, local officials, and regulators should consult with the environmental justice community members to determine what projects are needed in the communities. Also, they should ensure members of the existing community benefit from the redevelopment efforts. By being proactive and consulting with the affected community, the developer will likely experience less resistance from community members. If more municipalities would pass ordinances for EOZ, these ordinances may encourage more cleanup of contaminated sites in environmental justice communities and spur redevelopment that can trigger an economic recovery in these areas.

2018 Environmental Justice Initiative[47]

On December 6, 2018, Attorney General Gurbir S. Grewal and DEP commissioner Catherine R. McCabe announced a new statewide "Environmental Justice" initiative that includes civil actions, the creation of a new Attorney General Environmental Justice Section, and Community Listening Sessions.
Commissioner McCabe said,

Cleaner environments promote stronger communities. For too long the residents of urban areas and other communities have not had their voices heard and have had to bear the burden of disproportionate sources of pollution and the consequent health effects. It is imperative that we take actions such as these to substantively address these issues and restore the confidence of residents and their elected leaders that New Jersey is committed to improving day-to-day life for all New Jersey's people especially our most vulnerable populations.[48]

The new initiative began with DEP filing eight separate lawsuits targeting polluters in lower-income and minority communities. These lawsuits seek environmental justice for communities by using a variety of existing statutes and regulations. Some of cause of actions are as follows: claims for natural resource damages, the Spill Compensation and Control Act [N.J.S.A. 58:10-23.11], Water Pollution Control Act

[N.J.S.A. 58:10A-1 et. seq.], as well as common law causes of action public nuisance, trespass, negligence, and unjust enrichment.

In *NJDEP v. Novick Chemical, Inc., et. al.*, DEP in a civil action filed a notice of motion to enforce litigant's rights. This lawsuit was brought to enforce an executed administrative order that was ignored previously.

NJDEP, Commissioner of NJDEP and the Administrator of NJ Spill Compensation Fund v. SL Industries, Inc., et al. is a Pennsauken natural resource damages case filed by the State in 2018. "The lawsuit involves Puchack Wellfield, a series of wells that provided drinking water to Camden residents decades ago. The State alleges that the defendant was responsible for hazardous pollution that resulted in termination of the wells. The State is seeking NRD damages, as well as cleanup and removal costs that have been incurred and will be incurred at the site."[49]

In addition to the lawsuits, the Attorney General's Office is creating a new unit called the "Environmental Enforcement and Environmental Justice Section." The staff for this unit will be comprised of repurposed existing resources. Also, AG's office plans to hire more attorneys to bring enforcement actions and promote environmental justice across the state. The new office will be headed by Kevin Jespersen; he will oversee the Section while the AG's office conducts a national leadership search.

The initiative includes Community Listening Session. Attorney General Grewal and Commissioner McCabe plan to conduct listening sessions on environmental justice throughout the state where members of the public, community groups, and environmental groups will discuss their concerns and the environmental issues in their communities.

Implementation of Executive Order 23 by Governor Phil Murphy[50]

To implement the goals of Executive Order 23, draft guidance was issued for public comment and discussion from January 22, 2019, to March 22, 2019. The guidance document provides the framework for executive branch departments and agencies to incorporate environmental justice considerations (encompassing environmental, social, health, and economic concerns) in implementing their statutory and regulatory responsibilities. According to the draft guidance document, each state department or agency that has one or more programs affecting environmental justice communities will develop an EJ Action Plan and participate in the EJ Interagency Council (see description of EJ Interagency Council in the next section).

New Jersey DEP plans to use USEPA definition of environmental justice to help guide the purpose and goals of the directive in EO 23. Also, EPA has developed a screening tool called EJSCREEN to identify environmental justice communities. DEP has preliminarily recommended state agencies use EJSCREEN as well as other available state and community level data, for identifying environmental justice communities.

Environmental Justice Interagency Council

The draft guidance calls for the establishment of the New Environmental Justice (EJ) Interagency Council. The draft guidance states the EJ Interagency Council will collaborate and meet periodically with DEP's EJAC to identify environmental justice community concerns, develop priorities and action plans, and facilitate collaboration with environmental justice communities. Also, the EJ Interagency Council will establish a process to incorporate public input on environmental justice issues, challenges, and opportunities.

Workgroups will be formed to address issues affecting EJ communities. According to the draft guidance the first workgroups will address the following:

1. Use of screening tools and methodologies to identify EJ communities. The EJ Interagency Council will create a workgroup, led by DEP, to evaluate and make further recommendations on the use of screening tools to identify environmental justice communities. The workgroup will seek to maximize consistency among departments and agencies, while allowing appropriate flexibility to reflect programs' various purposes and goals.
2. Assessment of cumulative health risk. This workgroup, led by DEP and Department of Health, in consultation with the EJAC, will evaluate currently available tools, and methodologies and data sets to assess cumulative health risks in communities. The workgroup will make recommendations on how to promote access to data to help departments, agencies, and communities prioritize concerns, include health and environmental data in planning efforts, shape policy decisions, guide public health actions, and educate residents and local businesses.
3. Lead exposure. The workgroup will evaluate and develop cross-agency solutions to address disproportionate exposure to lead contamination in EJ communities, including exposure from lead paint in housing, in drinking water pipes, and in soil. Members shall include representatives of the DEP, Department of Health, Department of Community Affairs, Department of Children and Families, the Department of Education, and other appropriate departments and agencies.
4. Disproportionate exposure to the effects of climate change. This workgroup will identify special vulnerabilities of EJ communities to the effects of climate change, such as increased heat in urban areas, flooding, sewer overflows, lack of access to transportation and members may include, but are not limited to, DEP, Board of Public Utilities, Department of Community Affairs, Department of Health, DOT, Office of Emergency Management, and Economic Development Authority.

Each EJ Interagency Council workgroup should develop action plans with deliverables and milestones that include a focused community and stakeholder engagement strategy. The draft guidance states the EJ Interagency Council shall establish a transparent process for regular evaluation of the executive branch departments' and agencies' implementation of the Environmental Justice Executive Order No. 23 guidance. A final guidance document is anticipated by the end of 2019.

In conclusion, New Jersey will continue to strive to achieve EJ for all residents in the State. For more information or assistance, contact the EJ Program at:

Riche Outlaw, Coordinator
New Jersey Department of Environmental Protection
Deputy Commissioner's Office
Environmental Justice Program
401 East State Street, 7th floor East Wing

Mail Code: 402
Trenton, New Jersey 08625
Main Number: 609 – 633-0747
Fax Number: 609-984-3962

New Jersey continues to make strides toward its goal of addressing the historical impacts to our EJ communities.

The author gratefully acknowledges the assistance of Michael Gordon, Esq. in the preparation of this section. Gordon is adviser to the DEP commissioner and winner of the first-ever Lifetime Achievement Award presented by the *New Jersey Law Journal* for his lifetime commitment to environmental causes.

NOTES

1. United States Environmental Protection Agency, Environmental Justice, 3(2019) https://www.epa.gov/environmentaljustice.

2. *Id.*

3. Steve Lubetkin, NJEDA and DEP Expand Community Collaborative Initiative into Nine Additional Cities, GlobeSt.com (March 13, 2019), http://www.globest.com/2019/03/13/njeda-and-dep-expand-community-collaborative-initiative-into-nine-additional-cities/?slreturn=20 19023084435.

4. Thomas J. Belton, Protecting New Jersey's Environmental: From Cancer Alley to the New Garden State, 138 (2011).

5. 36 N.J.R. 1259(c)

6. *S. Camden Citizens in action v. N.J. Dep't of Envtl. Prot.*, Civil Action No. 01-702(FLW), 2006 U.S. Dist. Lexis 45765 at*6 (D.N.J. Mar. 31, 2006)

7. *Id.* at *9.

8. *S. Camden Citizens in Action v. N.J. Dep't of Envtl. Prot.*, 145 F. Supp. 2d 446.

9. *S. Camden Citizens in action v. N.J. Dep't of Envtl. Prot.*, Civil Action No. 01-702(FLW), 2006 U.S. Dist. Lexis 45765 at*35 (D.N.J. Mar. 31, 2006)

10. *Alexander v. Sandoval*, 532 U.S. 275, 121 S. Ct. 15111 (2001).

11. *S. Camden Citizens in action v. N.J. Dep't of Envtl. Prot.*, Civil Action No. 01-702(FLW), 2006 U.S. Dist. Lexis 45765 at*44 (D.N.J. Mar. 31, 2006)

12. *Id.* at *65.

13. *Id.* at *68.

14. *Id.* at *69.

15. *Id.* at *70.

16. *Id.* at *114, 115.

17. Thomas J. Belton, Protecting New Jersey's Environmental: From Cancer Alley to the New Garden State, 140 (2011).

18. State of New Jersey, Department of Environmental Protection, Community Collaborative Initiative, https://www.nj.gov/dep/cci (last visited March 25, 2019).

19. About-Camden Collaborative Initiative, http://www.camdencollaborative.com/about.html.

20. The Camden Salvation Army Kroc Center, http://www.camdenkroccenter.org/classes.html.

21. E-mail from Frank McLaughlin, New Jersey Department of Environmental Protection, Office of Brownfield Reuse, Community Collaborative Initiative, to Vanessa Day, Compliance and Enforcement (January 16, 2019, 15:15 EST) (on file with the author)

22. Steve Lubetkin, NJEDA and DEP Expand Community Collaborative Initiative into Nine Additional Cities, GlobeSt.com (March 13, 2019), http://www.globest.com/2019/03/13/njeda-and-dep-expand-community-collaborative-initiative-into-nine-additional-cities/?slreturn=20 19023084435.

23. *Id.*

24. New Jersey Department of Environmental Protection, Policy and Procedure, Standard Operating Procedures for Supplemental Environmental Projects into Settlement Agreement, Effective Date: December 5, 2011, page 1

25. NJDEP-News Release 16/23-DEP Partners with Groundwork Elizabeth and Kean University for Community-Based Sustainable Agriculture Initiatives, https://www.nj.gov/dep/newsrel/2016/16_0023.htm.

26. N.J.S.A. §2A:35A-2

27. *Township of Howell v. Waste Disposal, Inc.*, 207 N.J. Super. 80, 83 (1986).

28. *Township of Howell v. Waste Disposal, Inc.*, 207 N.J. Super. 80, 85 (1986).

29. *Id.* at *86.

30. *Id.* at *96

31. *Id.*

32. NJDEP-News Release 18/P084—New Jersey Moving Forward with Plans to Improve Air Quality using Volkswagen Settlement Funds, https://www.nj.gov/dep/newsrel/2018/18_0 084.htm.

33. NJDEP-News Release 19/P011- DEP To Use First Round of Volkswagen Settlement Funds for Electric Vehicle Charging Stations, NJ Transit Electric Buses, https://nj.gov/dep/newsrel/2019/19_0011.htm.

34. NJDEP-News Release 18/P084—New Jersey Moving Forward with Plans to Improve Air Quality using Volkswagen Settlement Funds, https://www.nj.gov/dep/newsrel/2018/18_0 084.htm.

35. NJDEP-News Release 19/P011- DEP To Use First Round of Volkswagen Settlement Funds for Electric Vehicle Charging Stations, NJ Transit Electric Buses, https://nj.gov/dep/newsrel/2019/19_0011.htm.

36. New Jersey Senate Bill S1700

37. New Jersey Senate Bill S1700 (amended) and New Jersey Assembly Bill 5094

38. N.J. Stat. §54:4-3.151

39. N.J.S.A. §54:4-3.153

40. N.J.S.A. §54:4-3.154

41. N.J.S.A. §54:4-3.155

42. N.J.S.A. § 54:4-3.156

43. NJSA §54:4-3.156 (c)

44. NJSA §54:4-3.156(b)

45. NJSA §54:4-3.158 (b) and (c)

46. State of New Jersey, Department of Law & Public Safety, Office of the Attorney General, Attorney General, DEP File Lawsuits Across New Jersey Targeting Polluters in Lower-Income and Minority Communities, https://www.nj.gov/oag/newreleases18/pr20181206a.html.

47. *Id.*

48. *Id.*

49. State of New Jersey, Environmental Justice Executive Order No. 23 Guidance Draft, https://www.nj.gov/dep/ej/eo23/docs/eo23-draft-guidance.pdf.

50. *Id.*

Chapter 5

Regulated and Protected Lands

Section 1

The Coastal Area/Waterfront Development

John (Jack) Van Dalen, Esq.

The coastal area of New Jersey and the State's tidal waterfront are heavily regulated by two principal laws: the Coastal Area Facility Review Act (CAFRA or Act) and the Waterfront and Harbor Facilities Act, commonly referred to as the Waterfront Development Act (WFD).[1] The WFD was enacted in 1914 with the primary purpose of promoting the development of New Jersey's waterfront to enhance commerce and navigation; today, that original purpose takes a backseat to environmental protection, with myriad environmental hurdles that must be cleared in order to undertake regulated waterfront development.[2] CAFRA, on the other hand, was always intended to be a widely encompassing environmental protection law. When originally enacted in 1973, CAFRA only applied to larger developments.[3] In 1994, however, a major amendment extended CAFRA's jurisdiction to even a single new home, if located within 150 feet of the mean high-water line, beach, or dune (with an exception if located landward of an existing qualifying structure).

CAFRA BACKGROUND

In recognition of the adverse environmental impacts to portions of the coastal area of the State, and in response to the Federal Coastal Zone Management Act, 16 U.S.C. 1451, et seq., CAFRA was enacted in 1973 to safeguard against inappropriate development within the coastal zone by granting NJDEP wide-ranging regulatory permitting authority in that area. CAFRA, N.J.S.A.13:19-1 et seq., declares the coastal area of the State to be "an exceptional, unique, irreplaceable and delicately balanced physical, chemical, and biologically acting and interacting natural environmental resource."[4] However, the Act does not aim to curtail all development in impacted areas but instead recognizes the "legitimate economic aspirations" of coastal area inhabitants and as such includes permitting procedures designed to encourage "compatible land uses."[5]

Nonetheless, a CAFRA permit may only be issued if the development meets a series of seven stringent environmental standards set forth in the Act:

> The commissioner shall review filed applications, including any environmental impact statement and all information presented at public hearings or during the comment period, or submitted during the application review period. A permit may be issued pursuant to this act only upon a finding that the proposed development:
>
> a. Conforms with all applicable air, water and radiation emission and effluent standards and all applicable water quality criteria and air quality standards.
> b. Prevents air emissions and water effluents in excess of the existing dilution, assimilative, and recovery capacities of the air and water environments at the site and within the surrounding region.
> c. Provides for the collection and disposal of litter, recyclable material and solid waste in such a manner as to minimize adverse environmental effects and the threat to public health, safety, and welfare.
> d. Would result in minimal feasible impairment of the regenerative capacity of water aquifers or other ground or surface water supplies.
> e. Would cause minimal feasible interference with the natural functioning of plant, animal, fish, and human life processes at the site and within the surrounding region. [N.J.S.A. 13-19-10].
> f. Is located or constructed so as to neither endanger human life or property nor otherwise impair the public health, safety, and welfare.
> g. Would result in minimal practicable degradation of unique or irreplaceable land types, historical or archeological areas, and existing public scenic attributes at the site and within the surrounding region.

These findings must be specifically made in issuing each CAFRA individual permit. But fortunately, there are many and various activities that qualify for CAFRA general permits, permits-by-certification, or permits-by-rule where some or all of the findings have already been made by NJDEP when it adopted those types of permits.

In *Toms River Affiliates v. Dep't of Envtl. Prot.*, 140 N.J. Super. 135 (App. Div. 1976), the court declared the Act's constitutionality, and in 1978, NJDEP promulgated a comprehensive set of regulations, amended many times since, that set forth the procedures and environmental standards governing CAFRA permitting. Today, those regulations can be found at N.J.A.C. 7:7-1 et seq.[6]

SCOPE OF REGULATED DEVELOPMENT

The 1973 version of CAFRA required a permit for the construction of a "facility," defined by a list of structures and uses, including pulp mills, slaughtering animals, quarrying, and other manufacturing structures and processes, which led to varying application of the Act. The amendments to CAFRA adopted in 1993 (effective July 19, 1994) replaced the term "facility" (and its long list of regulated activities) with "development," defined as "the construction, relocation, or enlargement of any building or structure and all site preparation therefore, the grading, excavation or filling on beaches or dunes, and shall include residential development [depending on location], commercial development, industrial development, and public development."[7]

The area covered by the Act constitutes approximately 18.3 percent of the state.[8] This Act delineates the sections of the state subject to CAFRA regulation by establishing boundaries based on existing roads, a primary example being the Garden State Parkway. Essentially, the coverage area extends "from the Raritan Bay south to Cape May and west and then north almost to the Delaware Memorial Bridge."[9] NJDEP takes the position that its jurisdiction extends to the inland boundary of the road.

The areas subject to the Act are classified under four subcategories.[10] The first subcategory imposes a permit requirement for a development located on a beach or dune. Those terms are defined broadly:

> "Beach" means a gently sloping unvegetated area of sand or other unconsolidated material found on tidal shorelines, including ocean, inlet, bay and river shorelines, and that extends landward from the mean high water line to either: the vegetation line; a manmade feature generally parallel to the ocean, inlet, bay or river waters such as a retaining structure, seawall, bulkhead, road or boardwalk, except that sandy areas that extend fully under and landward of an elevated boardwalk are considered to be beach areas; or the seaward or bayward foot of dunes, whichever is closest to the ocean, inlet, bay or river waters;

***

> "Dune" means a wind-or wave-deposited or man-made formation of vegetated sand that lies generally parallel to and landward of the beach, and between the upland limit of the beach and the foot of the most inland slope of the dune. Dune includes the foredune, secondary and tertiary dune ridges, as well as man-made dunes, where they exist.[11]

Thus, the definition of "beach" includes not just ocean beaches but also unvegetated sandy areas along any tidal shoreland and sandy areas that extend under an elevated boardwalk, unless the beach has already terminated. In at least one coastal town NJDEP has considered a virtually ground-level boardwalk to be "elevated." The definition of "dune" is much less precise than that of "beach" and includes natural formations of sand, as well as man-made ones, that can extend far inland.[12]

The second subcategory is comprised of areas up to 150 feet from the landward limit of any beach, dune, or the mean high-water line of tidal waters. Generally, a CAFRA permit will be required for any development in this region unless there is an intervening development with an aboveground structure between it and "the mean high water line of any tidal waters."[13] If an intervening development exists, up to two dwelling units or commercial development with up to four parking spaces may be constructed without a CAFRA permit.[14] Residential development involving three or more dwelling units, commercial developments involving five or more parking spaces, and any industrial or public development will require a CAFRA permit in the 150' zone even if behind an intervening development. NJDEP's regulations define what constitutes a qualifying intervening development, and many common aboveground structures including boardwalks, carports, and even roads are excluded.[15] NJDEP's regulations further require that the intervening structure has been in existence or under active construction as of July 19, 1994, the effective date of the CAFRA amendments.[16]

The third subcategory includes lands more than 150 feet beyond the mean high-water line or landward boundary of beaches or dunes. A permit is required for commercial development having fifty or more parking spaces, residential development having twenty-five or more dwelling units, and public and industrial developments.[17]

The fourth subcategory of CAFRA jurisdiction is development located beyond 500 feet landward of the mean high-water line, beach or dune and within the boundaries of a "qualifying municipality"[18] or "a city of the fourth class with a population of over 30,000 persons." Within any such city, only development with seventy-five or more dwelling units, commercial development having 150 or more parking spaces, or public or industrial development requires a CAFRA permit.[19]

While Section 5 of CAFRA sets forth what is regulated, Section 5.2 sets forth what is not regulated:

A permit shall not be required pursuant to section 5 of [CAFRA] for:

***

    b.   The reconstruction of any development that is damaged or destroyed, in whole or in part, by fire, storm, natural hazard or act of God, provided that such reconstruction is in compliance with existing requirements or codes of municipal, State and federal law;

    c.   The enlargement of any development if the enlargement does not result in:
        (1) the enlargement of the footprint of the development; or
        (2) an increase in the number of dwelling units within the development;

    d.   The construction of a patio, deck or similar structure at a residential development;

    e.   Services provided, within the existing public right-of-way, by any governmental entity which involve:
        (1) the routine reconstruction, substantially similar functional replacement, or maintenance or repair of public highways;
        (2) public highway lane widening, intersection and shoulder improvement projects which do not increase the number of travel lanes; or
        (3) public highway signing, lighting, guide rails and other nonintrusive safety projects;

    f.   The expansion of an existing, functional amusement pier, provided such expansion does not exceed the footprint of the existing, functional amusement pier by more than 25 percent, and provided the expansion is located in the area beyond 150 feet landward of the mean high water line, beach or dune, whichever is most landward; or

    g.   The enclosure of an establishment offering dining, food services and beverages that was in operation as of December 18, 2000 and is located upon a functional pier, provided the enclosure only includes an open area which was actively used in the operation of the establishment.[20]

Section 5's exemption for reconstruction of any development damaged or destroyed "by fire, storm, natural hazard or act of God" has been enormously important for the rebuilding of New Jersey's shore towns in the wake of Super Storm Sandy. NJDEP expanded and created additional permits-by-rule to further facilitate the rebuilding process through a set of CAFRA regulations adopted in 2013.[21]

No CAFRA permit is required for the enlargement of any development under Section 5.2, provided it is located within the same footprint and does not increase the number of dwelling units.[22] Under this provision of CAFRA, additional floors may be added to an existing home or commercial structure; however, the enlargement cannot increase the number of parking spaces.[23]

Section 5.2 also exempts the "construction of a patio, deck, or similar structure at a residential development." While NJDEP has provided a fairly extensive list of "similar structures," including porches, balconies and verandahs, fences, gravel or brick walkways, and even open carports, gazebos, hot tubs, and aboveground swimming pools not exceeding 500 square feet and not on pilings.[24] Whether these are exempt if located on a beach or dune is unclear. Indeed, when NJDEP first adopted regulations dealing with the exemptions in the 1993 amendments to CAFRA, it indicated that location did not matter (26 N.J.R. 2934(a), 2935, 2959), but later in 2000 amendments to the original exemption regulations it added the beach or dune limitation, blithely stating that it was just doing what the statute always required (32 N.J.R. 864(a), 866; 32 N.J.R. 3784(b)). However, DEP has recently begun viewing decks constructed on dunes on pilings with no excavation of the dune as exempt.

Finally, Section 5.2 of the Act exempts certain highway reconstruction, repairs, and improvements within an existing public right-of-way, as well as certain amusement pier expansions and a restaurant enclosure.

PERMITTING PROCEDURES

No person may engage in "development" inside the coastal zone without first obtaining a permit if the project does not qualify under any exemption provided for in the Act.[25] Persons seeking a permit shall apply to NJDEP, and such applications shall include an environmental impact statement (EIS) providing information "needed to evaluate the effects of a proposed development upon the environment of the coastal area," unless the need for an EIS has been waived or modified.[26] The procedures for reviewing a CAFRA application and the required contents of an application are set forth in N.J.A.C. 7:7-8 (individual permit) and N.J.A.C. 7:7-3 and 6 (simplified requirements called a Compliance Statement for some thirty-two various general permits ranging from construction of up to two homes or duplexes to spraying herbicides to control invasive species). DEP has also adopted twenty-three permits-by-rule which do not require an application but the criteria for the particular permit must be closely followed, NJAC 7:7-4, and three permits-by-certification which can be self-generated through DEP's online system. NJAC 7:7-5. The permits-by-rule allow such things as construction of a home on a man-made lagoon, and the permits-by-certification allow rebuilding a bulkhead, constructing a dock, or building a dune walkover in certain circumstances.

CAFRA grants broad discretion to the NJDEP in the issuance of individual permits, which are much harder to obtain than general permits, permits-by-certification, or in utilizing the many permits-by-rule. It is advisable to make your project fit, if possible, one of these three permit categories although some projects because of their size or other factors will require the more difficult and costly to obtain individual permit. In making individual permit determinations, NJDEP must consider many diverse factors and make the necessary findings laid out in Section 10 of the Act quoted earlier.[27] Section 10 requires NJDEP to consider whether the development in question "is located or constructed so as to neither endanger human life or property nor otherwise impair the public health, safety, and welfare," as well as other factors, including "trash disposal, interference with natural life processes, and degradation of unique or irreplaceable land types."[28]

Factors to be considered under Section 10 include, but are not limited to, whether or not the project conforms to applicable environmental standards; provides for disposal of waste in such a way that minimizes adverse impacts; would cause minimal impact upon the natural functioning of plant, animal, and human life at the site and in the surrounding region; and would not result in degradation of unique and irreplaceable land types, historical areas, or existing scenic attributes.[29] Even if the proposed development complies with the requirements set forth in the aforementioned section, the NJDEP may still deny a permit or attach conditions to an approval if it finds that the project "would violate or tend to violate the purpose and intent" of the Act.[30]

In practice, meeting the requirements of Sections 10 and 11 of CAFRA means meeting the numerous applicable standards set forth in the Coastal Zone Management Rules (CZM), N.J.A.C. 7:7-1, et seq. The CZM rules define and provide standards for development in some fifty Special Areas, ranging from Dunes, Bay Islands (islands between the barrier islands and the mainland), Wetlands and Wetland Buffers, Endangered or Threatened Wildlife or Plant Species Habitats, and Atlantic City (its own Special Area).[31] The CZM rules relevant to CAFRA permits also set forth standards for Beach and Dune Activities such as beach and dune maintenance,[32] Vegetative Requirements and Impervious Cover limitations,[33] Use Rules pertaining to activities such as housing and resort/recreational uses,[34] and Resource Rules pertaining such diverse things as water quality, traffic, public access to the waterfront, and the scale of development especially along a water area.[35] It should be noted that in a 2010 amendment to CAFRA, solar panels and arrays thereof were excluded from impervious surface limitations.[36]

Among the CZM rules relevant to CAFRA applications, some of the most controversial ones (in addition to Dunes and Endangered and Threatened Species) are those setting forth requirements for public access to privately owned land along the waterfront and limiting the scale or size of development along the waterfront.[37] While a full discussion of the Public Trust (public's right to use the tidal waters of New Jersey) and of the public's right of access to tidewaters, particularly ocean waters for bathing and fishing, is beyond the scope of this discussion, it is important to know that NJDEP has taken upon itself to define the Public Trust and extended the definition of the area impacted by the Public Trust to include not just the water but also all uplands fronting on tidal waters.[38]

The rule limiting the size and scale of development along the waterfront, known as the Scenic Resources and Design rule, N.J.A.C. 7:7E-8.12, requires that 30 percent of the preexisting water view across a parcel of property be preserved from development and that a structure more than 15' high be stepped back in a 2-1 ratio from the beach, dune, boardwalk, or waterfront. In other words, the floors of a building over fifteen feet high must be stepped back from the water in an Aztec pyramid-like fashion.[39]

Upon receipt of an application for an individual permit, the commissioner is required to notify the applicant regarding its completeness within twenty business days, and additional information is often requested at this point.[40] Within fifteen days of declaring the application complete, the commissioner shall then set a date for either public commenting (thirty-day comment period) or a public hearing, to be held no later than sixty days after declaring the application complete.[41] Within fifteen days following the comment period or the public hearing, NJDEP has another opportunity to require the submission of additional information.[42] Following the comment period or public hearing, NJDEP has sixty days to approve, approve with conditions, or disapprove the application; however, if additional information had been requested NJDEP has ninety days after receipt of that information to make a decision.[43] If the applicant or any other person is aggrieved by the permit decision, a request for an administrative hearing may be filed within thirty days of the decision or thirty days from publication of notice of the decision in the NJDEP Bulletin, whichever is later. Administrative appeals are routinely granted to applicants, but the process is agonizingly slow, sometimes taking two years or more before the Office of Administrative Law conducts a hearing and then almost a year before the administrative law judge issues an initial decision which then goes on to the commissioner of NJDEP for a final decision. For a permit applicant, the administrative appeal process is nonfunctional. Administrative hearings are only rarely granted to anyone else; a nonapplicant must show either a constitutional or statutory right to a hearing, a standard seldom met. Following a final decision on the administrative appeal, recourse can be sought through an appeal to the Superior Court, Appellate Division within the time period prescribed by the Rules of Court.

Waterfront and Harbor Facilities Act (WFD)

Until 1980, the WFD was only used to regulate projects at or below the mean high-water line of a navigable waterway. However, in 1978, NJDEP promulgated its first version of the Coastal Zone Management Program—Bay and Ocean Shore Segment regulations, primarily governing the issuance of CAFRA, WFD and Coastal Wetlands permits.[44] In order to have a complete CZM plan, NJDEP needed authority to regulate development of upland bordering the coast, including the coastal area upriver from the termination of CAFRA near the Delaware Memorial Bridge (up the Delaware River to the head of tide in Trenton) and the coastal areas north of CAFRA's termination in Raritan Bay and north to New York State. The WFD was the chosen vehicle for this new assertion of jurisdiction.[45]

Developments Regulated under the WFD

The principal regulatory section of the WFD is N.J.S.A. 12:5-3, which provides:

> All plans for the development of any waterfront upon any navigable water or stream of this State or bounding thereon, which is contemplated by any person or municipality, in the nature of individual improvement or development or as a part of a general plan which

involves the construction or alteration of a dock, wharf, pier, bulkhead, bridge, pipeline, cable, or any other similar or dissimilar waterfront development shall be first submitted to the Department of Environmental Protection. No such development or improvement shall be commenced or executed without the approval of the Department of Environmental Protection first had and received, or as hereinafter in this chapter provided.

NJDEP's coastal permitting procedural regulations define the WFD's geographic jurisdiction:

(a) The waterfront area regulated under this subchapter is divided into three sections, and will vary in width in accordance with the following rules:

    1. Within any part of the Hackensack Meadowland Development District delineated at N.J.S.A. 13:17-4.1, the area regulated by this section shall include any tidal waterway of this State and all lands lying thereunder, up to and including the mean high-water line.

    2. Within the "coastal area" defined by section 4 of CAFRA (N.J.S.A. 13:9-4), the regulated waterfront area shall include any tidal waterway of this State and all lands lying thereunder, up to and including the mean high-water line.

    3. In those areas of the State outside both the "coastal area" defined by CAFRA and outside of the New Jersey Meadowlands District, the regulated waterfront area shall include:

        i. All tidal waterways and land lying thereunder, up to and including the mean high-water line; and

        ii. Adjacent upland areas within 100 feet of the mean high-water line. For properties within 100 feet of the mean high-water line that extend beyond 100 feet from the mean high-water line, the regulated waterfront area shall extend inland to the lesser of the following distances:

            (1) 500 feet from the mean high-water line; or

            (2) To the first paved public road, railroad, or surveyable property line that:

                (A) Existed on September 26, 1980; and

                (B) Generally parallels the waterway.[46]

Thus, within the CAFRA area or within the Hackensack Meadowland Development District, you only need a WFD permit for development at or below the mean high-water line, but elsewhere in New Jersey, you need a WFD permit, whether in tidal water or up to 500 feet inland. Although N.J.S.A. 12:5-3 references "navigable water or stream" as the trigger for WFD jurisdiction, NJDEP has used the term "tidal waterway" to delineate the reach of the WFD.[47]

The WFD has two important exemptions:

(1) The repair, replacement or renovation of a permanent dock, wharf, pier, bulkhead or building existing prior to January 1, 1981, provided the repair, replacement or renovation does not increase the size of the structure and the structure is used solely for residential purposes or the docking or servicing of pleasure vessels;

(2) The repair, replacement or renovation of a floating dock, mooring raft or similar temporary or seasonal improvement or structure, provided the improvement or structure does not exceed in length the waterfront frontage of the parcel of real property to which it is attached and is used solely for the docking or servicing of pleasure vessels.[48]

Permitting Procedures and Substantive Standard

The procedures to be followed for an Individual WFD permit are governed by the same regulations as a CAFRA permit.[49] Notice is required to surrounding property owners, and a copy of the application shall be on file in the applicable municipality for public review and comment.[50] A WFD application for a general permit only has to include a Compliance Statement (instead of a full EIS), but the Compliance Statement must "address all coastal rules (N.J.A.C. 7:7) applicable to the proposed project."[51] In practice, NJDEP evaluates a WFD permit application under all the environmental standards set forth in the multitude of policies in N.J.A.C. 7:7-1 et seq., despite the admonition of the courts in the *Last Chance* cases and in Attorney General F.O. 6 that the WFD was enacted to protect and enhance water commerce and navigation.[52] Special Areas policies are drawn to protect areas such as Shellfish Habitat and Submerged Vegetation Habitat often present serious obstacles to building a bulkhead, pier, or dock.[53] However, in 2017 the Legislature enacted a law that exempts existing marinas and other water-dependent facilities from the Shellfish Habitat policy for certain dredging projects. P.L. 2017, c. 196. This exemption is in effect even though NJDEP has not yet incorporated it into its regulations. Certain permits-by-rule, general permits, and permits-by-certification are also available for some WFD developments, and it is always advisable to use one instead of seeking a WFD individual permit if at all possible. Finally, in order to obtain a WFD permit in a tide flowed area, it is necessary to obtain a tidelands grant, lease, or license to occupy the area, assuming the State owns the tide flowed area.[54]

NOTES

1. Wetlands laws and the Flood Hazard Area Control Act can also apply in these areas.

2. Did the New Jersey Legislature have protecting submerged aquatic vegetation, shellfish habitat, or intertidal areas in mind when it passed the law in 1914? NJDEP certainly does, and these and other environmental considerations must be taken into account when applying for a permit for a bulkhead, dock or other waterfront structure.

3. For example, housing developments over 24 units; unsurprisingly, this led to a proliferation of twenty-four unit developments.

4. N.J.S.A. 13:19-2.

5. *Id.*

6. The previous two sets of rules governing CAFRA which were found at NJAC 7:7 and NJAC 7:7E were consolidated in July 2015 as NJAC 7:7.

7. N.J.S.A. 13:19-3. "Commercial development" was defined as that which is "designed, constructed, or intended to accommodate commercial or office uses," essentially any structure purposed for providing commercial services. "Industrial development" is that which involves "manufacturing or industrial process," and N.J.S.A. 13:19-3 provides such examples as electric power production, food processing, storage facilities, and mining and excavation processes. "Residential development" is that which "provides one or more dwelling units." "Public development" includes public solid waste facilities, wastewater treatment facilities, public highways, airports, and utility pipelines; however, the section specifically excludes educational facilities, temporary or seasonal structures related to tourism, and power lines. It is also important to consider the section's definition of "person," which includes any individual, corporation,

company, association, society, firm, partnership, joint stock company, or governmental agency. Any "person proposing to construct or cause to be constructed" a non-exempt development in the coastal area is required to obtain a CAFRA permit. *N.J.S.A.* 13:19-6.

8. N.J.S.A. 13:19-4. See also 13C N.J. Prac., Real Estate Law and Practice § 46.33 (2d ed.).

9. See 50 N.J. Prac., Business Law Deskbook § 27:13 (2012-2013 ed.).

10. N.J.S.A. 13:19-5.

11. N.J.S.A. 13:19-3.

12. NJDEP's concept of what constitutes a dune is far more expansive than what would appear to an ordinary observer, so the agency and land owners fronting or near a beach are frequently at odds. In many areas, NJDEP considers all land between the beach and the first road (sometimes even landward of the first road) to be a dune. This reflects a view that much of the basic sandy geology of New Jersey's barrier islands and other shore areas is a "dune." At times, NJDEP has even taken the position that perfectly flat landscaped grass yards are part of a "dune."

13. N.J.S.A. 13:19-5(b)(1).

14. N.J.S.A. 13:19-5 (b) (2) and (3).

15. N.J.A.C. 7:7-2.2(b).

16. N.J.A.C. 7:7-2.2(b). The CAFRA statute does not contain any of these limitations.

17. N.J.S.A. 13:19-5 (e). See also *N.J.S.A.* 13:19-5 (c) which treats the area between 150' and 500' from the water, beach or dune similarly in certain cities.

18. See N.J.S.A. 52:27D-178.

19. N.J.S.A. 13:19-5(d).

20. N.J.S.A. 13-19-5.2.

21. For example, a damaged or destroyed home can be rebuilt in place under the statute or relocated laterally or further away from the water and its footprint expanded by up to 400 square feet (rules proposed May 5, 2013, 45 N.J.R. 1141(a), adopted June 20, 2013).

22. For example, NJDEP issued an exemption letter saying additional floors may be added to an existing hotel which was being rebuilt within the previous footprint but without expanded parking or an increase in dwelling units.

23. N.J.A.C. 7:7-2.2(c)(4).

24. N.J.A.C. 7:7-2.2(c)(5).

25. N.J.S.A. 13:19-5, 5.2, and 6.

26. N.J.S.A. 13:19-6.

27. N.J.S.A. 13:19-10.

28. *Matter of Egg Harbor Associates (Bayshore Ctr.)*, 94 N.J. 358, 365 (1983).

29. N.J.S.A. 13:19-10.

30. N.J.S.A. 13:19-11.

31. N.J.A.C. 7:7-9.

32. N.J.A.C. 7:7-10.

33. N.J.A.C. 7:7-13.

34. N.J.A.C. 7:7-15.2.

35. N.J.A.C. 7:7-16

36. N.J.S.A. 13:19-5.4.

37. N.J.A.C. 7:7-16.9 and 16.10

38. N.J.A.C. 7:7-9.48. Historically, the Public Trust in tidewaters was defined by the common law as applied and expanded by the courts. Emboldened by the New Jersey Supreme Court's decision in *Raleigh Avenue Beach Association v. Atlantis Beach Club, Inc.*, 185 N.J. 40 (2005), NJDEP set forth its definition of the Public Trust and the requirements for a public access and public use of a strip of land from the street to the water and then along the waterfront

of all properties in order to obtain a CAFRA permit. N.J.A.C. 7:7-16.9. The Appellate Division threw out the portion of the rules imposing various public accommodation requirements on municipalities, but in 2012, NJDEP adopted new rules with modified Public Trust/Public Access regulations for municipalities and more flexibility for small private developments in providing public access. *Id.* Later litigation briefly invalidated DEP's public access rules for lack of jurisdiction but the Legislature quickly enacted a law restoring DEP's jurisdiction over public access.

39. In practice, NJDEP has only applied the rule along the ocean or open bays, and not along other more narrow waterways. The 2-1 setback requirement has greatly influenced the shape of development (and sometimes stopped it) along the ocean front in places like the Wildwoods.

40. N.J.S.A. 13:19-8.

41. *Id.*

42. N.J.S.A. 13:19-9.

43. *Id.*

44. N.J.S.A. 13:9A *et seq.*, the Coastal Wetlands Act of 1970, won federal approval under the federal Coastal Zone Management Act, 16 U.S.C. §1451 *et seq.*, a federal law encouraging all coastal states to develop plans for managing their coastal areas.

45. Based upon advice from the Attorney General's office in 1980 (Formal Opinion No. 6, 1980), NJDEP adopted regulations applying the WFD to the "waterfront," defined as not only all tide flowed waters but also the lands bounding thereon no less than 100' or more than 500' inland. N.J.A.C. 7:7-2.3 (1980). The upland WFD rules were upheld by the Appellate Division in an unreported decision, *N.J. Builders Ass'n. v. New Jersey*, A-984-80T1, Nov. 30, 1982. With this enlargement of its jurisdiction filling the gap in CAFRA (and the Coastal Wetlands law), NJDEP quickly won federal approval of the complete CZM plan for New Jersey. *See generally* former versions of N.J.A.C. 7:7-1.1 for the history of the CZM plan. Thus beginning in 1980 the WFD applied to a fringe of upland bordering tidal waters throughout the State, excluding the CAFRA area and the Hackensack Meadowland District as defined in N.J.S.A 13:17-4. Later in 1988, NJDEP again sought to expand the use of the WFD, this time through the adoption of emergency regulations purporting to require a WFD permit in a varying area of upland bordering the water within the CAFRA zone. 20 N.J.R. 2815(a)(Nov. 7, 1988). This action was taken in response to extensive beach closings due to poor water quality and reports of medical waste washing ashore. If close enough to the water, all development, including those exempt from CAFRA, e.g., twenty-four dwelling units or less, needed a WFD permit. These expanded WFD regulations, and a succeeding set of more narrow regulations, were short lived. In *Last Chance Development Partnership v. Kean*, 119 N.J. 425 (1990), the Supreme Court struck down the 1988 set of regulations, holding that NJDEP had exceeded its authority under the WFD by regulating upland for environmental reasons and not for reasons related to commerce and navigation. A similar fate befell more narrow emergency regulations adopted in 1990. *Long Beach Tp. v. N.J. Dept. of Environmental Protection*, 245 N.J. Super 145 (App. Div. 1990). Finally, in 1993, the New Jersey Legislature put an end to this tug of war by amending the WFD to eliminate its applicability to upland within the CAFRA area, N.J.S.A. 12.5-3(b) (3), but also amending CAFRA to apply to even a single home if within 150 feet of the mean high water line, beach or dune, with no existing development between it and the water. *See* discussion of the scope of CAFRA in the preceding section.

46. N.J.A.C. 7:7-2.4(a).

47. See generally N.J.A.C. 7:7-2.4.

48. N.J.S.A. 12:5-3(b)(1) and (2). NJDEP has done its best to adopt regulations that purport to severely limit entitlement to these exemptions. See N.J.A.C. 7:7-2.4(d)(6) and (7).

49. N.J.A.C. 7:7-1.1 and 1.4(a)..

50. N.J.A.C. 7:7-24.1.

51. N.J.A.C. 7:7-23.6. See also N.J.A.C. 7:7-23.5 setting forth the requirements for a Compliance Statement.

52. See *supra* note 44.

53. N.J.A.C. 7:7-9.2 and 9.6.

54. See Section on Riparian Rights. The general rule is that the State owns naturally tide flowed areas but not man-made tidal areas.

Section 2

Wetlands

A. Vincent Agovino, PhD, P.W.S., L.S.R.P.

Wetlands are defined as "areas that are inundated or saturated by *surface or ground-water* at a frequency and duration sufficient to support, and that under normal circumstances do support, a prevalence of *vegetation* typically adapted for life in *saturated soil conditions*."[1] Wetlands can include bogs, swamps, coastal marshes, prairie potholes, and even your own front lawn. They offer several significant environmental benefits, including productivity, groundwater protection, flood protection, and aesthetics.

1. **Productivity**—Wetlands are among the most productive ecosystems in the world, productivity that is on a par with the tropical rain forest.[2] A wide variety of species of microorganisms, plants, insects, amphibians, reptiles, birds, fish, and other wildlife depend in some way on wetlands in their life cycles. Wetland plants provide breeding and nursery sites, stopovers for migratory species, and refuge from predators. Additionally, decomposed plant matter known as detritus is released into the water and becomes an important food for invertebrates and fish both in the wetland and in associated aquatic systems.

2. **Groundwater Protection**—Wetlands help maintain the level of the water table and exert control on the infiltration into the soil. This allows groundwater recharge and discharge to other waters as well. The amount of groundwater recharge by a wetland is largely dependent upon soil, vegetation and other characteristics, including the perimeter to volume ratio of the wetland. Most of the groundwater recharge occurs through soils around the edges of wetlands because the soil under most wetlands is relatively impermeable. Therefore, a high wetland perimeter to volume ratio, such as seen in small wetlands, means that the surface area through which water can infiltrate into the groundwater is high.

   Wetlands also protect the groundwater by nutrient removal, chemical detoxification, and sediment trapping. As water from an upland source or a stream channel enters a wetland, the water expands and flows through dense vegetation. The velocity of the flow is reduced, allowing suspended material in the water to settle to the wetland surface. The roots of wetland plants can then bind the accumulated sediments that are combined with the chemical constituents of the runoff. Estimates indicate that as much as 90 percent of the sediments that are present in runoff or in streamflow may be removed if the water passes through wetlands. Also, because pollutants, such as heavy metals, attach to soil particles, the settling of sediments in wetlands further improves water quality.

3. **Flood Protection**—Wetlands "function as natural sponges that trap and slowly release surface water, rain, snowmelt, groundwater and flood waters."[3] Tree roots and other wetland vegetation reduce the velocity of floodwaters and allow water to be more slowly distributed over the floodplain. Together, the improved water storage and deceleration lowers flood heights and reduces erosion in flood-prone areas.

4. **Aesthetics**—The recreational and cultural attributes of wetlands can be seen in the number of New Jerseyans who hunt, fish, bird-watch, or photograph wildlife. The financial benefits translate to multibillion-dollar expenditures annually for photography, art, hiking, fishing, boating and other recreational activities.

In New Jersey, wetlands are broadly defined as either *coastal wetlands* or *freshwater wetlands*, with specific parameters required for the regulation, identification, and disturbance of each.

THE WETLANDS ACT OF 1970

Background

The Wetlands Act of 1970 ("Wetlands Acts"), N.J.S.A. 13:9A-1 et seq., was enacted by the legislature in recognition of the importance of coastal wetlands, "one of the most vital and productive areas of our natural world."[4] Coastal wetlands, also called the "estuarine zone," are those lands "between the sea and land" that "protect the land from the force of the sea, moderate our weather, provide a home for waterfowl and 2/3 of all our fish and shellfish, and assist in absorbing sewage discharge by the rivers of the land."[5] The purpose of the Wetlands Act is to promote public health, safety, and welfare and protect both public and private property interests while maintaining the existing ecological balance.[6] The commissioner of Environmental Protection is specifically authorized to "adopt, amend, modify, or repeal orders regulating, restricting, or prohibiting dredging, filling, removing, or otherwise altering or polluting coastal wetlands" for the purpose of protecting the welfare of the public as well as public and private property.[7]

Effective July 6, 2015, the Coastal Permit Program rules and the Coastal Zone Management rules were consolidated into one chapter, N.J.A.C. 7:7-A. The consolidation of all the coastal rules in a single chapter is part of the New Jersey Department of Environmental Protection (NJDEP) effort to transform the operations of the Division of Land Use Regulation. With this and anticipated rulemaking, the NJDEP has proposed to align the rules governing the permitting processes of the coastal, freshwater and flood hazard permitting programs, to the extent the respective enabling statutes allow.

Boundaries

The Wetlands Act includes within the coastal wetlands

> any bank, marsh, swamp, meadow, flat or other low land subject to tidal action in the State of New Jersey along the Delaware bay and Delaware river, Raritan bay, Barnegat bay, Sandy Hook bay, Shrewsbury river including Navesink river, Shark river, and the coastal inland waterways extending southerly from Manasquan Inlet to Cape May Harbor, or at any inlet, estuary or tributary waterway or any thereof, including those areas now or formerly connected to tidal waters whose surface is at or below an elevation of 1 foot above local extreme high water, and upon which may grow or is capable of growing some, but not necessarily all, [of a listing of flora typical of wetlands ecosystems].[8]

The Wetlands Act required the NJDEP to take stock of all tidal wetlands within the state within two years of enactment and produce maps to be filed with the counties in which the coastal wetlands were located.[9] Coastal wetlands must be delineated and mapped based upon existing NJDEP aerial photographic mapping that provides an upper wetlands boundary line; if unmapped coastal wetland vegetation exists upland of the mapped upper wetlands boundary or there is no official map for the property, then the wetlands boundary determination is regulated under New Jersey Freshwater Wetlands Protection Act, N.J.S.A. 13:9B-1 et seq., discussed here.

Permitting

The Wetlands Act states that no "regulated activity" may be conducted in any wetland without first obtaining a permit.[10] A "regulated activity" is defined as including (but not limited to)

> draining, dredging, excavation or removal of soil, mud, sand, gravel, aggregate of any kind or depositing or dumping therein any rubbish or similar material or discharging therein liquid wastes, either directly or otherwise, and the erection of structures, drivings of pilings, or placing of obstructions, whether or not changing the tidal ebb and flow.[11]

In addition to applying for a permit, anyone wishing to engage in a regulated activity within the bounds of the wetlands must also provide notice to each gas and electric utility provider in the State as well as owners of real property located within the State and 200 feet of the property subject to permit review.[12] Permit applications are to include detailed descriptions of the proposed work as well as a map detailing the area of wetland affected by the project.[13] The Commissioner will then consider the application and the project's effect upon wildlife, public welfare, and the protection from coastal weather naturally afforded by wetlands.[14]

Additionally, to further prioritize and refocus its permitting efforts on the activities posing the most risk to the coastal environment, two new permits-by-rule, two general permits-by-certification (electronic permits), a new general permit and modifications to several existing general permits were developed. In addition, other rule changes were made in an effort "to further encourage appropriate redevelopment of more resilient coastal communities."[15]

Enforcement

Should the commissioner find a person to be in violation of the Wetlands Act or regulations adopted under the Wetlands Act (or any permit issued pursuant to the act), there are several avenues for enforcement. First, the commissioner may issue an administrative enforcement order for the violator to come into compliance.[16] Second, the commissioner may bring a civil action for remedies including injunction, recovery of costs, and compensatory damages.[17] Third, the commissioner may impose a civil administrative penalty assessment (CAPA) of not more than $25,000 per day per violation.[18] Fourth, the commissioner may bring an action in court for a civil penalty of up to $25,000 per day per violation.[19] Finally, the commissioner may petition the attorney general to pursue criminal action for crimes of the third degree.[20]

There is currently legislation proposed to amend the enforcement statute discussed earlier.[21] Rather than authorizing the Commissioner to "levy" a CAPA against violators directly, under the new legislation s/he would be authorized to "recommend [to an administrative law judge] the assessment of" a CAPA.[22]

FRESHWATER WETLANDS PROTECTION ACT

Background

Where the Wetlands Act of 1970 applies to "coastal wetlands," the freshwater wetlands of the State are protected by the New Jersey Freshwater Wetlands Protection Act (Freshwater Act), N.J.S.A. 13:9B-1 et seq. A "freshwater wetland" is defined as "an area that is inundated or saturated by surface water or groundwater at a frequency and duration sufficient to support, and that under normal circumstances does support, a prevalence of vegetation typically adapted for life in saturated soil conditions, commonly known as hydrophytic vegetation."[23] The purpose of the Freshwater Act is very similar to that of the Wetlands Act, although freshwater wetlands also play a significant role in protecting drinking water resources.[24]

Regulatory Basis

Freshwater wetlands in the State of New Jersey are regulated under state and federal law. The U.S. Army Corps of Engineers (ACOE) administers two permit programs that directly affect development in "waters of the United States," which includes wetlands and waterways. Section 10 of the Rivers and Harbors Act of 1899 requires a permit to construct structures in a navigable waterway of the United States.[25] Section 404 of the Clean Water Act regulates the discharge of dredged material and fill material in the waters of the United States.[26] Section 301 of the Clean Water Act prohibits the discharge of dredged or fill material into "waters of the United States" without a permit from the ACOE and, in New Jersey, the NJDEP.[27]

New Jersey is one of two states to which the ACOE has delegated authority to administer a permit program under the Clean Water Act for those wetlands covered by the federal statute.[28] The ACOE and NJDEP have signed a reciprocal agreement designating the NJDEP as the "lead agency with respect to delineations of . . . waters and wetlands" within the geographic boundaries of New Jersey.[29] The Division of Land Use Regulation (DLUR) of the NJDEP administers the Freshwater Act.

On December 18, 2017, the NJDEP adopted comprehensive amendments to the Freshwater Wetlands Protection Act Rules "to add appropriate flexibility, harmonize certain procedural provisions with the Department's other land use rules, provide better consistency with Federal, local, and other State requirements, implement statutory amendments related to agricultural exemptions and stream cleaning, and address implementation issues identified since the chapter's readoption with amendments in 2008."[30] The current rules, dated April 16, 2018, are posted at the DLUR web page.[31]

Freshwater Wetland Identification

The identification of freshwater wetlands within New Jersey is based upon the three-parameter approach enumerated in the *Federal Manual for Identifying and Delineating Jurisdictional Wetlands*.[32] Under this format, the three criteria—*vegetation, soil, and hydrology*—must be met under normal circumstances for an area to be considered a "wetland."

First, the dominant species of plant(s) must be *hydrophytic*. Hydrophyte means "any macrophyte that grows in water or on a substrate that is at least periodically deficient in oxygen as a result of excessive water content: plants typically found in wetlands and other aquatic habitats."[33] The presence or absence of hydrophytic vegetation at a site is determined by the "wetland indicator status (plant species' frequency of occurrence in wetlands)" as enumerated in the "National List of Plant Species That Occur in Wetlands."[34] A list of the wetland indicator status for plant species that occur in New Jersey has been prepared and characterizes the plants based upon the percent of the time that the plant species would be expected to be found in wetlands.[35] This characterization ranges from obligate (OBL) species that are found greater than 99 percent of the time in wetlands only, to upland (UPL) species that are found greater than 99 percent of the time in uplands only. Intermediate characterizations are known as "facultative" (FAC) species.[36]

Second, sites must have as their predominant substrates soils that exhibit hydric character. The National Technical Committee for Hydric Soils developed the following definition for hydric soils: "A hydric soil is a soil that is saturated, flooded, or ponded long enough during the growing season to develop anaerobic conditions that favor the growth of hydrophytic vegetation."[37]

Third, areas must meet the criteria for wetland hydrology. The term "wetland hydrology" encompasses all hydrologic characteristics of areas that are permanently or periodically inundated or have soils saturation for a significant period (usually a week or more) during the growing season.[38] When available, recorded data and aerial photographs can provide information on inundation and saturation of soils at a site. Field indicators include visual observation of inundation and saturation, oxidized root channels, watermarks, drift lines, and morphological plant adaptations.

Wetlands Resource Value

Three resource value categories are identified in the regulations governing freshwater wetlands: (1) exceptional resource value, (2) intermediate resource value, and (3) ordinary resource value.[39]

Freshwater wetlands of *exceptional resource value* are those which "discharge into FW-1 and FW-2 trout production waters and their tributaries; which are present habitats for threatened or endangered species; or those which are documented habitats for threatened or endangered species which remain suitable for breeding, resting, or feeding by these species during the normal period these species use the habitat."[40] A 150-foot transition area is assigned to freshwater wetlands of exceptional resource value.[41]

Freshwater wetlands of *intermediate resource value* are those not classified as having exceptional or ordinary resource value and have a 50-foot transition area.[42]

Freshwater wetlands of *ordinary resource value* exhibit none of the characteristics listed for wetlands of exceptional resource value mentioned earlier and are:

1. Isolated wetlands that are not surface water tributary systems discharging into an inland lake or pond, or a river or stream, and which are more than 50 percent surrounded by development and less than 5,000 square feet in size;
2. Drainage ditches;
3. Swales; or
4. Detention facilities.

Ordinary resource value wetlands have no transition area requirements.[43]

As it relates to coastal wetlands, a "buffer" or "buffer zone" is a transitional area of native vegetation that mitigates adverse impacts of development on adjacent wetlands.[44] The buffer zone is an area contiguous to coastal wetlands that is retained in a natural and undisturbed condition. Because buffers are valuable wildlife habitats, and the diversity and distribution of habitats can have critical impacts on wildlife, these are also regulated.

Permitting

Like the Wetlands Act of 1970, the Freshwater Wetlands Protection Act requires permitting for a number of regulated activities.[45] These permits are identified as either general permits or individual permits. General permits provide a means to perform a variety of activities within regulated freshwater wetlands, adjacent transition areas and/or State open waters, provided that the various restrictions are met for the type of general permit requested.[46] Included are activities related to minor road crossings, utility line installations, additions to and reconstruction of preexisting structures, hazardous site remediation and filling of isolated wetlands. The rules specify requirements and restrictions for all general permits, all of which must be considered prior to applying for a permit. Should these requirements not be met, an application for a general permit may be denied.[47] The general permits have been reorganized in the 2018 adoption, with several notable changes, including 7:7A-6.1 general permit-by-certification 8 for construction of an addition to a lawfully existing residential dwelling, and 7:7A-6.2

general permit-by-certification 24 for repair or modification of a malfunctioning individual subsurface sewage disposal (septic) system. At 7:7A-7.27, general permit 27 provides for application of herbicide within freshwater wetlands and transition areas to control invasive plant species. Other requirements to assure consistency with the most recent ACOE regulations have been included.[48]

Individual permits, in comparison, are for activities having substantial wetlands impacts that do not fall into one of the standard general permit or transition area waiver categories, and that propose to eliminate and/or reduce those impacts through an alternatives analysis.[49] If the proposed wetland disturbance cannot be eliminated or reduced to fit within a general permit category, the alternatives analysis is conducted to see if there are ways to achieve a project with a lesser wetland disturbance. Activities passing the alternatives analysis and having no viable alternatives are then issued an individual permit, and that permit will contain conditions for mitigation measures to restore wetland functions that would be lost by completing the project.

Applications are to include preliminary site plans, verification of notice of the application provided to the local municipality, verification that the proposed project has been published in a local newspaper, and a statement detailing potential adverse environmental impacts (as well as mitigating measures that may be taken).[50]

A permit will only be granted if the NJDEP finds that the activity (1) is dependent upon access to the freshwater wetlands, and has no viable alternative; (2) is not water-dependent, with no known alternative that would not involve a freshwater wetland; (3) will result in minimum practicable adverse impact or impairment upon the aquatic ecosystem; (4) will not jeopardize the continued existence of species protected under the Endangered and Nongame Species Conservation Act; (5) will not contribute to violation of any applicable state water standards; (6) will not contribute to violation of applicable toxic effluent standards under the Water Pollution Control Act; (7) will not violate any requirements imposed for the protection of marine sanctuaries under the Marine Protection, Research and Sanctuaries Act of 1972; (8) will not contribute to a significant degradation of ground or surface waters; and (9) is in the public interest and is otherwise lawful.[51]

Enforcement

The possible forms of enforcement under the Freshwater Wetlands Protection Act mirror those of the Wetlands Act and may be found at N.J.S.A. 13:9B-21. For cases where an administrative enforcement order for compliance has been issued, options including Alternate Dispute Resolution[52] have proven successful in resolving the violation.

NOTES

1. Federal Interagency Committee for Wetland Delineation, FEDERAL MANUAL FOR IDENTIFYING AND DELINEATING JURISDICTIONAL WETLANDS (Jan. 10, 1989), available at http://www.wetlands.com/pdf/89manv3b.pdf. (citing EPA Regulations at 40 C.F.R. 230.3) (emphasis added).
2. W. J. MITSCH & J. G. GOSSELINK, WETLANDS (2d ed. 1993).

3. EPA—Flood Protection, http://water.epa.gov/type/wetlands/flood.cfm.

4. N.J.S.A. 13:9A-1.

5. *Id.*

6. *Id.*

7. N.J.S.A. 13:19A-2.

8. Id.

9. N.J.S.A. 13:9A-1.

10. N.J.S.A. 13:9A-4.

11. *Id.*

12. *Id.*

13. *Id.*

14. *Id.*

15. https://www.nj.gov/dep/landuse/coastal/cp_main.html.

16. N.J.S.A. 13:9A-9(a)(1).

17. N.J.S.A. 13:9A-9(a)(2).

18. N.J.S.A. 13:9A-9(a)(3).

19. N.J.S.A. 13:9A-9(a)(4).

20. N.J.S.A. 13:9A-9(a)(5).

21. A. 1532, 215th Leg., 1st Sess. (N.J. 2012)

22. *Id.*

23. N.J.S.A. 13:9B-3

24. N.J.S.A. 13:9B-2

25. 33 U.S.C. § 403.

26. 33 U.S.C. § 1344(a)

27. 33 U.S.C. § 1311

28. See 50 N.J. Prac., Business Law Deskbook § 27:14 (2012-2013 ed.).

29. Army Corps Public Notice (Aug. 23, 1988).

30. https://www.nj.gov/dep/landuse/index.html.

31. https://www.nj.gov/dep/landuse/lawsregs.html.

32. *See* Federal Interagency Committee, *supra* note 1.

33. *Id.*

34. PORTER B. REED, *National List of Plant Species that Occur in Wetlands: 1988 National Summary*, U.S. FISH AND WILDLIFE SERVICE BIOLOGICAL REPORT (1988).

35. *Id.*

36. *Id.* at 9.

37. U.S. Dep't of Agriculture, Soil Conservation Service, 1987. *Hydric Soils of New Jersey.*

38. See Federal Interagency Committee, *supra* note 1

39. N.J.A.C. 7:7A-2.4(a).

40. N.J.A.C. 7:7A-2.4(b).

41. N.J.A.C. 7:7A-2.5(d).

42. N.J.A.C. 7:7A-2.5(e).

43. N.J.A.C. 7:7A-2.5(c).

44. *See* N.J.S.A. 13:9B-3.

45. N.J.S.A. 13:9B-9.

46. N.J.S.A. 13:9B-23; N.J.A.C. 7:7-1.4.

47. See, e.g., *In re Freshwater Wetlands Prot. Act Rules*, 180 N.J. 478 (2004).

48. N.J.A.C. 7:7A, 2018.

49. N.J.A.C. 7:7-1.4, -7.1

50. N.J.S.A. 13:9B-9.

51. *Id.*

52. ADR brings together parties to resolve disagreements without the need for legal or administrative intervention. The NJDEP's Office of Dispute Resolution utilizes two forms of ADR, facilitation and mediation. These are discussed on the NJDEP's website but both generally include an informal meeting between the individual or organization and the NJDEP program to determine if the parties can mutually resolve whatever issues are in dispute. Staff from the Office of Dispute Resolution preside over the meeting so that the action focuses on the issues and the ultimate goal, which may be to remediate a site, set a permit compliance schedule or resolve technical issues. The Office of Dispute Resolution also acts as an impartial third party to help solve the problems and explore options for resolution that may not previously have been considered.

Section 3

Flood Hazard Area

Brian Friedlich, P.E., and James Cosgrove, P.E.

EXECUTIVE SUMMARY

The Flood Hazard Area Control Act (FHACA) Rules, found at N.J.A.C. 7:13, were adopted on November 5, 2007, updated significantly on June 20, 2016, and most recently amended on April 16, 2018. The FHACA Rules replaced and significantly revised the previous regulatory approach, known as the "stream encroachment" regulations. The FHACA Rules impose more stringent standards and impact a broader range of properties in New Jersey, thereby affecting development and redevelopment projects statewide. Some of the major components of the FHACA Rules include regulating riparian zones (including 300-foot buffers on Category One waters), establishing methodologies for calculating design flood elevations, requiring 0 percent net fill for flood storage, and requiring new habitable buildings and roadways be raised 1 foot above the flood hazard area design flood elevation (FHADFE). The recent regulatory updates aimed to reduce unnecessary regulatory burden, add flexibility, provide better consistency with other regulations, and address implementation issues.

The areas regulated by the FHACA Rules include the flood hazard area (comprising the stream channel, floodway, and flood fringe) and the riparian zone. Regulated activities include: (a) the alteration of topography through excavation, grading, and/or placement of fill; (b) the clearing, cutting, and/or removal of vegetation in a riparian zone; (c) the creation of impervious surface; (d) the storage of unsecured material; (e) the construction, reconstruction, repair, alteration, enlargement, elevation, or removal of a structure; and (f) the conversion of a building into a single-family home or duplex, multi-residence building or critical building.[1] Applicants are encouraged to apply for applicability determinations, which are statements on whether a certain activity is regulated under the FHACA Rules.

Subchapters 3 and 4 of the FHACA Rules provide the methodologies that must be used to calculate the extent of the flood hazard area, floodway, and riparian zone. Applicants may apply for verifications, which are documents that contain NJDEP's approval of the regulated areas on a site. Verification is often required in order for NJDEP to issue an individual permit.

There are five main types of permits that can be used to authorize a regulated activity, including permits-by-rule, general permits-by-certification, general permits, individual permits, and emergency authorizations. Each of the permitting processes has its own application requirements, technical requirements and conditions, fee structure, and public notice requirements. Permits-by-rule are issued by NJDEP for activities that do not require review of detailed calculations and environmental impacts. Permits-by-rule do not require a formal application to be submitted to NJDEP and do not require prior NJDEP approval. General permits-by-certification is a new type of approval added in the 2016 update of the FHACA Rules that only requires an online application and generates an instant electronic permit. General permits and individual permits are issued for activities that require a more in-depth review of calculations, with individual permits requiring the longest review period and most expensive review fees. Emergency authorizations can be issued when conditions warrant immediate action to protect the environment and/or public health, safety and welfare. Hardship exceptions to individual permits may be applied for in cases where the applicant cannot meet the requirements of the FHACA Rules.

HISTORY OF RULES

The FHACA Rules implement the New Jersey Flood Hazard Area Control Act, N.J.S.A. 58:16A-50 et seq., and satisfy the State's statutory directive to

> adopt land use regulations for the flood hazard area, to control stream encroachments, to coordinate effectively the development, dissemination, and use of information on floods and flood damages that may be available, to authorize the delegation of certain administrative and enforcement functions to county governing bodies and to integrate the flood control activities of the municipal, county, State and Federal Governments.[2]

The FHACA Rules have been updated several times. The 2007 rule adoption replaced and significantly revised the previous regulatory scheme, known as the "stream encroachment" regulations. The FHACA Rules impose more stringent standards and impact a broader range of properties in New Jersey, thereby affecting development and redevelopment projects statewide. Some of the major changes include introducing new regulated riparian zones (including 300-foot buffers on Category One waters), establishing new methodologies for calculating design flood elevations, requiring 0 percent net fill requirements for flood storage, and requiring new buildings/roadways be raised one foot above the FHADFE.

The recent FHACA rule amendments, including substantial updates adopted on June 20, 2016, aimed to reduce unnecessary regulatory burden, add flexibility, provide better consistency with other regulations, and address implementation issues. Some of the key changes include removal of requirements for areas containing acid-producing soil, modifications to allowable riparian vegetation disturbance limits under individual permits, increased riparian zone mitigation options, consolidation of requirements for special water resource protection areas from the Stormwater Management Rules (N.J.A.C. 7:8) into a hybrid 300-foot riparian buffer in the FHACA Rules, expansion of allowable activities under permits-by-rule, creation of a new approval type called a general permit-by-certification, modifications to the general permit types and application process, and new individual permit standards for certain activities, such as bridges and culverts.

THE REGULATED AREAS

The FHACA Rules govern "regulated activities" in a "regulated area." The term "regulated activities" includes (a) the alteration of topography through excavation, grading, and/or placement of fill; (b) the clearing, cutting, and/or removal of vegetation in a riparian zone (as defined here); (c) the creation of impervious surface; (d) the storage of unsecured material; (e) the construction, reconstruction, repair, alteration, enlargement, elevation, or removal of a structure; and (f) the conversion of a building into a single-family home or duplex, multi-residence building, or critical building.[3]

The FHACA Rules define a regulated water as any water except man-made canals, coastal wetlands, and waters with a drainage area less than 50 acres that do not have a discernible channel, are not man-made conveyance structures, or are disconnected (such as an isolated pond or depression with no outlet). A regulated water may possess two types of regulated areas:

1. The Flood Hazard Area (including channel, floodway, and flood fringe)
2. The Riparian Zone

The Flood Hazard Area

All regulated waters with a drainage area greater than 50 acres have an associated regulated flood hazard area, defined as the area submerged by water during the flood hazard area design flood. Regulated waters with a drainage area less than 50 acres do not have a regulated flood hazard area. The flood hazard area typically contains a channel, floodway, and flood fringe. The only exceptions are the Atlantic Ocean and other nonlinear tidal features such as inlets and bays, which do not possess a floodway. The floodway is defined as the inner portion of the flood hazard area which is required to carry and discharge floodwaters resulting from the 100-year flood. The flood fringe is the outer portion of the flood hazard area outside of the floodway. The floodway is characterized by faster and deeper flows than the flood fringe. The regulated water itself is considered part of the floodway.

The flood hazard area is determined by one of six defined methodologies in the FHACA Rules:

1. **Method 1: Department Delineation Method**—Floodway and FHADFE defined based on published Department delineation maps. The floodway is the spatial extent shown on the map, while the FHADFE is the elevation shown on the flood profile adopted along with the map.
2. **Method 2: FEMA Tidal Method**—Floodway equal to the floodway shown on the FEMA mapping, or if a FEMA floodway map does not exist, then equal to the

extent of the channel (i.e., equal to the top of bank). The FHADFE is equal to the 100-year flood elevation.

3. **Method 3: FEMA Fluvial Method**—Floodway equal to the floodway shown on the FEMA mapping. FHADFE is equal to one foot above the 100-year flood elevation.

4. **Method 4: FEMA Hydraulic Method**—Floodway and FHADFE defined based on a standard step backwater analysis using FEMA flow rates. For tidal areas, the 100-year flow rate is used. For fluvial areas, 125 percent of the 100-year flow rate is used. The floodway limit is calculated using the 100-year flow rate, assuming a maximum rise of 0.2 feet in the 100-year flood elevation.

5. **Method 5: Approximation Method**—The FHADFE can be defined using the Approximation Method, as detailed in Appendix 1 of the FHACA Rules. A combination of data is required, including the contributory drainage area, the Watershed Management Area in which the site is located, and the low point elevation of downstream roadways within 1 mile from the site. The floodway cannot be determined using this method, which limits the types of regulated activities in which the Approximation Method can be used (see N.J.A.C. 7:13-3.5(f)).

6. **Method 6: Calculation Method**—Floodway and FHADFE defined based on a standard step backwater analysis and flow rates calculated with a hydrologic model. The FHADFE is based on the 100-year flow rate for tidal areas and 125 percent of the 100-year flow rate for fluvial areas. The floodway limit is calculated using the 100-year flow rate, assuming a maximum rise of 0.2 feet in the 100-year flood elevation.

The selection of a methodology is based on a number of factors, such as whether a Department delineation or FEMA map exists, whether the applicant prefers to calculate the flood hazard area or floodway limits, and what type of project is proposed.[4] Detailed requirements for selecting a methodology are listed at N.J.A.C. 7:13-3.2. The flood hazard area is never defined based on the spatial extents shown on a Department delineation map or a FEMA flood map. Instead, the FHADFE indicated on the flood profiles, along with on-site topographic data, is used to determine the flood hazard area or the area that lies below the FHADFE.

Riparian Zone

The vast majority of regulated waters also have a riparian zone, including regulated waters with a drainage area less than 50 acres. The riparian zone is defined as the area within and adjacent to regulated waters. Exceptions include the Atlantic Ocean, man-made lagoons, stormwater management basins, wastewater treatment ponds, barrier island complexes, regulated waters enclosed in pipes, and man-made open channels.

The riparian zone varies from 50 feet to 300 feet wide on both sides of the regulated water, depending on the classification as shown in Table 5.3.1.

If the regulated water has a defined bed and bank, the riparian zone is measured from the top of the bank. If there is no discernible bed and bank, the riparian zone is measured from an alternative point, such as the stream centerline (for linear features), normal water surface limit (for nonlinear, nontidal waters), or mean high water level (for nonlinear tidal waters). The riparian zone is separate from and in addition to other

Table 5.3.1   Riparian Zone

Type of Regulated Water	Riparian Zone Width (feet)
Category one waters and all upstream tributaries within the same HUC-14 watershed	300
Trout production waters and all upstream tributaries	150
Trout maintenance waters and all upstream tributaries within 1 linear mile measured along the length of the regulated water	150
Any segment of water flowing through an area with water dependent t&e species habitat and all upstream tributaries within 1 linear mile measured along the length of the regulated water	150
All other waters	50

regulated buffer areas, such as wetland transition areas (regulated under N.J.A.C. 7:7A) and special water resource protection areas (regulated under N.J.A.C. 7:8).

The "grandfathering" provisions of the FHACA Rules are listed at N.J.A.C. 7:13-2.1(c). One important grandfathering provision is that a regulated activity that was part of a project that was subject to neither the requirements of the FHACA Rules nor Coastal Area Facility Review Act Rules prior to November 5, 2007, does not require a permit if one of the following conditions applies:

1. The project received municipal approval prior to November 5, 2007, which enables construction of the regulated activity; or
2. The project did not require municipal approval, but a building/structure foundation, subsurface improvement for a roadway, or installation of all bedding materials for a utility line have been constructed prior to November 5, 2007.

APPLICABILITY DETERMINATIONS AND VERIFICATIONS

Applicants may apply for applicability determinations from NJDEP, which are statements on whether a certain activity is regulated under the FHACA Rules. While applicability determinations are optional, NJDEP encourages applicants to obtain them, especially if it is unclear whether or not an activity falls under the jurisdiction of the FHACA Rules. Applicability determination applications must contain an application form, USGS quad map, flood mapping, topographic mapping, written descriptions of the site/project, site photographs, and site plans[5]. Applications for applicability determinations do not require a fee. NJDEP will generally review applicability determinations within thirty days of receiving the application, workload permitting. Based on their review, NJDEP may respond in one of the following ways:

1. Not issue an applicability determination because NJDEP cannot determine if the FHACA Rules apply because the limits of the flood hazard area and/or the riparian zone cannot be determined without additional information. In this situation, NJDEP requires that the applicant first obtain a verification under N.J.A.C. 7:13-5.

2. Issue an applicability determination that the FHACA Rules do not apply and that no permit is required. This determination is subject to any future amendments to the Rules. If future changes to the Rules put in place stricter standards such that the activity becomes regulated, or NJDEP amends the flood hazard area or riparian zone limits such that the activity now lies within a regulated area, the applicability determination shall become void.

3. Issue an applicability determination that the FHACA Rules do apply to the proposed activity. NJDEP will generally inform the applicant whether the activity would be permitted under a permit-by-rule, general permit-by-certification, general permit or individual permit.

Applicants may also apply for verifications. Verifications are documents that contain NJDEP's approval of a FHADFE on a site, as well as the flood hazard area limit or an indication that the entire site is within the flood hazard area. Verifications may also include the riparian zone limit and/or floodway limit if applicable. Applications for verifications require a number of supporting documents, including an application report, engineering report (for Methods 4, 5, or 6 only), and site plans. They also require public notice for Methods 4, 5, and 6, and an application fee in accordance with the FHACA Rules. Verifications are typically valid for five years except when issued concurrently with an individual permit that is valid for 10 years. There are several cases where verifications are required to issue a general or individual permit.[6] If NJDEP issues a verification for a site and within five years issues a general permit or individual permit for an activity that relies on the verification, NJDEP automatically reissues the verification such that the verification and permit authorization have the same expiration date. Verifications may be transferred to new property owners at the time of sale pursuant to N.J.A.C. 7:13-22.4.

PERMITTING PROCEDURE AND REQUIREMENTS

The FHACA Rules provide for five types of permits and permitting processes:

1. Permits-by-Rule
2. General Permits-by-Certification
3. General Permits
4. Individual Permits
5. Emergency Permits

Activities may be authorized by multiple permits on a single site, provided that the individual limits and conditions of each permit are not exceeded, either individually or cumulatively. A detailed description of conditions for using more than one permit on a single site is provided at N.J.A.C. 7:13-6.4.

Permits-by-Rule

Permits-by-rule are available for a number of activities that do not require a detailed review of engineering calculations or environmental impacts. A total of sixty-three permits-by-rule are listed at N.J.A.C 7:13-7. Permits-by-rule do not require prior notification. Each of the sixty-three permits-by-rule contains detailed requirements that must be satisfied in order to be eligible. In addition, the general provisions at N.J.A.C. 7:13-6 must be met for all permits-by-rule.

General Permits-by-Certification

General permits-by-certification are a new type of approval included in the amendments to the FHACA Rules that were adopted on June 20, 2016. There are sixteen general permits-by-certification listed at N.J.A.C. 7:13-8, along with detailed requirements that must be satisfied in order to be eligible. In addition, the general provisions at N.J.A.C. 7:13-6 must be met for all general permits-by-certification. Applications for general permits-by-certification are submitted online, and require project information, contact information, and a certification that the requirements and conditions of the permit have been satisfied. While there is no fee for general permits-by-certification 4 and 5, there is a $1,000 fee for all other general permits-by-certification. Once the application is completed, the permit authorization is instantly made available electronically through NJDEP's online permitting system (www.nj.gov.dep/online). General permits-by-certification are valid for five years and can be extended one time for five years.

General Permits

A total of fourteen general permits are listed under Subchapter 9 of the FHACA Rules. General permits require less review time and a reduced review fee as compared to individual permits. Detailed requirements for each of the general permits are listed at N.J.A.C. 7:13-9.1 through 9.14, while general provisions for all general permits are listed at N.J.A.C. 7:13-6. Applications for general permits must contain an application report, proof of public notice, site plans, project location, an application fee, and documentation, calculations, and analyses demonstrating compliance with all standards and provisions in the particular general permit. NJDEP publishes checklists for all general permit applications online.

A general permit authorization is generally valid for five years and may be extended one time for five years as per N.J.A.C. 7:13-22.3; however, a new general permit to replace an expired one may be requested by submitting a new application. A general permit can also be transferred with the sale of a property. There is no review fee for general permits 1, 4, and 5, and a review fee of $1,000 for all other general permits.

Individual Permits

Applications are filed under the individual permitting process when the proposed activities do not fall under the provisions for the permits-by-rule, general permits-by-certification or general permits. Individual permits typically involve more detailed engineering calculations and consideration of environmental impacts. Individual permit applications require more detailed information, including a project checklist, application report, engineering report, environmental report, project drawings, proof of public notice and an application fee. Application fees for individual permits are based on the fee schedule in Subchapter 20 of the FHACA Rules.

Individual permits are typically valid for five years, with the exception of linear activities or projects that are greater than 10 miles in length, flood control projects, or quarry or mining operations, which are valid for 10 years. The individual permit general conditions are listed at N.J.A.C. 7:13-22.2. Subchapter 11 of the FHACA Rules breaks down the individual permit requirements based on regulated area (i.e., channel, riparian zone, floodway, and flood fringe).

Requirements for Regulated Activities in a Channel

The FHACA Rules discourage regulated activities in a channel. NJDEP will only issue an individual permit for work in a channel if the requirements at N.J.A.C. 7:13-11.1(b) are satisfied.[7]

Requirements for Regulated Activities in a Riparian Zone

The FHACA Rules regulate the amount of riparian zone vegetation that can be disturbed. Riparian zone vegetation includes the area within the limit of disturbance, the area under the tree canopy of trees to be disturbed, and the area of all other vegetation to be temporarily or permanently disturbed. Table 11.2 in the FHACA Rules sets forth the maximum allowable disturbance to riparian zone vegetation for various activities, such as roadways, utility lines, and private residences. The amount of allowable disturbance depends on the type of activity and the width of the riparian zone, with larger amounts of disturbance allowable for wider riparian zones. Each regulated activity has its own specific requirements for riparian zone disturbance, listed at N.J.A.C. 7:13-11.2(g) through (y). It should be noted that section (y) is provided for "all other regulated activities" not listed at sections (g) through (x), and that mitigation is required for some activities in accordance with N.J.A.C. 7:13-13.4. Riparian zone mitigation can be accomplished through creation, restoration, enhancement, preservation and/or banking. Detailed requirements and standards for providing riparian zone mitigation are included at N.J.A.C. 7:13-13. Mitigation plans must be submitted to NJDEP for review and approval. Furthermore, there are requirements for monitoring, reporting, and preservation of mitigation areas listed at N.J.A.C. 7:13-13.12 and N.J.A.C. 7:13-13.13.

Requirements for Regulated Activities in a Floodway

For regulated activity in a floodway, individual permits are not available for activities involving the placement of aboveground structures or fill in a floodway, activities that raise the ground elevation in a floodway, or activities that would obstruct the passage of floodwaters in a floodway. However, notwithstanding these prohibitions, NJDEP will issue individual permits for certain regulated activities in a floodway, including but not limited to the reconstruction of or addition to a lawfully existing building, the construction of a water control or stormwater outfall structure, and the placement of fill in the floodway under certain circumstances. A complete list of allowable activities and the requirements for these regulated activities in a floodway are listed at N.J.A.C. 7:13-11.3(c).

Requirements for Regulated Activities in a Flood Fringe

For regulated activity in a flood fringe, NJDEP's requirements focus primarily on the volume of material that may be placed aboveground as well as other activities that would reduce flood storage volume on a site. For example, if construction activities cut off a section of the site from the floodplain, the storage volume over that section would no longer be effective flood storage and would be considered displaced. Alternatively, if an open garage were constructed to allow floodwaters to easily flow in and out of the building, it would not be considered to displace flood storage volume. For most sites, NJDEP will only issue an individual permit if the regulated activity will displace no more than 20 percent of the effective flood storage volume on-site, and all flood storage displacement on-site is compensated offsite. The flood storage volume is calculated by both the volume between the FHADFE and the ten-year flood elevation, and the volume between the ten-year flood elevation and the ground. The net fill requirements must be satisfied for both of these sections of flood storage. There are several activities that are not subject to the requirements for flood storage volume limits and are listed at N.J.A.C. 7:13-11.4(d). Some examples of these activities are fill material in a tidal floodplain, reconstruction of a public railroad or roadway, and construction of one private residence that is not part of a larger subdivision. N.J.A.C. 7:13-11.4 provides additional details and requirements regarding methods for calculating flood storage volume and creating flood storage volume on-site and off-site.

N.J.A.C. 7:13-11.5 and 11.6 provide special requirements for regulated activities within or along waters with fishery resources and within habitat for threatened and endangered species.

Individual Permit Requirements for Specific Regulated Activities

Subchapter 12 of the FHACA Rules sets forth design and construction standards that apply to various regulated activities, including stormwater management; excavation, fill, or grading activities; construction of a structure, building, railroad, roadway, or parking area; construction of a bridge, culvert, utility line, stormwater outfall structure, low dam, dam, flood control project, retaining wall, or bulkhead; bank stabilization; channel restoration; removal of sediment and debris; storage of unsecured material; investigation, cleanup, or removal of hazardous substances; placement, storage, or processing of hazardous substances, solid waste or recyclable materials; solid waste landfill closure; and removal of existing fill or an existing structure. For all regulated activities, NJDEP will issue an individual permit only if it determines that the activity is not likely to cause significant and adverse effects on water quality or supply, aquatic biota, flooding, drainage, channel stability, threatened and endangered species, navigation, energy production, and fishery resources.

Hardship Exceptions for Individual Permits

Notwithstanding the strict guidelines for individual permits, NJDEP may issue waivers from the requirements of the FHACA Rules by granting a hardship exception.[8] NJDEP considers hardship exception applications if there is no feasible or prudent alternative to the proposed project, if the costs to comply with the regulations are unreasonably high, or if the applicant and NJDEP agree to alternative requirements that provide equal or better protection to public health, safety, and welfare of the environment. In order for NJDEP to grant a hardship exception, the applicant must demonstrate that compliance with the FHACA Rules will result in an exceptional and/or undue hardship, that the proposed activities will not adversely affect the use of contiguous or nearby property, and that the proposed activities will not pose a threat to the environment or public health, safety, and welfare. NJDEP also considers whether the hardship claimed by the applicant is not due to the applicant's own actions.

Application Process for Verification, General Permits, and Individual Permits

NJDEP follows a similar process for review of verifications, general permits and individual permits. Within twenty days of receipt of an application, NJDEP is required to determine whether an application is administratively complete. If NJDEP determines that it is not complete and that additional information is required, the applicant then typically has ninety days to submit the additional material. NJDEP then has an additional fifteen days to deem the application administratively complete. Within ninety days of deeming an application administratively complete, NJDEP must act in one of the following two ways:

1. Determine that the application meets the requirements of the Rules and approve the application in writing.
2. Determine that the application does not meet the requirements of the Rules and deny the application in writing.

The ninety-day deadline for NJDEP's action may be extended for thirty calendar days by mutual agreement between NJDEP and the applicant.

Emergency Authorizations

NJDEP has the ability to issue emergency authorizations when a threat to life, a severe loss in property, or environmental degradation exists or is imminent, and the threat of severe loss or degradation can only be prevented through a regulated activity. The applicant must demonstrate extraordinary risk if the emergency permit is not issued and that the damage would likely occur prior to a flood hazard area individual or general permit authorization being issued. The applicant must submit the information listed at N.J.A.C. 7:13-16.2(a)[9] by telephone, and in addition by fax, email, or letter, if possible.

In general, regulated activities approved under an emergency authorization must commence within thirty calendar days of NJDEP's verbal approval (unless NJDEP establishes a different timeline). If they do not commence in that time period, the emergency permit is void. Once commenced, the regulated activities typically must be completed within sixty calendar days of NJDEP's verbal approval. If they are not completed, the activities must cease until an individual permit, general permit authorization or another emergency permit is issued. The applicant must still apply for the appropriate general permit or individual permit authorization within ninety days of NJDEP's verbal approval of the emergency permit. The application should include a demonstration that the regulated activities comply with the FHACA Rules and "as-built" drawings, as applicable. NJDEP can extend the thirty-, sixty-, and ninety-day timeframes for emergency permits if the applicant demonstrates that the requirements cannot feasibly be satisfied, or the activities cannot feasibly be completed in that time. While the applicant must comply with the FHACA Rules to the fullest extent practicable, NJDEP may require additional modification, restoration and/or stabilization measures as necessary.

NOTES

1. N.J.A.C. 7:13-2.4.
2. N.J.S.A. 58:16A-50b.
3. N.J.A.C. 7:13-2.4.
4. See Appendix 2 of the FHACA Rules for a list of Department delineated waters.
5. N.J.A.C. 7:13-2.5.
6. N.J.A.C. 7:13-5.5.
7. The following is a sample of some of the requirements: The basic purpose of the project cannot be accomplished without work in the channel. Disturbance to the channel is eliminated where possible, and otherwise minimized by relocating the project or reducing the size/scope of the project. Aquatic habitat is preserved where possible, and otherwise restored/enhanced where disturbance is required. Stabilization measures, such as rip-rap or scour holes, are only used where necessary and cannot be avoided through alternative designs. Rip-rap must be embedded in the channel in such a way as to not impede low-flow aquatic passage and withstand velocities associated with bank-full flows. See N.J.A.C. 7:13-11.1 for full list of requirements.
8. N.J.A.C. 7:13-15.1.
9. That is, property location, nature and cause of emergency, nature and extent of proposed regulated activities, contact information of owner, proposed dates of regulated activities, and so on.

Section 4

Riparian Lands

Daniel E. Horgan, Esq.

New Jersey's riparian lands are managed under provisions of the N. J. Constitution and statutes.[1] The agency with exclusive jurisdiction is the Tidelands Resource Council (TRC), twelve citizens appointed by the governor.[2] The TRC's administrative functions are performed by the Bureau of Tidelands within the N.J. Dept. of Environmental Protection (Tidelands). The intent of this section is to provide practitioners with basic tools to identify riparian issues in New Jersey, advise clients, and resolve riparian claims successfully. As with any other real property, riparian lands are also subject to local, regional, state, and federal regulations, everything from local zoning to Federal Clean Water Act and NJDEP environmental limitations and permit requirements. These must not be overlooked; a riparian conveyance from the State gives only a property interest. A property owner must still pay taxes, obtain permits, and comply with all other rules. Obtaining a grant, lease, or license for riparian property may be a necessary prerequisite to applying for or receiving permits to use the riparian property interest. Other sections of this volume deal with those regulatory issues; this section is fundamentally about how to acquire real property interests from the State, whether those interests are in "land under water" or developed upland sites that have been high and dry for hundreds of years. A surprising number of properties may still have a state riparian claim attached to them.

IDENTIFYING RIPARIAN CLAIMS

Riparian lands are defined as those lands now or formerly flowed by the tide. Since the natural location of tidal shorelines is in a constant state of change, erosion and accretion will occur unless some man-made structure like a bulkhead fixes the location of the high tide. When upland is lost by tidal erosion, the State has a new claim to the land newly washed by the tide. Conversely, the State's claim is lost through accretion, the gradual build-up of a shore that pushes the high tide line farther out. But the mere presence or absence of tidal water is not the only factor considered. The first exception to erosion or accretion is avulsion, the unnatural change in a shoreline, usually due to a storm or some other sudden force.[3] For example, a hurricane could wash away some (or all) of an upland owner's property, but that would not give the State riparian ownership. Nor would a storm extend an owner's property into a former riparian area. Reliance on any of these factors can be a risky business because they are very fact sensitive. The TRC and the deputy attorney general advising it in its role as a trustee of the State's riparian lands must be convinced before they will agree to "give up" a claim. For example, the Tidelands website[4] discussing Statements of No Interest (SNI), which have the effect of relinquishing a potential claim, advises that a SNI will "only be issued when an applicant can prove beyond all doubt that the State of New Jersey has no Tidelands claim."

These tide-related concepts are difficult to resolve and have led to disputes and uncertainty, culminating in *O'Neill v. State Highway Department*, which set forth the fundamental principles of riparian law and called for a better system of identifying the areas claimed by the State.[5] *O'Neill* also made it clear that a landowner faced with a claim had a right to litigate to quiet title and discussed the burdens of proof. Not long afterward, the legislature required the TRC to investigate and map its claims and publish the maps.[6] A 1981 amendment to the State Constitution created a statute of repose of sorts for lands which had not been tide flowed for forty years prior and which were claimed as state riparian lands on the claim maps. Today, the State's riparian claims are shown on adopted and filed claim maps which offer a fixed and reliable starting point in determining whether a particular property is subject to a claim. But, except in clear cases, it is only a starting point.

RIPARIAN APPLICATIONS

The claim maps only assert claims by showing areas where the State believes it has an interest, placing the burden of showing that there is no claim on the landowner. Like much of the State's geophysical information and data, the map's claim lines are available to surveyors in digital format and can be easily plotted on a survey. If the property under consideration is on the landward side of the claim line, the State has no claim. Even if the property is on the water side of the claim line(s) it does not necessarily mean that the State has a valid claim. At this point, unless there is a former riparian grant unambiguously shown to convey the full riparian rights to the upland owner or someone in the owner's chain of title, a cloud on title exists. Title insurance policies will almost certainly include a riparian exception in the absence of a prior grant and, depending on the extent of the claim, financing may be difficult or impossible. The owner may find that improvements within claimed areas are subject to state claims for use and occupancy, thereby making it necessary to address the claim with the Bureau of Tidelands.

Applications for riparian grants, SNI, or major riparian leases[7] generally move slowly, but there are some steps one can take to alleviate the delays, such as applying for revocable riparian licenses while a grant is being considered. However, this process is also time consuming and uncertain. The State has virtually absolute discretion in some riparian matters and, while you may be able to question and challenge the State's claim to ownership, there is no review of discretionary acts. This means that the TRC sets the price to be paid for grants, leases, and licenses and can refuse to approve virtually any application. The NJDEP commissioner can refuse to approve any action by the TRC, and the governor may delay consideration and ultimately refuse to sign a riparian grant.[8]

Against this backdrop, it is important to keep in mind that challenging a riparian claim through a quite title action in chancery court can be a poor alternative because the burden of proof will fall on the landowner. An unsuccessful challenge will put the applicant in the unenviable position of seeking a grant but without the possibility of arguing for a discount in price which may have been possible due to "litigation risk." For this reason it is not advisable to initiate quite title proceedings. The result of an unsuccessful challenge could be an expensive and restrictive grant on top of expensive litigation. In the alternative, the state might keep the riparian interest and not sell it at all.

PREPARING TO APPLY FOR A GRANT
SNI, LEASE, OR LICENSE

The first step is to review the State's "grant maps" to find any past grants, leases, or licenses that the State has located on its mapping.[9] The most up-to-date versions of these are found at the Bureau of Tidelands in Trenton and should show past riparian conveyances within the claim areas shown on the claims maps. Things to look for on the grant maps include the following.

Riparian Grants

Past grants may have covered some or all of the subject property, recited adjoining grants not plotted on the maps, or referred to other things such as past riparian titles and legislative grants or enactments. Get a copy of any such grant and read it carefully to determine if it vested title in a prior upland owner and whether it has limitations, preconditions to vesting title or reverter clauses. Some old grants are no longer valid for a variety of reasons. A title company can provide guidance on most of these issues. If the grant is still good and valid, have it plotted on a current survey to insure that it covers the property without exception. Exceptions can include gaps (gores) between old grants and gaps between the State's current claim line and the inland tidal line of conveyance on the grant. Also, the grant may not have extended outward as far as the present outward limit of the current owner's property. Any shortfall in these areas will have to be cured by a new riparian instrument. Despite current policies against conveyances of lands that are currently tide flowed, exceptions are sometimes made where a grant would fill in small gaps and allow the applicant to enjoy the full use of past grants, but extensions simply to add areas under water are highly unlikely.

Leases

Leases should be scrutinized in the same manner as grants, described earlier but with an additional look at the economic terms and end of lease provisions. Some old leases allowed for the lease to be converted to a grant, with or without specifying the time to do so or the economic consideration to be paid. Terms in an old lease which are still viable may be enforceable against the State by the current owner, but this is a matter of interpretation of the lease contract, and the TRC is averse to accepting economic terms set in the past. While such terms are an unusual find, it is worth looking for, particularly in older leases in port and river areas in prior industrial areas.

Other Information on Grant Maps

Grant maps may contain clues to other useful inquiries but may not contain everything. For example, the information plotted on a grant map may (or may not) tell the whole story about old legislative grants to railroads or canal companies. Prior to the current riparian legislation it was common for the legislature to issue a grant to a railroad or canal company allowing the grantee to gain title to tide flowed lands provided it met certain conditions. Those conditions would include filling and improving lands for their respective businesses and (sometimes) filing proofs of such filling. The grant maps may show the areas where the grantee could have acquired title, but that does not mean that title was perfected by performance and/or recording. Also relevant to further inquiries as to the validity of the State's mapping are the date put on the inland claim line, which may or may not agree with the information used to produce the claim maps.

Claim File

Another source of useful information can be the "claim file" which may contain the notes, maps, and resources used to produce the maps. Some sources of information are inherently more reliable than others in establishing the location of historical high water and prior filling. For example, the location of a shoreline on a historic Sandborn© fire insurance map[10] showing existing structures on an established, filled waterfront may be a more reliable map of the actual shoreline than a navigation chart drawn for purposes of locating a channel in a river or inlet. But most important may be what *is not* in a claim file. Historical research on a particular piece of property may yield maps, overlooked by the State, which can be shown to be more accurate than those in the grant file and more favorable to the applicant. In such a case, if the new map defeats a claim, particularly a significantly valuable one, the applicant can expect a delay while the TRC staff exhaustively reviews the matter and looks everywhere possible to support its claim with additional material.

HISTORICAL, LEGAL, AND OTHER RESEARCH

In the author's experience, sound research with full documentation can win a SNI, even where the claim value is high. To be taken seriously in a debate on the validity of a riparian claim, an applicant needs to know the facts in his or her favor and present them with well-researched documentation. It is also necessary to know the terms, conditions, and history of any prior grant, legislative grant, or litigated decision affecting the specific area (not only the specific property) in question. Some of this, as discussed earlier, is available through research at Bureau of Tidelands' offices, and going there is a good way to impress the TRC staff that your applicant is serious. The Tidelands pages of the NJDEP website contain information on current forms and issues, from jet-skis, to utilities, to aquaculture, and should be read carefully. Other sources include historical maps, aerial photos, and similar documents that can be found online, at local libraries, historical societies, government archives, newspapers, and other sources. Anything of value that can be authenticated should be used. The author once used an aerial photo of an industrial section of the Passaic River in Harrison, New Jersey, to justify a claim of filling under the mid-nineteenth-century Wharf Acts.[11] The picture was taken over forty years before the invention of the airplane by an enterprising civil war era photographer from a hot air balloon. It was better evidence than anything the State had in its files and accomplished its purpose.

VALUING RIPARIAN CLAIMS

The TRC is bound to receive full value for what it gives and that starts with the State's assessment of that value. Applicants are asked to submit appraisals for review, but there is little bargaining on the price which is usually established as a unit value based on the owner's upland value. An exception arises when the claim can be brought into question through credible scrutiny based upon factual knowledge and good research. This should always be done carefully and put into a well-supported written submission. Remember, as the Tidelands website says, you have to prove your point "beyond all doubt." It can be done.

Payments for leases are determined by fair market value, usually with escalations, on a fixed schedule. Renewals will be at market value as determined by the State through review of appraisals at the time of renewal. If the riparian interest is to be used for a specific, limited purpose, it may be possible to control the cost by proposing and agreeing to a use limitation in the grant or lease.

RIPARIAN GRANT APPROVAL

Once the claim area and price have been set, the TRC should be willing to give a "sweep grant" covering all State claims to the property, avoiding the chance that some small area or sliver of land was overlooked. Once the TRC and DEP commissioner have approved the grant and it is awaiting the governor's signature, the TRC is usually willing to issue an interim, revocable license to use the property. Licenses can be granted by the TRC without the governor's approval; however, there is no guarantee that the grant will ultimately issue. Title companies may insure title on conditions, such as the posting of the cost of the grant and an opinion letter as to the likelihood of the grant issuing, something that should happen in the absence of potentially controversial issues.

NOTES

1. N.J.S.A. Const. Art. 8§V, ¶1; N.J.S.A. 13:1B-13 through 13:1B-13.14. N.J.S.A. 13:1B-13-13 dedicates revenues derived from riparian transactions to the Fund for the Support of Free Public Schools. See N.J.S.A. Const. Art. 8,§IV, ¶2 establishing the school fund.

2. N.J.S.A. 13:1B-10. Statutes and cases are not extensively cited in this Section, both for reasons of economy and because a practitioner undertaking a riparian application should first review the relatively short body of statutory and case law as suggested later in this Section.

3. See *Borough of Wildwood Crest v. Masciarella, et al.*, 51 N.J. 352 (1968).

4. See Tidelands, available at http://www.nj.gov/dep/landuse/tl_main.html [*emphasis added*].

5. 50 N.J. 307 (1967).

6. N.J.S.A. 13:1B-13.2 *et seq.*

7. Statutory requirements for decisions within specific time frames to the contrary notwithstanding. See, e.g., N.J.S.A. 13:1B-13.7 and 13.8. Forced to a quick decision, the TRC would likely say "NO." One of the most important things to remember is that you are dealing with the sovereign that makes the laws, so the playing field is not always level. Your client may be a land baron, but they are not the king.

8. This is not to say that the TRC or its staff act arbitrarily or unreasonably; to the contrary, they are committed to securing the best financial result for the State's School Fund to which the money earned is dedicated. They act as property managers and stewards of the State's interest, and generally leave considerations of environmental policy to the agencies charged with making those judgments.

9. The technically oriented can view claim maps online, but beware the disclaimers, and be sure that any line relied upon is accurately plotted with respect to the applicant's property. See Tidelands GIS, available at http://www.state.nj.us/dep/gis/tidelandsshp.html.

10. See Sanborn, available at http://www.sanborn.com/ as just one example of such sources that may be found online.

11. The Wharf Acts allowed for acquisition of riparian rights by upland owners if the owner constructed improvements such as solid fill piers, and bulkheads. When they were repealed, circa 1871, they grandfathered the rights to those owners who had complied with their terms prior to repeal. Some areas of the state covered by such acts had significant filling in the nineteenth century, mostly for industrial purposes and those riparian titles are still good against state claims. An examination of this subject in any detail is beyond the scope of this section.

Section 5

Highlands

William J. Beneduce, Esq., Kim Ball Kaiser, Esq., and Christine A. LaRocca, Esq.

The Highlands Region is a 3.5 million-acre, four-state physiographic area that extends from northwestern Connecticut, across the lower Hudson River Valley in New York and northern New Jersey, into east-central Pennsylvania.[1] The New Jersey Highlands is an area of 859,358 acres in the northern portion of the state which serves as a vital source of drinking water for over half of New Jersey residents. State and federal agencies have recognized the value of the Highlands Region and have studied it for over 100 years, resulting in a number of reports including the 1907 Potable Water Commission Report and the U.S. Forest Service bistate study conducted in 1992 and updated in 2002. Building upon these efforts, New Jersey established the New Jersey Highlands Task Force in 2003 for the purpose of reviewing detailed information on resources in the Highlands and the tools that could be utilized to achieve appropriate land acquisition, regional planning, and regulatory authority to protect these vital resources.

THE HIGHLANDS WATER PROTECTION AND PLANNING ACT

As a result of the Highlands Task Force recommendations, the New Jersey Legislature enacted the Highlands Water Protection and Planning Act (Act) on August 10, 2004.[2] The Act finds that "the protection of the New Jersey Highlands, because of its vital link to the future of the State's drinking water supplies and other key natural resources, is an issue of State level importance that cannot be left to uncoordinated land use decisions" of eighty-eight municipalities and seven counties (Bergen, Hunterdon, Morris, Passaic, Somerset, Sussex, and Warren) in the region.[3]

The Highlands Act divides the Highlands Region into the Preservation Area and the Planning Area and delineates the boundary of the Preservation Area finding that "because of the imminent peril that the ongoing rush of development poses for the New Jersey Highlands, immediate, interim standards should be imposed on the date of enactment in the Preservation Area."[4] The Preservation Area is approximately 415,000 acres. Fifty-two municipalities have land in the Preservation Area; five municipalities are located entirely in the Preservation Area, while forty-seven municipalities have lands in both the Preservation and Planning Areas.

The Preservation Area was subject to immediate environmental standards in the Highlands Act.[5] These standards were later codified by the New Jersey Department of Environmental Protection (NJDEP) as the Preservation Area rules.[6] These rules govern development activity in the Preservation Area. The standards in the rules include prohibition on development within 300 feet of any Highlands open water; measures to ensure that existing water quality be maintained, restored, or enhanced; regulation of water diversions of more than 50,000 gallons per day; a septic system density standard to prevent degradation of water quality; a zero net fill requirement for flood hazard area; anti-degradation provisions for surface water quality and storm water regulations; a prohibition on more than 3 percent impervious surface of an existing lot; and a prohibition on development that disturbs upland forested areas to protect forest resources, water quality and quantity, and critical habitat.[7]

Eighty-three municipalities have land located in the Planning Area, which is approximately 445,000 acres. Thirty-six municipalities are situated entirely in the Planning Area. Both the Preservation and Planning Areas have regional goals, many of which apply to both areas, including protecting, restoring, and enhancing the quality and quantity of surface and groundwater; promoting water conservation; preserving farmland; and promoting brownfields remediation and redevelopment.[8]

THE ROLE OF THE NEW JERSEY DEPARTMENT OF ENVIRONMENTAL PROTECTION

No person shall undertake a "major Highlands development"[9] proposed in the Preservation Area without first obtaining approval from NJDEP in accordance with the NJDEP Preservation Area rules.[10] However, the Highlands Act also creates seventeen exemptions for certain projects and activities that are excepted from the provisions of the Highlands Act, the Highlands Regional Master Plan, the NJDEP Preservation Area rules, and conforming local ordinances.[11] NJDEP issues a Highlands Applicability Determination to decide if a project is a major Highlands development or whether it qualifies for one of the exemptions under the Highlands Act. The definition of major Highlands development does not include agricultural or horticultural use or development[12] in the Preservation Area. However, the NJ Department of Agriculture's "Agricultural Development in the Highlands" rules govern those activities rather than the NJDEP.[13]

The NJDEP Preservation Area rules establish a two-step permitting process for development in the Preservation Area. First, a Highlands Resource Area Determination is required that identifies the location of any Highlands Resources. Then, a Highlands Preservation Area Approval (HPAA) permit must be obtained where the stringent statutory environmental standards of the Highlands Act as well as regulatory standards, such as the septic system density requirements, are applicable.

When a proposed project is not exempt, the permitting system may allow relief from the requirement to obtain an HPAA. Three HPAA with waivers are available:

a waiver to protect public health and safety; a waiver to permit redevelopment of NJDEP brownfield sites and areas with at least 70 percent impervious surface (Highlands Redevelopment Areas are designated by the Highlands Council); and a waiver to avoid the taking of property without just compensation. All waiver determinations are made by NJDEP.[14]

THE HIGHLANDS WATER PROTECTION AND PLANNING COUNCIL

The Highlands Act also created the Highlands Water Protection and Planning Council (Highlands Council) comprised of fifteen members, charged with preparing a Highlands Regional Master Plan (RMP). The RMP was approved by the Council on July 17, 2008, and became effective September 8, 2008. Its primary goal is to "to protect and enhance the significant values of the resources" of the entire Highlands Region.[15] The Highlands Act identifies specific components that are required in the RMP, including a resource assessment to determine the amount and type of human development and activity that the Highlands ecosystem can sustain while maintaining overall ecological values; a smart growth component; a transfer of development rights program; a transportation component; a financial component; a local participation component; and a coordination and consistency component.[16] Additionally, as elements of the RMP, the Highlands Council also prepared a Land Use Capability Map and comprehensive policies for planning and development based on the stringent environmental standards adopted by NJDEP and the RMP resource assessment; identified zones in the Preservation Area which are to be permanently preserved in order to protect water and other sensitive resources; developed minimum standards governing master planning; and established development regulations for municipal and county lands in the Preservation Area.[17]

HIGHLANDS RMP CONFORMANCE PROCESS

Conformance with the RMP (Plan Conformance) is mandatory in the Preservation Area and voluntary in the Planning Area. Plan Conformance includes the revision of local master plans and land-use and development regulations necessary to conform to the RMP.[18] It also requires a municipality to prepare and adopt a municipal build-out analysis, Housing Element and Fair Share Plan, Highlands Environmental Resource Inventory, Highlands Municipal Master Plan Element, and Highlands Land Use Ordinance and implementation schedule. Importantly, the Plan Conformance process incorporates the goals, policies, and objectives of the RMP into local planning and brings about the implementation of the RMP.

Plan Conformance Guidelines were adopted along with the RMP in 2008. The guidelines have since undergone revision to simplify the process. Additionally, the Highlands Council has designated a staff liaison for each municipality to assist with Plan Conformance activities and generally provide assistance on all Highlands-related matters.

TRANSFER OF DEVELOPMENT RIGHTS PROGRAM

The Highlands Act also required the Highlands Council to develop a Transfer of Development Rights (TDR) program for the Highlands Region.[19] The Highlands Council adopted the TDR program as part of the RMP and established the Highlands Development Credit (HDC) Bank in June 2008 to effectuate the TDR program.

The Highlands TDR program identifies sending zones in the Preservation Area, where development is restricted, and allocates TDR credits called HDCs to sending zone property owners to provide landowner equity in those areas. HDCs may be sold to developers for use in building in areas identified as voluntary receiving zones, which have the infrastructure and land use capacity to support additional growth. Any municipality in the Planning Area whose municipal master plan and development regulations have conformed with the RMP can petition the Highlands Council to create a voluntary receiving zone.[20] If a receiving zone provides for a minimum residential density of five dwelling units per acre, then the municipality is eligible for an enhanced planning grant from the council of up to $250,000; is eligible for a grant to reimburse the reasonable costs of amending the municipal development regulations to incorporate the receiving zone; is authorized to impose up to $15,000 per unit impact fee for new development within the receiving zone; is accorded priority status in the Highlands Region for any state capital or infrastructure programs; and could obtain the ability to control the design of the receiving area.[21] The HDC Bank has a nine-member board of directors and works in conjunction with the Highlands Council to implement the Highlands TDR program.[22]

HIGHLANDS OPEN SPACE PARTNERSHIP FUNDING AND DEVELOPMENT CREDIT PURCHASE PROGRAMS

The Highlands Council currently administers two preservation programs authorized under N.J.A.C. 7:70, the Highlands Open Space Partnership Funding Program (OSP), and the Highlands Development Credit Purchase Program (HDCPP).

The Highlands Open Space Partnership Funding Program

The OSP is a matching grant program that provides up to 50 percent of land acquisition funds to eligible funding partners for the preservation of land throughout the Preservation and Planning Areas of the Highlands Region.[23] Eligible partners include (1) the State of New Jersey, (2) any of the seven counties located in the Highlands Region, (3) any of the eighty-eight municipalities located in the Highlands Region, and (4) charitable conservancies.[24] Funding can be awarded for fee simple acquisition of land for conservation and/or passive recreation purposes or for the purchase of conservation easements.[25]

Under N.J.A.C. 7:70-3.1.c, the following projects, properties, and expenses are not eligible for OSP funding:

• Properties to be held in fee simple title by the Highlands Council;
• Properties which require condemnation;

- Properties containing significant environmental contamination, including, but not limited to, former landfill sites, sites having a history of operating as a facility with a substantial likelihood for on-site contamination, and sites listed on the NJDEP's Known Contaminated Sites List;
- Properties already preserved or acquired during the application process;
- Administrative or operational costs of the applicant or current or former owners;
- Construction or development projects, including capital improvements, recreation improvements, infrastructure projects, and the restoration, rehabilitation, or reconstruction of any structure (however, this shall not preclude the purchase of the eligible underlying lands);
- Maintenance, care, custodial, or policing expenditures, including, but not limited to, grounds maintenance, restoration, or reconstruction;
- Ceremonial or publicity expenses;
- Interest, bonding expenses, or other financing costs;
- Fundraising or lobbying expenses; and
- Interpretive activities, such as displays or signs.

Following the review of OSP applications by Highlands Council staff for administrative completeness, the applications are reviewed by the Highlands Council's Landowner Equity and Land Preservation (LELP) Committee.[26] The LELP Committee prepares a final recommendation for the Highlands Council, which may then adopt a resolution authorizing funding for specific OSP applications. From the date of approval of the application,[27] the applicant will have twelve months (with up to two six-month extensions) to close on the acquisition, pending review and approval of final documents by Highlands Council staff.[28] Throughout the OSP process, the burden remains on the funding partner to secure additional funding and work with the landowner to close the transaction.

HDC Purchase Program

The HDCPP authorizes the Highlands Development Credit Bank Board to purchase development rights from private landowners in the Highlands Region. The HDCPP process includes three steps:

1. *HDC Allocation.* The Allocation is effectively an appraisal of HDCs. Highlands Council staff determines how many HDCs a property is entitled to, based on its development potential prior to the enactment of the Highlands Act. This review includes local zoning considerations, environmental constraints, location, and zoning factors. An HDC Allocation is tied to the land, not to a property owner. It can be obtained at any time at no cost.
2. *HDC Certification.* A property owner can obtain an HDC certificate that establishes the landowner's rights to the HDCs through the certification process. The Highlands Council will issue a certificate for the HDCs to the landowner in exchange for recording a conservation deed of easement restricting the land from future development of the property. Certain activities (e.g., certain exemptions and agriculture) are permitted under the conservation easement. The landowner

may still retain the underlying fee and other property rights or may sell those rights to another owner but still retain ownership of the HDC certificate.
3. *HDC Purchase*. The HDC Bank may purchase HDCs from landowners through the HDCPP. The HDC Bank purchases HDCs at a rate of $16,000 per credit. Following the review of HDC purchase applications by Highlands Council staff for administrative completeness, the applications are reviewed by the Highlands Council's LELP Committee.[29] The LELP Committee prepares a final recommendation for the Highlands Council, which may then adopt a resolution authorizing funding for specific HDC purchase applications. The transaction is completed when the owner of the HDC certificate signs it over to the HDC Bank in exchange for the purchase price of the HDCs.[30]

STRONG PRESUMPTION OF VALIDITY AND BURDEN OF PROOF

The Highlands Act provides that the municipal master plan and development regulations of any municipality, and any county located in the Highlands Region, which has been approved by the Highlands Council to be in conformance with the RMP, shall be entitled to a strong presumption of validity. In any cause of action contesting an act or decision of the local government unit taken or made under authority granted pursuant to the Municipal Land Use Law,[31] the State Uniform Construction Code Act,[32] or the Highlands Act, the court is required to give extraordinary deference to the local government unit. Additionally, the plaintiff shall have the burden of proof to demonstrate by clear and convincing evidence that the act or decision of any such local government unit was arbitrary, capricious, or unreasonable or a patent abuse of discretion.[33]

ENFORCEMENT

The Highlands Act provides the NJDEP with an array of enforcement options for violations of the Act, including the following: (1) issue an order requiring compliance or restoration of the area in violation, (2) bring a civil action, (3) levy a civil administrative penalty up to $25,000 per day, and (4) bring an action for a civil penalty up to $10,000 per day, or petition the State attorney general to file a criminal action.[34] The person alleged to have been in violation is granted notice of a right to a hearing to contest the allegations set forth in the order. In addition, a notice of violation shall be recorded on the deed of the property wherein the violation occurred, on order of the NJDEP, by the clerk or register of deeds and mortgages of the county wherein the property is located and with the clerk of the Superior Court and shall remain attached thereto until such time as the violation has been remedied and the NJDEP orders the notice of violation removed.[35] The Highlands Act gives NJDEP the authority to enter any property, facility, premises, or site for the purpose of conducting inspections or sampling of soil or water, and for otherwise determining compliance with any Highlands approval or Highlands rule or regulation.[36]

NOTES

1. N.J.S.A. 13:20-2.
2. N.J.S.A. 13:20-1 et seq.; P.L. 2004, c.120.
3. N.J.S.A. 13:20-2.
4. N.J.S.A. 13:20-2.
5. N.J.S.A. 13:20-2.
6. N.J.A.C. 7:38-1 et seq.
7. N.J.S.A. 13:20-32.
8. N.J.S.A. 13:20-10.
9. N.J.S.A. 13:20-3. "Major Highlands development" means, except as otherwise provided pursuant to subsection a. of section 30 of this act, (1) any nonresidential development in the preservation area; (2) any residential development in the preservation area that requires an environmental land use or water permit or that results in the ultimate disturbance of one acre or more of land or a cumulative increase in impervious surface by one-quarter acre or more; (3) any activity undertaken or engaged in the preservation area that is not a development but results in the ultimate disturbance of one-quarter acre or more of forested area or that results in a cumulative increase in impervious surface by one-quarter acre or more on a lot; or (4) any capital or other project of a state entity or local government unit in the preservation area that requires an environmental land use or water permit or that results in the ultimate disturbance of one acre or more of land or a cumulative increase in impervious surface by one-quarter acre or more. Major Highlands development shall not mean an agricultural or horticultural development or agricultural or horticultural use in the preservation area. Solar panels shall not be included in any calculation of impervious surface.
10. N.J.A.C. 7:38-1.1.f.
11. N.J.S.A. 13:20-28.
12. N.J.S.A. 13:20-3.
13. N.J.A.C. 2:92 et seq.
14. N.J.S.A. 13:20-33.b.
15. N.J.S.A. 13:20-10.a.
16. N.J.S.A. 13:20-11.
17. N.J.S.A. 13:20-12.
18. N.J.S.A. 13:20-14; N.J.S.A. 13:20-15.
19. N.J.S.A. 13:20-13.
20. An amendment to the Highlands Act in 2010 allows any municipality outside the Highlands Region in the State to serve as a receiving zone. See the criteria at N.J.S.A. 13:20-13.1.
21. N.J.S.A. 13:20-13.k.
22. N.J.S.A. 13:20-13.
23. N.J.A.C. 7:70-3.3.e.1.
24. N.J.A.C. 7:70-3.1.a.
25. N.J.A.C. 7:70-3.1.b.
26. N.J.A.C. 7:70-3.3.
27. The effective date of the approval shall be the date of the adoption of the resolution following the expiration of the governor's statutory period of review. N.J.A.C. 7:70-3.3.g.
28. N.J.A.C. 7:70-3.4.a.
29. N.J.A.C. 7:70-4.2.
30. N.J.A.C. 7:70-4.4.d.
31. N.J.S.A. 40:55D-1 et seq.

32. P.L. 1975, c.217 (C.52:27D-119 *et seq.*); N.J.S.A. 52:27D-119 et seq.
33. N.J.S.A. 13:20-22.
34. N.J.S.A. 13:20-35.
35. N.J.S.A. 13:20-35.g.
36. N.J.S.A. 13:20-35.k.

Section 6

Pinelands

Jeffrey I. Baron, Esq.

The Pinelands Protection Act, N.J.S.A. 13:18A-1 et seq. (herein referred to as the "Act") was adopted in 1979 to protect "pine-oak forest, cedar swamps, and extensive surface and groundwater resources of high quality which provide a unique habitat for a wide diversity of rare, threatened and endangered plant and animal species."[1] Declaring that the continued viability of "significant and unique natural, ecological, agricultural, scenic, cultural and recreational resources" within the Pinelands was "threatened by pressures for residential, commercial and industrial development," the Act was adopted to control or preclude such development.[2]

PINELANDS COMMISSION

The Act is implemented by a separate agency known as the Pinelands Commission, a political subdivision of the State exercising public and essential governmental functions, including planning authority under the enabling Federal legislation and the Act. The Pinelands Commission essentially oversees any disturbance of land and all development within the Pinelands Region, an area encompassing portions of fifty-two municipalities within Atlantic, Burlington, Camden, Cape May, Cumberland, Gloucester, and Ocean Counties.[3] It is notable, however, that the Pinelands Commission has no enforcement authority.

The Pinelands Commission was initially mandated to prepare and adopt a Comprehensive Management Plan (herein referred to as the "Plan") for the Pinelands Area. Certain portions of the Plan were applicable to the Preservation Area, while other portions were applicable to the Protection Area.[4] The Plan was to include a resource assessment addressing numerous environmental concerns including, inter alia, a determination of "the amount and type of human development and activity which the ecosystem of the pinelands area can sustain while still maintaining the overall ecological values."[5] The goals of the Plan with respect to the Protection Area were to "preserve and maintain the essential character of the existing pinelands environment, protect and maintain the quality of surface and groundwaters, promote continuation and expansion of agricultural and horticultural uses, discourage piecemeal and scatter development and encourage appropriate patterns of compatible residential, commercial and industrial development."[6] The goals of the Plan with respect to the Preservation Area were to "preserve an extensive and contiguous area of land in its natural state, thereby ensuring the continuation of a pinelands environment."[7] The Act and the Plan were enacted to preserve and protect the unique environment of the Pinelands Area.

To ensure consistency with the Plan, each county within the Pinelands Area was required to submit a county master plan which implemented the objectives of the Plan.[8] Each municipality within the Pinelands Area was similarly required to submit a master plan and local land-use ordinances to implement the objectives of the Plan.[9]

The Act incorporated a density transfer program unique to New Jersey, mandating a program for the allocation and transfer of Pinelands Development Credits.[10] The Development Credit Program was to be implemented by a Pinelands Development Credit Bank (herein referred to as the "Bank") which was authorized to purchase and sell pinelands development credits.[11] Essentially, property owners with development rights could sell development credits to the Bank which could thereafter sell such credits to developers.[12]

THE COMPREHENSIVE MANAGEMENT PLAN

The provisions of the Plan are often included verbatim in the master plans and/or development ordinances of municipalities within the Pinelands Region.[13] Prior to pursuing any development action in the Pinelands Area, the definitions governing the interpretation of the Plan should be carefully reviewed.[14] The definitions in the Plan are somewhat different from those contained in other land development legislation, including the Municipal Land Use Law, N.J.S.A. 40:55D-4 et seq. Further, the definitions in the Plan supersede those in other legislation when dealing with property in the Pinelands.[15]

The Plan is organized into seven "Parts." The Parts are briefly described in N.J.A.C. 7:50-4. Part I includes, inter alia, the procedure for requesting a pre-application conference with the executive director of the Pinelands Commission.[16] Applicants seeking development approvals pursuant to the Plan are encouraged to discuss the application with the appropriate municipal officials prior to requesting a conference with the executive director.[17] The procedure for scheduling a pre-application conference, the conduct of such conference, and other informational items are contained in N.J.A.C. 7:50-4.2(a)1.-5. It should be noted that no representation made by the executive director or any member of the Pinelands staff at a pre-application conference shall be binding on the Pinelands Commission or the executive director.[18] Nevertheless, a pre-application conference may ensure that an applicant is seeking the appropriate relief and may provide some insight into the application's viability based upon the commission's professional staff's comments.

Part III of the Plan establishes procedures and standards governing the Pinelands Commission's review of municipal or county approvals of applications for development in certified Pinelands municipalities.[19] In addition to ensuring that applications are consistent with the Plan, consideration may be given to "critical on-site and off-site engineering, planning and design elements so as to preserve and maximize the benefits to the wide diversity of rare, threatened and endangered plant and animal species and the many significant and unique natural, ecological, agricultural, scenic, archaeological, historic, cultural and recreational resources found in the Pinelands Area."[20] The Plan specifically authorizes Pinelands Commission review of all municipal development approvals and of all permits issued by local permitting agencies in certified municipalities except for specifically exempted activities.[21]

Prior to filing any application for development of land in the Pinelands, an applicant must complete and submit an application to the Pinelands Commission in accordance with N.J.A.C. 7:50-4.2(b).[22] Upon a determination that an application is complete, a Certificate of Filing shall be issued. No local permitting agency shall determine that any application for development is "complete" unless it is accompanied by a Certificate of Filing from the Pinelands Commission.[23] The Certificate may identify inconsistencies of the proposed development with the Plan or local certified land-use ordinances and may indicate that if such inconsistencies are not resolved by a local approval, that local approval will be subject to review by the Pinelands Commission.[24] At the time of submission of a development application to any Pinelands certified municipality, it is recommended that the applicant also submit a complete copy of the municipal application (including any plans, reports, and studies) to the Pinelands Commission.

Upon receiving notice of any local preliminary approval from a municipality, the executive director shall review the application for development and any recommendations made by the Commission staff to determine whether the grant of preliminary approval raises substantial issues with respect to "conformance of the proposed development with the minimum standards of [the] Plan."[25] Within thirty days of receiving a notice of preliminary approval, the executive director shall provide his determination by mail to the applicant and the local permitting agency along with other specified individuals.[26] If the executive director determines that the preliminary approval should be reviewed by the Commission, the Pinelands Commission shall "call up" the approval by written notice to the applicant. Either the applicant, the local permitting agency, or any interested party may within twenty-one days of mailing of the executive director's determination, request a hearing before an administrative law judge.[27] No person shall carry out any development pursuant to a preliminary approval granted by a local permitting agency until an approval has been obtained pursuant to N.J.A.C. 7:50-4.37(b).[28]

The procedure for final development approvals is very similar to that for preliminary approvals. An applicant is encouraged to submit an application for final development approval (including all plans, reports, and studies) to the Pinelands Commission at the time of application to the municipal agency. Upon notice of final approval by a certified municipality, the executive director shall review the final application with respect to the Commission staff's recommendations and any decision on preliminary review and determine whether the final approval "raises substantial issues with respect to the conformance of the proposed development with the minimum standards of [the

Plan] and the provisions of the relevant certified local ordinance."[29] If "substantial issues" are raised the final application will be "called up." The executive director shall give his determination on the final approval within fifteen days of receipt to the applicant, the local permitting authority and other interested parties.[30] If applicable, the notice shall set a date, time, and place for a public hearing if the Pinelands Commission does not issue an approval.[31] Again, no development can be pursued pursuant to a final municipal development approval unless the local permitting agency has received an approval from the Pinelands Commission.[32]

The public hearing procedure for a denied approval is set forth in N.J.A.C. 7:50-4.41. An applicant is encouraged to attempt to resolve any objections or disputes with the Pinelands Commission prior to a public hearing, since the executive director's determinations are not often overturned. As a reminder, all applications for permits (such as zoning permits, construction permits, demolition permits) must be submitted to the Pinelands Commission as well as any permits actually issued by a certified municipality.

Part V of the Plan establishes the procedures and standards by which the Pinelands Commission may waive strict compliance with the Plan.[33] Waivers are "intended to provide relief where strict compliance with [the] Plan will create an extraordinary hardship or where the waiver is necessary to serve a compelling public need."[34] The standards for the grant of waivers are set forth in N.J.A.C. 7:50-4.62. Careful review and research should be undertaken to determine whether justification exists for a Waiver of Strict Compliance. A Waiver of Strict Compliance is required for relief from each individual standard or condition in the Plan. In other words, to obtain approval for overall development, the applicant must obtain a Waiver of Strict Compliance for each deficiency or nonconformance. Waivers of Strict Compliance are not routinely granted and the provisions of N.J.A.C. 7:50-4.63 through 4.65 should be carefully reviewed.

An applicant may obtain a letter of clarification or interpretation from the Pinelands Commission for a proposed development, use, standard, and so on. To do so, an applicant must request a pre-application conference which sets forth the clarification or interpretation requested and the facts and circumstances which are the basis of the request for an interpretation.[35] While a request for a letter of clarification or interpretation is discretionary with the executive director, the discussion of the clarification or interpretation at a pre-application confirmation may be helpful. The executive director's position regarding the clarification or interpretation is normally conveyed at the pre-application conference and can assist in the preparation of a development application.

The eight management areas governing the general distribution of land uses and intensities in the Pinelands are described and discussed in N.J.A.C. 7:50-5.11. The standards and provisions of each management area are detailed and unique. In most cases, the provisions of the management areas are mirrored in a certified municipality's master plan and/or zoning ordinance. After determining the management area in which a property sought for development is located, the standards in the Plan should be carefully reviewed with those in the municipal development ordinance to ensure compliance with the Plan.

The purpose and operation of the Pinelands Development Credit Purchase Program are described in N.J.A.C. 7:50-5.51 et seq. If permitted, the purchase of Pinelands Development Credits may be critical to permit the density desired by an applicant in certain management areas. The provisions are detailed and should be carefully reviewed.

The Pinelands Commission has exclusive jurisdiction and control over wetlands in the Pinelands. The provisions involving the identification, preservation, buffering, and so on relating to pinelands are found at N.J.A.C. 7:50-6.1. In most instances, the provisions as to wetlands in the applicable municipal development regulations will mirror those in the Plan. Once again, an applicant should review the specific provisions and language in the Plan against those in a municipal ordinance to ensure that a development application will be consistent with the Plan. Also note that N.J.A.C. 7:50-6.14 prohibits any development, except that permitted by the Plan, to be carried out within 300 feet of any wetlands without a demonstration that the proposed development will not result in a significant adverse impact on the wetland.[36] The criteria that must be reviewed to determine significant adverse impact upon wetlands are found at N.J.A.C. 7:50-6.7. If wetlands or wetlands buffers are disturbed without Pinelands Commission approval, the Pinelands Commission and/or the New Jersey Department of Environmental Protection will normally require mitigation and may also impose mandatory penalties for such action.

A municipal master plan or land-use ordinance must include the standard for protection of fish and wildlife contained in N.J.A.C. 7:50-6.32. The Plan adopts the designation of threatened or endangered animal species designated in N.J.S.A. 23:2A-1 et seq. If an endangered species is discovered in an area proposed for development, careful attention to the provisions in the applicable municipal development ordinances is essential. Retention of experts familiar with threatened and endangered species found in the Pinelands Area is a necessity since negotiations with the Pinelands Commission regarding delineation of habitats, appropriate buffers, and so on requires significant expertise.

Each certified municipal master plan and land-use ordinance must provide for the protection of surface and groundwater quality in the Pinelands.[37] Complex standards and substantial details regarding the design, location, installation, and maintenance of septic systems in the Pinelands are found at N.J.A.C. 7:50-6.82. Again, retention of an experienced and knowledgeable expert as to the design, installation, and maintenance of septic systems is critical to ensure compliance with the Plan's provisions. Since the Pinelands Commission mandates the use of "alternate septic systems," an applicant should be diligent in selecting an experienced and knowledgeable septic expert.

As originally noted, the Act and Plan were adopted to protect and preserve the unique environmental character of the Pinelands Area. This chapter has reviewed the most salient environmental conditions and the procedure which must be followed to obtain development approvals in the Pinelands. The Act and Plan encompass hundreds of pages; therefore, careful research, consultation with the Pinelands Commission's staff, and the retention of experienced, knowledgeable experts are critical to the successful navigation of this environmentally oriented legislation.

NOTES

1. N.J.S.A. 13:18A-2.
2. *Id.*
3. N.J.S.A. 13:18A-5a(2).
4. N.J.S.A. 13:18A-8.
5. N.J.S.A. 13:18A-8a(1).
6. N.J.S.A. 13:18A-9a(1)-(5).
7. N.J.S.A. 13:18a-9c(1).
8. N.J.S.A. 13:18A-12a.
9. N.J.S.A. 13:18A-12b.
10. N.J.S.A. 13:18A-31.
11. *Id.*
12. *Id.*; N.J.S.A. 13:18A-35.
13. N.J.A.C. 7:50-3.11.
14. N.J.A.C. 7:50-2.11.
15. See *Uncle v. N.J. Pinelands Commission*, 275 N.J. Super. 82 (App. Div. 1994).
16. N.J.A.C. 7:50-4.2(a).
17. *Id.*
18. N.J.A.C. 7:50-4.2(a)5.
19. N.J.A.C. 7:50-4.31(a).
20. *Id.*
21. N.J.A.C. 7:50-4.31(b).
22. N.J.A.C. 7:50-4.33.
23. N.J.A.C. 7:50-4.34.
24. N.J.A.C. 7:50-4.34.
25. N.J.A.C. 7:50-4.37(a).
26. N.J.A.C. 7:50-4.37(b).
27. N.J.A.C. 7:50-4.37(b).
28. N.J.A.C. 7:50-4.37(d).
29. N.J.A.C. 7:50-4.40(a).
30. N.J.A.C. 7:50-4.40(b).
31. N.J.A.C. 7:50-4.40(b).
32. N.J.A.C. 7:50-4.40(c).
33. N.J.A.C. 7:50-4.61.
34. N.J.A.C. 7:50-4.61.
35. N.J.A.C. 7:50-4.73(a).
36. N.J.A.C. 7:50-6.14.
37. N.J.A.C. 7:50-6.82.

Section 7

Meadowlands

Steven R. Gray, Esq., and Thomas J. O'Connor, Esq.

The Hackensack Meadowlands Reclamation and Development Act[1] ("Act"), effective January 13, 1969, identified the Meadowlands of the Lower Hackensack River ("Meadowlands") as "a land resource of incalculable opportunity for new jobs, homes and recreational sites" but also recognized the need for a comprehensive and balanced approach to regulation and protection of the important, environmentally sensitive natural features of the area.[2] The Act balances and regulates these two competing interests, along with regional coordination of the local governments in fourteen[3] municipalities, which fall into the territory covered by the Act ("District").

The Hackensack Meadowlands Development Commission was renamed the New Jersey Meadowlands Commission (NJMC) in 2001 when preservation, rather than development, became the agency's focus.[4] Pursuant to the Hackensack Meadowlands Agency Consolidation Act, adopted in 2015 (the "2015 Consolidation Act"),[5] the NJMC was dissolved and all powers of the NJMC were vested in the New Jersey Sports and Exposition Authority (NJSEA).[6] The NJSEA currently oversees the growth and development of the District by interpreting and enforcing the Act. NJSEA's mission and goals include: (1) the preservation of the delicate balance of nature; (2) the provision of special protection from air and water pollution and special provision for solid waste disposal; and (3) the orderly, comprehensive development of the Hackensack Meadowlands to provide more space for industrial, commercial, residential, public recreational, and other uses.[7]

SOLID WASTE DISPOSAL SITES
RECLAIMED FOR DEVELOPMENT

Under the Act, NJSEA must provide for continued use of the region to meet the solid waste needs of the area and is authorized to build facilities with capacity to receive additional solid waste from outside the District to generate revenue.[8] The designation of an area as environmentally sensitive and valuable and its concurrent use for solid waste disposal are seemingly at odds. But the revenue generated from the solid waste disposal services has been a source of NJSEA's funding.[9] Moreover, the Act authorizes NJSEA to issue bonds to pay for these solid waste disposal facilities[10] and sets forth a tax-sharing plan[11] to balance the shares of tax revenue from development of the area among the municipalities in the District.[12]

At its inception, the Act charged NJSEA with the obligation to provide disposal facilities for solid waste entering the District in 1969. This comprised the waste generated by all or a portion of five counties (Hudson, Bergen, Union, Morris, and Essex), as well as an unspecified amount entering the District from outside the state. To plan for such facilities, NJSEA had to close many disposal facilities that had outlived their usefulness, presented environmental hazards, and stood as obstacles to the orderly development of land in the District.[13]

In the early 1970s, the Solid Waste Management Act ("Solid Waste Act")[14] designated the District as one of the twenty-two solid waste planning districts in the state so anyone proposing a new or enlarged landfill disposal facility in the District had to obtain the approval of NJSEA and either Hudson or Bergen County. To preserve valuable landfill space, many counties and NJSEA banned out-of-state wastes from their Districts by means of waste flow direction. This was initially approved by New Jersey Department of Environmental Protection (NJDEP), but it was eventually overturned by the U.S. Supreme Court as contrary to the "interstate commerce" clause of the U.S. Constitution.[15]

Presently, NJSEA has limited the number of disposal facilities in the District[16] and has planned for productive uses for these properties, some of which are privately owned, or located in Redevelopment Districts intended for mixed residential, commercial, and recreational uses. Other properties are publicly owned and, on an interim basis, are used to generate revenues from utility companies eager to reclaim gas and solar energy for electricity.

DEVELOPMENT ON OR ADJACENT TO WETLANDS AND OPEN WATERS

A large portion of the landmass in the Meadowland District is wetlands influenced by tidal (salt) waters (as the Meadowlands have been historically thought of as swampland). Some of these tidal wetlands have been drained for mosquito control, filled for reclamation, or else used for solid waste landfilling—all before becoming subject to regulation by the U.S. Army Corps of Engineers ("Corps") under the Federal Clean Water Act ("CWA") in 1975. Tide gates were installed at the mouth of many rivers and streams; therefore, freshwater wetlands also can be found in the District.

The Corps, in the first instance, has jurisdiction to determine the Federal jurisdiction over activities proposed within "waters of the United States," including wetlands.[17] However, the extent of this jurisdiction is by no means clear, as evidenced most recently by a divided U.S. Supreme Court in *Rapanos v. U.S*, which considered whether the term "navigable waters" or "waters of the United States" in the CWA covered wetlands that are not located adjacent to waters that are navigable in fact.[18] Four justices joined in a plurality opinion written by Justice Scalia, delivering the judgment of the Court that the language, structure, and purpose of the CWA required limiting federal authority to relatively permanent, standing, or continuously flowing bodies of water traditionally recognized as streams, oceans, rivers, and lakes connected to traditional navigable waters or in the case of wetlands, with a continuous surface connection to such water bodies.[19] Four dissenting justices opined that the agencies could regulate any waters to advance the statutory goal of maintaining the chemical, physical, and biological integrity of the nation's waters.[20] Justice Kennedy alone, in a separate concurring opinion, proposed a "significant nexus" test, where a water body would be subject to federal regulation only if that water body would significantly affect a navigable in fact waterway. Justice Kennedy would exclude from regulation remote drains, ditches, and streams with insubstantial flows, and reject speculative evidence of a "significant nexus."[21]

In 2015, the Corps adopted rules ("2015 Rule") which purported to clarify the criteria to determine whether proposed activities in wetlands are within its regulatory jurisdiction. 33 C.F.R. §328. The 2015 Rule remains in effect in New Jersey.[22] Wetlands adjacent to five categories of "navigable" water bodies are regulated. Non-adjacent wetlands within the 100-year flood plain or within 4,000 feet of the high tide line or ordinary high watermark of a water body are regulated on a case-by-case basis according to the "significant nexus" test. The 2015 Rule also excludes certain types of wetlands created by man-induced activities. 33 C.F.R. 328.3(b).

The Corps' jurisdiction overactivity in wetlands is not exclusive. The Corps retained jurisdiction over wetlands in the District when it delegated authority to NJDEP in the 1980s to regulate freshwater wetlands elsewhere in the State. But under parallel Federal authority, NJDEP has been delegated authority under Section 401 of the CWA, 33 U.S.C. 1341, to issue water quality certificates for activities which have the potential to impair water quality as a result of a proposed discharge of fill material to "navigable waters"[23] or to wetlands in connection with a development. Thus, NJDEP indirectly regulates wetlands in this process. Also, the State has been delegated authority[24] to issue determinations that a proposed land use or activity requiring Federal action (e.g., permit approval by the Corps) is consistent with the State's Coastal Management Plan that includes the District.

Applications to the Corps proposing—in conjunction with development projects— to fill or disturb wetlands pursuant to CWA, or to build or rehabilitate structures located in open waters pursuant to the Rivers and Harbors Appropriation Act, are reviewed either as "individual permit" applications or in accordance with a more abbreviated "Nationwide Permits" process in the case of minor fills or disturbances (e.g., related to maintenance). Individual permits require an applicant to demonstrate that there is "no practicable alternative" to the proposed fill or disturbance—including a consideration of the "no action" alternative requiring the applicant to show why the proposed project cannot be built on another parcel with less or no wetlands impacts at all.

At the Federal level, the Corps must consider comments on a permit application by its sister agencies prior to determining, for example, that the environmental impacts associated with a particular project are not significant enough to warrant requiring the preparation of a full-fledged environmental impact statement.[25] Moreover, the CWA, Section 404(c)[26] gives the U.S. Environmental Protection Agency (EPA) the final word on Section 404 permits, should it contest the Corps' decision.

To facilitate coordinated decision-making on projects involving wetlands within the District, NJDEP and NJSEA have signed a memorandum of understanding to delineate their respective roles where their respective jurisdictions may overlap.[27] The affected Federal and State agencies also have formed an interagency task force or advisory committee (known as MIMAC).[28] MIMAC discusses project applications in public session (1) in their early stages, to solicit comments to provide guidance to the applicant, and (2) in their later stages, after the Corps has preliminarily determined that the wetlands impacts associated with a project are unavoidable, have been minimized, and mitigation is required to compensate for such impacts.[29] Wetlands mitigation can be done on-site but is discouraged to compensate for the minor wetlands "fills" on the site of a proposed development project. In this latter case, mitigation is often fulfilled through the purchase of credits at a mitigation bank ("Bank") located within the District, which uses these funds to enhance the quality of wetlands that the Bank owns. Due to the scarcity of Banks in the Meadowlands, the cost of mitigation within the District can be an order of magnitude higher than elsewhere in the southern portion of the State.

Despite the attempts to delineate the respective roles of the different agencies and to designate a "lead agency" responsible for final permit determinations, it is often difficult to harmonize the criteria applied to the same project by different Federal and State agencies; consequently, the Corps defers its decisions on permit applications until the applicant has obtained State clearances in the form of a water quality certificate or a Federal consistency determination, which are issued by NJDEP as a component of a Waterfront Development Permit (WDP) or a Flood Hazard Area Permit (FHAP).

The WDP Law[30] is applied by NJDEP differently within the District than it is elsewhere in the State. On properties subject to the influence of tidal waters, there is a clear line of demarcation between WDP and FHAP jurisdiction, namely the elevation of "mean high" tidal waters (i.e., the average height of tidal waters along a riverbank). Activities undertaken in "open waters" below the mean high tidal elevation require a WDP; activities proposed to be undertaken above that elevation require a FHAP. In the latter case, in times of storms, the "surge" of tidal waters as opposed to the rainwater from storms usually governs the amount of flooding, and NJDEP's FHAP review of proposed activities on the portion of lands located within the regulated flood plain is often a limited one. NJDEP requires stormwater runoff to be detained and filtered to protect water quality, and the lowest floor of occupied buildings must be elevated at least one foot above the flood hazard area's 100-year flood elevation. However, where proposed activities also have the potential to affect freshwater wetlands, NJDEP conducts an independent environmental review of a project in the context of a FHAP application; this permit constitutes the water quality certificate required by the Corps for the issuance of its permit. The NJDEP and the Corps make every effort to coordinate their decision-making.[31]

REDEVELOPMENT AREAS

NJSEA has exclusive power to declare any portion of the District to be a renewal area.[32] The procedure for declaring an area in need of redevelopment, and thereafter adopting a redevelopment plan, follows much the same course as municipal action under the Local Redevelopment and Housing Law,[33] including notice to affected property owners and a public hearing.[34] Owners of property within the investigation area who submit a written objection to NJSEA's need determination may appeal to the Superior Court Appellate Division.[35] The substantive criteria for determination of the need for redevelopment do differ in some ways from the Local Redevelopment and Housing Law, so a practitioner should be careful to refer to the specific criteria listed at N.J.A.C. 19:3-5.7.[36]

Conversely, municipalities may *not* exercise redevelopment authority over any lands within the District. Courts have summarily dismissed such efforts.[37] It is noteworthy that redevelopment plans, and amendments thereto, are adopted by resolution of NJSEA commissioners based upon the recommendations of staff,[38] and are not subject to the more rigid procedures governing adoption of agency regulations under the Administrative Procedures Act.[39]

APPLICATIONS FOR DEVELOPMENT/NJSEA'S PREEMPTIVE ZONING AUTHORITY

NJSEA has preemptive zoning jurisdiction over all properties located within the District boundaries. Under the 2015 Consolidation Act, constituent municipalities may opt to assume authority to review and approve the site plan and subdivision applications, with certain exceptions, provided that the municipality adopts applicable NJSEA regulations.[40] Thus, regardless of whether a municipality assumes the site plan and subdivision review, the NJSEA's use and bulk standards must be applied by the municipality. The NJSEA retains jurisdiction over any application requiring a use variance, a special exception, or any project it deems, in its sole discretion, to be vital to the public safety, general welfare, development, or redevelopment of the District.[41]

With the exception of properties within municipalities that have assumed jurisdiction over site plan and subdivision review as permitted by the 2015 Consolidation Act,[42] every application for subdivision, site plan, and building permit must be submitted to NJSEA for review and approval by the NJSEA prior to action by the municipal approving authority.[43] Even in those municipalities that have assumed jurisdiction over site plan and subdivision review, all applications must be submitted to the NJSEA for initial review, after which the NJSEA will transmit the application to the municipality within three business days.

Zoning Certificate/Subdivision

Applications for development that require site plan review are processed administratively by qualified NJSEA staff engineers and planners.[44] The required form and content of the site plan is similar to site plan applications under the MLUL. The NJSEA approval is referred to as a "zoning certificate." Applications for a zoning certificate must also demonstrate compliance with applicable environmental performance standards established by NJSEA regarding noise, vibrations, airborne emissions, as well as hazardous materials, liquids, and chemicals.[45]

Most municipalities conduct a limited "informal" review of the project plans and provide comments, if warranted, to NJSEA in response to notice of the application. A 1992 statutory amendment formalized the procedure for written notice of all applications for development and consultation by NJSEA with the constituent municipality, providing the municipality with an opportunity to convey concerns or objections to NJSEA regarding the application.[46]

Local zoning ordinances are preempted by the NJSEA master plan and zoning regulations and a municipal planning board may take no action that would contravene the NJSEA master plan.[47] A municipal construction official may ultimately be compelled to issue building permits for a project based upon a NJSEA zoning certificate regardless of municipal review or approval. Nonetheless, in any major application for development, it is advisable that an applicant's attorney confirm with the appropriate municipal official (e.g., a zoning officer or municipal attorney) the current practice of the municipality regarding municipal review.

Applications for subdivision are reviewed and approved by NJSEA. Signatures of the municipal planning board and the municipal engineer must be obtained to comply with the recording requirements under the Title Recordation Law.[48]

Variance/Special Exception

Applications for a variance or special exception from applicable NJSEA regulations require a public hearing.[49] Public hearings are conducted by NJSEA staff, usually chaired by the chief engineer. There is a provision for waiver of hearing, but this is, in practice, exercised sparingly. NJSEA standards for granting a variance differ from the MLUL in several respects, the primary difference being the absence of the C(2) or "flexible C" variance, which employs a balancing of the relative benefits and detriments of the variance. NJSEA variance standards are limited to demonstration of undue hardship akin to the C(1) variance under the MLUL. On occasion, planners and attorneys have been caught off guard by the significantly stricter variance standards of NJSEA.[50] The proofs for a special exception are similar to a conditional use under the MLUL.[51]

Construction Permits/Occupancy Certificates

All construction plan review is performed by NJSEA sub-code officials.[52] Building permits are issued by the building department of the constituent municipality upon NJSEA plan release. Municipal building officials conduct inspections. NJSEA requires the issuance of a certificate of occupancy upon any change in tenant but not upon change in ownership only.[53]

PROJECT IMPACT ASSESSMENT

Applicants must submit a Project Impact Assessment (PIA) for any development of twenty-five dwelling units; 75,000 square feet of retail; 100,000 square feet of office or other commercial space; 15 acres of industrial development; or any project that, in the opinion of the chief engineer, may have substantial impact on the environment.[54] Depending upon the nature and size of the proposed development, the PIA can be a time-consuming and costly endeavor, requiring the applicant to assemble a comprehensive, multidiscipline report.[55]

The PIA must be prepared by qualified professionals and provide a comprehensive analysis of the impact of the development on wetlands, including a wetlands delineation and jurisdictional determination from the Corps; floodplain mapping; drainage and water quality; riparian lands; and wildlife and vegetative habitats. The PIA must address traffic impacts and compliance with NJSEA's aforementioned performance standards concerning noise, vibrations, and air quality. The applicant must also address any required remediation of contamination related to soil, air, or water. NJSEA staff will frequently contact the NJDEP case manager regarding the project's status. The PIA must also address cultural and historic resources, and the availability of public services, such as wastewater treatment, water supply, energy supply, and solid waste.

A significant component of the PIA is the fiscal impact analysis, which includes an evaluation of projected ratables, estimated taxes, and municipal and school budget increases due to the proposed development. In order to assess properly the project's net fiscal impact, it is imperative to factor in NJSEA's Intermunicipal Tax Sharing Formula, which is intended to equalize the costs and benefits of development among the constituent municipalities. NJSEA staff will assist in the calculation of the complex tax sharing formula.

A copy of the PIA is forwarded by NJSEA to the municipality in which the project is located. The municipality has thirty days to review the PIA and provide comments, though extensions are routinely granted.[56] To enhance the prospect of a positive and timely response from the municipality, it is best to have reviewed the net fiscal impact of the project with the municipality's chief financial officer or other designated official in advance of NJSEA forwarding the PIA for comment. It is also advisable to coordinate the availability of public services and utilities in advance with the municipal engineer.

HACKENSACK MEADOWLANDS MUNICIPAL COMMITTEE

To balance the relatively broad and comprehensive nature of NJSEA's jurisdiction, NJSEA is advised by a Hackensack Meadowlands Municipal Committee ("Committee") which consists of the chief elected executives of each constituent municipality.[57] The Committee reviews all plans and regulations of NJSEA prior to their enactment, but its rejection of a proposed action can be overridden by a majority of the members of NJSEA.[58]

CONTEST OF NJSEA ACTIONS

NJSEA wields broad power to delegate decision-making internally, though the final decision on whether to grant or deny a variance or special exception application must be made by the Board of Commissioners.[59] Decisions of NJSEA staff, including staff recommendations to the Board of Commissioners regarding variances or special exceptions, may be appealed through the Office of Administrative Law (OAL) for a hearing under the Administrative Procedures Act.[60] A final decision of the Board of Commissioners is appealable to the Appellate Division.[61] However, a third party may not appeal a permit decision unless there exists a particularized property interest sufficient to require a hearing on constitutional or statutory grounds.[62] *In re Amico/ Tunnel Carwash* further affirmed that third party owners of property who reside close to a proposed residential development site and are fearful of resultant injury to their property did not necessarily have a particularized property interest that gave them a constitutional right to a hearing.[63]

The appellate court displayed significant deference to NJSEA's authority in *Infinity Broadcasting Corporation vs. New Jersey Meadowlands Commission*.[64] Two local radio stations argued that NJSEA did not fully consider expert reports, did not account for the property values affected by the proposed construction, and failed to consider whether the purposes of the redevelopment plan could be accomplished by relocating structures of a height that interfered with the radio signals.[65] The court found NJSEA's action was quasi-legislative, similar to a municipality's adoption of a zoning ordinance or a redevelopment plan, and therefore, was only subject to review if "arbitrary or capricious, contrary to law, or unconstitutional."[66] Likewise, the court held that NJSEA had fulfilled its due process requirements by delegating to its staff public hearings on the amendments, by providing enough information about the amendments for Infinity and Inner City to oppose them, and by receiving their comments and objections. The plaintiffs also argued that the amendment violated basic principles of land use law and amounted to a taking, but the trial court, which heard the appeal, dismissed the claim, citing that such an administrative action was not open for review.[67]

In another case, *In re Hartz/Damascus Bakery, Inc.*,[68] the appellate court ruled that a town can have sufficient stake in the outcome of a zoning matter and "real adverseness" to have standing to challenge NJSEA's zoning certificate approval. But absent clear language to the contrary, legislatively created agencies authorized by the superior governmental authority of the State may not be subject to rules and regulations of local governing boards and agencies.[69] In *Hartz/Damascus*, NJSEA complied with the Act's requirement in that it had consulted with the town before approving an application. Having failed to object within the ten-day statutory period,[70] the town lost its opportunity to comment on the pending application.[71] The Act confers extremely broad authority to NJSEA in the regulation, management, and development of the Meadowlands District, and makes it very difficult to challenge decisions and actions by NJSEA unless the decision or action can be found arbitrary and capricious, contrary to law, or unconstitutional.

NOTES

1. N.J.S.A. 13:17-1 *et seq.*
2. N.J.S.A. 13:17-1.
3. The Act's territory includes ten municipalities in Bergen County (Carlstadt, East Rutherford, Little Ferry, Lyndhurst, Moonachie, North Arlington, Ridgefield, Rutherford, South

Hackensack, and Teterboro) and four municipalities in Hudson County (Jersey City, Kearny, North Bergen, and Secaucus). N.J.S.A. 13:17-3.

4. New Jersey Meadowland Commission Website, *History of the District*, available at https://www.njsea.com/history/.

5. Effective February 5, 2015, and amended July 6, 2015.

6. All references to actions previously applicable to the "HMDC" or "NJMC" are hereinafter cited as "NJSEA" for consistency.

7. New Jersey Meadowland Commission Website, *Master Plan*, available at http://www .njmeadowlands.gov/about/missions.html. N.J.S.A. 13:17-1.

8. N.J.S.A. 13:17-10.

9. New Jersey Meadowland Commission Website, *Financial Information*, available at https://www.njsea.com/financial-information/.

10. N.J.S.A. 13:17-10.

11. Challenged and upheld under *Township of North Bergen v. Township of Teterboro*, 254 N.J. Super. 704 (Law Div. 1991).

12. See *Town of Secaucus v. Hackensack Meadowlands Development Com'n*, 267 N.J. Super. 361, 368 (App. Div. 1993).

13. New Jersey Meadowland Commission Website, *Solid Waste*, available at https://www. njsea.com/solid-waste/.

14. N.J.S.A. 13:1E-1 *et seq.*

15. *Philadelphia v. New Jersey*, 437 U.S. 617 (1978).

16. NJSEA owns and has retained a contractor to operate a construction waste landfill in Kearny; the former NJSEA Baler in North Arlington now operates as a transfer station to consolidate and ship solid waste out of the District. See *NJ DEP Statewide* Solid Waste *Management Plan 2006*, available at www.state.nj.us/dep/dshw/recycling/swmp/pdf/swmp2006. pdf. See also New Jersey Meadowland Commission Website, *Solid Waste*, *available at* https:// www.njsea.com/solid-waste/.

17. The Corps' jurisdiction over filling of wetlands stems from Section 404 of the Clean Water Act, 33 U.S.C. § 1344. It also regulates the placement of structures in "waters of the United States" under Section 10 of the Rivers and Harbors Appropriation Act of 1899, 33 U.S.C. § 403.

18. 547 U.S. 715 (2006).

19. *Id.* at 732-33.

20. *Id.* at 788.

21. *Id.* at 759-87.

22. The Trump administration recently attempted to rescind the 2015 Rule pending adoption of new rules which would more closely follow the Scalia "test" but, in 2018, a federal court enjoined the proposed suspension of the rule in a majority of states, including New Jersey, because the agency had not followed proper administrative procedures. *South Carolina Coastal Conservation League v. Pruitt*, Docket No. 2-18-CV-330-DCN (D.S.C., December 4, 2018). As a result, in New Jersey, the 2015 Rule still governs.

23. For a definition of "navigable waters," see *United States v. Riverside Bayview Homes, Inc.*, 474 U.S. 121 (1985).

24. See Coastal Zone Management Act, 16 U.S.C. § 1451 *et seq.*

25. Such a determination by the Corps is known as a "Finding of No Significant Impact" (FONSI).

26. 33 U.S.C. § 1344.

27. *Memorandum of Agreement between DEP and NJSEA*, dated November 9, 2005, available at http://www.nj.gov/dep/cmp/section-6-table-d.pdf.

28. Meadowlands Interagency Mitigation Advisory Committee (MIMAC) is composed of representatives from NJSEA, NJDEP, the Corps (New York District), EPA, U.S. Fish and Wildlife Service (USFWS), National Oceanic and Atmospheric Administration (NOAA), and National Marine Fisheries Service.

29. In an attempt to guide and streamline the Corps' decisions involving wetlands, in the 1990s, NJSEA sponsored the preparation of a Special Area Management Plan (SAMP) and a District wide environmental impact statement evaluating impacts to wetlands in areas identified for future development in the District Master Plan. The goal was to evaluate potential wetlands in a District wide rather than an individual project basis. The proposed SAMP was withdrawn after public hearings.

30. N.J.S.A. 12:5-3.

31. The practitioner is advised to compare the criteria (a) utilized by the Corps to decide there is no practicable alternative to a proposed wetlands impact under the Clean Water Act, Section 404(b)(1) guidelines (40 C.F.R. § 230.10), and (b) applied by NJDEP (N.J.A.C. 7:7A-10.2) to evaluate non-wetlands alternatives to a proposed project in the context of its water quality certificate review. The Corps' guidelines, in accordance with its statutory charge, balance development with environmental impacts and consider the cost of an alternative as a factor in its decisions.

32. The statute uses the historic term "renewal area" but current regulations refer to an "area in need of redevelopment"; see N.J.A.C. 19:3-5.1.

33. N.J.S.A. 40A:12A-1 *et seq.*

34. N.J.A.C. 19:3-5.5—5.10.

35. N.J.S.A. 5:10A-23(f).

36. See *Gallenthin Realty Development, Inc. v. Borough of Paulsboro*, 191 N.J. 344 (2007), clarifying and limiting application of redevelopment criteria.

37. See *Infinity Broadcasting Corp. v. New Jersey Meadowlands Comm'n*, 187 N.J. 212 (2006); *Nuckel v. New Jersey Meadowlands Comm'n*, 2006 N.J. Super. Unpub. LEXIS 1593 (App. Div. Aug. 8, 2006).

38. N.J.A.C. 19:3-5.10(c).

39. N.J.S.A. 52:14B-1 *et seq.*

40. N.J.S.A. 5:10A-11.

41. N.J.S.A. 5:10A-11(d),(f).

42. N.J.S.A. 5:10A-11.

43. N.J.S.A. 13:17-14(a); N.J.S.A. 5:10A-12—13.

44. See New Jersey Meadowland Commission Website, *Site Plan Review and Zoning Certificates*, available at https://www.njsea.com/applications/.

45. N.J.A.C. 19:4-7.1 *et seq.*

46. N.J.A.C. 19:5-7.12.

47. N.J.A.C. 19:4-3.2(5)(i).

48. N.J.S.A. 46:26A-1 *et seq.*, adopted in 2012 to replace the former Map Filing Law.

49. N.J.A.C. 19:4-4.13—4.14; Conditional uses, referred to in NJSEA parlance as "special exceptions" (dating back to older zoning terminology), require a public hearing. *See* N.J.A.C. 19:4-4.13(d).

50. *Compare* N.J.A.C. 19:4-4.14 *to* N.J.S.A. 40:55D-62—66.

51. N.J.A.C. 19:4-4.13; N.J.S.A. 40:55D-67.

52. N.J.A.C. 19:6-1.6.

53. N.J.A.C. 19:4-4.8(b).

54. N.J.A.C. 19:4-10.1—10.10.

55. See N.J.A.C. 19:10-4 *et seq.* for the content of the PIA.

56. N.J.A.C. 19:4-10.10(b).

57. N.J.S.A. 13:17-7, 8.

58. *Id.*

59. N.J.A.C. 19:4-4.13—4.14.

60. N.J.S.A. 52:14B-1 *et seq.*

61. N.J.A.C. 19:4-4.19(e)

62. N.J.S.A. 52:14B-3.2(c); N.J.S.A. 52:14B-3.3. See also *In re AMICO/Tunnel Carwash,* 371 N.J. Super. 199 (App. Div. 2004).

63. *In re AMICO/Tunnel Carwash,* 371 N.J. Super. 199, 211 (App. Div. 2004) ("[S]imply because some of the plaintiffs reside close to the . . . site and are fearful of resultant injury to their property, does not mean that they are entitled to an adjudicatory hearing. Fear of damage to one's . . . generalized property rights shared with other property owners is insufficient to demonstrate a particularized property right.") (citations omitted). In addition, the court in this case also ruled that NJSEA staff do not have the statutory authority to decide a variance application; the final decision to grant or deny a variance application must be made by the members of the NJSEA themselves and not by the staff. See id., at 212-15.

64. *Infinity Broadcasting Corp. v. New Jersey Meadowlands Comm'n.,* 377 N.J. Super. 209 (App. Div. 2005), affirmed in part and reversed in part, *Infinity Broadcasting Corp. v. New Jersey Meadowlands Comm'n.,* 187 N.J. 212 (2006).

65. *Id.*

66. *Id.* at 225, citing *Downtown Residents for Sane Devel. v. City of Hoboken,* 242 N.J. Super. 329, 332 (App. Div. 1990); *see also Kelly v. Hackensack Meadowlands Dev. Com.,* 172 N.J. Super. 223 (App. Div. 1980).

67. *Id.* at 229–30.

68. *In re Hartz/Damascus Bakery, Inc.,* 404 N.J. Super. 49 (App. Div. 2008).

69. *Id.* at 65–67.

70. *Id.* at 57, citing N.J.S.A. 13:17-14.1.

71. *Id.*

Section 8

Farmland

William L. Horner, Esq.

There seems to be no definitive explanation for New Jersey's official state nickname "The Garden State." The nickname was actually opposed in 1954 when then-governor Robert B. Meyner issued the following veto message in response to Assembly Bill No. 454, which proposed printing it on all New Jersey passenger car license plates:

> My investigation discloses that there is no official recognition of the slogan "Garden State" as an identification of the State of New Jersey. It is, moreover, obvious that New Jersey's place in the economy and life of the nation is today attributable to its preeminence in many fields, in addition to its acknowledged high standing in agricultural pursuits. Statistically, only 2.4 percent of our workers are employed on farms while 97.6 percent are engaged in non-agricultural occupations. New Jersey is noted for its great strides in manufacturing, mining, commerce, construction, power, transportation, shipping, merchandising, fishing and recreation, as well as in agriculture. I do not believe that the average citizen of New Jersey regards his state as more peculiarly identifiable with gardening for farming than any of its other industries or occupations. Indeed, many of our people regard the state as preeminently a residential community.[1]

Nevertheless, there seems to have been general agreement as to the importance of defending New Jersey's farmlands. By 1960, the State Legislature had commenced efforts to protect and promote New Jersey agriculture by amending the tax laws to include a provision that reduced assessments on farmland by disregarding farmland's potential development value: "In the assessment of acreage which is actively devoted to agricultural use, such value (taxable value) shall not be deemed to include prospective value for subdivisions or non-agricultural use."[2] However, this enactment was promptly declared invalid in *Switz v. Kingsley*[3] because it violated the State Constitution's requirement for uniform real estate tax valuation.[4]

Within the next year, New Jersey Constitution Article VIII, § I, paragraph 1 was amended to include a new subpart (b) that authorized reduced assessment for farmland and imposed a "rollback" tax when property assessed as farmland is changed to non-agricultural use.[5] The Legislature promptly implemented the constitutional amendment by enacting the Farmland Assessment Act of 1964, N.J.S.A. 54:4-23.1 et seq.

Other pro-agriculture legislation followed. Seventeen years after the institution of farmland tax assessment, New Jersey voters approved the Farmland Preservation Bond Act of 1981[6] which authorized bond sales to fund farmland preservation initiatives. The Right to Farm Act, N.J.S.A. 4:1C-1 et seq., was enacted in 1983 to help protect properly conducted commercial farm operations from nuisance suits and undue limitations imposed by municipal land use and development regulations. The Agricultural Retention and Development Act, N.J.S.A. 4:1C-11 et seq., enacted simultaneously with the Right to Farm Act, authorized the formation of county agriculture development boards, and established requirements for the creation and administration of county and municipal farmland preservation programs. County agriculture development boards were also given jurisdiction to hear and decide certain cases arising under the Right to Farm Act.

Farmland assessment, farmland preservation, and the Right to Farm Act will all be discussed in greater detail in this section.

ENVIRONMENTAL DUE DILIGENCE

Like all purchasers of real estate, buyers of farmland should exercise an appropriate degree of due diligence with respect to potential environmental problems. If the farmland includes areas presently or formerly occupied by buildings or other structures, the usual investigations should be done for fuel tank leakage and harmful construction materials, such as asbestos. Work areas where fuels, lubricants, and chemical applications such as fertilizers, pesticides, and herbicides have been stored, staged, or processed should be inspected to ascertain the degree to which such materials might have accumulated in soils. Wells, whether for potable water supply or irrigation, should be located and tested. Inquiries and inspections should be made as to the presence of any old farm dumps or other buried refuse, particularly in and near slopes, woods, waterways, and other areas of the farm that historically have not been cultivated as farmland, and in remote areas of the farm where contamination and debris might have been deposited by trespassers. These sorts of noncultivated lands should also be inspected for evidence of previously existing buildings or structures near which otherwise hidden tanks, dumps, and so on might be located. The extent of wetlands and other environmentally regulated areas should be ascertained to the buyer's satisfaction.

If the farm being purchased has been preserved as discussed here, the existence in cultivated soils of residues from customary farm-related chemical fertilizers, pesticides, and herbicides might not cause great concern because the land will be used in perpetuity only for agricultural purposes. On the other hand, such residues should be of concern for farms having development potential, particularly if for residential purposes. So, whether to help ensure that one's intended development plans will not be unexpectedly impeded, or simply to confirm that the farm's estimated development-potential value is consistent with the purchase price being paid, farm buyers should test the cultivated soils in various locations to ascertain whether and to what extent such chemical residues exist, and obtain professional advice as to whether and how they can be remediated if necessary.

TITLE/SURVEY/LEASES

Quality and Quantity of Title

It is not uncommon for a working farm to have been owned by one or more extended families for generations, with ownership transferred only periodically by interfamily deeds, wills, or intestacy, and therefore never subjected to the degree of scrutiny that typically attends an arms-length transaction. It is also not uncommon for a family farm under such circumstances to have been the subject of other types of conveyances over time, such as access easements granted to adjoining owners, utility easements granted to power and gas companies, road and drainage easements granted to government entities, and out-parcels deeded to family members or others prior to the enactment of modern subdivision laws. For these reasons, it is advisable for both the seller and buyer to obtain reasonable certainty as to the quality and quantity of a farm seller's title before entering into a contract for sale.

The cost of a title search is small compared to the time and effort required to negotiate, enforce, and comply with contingencies for title quality disclosure and cure that may be necessitated by lack of certainty on these points. On the other hand, once the advance title search results have been obtained, and if the parties are satisfied with the results, the title exceptions appearing in title report can be cited specifically in the contract as either acceptable to the buyer or as unacceptable and requiring removal by seller prior to closing. If the buyer and the seller agree in the contract that the buyer will purchase a title insurance policy from the company that prepared the search, the report can easily be converted into a title insurance commitment, and the cost of the search can be paid or reimbursed by buyer at closing as part of the buyer's customary title insurance costs.

Survey

The sorts of family farm grants and conveyances discussed earlier are often effectuated by deeds or other instruments that contain generalized or otherwise imprecise property descriptions. Therefore, unless the farm has been surveyed recently, it is advisable for the contract to contain a mutually acceptable survey-related cancellation contingency, and for the survey, if to be included in the deed of conveyance, to be certified to the seller as well as the buyer, lender, title insurer, and so on. Such a contingency can include a cancellation "floor" on acreage amount for the protection of the buyer (if the survey reveals considerably less acreage than expected), and a cancellation "ceiling" for the benefit of the seller (if the survey reveals considerably more acreage than expected).

A survey will also reveal the exact locations of improvements and features on the farm and adjoining lands relative to the farm's property boundaries, sometimes with unexpected results. Farm roads, irrigation equipment, and even buildings might be found to encroach or to be located entirely upon, adjoining lands. A survey might also help disclose the existence of unrecorded rights that others may have or claim relating to these sorts of improvements and features. To avoid a breach of contract controversies between buyer and seller in these instances, it may be advisable for both parties to have the benefit of cancellation in the event such previously unknown conditions, rights or claims are disclosed by the buyer's survey and deemed unacceptable to the buyer.

Farm surveys can be expensive, particularly if the acreage is large and the property boundaries are wooded, sloped, or wet. It is therefore reasonable for a survey cancellation clause to include a requirement for apportionment of survey cost between buyer and seller in the event of cancellation, and for seller to receive all post-cancellation rights to the survey by assignment (with advance consent from the surveyor) for use in future transactions or other endeavors (such as attempts to resolve any adjoining-owner encroachment issues, rights, or claims by negotiated agreement, settlement, or litigation).

Leases

Farm sale contracts should be very clear on issues pertaining to leases, and the buyer should review all leases prior to signing a purchase contract. In addition to leases with tenant farmers, it is not unusual for farms to include residential leases for tenant-occupied housing, and areas that are subject to hunting or woodlot leases.

A buyer should carefully consider the term of a farm lease in the context of the buyer's plans for the property, including any periods within which notices of nonrenewal or lease modification may be given. A buyer desiring to farm the property will obviously want any existing farm lease to expire in time for the buyer to commence intended farming operations, and for the lease to require the farm tenant to leave the property in good farmable condition upon termination. For this reason, the timing for planting and harvest of the tenant's existing or proposed crop vis-à-vis the buyer's proposed crop may be an important factor in the timing of the transaction closing, as well as any tenant obligations to remove and dispose of the detritus from completed farming activities, such as drip irrigation tubing and plastic mulch, and to plant cover crops.[7] On the other hand, a buyer who wants a farm lease to continue for purposes of ongoing rental income and farmland assessment qualification should make sure that the lease will remain in effect subject to appropriate automatic renewal and cancellation notice requirements.

A farm lease should specify whether and to what extent the tenant can use existing structures, facilities and installations at a farm, and what responsibilities pertain to such use. Any buildings available for use by the tenant should be identified in the lease, along with any restrictions or limitations on use, or any shared use with the owner or other persons. The tenant's use of facilities such as irrigation wells, ponds, and equipment would likely include the responsibility to pay for water pump electricity, fuel, and maintenance, and to keep accurate water usage logs in order to comply with any applicable reporting requirements. A farm lease should also specify whether and to what extent the tenant can construct or install new structures and facilities at the farm, and whether, and on what terms, they may be removed prior to, at, or within a reasonable time following the expiration or termination of the lease. If there are woods, marshes, waterways, or other areas suitable for hunting, wood-gathering, or other nonfarm activities, the buyer should ascertain whether and to what extent the farm tenant is entitled to use them, and whether and to what extent the owner has reserved rights to use any portions of the farm. A farm buyer should review and be satisfied with all such lease provisions prior to contracting or purchase.

Ideally a farm lease will include a provision allowing the owner to reenter the farm to plant and/or harvest crops, and take any other actions necessary to preserve the property's farmland tax assessment qualification in the event of any act or omission by the tenant that could jeopardize it, together with an obligation by the tenant to indemnify the owner for any costs resulting from such loss of assessment or rollback taxes. There may be rights of reentry for other purposes as well.

If the farm is subject to a development easement for farmland preservation the lease should provide that the tenant may not, by act or omission, violate its requirements, and the buyer should review the easement's provisions and inspect the property as necessary to confirm that there are no violations. If any lease includes insurance requirements, the buyer should confirm that the tenant is in compliance with them and should also confer with buyer's own insurance provider in order to obtain such policies of insurance as may be required or otherwise appropriate in the context of the lease. If the lease contains no insurance provisions, it is advisable for the buyer to find out what policies of insurance might be appropriate in the context of the lease.

FARMLAND ASSESSMENT

Generally speaking, land will qualify for reduced assessment under the Farmland Assessment Act of 1964 if it consists of at least 5 acres from which a certain amount of annual income (currently $1,000 per year for the first 5 acres) has been generated from the production of agricultural products for three or more consecutive years.[8] These requirements must be confirmed annually, on or before August 1, by application to the municipal tax assessor, in order for the farmland assessment qualification to continue.[9] Once qualified, a farm or part of it can lose its farmland assessment and be subject to rollback taxes if changed to a nonagricultural use.[10] Rollback tax is calculated based on the difference between the tax paid at the farmland assessment rate and the tax that would be payable at the regular non-farmland assessment rate for the year in which the change of use occurs and the two prior years. It is also possible for a qualified farm to lose its farmland assessment for failure to file the forms that are due on August 1, but if the farm continues to be used for agricultural purposes there will be no rollback. The consequence is taxation at the regular rate for the years in which the farmland assessment qualification is lost.

Farm buyers should obtain confirmation that the farmland assessment qualification is in effect, and if the purchase transaction is to occur on or about August 1, the contract should clearly provide who—seller or buyer—will be responsible for causing the required annual filing to be timely and properly accomplished so that the farmland assessment qualification will continue for the next year. If the farm is leased to a tenant farmer it is important to get reasonable assurance the tenant will cooperate in providing information necessary for the renewal of the farmland assessment each year, including any supplemental forms that the assessor may require to confirm farm income from the sale of crops or livestock.

The contract should also confirm that the seller will be responsible to the buyer for any loss of farmland assessment or rollback taxes that are occasioned by actions or omissions of the seller, and that the buyer will be responsible for any loss of farmland assessment or rollback taxes that are occasioned by actions or omissions of the buyer.

FARMLAND PRESERVATION

Development Easements

Whether accomplished through public or private nonprofit agencies, the purchase of a farm's development rights for permanent preservation using public funds pursuant to the Agricultural Retention and Development Act (cited earlier) requires approval by the State Agriculture Development Committee (SADC). Permanent preservation is effectuated by the farm owner granting a "development easement" that effectively sells and relinquishes all of the farm's nonagricultural development rights. The purchase price paid to the owner is based on the appraised value of those rights.

Development easements having a shorter duration—a minimum of eight years—may be approved by county agriculture development boards. Although no payment is made to the farmer for such short-term development easements, the farmer can benefit through eligibility for farm-related soil and water conservation programs which include state-funded cost-sharing for improvements such as irrigation and water impoundment facilities, alteration of field grading and hedgerows, and other initiatives that can help improve farmland management and increase agricultural production (these benefits are also available to permanently preserved farms). The issues discussed in this section are to be considered primarily in the context of permanently preserved farms.

The most important thing to understand, whether deciding to preserve a farm or to purchase one that has already been preserved, is the great extent to which use of the land is limited by the development easement. Essentially, preserved farms may be used only for agricultural purposes, and any nonagricultural use or development is prohibited. The definition of "agricultural use" as set forth in the SADC's required form of development easement (derived from the New Jersey Administrative Code at N.J.A.C. 2:76-6.15) is "the use of the Premises for *common farmsite activities*" and includes a list of examples. Accordingly, it is critical for the owner or potential purchaser of a preserved farm to conduct an appropriate inquiry before engaging in any activity that might not fall squarely within the definition. Further, the owner or potential purchaser should bear in mind that even though a proposed activity might qualify as permitted agriculture, the manner in which it is conducted could violate the terms of the development easement.[11]

Development easements will often contain some limited exceptions to the agriculture-only rule. Nonagricultural structures and uses in existence as of the time a farm is preserved may be continued if so, specified in the development easement, but such structures and uses cannot be enlarged or expanded, and if they cease, they will be deemed abandoned. A preserved farm owner may also derive income from "certain recreational activities such as hunting, fishing, cross country skiing, and ecological tours" if such activities do not interfere with agricultural production or involve changes to the farm (golf courses and athletic fields are expressly prohibited).

A preserved farm may be the site of an existing farmhouse or housing for agricultural laborers who work at the farm, and these may continue to be maintained, occupied and used as such. The sorts of structures and uses that would normally be regarded as "accessory" to these residential uses are also permitted, but careful advance inquiry should be made in connection with any proposal to develop new or expanded residential uses or structures (building additions, garages, pools, etc.). Existing residential structures may be replaced with SADC approval. Development easements contain no restrictions against constructing new buildings for agricultural purposes.

A preserved farm might also have allowances for *areas* that are not so strictly limited by restrictions against nonagricultural use. One such allowance is an "exception area," which is a specifically described portion of the farm that is not subject to most of the use restrictions of the development easement. As such, an exception area may be used as a residential dwelling site or for other nonagricultural purposes that do not interfere with the agricultural use of the preserved farm.[12]

There are two types of exception areas—severable and non-severable. A "severable" exception area is one that may be subdivided and transferred separately from the preserved farm to another owner without further SADC approval. A "non-severable" exception area may not be subdivided or transferred to separate ownership but rather must remain as part of the preserved farm.[13]

The other type of allowance by which an area of a preserved farm might not be so severely limited by restrictions against nonagricultural use is a "residential dwelling site opportunity" or "RDSO."[14] An RDSO is the right to develop and use a portion of a preserved farm as a residential homesite that cannot be subdivided from the farm. The location, size, and configuration of an RDSO are not specified in advance, and an RDSO cannot be developed without prior SADC approval confirming compliance with regulatory requirements to minimize adverse impact on agricultural operations at the preserved farm.

Owners and potential purchasers of preserved farms should bear in mind that any subdivision or nonagricultural use of an exception area, or development of an RDSO, will also be subject to normally applicable municipal, county, and state ordinances, approvals, and requirements. For this reason, it is advisable to subdivide exception areas and exercise any other of the aforesaid nonagricultural development and use rights as promptly as possible, particularly if applicable zoning requirements and other regulations are favorable. For example, even though the size and configuration of a severable exception area may conform to all zoning requirements in effect at the time the development easement is granted, a change in zoning to require a larger minimum lot size, width, or depth would mean that the municipal subdivision approval necessary to "sever" the exception area as a separate lot could not be granted without variance approval.

It should also be borne in mind that even if a preserved farm may be comprised of several municipal tax lots, no part of the farm may be transferred separately, even with subdivision approval, unless approved in advance by the SADC.[15] In determining whether to approve the division of a preserved farm, the SADC will look primarily for

whether all of the resulting separate farm parcels will be independently "agriculturally viable," meaning "capable of sustaining a variety of agricultural operations that
yield a reasonable economic return under normal conditions, solely from each parcel's
agricultural output."[16]

     There are also some qualified statutory allowances for nonagricultural uses and
structures at preserved farms, including personal wireless service facilities; biomass,
solar, or wind energy generation facilities, structures, and equipment; rural micro-
enterprise activities; and "special occasion events" at wineries.[17] Also, as will be
discussed here, the list of activities that are authorized as agriculture under the Right
to Farm Act continues to expand, thus increasing the overall utility of New Jersey's
preserved farms.

Unspecified Utility Easements and USEMs

The term "unspecified utility easement" is used by the SADC to refer to utility easements that are typically prepared on preprinted forms, a page or two in length, with
spaces where the owner's name, address, and property information can be filled in
when a utility installation project—such as new or rerouted electrical service to a
house or outbuilding, or installation of poles and wires along a public road—is about
to commence. Unspecified utility easements usually do not include maps or surveyed
metes and bounds descriptions but instead only identify the subject property generally, by street address, municipal lot and block, and outbound references to roads and
other properties that border it on the North, South, East, and West. In this respect,
the significant feature of unspecified utility easements is that they generally identify
the property that is subject to the easement, rather than designating a specifically
described area within the property where utility improvements will be installed.

     The generalized property descriptions contained in unspecified utility easements
might suggest that such easements constitute "blanket" easements which give the
utility company a perpetual right to place poles and wires upon and over all or any
part of the property at any time in the future without further owner consent. Such
an interpretation would obviously be contrary to the reasonable expectations of any
landowner who signs an easement form at the request of a utility company representative in order to accomplish a specific proposed installation, but it would also be
contrary to applicable law. New Jersey court decisions provide that, in the absence of
a specifically described easement area, it is the conduct of the parties that confirms
their mutually agreed intent as to the nature and location of structures and facilities.[18]
Further, a statute that was enacted in 1957 provides that recorded utility easements
without specific location descriptions (i.e., unspecified utility easements) are valid as
record notice for only one year.[19] So, when a landowner executes an unspecified utility
easement, perhaps in connection with his or her own request for electrical service to
a new structure on his or her property, or in response to a utility company's request
to install a new utility line along or across a portion of his or her property to serve
others, it is the actual installation that immediately follows the easement's signature
that defines the location, and the nature and extent of usage, of the new utility easement area. As time passes following such initial installation without any noticeable
change in facilities or activities, it becomes ever more apparent that nothing more

than the initial installation was intended or authorized, and that another easement must be obtained if the utility company later wants to install additional facilities on the property. (This may be why it is not unusual for a title search to reveal multiple, successive, and for the most part identical unspecified utility easements to the same utility company grantee.) Easement areas for more substantial utility installations, on the other hand, such as high-voltage electric tower corridors, are typically not obtained via unspecified utility easement forms but rather are particularly described by metes and bounds based on actual field surveys.

Whenever the SADC acquires a farmland preservation easement it must ensure that there are no previously recorded instruments that could interfere with future agricultural use of the land, or SADC's ability to enforce the requirements for such use. Accordingly, SADC obtains title searches and title insurance for all farmland preservation easement transactions; requires mortgages to be discharged or subordinated; and typically, does not pay for acreage that is subject to existing road-widening or other easements.

For many years, the SADC was unconcerned about unspecified utility easements, and routinely preserved farms without requiring such easements to be extinguished or subordinated. However, in the early 2010s, the SADC became concerned about the possibility that unspecified utility easements held by the Atlantic City Electric Company (ACE) might actually give ACE perpetual "blanket" rights to install additional future utility infrastructure anywhere, at any time, on farms that have been preserved with public funds, in a manner that might interfere with agricultural activities. As a result, several farmland preservation transactions were stalled while SADC decided what to do about this newly perceived problem.

During this period SADC engaged in discussions with ACE that resulted in an agreement that was memorialized between SADC and ACE on April 24, 2014, in a memorandum of understanding (MOU) which was intended to govern all future preservation transactions for farms that are subject to ACE's unspecified utility easements. The MOU provides that, whenever a farmland preservation transaction requiring SADC approval involves land that is subject to one or more of ACE's unspecified utility easements, SADC will require the landowner to enter into an agreement with ACE called a Utility Service Easement Modification (USEM) by which the unspecified utility easements are modified to become more specified. The modification involves a trade of sorts—the landowner gives ACE a variety of new "specified" utility easement rights over the farmland in return for ACE's release of its unspecified utility easement rights:

1. The USEM gives ACE a "floating" 40-foot-wide easement area along all public roads that abut the property wherever roadside poles and wires have been previously installed, as measured from the present roadway edge, or any future roadway edge if the roads are ever widened.
2. The USEM gives ACE a 30-foot-wide right-of-way centered on any poles and wires that were previously installed anywhere on the property (i.e., 15 feet on each side of the poles).
3. The USEM gives ACE a 200-foot-wide right-of-way centered on any poles and wires (i.e., 100 feet on each side of the poles) that were previously installed anywhere on the property and which carry 69,000 volts or more of electricity.

4. The USEM gives ACE the right to increase and add to the facilities that are already located within the mentioned easement areas, and also to install new facilities in those areas, for "electric utility service" (see the definition of this term in endnote 20).

5. The USEM gives ACE the right to acquire, in consideration for payment to the landowner, additional utility easements having widths 30, 40, and 200 feet, along and within the property, and perhaps even against the landowner's wishes by eminent domain. This is suggested by language in the USEM that allows ACE to "negotiate" and "acquire" such additional utility easements but which makes no mention that the terms of sale must be voluntarily accepted by the landowner. Normally a utility company could not lawfully accomplish a taking of preserved farmland by eminent domain, at least not without great difficulty, but perhaps the advance authorization for such acquisition contained in a USEM that has been signed and agreed to by SADC, ACE, and the landowner, might facilitate this sort of taking.

Whenever a farmland preservation transaction involving a USEM is consummated, the SADC pays the landowner the agreed-upon per-acre development value for all of the new USEM utility easement areas along with the rest of the approved farm acreage, but the landowner is paid nothing extra by SADC or ACE for the *additional future utility installation rights* given to ACE in the USEM. Nor, for that matter, is the landowner compensated for the potentially severe limitations on land use within the USEM easement areas that might result if such future installations were to impede agricultural activities, or for the impacts on property value that might result if such future installations were aesthetically displeasing. Indeed, the USEM definition of "electric utility service" is very broadly drafted, and could result in a wide variety and vast extent of future installations within the USEM utility easement areas.[20] Moreover, given the likelihood and unpredictability of ongoing changes in electric distribution/transmission and communication technologies, such future installations might involve structures and facilities, whose appearance and number simply cannot be presently envisioned with any reasonable degree of accuracy.

Unfortunately, many landowners who enter into farmland preservation transactions, particularly those without independent legal counsel, might not understand what they are giving up when they sign a USEM; others, whether they understand or not, might be under sufficient financial pressure by the time closing approaches to sign anything just to receive payment. To make matters more difficult (even for independent legal counsel), SADC's farmland preservation easement contracts and advance informational brochures do not include any explanation of the USEM requirement, perhaps because of the rather esoteric legal issues involved, or maybe because the USEM requirement was not implemented through the typical SADC rulemaking process. For example, an SADC farmland preservation contract recently reviewed by this author contained only one innocuous reference to "unspecified utility easements," with no definition of the term.[21] A landowner who refuses to execute a USEM after signing such a contract may be declared in breach or required to pay high transaction costs in the event of SADC cancellation.

For all of the above reasons, any owner of farmland who intends to sell a development easement for its preservation, and who is concerned about the possible applicability of USEM requirements, should obtain and carefully review an advance title search of his or her property to ascertain the existence of any unspecified utility easements before signing a contract.

RIGHT TO FARM ACT

The Right to Farm Act (RTFA) authorizes the SADC

> to aid in the coordination of State policies which affect the agricultural industry in a manner which will *mitigate unnecessary constraints on essential farming practices* by recommending to appropriate State departments a program of *agriculture management practices* which, if consistent with relevant federal and State law, and non-threatening to the public health and safety, would afford the farmer *protection against municipal regulations and private nuisance suits.*[22]

The RTFA further provides that "notwithstanding the provisions of any municipal or county ordinance, resolution, or regulation to the contrary," the owner or operator of a qualifying commercial farm whose farming operation conforms to the SADC's agricultural management practices (AMPs) and applicable federal or state laws, and "does not pose a direct threat to public health and safety," may continue such operation even if it would otherwise violate municipal land use requirements or constitute public or private nuisance.[23] Stated more simply, the SADC is supposed to identify and provide operating standards for various types of farming activities, and if a farmer's operation qualifies as a "commercial farm" and conforms to the standards, the farmer will not be constrained by claims of nuisance or zoning violation.

The primary list of permitted agricultural activities is set forth in the statute itself and includes operations that are customarily recognized as traditional farming, such as production, processing, and packaging of crops; field and soil management; pest, weed, and disease control; and disposal of agricultural waste. There are also a few listed activities that might not be as readily recognized as traditional farming, such as the operation of farm markets, "agriculture-related educational and farm-based recreational activities," and "generation of power or heat from biomass, solar, or wind energy."

In addition to the statutorily listed agricultural activities, and pursuant to the mentioned statutory mandate, the SADC has promulgated AMPs for several other types of agricultural operations, some of which are rather detailed, including apiary and poultry manure management; "food processing by-product land application"; commercial vegetable and tree fruit production; natural resource conservation; on-farm composting; fence installation for wildlife control; equine activities; aquaculture; solar energy generation facilities; pick-your-own operations; and, most recently, "on-farm direct marketing facilities, activities, and events," which include a wide array of activities that might not otherwise be regarded as typical to farming.[24] The list will no doubt continue to grow over time.

Finally, the RTFA provides a procedure by which commercial farm operations that are not specifically addressed by the statute or AMP regulations can be reviewed on a case-by-case basis by county agriculture development boards (CADBs) (or by the SADC in counties where no CADB exists) to determine whether they nonetheless qualify for RTFA protection as "site-specific agriculture management practices" (SSAMPs).[25] Generally speaking, this requires proof that the structure or use in question constitutes "a generally accepted agricultural operation or practice," and does not pose a direct threat to public health and safety. These requirements have been interpreted by the New Jersey Supreme Court to mean, more specifically, that CADBs must take into account the interests of farmers while simultaneously considering the extent of the use of AMPs and the limitations imposed on such uses by a municipality in the interest of public health and safety, and to balance these potentially competing interests on a case-by-case basis.[26]

New Jersey courts have consistently held that the RTFA preempts municipal land use requirements and public and private nuisance claims with respect to commercial farms, and that the CADBs (or SADC where no CADB exists) have primary jurisdiction over such matters, with appeals to be taken first to the SADC and then to the Appellate Division of the New Jersey Superior Court.[27]

So, as a practical matter, any commercial farm operator who seeks to build a structure or commence a use that is alleged by a municipality or any other party as requiring site plan or variance review by a planning or zoning board, or as constituting a nuisance, should consider making application to the applicable CADB for a determination that the structure or use qualifies for RTFA protection. At a public hearing (for which notice should be given by newspaper publication and by certified mailing to owners of land within 200 feet of the property in question),[28] the farmer will be required to prove that the farm is, in fact, a "commercial farm,"[29] and that the operation in question either meets standards specified in the RTFA or the SADC-promulgated AMPs, or qualifies for CADB approval as an SSAMP. The farmer must also prove that the manner in which the operation is to be conducted will not pose a direct threat to public health and safety using the balancing test described earlier.

The court decisions cited earlier have made it clear that CADBs are not given carte blanche authority to override municipal and private concerns but rather must consider these concerns, along with the intent and purpose of municipal land use regulations, in reaching a decision. This means, for example, that a farmer who seeks to avoid the expense of municipal site plan and variance review to construct an agricultural building within minimum municipal yard setbacks at an intersection of public roads might be required to provide some degree of formal site planning and engineering testimony at the CADB hearing to show that adequate ingress, egress, parking, drainage, and sight distances will be established in order to protect the health, safety, and welfare of nearby property owners and the public at large.[30] To that end, the aforementioned AMP for "on-farm direct marketing facilities, activities, and events" includes site-plan-type review requirements for many aspects of development, including hours of operation, lighting, sanitary facilities, safety procedures, signs, parking, buffering and screening, and setbacks.[31]

Anyone purchasing a farm should be aware of the RTFA protections and, if proposing to engage in any activities not specifically listed in the statute or AMPs, should seriously consider making the farm purchase contingent upon advance SSAMP approval for such activities. The SADC maintains chronologically organized, topically summarized online databases at which SADC and CADB decisions on nuisance (conflict) and SSAMP cases can be reviewed and downloaded.[32]

NOTES

1. See "Why is New Jersey called 'The Garden State?'" available at https://www.quora.com/Why-is-New-Jersey-called-The-Garden-State, citing "The Garden State and Other New Jersey State Nicknames," previously (but no longer) available at The Official Website for the State of New Jersey (http://www.state.nj.us/njfacts/garden.htm). Despite the Governor's veto, the law passed on December 6, 1954, and is currently codified as N.J.S.A. 39:3-33.2.

2. N.J.S.A. 54:4-1.

3. 37 N.J. 566 (1962).

4. "The provision of section 23 that in the assessment of acreage actively devoted to agricultural use, the taxable value 'shall not be deemed to include prospective value for subdivisions or nonagricultural use,' is plainly invalid. . . . However the provision may be viewed, it is inescapable that the Legislature intended some impact upon the 'standard of value' favorable to this class of real property. [New Jersey Constitution] Art. VIII, s I, par. 1, plainly requires the application of the same standard of value and the same rate of tax, to all real property taxable for local use." *Id.* at 585.

5. Article VIII, § I, paragraph 1 (b) provides:

The Legislature shall enact laws to provide that the value of land, not less than 5 acres in area, which is determined by the assessing officer of the taxing jurisdiction to be actively devoted to agricultural or horticultural use and to have been so devoted for at least the 2 successive years immediately preceding the tax year in issue, shall, for local tax purposes, on application of the owner, be that value which such land has for agricultural or horticultural use.

Any such laws shall provide that when land which has been valued in this manner for local tax purposes is applied to a use other than for agriculture or horticulture it shall be subject to additional taxes in an amount equal to the difference, if any, between the taxes paid or payable on the basis of the valuation and the assessment authorized hereunder and the taxes that would have been paid or payable had the land been valued and assessed as otherwise provided in this Constitution, in the current year and in such of the tax years immediately preceding, not in excess of 2 such years in which the land was valued as herein authorized.

Such laws shall also provide for the equalization of assessments of land valued in accordance with the provisions hereof and for the assessment and collection of any additional taxes levied thereupon and shall include such other provisions as shall be necessary to carry out the provisions of this amendment.

6. P.L.1981, c. 276.

7. The types of crops that the tenant is permitted to grow, or intends to grow, should also be taken into account. Some crops like asparagus, hay, orchards, and vineyards can be expensive to plant and require more than a single season of growth before harvest, in which case a lease should include a term that is reasonable for the yield duration that the plantings, with appropriate periodic rent increases, and provisions that govern what will become of the plantings and any unharvested crops, upon termination of the lease (i.e., whether removed by the tenant at tenant's expense, or becoming the property and responsibility of the owner). A tenant who raises livestock may also need longer lease terms and advance notice periods due to the difficulty and expense that can be involved in moving a herd of animals, and the structures, facilities and installations that serve them, to another farm. The potential buyer of a farm that is subject to any of these sorts of farm tenancies, but for which the terms are unclear, should require them to be satisfactorily formalized before the purchase.

8. N.J.S.A. 54:4-23.1 *et seq.*; see N.J.S.A. 54:4-23.5 for acreage and income requirements.

9. N.J.S.A. 54:4-23.6.

10. N.J.S.A. 54:4-23.8.

11. An example of this can be found in *State of New Jersey v. Quaker Valley Farms*, 235 N.J. 37 (2018), in which a farmer was found to have violated the soil conservation provisions of a development easement by engaging in a vast earth movement project that attended the construction of several greenhouses.

12. The easement language currently refers only to "residential units" so anyone desiring to use an exception area for purposes that are both non-agricultural and non-residential should make careful inquiry prior to any such development or use.

13. See reference to exception areas in definition of "farm" at N.J.A.C. 2:76-24.3; other references at N.J.A.C. 2:76-17.9, -17A.9, and -24.6.

14. N.J.A.C. 2:76-6.17.

15. Conveyances, however, might nonetheless occur. See, for example, *Birch Investments LLC v. Keymer*, No. A-1840-16T42018, WL 1954771 (N.J. App. Div. Apr. 26, 2018), an unpublished opinion in which the Appellate Division determined that the holder of a municipal tax sale certificate affecting only one of three tax lots that comprised a preserved farm was entitled to foreclose that certificate, and thus acquire independent ownership of that single lot, despite the restriction against division that was set forth in the farmland preservation easement.

16. N.J.A.C. 2:76-6.2 and -6.15.

17. N.J.S.A. 4:1C-32.1 through -32.14.

18. See *Sked v. Pennington Spring Water Co.*, 72 N.J. Eq. 599 (1907), *McLaren v. AT&T*, 1 N.J.Super. 600 (Law Div. 1948), and *Sussex Rural Electric v. Wantage*, 217 N.J.Super. 481 (App. Div. 1987).

19. N.J.S.A. 48:3-17.3.

20. The USEM defines "electric utility service" as "a line or lines for the distribution and/or transmission of electric energy, together with communications and cable television, and all necessary poles, wires, cables, fiber optic cables, fixtures, appliances, guy wires, stubs, anchors, brace poles, and other appropriate facilities, accessories and appurtenances thereto." It should be noted that the terms "distribution" and "transmission" have distinct meanings, as "distribution" of electricity is accomplished at low voltage using small lines over short distances (for example between substations and customers' homes), while "transmission" involves sending higher voltages via larger lines over longer distances.

21. The contract paragraph in question read: "In the event that there are any outstanding mortgage liens or any other encumbrances or claims against the Property including verbal and written lease agreements and unspecified utility easements, this Agreement shall be contingent upon the consent of all mortgagees and all other claimants against the Property to subordinate their claims to the Deed of Easement to be executed by Seller. If such mortgagees or claimants are unwilling to subordinate their claims to the Deed of Easement, the SADC may terminate this Agreement, in which case, the Seller agrees to reimburse the SADC for the Application Processing Costs incurred with respect to Seller's application."

22. N.J.S.A. 4:1C-1 (italics added).

23. See N.J.S.A. 4:1C-9.

24. See N.J.A.C. 2:76-2A.13, which includes the following definitions that show the variety of uses and structures to be permitted as, or in connection with, agriculture:

"Agriculture-related educational activities" means on-farm educational offerings that have an agricultural focus and are related to marketing the agricultural or horticultural output of the commercial farm. Such activities are accessory to, and serve to increase, the direct-market sales of the agricultural output of a commercial farm by enhancing the experience of purchasing agricultural products for the purpose of attracting customers to the commercial farm. Examples of agriculture-related educational activities may include, but are not limited to: school trips, hands-on farming activities, educational displays, farm tours, farm task experiences, wine tastings, agriculture-related lectures for clubs, farm open house days, and agriculture-related classes on topics, such as, but not limited to: canning, freezing, cooking with fresh produce, pie making, pruning, beekeeping, animal care, and gardening.

"Ancillary entertainment-based activities" means non-agricultural offerings, commonly used as incidental components of on-farm direct marketing activities, that are accessory to, and serve to increase, the direct-market sales of the agricultural output of a commercial farm. Such activities are designed to attract customers to a commercial farm by enhancing the experience of purchasing agricultural products. Examples of ancillary entertainment-based activities include, but are not limited to: background live or recorded music, face painting, story-telling, sandbox area, small swing set or playground equipment, pedal carts for children, and picnic tables. Such activities may have a fee associated with them, but such fees shall be *de minimis* compared to the income generated from the sale of the agricultural output of the commercial farm.

"Farm-based recreational activities" means recreational offerings that are uniquely suited to occurring on a farm and also may include common outdoor recreation activities that are compatible with the agricultural use of the farm, where such offerings and activities are related to marketing the agricultural or horticultural output of the commercial farm. Such activities are accessory to, and serve to increase, the direct-market sales of the agricultural output of the commercial farm by enhancing the experience of purchasing agriculture products for the purpose of attracting customers to the commercial farm. Examples of farm-based recreational activities uniquely suited to occurring on a farm may include, but are not limited to: corn, sunflower, and other crop mazes; hayrides and wagon rides; agricultural animal display or petting areas; farm tours; horseback riding; pony rides; and tractor pulls. Examples of farm-based recreational activities considered common outdoor recreation activities that are compatible with the agricultural use of the farm include, but are not limited to: hiking; bird watching; sleigh rides; hunting and fishing; and bonfires. Activities and related infrastructure not considered farm-based recreational activities include, but are not limited to: athletic fields; paintball; go-karting and other similar racetracks; carnival-type amusement rides; and the flying of hobby, private, or commercial aircraft.

25. N.J.S.A. 4:1C-9; *N.J.A.C.* 2:76-2.3 and -2.4.

26. *Franklin Tp. v. Den Hollander*, 172 N.J. 147, 153 (2002).

27. See *Franklin Tp. v. Den Hollander*, 338 N.J. Super. 373 (App. Div. 2001), *affirmed* 172 N.J. 147 (2002) (municipal land use regulations); *Bor. of Closter v. Abram Demaree Homestead, Inc.*, 365 N.J. Super. 338 (App. Div. 2004) (public nuisance); and *Curzi v. Raub*, 415 N.J. Super. 1 (App. Div. 2010) (private nuisance).

28. The Appellate Division initially asserted the logical importance of such notice in *Curzi v. Raub, supra,* at 23; later, in 2014, the SADC adopted notice requirements by rule for all CADB nuisance and SSAMP hearings (see N.J.A.C. 2:76-2.7(d) and -2.8(c)1).

29. N.J.S.A. 4:1C-3 defines a "commercial farm" as (1) a farm management unit of no less than five acres producing agricultural or horticultural products worth $2,500 or more annually, and satisfying the eligibility criteria for differential property taxation pursuant to the "Farmland Assessment Act of 1964," [N.J.S.A. 54:4-23.1 *et seq.*], or (2) a farm management unit less than five acres, producing agricultural or horticultural products worth $50,000 or more annually and otherwise satisfying the eligibility criteria for differential property taxation pursuant to the Farmland Assessment Act, and a "farm management unit" as a parcel or parcels of land, whether contiguous or noncontiguous, together with agricultural or horticultural buildings, structures and facilities, producing agricultural or horticultural products, and operated as a single enterprise.

30. In 2014, the SADC adopted procedures for CADB review of RTFA applications, codified as N.J.A.C. 2:76-2.3 through -2.5, -2.7, and -2.8, including checklists similar to those typically required for development applications pursuant to the Municipal Land Use Law.

31. See, generally, N.J.A.C. 2:76-2A.13.

32. See https://nj.gov/agriculture/sadc/rtfprogram/formdet/conflictres/ and https://nj.gov/agriculture/sadc/rtfprogram/formdet/ssamp/

Section 9

Green Acres Diversions

Brent Carney, Esq., and Andrew Brewer, Esq.

In striking a balance between preservation and development, the law recognizes the need for development of parkland that was originally intended to be preserved for recreation and conservation purposes in limited circumstances. Lands that are acquired by a local government unit or a nonprofit with Green Acres funding are referred to as funded parkland. Unfunded parkland refers to all other land held by a local government unit for recreation and conservation purposes at the time of receipt of Green Acres funding.

THE GOAL OF THE GREEN ACRES PROGRAM

The goal of preservation set forth by the Green Acres program is as follows: "[T]o achieve, in partnership with others, a system of interconnection open spaces, whose protection will preserve and enhance New Jersey's natural environment and its historic, scenic, and recreational resources for public use and enjoyment." The general rule is that funded parkland and unfunded parkland are to be held in perpetuity for recreation and conservation purposes. Specifically, these lands are subject to Green Acres restrictions which limit the use, maintenance, and disposal of the property. Additionally, funded and unfunded parkland are to be identified by the local government unit on the Recreation Open Space Inventory (the ROSI). The Green Acres program within the New Jersey Department of Environment Protection (NJDEP) also provides an online ROSI.

Properties that are not on the ROSI, however, are also subject to Green Acre restrictions if at the time the local government unit received the Green Acres funding or anytime thereafter, the local government unit utilized its property for recreation and conservation purposes. This is true, even if the local government unit identified such property for non-recreation and conservation purposes in its master plan, zoning ordinances, or such other planning documents but utilized the property as a park. *Cedar Cove, Inc. v. Stanzione*, 122 N.J. 202, 215 (1991) ("Thus, in this case, such official municipal determinations, e.g., those reflected in master plans, zoning ordinances, or tax maps, that do not coincide with actual use cannot alone establish the character or nature of properties sufficiently to exempt them from the sales restrictions of the 1975 Act.").

EXCEPTIONS TO THE RULE

Certain exceptions to the general rule, however, apply. The following activities do not constitute a diversion or disposal of funded or unfunded parkland pursuant to N.J.A.C. 7:36-25.2(d):

1. Construction of a regional flood control project that is part of a regional flood control plan and that will, as a significant design element and purpose of the project, create or enhance a permanent water body suitable for water-dependent public recreation, provided the project does not have any significant adverse impact on the natural resource or recreational value of the affected parkland;

2. The continued operation of a municipal or county leaf-composting facility that existed as of the time of receipt of Green Acres funding, provided that the facility is in compliance with all applicable state and local regulations; however, any expansion of the facility (including the use of adjacent parkland as a regulatory buffer for the composting facility), any use of the composting facility for materials other than leaves, or any use of the facility for another non-recreation or nonconservation purpose requires the approval of the commissioner and the State House Commission as a diversion under N.J.A.C. 7:36–26. In addition, in the event the local government unit ceases operation of the facility, the underlying land shall be subject to the Green Acres restrictions to the same extent as it would have been had the leaf composting facility not existed;

3. The removal of a nonhistoric structure from funded or unfunded parkland to facilitate or expand the recreation or conservation use of the parkland, whether or not the structure was purchased with Green Acres funding;

4. The administrative transfer of parkland by a local government unit or nonprofit to another local government unit, the state, the federal government, or a nonprofit for recreation and conservation purposes, provided such transfer complies with the procedural requirements of *N.J.A.C.* 7:36–25.5;

5. The use of a parking lot as a designated commuter parking lot, provided the parking lot was constructed on parkland prior to June 30, 1999, and was not constructed with Green Acres funding and that such use is approved by the commissioner under *N.J.A.C.* 7:36–25.15;

6. Replacement or enlargement of an existing municipally owned or county-owned drainage structure or sewer or water pipeline within a 20-foot assumed easement width (as calculated by measuring ten feet on each side from the center of the pipe or drainage structure). However, construction of new privately owned utilities or construction of new roads to service municipal or county utilities within the assumed easement shall constitute a diversion of parkland;

7. Replacement or enlargement of a highway or pedestrian bridge within an existing road right-of-way or, if no right-of-way is formally delineated, within an assumed

right-of-way corridor created by a connection of the road rights-of-way on either end of the bridge;

8. Any lease or use agreement, or renewal thereof, which supports or promotes the use of parkland for recreation and conservation purposes, has a term of fewer than twenty-five years and is approved by the Department under *N.J.A.C.* 7:36-25.13 and any concession agreement meeting the requirements of *N.J.A.C.* 7:36-25.13(f); and

9. Any lease or use agreement for the use of parkland for a beneficial public purpose other than recreation and conservation purposes which is approved by the Department under, and subject to the limitations of, *N.J.A.C.* 7:36-25.14.

THE GREEN ACRES PROGRAM

The law also recognizes that the goal of the Green Acres program must be balanced with development of parkland when there is a compelling public need, or such disposal or diversion of Green Acres restrictions will yield a significant public benefit. Specifically, there is a disposal/ diversion process, albeit cumbersome, that delegates to the NJDEP commissioner and the State House Commission the power to divert the use or control of parkland for other than recreation and conservation purposes. Specifically, the Green Acres Land Acquisition and Recreation Opportunities Act of 1975 (the "1975 Act") states, "A local unit which receives a grant under this act shall not dispose of or divert for a use for other than recreation and conversation purposes any lands held by such local unit for such purposes at the time of receipt of said grant without the approval of the commissioner [of the DEP] and the State House Commission and following a public hearing by the local unit at least 1 month prior to any such approvals." *N.J.S.A.* 13:8A-47b. The regulations promulgated in accordance with this statute impose a penalty on those that ask for forgiveness for a diversion, rather than permission.

Pursuant to the regulations promulgated by the Green Acres, the disposal (the conveyance of permanent possession of property in fee simple or by easement contrary to Green Acres restrictions) or diversion (the use of parkland contrary to Green Acres restrictions) is classified as either "major" or "minor."

Minor Disposals or Diversions

A minor disposal or diversion is defined pursuant to *N.J.A.C.* 7:36-26.2, and generally applies to (1) easements that occupy less than ten percent of the parkland parcel granted to a public entity; (2) the conveyance or lease of up to one-half acre of parkland if it is less than five percent of the parkland parcel for a project that serves a public purpose; (3) the conveyance of up to one-half acre of parkland to the owner of an adjacent property in order to resolve a boundary dispute if it existed prior to the receipt of Green Acre funding and does not create access that did not exist as of the time of receipt of Green Acre funding; (4) the exchange for other land of equal acreage and located within the same block and lot that supports a public purpose such as relocation of roads or utilities within a park to improve the functioning of a park; or (5) a diversion for the construction of a building for public indoor recreation on funded parkland provided the diversion is less than 50,000 square feet of disturbance. All of these diversions are subject to further specific conditions as set forth in *N.J.A.C.* 7:36-26.2 in order to be classified as a minor diversion.

While this section is not intended to provide the full detailed requirements, if the diversion is classified as minor, the minor diversion requirements generally include the following: (1) a pre-application conference with the Green Acres program; (2) the submission of a pre-application to the Green Acres program that includes a detailed description of the proposed minor diversion, an alternatives analysis for each alternative that could be taken to fulfill the compelling public need or yield significant public benefit which is feasible, reasonable and available including the alternative of "no build" or "no action," an environmental assessment report, a value statement based on the highest and best use or the use intended subsequent to the diversion, a compensation proposal, a listing of other federal, interstate, state, county, and local approvals and permits required for the project, certain mapping including aerial or GIS-based maps of the property to be diverted and the replacement land, and any other information requested by the Green Acres program; (3) the submission of a final application if the Green Acres program after reviewing the pre-application authorizes the submission of the final application; (4) a public hearing on the complete application and a written public comment period which requires a thirty day notice period published in the official newspaper of the municipality in which the parkland proposed for diversion is located, notice on the official website, written notice to Green Acres, the governing body, local planning boards, environmental commissions and open space advisory committees, certified mail to all persons who own land within 200 feet of the parkland, a sign posted on the property meeting certain size and notice requirements, and no later than fifteen days prior to the hearing a display advertisement in the official newspaper of the municipality (the hearing must be transcribed and written public comment must be accepted until two weeks after the hearing); (5) thereafter if the NJDEP commissioner approves the final application it will be sent to the State House Commission which meets four times per year; (6) if the State House Commission approves the same, the applicant must remit any monetary compensation required pursuant to the approval prior to implementing the diversion; and (7) thereafter the NJDEP commissioner shall execute a release of the Green Acres restrictions as to the minor diversion.

Major Disposals or Diversions

If a diversion is not classified as minor, then by definition the diversion is classified as a major diversion. A major diversion is a much more cumbersome process than a minor diversion. While this section is not intended to provide the full detailed requirements, a major diversion generally consists of the following: (1) a pre-application conference with the Green Acres program; (2) a scoping hearing to solicit public comment on the proposed diversion and written public comment which requires a thirty-day notice published in the official newspaper of the municipality in which the parkland proposed for diversion is located, notice on the official website, written notice to Green Acres, the governing body, local planning boards, environmental commissions and open space advisory committees, certified mail to all persons who own land within 200 feet of the parkland, a sign posted on the property meeting certain size and notice requirements, and no later than fifteen days prior to the hearing a display advertisement in the official newspaper of the municipality (the scoping hearing must be transcribed and written public comment must be accepted until two weeks after the hearing); (3) the submission of a pre-application to the Green Acres program that includes a detailed description of the proposed minor diversion, an alternatives analysis for each alternative that could be taken to fulfill the compelling public need or yield significant public benefit which is feasible, reasonable, and available including the alternative of "no build" or "no action," an environmental assessment report, a preliminary compensation proposal, and value statement based on the highest and best use or the use intended subsequent to the diversion, a description of how the proposed project will support the State Development and Redevelopment Plan Goals and will be consistent with the State Development and Redevelopment Plan's Policy Map and the Statewide Policies, a listing of other federal, interstate, state, county, and local approvals and permits required for the project, a copy of the deed for the parkland, certain mapping including aerial or GIS-based maps of the property to be diverted and the replacement land, proof of proper notice of the scoping hearing, a resolution of the governing body endorsing the diversion of parkland, and any other information requested by the Green Acres program; (4) the submission of a final application if the Green Acres program after reviewing the pre-application authorizes the submission of the final application; (5) a public hearing on the complete application and a written public comment period which requires a thirty-day notice period published in the official newspaper of the municipality in which the parkland proposed for diversion is located, notice on the official website, written notice to Green Acres, the governing body, local planning boards, environmental commissions and open space advisory committees, certified mail to all persons who own land within 200 feet of the parkland, a sign posted on the property meeting certain size and notice requirements, and no later than fifteen days prior to the hearing a display advertisement in the official newspaper of the municipality (the hearing must be transcribed and written public comment must be accepted until two weeks after the hearing); (6) thereafter if the NJDEP commissioner approves the final application it will be sent to the State House Commission which meets four times per year; (7) if the State House Commission approves the same, the applicant must remit any monetary compensation required pursuant to the approval prior to implementing the diversion; and (8) thereafter the NJDEP commissioner shall execute a release of the Green Acres restrictions as to the major diversion.

Additionally, major disposals or diversions require replacement land for the disposal or diversion in certain ratios that range from a minimum of 1:1 to 6:1 for general disposals or diversions. The ratio represents the area of replacement land necessary that will become Green Acre restricted as compared to the area of the subject property for which the disposal or diversion of Green Acre restrictions is sought. Notwithstanding the land replacement ratio, the fair market value of the replacement property must always be at least equal to the property being diverted or disposed of. Green Acres defines fair market value to mean "the market value of the parkland proposed to be disposed of or diverted shall be based on the highest and best use or the use intended for the land subsequent to its disposal or diversion, whichever would result in higher market value." *N.J.A.C.* 7:36-26.10(f). In the event that replacement land is not available, the minimum ratios for monetary compensation range from ratios of 2:1 to 10:1. Monetary compensation is not an option for legalizing past disposals or diversions. Legalizing past disposals or diversions has a minimum land replacement ratio of 20:1. Thus, the regulations are designed so that asking permission for disposal or diversion is better than asking for forgiveness for prior illegal disposal or diversion of parkland.

SIGNIFICANT CASE LAW

The significance of the importance placed on the developmental restrictions is evident from the language of the statutory provision as well as the impact of violations of those provisions as determined by both State and Federal courts. The Green Acres statute and regulations unambiguously prohibit the diversion of restricted parkland without first having obtained NJDEP and State House Commission approval. *N.J.S.A.* 13:8A-47(b). The intention of the legislature is unmistakable—there is no authority to divert parkland until NJDEP approval is obtained. The courts faced with this question have held that any attempt to do so is not merely an "irregular exercise" of authority, because the authority does not exist until NJDEP approval is obtained. See, *First American Title Insurance Co. v. Township of Rockaway*, 322 N.J. Super. 583 (Ch. 1999) citing *Samco Rockaway 90 Inc. v. Lawyers Title Ins.*, 1995 WL 328141 (D.N.J. 1995). ("In this case, it is undisputed that Lot 36 was subject to Green Acres restrictions. Therefore, Rockaway did not have the statutory authority to sell Lot 36 to Barki. Without statutory authority, Rockaway's attempted sale of Lot 36 is *ultra vires* and *void ab initio*.") In other words, in the eyes of the law, a transaction in violation of a Green Acres restriction never happened, which can lead to unique problems suffered by the unwary.

In *First American*, the Township of Rockaway had accepted Green Acres funds in 1981, and in the process had designated the property in question as recreation and open space, subject to Green Acres restrictions. In 1985, Rockaway, without any approval from the DEP, adopted a resolution authorizing the sale of the property. Following an auction in September 1985, the property was sold to defendant Zibaee. In 1988, Zibaee obtained a subdivision of the property by the Rockaway Planning Board and recorded a deed to himself. The DEP had sent Rockaway a letter in 1991 directing the Township to notify the persons in the purported chain of title that the conveyances were prohibited. The Township failed to notify any of the participants. In 1995, Zibaee sold the property to defendant Erickson.

Defendant Erickson was advised in December 1995 of the Green Acres encumbrance and that it prohibited the issuance of any construction permits. First American paid Erickson under its title policy, then sued the parties in the chain of title to unravel the transactions. As a preliminary issue to proceed with the action to quiet title, the Court first analyzed the initial conveyance from Rockaway to Zibaee. That analysis resulted in the following:

Because the approval of the New Jersey Department of Environmental Protection ("NJDEP") is a mandatory requirement before a municipality may convey a property subject to Green Acres restrictions, Rockaway's conveyance of the subject premises is void ab initio. Id. at 592.

After citing the prohibition against diversion contained in *N.J.S.A.* 13:8A-47(b), the court noted that under that provision the Township was "prohibited from selling or conveying the subject premises without the requisite State approvals." Id. at 578, *citing Cedar Cove Inc. v. Stanzione*, 122 N.J. 202 (1991). In *Cedar Grove Inc. v. Stanzione*, 122 N.J. 202, 214 (1991), the New Jersey Supreme Court held that "The purpose of the additional restriction of the 1975 [Green Acres] act (N.J.S.A. 13:8A–47b) is to prevent municipalities from selling existing recreational or conservation land on receipt of Green Acres funding for the acquisition or improvement of additional sites." The Court voided a sale by the Borough of Toms River of recreational land as a result of Green Acres restrictions.

The same concern has been voiced by the Law Division on this issue. In *Kaufman v. North Haledon Borough*, 229 N.J. Super. 349, 359 (Law Div. 1988), the court held that

> The language of the statute is mandatory and would appear, the Court concludes, to be self-implementing and not require any further administrative action by the NJDEP. Any lands held by a municipality for either recreation or conservation purposes at the time of Green Acres funding are made subject to this statutory restriction and cannot be sold or otherwise diverted from their existing use unless statutory requirements have been met.

After reviewing this, in *Samco* Judge Wolin held, "In this case, it is undisputed that Lot 36 was subject to Green Acres restrictions. Therefore, Rockaway did not have the statutory authority to sell Lot 36 to Barki." *Id.* at 3. This holding was cited with approval by the court in *First American* when it came to the same conclusion, holding that such a conveyance was void ab initio.

Similar difficulties were encountered by a developer in the Township of Millburn following a subdivision which ran afoul of the Green Acres restrictions. *Haykell Development LLC v. Township of Millburn, et al.* (Dkt. ESX-L-6339-09). A subdivision application adjacent to a Green Acres restricted park involved a newly created lot with unique access issues. The developer proposed and was ultimately granted the right to access the property by way of an existing driveway in the park, albeit without first obtaining DEP approval. The developer proceeded to construct a luxury single-family home and placed it on the market at an initial list price of $5.5M, prior to the economic downturn in 2008. While the new home was being marketed, NJDEP learned of the unauthorized use of the driveway for access and directed that no sale take place until new access was obtained, or the Green Acres violation remedied. The Township commenced proceedings to obtain approval for the disposal/diversion, but litigation ensued wherein the developer sought damages related to its inability to sell the property while the disposal/diversion process proceeded.

The trial court ultimately dismissed the claims against the Township based on two principles. First, as in the cases cited earlier, the court held that the "permission" to use the park driveway was not within the power of the Township, and thus had no legal effect. Second, the court held that because the Green Acres restrictions were filed with the county clerk, the developer had constructive, if not actual notice, of the impediment and therefore was charged with knowledge that any "permission" without explicit DEP approval would not be effective. Once the approval for the disposal/diversion was provided by the DEP, the home was sold in late 2012.

Section 10

Historic Preservation

Michele R. Donato, Esq.

ESTABLISHING A HISTORIC PRESERVATION COMMISSION

Municipal agencies, including historic preservation commissions, are created by the Legislature, and their powers are conferred by the Municipal Land Use Law (MLUL). *In re Estate of Neuberger v. Middletown Tp.*, 215 N.J. Super. 375 (App. Div. 1987).

In some communities, the historic preservation commission ("commission") is created by ordinance to spearhead initial planning efforts to evaluate properties eligible for historic designation. In other communities, the planning board engages in studies to identify historic resources in the master plan. The MLUL does not dictate the process but instead gives municipalities the flexibility to engage in historic preservation planning to regulate historic properties and provide design guidelines as best suited for the community.

ORDINANCE REQUIREMENTS

In 1985, the Legislature first enabled municipalities to adopt historic preservation ordinances and imposed important planning requirements in order to do so. To address concerns that properties would be arbitrarily designated as historic, after July 1, 1994, the MLUL mandates the identification of historic sites and districts in the historic preservation plan element of the master plan before adopting a regulatory ordinance. The 1991 amendments to the MLUL require that the historic preservation element or other master plan element indicate the location and significance of historic sites and districts, identify the standards used to assess worthiness, and analyze the impact of each component element of the master plan on the preservation of historic resources. N.J.S.A. 40:55D-65.1.

The definition of the term "historic site" reaches beyond architectural and historic importance and includes natural objects of historical, archaeological, cultural, or scenic significance. N.J.S.A. 40:55D-4. Some recent municipal and state efforts have broadened the meaning of historic to include industrial properties and other sites due to their association with a community's cultural history. The success of this expanded approach is yet to be tested in court.

Initially, the MLUL simply required listing historic sites in the master plan. The 1991 adoption of N.J.S.A. 40:55D-65.1 creates a procedure for an exception parallel to that applicable to land use ordinances and allows an ordinance to be adopted without planning support in the master plan, provided that the governing body provides a statement of reasons in a resolution, records the reasons in the minutes and passes the ordinance by a weighted majority. In the land use field, the Supreme Court has questioned the validity of a resolution of reasons that is not supported by planning. *Riya Finnegan v. South Brunswick Township*, 197 N.J. 184 (2008)

Since enactment of the enabling provisions for historic preservation, there have been no reported cases in New Jersey in which a municipality has designated a historic site or district without complying with N.J.S.A. 40:55D-65.1.

DESIGN CRITERIA AND GUIDELINES

When a municipality designates and regulates historic sites and districts, the ordinance must provide design criteria and guidelines in addition to the zoning designations. The guidelines can be inherently flexible to address the architectural mélange that often exists. In *Nadelson v. Township Of Millburn*, 297 N.J. Super. 549 (Law Div. 1996) the court rejected a challenge to guidelines as impermissibly vague.

There are many examples of well-written and informative guidelines that aid the commission and the regulated community in a constructive manner. Communities should adopt guidelines with graphics and other design tools to facilitate preservation. It is also advisable to implement a tiered system of review. The MLUL permits the ordinance to define a minor application that the chairman of the commission can approve. For example, fences, lighting, and requests for field changes that comply with the design guidelines can efficiently be placed in this category. A monetary threshold for minor work is not recommended since it does not relate to historic integrity. The ordinance should also provide a mechanism for emergency repairs.

A well-written ordinance should contain a definition of ordinary maintenance and repair to allow the repair and replacement of deterioration, wear, or damage to a structure with material and workmanship of the same quality and appearance. If a designated official certifies that the work to be performed meets this definition, then no permit should be required.

These types of provisions encourage preservation yet relieve property owners of unnecessary administrative review.

HYBRID NATURE OF AN HPC

N.J.S.A. 40:55D-109 specifies the powers and duties of historic preservation commissions. These powers are often described as hybrid since an HPC has both land use and construction-related functions. The MLUL spells out these distinct powers— one being the function of commissions with respect to planning and development applications and the other being the permit review function. These hybrid powers are frequently misunderstood.

A commission is authorized to perform planning activities by preparing a survey of historic sites and by coordinating with the planning board regarding the master plan. A commission can also recommend the inclusion of historic sites in the capital improvement program. Broad advisory and educational and informational functions are authorized. In addition to these planning functions, the commission advises the planning board and board of adjustment on applications for development.

N.J.S.A. 40:55D-110 provides for the commission's purely advisory role regarding development applications and applies regardless of whether the historic resource is specifically regulated in the ordinance. Advisory review of applications applies to all sites or districts identified on the official map or in any component element of the master plan.

Failure to refer the application to the commission does not invalidate the development application. The commission may provide its advice by submitting a written report, but the MLUL specifies that the advice must be conveyed orally by one of the commission members or staff, even if a written report is submitted.

The hybrid aspect of the commission is its power to report on permits *not approved by an application for development*. The permit review function can apply to an activity such as demolition or construction of an addition that does not require the approval of an application for development, that is, where there is no MLUL involvement. It can also apply to those aspects of an application not approved by the planning or zoning board, it being the Legislature's assumption that land use boards do not regulate architectural style.

Planning and zoning boards have no authority to act on demolition permits since none of the standards of a subdivision or site plan ordinance authorize either board to consider demolition. N.J.S.A. 40:55D37 to 40. In a comprehensive but unpublished decision, Maurice J. Gallipolli, former Assignment Judge of Hudson County, ruled that a planning board had no authority to deny a conforming application based on the commission's report that demolition should not be permitted. If a municipality seeks to restrict demolition of historic structures, it must do so through historic preservation.

N.J.S.A. 40:55D-111 addresses applications for permits pertaining to historic properties and imports a new function into the MLUL. If the ordinance regulates historic sites or districts, the governing body *shall* provide for referral of permits to the commission for a written report regarding "any of those aspects of the change proposed, which aspects were not determined by approval of an application for development by a municipal agency." This power can relate to permits required by other statutes even if no land use application is required.

The permit review function is commonly referred to as a "certificate of appropriateness." Although not specifically defined in the MLUL, N.J.S.A. 40:55D-18, which pertains to enforcement, authorizes a governing body to require "specified permits, certificates or authorizations" prior to construction, alteration, repair, remodeling, removal, destruction, and other activities.

A common example of the permit review function when no land use application is involved is for an addition to a single-family house that is a designated historic site or located in a historic district. If the addition conforms to the zoning ordinance, no variances are required. As a single-family house, no site plan review is required. N.J.S.A. 40:55D-37a. As a freestanding preexisting lot, no subdivision approval is required. *See* the definition of "subdivision" in N.J.S.A. 40:55D-7. Because the house is regulated by the historic preservation ordinance, permit review by the commission *is* required.

Another instance of a permit that has no land use component is demolition. The construction official issues the permit under the Uniform Construction Code and the official is required to refer the permit to the commission for its report. The review of a permit for demolition is within the exclusive jurisdiction of the commission under the MLUL, subject to possible appeal to the zoning board of adjustment pursuant to N.J.S.A. 40:55D-70a.

STRONG OR WEAK COMMISSION

In connection with permit review, a municipality can create either a strong or a weak commission. A strong commission reports directly to the administrative officer, whereas a weak commission reports to the planning board, which in turn reports to the administrative officer. The report of the commission, or the planning board, as the case may be, is binding on the administrative officer.

The permit review function provides that the commission, or the planning board in the case of a weak commission, shall report to the administrative officer within forty-five days of referral of the application to the commission. If the commission recommends against the permit or recommends conditions, the administrative officer must deny the permit or include the conditions. Failure to report within the forty-five-day period constitutes a favorable report without conditions. As a result of these procedures, the decision is actually that of the administrative officer and not the commission. Since the commission speaks through the administrative officer, there is a *de novo* appeal from the decision pursuant to N.J.S.A. 40:55D-70a.

The MLUL does not authorize proceedings before a commission to be treated as applications for development. There is no provision for maintaining a verbatim record, for determining completeness or incorporating other procedural features applicable to applications for development.

INVERSE CONDEMNATION CONCERNS

A municipality is not allowed to zone property into idleness by restraint against all reasonable use. As Justice Holmes noted, "A strong public desire to improve the public condition is not enough to warrant achieving the desire by a shorter cut than the constitutional way of paying for the change." *Pennsylvania Coal Co. v. Mahon*, 260 N.J. 393 (1922). Case law recognizes that when historic properties cannot feasibly and reasonably be developed, demolition is appropriate. *In re Register of Historic Places Act*, 408 N.J. Super. 54 (App. Div. 2009).

Some municipalities have incorporated a hardship provision into their ordinances to provide relief for historic properties seeking approval for demolition or adaptive reuse. The issue arises when slate roofs, siding or other expensive historic features are to be replaced. An attorney general's opinion dated January 29, 1997, finds that hardship procedures are not authorized by the MLUL.

Sound governance requires a balance that does not allow the public to dominate the discourse by preventing the reasonable use of land. Preventing demolition of structures that lack historic beauty and depriving a property owner of just compensation can undermine the legitimacy of preservation efforts for meaningful architectural gems. Preservation regulation is still a young aspect of land use law, and it should concentrate on properties of enduring value to strengthen the core value of preservation.

Chapter 6

Air Quality Regulations

Manko, Gold, Katcher & Fox LLP

Air quality in New Jersey is protected under an overlapping regulatory scheme involving federal and state-level requirements. At the federal level, the Clean Air Act (CAA), 42 U.S.C.A. § 7401 et seq., establishes air quality standards that states are required to meet, as well as the permitting standards applicable to larger emission sources. Those federal requirements may be implemented by the U.S. Environmental Protection Agency (EPA), but are typically also delegated to state or local air pollution control agencies.

At the state level, the Division of Air Quality of the New Jersey Department of Environmental Protection (NJDEP or Department) manages air quality pursuant to the Air Pollution Control Act (APCA), N.J.S.A. 26:2C-1 et seq. The regulatory subchapters implementing the APCA found at N.J.A.C. 7:27 provide the State's air pollution control regulations and "govern the emitting of and such activities as result in the introducing of contaminants into the ambient atmosphere."[1] Additional requirements provided at N.J.A.C 7:27A detail air administrative procedures and penalties, and the provisions of N.J.A.C. 7:27B mandate specific air sampling and analytical procedures. Collectively, these regulations comprise a comprehensive program including air monitoring, inventories of sources, emission reduction plans, rules, permits, stack testing, air quality modeling and risk assessment, vehicle testing, inspections and enforcement.

FEDERAL CLEAN AIR ACT

Because NJDEP's air quality program seeks, at least in part, to satisfy federal standards, an understanding of the federal statutory structure is necessary for any analysis of air pollution control in New Jersey. Congress first signed the CAA into law in 1970, with the stated purpose of "protect[ing] and enhance[ing] the quality of the Nation's air resources so as to promote the public health and welfare and the productive capacity of [the United States] population."[2]

EPA is the federal agency charged with administering the CAA. In 1990, Congress dramatically expanded the scope of the CAA, giving EPA greater authority to administer the Act and subjecting more sources of air pollution to the CAA's permitting requirements.[3] The CAA's six titles require EPA to set air quality standards for stationary and mobile sources of air pollution, establish programs for acid rain control and ozone protection, and set forth a comprehensive air permitting program jointly administered by the States and EPA.

National Ambient Air Quality Standards

The CAA relies on "cooperative federalism" to achieve its air quality goals, requiring EPA to set national air quality standards and the states to achieve such national standards through adoption of their own air quality regulations.[4] Section 108 of the CAA obligates EPA to publish and "from time to time" revise a list which includes each "air pollutant" that "cause[s] or contribute[s] to air pollution which may reasonably be anticipated to endanger public health or welfare" and which are produced by "numerous or diverse mobile or stationary sources."[5] Air pollutants listed under Section 108 are referred to as "criteria pollutants" and are chosen for their wide-spread presence throughout the country. Since the passage of the CAA, EPA has listed six criteria pollutants:

- Carbon Monoxide (CO)
- Lead (Pb)
- Nitrogen Oxides (NO_x)
- Ozone (O_3)
- Particulate Matter (PM)
- Sulfur Dioxide (SO_2)

EPA has further defined PM in two different forms: coarse particulate matter (PM_{10}) and fine particulate matter ($PM_{2.5}$).

For each criteria pollutant, EPA must set National Ambient Air Quality Standards (NAAQS), which are limits on the concentration of each criteria pollutant that may be present anywhere in the United States. The NAAQS themselves are not directly enforceable under the CAA but rather set the standards that define the states' obligations to limit pollutants through the adoption of state-specific air quality programs.

The CAA requires EPA to set both "primary" and "secondary" NAAQS.[6] Primary NAAQS must be set at a level "requisite to protect public health with an adequate margin of safety."[7] Secondary NAAQS must be set at a level "requisite to protect the public welfare from any known or anticipated adverse effects associated with the presence of such air pollutant in the ambient air."[8] EPA is required to review each NAAQS every five years and make any revisions to the NAAQS which are necessary to ensure that the standards continue to protect the public health and welfare. Thus far, EPA has expressed all NAAQS in terms of concentrations of the given criteria pollutant in the ambient (i.e., outdoor) air, which are measured over a specific time period. For example, the primary NAAQS for SO_2 is 75 parts per billion (ppb) measured over a one-hour period,[9] and the secondary NAAQS for SO_2 is 0.5 parts per million (ppm) measured over a three-hour period.[10] The NAAQS are codified in 40 C.F.R. Part 50.

State Implementation Plans

The primary mechanism for enforcing the NAAQS is through State Implementation Plans (SIPs), which are plans that the CAA requires each state to prepare to demonstrate how it will achieve a given NAAQS. States are required to submit their SIPs to EPA for approval, and each SIP must identify legally enforceable regulations with which sources of air pollution must comply.[11]

After setting a NAAQS, EPA is required to designate, within two years, areas in each state that either meet or exceed the given NAAQS.[12] An area of a state that meets the NAAQS is said to be in "attainment," whereas an area of a state that does not meet the NAAQS is referred to as a "nonattainment" area.[13] After EPA designates areas of each state as either attainment or nonattainment areas (or unclassifiable), each state is required to submit to EPA its SIP governing the relevant criteria pollutant.[14] The CAA allows states more time to submit SIPs for the areas of a state that are in nonattainment.[15]

In New Jersey, the Department's Bureau of Air Quality Planning (BAQP) is responsible for developing SIPs designed to bring the State's remaining nonattainment areas into attainment and to maintain the air quality of areas already in attainment. The plans are all available through the Bureau's website, www.state.nj.us/dep/baqp, and include components such as emission inventory development, control strategy evaluation, coordination with other states and regional organizations, and public participation in the process. As a general matter, New Jersey's SIPs consist of all the various permitting, control, monitoring, and enforcement conditions applicable to sources of air pollution through the regulations set forth at Title 7, Chapter 27 of the New Jersey Administrative Code.

The Bureau of Air Monitoring within the Department's Division of Air Quality monitors air quality at monitoring sites throughout the State and makes the resulting data available at www.njaqinow.net. With the exception of ozone, New Jersey has attained the NAAQS for all criteria pollutants. Most recently, EPA redesignated the entire state as unclassifiable/attainment for the 2010 1-hour SO_2 standard in January 2018.[1617] All of New Jersey is designated as a moderate nonattainment area for the 8-hour ozone standard of 0.075 ppm.[18]

NEW JERSEY AIR QUALITY PERMITTING

New Jersey's air quality permitting programs are intended to satisfy both CAA permitting program requirements and the permitting requirements set forth in the APCA. Air permits are administered by the Department's Bureau of Air Permits (BAP). BAP implements the State's air permitting programs through the issuance of two primary types of permits that incorporate both federal- and state-based applicable requirements: preconstruction permits and operating permits. Operating permits or certificates issued to "minor facilities" are governed by Subchapter 8 of the APCA regulations.[19] Operating permits issued to "major facilities" are governed by Subchapter 22.[20] Specific and additional permitting requirements may also result from the application to a given facility of federal requirements such as those found in the New Source Review program of the CAA.

Applicability—"Significant Sources"

New Jersey's permitting requirements apply to certain "sources of air contaminant emissions," some of which are individual pieces of equipment, others of which entail operations or processes that result in emissions. "Air contaminant" is defined very broadly by the New Jersey air quality regulations to include any substance, other than water or distillates of air, present in the atmosphere as solid particles, liquid particles, vapors, or gases.[21] However, only "significant sources" of air contaminants fall under New Jersey's permitting framework, with any sources not meeting this threshold being deemed an "insignificant source" not required to have a permit or operating certificate. It is critical to recognize the distinction between "significant" sources and "major" sources for purposes of New Jersey's air permitting scheme. A significant source merely is not insignificant and may be a "minor" source of air emissions. Similarly, the significance thresholds used for New Jersey air permitting purposes are substantially less than the "significance" thresholds applied under federal New Source Review regulations.

The scope of significant sources requiring permitting under the regulations extends to any equipment or operation that emits air contaminants other than carbon dioxide and which belongs to a number of listed categories. These categories include, but are not limited to certain types of

- commercial fuel burning equipment
- emergency generators
- equipment emitting toxic substances
- dry cleaning equipment
- surface cleaners
- equipment used in graphic arts operations
- gasoline transfer operations
- stationary storage tanks

The commercial fuel burning category is quite broad, as it covers units having a maximum rated heat input capacity of 1 MMBtu/hr, including emergency generators.[22] Another category of significant sources, covering equipment in which the combined weight of all raw materials used exceeds 50 pounds in any one hour, is generally viewed as a catchall for certain sources not otherwise falling into significant source categories.[23]

The regulations also notably contain specific exclusions from the definition of significant source for listed sources that do not need a permit or operating certificate.[24] These exempted sources include equipment and sources such as certain[25]

- photocopiers
- hand-held polishing equipment
- storage tanks meeting specific criteria
- basins and lagoons at treatment works
- smaller incinerators serving limited dwelling units
- smaller fuel cell systems
- dry cleaning equipment that uses only liquid carbon dioxide

Accordingly, when evaluating the applicability of air permitting obligations in New Jersey, a necessary first step is to review both the listed significant and the exempted sources to determine how a particular activity or piece of equipment will be treated under the regulations.

Minor and Major Facilities

For any significant source, the applicable permitting framework will be determined in part by whether the source is part of a "Minor Facility" or a "Major Facility." Minor facilities are those facilities which exhibit potential emission rates below the applicable major source thresholds, and which do not otherwise trigger the operating permit requirements established under Subchapter 22. A facility can also qualify as a minor source by accepting federally enforceable permit limitations in order to avoid triggering the major source standards under Subchapter 22, in which case the source is known as a synthetic minor source.

Major facilities are those facilities for which total emissions of certain pollutants (hazardous air pollutants and/or criteria pollutants) exceed the major source thresholds established in Title V of the CAA and further detailed at N.J.A.C. 7:27-22.2. Major facilities further include those facilities regulated under the acid rain program in Title IV of the CAA. Facility owners and operators can also voluntarily elect to obtain a major source operating permit.[26] As the identification of significant source operations in Subchapter 8, Subchapter 22 identifies significant source operations subject to the operating permit requirement.[27]

Preconstruction Permits and Operating Certificates

Owners and operators of proposed new or modified sources are required under most circumstances to obtain a preconstruction permit and operating certificate before initiating construction, installation, reconstruction, or modification of any stationary source of air emissions (or control apparatus serving the source) that qualifies as a "significant source" under Subchapter 8 of the APCA regulations.[28]

Applications. In order to obtain a preconstruction permit and operating certificate, a facility owner or operator must submit an application to the Department in accordance with N.J.A.C. 7:27-8.4. Completed applications should be submitted in electronic format, using the Department's Remote AIMS Data User System (RADIUS) or Electronic New Jersey Environmental Management System (e-NJEMS), if available.[29] A permit application must include details regarding the equipment or control apparatus as necessary to determine whether such equipment is designed to operate without causing a violation of any relevant State or Federal laws or regulations.[30] Such information generally describes the processes, raw materials used, operating procedures, physical and chemical nature of any air contaminant, the volume of gas discharged, and such other information as the Department considers necessary.[31] In some cases, an application may cover more than one source, depending on whether a logical grouping can be established, considering how each source is vented or how a particular product is made.[32]

Permit Requirements / State of the Art Technology. To obtain approval of a permit and certificate, an applicant is required to demonstrate that each significant source at issue meets the appropriate standard for emission control.[33] Depending on the location and the type of source, the applicable standard could include the Reasonably Available Control Technology (RACT) requirements under N.J.A.C. 7:27-16 or 19, the federal New Source Performance Standards (NSPS) under the CAA,[34] the Best Available Control Technology (BACT) requirements under the federal Prevention of Significant Deterioration (PSD) program,[35] or any other applicable State or Federal pollution control standards.

Even for those sources that exhibit emission rates below thresholds triggering any federal emission control requirements, New Jersey regulations establish a program requiring evaluation of control options. The APCA requires the owner or the operator of a source whose potential emissions exceed applicable thresholds listed in Tables A and B of Appendix 1 to Subchapter 8 to incorporate "advances in the art of air pollution control," commonly referred to as "State of the Art" or "SOTA."[36] These emission thresholds are generally substantially less than emission triggers under federal regulations. The Department states that the SOTA requirement is intended to minimize the degradation of air quality from new sources, improve air quality when existing sources are replaced or reconstructed, maximize economic growth opportunity, and promote pollution prevention.[37]

Both the applicability and the requirements of SOTA can entail a complex analysis because the regulations identify a number of ways in which SOTA can be demonstrated. For instance, for a source that is subject to Lowest Achievable Emissions Rate (LAER) requirements for a particular air contaminant (see New Source Review (NSR) section below), compliance with LAER represents SOTA for the source.[38] Similarly, if a source is subject to federal National Emission Standards for Hazardous Air Pollutants (NESHAP) and/or NSPS, compliance with the applicable requirements under these regulatory programs satisfies SOTA for the source.[39] Alternatively, if a source is not otherwise subject to any NSR-based control technology standards, or any NESHAP or NSPS requirements, then the applicant must document SOTA using one of the alternative options established by the Department, which include demonstrating compliance with a Department-approved SOTA Manual and performing a case-by-case "top-down" SOTA demonstration.[40]

Source Testing. Facility owners and operators will generally be required to perform certain emissions testing pursuant to the preconstruction permit and operating certificate. Such testing must be conducted under the oversight, in accordance with the standards and procedures of the Department's Emission Measurement Section (EMS)—formerly the Bureau of Technical Services, which is responsible for overseeing the quality assurance/quality control of air emissions measurements in New Jersey. EMS has three primary programs, including oversight and review of all single event stack emission tests conducted by source facilities, certification of the accuracy and reliability of continuous emissions monitoring systems (CEMS), and conducting confirmatory and research testing utilizing EMS's mobile analyzing equipment. EMS has issued Technical Manual 1004 establishing guidelines for compliance stack testing programs to be followed by affected facility owners and operators in New Jersey, and Technical Manual 1005 establishing guidelines on CEMS, Continuous Opacity

Monitoring Systems (COMS), Periodic Monitoring Procedures (PMPs), and Annual Combustion Adjustments.[41]

General Permits

As an alternative to applying for a source-specific preconstruction permit and operating certificate, owners and operators of certain classes of significant sources have the option of applying for a general permit.[42] General permits are available to owners and operators of a number of significant source categories, including certain fuel dispensing facilities, emergency generators, stationary storage tanks, boilers and/or heaters having a capacity less than 10 MMBtu/hr, dry cleaning equipment, and portable engines, among others.[43] NJDEP has recently made available for use revised general permits for Plating, Etching, Pickling, and Electropolishing Operations, Manufacturing and Materials Handling Equipment, and Non-Hazardous Dry Cleaning Equipment. Additional revisions to the general permits for Boilers and Heaters between 10 MMBTU/hr and 50 MMBTU/hr and Temporary Equipment are expected sometime in 2019. General permits are not available to sources that are subject to federal PSD standards pursuant to 40 C.F.R. Part 52, or the Nonattainment NSR emission offset requirements under Subchapter 18.[44]

In issuing a general permit, the Department confirms that it approves the activities authorized by the general permit (thereby satisfying the requirements at N.J.A.C. 7:27-8.3 for a preconstruction permit and operating certificate), provided that the owner or the operator of the source registers with the Department and meets the requirements of the general permit.[45] Note, however, that while the Department will acknowledge receipt of a registration for a general permit, such acknowledgment only indicates that the Department received the registration, and does not mean that the Department has reviewed or approved the registration.[46] As such, if the registration is incorrect or deficient, the Department's acknowledgment does not relieve the owner or operator from liability for penalties for any unauthorized activities.[47] Accordingly, construction/operation pursuant to a general permit is undertaken at the permittee's own risk.

Operating Permits/Title V

Title V of the CAA was added by Congress in 1990 and directed each state to establish an operating permit program for certain "major" sources of air pollution.[48] Title V operating permits address all applicable pollution control obligations under the SIP or any relevant federal implementation plan (FIP), the acid rain program, the air toxics program, or other applicable provisions of the CAA.[49] Title V, on its own, did not create new substantive requirements but was meant to facilitate compliance with and enforcement under the CAA. Since its establishment, the Title V program has become the primary mechanism for imposing CAA stationary source requirements on major sources of air emissions.

New Jersey administers its Title V program through Subchapter 22 of the APCA regulations, N.J.A.C. 7:27-22, and requires all Major Facilities to obtain and comply with detailed operating permits.

Applicability. The New Jersey Title V permit program requires permits for certain types of facilities, including (1) all "major" sources of air pollution; (2) certain sources subject to categorical standards promulgated under Sections 111 or 112 of the CAA; (3) sources subject to Title IV's acid rain program; (4) sources subject to the NSR Program; and (5) any other "stationary source in a category designated . . . by regulations promulgated by EPA."[50] Generally, a "major" source subject to the Title V regulations is one with potential to emit 100 tpy or greater of any regulated pollutant, or one with potential to emit 10 tpy of a particular hazardous air pollutants (HAP), or 25 tpy of any combination of HAPs.[51]

The general provisions of Title V operating permits in New Jersey echo many of the general provisions applicable to permits issued under Subchapter 8 of the APCA regulations discussed above but also reflect all the requirements to which a major source is subject under the CAA, such as monitoring, recordkeeping, reporting, and compliance certification requirements.[52]

Electronic Permit Application Requirements. Construction and operating permit applications (excluding any information for which a confidentiality claim is being asserted), including both initial applications and modification applications, must be completed using New Jersey's software for electronic preparation and submittal of air permit applications, known as RADIUS.[53] The Department designed RADIUS to interact with the Department's environmental regulation database, NJEMS. The current version of RADIUS (Version 5.0) allows users as of January 2013 to submit online electronically prepared applications. Users may also submit completed applications via mail with a paper certification, but even mailed applications must be prepared under the RADIUS format. The Department has prepared a user guide for preparing permit applications using RADIUS, which is available at the Department's website.[54]

RADIUS has long been the processing vehicle for securing an air permit in New Jersey. However, the Department recognizes that there are still several thousand permits outstanding whose issuance predated NJEMS. Some of these permits have expired, while others have been renewed over time. The Department is concerned that such permits are outdated and, therefore, are missing certain applicable requirements and/or reflect inaccurate equipment inventories. In early 2019, the Department listed among its objectives the need to address these pre-NJEMS permits, including by ensuring they are up-to-date and referring noncompliant permits to the Department's enforcement division where appropriate.

Permit Issuance Process. After receiving a permit application and determining that it is administratively complete,[55] the Department will complete its technical review and eventually prepare a draft permit. Depending on the type of permit requested, the Department may be required to issue the draft permit for public review and comment. Drafts of construction permits that are subject to federal PSD requirements, which require EPA approval due to a revision to the SIP, or permits subject to emission offsets under Subchapter 18, must be made available for public review and comment.[56] In the operating permit context, the Department must allow for public comment on draft permits for initial source operations, significant modifications to existing operating permits, and operating permit renewals.[57] The Department may also publish a draft permit (construction or operating) for public comment or hold a public hearing on a draft permit whenever the Commissioner finds a significant degree of public interest in the application.[58] For example, the Department generally seeks public comment on proposed projects in "environmental justice" areas within the State.[59] The public comment period for a draft operating permit will be specified in the public notice announcing the comment period and will be at least thirty days.[60]

After the close of the public comment period and the consideration of comments on a draft operating permit, the Department will prepare a proposed operating permit for EPA review (along with copies of any comments received from the public).[61] EPA will then have forty-five days to review the proposed permit.[62] The Department retains the responsibility to ultimately issue (or deny) a final operating permit for the permittee.[63]

Permit Appeal Process. To the extent that a permittee wishes to challenge one or more provisions within a final permit issued by the Department, the permittee may do so by filing a request for an adjudicatory hearing with the Department's Office of Legal Affairs.[64] All requests must be filed within twenty days from the date the final permit was received by the permittee.[65] Each request for a hearing must contain specific information, including information identifying the permittee raising the challenge, a statement of the legal authority and jurisdiction under which the request for a hearing is made, a brief statement of specific facts describing the Department decision being appealed, as well as the nature and scope of the interest of the party challenging the decision, and a statement of all facts (including any associated legal issues) alleged to be at issue and their relevance to the Department decision for which a hearing is requested.[66] If the Department grants the request for a hearing, the matter will be transferred to the Department's Office of Administrative Law and will be assigned to an administrative law judge and scheduled for a hearing.

Changes to Permits and Certificates

There are several ways in which an existing operating permit (for major facilities) or operating certificate (for minor facilities) can be changed. In order from the least to the most formal and comprehensive, options for changing a permit or certificate include (1) an administrative amendment; (2) a seven-day notice change; (3) a compliance plan change; and (4) a permit revision.[67] First, an *administrative amendment* can be requested where the facility owner or operator is seeking to make certain types of changes that do not increase actual emissions, cause the emission of a new air contaminant or class of air contaminants, violate an applicable permit requirement, or result in the source as subject to an applicable requirement to which it was not previously subject.[68] These types of changes include but are not limited to, correcting typographical errors, revising a permit to accomplish a change in ownership or operational control, increasing the frequency of monitoring, recordkeeping and/or reporting requirements required by the permit, and amending the permit to reflect certain limited changes in the contents of a storage tank or raw materials associated with a permitted process.[69] As a general matter, if the relevant regulatory requirements for seeking an administrative amendment are satisfied, the permittee may, at its own risk, make the proposed change at the facility upon submittal of the amendment but no sooner.[70]

Like an administrative amendment, the *seven-day-notice change* procedure can be utilized where the proposed change does not require an increase in any allowable emissions limit established in the operating permit or certificate, cause the emission of a new air contaminant or class of air contaminants, or make less stringent a monitoring, recordkeeping, or reporting requirement already included in the operating permit or certificate.[71] The specific types of changes that are allowed as seven-day-notice changes include any reconfiguration to an operating scenario, a change related to an emissions trading program attached to an operating permit, and a change to a significant source operation which is not already authorized by the operating permit, provided the change does not cause actual emissions to exceed applicable emission limits in the permit.[72] If the relevant requirements for making a seven-day-notice change are satisfied, the permittee may make the proposed change seven days after the Department has received the change request.[73] The Department shall attach the notice of the seven-day-notice change to the operating permit but shall not revise the operating permit until the next application for renewal.[74] However, on several occasions, the Department has notified sources substantially after the seven-day period has elapsed that the Department does not agree that the change was governed by the seven-day-notice provisions of the regulations. Under the Department's approach in these cases, the source would face risk in relying upon a seven-day notice by proceeding with the change in the absence of any response by the Department (although the regulatory text would appear to protect the source from enforcement exposure).

In the context of operating permits, a *minor modification* allows a permittee to make certain changes to an operating permit that would increase actual emissions by insignificant amounts, and other changes that do not increase emissions, but may increase ambient concentrations of air contaminants.[75] The types of changes that can be made as minor modifications include but are not limited to the construction or installation of any new significant source operation, a change in the location of the point of discharge of any air contaminant from a significant source operation into the outdoor atmosphere, and changes in raw materials or production processes if the change would increase actual emissions over the allowable limit already in effect.[76] Upon the approval of a minor modification application, the Department will incorporate the changes into the permit (a separate preconstruction permit is not required).[77] The permittee has the option of implementing the proposed change at its own risk once the administratively complete application is received by the Department.[78] However, if the minor modification is not approved, the existing permit provisions the permittee sought to modify shall be enforced.[79]

Finally, a major facility permittee may submit an application for a *significant modification* of an existing operating permit to accomplish more substantial changes. In the same manner, minor facilities can seek formal *permit revisions* to their permits and operating certificates.[80] These more comprehensive procedures are required where a change will cause a facility to emit a new, unpermitted air contaminant, will increase the facility's emissions above applicable maximum allowable emission limits, or will cause the facility to be subject to the emission offset requirements under Subchapter 18, the federal NSPS or NESHAP standards, the federal PSD regulations, or any federal visibility regulations.[81] Significant modifications can also be used to accomplish permit revisions which change the applicable monitoring method from continuous to parametric monitoring or relax federally enforceable recordkeeping or reporting requirements, among other changes.[82] As with a minor modification, the Department shall incorporate the requested changes into the permit upon the approval of the application for a significant modification and, therefore, a separate preconstruction permit application is not required.[83] The permittee may not make the change proposed in a significant modification until the Department has approved the application; there is no at-risk provision associated with a major modification.[84]

New Source Review Permitting

A primary means of achieving the CAA's goal of attaining and maintaining the NAAQS is the NSR Program, which is comprised of two main components: (1) the PSD Program and (2) Nonattainment NSR.[85] The PSD Program applies to new major stationary sources or major modifications of stationary sources in attainment areas.[86] Nonattainment NSR applies to new major stationary sources or major modifications of stationary sources in nonattainment areas.[87]

A major source under the PSD Program is either (1) one of twenty-eight specified classes of sources with the potential to emit 100 tons per year (tpy) of any pollutant regulated under the CAA other than HAPs regulated under Section 112 or (2) any other source that has potential to emit 250 tpy of any pollutant regulated under the CAA.[88] A major source under the Nonattainment NSR program is generally defined as a source with the potential to emit 100 tpy or more of a given criteria pollutant. However, sources of nitrogen oxides (NOx) and volatile organic compounds (VOCs), which are precursors to ground-level ozone, may be subject to lower major source threshold applicability levels depending on the nonattainment area classification area in which the facility is located.[89]

The NSR Program is designed to ensure that air quality in attainment areas will not degrade due to increased emissions from new or reconstructed sources of air pollution and that nonattainment areas continually improve their air quality by requiring new or modified sources to comply with stringent emission limits.[90] To accomplish these objectives, the NSR Program requires new or modified major stationary sources of air pollution to obtain preconstruction and operating permits which set forth the conditions and standards under which a facility must operate.[91]

New Jersey's Nonattainment NSR Program. New Jersey's nonattainment NSR regulations are contained in Subchapter 18 of the APCA regulations and require the imposition of additional permitting requirements if a proposed project triggers NSR. New Jersey is authorized to administer its NSR permit program in nonattainment areas pursuant to its EPA-approved SIP.

Evaluating the applicability of NSR to a new source or the modification of an existing source involves a complex analysis of the nature of the project, the potential emissions associated with the proposed project, the net emissions increases evaluated over a contemporaneous time period, and, in some cases, air quality modeling.

In order to determine whether the additional NSR-based requirements apply, the applicant will generally need to evaluate its facility's preexisting total emissions of any of the New Jersey–regulated criteria pollutants for which the area is designated as nonattainment and compare these emission rates to the regulatory standard for such pollutant for major stationary sources. This evaluation allows for the classification of the source as an existing major stationary source; such classification dictates the significance levels applicable for each pollutant under the next phase of the analysis.

The applicant must then calculate the projected increase in emissions of any of the criteria pollutants attributable to the proposed project. NSR requirements apply where the new facility as a whole, or the emission increase proposed in a given application, would equal or exceed specified thresholds, and the proposed emissions would also result in a "significant net emissions increase" of any air contaminant above the specified significance levels. Potential regulatory changes addressing this emissions accounting methodology are afoot at the federal level that may ultimately be reflected in New Jersey's own NSR program. For now, however, the Department has not signaled any intention to revise the State's regulations (or the application thereof), notwithstanding several recent policy directives from President Trump's EPA supporting changes in the permitting authority's approach to NSR applicability.

If a proposed project in a nonattainment area triggers NSR permitting requirements under Subchapter 18, then the applicant must demonstrate through the application process satisfaction of the following enhanced requirements: (1) installation of technology providing for LAER on the new or modified equipment emitting the relevant air pollutant, (2) emissions offsets, and (3) public involvement. LAER is based on either the most stringent emission limitation in any SIP for the same class or category of sources, or the most stringent emission limitation achieved in practice by a source in the same class or category.[92] Emissions offsets are essentially emissions reduction credits that a Nonattainment NSR source must obtain from existing sources, typically from the same air quality control region. To satisfy regulatory standards, emissions offsets must meet multiple criteria to be "creditable."[93]

New Jersey's PSD Program. If a proposed project is located in an attainment area, it may be subject to the federal PSD requirements, which apply to new major stationary sources or to major modifications to existing major sources in attainment areas. Similar to Nonattainment NSR, PSD will apply if the potential emission increase from the new or modified source exceeds specific levels published for each criteria pollutant under the federal regulations. If the PSD program is triggered, then the facility may not commence the construction of the new major source or major modification to an existing source without first obtaining a PSD permit.

The PSD Program generally requires the following from applicants: (1) installation of BACT on all equipment that emits air pollutants; (2) an air quality analysis that demonstrates that the new or modified source will not contribute to a violation of the NAAQS or any PSD requirement; (3) an additional impact analysis that assesses the impact on air, soil, water, vegetation, and visibility caused by a proposed increase of any regulated pollutant emitted by the source; and (4) public involvement in the permitting process.[94] One of the most critical components of the PSD Program is the BACT requirement, which EPA defines as an emission limitation based on the maximum degree of control that a source can achieve.[95]

While the federal regulations establish the requirements for NSR programs (both Nonattainment NSR and PSD), States may either adopt their own program for approval by EPA (as is the case with New Jersey's nonattainment NSR program), incorporate the federal program directly into the SIP, or rely directly on the federal program through a direct delegation of authority from EPA. In New Jersey, PSD permits are issued by NJDEP pursuant to such a delegation of authority from EPA.[96] The delegation of authority is significant because NJDEP-issued PSD permits are considered federal permits and remain subject to federal procedural and administrative review before the federal Environmental Appeals Board. By contrast, Nonattainment NSR permits are issued pursuant to New Jersey law (N.J.A.C. 7:27-18), and therefore, such permits are not subject to administrative review by EPA on appeal.

AIR POLLUTANT REGULATORY PROGRAMS

Specific pollutants or groups of pollutants may be subject to emissions limitations under one or more federal or state regulations, including NSPS, NESHAPs, NSR, and the federal acid rain program. Where a pollutant is subject to multiple emission limitations, the most stringent limitation governs, but all such limitations legally remain applicable. In addition to these broad federal programs, New Jersey has promulgated several regulatory programs that target specific pollutants, some of which are discussed in the following subsections.

Air Toxics/Hazardous Air Pollutants

Pursuant to Section 112 of the CAA, EPA has promulgated NESHAPs for certain categories and subcategories of industrial sources that emit one or more HAPs. The federal NESHAPs establish emissions limitations or work practice requirements for particular source categories and subcategories that are based on the maximum achievable control technology (MACT) as determined by EPA.

NJDEP does not have delegated authority to implement the NESHAPs. However, even without the delegation of authority, NJDEP is authorized to enforce NESHAP standards by including such obligations in a state-issued operating permit.[97] For minor sources, NJDEP requires any person applying for a preconstruction permit or permit revision to submit, as part of the permit application, a NESHAP applicability determination and compliance demonstration.[98]

In addition to the federal MACT standards, NJDEP has established its own Air Toxics Program applicable to operations and equipment that emit certain state-defined toxic substances (referred to as TXS).[99] NJDEP requires any person emitting a listed TXS from any source operation, storage tank, or transfer operation to register with NJDEP and provide information relating to storage vessel size, transfer rates, emission rates, operating procedure, and any other information requested by NJDEP.[100] NJDEP may also require the source operation to implement SOTA for control of the TXS.[101]

NJDEP has also established a risk assessment policy, which is designed to address the potential risk posed by air toxics after the application of SOTA or MACT pollution controls.[102] Risk assessment is ordinarily conducted following the submission of a permit application in one of two ways: risk screening or comprehensive risk assessment. In NJDEP's January 2018 Resiliency, Air Toxics and Exemptions (RATE) rulemaking, NJDEP changed the reporting thresholds for many HAPs, and the majority of the thresholds were lowered. These revised thresholds will determine whether potential emissions of HAP identified through the permitting process for new or modified sources will be subject to NJDEP's risk assessment procedure.

Most facilities that are required to conduct a risk assessment can make use of NJDEP's risk screening process, which begins with a simplified first-level screening analysis using NJDEP's Risk Screening Worksheet for Long-Term Carcinogenic and Noncarcinogenic Effects and Short-Term Effects (Risk Screening Worksheet). The Risk Screening Worksheet uses generalized worst-case assumptions to estimate cancer and non-cancer risks from the inhalation of emissions proposed in the application.[103] In 2018, NJDEP updated the Risk Screening Worksheet to incorporate updated EPA and California risk factors that include more stringent toxicity values for many listed substances, as well as Technical Manual 1003 (Guidance on Preparing a Risk Assessment for Air Contaminant Emissions). The effect of NJDEP's reduction in reporting thresholds and revisions to the risk screening worksheet may make it more likely for a facility to have to conduct a more detailed "refined risk assessment." In the event that a comprehensive risk assessment is required, the permit applicant will be required to perform a detailed risk assessment based on a protocol approved by NJDEP's EMS. If risk targets are still exceeded after the performance of a refined risk assessment, then additional site-specific modeling may be required, or in some cases, additional air toxic emission reductions may be required before a permit is issued. NJDEP also completed updates to Technical Manual 1002 (Guidance on Preparing an Air Quality Modeling Protocol) that may impact methods for modeling and air quality impact analyses under various permitting-related requirements, including PSD.

In 2019, NJDEP announced its intention to undertake a rulemaking that would add hydrogen sulfide, N-propyl bromide, and sulfuryl fluoride to its Air Toxics Program. The rulemaking is also anticipated to include categorical requirements for commodity fumigation operations and to increase the number of air toxics required to be included in annual emission statements.

Volatile Organic Compounds

VOCs and NOx are the primary precursor pollutants to the formation of ground-level ozone. As part of New Jersey's effort to attain and maintain the NAAQS for ozone, NJDEP has established comprehensive requirements and procedures governing the control of VOC emissions in Subchapter 16.[104] Subchapter 16 generally establishes New Jersey's determination of RACT standards for certain source operations. RACT is the lowest emission limitation that a particular source is capable of meeting by the application of air pollution control technology and/or pollution prevention measures that are reasonably available considering technological and economic feasibility.[105]

Subchapter 16 establishes specific VOC RACT requirements for several different source categories and activities including VOC stationary storage tanks, gasoline transfer operations, VOC transfer operations (other than gasoline), marine tank vessel loading and ballasting operations, open top tanks and solvent cleaning operations, surface coating and graphic arts operations, boilers, stationary combustion turbines, stationary reciprocating engines, asphalt pavement production plants, surface coating operations at mobile equipment repair and refinishing facilities, flares, application of cutback and emulsified asphalts, petroleum solvent dry cleaning operations, and natural gas pipelines.[106] In addition, VOC RACT requirements apply to "other source operations," which include twenty-one additional source categories (not limited to manufacturing).[107]

Subchapter 16 also imposes leak detection and repair requirements on petroleum refineries, natural gas/gasoline processing plants, synthetic organic chemical or polymer manufacturing facilities, or any chemical plant, other than a synthetic organic chemical or polymer manufacturing facility, which is a major VOC facility (a facility with the potential to emit twenty-five or more tons of VOC per year).[108]

NOx Emissions

Similar to VOCs, NJDEP has established RACT requirements in Subchapter 19 of the New Jersey air regulations concerning the control of NOx emissions. Subchapter 19 requires certain stationary source operations located at a major NOx facility to use RACT to reduce NOx emissions. A major NOx facility is defined for these purposes as any facility that has the potential to emit twenty-five or more tons of NOx per year.[109] Specified types and sizes of sources at minor facilities are also required to meet RACT emissions limits. The source categories covered by Subchapter 19 include, among others, boilers serving electric generating units, stationary combustion turbines, industrial/commercial/institutional boilers and other indirect heat exchangers, stationary reciprocating engines, asphalt plants, municipal solid waste incinerators, and glass manufacturing facilities.[110] Specific applicability thresholds and emissions standards for each of the regulated source categories are provided within Subchapter 19.

Sulfur in Fuels

NJDEP regulates the emission of sulfur dioxide, in part, through limitations on the sulfur content in fuel oil as well as through output-based performance standards for solid fuels. For fuel oil, NJDEP has established limits on the maximum allowable sulfur content depending on the type of fuel oil, where it is sold within the State and the date of purchase.[111] For solid fuels, NJDEP transitioned from a sulfur content requirement (similar to the fuel oil standard) to an output-based performance standard. Specifically, as of December 15, 2012, any source that combusts solid fuel must meet both the twenty-four-hour emission rate and the thirty-calendar-day rolling average emission rate for SO_2.[112] The output-based performance standard allows each facility to choose how to control SO_2 emissions.

Malodors and Nuisance

NJDEP prohibits any person from allowing any air contaminant, including odors, to be present in the outdoor atmosphere in such quantity and duration which is, or tends to be, injurious to human health or welfare, animal or plant life or property, or which would unreasonably interfere with the enjoyment of life or property.[113] This broad prohibition against malodors does not apply to areas over which the owner or operator has exclusive use or occupancy. NJDEP is given broad discretion to determine whether an odor "unreasonably interferes with the enjoyment of life or property" and may consider such factors as the character, severity, frequency, and duration of the odor, as well as the number of persons affected.

Particulate Matter

Subchapter 6 of New Jersey's air regulations contains general particle emission standards for emissions from manufacturing processes.[114] In addition, Subpart 4.2 contains particle emission standards for the combustion of fuel, including specific emission standards for new and existing coal-fired boilers.[115] NJDEP has not established source-specific particle emission standards (besides the coal-fired boiler standards in Subpart 4.2); however, such standards may be established as part of the permitting process.[116]

Visible Emissions and Opacity

NJDEP prohibits visible emissions of greater than 20 percent opacity, exclusive of visible condensed water vapor, for more than three minutes in any consecutive thirty-minute period.[117] This general opacity requirement constitutes a "state only" standard, and therefore is generally not federally enforceable even when incorporated into a Title V operating permit. NJDEP may impose more stringent visible emission standards through the application of SOTA.

Greenhouse Gas Regulation

Passed in 2007, the New Jersey Global Warming Response Act sets statewide limits on greenhouse gas emissions.[118] The law mandates reductions in greenhouse gas emissions to 1990 levels by 2020, approximately a 20 percent reduction below estimated 2020 business-as-usual emissions, followed by a further reduction of emissions to 80 percent below 2006 levels by 2050. Under the statute, NJDEP is tasked with evaluating methods to meet and exceed the mandated limits and is also required to conduct a statewide greenhouse gas emissions inventory and establish a greenhouse gas emissions monitoring and reporting program.

NJDEP conducted the required greenhouse gas evaluation and in December 2009 released a report detailing significant sources of greenhouse gases and providing a proposed framework for how the State can meet its greenhouse gas goals of the Global Warming Response Act.[119] Steps taken by New Jersey to meet its greenhouse gas goals have included the adoption of the California Low Emission Vehicle program, the adoption of Renewable Portfolio Standards requiring utilities to meet increasing amounts of their customers' needs through renewable energy sources, and the implementation of the New Jersey Clean Energy Program to provide incentives to encourage more efficient energy usage.[120] At the end of 2018, the state senate introduced proposed amendments to the Global Warming Response Act that would require NJDEP to establish a greenhouse gas monitoring and reporting program and would impose specific timeframes for NJDEP to prepare a report that recommends further measures the state can take to reduce greenhouse gas emissions.

While New Jersey also initially participated in the development of a cap-and-trade program for greenhouse gas emissions from power plants through the Regional

Greenhouse Gas Initiative (RGGI), the State ceased participation in the initiative in 2011.[121] On December 17, 2018, however, NJDEP proposed a set of rules meant to establish a framework for the estate's reentry into RGGI. The proposed rulemaking package would establish the New Jersey Carbon Dioxide (CO_2) Budget Tracking Program, a cap-and-trade program that would set a statewide carbon budget for large fossil fuel electric generating limits (EGUs) and would require subject EGUs to possess CO_2 allowances equivalent to their annual emissions. On December 18, 2018, New Jersey also announced its intention to participate in the nascent Transportation Climate Initiative, which is a regional program similar to RGGI that will attempt to reduce greenhouse gas emissions from module sources. These regulatory initiatives are expected to continue to play out over the coming months and years.

INSPECTIONS, ENFORCEMENT, AND PENALTIES

To ascertain compliance with the various air-related statutory, regulatory and permitting requirements, NJDEP's Bureau of Air Compliance and Enforcement conducts site inspections and detailed reviews of reported information. Where the Department identifies alleged violations, it provides notice to the alleged violator and may take additional administrative actions and levy penalties where necessary. The Department also works cooperatively with criminal prosecutors to address identified criminal violations.

Inspections

The Department attempts to inspect all major facilities at least every other year and minor facilities at least once every five years. Inspections can also be prompted by reports of incidents or complaints made to the Department, referrals received from other government agencies, in response to emissions testing results or facility self-disclosures of noncompliance, or even as part of a broader, multimedia enforcement effort.

The Department asserts broad authority to conduct investigations as its inspectors are generally authorized to enter facilities to enforce environmental laws and regulations.[122] The APCA further states that NJDEP may "[e]nter and inspect any building or place, except private residences, for the purpose of investigating an actual or suspected source of air pollution and ascertaining compliance or noncompliance with any codes, rules, or regulations" of the NJDEP.[123] Denying Department inspectors' entries or inhibiting their inspection can result in the issuance of an enforcement order and the assessment of a penalty, with each day that entry is denied constituting a separate and distinct offense.[124]

Where the facility being investigated is operating under a permit, investigators will review its operations to ensure that the facility is operating in compliance with its permitted obligations, that the facility's equipment matches what was identified in its air permit application, and that no modifications have been made to the facility that would trigger additional requirements such as an NSR review. Facility managers would be well advised to review their permits in advance of any scheduled inspection and to have required records available during the inspection in the event that any compliance questions arise.

Where the Department investigates a property or facility as a result of receiving a complaint, it looks to determine whether the site is emitting air pollutions "in such quantities and duration as are, or tend to be, injurious to human health or welfare, animal or plant life or property, or would unreasonably interfere with the enjoyment of life or property."[125] Complaints received by the Department frequently involve the issues of odor. If the Department determines that an odor is being generated, and the character, severity, frequency, and the duration of the odor are such that it unreasonably interferes with the enjoyment of life or property in the area, then the alleged violator can be cited, and penalties can result.

Examples of violations identified through inspections include:

- Exceedances of permit emission limits;
- Unpermitted installation or operation of significant sources;
- Operating under an expired permit;
- Failure to transfer ownership of an air permit upon the sale of a facility, which results in the termination of the permit;
- Use of new raw materials that are not permitted;
- Filing incorrect information in an original air permit application (e.g., incorrect BTU/hr rating for a boiler);
- Emissions of air contaminants above major facility thresholds without having a Title V Operating Permit;
- Recordkeeping and reporting failures;
- Insufficient monitoring of emissions, including excessive downtime for a facility's Continuous Emissions Monitors;
- Emissions determined to be injurious to human health or welfare or that unreasonably interfere with the enjoyment of life or property.

Enforcement

Once the Department determines that noncompliance has occurred, several different types of enforcement actions are available to the Department. The most typical first step is the issuance of a Notice of Violation (NOV). The NOV contains no penalty assessment but instead serves to notify the facility of the alleged violation. An NOV typically lists the date of discovery of the violation, a description of the violation, and a date by which the Department requires the violator to come into compliance. While an NOV typically allows a violator thirty to sixty days to reach compliance, specific deadlines vary depending on the situation.

New Jersey categorizes violations as either "minor" or "non-minor." Under the State's Grace Period Law, N.J.S.A. 13:1D-125 et seq., entities accused of specified minor violations are afforded a "Grace Period" to correct the violation in order to avoid the imposition of a penalty that would otherwise apply. Minor violations are typically those that pose minimal risk to human health or the environment and include certain recordkeeping and reporting requirements such as the recording and maintenance of emission testing data. If a minor violation is corrected within the relevant Grace Period, then no further enforcement action or penalty assessment should follow.

Where a violation is categorized as non-minor, no grace period applies to the imposition of penalties. Non-minor violations include any action posing a threat to human health or the environment, such as major exceedances from permit limits. If the Department finds a non-minor violation, one or more of the following actions may result: issuance of an Administrative Order, with or without a penalty assessment; entry of an Administrative Consent Order; filing of a request for judicial relief; or referral of criminal charges to the Attorney General.

If a facility fails to achieve the compliance required under an NOV or Administrative Order, or where the violation at issue has mandated penalties, then the Department may issue an Administrative Order and Notice of Civil Administrative Penalty Assessment (AONOCAPA). An AONOCAPA typically identifies the relevant statutory, regulatory, or permit provision being violated, provides a description of the violation, orders that the violation ceases, specifies additional corrective actions, if any, and imposes a civil administrative penalty.[126]

Penalties

Penalty assessments are calculated based on the Civil Administrative Penalty Schedule found in N.J.A.C. 7:27A-3. The penalty calculation begins with a base penalty amount dictated by the particular violation at issue, which may then be modified to account for factors such as the compliance history of the violator, the number of times, frequency and severity of the violation, and the nature and effectiveness of remedial and preventative steps taken by the violator.[127] The resulting penalties can range significantly in amount depending on the type and duration of the violation. The Department may, for example, assess a civil administrative penalty of not more than $10,000 for a first offense, but each day during which a violation continues constitutes an additional distinct offense so that a single, repeated emission exceedance can result in a large penalty assessment. Pursuant to the Department's self-disclosure policy, in certain instances, a regulated entity may be eligible for a 75 to 100 percent penalty reduction from the calculated penalty assessment for violations that it voluntarily discovers as part of an audit, discloses, and corrects.[128] However, certain conditions must be present for an affected entity to avail itself of the self-disclosure policy.

Affirmative Defenses to Penalty Liability. The APCA establishes an affirmative defense to penalty liability where air pollution violations result from: a non-recurring equipment malfunction, equipment start-up, equipment shut-down, or necessary equipment maintenance.[129] To successfully assert an affirmative defense, a facility also must demonstrate that the facility was being operated with due care, that the violation was not caused by operator error or maintenance failures, and that reasonable steps were taken to minimize emissions.[130] Where a violation was the result of equipment malfunction, it must further be shown that the malfunction was not part of a recurrent pattern. Finally, parties asserting an affirmative defense must strictly adhere to the initial notification requirements related to the violation and must submit, within thirty days of the occurrence, written documentation demonstrating that the affirmative defense criteria have been met. To the extent that affected parties do qualify for an affirmative defense, they are advised to identify such qualification in the context of any subsequent compliance-based reports required to be submitted for the relevant period.

Appealing an Enforcement Action

While the Department has asserted that NOVs constitute informal agency actions, administrative orders and AONOCAPAs are formal actions subject to appeal. In fact, the Department is required to include within each AONOCAPA a statement advising the alleged violator of the right to request an adjudicatory hearing, as well as a form that can be used to submit a hearing request to the Department's Office of Legal Affairs. Such hearing requests must be submitted within twenty days of receiving the enforcement document. If the Department does not receive a hearing request within twenty days, then the AONOCAPA becomes a Final Order. Note that the filing of a hearing request does not stay any actions required to be undertaken by the Department's action, absent an express decision by the Department to stay such action. The burden is on the party requesting a hearing to explicitly request a stay of action within the same document and to describe reasons why such stay should be granted.[131]

Payment of a civil penalty is due in the timeframe set out in the AONOCAPA. However, where a hearing request is submitted, payment is not required until the Department either denies the hearing request or following the issuance of a Final Order after an adjudicatory hearing.[132]

Local and Federal Inspections and Enforcements

In addition to inspections and enforcement action taken by the Department, facilities may also be subject to enforcement by local agencies as well as EPA. County health agency personnel may perform investigations under the authority delegated by the Department pursuant to the County Environmental Health Act, N.J.S.A. 26:3A2-21 et seq. Local government entities also perform investigations pursuant to municipal pollution control ordinances.

The APCA prohibits local agencies from regulating or collecting fees from any facility required to obtain an operating permit under the statute or from any research and development facility. The APCA also bars counties and municipalities from enacting requirements more stringent than those found in the APCA, but county or municipal requirements in effect as of August 2, 1995 (when the APCA was amended) continue to be in effect even if they established more stringent requirements.[133] Penalties for violations of ordinances or requirements of municipalities or counties cannot exceed $2,500.

At the federal level, while EPA delegates significant authority to the Department to implement federal air programs, the Agency maintains concurrent authority and can conduct inspections and take enforcement actions based on alleged violations of the CAA or state requirements incorporated in New Jersey's SIP.

Citizen Suits

Emitters of air pollution in New Jersey may also be subject to action by private persons. The CAA specifically contains a citizen suit provision authorizing "any person" to commence an action "against any person" who is alleged to have violated an emission standard or limitation set out in the CAA.[134] While the APCA does not contain a parallel citizen suit provision, New Jersey's Environmental Rights Act, N.J.S.A. 2a:35a-1 et seq., authorizes citizens to seek injunctive or other equitable relief to compel compliance with the State's environmental laws. Private actions claiming damages from air emissions have also been grounded in traditional common law claims, including negligence, nuisance and trespass.

Criminal Penalties

While the great majority of the Department's air-related enforcement activities are administrative actions, the APCA also authorizes criminal penalties. Purposeful or knowingly false material statements to the Department or violation of regulatory requirements or permit provisions are categorized as crimes of the third degree.[135] Reckless violating conduct is categorized as a crime of the fourth degree.[136]

NOTES

1. N.J.A.C. 7:27-1.1
2. 42 U.S.C. § 7401(b)(1). Congress has twice amended the CAA in 1977 and 1990.
3. EPA, Plain English Guide to the Clean Air Act, available at http://epa.gov/sites/production/files/2017-08/documents/peg.pdf.
4. 42 U.S.C. §§ 7409-7410. Whereas the regulation of stationary sources of air pollution is a joint effort between the EPA and the states, the regulation of mobile sources of air pollution is left primarily to the EPA.
5. 42 U.S.C. § 7408(a)(1).
6. 42 U.S.C. § 7409.
7. 42 U.S.C. § 7409(b)(1).
8. 42 U.S.C. § 7409(b)(2).
9. 40 C.F.R. § 50.17.
10. 40 C.F.R. § 50.5.
11. 42 U.S.C. § 7410(a)(1).
12. 42 U.S.C. § 7407(d)(1)(B).
13. 42 U.S.C. § 7407(d)(1)(A).
14. 42 U.S.C. § 7410(a)(1).
15. 42 U.S.C. § 7502(b).
16. 83 Fed. Reg. 1098, 1144 (January 9, 2018).
17. 78 Fed. Reg. 54,396 (September 4, 2013).
18. NJDEP, Attainment Area Status, http://www.nj.gov/dep/baqp/aas.html#eighthour.
19. N.J.A.C. 7:27-8.
20. N.J.A.C. 7:27-22.2(a) (applicability provisions for major sources requiring operating permits under Subchapter 22).

21. N.J.A.C. 7:27-8.1.

22. N.J.A.C 7:27-8.2(c)(1).

23. N.J.A.C 7:27-8.2(c)(19).

24. N.J.A.C. 7:27-8.2(d).

25. N.J.A.C. 7:27-8.2(d)(1)-(14).

26. N.J.A.C. 7:27-8.2(j).

27. N.J.A.C. 7:27-22.1.

28. N.J.A.C. 7:27-8.3(a)-(b).

29. N.J.A.C. 7:27-8.4(b)-(c).

30. N.J.A.C. 7:27-8.4(d).

31. *Id.*

32. N.J.A.C. 7:27-8.4(h).

33. N.J.A.C. 7:27-8.11(a).

34. 40 C.F.R. Part 60.

35. 42 U.S.C.A. § 7475(a)(4); 40 C.F.R. § 52.21(b)(12). See also EPA RACT/BACT/LAER Clearinghouse, available at https://cfpub.epa.gov.rblc.

36. N.J.A.C. 7:27-8.12(a).

37. https://www.state.nj.us/dep/aqpp/sota.html.

38. N.J.A.C. 7:27-8.12(e)(1).

39. N.J.A.C. 7:27-8.12(e)(3)-(4).

40. N.J.A.C. 7:27-8.12(e)5, (f); see also SOTA Technical Manuals, available at http://www.nj.gov/dep/aqpp/sota.html.

41. Available at https://www.state.nj.us/dep/aqpp/techman.html.

42. N.J.A.C. 7:27-8.8(a).

43. N.J.A.C. 7:27-8.8(c).

44. N.J.A.C. 7:27-8.8(b).

45. N.J.A.C. 7:27-8.8(a), (d), (e), (i), (j), (l), (o).

46. N.J.A.C. 7:27-8.8(j) (registration might be incorrect or deficient, for example, "if the registered source does not qualify for the general permit; if the registration was improperly completed; or if the registration did not include a key element such as required information or the correct fee.").

47. N.J.A.C. 7:27-8.8(k).

48. 42 U.S.C. § 7661a(b).

49. See 40 C.F.R. Part 70 (State Operating Permit Program).

50. 42 U.S.C. § 7661a; N.J.A.C. 7:27-22.2.

51. 40 C.F.R. § 70.2.

52. 40 C.F.R. § 70.6; N.J.A.C. 7:27-22.16.

53. N.J.A.C. 7:27-8.4(b)-(c).; N.J.A.C. 7:27-22.4(c).

54. See http://www.state.nj.us/dep/aqpp/radius.html.

55. N.J.A.C. 7:27-22.10(a).

56. N.J.A.C. 7:27-8.10(a).

57. N.J.A.C. 7:27-22.11(a).

58. N.J.A.C. 7:27-8.10(b); N.J.A.C. 7:27-22.11(l).

59. Governor Murphy signed Executive Order No. 23 on April 20, 2018. In accordance with this order, the Department is taking the lead in developing guidance for all executive branch departments and agencies for the consideration of environmental justice in implementing their statutory and regulatory responsibilities, reflecting environmental, social, health, and economic concerns. Comments on the draft guidance were accepted through March 2019, and a final guidance document is expected to follow.

60. N.J.A.C. 7:27-22.11 (b).

61. N.J.A.C. 7:27-22.12(a), (b).

62. N.J.A.C. 7:27-22.12(d).

63. N.J.A.C. 7:27-22.13.

64. N.J.A.C. 7:27-1.32(a), (b)

65. N.J.A.C. 7:27-1.32(c).

66. N.J.A.C. 7:27-1.32(d).

67. N.J.A.C. 7:27-8.17; N.J.A.C. 7:27-22.20 to 25.

68. N.J.A.C. 7:27-8.21; N.J.A.C. 7:27-22.20(b).

69. *Id.*

70. N.J.A.C. 7:27-8.21(a); N.J.A.C. 7:27-22.20(a).

71. N.J.A.C. 7:27-8.20; N.J.A.C. 7:27-22.22(b).

72. N.J.A.C. 7:27-8.20; N.J.A.C. 7:27-22.22(c).

73. N.J.A.C. 7:27-8.20(g); N.J.A.C. 7:27-22.22(a).

74. *Id.*

75. N.J.A.C. 7:27-22.23(a).

76. N.J.A.C. 7:27-22.23(c).

77. N.J.A.C. 7:27-22.23(a).

78. N.J.A.C. 7:27-22.23(a)2.

79. N.J.A.C. 7:27-22.23(a)3.

80. N.J.A.C. 7:27-8.18.

81. N.J.A.C. 7:27-8.18(a); N.J.A.C. 7:27-22.24(b).

82. *Id.*

83. N.J.A.C. 7:27-22.24(a).

84. *Id.*

85. See 42 U.S.C. 7501 to 7515 (Nonattainment NSR Program) 42 U.S.C. §§ 7470 to 7479 (PSD Program).

86. 42 U.S.C. § 7475.

87. 42 U.S.C. § 7503.

88. 40 C.F.R. § 51.166(b)(1)(i), 52.21(b)(1)(i).

89. 40 C.F.R. §51.165(a)(1)(iv)(A).

90. 42 U.S.C. § 7470.

91. 42 U.S.C. §§ 7475, 7503.

92. N.J.A.C. 7:27-18.3.

93. N.J.A.C. 7:27-18.5 (To qualify as an emission reduction eligible for offset, the decrease in emissions must be (1) quantifiable; (2) federally enforceable; (3) not required by any law, rule, permit, order, or other legal document; (4) not relied upon by NJDEP in the SIP to demonstrate attainment or maintenance of a NAAQS or to demonstrate reasonable further progress toward attainment of a NAAQS; and (5) verifiable to NJDEP's satisfaction). As defined in N.J.A.C. 7:27-18.1.

94. 42 U.S.C. § 7475(a); see also EPA, Prevention of Significant Deterioration (PSD) Basic Information, available at http://www.epa.gov/NSR/prevention-significant-deterioration-basic-information.

95. *Id.*

96. 40 C.F.R. § 52.1603(b) (NJDEP accepted delegation of the PSD program from EPA on February 22, 1983).

97. N.J.A.C. 7:27-22.26(b).

98. N.J.A.C. 7:27-8.4(i).

99. N.J.A.C. 7:27-17.3, Table 1; see also NJDEP, Air Toxics Program, available at http://www.nj.gov/dep/airtoxics/njatp.htm.

100. N.J.A.C. 7:27-17.3(a). Note that the submission of a permit application satisfies the registration requirements for sources emitting a listed TXS. N.J.A.C. 7:27-17.3(f).

101. N.J.A.C. 7:27-17.3(b)-(e).

102. NJDEP, Air Toxics Program: NJ's Multi-Pronged Approach to Decreasing Air Toxics Emissions, *available at* http://www.nj.gov/dep/airtoxics/njatp.htm.

103. NJDEP, *Technical Manual 1003 – Guidance on Risk Assessment for Air Contaminant Emissions § 2.1*, December 2018.

104. N.J.A.C. 7:27-16.1 et seq.

105. N.J.A.C. 7:27-16.1A.

106. N.J.A.C. 7:27-16.2 to16.13, 16.17, 16.19, 16.21.

107. N.J.A.C. 7:27-16.16.

108. N.J.A.C. 7:27-16.18.

109. N.J.A.C. 7:27-19.1.

110. N.J.A.C. 7:27-19.4, 19.5, 19.7-19.10, 19.12.

111. N.J.A.C. 7:27-9.2.

112. N.J.A.C. 7:27-10.2(h).

113. N.J.A.C. 7:27-8.3(j) and 22.16 (g).

114. N.J.A.C. 7:27-6.2.

115. N.J.A.C. 7:27-4.2.

116. While fine particulate emissions are not specifically subject to RACT, the RACT measures for VOCs and NOx often result in reductions in particulate emissions.

117. N.J.A.C. 7:27-6.2(d)-(e).

118. N.J.S.A. 26:2c-37 et seq.

119. See New Jersey's Global Warming Response Act Recommendations Report, available at www.NJ.gov/dep/sage/docs/NJGRWA_final-report-dec2009.pdf)

120. See N.J.A.C. 7:27-29.2; www.state.nj.us/dep/aqes/climate/action.html.)

121. See http://www.rggi.org/.

122. N.J.S.A. 13:1D9(d).

123. N.J.S.A. 26:2C-9(b)(4). *See also* N.J.A.C. 7:27-1.31.

124. N.J.A.C. 7:27A-3.7.

125. N.J.S.A. 26:2C-2 (as defining "air pollution"); N.J.A.C. 7:27-5.2.

126. N.J.A.C. 7:27A-3.3(a).

127. N.J.A.C. 7:27A-3.5(e).

128. See http://www.nj.gov/dep/enforcement/self-disclosure.htm.

129. N.J.S.A. 26:2C-19.2.

130. *Id.*

131. N.J.A.C. 7:27-1.33(b).

132. N.J.A.C. 7:27A-3.3(b).

133. N.J.S.A. 26:2C-22.

134. 42 U.S.C.A. § 7604.

135. N.J.S.A. 26:2C-19(f).

136. *Id.*

Chapter 7

Water Quality and Water Supply

Marty M. Judge, Esq.

HISTORICAL BACKGROUND

No discussion of the regulation of water quality and water supply in New Jersey would be complete without reference to the historical and common law antecedents to modern regulation. Whereas modern water regulation is largely a matter of statutory law and the adoption of administrative agency rules implementing those statutes, the history of water regulation goes back much farther in New Jersey. In fact, some degree of regulation of water has been a feature of New Jersey since its colonial days, the State having inherited its original laws from the common law of England.

Contrary to modern water law, where there is probably a greater emphasis in the statutes and regulations on preventing pollution and preserving the quality of water resources than on the issue of water allocation and supply,[1] the emphasis of the law in earlier times focused on who had the right to use or "take" water for consumption—originally for agricultural and later for industrial purposes. It was not until the middle of the twentieth century the law began to focus attention on the issue of water quality.[2]

For centuries, water in its naturally occurring state has been considered to be a natural resource in New Jersey, and it is therefore subject to the public's (or sovereign's) ownership, control, and allocation under the Public Trust Doctrine. The gist of this doctrine is that public lands, waters, wildlife, and other natural resources of the State, as distinguished from purely private property, are "common property"[3] and are held in trust by the government for the benefit of its citizens—that is, the citizens get the benefit of the use of these resources, but only the sovereign owns and, ultimately controls, the resources for the good of all citizens. Therefore, the sovereign has the inherent power to restrict, limit, condition, allocate, and otherwise regulate and control the use by citizens of its natural resources, including water.[4] This is the bedrock principle on which all modern laws affecting water quality and water allocation are based.

At common law, the allocation of water resources and the resolution of water rights disputes in New Jersey were controlled by the so-called American or "reasonable use" doctrine of riparian law.[5] The reasonable use rule permits each riparian proprietor to use "water for any lawful purpose so long as the use is reasonable and does not unreasonably interfere with the legitimate uses and needs of other proprietors on the stream."[6]

A hodgepodge of statutes was enacted throughout the first half of the twentieth century that increasingly required permits for certain categories of water diversions and by which the common law riparian system was slowly eroding.[7] However, these earlier statutes all retained limitations and exemptions which allowed vestiges of the riparian system to remain intact. Notably, this included a substantial number of so-called "legislative grants" and "grandfather rights" to water resources which were exempt from the permit process altogether.[8] In 1981, New Jersey enacted the Water Supply Management Act ("WSMA"),[9] which comprehensively revised the entire system for allocating water resources in New Jersey and now empowers NJDEP to issue "water allocation permits" for nearly all uses of water. The Legislature specifically found that

- "the water resources of the State are public assets of the State held in trust for its citizens";
- "ownership of these assets is in the State as trustee of the people";
- the State's water resources "must be planned for and managed as a common resource"; and
- "it is necessary that the State, through its Department of Environmental Protection, have the power to manage the water supply by adopting a uniform water diversion permit system."[10]

While the law of water supply in New Jersey was evolving in the manner just discussed, the modern law respecting water quality did not really begin to take shape until the mid-twentieth century, with increasing recognition of the deplorable conditions of the nation's water supplies due to years of indiscriminate release of pollutants into the State's water bodies. At common law, the earliest cases respecting water pollution claims tended to follow the same legal principles that governed water consumption—that is, pollution of water was viewed as another aspect of "use" such that there was no absolute restriction on polluting, but it might be prohibited if the pollution "unreasonably" interfered with the water usage rights of another individual or the public at large. There was no administrative agency, like the NJDEP, to prevent and clean up pollution in the State's waters.[11]

WATER POLLUTION CONTROL

Today, the regulation of water pollution in New Jersey is governed principally by the Water Pollution Control Act ("WPCA").[12] This statute prohibits the discharge of any pollutant into the waters of the state without a valid permit. The WPCA broadly defines the term "pollutant" to include almost any released material or discarded waste[13]; "discharge" to include releases to waters of the State and to municipal treatment works[14]; and "Waters of the State" to include surface or groundwater.[15] The WPCA provides NJDEP with broad authority to restore, enhance, and maintain the integrity of New Jersey's waters.

A second goal of the WPCA is to provide NJDEP with sufficient authority to qualify to administer the discharge permit system required under the Federal Water Pollution Control Act.[16] To this end, the NJDEP developed a regulatory program which governs discharges of pollutants to surface waters (including discharges onto land from which the pollutant might flow into surface waters) and which incorporates all the necessary requirements of the Federal Act. The NJDEP has been authorized by USEPA to administer the federal water pollution program.[17]

In addition to regulating discharges to surface waters pursuant to the Federal Act, the New Jersey Act also prohibits discharges to groundwater without a permit; thus NJDEP's regulatory program extends to groundwater releases. The NJDEP has interpreted its authority over groundwater discharges to include "all discharges, past or present, actual or potential, of pollutants, including hazardous and non-hazardous waste to groundwater,"[18] including past releases onto land or into wells from which the pollutant might flow or drain into groundwater. Thus NJDEP's regulation of discharges to groundwater encompasses even discharges or leachate from old spills or nonoperational waste disposal sites.

The NJDEP's Water Pollution Control Regulations also govern the discharge of industrial pollutants to municipal or privately owned treatment works. A "treatment works" is defined as a system used in the "storage, treatment, recycling or reclamation of municipal or industrial waste of a liquid nature."[19] Therefore, any industrial pollutant that is discharged to essentially any water-related medium, surface or groundwater or to a sewage treatment system, is governed by the New Jersey WPCA and the regulations promulgated under it by NJDEP.

Permit Program

The regulation of water pollution is accomplished primarily through the requirement that all discharges be pursuant to a New Jersey Pollutant Discharge Elimination System ("NJPDES") permit, unless specially exempted from the permit requirement by regulation. The regulations also require that no person may "build, install, modify or operate any facility for the collection, treatment, or discharge of any pollutant" except in conformance with a valid NJPDES permit.[20]

While there are specialized regulations and conditions applicable to specific permits for discharge to surface water, groundwater discharge permits, and for discharges to treatment works, certain requirements are applicable to all NJPDES permits. In general, all NJPDES permits must contain detailed conditions which ensure compliance with all applicable federal and state effluent limitations[21] and water quality standards.[22] The permits also include schedules of compliance leading to compliance with state and federal regulations and requirements for the installation, maintenance, and the use of discharge monitoring equipment or methods as well as requirements for periodic reporting of monitoring results to NJDEP.

Permits are issued after a lengthy administrative process which begins with submission of the discharger's application.[23] The NJDEP then tentatively decides whether to issue a permit or to deny the application. If the NJDEP tentatively decides to issue a permit, a draft permit containing proposed conditions is prepared. The public then is given notice of the draft permit, or of the denial of the application, and an opportunity for a public hearing. The NJDEP then responds to the public comments and issues a final decision on the permit.[24] Within thirty days of the final decision, the applicant can request an adjudicatory hearing to contest the final decision, including any particular conditions in the permit.[25]

NJPDES permits are issued for fixed terms, up to five years. However, permits can be modified, or reopened for a number of reasons, including the occurrence of material and substantial alterations to the permitted facility or its discharge, or whenever required by "reopener" conditions found in the permit. A common reopener is for categorical federal effluent limitation guidelines for toxic pollutants. Permits may be transferred, as for example when a facility is sold, only upon meeting certain conditions such as prior notice to NJDEP. Permits may be renewed at the end of the fixed term; however, the application for renewal must be made at least 180 days prior to the expiration of the existing permit. Permits may be terminated, or a renewal application denied for several reasons including, for example, noncompliance with any condition of the permit, failure to pay permit fees, or failure by the applicant, during the permitting process, to disclose fully all relevant facts.[26]

The NJDEP is required under the New Jersey Act to assess annual permit fees which are designed to recover the estimated cost of processing, monitoring, and administering the NJPDES permit program.[27] Currently, annual permit fees are assessed based upon a complicated formula which considers the Department's assessment of the discharge's environmental impact.[28]

Discharges to Surface Water

The water pollution control regulations require a NJPDES Discharge to Surface Water ("DSW") permit for the discharge of a pollutant from any "point source" into surface waters of the state.[29] The term "point source" means a discernible, confined, and discrete conveyance such as a pipe, ditch, channel, tunnel, or conduit from which pollutants are discharged. The regulations also require a DSW permit for concentrated animal feeding operations and concentrated aquatic animal production facilities, even though releases from these operations are not necessarily from a point source. DSW permits are also required for "separate storm sewers" which are pipes, conduits, or ditches used for collecting and conveying storm water runoff which are located in an urbanized area or, if not in an urbanized area, where the NJDEP specifically determines that a particular storm sewer is a significant contributor of pollution to State waters.

All DSW permits contain conditions requiring the facility to meet the technology-based effluent limitations and standards of the Federal Act, as well as any more stringent State requirements or water quality standards.[30] Because of increasing concerns regarding the releases of toxic pollutants,[31] all DSW permits contain special conditions relating to toxics. For example, both the New Jersey Act and the implementing regulations specifically require that where a toxic effluent limitation has been promulgated under the Federal Act which is more stringent than any such limitation in an existing permit, the NJDEP must revise or modify the permit in accordance with the stricter limitation on toxic pollutants.[32]

Any person planning to undertake an activity that will require a DSW permit must first apply for a Discharge Allocation Certificate ("DAC") at least ninety days prior to initiation of final engineering design specifications and plans for the entire facility (or for the specific pollution collection and treatment equipment in an existing facility).[33] The DAC is designed to assist the applicant in planning and engineering the facility because the DAC sets out the permit conditions that will apply to the facility including any waste load allocation the Department may require. Thus, the facility can be designed to meet the conditions and requirements that NJDEP ultimately will impose under the water pollution control program.

Upon acquiring the DAC, design and construction of the facility can proceed. At least sixty days prior to the beginning of actual discharges to surface water, the holder of the valid DAC must submit an application for the final DSW permit, which will reflect the conditions and requirements found in the DAC. Finally, all applicants and DSW permit holders are required to submit an emergency plan report which must consider various emergency situations that may impact on the facility's discharges and ability to meet permit conditions. The plan must ensure effective operation of the facility under those emergency conditions.[34]

Discharges to Groundwater

The water pollution control regulations require that persons discharging pollutants to groundwater obtain a NJPDES Discharge to Groundwater ("DGW") permit.[35] The term "discharge" includes releases directly to groundwater or onto land or into wells from which the pollutant might flow or drain into groundwater. In addition to current, intended discharges to groundwater, NJDEP has interpreted this to cover all discharges of pollutants "past or present, actual or potential" which could include any activity or operation where current or even past practices have resulted in actual or potential discharges to groundwater. Thus, NJDEP may require DGW permits for past chemical spills or old waste disposal sites even if it determines that there is only a "potential" discharge to groundwater.

DGW permits set groundwater concentration limits for both hazardous and nonhazardous pollutants. All DGW permits require the permittee to undertake a groundwater monitoring program, which consists of the installation of monitoring wells as well as periodic groundwater sampling to ensure compliance with permit limits and to determine whether there has been any contamination of groundwater. At a minimum, the groundwater monitoring program requires the installation of upgradient wells in order to determine background groundwater quality and at least three monitoring wells downgradient to detect any migration of pollutants from the facility into the groundwater.[36]

If the samples from the monitoring wells show that the releases from the facility have contaminated groundwater in excess of permit levels, a more comprehensive groundwater assessment plan must be submitted.[37] Furthermore, the facility may be required to undertake a "corrective action program" to remediate or reverse the contamination of groundwater caused by the facility's discharges.

An application for a DGW permit must be submitted at least ninety days prior to the planned discharge, but if the facility will require the building of waste collection or treatment equipment, application must be made 180 days prior to the building, installing, or modifying of the equipment.

Underground Injection Control

Underground injection, which is the subsurface emplacement of fluids by well injection, is also governed by the water pollution control regulations through the Underground Injection Control ("UIC") program.[38] Because the UIC program governs the injection of "fluids," it also covers underground storage of fluids and gases in geologic formations in addition to the disposal or discharge of waste through underground injection.[39]

A NJPDES permit is required for any underground injection well that includes any well (even a dug hole) that is deeper than its widest surface opening where the principal function is the emplacement of fluids. The UIC program also covers septic tanks, seepage pits, or cesspools that are used by the owner or operator of a hazardous waste facility to dispose of hazardous waste, or by an industrial facility, a multiple dwelling, or a community system for the subsurface emplacement of wastes.[40]

Injection wells are divided into and regulated by five classes: Class I wells are those that inject hazardous, municipal, or industrial waste (as long as there is no formation containing an underground source of drinking water within two miles of the injection well); Class II wells are those that inject fluids that are brought to the surface during the production of oil or natural gas, or which inject hydrocarbons for underground storage; Class III wells inject fluids in connection with the extraction of minerals or energy (e.g., geothermal energy); Class IV wells are those that inject hazardous, municipal, or industrial wastes into geologic formations which contain a source of drinking water within two miles of the well; and Class V wells which are all other injection wells, including mostly those that inject relatively clean water (e.g., salt water intrusion barrier wells used to inject water into fresh water aquifers to prevent saltwater intrusion). Class V wells also include industrial septic tanks.[41]

By regulation, NJDEP has prohibited any new wells that inject hazardous, municipal, and industrial waste into a formation that contains underground sources of drinking water within two miles of the well, that is, Class IV wells, and has phased out the use of existing Class IV wells.[42]

Also, by regulation the NJDEP has provided a permit-by-rule for all Class V wells.[43] A permit-by-rule allows the facility to avoid the requirement of obtaining an individual permit, as long as it complies with special regulations regarding reporting to NJDEP and certain construction and abandonment requirements. If a facility with a Class V well does not comply with those special requirements, it can lose its permit-by-rule status and must obtain an individual NJPDES permit.

The UIC regulations prohibit the movement of fluids from any injection well into underground sources of drinking water. If movement of fluids into drinking water is detected, NJDEP can require the operator to take corrective action to prevent contamination of the drinking water source.[44]

All Class I, II, and III injection wells are required to have an individual UIC permit which contains conditions and standards specific to that class of well. These standards

relate to the construction, operation, and monitoring of the well, together with requirements for periodic reporting to NJDEP.[45]

Discharges to Domestic Treatment Works

The Water Pollution Control regulations govern facilities that discharge, primarily
nondomestic pollutants to a domestic treatment works.[46] Such facilities, although they
do not discharge directly to waters of the state, are regulated as "indirect dischargers"
to domestic treatment works. A domestic treatment works is a publicly or privately
owned facility for the treatment, prior to discharge, of municipal or industrial waste
of a liquid nature.

Pretreatment Standards

Domestic treatment works are themselves subject to the conditions of an NJPDES
permit for the discharge of liquid wastes. Levels of contaminants in the sludge produced from these treatment works are also regulated. The uncontrolled introduction
of pollutants into the treatment works might allow the pollutants to pass through the
treatment process untreated, or the pollutants might interfere with the waste treatment
process, resulting in either a violation of the treatment works' NJPDES permit, or a
violation of the sludge contamination limitations. To avoid these problems, the Water
Pollution Control Regulations require all non-household users of domestic treatment
works to meet certain pretreatment standards before discharging to the treatment,
works.[47] The NJDEP has adopted the pretreatment standards promulgated by the
USEPA pursuant to the Federal Act.[48] Those pretreatment standards absolutely prohibit some contaminants in discharges to treatment works and require pretreatment
prior to discharge of other contaminants. The pretreatment regulations set limits on
discharges on an industry-by-industry basis. In addition, the New Jersey regulations
provide that no indirect discharger may release any pollutant in sufficient quantity so
that the individual release alone causes the treatment works' discharge to exceed set
limits for toxic substances, or causes the treatment works' sludge to exceed established criteria for the disposal of sludge. The New Jersey Act empowers municipally
owned treatment works to set terms and conditions on the discharge of pollutants
into their treatment works, and grants investigatory powers to ensure compliance by
indirect dischargers. The regulations require all users of domestic treatment works to
comply with any ordinances, rules, or regulations promulgated by the domestic treatment works.

Significant Indirect Users

Because the definition of discharge in the New Jersey WPCA includes releases to
treatment works, all such dischargers are required to have an NJPDES permit. The
NJDEP has provided a permit-by-rule for most users of domestic treatment works,
except for "Significant Indirect Users." In order to qualify for the permit-by-rule,
and thus be exempted from the requirement of an individual NJPDES permit, the
user must comply with specific regulations which include the user obtaining prior
written authorization for the discharge to the treatment works. Eligibility for the

permit-by-rule can be withdrawn or refused by the Department for a number of reasons, which include the user having been found to be in significant violation of State environmental laws or regulations.[49]

Significant Indirect Users are required to obtain individual NJPDES permits for the discharge to a treatment works. The regulations provide a laundry list of users that are deemed to be Significant Indirect Users. In general, a Significant Indirect User is one who discharges significant quantities of effluent to the treatment works, or whose discharges may contain toxic or hazardous substances (e.g., discharges from hazardous waste facilities or discharges of landfill leachate).[50]

SEWAGE AND WASTEWATER TREATMENT

The control of water pollution from sewage and wastewater treatment is accomplished through several related statutes that either compliment or implement the NJDEP's regulatory program under the WPCA.

Water Quality Planning

The Water Quality Planning Act[51] mandates an area-wide waste treatment planning process which ensures adequate sewage and wastewater treatment systems and which provides for, to the extent feasible, the control of all sources of water pollution in order to maintain water quality.[52] The Act provides for the establishment of planning areas, which generally conform to county boundaries with modifications made to account for major watersheds, and for the designation of area-wide planning agencies authorized to undertake the planning process.[53]

Each designated planning agency, and the NJDEP for areas without a designated agency, must conduct the area-wide planning process and submit the area-wide plan to the Governor. Each planning agency must coordinate its work with every other planning agency with which it shares a river basin, and any conflicts that occur must be submitted to the NJDEP for mediation.

The area-wide plan must include the following:

(1) the identification of treatment works, including wastewater collection and urban stormwater runoff systems, necessary to meet the anticipated municipal and industrial waste treatment needs of the area for a twenty-year period (updated annually) and to establish construction priorities for such treatment works;

(2) the establishment of a regulatory program to ensure that all types of water pollution are controlled to the extent feasible and that industrial or commercial wastes discharged into any treatment works meet the applicable pretreatment requirements;

(3) the identification of existing or required agencies necessary to construct, operate, and maintain sewage and wastewater treatment facilities required by the plan and otherwise necessary to carry out the plan;

(4) a process to identify and control agriculturally and silviculturally related non-point sources of water pollution;

(5) a process to identify construction activity–related sources of pollution and procedures and methods, including land use requirements, to control such pollution.[54]

The actual implementation of the area-wide plan, such as the construction of wastewater treatment facilities or the enforcement of industrial pretreatment regulations is
left to independent agencies. These independent agencies include local sewage treatment authorities, established pursuant to the Sewage Authorities Law[55]; the Passaic
Valley Sewerage District[56]; and local municipal utilities authorities established pursuant to the Municipal and County Utilities Authorities Law.[57]

Perhaps the most direct impact upon the public of the area-wide waste treatment
planning process is the requirement in the Act that all projects and activities affecting
water quality in the planning area must be developed and conducted in a manner consistent with the area-wide plan, and that the NJDEP may not grant any permit (such
as a NJPDES permit) which is in conflict with an adopted area-wide plan.[58] Thus,
for example, the NJDEP could not grant a permit for a direct DSW if the area-wide
plan requires that all discharges in that area be directed to the local sewage treatment
works.

Another impact upon the public of the process of planning for sewage treatment
facilities arises from the Realty Improvement Sewerage and Facilities Act.[59] This
Act provides that no building permit can be issued for the construction of any realty
improvement[60] until the local board of health certifies that the proposed water supply
system and sewerage facilities are in compliance with the standards for the construction of such systems promulgated by the NJDEP.[61]

The Act also provides that no municipality may issue a subdivision approval
for any subdivision of fifty or more realty improvements until the NJDEP certifies
that the proposed water supply and sewerage facilities comply with the applicable
standards.

Wastewater Treatment Works

A person planning to build, install, or substantially modify a facility for the collection or treatment of a pollutant, that is, a treatment works, must apply to the NJDEP
for approval pursuant to the Water Pollution Control Regulations.[62] Within twenty
working days of submission of the application, the NJDEP determines whether the
discharger will be required to comply with the requirements for a treatment works
approval. In deciding whether treatment works approval will be required, the Department considers the degree of risk to public health posed by the proposed discharge, the
characteristics and quality of both the discharge and the receiving waters, the quantity
of the discharge, and the site of the discharge.

If the Department decides that treatment works approval is required, the applicant
proceeds through a three-stage procedure to obtain final approval: Stage 1 is a preliminary review of the proposed treatment works; Stage 2 is review and approval to
construct or modify the treatment works; and Stage 3 is approval to operate the treatment works if it has been built in conformance with Stages 1 and 2.

In addition to receiving approval to build or modify a treatment works, each domestic treatment works must monitor the amount of committed flow of effluent being

discharged to it.[63] If the committed flow reaches or exceeds 80 percent of the permitted capacity, a plan for avoiding overloading the facility or for avoiding a violation of the NJPDES permit must be submitted. If the facility's committed flow reaches 100 percent of design capacity or if the facility consistently violates effluent limitations in its NJPDES permit, NJDEP may impose a sewer connection ban.

The NJDEP also has promulgated construction standards for wastewater treatment facilities.[64] The standards designate no delegable responsibilities for various construction tasks between the owner and the contractor, designate appropriate payment schedules and establish certain construction and inspection standards for the construction of treatment works and piping systems.

Sludge Management

The Water Pollution Control Regulations include a Sludge Quality Assurance Program which is designed to determine the degree of contamination, by chemicals, metals, and toxic organic compounds, in the sludge produced by domestic and industrial treatment or pretreatment works.[65] All domestic and industrial treatment works, as well as Significant Indirect User pretreatment works, are required to periodically sample their sludge. These samples are tested for heavy metals, selected chemicals, and certain toxic organic compounds, using specified procedures. Facilities must report to NJDEP the results of the sampling and testing as well as the method of disposal of the sludge.

Anyone who plans to dispose of sludge or seepage by application onto land must obtain a NJPDES permit.[66] The NJPDES permit for land application of sludge or seepage contains conditions relating to application rates, operational procedures, restricted areas and buffer zones, groundwater monitoring through the use of monitoring wells, soil monitoring, sludge quality monitoring, transport of sludge to the disposal site, and record keeping provisions.

Treatment works whose sludge is disposed of by ocean dumping are required to submit a sludge management plan to insure that land-based alternatives to ocean dumping will be available before the federal ban on ocean dumping of sludge takes effect. The facility must also submit a task schedule with specifications and a construction schedule for the alternatives chosen under the sludge management plan.[67]

ENFORCEMENT AND PENALTIES

The NJDEP is charged, under the New Jersey WPCA, with the responsibility for determining compliance with the Act or any applicable State or federal regulation. The NJDEP is given the right to enter all premises where a discharge source is or might be located, for the purposes of inspection, sampling, copying, or photographing or to enter any premises in which monitoring records or equipment required by a permit are kept.[68] In addition to the investigatory powers authorized by statute, the Water Pollution Control Regulations require all holders of NJPDES permits to furnish to the Department, within a reasonable time, any information the Department may request in order to determine compliance with the permit. Moreover, information in reports required to be submitted to the NJDEP on a regular basis, such as Discharge Monitoring Reports, can be used to determine compliance with the Act, its regulations or permit conditions.

If the Department determines there has been a violation of the Act, regulations, or a permit condition, it has several enforcement options.[69] The Commissioner may issue a compliance order requiring the facility to comply with the applicable regulation or permit condition and may assess a civil administrative penalty of up to $50,000 per violation. If a violation is of a continuing nature, each day constitutes a separate violation. The environmental impact of the violation and the seriousness of the violator's conduct are considered when administrative penalties are imposed.[70]

In addition, the NJDEP may bring a civil court action seeking an injunction against the violator as well as assessment of costs in investigating the violation and litigating against the violator. Moreover, it may seek costs incurred by the State in correcting the adverse effects on the environment caused by the violation and compensatory damages for the loss of wildlife, fish, or other aquatic life. Additionally, the court may also impose a civil penalty of up to $50,000 per day for violations of the Act or any administrative or court order issued pursuant to the Act, or for the failure to pay an administrative penalty.

There are also criminal penalties for willful or negligent violations of the Act or its regulations.[71] First offenders are guilty of a crime in the fourth degree punishable by fines ranging from $5,000 to $50,000 per day, or imprisonment for up to one year, or both. Subsequent offenses are punishable by fines ranging from $10,000 to $100,000 per day, or imprisonment for up to two years, or both. A person who knowingly falsifies a statement or document required under the Act or who tampers with a monitoring device is subject to a fine of up to $20,000 or up to six months imprisonment, or both. Moreover, any conveyance or equipment used in a willful discharge in violation of the Act is subject to forfeiture to the State. Finally, it should be noted that in any of these enforcement actions, it is not a defense that cessation of operations would have been necessary to comply with conditions in the permit.[72] Therefore, in some instances, operations may have to be stopped or reduced in order to avoid penalties and fines under the Act.

The NJDEP also has enforcement authority under the Fish and Game, Wild Birds and Animal statute,[73] which prohibits the discharge, into any fresh or tidal waters, of any petroleum products, debris, and hazardous, deleterious, destructive, or poisonous substances of any kind. Violations of this Act are subject to a penalty of up to $6,000 per day for each violation.

WATER SUPPLY AND QUALITY

New Jersey has enacted a series of related statutes designed to ensure an adequate supply of high-quality water. The statutes seek to accomplish this goal by (1) protecting the amount of water supplies under normal as well as drought conditions, (2) regulating the quality of drinking water supplied by public water systems, and (3) establishing surface and groundwater quality standards and criteria.

Water Supply and Diversion

Because New Jersey holds that the water resources of the State are public assets held in trust for the State's citizens, the State manages the waters of the State[74] as a common resource to assure the fair allocation of the water supply. The protection of the State's water supplies during drought conditions and the assurance of a fair allocation of waters of the State during normal conditions, through the use of water diversion permits, are accomplished primarily through the Water Supply Management Act.[75]

Drought Emergencies

The Water Supply Management Act empowers the Governor to declare, by executive order, a state of water emergency upon a finding by the NJDEP that there is a water supply shortage which endangers the public health, safety, or welfare in all or part of the State.[76] The NJDEP has adopted, as required by the Act, an Emergency Water Supply Allocation Plan,[77] to be utilized as the basis for imposing water usage restrictions during a declared state of water emergency.

During a declared State Water Emergency, the NJDEP may take steps to alleviate the adverse effects of the emergency such as:

(1) order any person to reduce by a specified amount the use of any water supply, to make use of an alternative water supply, to make emergency interconnections between systems, to transfer water between public or private systems, or to cease the use of any water supply;
(2) order any water distribution and supply systems to reduce or increase by a specified amount the distribution of water to certain users, or to share any water supply with other distributors;
(3) establish priorities for the distribution of any water supply;
(4) direct any person engaged in retail distribution of water to impose surcharges as a penalty for the violation of any order to reduce usage.[78]

The NJDEP has promulgated regulations pursuant to the Act which establish a system for prioritizing the allocation of water supplies during an emergency. This priority system is based upon a phased approach to drought emergencies ranging from Phase I conditions (available water supplies below normal) through Phase IV (disaster stage).[79] The NJDEP has authority to order curtailment of certain activities depending upon which drought emergency phase has been declared, and the water use restrictions become more stringent as the State moves from Phase I through Phase IV.[80]

Water Diversion

In order to ensure a fair allocation of water during normal conditions, the Act requires the NJDEP to regulate persons who divert more than 100,000 gallons per day of State waters, including surface or groundwater. Thus a person who diverts or plans to construct any building which may require the diversion of more than 100,000 gallons of surface or groundwater, per day, for non-agricultural or horticultural purposes must obtain a permit from the NJDEP.[81] The Department may also establish standards and procedures that diverters must follow to ensure that proper diversion methods are used, that only the permitted quantity is diverted, that the water is used only for its permitted purpose, that the water quality of the water source is maintained, and for the submission of reports concerning the diversion and use of the water.[82]

A person who diverts 100,000 or more gallons of surface or groundwater, per day, for agricultural or horticultural purposes must obtain approval of a five-year water usage certification program from the appropriate county agricultural agent.[83] The county agent's approval is based on standards and procedures established by the NJDEP.[84]

Before the issuance of a diversion permit or water usage certificate, the public must be given notice of the application and the opportunity for a public hearing. Each permit and water usage certificate will be renewed by the Department upon expiration except that the Department may, after notice and hearing, limit the quantity to the amount currently diverted or reasonably required for demonstrated future needs.[85]

Finally, the Act prohibits the transport of water from the Pinelands National Reserve to more than 10 miles outside the boundary of the Pinelands. This prohibition does not apply to water previously transported out of the Pinelands for public water supply purposes prior to the effective date of the Act.[86]

No tax, fee, or other charge is imposed on a diversion of surface or groundwater for agricultural or horticultural purposes. However, the Department may impose a fee for the cost of processing, monitoring, and administering the water usage certification program.[87]

Violations of the Water Supply Management Act or of any rule, regulation, or order are subject to injunctive action and administrative penalties of not more than $5,000 for each offense. In addition, civil penalties of not more than $5,000 for each offense can be collected in a civil action by a summary proceeding.[88]

WATER SUPPLY AUTHORITIES

The supply of water in New Jersey is also protected and enhanced pursuant to several statutes relating to water supply authorities. The New Jersey Water Supply Authority Act[89] established the New Jersey Water Supply Authority and transferred to the Authority, all past and future State-owned water supply facilities, such as the Delaware and Raritan Canal Transmission Complex and the Spruce Run-Round Valley Reservoir Complex. The Authority is empowered to design, initiate, acquire, construct, maintain, and operate water supply projects.

The North and South Jersey Water Supply Districts[90] law divided the State into two water supply districts and established the potential creation of a water supply commission for each district, based on a petition process to be followed by municipalities. However, in actual effect, only the North Jersey District Water Supply Commission presently exists. Under the law, these commissions develop, acquire, and operate a new water supply or an additional water supply for the participating municipalities located within the district.

Under an act that provides for the improvement and acquisition of small water companies,[91] whenever any small water company is found to have failed to comply with an order from the NJDEP concerning the availability or portability of water or the provision of water at adequate volume and pressure, the NJDEP together with the Board of Public Utilities must conduct a public hearing to determine the appropriate actions to be taken. Such actions authorized by the statute included making all improvements necessary to meet the orders or an order requiring the acquisition of the small water company by a suitable public or private entity.

Finally, the Safe Dam Act[92] authorizes the NJDEP to regulate the construction, inspection, repair, and safety of dams and reservoirs and requires the Department to establish a periodic dam safety inspection and reporting procedure. In addition, the statute provides for a hearing on petitions protesting the abandonment or removal of any reservoir, body of water, or dam.

SAFE DRINKING WATER ACT

The regulation of pollutants in drinking water supplies is governed by the New Jersey Safe Drinking Water Act.[93] The goals of the Act are to empower the NJDEP to promulgate and enforce regulations to purify drinking water prior to its distribution and to authorize the NJDEP to assume primary enforcement responsibility under the Federal Safe Drinking Water Act.[94] The goals of the Act are accomplished through the imposition of primary and secondary drinking water standards upon drinking water suppliers, through the imposition of limits on hazardous contaminants in drinking water, and through standards for the construction of public water systems.

Primary Drinking Water Standards

The NJDEP has adopted the National Primary Drinking Water Standards[95] as New Jersey's primary standards. The federal primary drinking water standards generally apply to all "public water systems" which provide piped water for human consumption and which have at least fifteen service connections or regularly serve an average of at least twenty-five individuals daily, at least sixty days per year.

The primary drinking water standards establish Maximum Contaminant Levels ("MCLs") for turbidity, microbiological contaminants, certain organic and inorganic chemicals, and radioactivity in drinking water supplied by public water systems. The standards also establish treatment techniques to be used to meet the MCLs, as well as schedules for required periodic testing of drinking water supplies to determine compliance with these MCLs, and subsequent reporting of results to the State. The primary drinking water standards also contain special MCLs and monitoring requirements for a specific list of volatile organic compounds. These special regulations are only applicable to community water systems, defined as public water systems which serve at least fifteen service connections used, by year-round residents or regularly serve at least twenty-five year-round residents, and non-transient, non-community water systems which are public water systems that regularly serve at least twenty-five of the same persons over six months per year.

The NJDEP has established more stringent MCLs and testing schedules for a few of the contaminants covered by the federal standards and also has required non-public water systems to meet more stringent MCLs and testing standards for coliform bacteria.[96] The standards require that any public water system report to the State any failure to comply with primary drinking water regulations, within forty-eight hours of discovery. If a public water system fails to comply with applicable MCLs or applicable monitoring requirements, notification must be given to customers, by direct mail, and to the general public. Furthermore, this notification must be repeated every three months for as long as the system is not in compliance.

Secondary Drinking Water Standards

The NJDEP has established secondary drinking water standards[97] which set upper and lower limits for substances in drinking water that affect the taste, odor, or appearance of the water, such as color or pH. The secondary limits are not enforceable but are only recommended standards that water supply authorities may refer to in determining the suitability of drinking water supplies. However, the NJDEP has established a schedule under which public water systems must at least test their drinking water supplies for the substances covered by the secondary limits.

Hazardous Contaminants Requirements

The Safe Drinking Water Act requires the owner or operator of a "public community water system" to test its water to determine the presence of certain hazardous organic compounds and to require compliance with MCLs established for those hazardous contaminants.[98] A public community water system is a public water system which serves at least fifteen service connections used by year-round residents or regularly serves at least twenty-five year-round residents.

The NJDEP has promulgated regulations which establish periodic testing schedules which public community water systems must follow to determine the presence of hazardous organic compounds.[99] The Department just recently promulgated MCLs for these hazardous organic contaminants.[100] If the results of the required testing show that the water system exceeds the MCL for a hazardous contaminant, the water system must provide public notice in accordance with the procedures established under the primary drinking water standards. In addition, within one year of receipt of the test results showing a violation of the MCL, the water system must take all actions necessary to bring its water into compliance. The NJDEP may require remedial action in less than one year if it determines that there is an immediate public health threat, or the Department may grant an extension for compliance if new construction is required.[101]

Standards for the Construction of Public Water Systems

The NJDEP has promulgated regulations which govern the design and the construction of water supply systems. Public community water systems are required to seek prior approval from the NJDEP for any construction of a new water system or for any substantial modification of an existing water system.[102]

The regulations also provide standards for the construction of public community water systems which cover well installation, pumping station specifications, distribution system standards, chemical handling and feeding as well as filtration, disinfectant, and pretreatment standards. While public non-community and non-public water systems do not need NJDEP approval prior to the construction of a new water system, such water systems are subject to a separate set of construction standards.[103]

Enforcement and Penalties

The NJDEP is empowered to issue orders requiring compliance with the Safe Drinking Water Act and to assess civil administrative penalties of up to $5,000 for the first offense, $5,000 to $10,000 for the second offense and up to $25,000 for subsequent offenses. Each day a continuing violation is not corrected, subsequent to receipt of an order to cease the violation, constitutes a separate violation. The NJDEP also may institute a civil action for injunctive relief to prohibit or prevent violations of the Act or its regulations and the court may impose a fine of up to $10,000 for any violation of the Act, an administrative or court order, or for failure to pay an administrative penalty.[104]

SURFACE WATER QUALITY CRITERIA

Pursuant to its authority under both the WPCA[105] and the Water Quality Planning Act,[106] the NJDEP has established water quality standards and criteria for all surface waters, including both fresh and salt water, in order to protect and enhance the quality of those waters.[107]

The regulations establish various classes of waters to which the applicable water quality standards and criteria are applied. For example, there are two classes of fresh water: FW1 which are fresh waters originating in relatively pristine areas such as state or federal parks, and which are not subject to any man-made wastewater discharges. These FW1 waters are highly protected by the water quality criteria which require that these waters be maintained in their natural state.[108] FW2 waters are all other fresh surface waters that do not qualify as FW1 waters. While the quality of these waters is protected so that no degradation of existing water quality occurs, the standards are less stringent than for FW1 waters.

With regard to each classification, the regulations also establish appropriate uses for which the quality of such water should be maintained. For example, NJDEP applies the relevant water quality criteria so that the quality of FW1 waters are maintained to allow for the following uses:

(1) set aside for posterity to represent the natural aquatic environment and its associated biota;
(2) primary and secondary recreation;
(3) maintenance, migration, and reproduction of the natural and established aquatic biota; and
(4) all other reasonable uses.[109]

Every river, stream, or other body of water or segments of water bodies are assigned to an appropriate classification. The surface water quality criteria are applied to the specific classifications. These criteria vary depending upon which classification the stream segment qualifies for. The criteria generally are expressed in terms of maximum contamination limits for specific pollutants. For example, for FW2 waters, the water quality criteria provide maximum concentration limits for pollutants such as bacteria, chloride, cadmium, and chlordane.

The most direct impact upon the public of these surface water quality regulations is through the NJPDES DSW permits for point sources of pollution. Normally, the conditions of such individual discharge permits include technology-based effluent limitations. However, if the technology-based effluent limitations are insufficient to meet or maintain the water quality standards applicable to the classification assigned to the particular stream, the NJDEP must impose the more stringent water quality effluent limitations that have been established.[110] These water quality effluent limitations are designed so that the quality of the waters receiving a discharge will meet the standards and criteria established for that classification after the introduction of the proposed discharge.[111]

The regulations provide mechanisms for either modifying the established water quality–based effluent limitations or for reclassifying specific segments for less restrictive uses or classifications.[112] The regulations set out the standards that must be met to obtain a modification of an effluent limitation or to reclassify a segment of stream. The reasons that will support such a change include, among others:

(1) The water quality criteria, or the existing designated use, are not attainable because of natural background;
(2) The water quality criteria or existing designated use are not attainable because of irretrievable man-induced conditions.[113]

GROUNDWATER QUALITY CRITERIA

In order to protect the quality of groundwater resources, NJDEP has promulgated groundwater quality standards and criteria similar to those applicable to surface water.[114] The regulations establish groundwater classifications which are based upon natural concentrations of dissolved solids. For example, GW2 is the class of groundwater having a natural total dissolved solids concentration of 500 mg/l or less. The regulations also designate appropriate uses for each class of groundwater.[115]

The groundwater quality regulations are thus designed to protect the quality of water in each class, such that the designated uses will be maintained. This is accomplished through the groundwater quality criteria which set specific concentration limits for certain pollutants.[116] For example, the criteria for GW2 waters set maximum concentration limits for such pollutants as Arsenic, Cadmium, Lead, and Mercury.

Because every discharger to groundwater must obtain a NJPDES permit, the application of groundwater quality–based effluent limitations in the form of permit conditions is the regulatory mechanism whereby NJDEP ensures that the groundwater quality criteria are met. For new dischargers or existing dischargers seeking to modify their discharge, where existing groundwater quality is consistently better than the applicable criteria limits, the NJDEP imposes, as permit conditions, effluent limitations designed to protect the high quality of that groundwater. Where the existing quality is equal to or worse than the applicable criteria, the NJDEP may impose effluent limitations on permits for new or modified discharges designed to attain or maintain the applicable quality criteria limits.[117] Where existing groundwater quality does not meet the quality criteria for that class, primarily because of human activities, the NJDEP is authorized to require all or some existing dischargers to undertake remediation efforts to restore the water quality or to contain the contamination to a small area.[118]

There are procedures for obtaining a modification to the groundwater quality–based effluent limitations that NJDEP proposes to impose on a discharger.[119] In cases where the groundwater quality exceeds the applicable criteria, in order to obtain a modification to the effluent limitation the discharger must show that (1) there is no reasonable relationship between the economic and the social costs of meeting such limitations and the benefits of maintaining the existing high groundwater quality; (2) some degradation of high-quality water should be allowed for necessary and justifiable economic or social development; and (3) the modified effluent limitations will not interfere with designated groundwater uses for that class.

Where groundwater quality is equal to or worse than applicable standards, the discharger may seek a modification for the proposed effluent limitation by showing that (1) the existing designated use is not attainable because of natural background; (2) the existing designated use is not attainable because of irretrievable man-induced conditions; or (3) there is no reasonable relationship between the costs in achieving the limitation and the benefit of maintaining or attaining the water quality criteria for that class.

There also is a procedure for reclassifying an area of groundwater so that less restrictive designated uses and thus less stringent criteria will apply.[120] In order to obtain a reclassification of groundwater, the discharger must show that (1) the designated use is not being achieved because of the presence of pollutants, except total dissolved solids; (2) the designated use is not attainable because of irretrievable man-induced conditions; or (3) the costs of restoring water quality bear no reasonable relationship to the benefits to be obtained.

NOTES

1. Although, as will be noted, the latter is not ignored.

2. The public became increasingly aware of the effects of decades of indiscriminate discharging of pollutants into our waters, from publications like Rachel Carson's Silent Spring.

3. The first New Jersey case recognizing so-called common property, or natural resources, was *Arnold v. Mundy,* 6 N.J.L. 1 (Sup. Ct. 1821). The Court famously declared:

> Every thing susceptible of property is considered as belonging to the nation that possesses the country, and as forming the entire mass of its wealth. But the nation does not possess all those things in the same manner. By very far the greater part of them are divided among the individuals of the nation, and become Private property. Those things not divided among the individuals still belong to the nation, and are called Public property. Of these, again, some are reserved for the necessities of the state, and are used for the public benefit, and those are called "the domain of the crown or of the republic"; others remain common to all the citizens, who take of them and use them, each according to his necessities, and according to the laws which regulate their use, and are

called Common property. Of this latter kind, according to the writers upon the law of nature and of nations, and upon the civil law, are the air, the ***running water***, the sea, the fish, and the wild beasts. . . . But inasmuch as the things which constitute this Common property are things in which a sort of transient usufructuary possession, only, can be had; and inasmuch as the title to them and to the soil by which they are supported, and to which they are appurtenant, cannot well, according to the common law notion of title, be vested in all the people; ***therefore, the wisdom of that law has placed it in the hands of the sovereign power, to be held, protected, and regulated for the common use and benefit. But still, though this title, strictly speaking, is in the sovereign, yet the use is common to all the people.***

6 N.J.L. at 71 (emphasis added).

4. See *Borough of Neptune City v. Borough of Avon-By-The-Sea*, 61 N.J. 296 (1972).

5. See *Armstrong v. Francis*, 20 N.J. 320 (1956); *Borough of Westville v. Whitney Home Builders*, 40 N.J. Super 62 (App. Div. 1956).

6. 5A *Powell on Real Property*, ¶ 713[4][b], p. 65-77. This is to be contrasted with the so-called English rule (or "natural flow" theory) that all riparian owners are entitled to water absolutely undiminished in quantity and quality. See Lechner, "Riparian Rights to Water Quality," 6 *Seton Hall Legislative Journal* 339, 340 (1983). Application of this doctrine "severely limits the consumptive uses that may be made of the water since virtually any consumptive use will diminish the quantity or quality of the water available to other users downstream." 5A *Powell on Real Property*, ¶ 713[4][a], p. 65-75. As a result, the "natural flow" doctrine has been abandoned by most riparian jurisdictions. *Id.* at p. 65-77. The "natural flow" theory is similar to, but is to be distinguished from, the rule followed mainly in Western states, that the party "first in time" generally has water rights to the exclusion of all others.

7. See English, "A New Approach to New Jersey's Water Supply Problems," 6 *Seton Hall Legislative Journal* 349 (1983).

8. *Id.* at 350.

9. N.J.S.A. 58:1A-1 et seq. See *infra* for a more fulsome discussion of this statute.

10. N.J.S.A. 58:1A-2.

11. Therefore, to the extent that the prevention or cleanup of water pollution was addressed by the law at all, it tended to be in court cases brought by individual water "users" against other water "users" alleging that the first party's rights of "reasonable use" had been interfered with due to the second party's acts causing pollution. Consequently, there are various cases from the 1800s and early 1900s in which downstream water users, often farmers, won both injunctions and monetary damages against upstream water users, sometimes other farmers, sometimes businesses like abattoirs, for dumping animal waste, animal parts and the like into streams, thereby rendering the water contaminated and unfit for use by the downstream user.

12. N.J.S.A. 58:10A-1 et seq.

13. The Act defines "pollutant" as any "dredged spoil, solid waste, incinerator residue, sewage, garbage, refuse, oil, grease, sewage sludge, munitions, chemical wastes, biological materials, radioactive substance, thermal waste, wrecked or discarded equipment, rock, sand, cellar dirt, and industrial, municipal or agricultural waste or other residue discharged into the waters of the State." N.J.S.A. 58:10A-3n.

14. The Act defines "discharge" as "the releasing, spilling, leaking, pumping, pouring, emitting, emptying or dumping of a pollutant into the waters of the State or onto land or into wells from which it might flow or drain into said waters, and shall include the release of any pollutant into a municipal treatment works." N.J.S.A. 58:10A-3e.

15. The Act defines "Waters of the State" as "the ocean and its estuaries, all springs, streams and bodies of surface or ground water, whether natural or artificial, within the boundaries of this State or subject to its jurisdiction." N.J.S.A. 58:10A-3t.

16. 33 U.S.C. §1251 et seq.

17. 47 Fed. Reg. 17331 (April 22, 1982).

18. N.J.A.C. 7:14A-6.1(a).

19. N.J.A.C. 7:14A-l.9.

20. N.J.A.C. 7:14A-l.2(b).

21. An effluent limitation is a restriction on quantities, quality, rates, and concentration of chemical, physical, thermal, biological, and other constituents of pollutants. N.J.S.A. 58:10A-3f.

22. N.J.S.A. 58:10A-6(f)2.

23. However, NJDEP has reserved the authority to unilaterally issue a NJPDES permit, based upon information the Department possesses, which the permittee must comply with even though no application is submitted. *See* N.J.A.C. 7:14A-2.1(d). This authority was challenged in *VI-Concrete Co. v. Dep't of Environmental Protection*, 220 N.J. Super. 176, 531 A. 2d 1039 (App. Div. 1987). In that case, the New Jersey Appellate Division upheld the NJDEP's issuance of a NJPDES permit to the owner of land which had been used by a prior owner as a landfill. That permit required the current landowner to undertake a groundwater monitoring program. The court found that the Department had the authority to issue such a permit requiring groundwater monitoring at the former landfill, even though no application for a permit had been made. The court also found that the permit was properly directed to the current landowner even though it was the prior landowner that had operated the landfill. On appeal, the New Jersey Supreme Court reversed, finding that NJDEP's lack of a duly promulgated regulation governing groundwater monitoring requirements at old landfills invalidated the NJPDES permit, *VI-Concrete Co. v. Dep't of Environmental Protection*, Docket No. 27,754 (April 19, 1989). Since the Supreme Court did not expressly address the issue of whether NJDEP may unilaterally issue a NJPDES permit without the permittee submitting an application, the Department's authority has not been conclusively established.

24. N.J.A.C. 7:14A-7.6.

25. N.J.A.C. 7:14A-8.9.

26. N.J.A.C. 7:14A, Subchapter 2.

27. N.J.S.A. 58:10A-9.

28. N.J.A.C. 7:14A-l.8.

29. N.J.A.C. 7: 14A, Subchapter 3.

30. N.J.A.C. 7:14A-3.13(a).

31. A "toxic pollutant" means "those pollutants, or combinations of pollutants, including disease causing agents, which after discharge and upon exposure, ingestion, inhalation or assimilation into any organism, either directly or indirectly by ingestion through food chains, may, on the basis of information available to the Commissioner, cause death, disease, behavioral abnormalities, cancer, genetic mutations, physiological malfunctions, including malfunctions in reproduction, or physical deformation, in such organisms or their offspring," N.J.S.A. 58:10A-3r, and includes any toxic pollutants identified pursuant to the Federal Act.

32. N.J.S.A. 58:10A-7(a)(3); N.J.A.C. 7:14A-2.12.

33. N.J.A.C. 7:14A-3.2, 3.3.

34. N.J.A.C. 7:14A-3.12.

35. N.J.A.C. 7:14A, Subchapter 6.

36. N.J.A.C. 7:14A-6.3 to 6.9.

37. N.J.A.C. 7:14A-6.10, 6.15.

38. N.J.A.C. 7:14A, Subchapter 5.

39. However, the UIC program does not cover the underground storage of fluids in preconstructed underground storage tanks, N.J.A.C. 7:14A-5.1(b)(2)(iv).

40. Single family residential disposal systems such as septic tanks or cesspools are not covered by the UIC program, N.J.A.C. 7:14A-5.1(b)(2)(ii). Regulations setting out construction standards for individual subsurface disposal systems can be found at N.J.A.C. 7:9-2.1.

41. N.J.A.C. 7:14A-8.2.

42. N.J.A.C. 7:14A-8.7.

43. N.J.A.C. 7:14A-8.8.

44. N.J.A.C. 7:14A-5.4.

45. N.J.A.C. 7:14A-5.13 to 5.17.

46. N.J.A.C. 7:14A, Subchapter 13.

47. N.J.A.C. 7:14A-13.3, 13.5.

48. 40 C.F.R. §403.

49. N.J.A.C. 7:14A-13.5.

50. N.J.A.C. 7: 14A-1.9, 10.5.

51. N.J.S.A. 58:11A-1 to 11.

52. Because such area-wide plans also are undertaken pursuant to Section 208 of the Federal Water Pollution Control Act, 33 U.S.C. §1288, they are sometimes called "Section 208 plans."

53. N.J.S.A. 58:11A-4.

54. N.J.S.A. 58:11A-5.

55. N.J.S.A. 40:14A-1 et seq. The Act authorizes counties and municipalities to create sewer authorities that are empowered to construct, operate, and maintain sewage facilities; to impose rates and service charges; and to control pollutants in discharges to sewage treatment works.

56. N.J.S.A. 58:14-1 et seq.

57. N.J.S.A. 40:14B-1 et seq. The Act authorizes counties and municipalities to create independent utilities authorities to distribute an adequate water supply for public or private use, relieve state waters from pollution, provide sewage collection and disposal services and to provide solid waste services.

58. N.J.S.A. 58:11A-10.

59. N.J.S.A. 58:11-23 et seq.

60. The term "realty improvement" is defined as any proposed new residence or other building the useful occupancy of which shall require the installation or erection of a water supply system or sewerage facility, other than one which is to be served by an approved water supply and an approved sewerage system. N.J.S.A. 58:11-24(e).

61. See Section 3.2, Wastewater Treatment Works and Section S.3.4, Standards for the Construction of Public Water Systems, for a discussion of the appropriate construction standards.

62. N.J.A.C. 7:14A, Subchapter 12.

63. N.J.A.C. 7:14A-12.20, 12.21.

64. N.J.A.C. 7:14, Subchapter 2.

65. N.J.A.C. 7:14, Subchapter 4. The term "sludge" refers to the solid residue resulting from physical, chemical, or biological treatment of domestic or industrial wastewater.

66. N.J.A.C. 7:14A-10.8.

67. N.J.A.C. 7:14, Subchapter 7.

68. N. J .S.A. 58:10A-6(g).

69. N.J.S.A. 58:10A-10.

70. N.J.A.C. 7:14-8.5.

71. N.J.S.A. 58:10A-10(f).

72. N.J.A.C. 7:14A-2.5(a)(5).

73. N.J.S.A. 23:5-28.

74. The term "waters of the state" is defined, for the purposes of water supply control, to include all surface and groundwater of the State, N.J.S.A. 58:1A-2.

75. N.J.S.A. 58:1A-1 et seq.

76. N.J.S.A. 58:1A-4a.

77. N.J.S.A. 58:1A-4.

78. N.J.S.A. 58:1A-4.

79. N.J.A.C.7:19A, Subchapter 5.

80. For example, in Phases III and IV, NJDEP may order selective curtailment of water use by large industrial users. In Phase IV, NJDEP can even order selective closings of large industrial users. N.J.A.C. 7:19A, Subchapter 6.

81. N.J.S.A. 58:1A-5; N.J.A.C. 7:19, Subchapter 2.

82. N.J.S.A. 58:1A-8.

83. N.J.S.A. 58:1A-6.

84. N.J.A.C. 7:20A-1.1 et seq.

85. N.J.S.A. 58:1A-7.

86. N.J.S.A. 58:1A-7.1.

87. N.J.S.A. 58:1A-7.2.

88. N.J.S.A. 58:1A-16.

89. N.J.S.A. 58:1B-1 et seq.

90. N.J.S.A. 58:5-1 et seq.

91. N.J.S.A. 58:11-59 et seq.

92. N.J.S.A. 58:4-1 et seq.

93. N.J.S.A. 58:1A-1 et seq.

94. 42 U.S.C. §300f et seq.

95. 40 C.F.R. §141.

96. See, N.J.A.C. 7:10, Subchapter 5.

97. N.J.A.C. 7:10, Subchapter 7.

98. N.J.S.A. 58:12A-12, 15.

99. N.J.A.C. 7:10-14, 16.9.

100. N.J.A.C. 7:10-16, 21 N.J. Reg. 46a (January 3, 1989).

101. N.J.A.C. 7:10, Subchapter 16.

102. N.J.A.C. 7:10, Subchapter 11.

103. N.J.A.C. 7:10, Subchapter 12.

104. N.J.S.A. 58:12A-10.

105. N.J.S.A. 58:10A-6.

106. N.J.S.A. 58:11A-7b.

107. N.J.A.C. 7:9, Subchapter 4.

108. N.J.A.C. 7:9-4.14(a).

109. N.J.A.C. 7:9-4.12(a).

110. N.J.A.C. 7:9-4.6; 7:14A-3.13.

111. N.J.A.C. 7:9-4.4.

112. N.J.A.C. 7:9-4.8 to 4.10.

113. N.J.A.C. 7:9-4.8(a), 4.9(a), 4.10(e).

114. N.J.A.C. 7:9, Subchapter 6.

115. N.J.A.C. 7:9-6.5.

116. N.J.A.C. 7:9-6.6.

117. N.J.A.C. 7:9-6.9

118. N.J.A.C. 7:9-6.5(b).

119. N.J.A.C. 7:9-6.9.

120. N.J.A.C. 7:9-6.10.

Chapter 8

Sewage/Wastewater Treatment

Diane Alexander, Esq., and James Cosgrove, P.E.

The Federal Water Pollution Control Act (FWCPA or Clean Water Act), 33 U.S.C.A. 1251 et seq., institutes national policy for the control of water pollution and establishes the national goal to restore and maintain the chemical, physical, and biological integrity of the nation's water.[1] The Clean Water Act prescribes technology-based effluent limitations and effluent limitations for point source discharges, as well as nonpoint source management programs. The Clean Water Act also prohibits the discharge of any pollutant except as permitted by the Clean Water Act[2] and establishes the national policy governing water quality standards and total maximum daily loads (TMDLs) for pollutants. With respect to planning, it is the Clean Water Act that encourages and facilitates the development and implementation of area-wide waste treatment management planning (area-wide waste treatment plan or "§ 208 Plan") and dictates the use of a continuing planning process.

SEWAGE/WASTEWATER PLANNING IN NEW JERSEY

The New Jersey Water Quality Planning Act, N.J.S.A. 58:11A-1 et seq., and the regulations adopted pursuant thereto at N.J.A.C. 7:15-1 et seq. implement the federal scheme and mirror the federal requirements. As such, the New Jersey Water Quality Planning Act prescribes water quality management policies and procedures concerning water quality management planning. As stated in the Federal Clean Water Act, the objective of the State Act is to, wherever attainable, restore and maintain the chemical, physical, and biological integrity of the waters of the State. The Water Quality Planning Act and implementing regulations at N.J.A.C. 7:15 dictate that the Statewide Water Quality Management Plan be prepared by the NJDEP. Area-wide waste treatment management planning processes must be developed and implemented to achieve the objective of the Act and to control the sources of pollutants in the waters of the State. The Water Quality Planning Act dictates that the governor designate areas, to the maximum extent feasible consistent with county boundaries with appropriate modifications to account for major watersheds, for area-wide water treatment planning and designate the county board of chosen freeholders as the designated area-wide planning agency.[3]

The designated area-wide planning agencies, or the NJDEP in areas without a designated agency, must develop the area-wide plans after coordination with other planning agencies. These plans must include the identification of treatment works necessary to meet the anticipated municipal and industrial waste treatment needs of the area over a twenty-year period and must be updated annually. The area-wide plan must include an analysis of alternative waste treatment systems and any requirements for the acquisition of land for treatment purposes; the identification of the necessary wastewater collection and urban stormwater runoff systems; and the determination of a program to provide the necessary financial arrangements for the development of such treatment works. The plan must also include construction priorities and time schedules for the initiation and completion of all treatment works; the establishment of a regulatory program to control or treat all point and nonpoint sources of pollution; regulate facilities in the area which may result in any discharge; and assure that any industrial or commercial wastes discharged into any treatment works meet applicable pretreatment requirement.[4] Requirements for mapping features are defined at N.J.A.C. 7:15-5.17, and specifications for text and graphics are set forth at N.J.A.C. 7:15-5.20. In addition, the regulations provide a procedure for an applicant to request a habitat suitability determination relevant to areas designated as environmentally sensitive[5] and requires the development of TMDLs for water quality limited segments pursuant to N.J.A.C. 7:15-6.3.

Once adopted, the Water Quality Planning Act prohibits the commissioner of the NJDEP from granting any permit which is in conflict with an adopted area-wide plan.[6] In order to determine if a project is consistent with the applicable area-wide plan, procedures for consistency determinations have been established and codified at N.J.A.C. 7:15-3.2. N.J.A.C. 7:15-3.5 sets forth procedures for Plan revisions, and N.J.A.C.7:15-3.4 proscribes the procedures for Plan amendments.[7]

PUBLICALLY OWNED WASTEWATER TREATMENT PLANTS

Enabling legislation for Municipal and County Sewerage Authorities and Municipal and County Utilities Authorities is found at N.J.S.A. 40:14A-1 et seq. ("The Sewerage Authorities Law") and at N.J.S.A. 40:14B-1 et seq. ("The Municipal and County Utilities Authorities Law"), respectively. The Sewerage Authorities Law, N.J.S.A. 40:14A-1 et seq., allows the governing body of a county or municipality to create a sewerage authority[8] for the purpose of, among other things, relieving pollution.[9] The Sewerage Authorities Law defines the powers of the Authority,[10] including the power to acquire, construct, maintain, operate, or improve works for the collection, treatment, purification, or disposal of sewage or other wastes, and "to enter into any and all contracts, execute any and all instruments, and do and perform any and all acts or things necessary, convenient, or desirable for the purposes of the sewerage authority or to carry out any power expressly given in this act subject to the Local Public Contracts Law."[11] It authorizes service charges and collection and enforcement of such charges, including the assessment of connection fees.[12]

The Sewerage Authorities Law regulates boards, members, terms, quorum, compensation, and conflicts of interest.[13] The Municipal and County Utilities Authority Law[14] provides for the creation of a utility[15] for the purposes set forth at N.J.40:14B-19, with the power to acquire, construct, maintain, operate, or improve works for the collection, treatment, recycling, and the disposal of solid, sewage, or other wastes, and includes the generation of hydroelectric power[16] and "to enter into any and all contracts, execute any and all instruments, and do and perform any and all acts or things necessary, convenient or desirable for the purposes of the sewerage authority or to carry out any power expressly given in this act subject to the Local Public Contracts Law."[17] The Municipal and County Utilities Authority Law also authorizes service charges and connection fees and the collection and enforcement of such charges,[18] and authorizes the creation or reorganization of an authority,[19] terms,[20] compensation,[21] and conflicts of interest,[22] and establishes the powers of said boards.[23]

Two other statues exist to address the disposal of sewage by local government entities. Joint Meetings may be formed pursuant to N.J.S.A. 40:48B-2.1 et seq., which allows for the creation of a joint meeting for the collection and the disposal of wastewater. Also, local units may operate either a county or a municipal sewerage facility under the Municipal and County Sewerage Act, N.J.S.A. 40A:26A-1 et seq.

These local government entities are independent public agencies and subject to the Local Authorities Fiscal Control Law,[24] which provides for State review of project financing of local authorities and for State supervision over the financial operations of local authorities; N.J.A.C. 5:31-1.1 governs the preparation, introduction, approval, adoption, and execution after the adoption of any budget by a local authority, the accounting principles and policies for such authorities, the administration of financial affairs of such authorities, the annual audit of the financial statements of such authorities, and the financial reporting practices of such authorities. Funding is available from the New Jersey Wastewater Treatment Trust,[25] which provides financial assistance for the construction of wastewater treatment system projects, sets forth the rules governing the administration of financial assistance programs for a wide variety of water supply, wastewater, stormwater, and nonpoint source management projects as well as the rules regarding State matching grants that were formerly provided to public entities receiving Federal Construction Grants. Also included are the rules that apply to the Environmental Infrastructure Financing Program that is jointly administered by the New Jersey Department of Environmental Protection (NJDEP) and the New Jersey Environmental Infrastructure Trust (Trust), as well as the Pinelands Infrastructure Trust Financing Program rules—a combined grant/loan program.[26] They are also subject to the Local Government Ethics Law,[27] which establishes a statutory code of ethics covering the officers and employees of most local governments and their agencies and instrumentalities. It requires certain officers of such local public entities to file financial disclosure statements, as well as the Local Public Contracts Law,[28] the Open Public Meetings Act,[29] and the Open Public Records Act.[30]

THE REALTY IMPROVEMENT SEWERAGE AND FACILITIES ACT (1954)

The Realty Improvement Sewerage and Facilities Act, N.J.S.A. 58:11-23 et seq. and implementing regulations governing standards for individual subsurface sewage disposal systems at N.J.A.C. 7:9A-1.1 et seq. direct that no building permit for the construction of a realty improvement[31] shall be issued by any municipality or other authority nor shall construction begin until the board of health having jurisdiction shall have certified that the water supply and sewerage facilities for the project are compliant.[32] Procedural requirements for certification are set forth at N.J.S.A. 58:11-26-31. The Act further directs that the NJDEP adopt standards for the construction of water supply systems and for sewerage facilities for realty improvements[33] and authorizes the NJDEP, among other things, to establish a septic density standard as necessary to prevent the degradation of water quality or to require that water quality be restored.[34] The NJDEP is further authorized to designate by regulation areas that are essential to the public health and well-being and to restrict or regulate the types of sewerage facilities that may be constructed in these areas[35] and provides for the installation and use of an alternative waste treatment system and greywater systems subject to local health department regulation and inspection.[36] Subdivision approval for less than fifty realty improvements may be granted at the local level; however, with respect to subdivision approval covering fifty or more realty improvements, NJDEP must approve the proposed facilities.[37] The minimum uniform technical standards for the proper location, design, construction installation, alteration, repair, and operation of individual subsurface sewage disposal systems with an expected volume of sanitary sewage less than or equal to 2,000 gpd are at N.J.A.C. 7:9A.

TREATMENT WORKS APPROVALS

The Treatment Works Approval (TWA) program regulates the construction and operation of industrial and domestic wastewater collection, conveyance, and treatment facilities, including treatment plants, pumping stations, interceptors, sewer mains, and other collection, holding, and conveyance systems.[38] N.J.A.C. 7:14A-22.2 et seq. establishes the rules regarding TWAs, Capacity Assurance Programs, Sewer Bans, and Sewer Ban Exemptions. N.J.A.C. 7:14A-23.1 et seq. contains the technical requirements for TWAs.

TWAs are a type of construction permit. No person shall build, install, modify, or operate any facility (including any sewer extension) for the collection, conveyance, treatment, or discharge of any industrial or domestic wastewater except in conformance with N.J.S.A. 58:10A-6 and N.J.A.C. 7: 14A-22.2. Activities for which a TWA is required are set forth at N.J.A.C. 7:14A-22.3, and those for which a TWA is not required are listed at N.J.A.C. 7:14A-22.4.

There are three stages of TWA. Stage I is an optional preliminary or conceptual review; Stage II is an approval to construct, install, or modify a treatment works; and Stage III is an approval to operate a treatment works that have received Stage II approval. Stage II and III approvals are generally issued concurrently, except in sewer ban areas or where no downstream sewers exist or other circumstances where the operation of the treatment works cannot occur immediately following construction.[39]

An evaluation of the design of the proposed collection, conveyance, or treatment facility is conducted on a local level prior to endorsement and submission to the NJDEP for its review and approval. Upon submission to the NJDEP, the design is reviewed to determine if the project is able to perform the tasks for which it is intended. An assessment is also made relative to the sufficiency of downstream conveyance and treatment capacity. In the case of a treatment facility, a TWA is issued after a discharger has obtained a New Jersey Pollutant Discharge Elimination System (NJPDES) Permit and subsequent to NJDEP's review and determination that, as designed, the facility is able to meet the effluent standards specified in the NJPDES permit. The regulations establish that within twenty business days of receipt of an application, the NJDEP must perform a review of the application to determine if it is administratively complete and notify the applicant, in writing, of the administrative status of the application and any additional information that is necessary to make the application complete.[40] The NJDEP must approve condition or deny an application for a TWA within ninety days of receipt of an administratively complete application. This deadline may be extended for one 30-day period upon mutual consent. If the NJDEP fails to act within ninety days of receipt of an administratively complete application, the application is deemed approved, provided that the application does not violate any other statues or regulations.[41] For Stage II TWAs, written statements of consent are required on the WQM003 form from the affected municipality, sewerage authority, owner of the receiving treatment plant, owner/operator of the wastewater conveyance system and district sludge management lead planning agency if applicable.[42] The statement of consent must be submitted to the NJDEP within 60 days of the request for consent. This period may be extended for an additional thirty days upon request.[43] If the affected municipality or sewerage authority expressly denies the request for consent, it must state its reasons,[44] and the permit application may be deemed incomplete for processing or, in the alternative, the NJDEP may review the reasons for the denial and consider the reasons stated in its determination.[45] If no written statement of consent or denial is issued, upon receipt of proof of written request for a written statement of consent, the NJDEP will review the reasons for the lack of response if known on the basis of reasonably reliable information and consider such reasons in its determination.[46] The procedure for a modification or a revocation of a TWA is set forth at N.J.A.C. 7:14A-22.1. Stage II approvals are valid for an initial period of two years unless otherwise stated and expire unless building, installing, or modifying the treatment works has begun. At the discretion of the NJDEP, the approval may be extended to a maximum period of five years. Extensions, if granted, will be for a maximum of one year each. An applicant must submit a request for an extension prior to expiration and in accord with N.J.A.C. 7:14A-22.12. A TWA may otherwise be extended pursuant to the provisions of the Permit Extension Act, if applicable.[47] The third and most recent amendment to the Permit Extension Act extends certain development approvals until December 31, 2014.

   Civil administrative penalties for conducting unapproved activities are assessed against the violator who approves, endorses, allows construction or operation to commence or proceed, builds, modifies, installs, replaces, expands, or operates a facility or treatment works without proper authorization or in violation of any rule, administrative order, sewer connection ban, or permit issued pursuant to the Water Pollution Control Act[48] and are assessed in accordance with N.J.A.C. 7:14-8.8(b) based upon the seriousness of the violation and the conduct of the violator. Each day or part of a day that the operation of the facility or treatment works continues without the required NJDEP approval is considered an additional, separate, and distinct violation.[49]

CAPACITY ASSURANCE PROGRAM

The Capacity Assurance Program ("CAP") regulations at N.J.A.C. 7:14A-22.16 et seq. require that facilities plan for reaching the limits of their permitted capacity in advance of doing so. When the average flow over twelve consecutive months, as reported in Discharge Monitoring Reports (DMRs), reaches or exceeds 95 percent of the permitted flow of the treatment plant, the regulations require the development of a program and the implementation of measures to reduce the flow to the facility and/or plan for an increase in the capacity of the facility before the facility exceeds its ability to adequately treat the flows received.

When triggered, the Capacity Assurance Program requires that the permittee, in coordination with participating municipalities and sewerage authorities, conducts a capacity analysis that assesses the treatment works; evaluates alternative measures that would maximize conveyance and the treatment of existing flows, reduce, or maintain existing flows below permitted flow, and/or increase the capacity of the treatment works; identifies the alternative(s) that will be implemented; establishes an implementation schedule; and identifies the financing mechanism(s) for the selected alternatives. Thereafter, the permittee must submit a Capacity Analysis Report to the NJDEP within 180 days after the last day of the final month of the 12-consecutive-month period. A completed WQM007 Form must be submitted quarterly beginning the last day of the month following the date the program was triggered. NJDEP may also notify a permittee, or operator of a conveyance system, that they must conduct a capacity analysis and submit a Capacity Analysis Report, including in circumstances where flows are occasionally exceeded during wet weather events.

The Capacity Analysis Report must evaluate the following: an assessment of the treatment works, including dry weather treatment capacity and wet weather treatment capacity at the plant; sources and extent of inflow and infiltration; amount of flow for connections for which TWAs have been issued but which are not yet in operation, and projected flows to accommodate growth within the service area over the next twenty-year period; current operation and maintenance practices that maximize conveyance and treatment; planned improvements to the treatment works; pending applications for NJPDES permits and TWAs related to the capacity of the treatment works; and compliance status, including NJPDES permit violations and known sanitary sewer overflows. An evaluation of alternative measures that would maximize conveyance and treatment of existing flows, reduce existing flows below permitted flow at the treatment plant and ensure adequate conveyance capacity, and/or increase the capacity of the treatment works, as well as an implementation schedule for selected alternatives, a description of the mechanisms to be used to finance the selected alternative(s) and submittal of quarterly progress reports may also be required.

Upon receipt of NJDEP approval of a Capacity Assurance Program, the permittee or owner of the conveyance system must give public notice of the program in the manner set forth in the regulations; in accordance with N.J.A.C. 7:14A-22.16, including a statement that informs local residents, developers, local planning boards, and other affected persons that the treatment plant is approaching its permitted capacity, and the possibility exists that a sewer connection ban will be imposed if the plant is unable to maintain compliance with its discharge limits. If it is anticipated that additional flows will cause violations of any pollutant parameter limits contained in the plant's NJP-DES permit or its federal counterpart, the National Pollutant Discharge Elimination System (NPDES) permit, the permittee must prepare for the imposition of a sewer connection ban in accordance with N.J.A.C. 7:14A-22.18.

If the permittee, any of the participating municipalities, a sewage authority, or the owner or operator of a conveyance system does not comply, NJDEP may cease the further issuance of TWAs for additional flow to the treatment facility.

IMPOSITION OF SEWER BANS

Under the Capacity Assurance Program, a sewer connection ban is not imposed automatically when the flow to a treatment plant reaches 100 percent of its design capacity, but only in the event that the downstream sewerage facilities do not have adequate conveyance capacity as defined in N.J.A.C. 7:14A-1.2, or where it is anticipated that additional flows will result in violations of any pollutant parameter limits contained in the plant's NJPDES or NPDES permit, or where for a three-month period the treatment plant has discharged effluent in violation of the plant's NJPDES permit. In the event that the flow to a sewage treatment plant is at or above 100 percent of the plant's permitted capacity, and the Department determines that issues above have not been appropriately addressed and that additional flows above the plant's permitted capacity may result in violations of their NJPDES permit, the Department may cease the further issuance of TWAs for additional flow to the plant.[50] Consequently, flow alone does not result in the imposition of a ban; however, the inability to meet permit limitations or inadequate conveyance capacity will trigger a sewer connection ban.

SEWER BAN EXEMPTIONS

N.J.A.C. 7:14A-22.19 establishes the general policy and procedure for the review and granting of sewer connection ban exemptions, and N.J.A.C. 7:14A-22.20 lists those activities which do not require an exemption from the Department. The application procedures for obtaining a sewer connection ban exemption from the Department are set forth at N.J.A.C. a7:14A-22.21 and include the requirement that an applicant requesting an exemption must submit the application for an exemption from a sewer connection ban, and any other appropriate documentation, to the appropriate sewerage authority or municipality, who shall review the request for compliance with the applicable criteria. If the affected sewerage authority or municipality determines that the applicant meets the criteria specified in N.J.A.C. 7:14A-22.22, or more stringent criteria that may be locally adopted, the authority will forward the application package and a written letter of consent to the NJDEP for a final decision. If the sewerage authority or municipality denies the sewer ban exemption request, that decision cannot be appealed to the Department.

RESIDUALS MANAGEMENT

Residuals result from the series of physical, chemical, and biological processes that occur at a domestic or industrial wastewater treatment plant. Residual means "a solid waste that consists of the accumulated solids and associated liquids which are by-products of a physical, chemical, biological or mechanical process or any other process designed to treat wastewater or any other discharges subject to regulation under the State Act. . . . [R]esidual includes, but is not limited to, marketable residual product, sludge and sewage sludge. Residual excludes screened vegetative waste and grit and screenings."[51] N.J.A.C. 7:14C and the NJPDES Permit issued to facilities discharging wastewater and generating residuals contain conditions that require monitoring and reporting of the quantity and the quality of residual generated.[52]

The residual is regulated under the NJPDES regulations at N.J.A.C. 7:14A; N.J.A.C. 7:14A-20 establishing standards for the use or disposal of residual; N.J.A.C. 7:14C the Sludge Quality Assurance Regulations; and USEPA 40 CFR Part 503. These rules regulate how residuals can be applied and used,[53] incinerated,[54] or managed at facilities that are designed and permitted to accept and dispose of residuals. Residual is also incinerated and managed in a variety of ways at out-of-state facilities. While residual managed in other states is regulated by the receiving state, the generator must demonstrate compliance with the receiving state's law.

The regulations dictate the analytical procedures and reporting and sampling procedures that must be followed. This is also reflected in the NJPDES permit. General reporting requirements are set forth at N.J.A.C. 7:14C-1.7, and reporting requirements specific to domestic treatment works are found at N.J.A.C. 7:14C-1.8, and for industrial treatment works, N.J.A.C. 7:14C-1.9. Noncompliance is addressed at N.J.A.C. 7:14C.1.11. Failure to submit Sludge Quality Assurance Reports (SQARs) to the NJDEP or willful falsification of information will subject the violator to penalties as contained at N.J.A.C. 7:14-8 pursuant to N.J.A.C. 7:14C-1.11. The facility receiving the residuals is also required to report to the NJDEP the quantity and quality of residuals received. Monitoring Parameter Tables are included in the Appendix to N.J.A.C. 7:14C. The requirements and procedures by which the NJDEP will determine whether further treated effluent can be beneficially reused and whether a determination of environmental benefit (DEB) will be issued by the NJDEP allowing the applicant to claim a corporate tax credit pursuant to N.J.S.A. 54:10A-5.31 and/or of obtaining a sales tax refund pursuant to N.J.S.A. 54:32B-8.36, is set forth at N.J.A.C. 7:14D, DEB of the Reuse of Further Treated Effluent in Industrial Facilities.[55]

STORMWATER MANAGEMENT AND STORMWATER UTILITIES

The standards, criteria, and best management practices relative to stormwater from new development are contained in the Stormwater Management Act N.J.S.A. 40:55D-93 and the Stormwater Management Rules, N.J.A.C. 7:8. The Municipal Stormwater

Regulation Program for existing development as regulated in Municipal Stormwater Permits is addressed in the NJPDES Rules, N.J.A.C. 7:14A-25. Stormwater is also addressed in more than a dozen laws and regulations; however, none of these statutes or regulations provided for the creation of a stormwater utility or established a dedicated funding source for stormwater, until now. On March 18, 2019, NJ's ability to improve water quality, and more quickly recover from weather-related disasters, took a giant leap forward when the governor signed the Clean Stormwater and Flood Reduction Act—A2694/S1073.

The Clean Stormwater and Flood Reduction Act, authorizes, but does not require, the establishment of stormwater utilities and provides for a dedicated funding source to be used only in furtherance of stormwater management.

The Existing Plan

Pursuant to the Clean Water Act and N.J.A.C. 7:14A-25, municipalities must develop Stormwater Management Plans and must manage stormwater emanating from within the municipality pursuant to a Municipal Stormwater Permit (i.e., MS4 Permit) issued and enforced by the NJDEP. Many municipalities have struggled with staffing and funding necessary to address and be proactive with respect to stormwater management in the face of the myriad of other issues facing the municipality. The Clean Stormwater and Flood Reduction Act was designed to provide relief to those struggling with their stormwater responsibilities through the ability to delegate critical tasks and through the creation of a dedicated funding source, which expectantly will allow for efficient, effective, and proactive stormwater planning and management.

Formation of a Utility

The Clean Stormwater and Flood Reduction Act and Flood Defense Act amends existing statutes to allow municipalities, counties, sewerage authorities, municipal and county utility authorities, and county improvement authorities to, by resolution or ordinance, establish a Stormwater Utility. (The Act amends the following statutes: Sewerage Authorities Law, Municipal and County Utilities Authorities Law, County Improvement Authorities Law, Municipal and County Sewerage Act, and the Municipal and County Flood Control Financing Act.) The limited purpose of the Stormwater Utility would be to control stormwater runoff and pollution in the county/counties or municipality/municipalities creating it.

Stormwater includes precipitation, including rain and snow, and includes precipitation conveyed by snow removal equipment. Under the Clean Stormwater and Flood Reduction Act, the governing body of any county or municipality (or governing bodies of any two or more counties or municipalities) may by resolution or ordinance establish a stormwater utility, or request that a sewerage authority establish a stormwater utility, for the purposes of acquiring, constructing, improving, maintaining, and operating stormwater management systems in the county or municipality, consistent with State and federal laws, rules, and regulations.

Powers Conferred

The county, municipality, sewerage authority, municipal and county utility authority, and county improvement authority establishing a Stormwater Utility would be empowered to charge and collect reasonable fees and other charges to recover the stormwater utility's costs for stormwater management. These fees and other charges may be charged to and collected from the owner or occupant, or both, of any real property from which originates stormwater runoff which directly or indirectly enters the stormwater management system or the waters of the State. Any fee or other charges that a county, municipality, or authority charges and collects must be based on a fair and equitable approximation of the proportionate contribution of stormwater runoff from a real property. Credits and exemptions are also provided for with respect to properties that maintain their own stormwater systems, that employ green infrastructure, and that are actively devoted to agricultural or horticultural use. No particular methodology is mandated in the law; however, guidance regarding the means and methods for calculating fees will be provided in a forthcoming Guidance Manual.

A Stormwater Utility may acquire by gift, grant, purchase, or condemnation, or in any other lawful manner, any privately owned stormwater management system, or any real property necessary for the construction, improvement, operation, or maintenance of a stormwater management system and may contract with others for the construction, improvement, maintenance, and operation of the Stormwater Management System. It may also bond for the purpose of paying all or any part of the cost of the Stormwater Management System, and may enact and enforce resolutions, ordinances, and regulations governing the planning, management, implementation, construction, maintenance, and operation of the Stormwater Management System, provided that they are consistent with federal and state law and regulation. Stormwater Utilities may utilize competitive contracting to enter into contracts for the construction, improvement, operation, or maintenance of stormwater management systems.

Stormwater Utility Account

The money collected pursuant to this law must only be used to pay for or recover all or a portion of the cost of enumerated purposes: establishment of a stormwater utility and related administrative expenses; capital expenditures, including acquisition, construction, and improvement of a stormwater management system; operation and maintenance of a stormwater management system; development and implementation of asset management programs for stormwater management systems; development and implementation of a stormwater management plan and stormwater control ordinances; actions required by any NJPDES Permit; any long-term control plan to mitigate combined sewer overflows pursuant to State or federal law, rule, regulation, permit, or consent decree; monitoring, inspection, and enforcement activities; public education and outreach related to stormwater management; and any other purpose related to stormwater management as may be authorized by the department, the Division of Local Government Services in the Department of Community Affairs, or the Local Finance Board pursuant to rules, regulations, or permits.

Annually, 5 percent of all fees collected, up to $50,000, must be remitted to the State Treasury to be deposited into a newly created "Clean Stormwater and Flood Reduction Fund."

Guidance

NJDEP, in consultation with the Board of Public Utilities and Division of Local Government Services, and with the input of stakeholders, must develop and periodically update a Stormwater Utility Guidance Manual. The Guidance Manual must include Stormwater Utility reporting requirements, technical assistance for the establishment of a stormwater utility, means and methods for calculating and revising fair and uniform stormwater utility fees and appropriate credits and exemptions, information on developing an asset management program and incorporation of green infrastructure, as well as public education and outreach guidance.

NOTES

1. FWPCA §101(a).
2. FWPCA § 301(a).
3. N.J.S.A. 58:11A-4.
4. Additional area-wide plan requirements are set forth in N.J.S.A. 58:11A-5. N.J.A.C. 7:15-5.15 et seq. sets forth the contents required.
5. N.J.A.C. 7:15-5.26.
6. N.J.S.A. 58:11A-10 and N.J.A.C. 7:15-3.1.
7. Guidance and application forms for Amendments and Revisions to a WQM Plan can be found at: http://www.nj.gov/dep/wqmp/applications.html. Guidance and application forms for Consistency Determinations can be found at: http://www.nj.gov/dep/wqmp/docs/cd_appli cation_form20051019.pdf.
    and http://www.nj.gov/dep/wqmp/docs/cd_fact_sheet.pdf.
8. N.J.S.A. 40:14A-4.
9. N.J.S.A. 40:14A-6(a).
10. N.J.S.A. 40:14A-7.
11. N.J.S.A. 40:14A-7(13).
12. N.J.S.A. 40:14A-8 and *White Birch Realty Corp. v. Gloucester Twp. Mun. Utils. Auth.*, 80 N.J. 165, 176-77 (1979) ("There may be any number of ways in which a computation of a fair share can be fixed, and a utilities authority is free to adopt any one which will accomplish the result of fairly apportioning system costs among the users."). See also *Spectraserv, Inc. v. Kearny Mun. Utilities Auth.*, 2008 WL 4790978 (App. Div. November 5, 2008) (A court will not overturn a rate structure simply because there may be a preferable alternative, so long as the operative structure is not arbitrary, capricious, or unreasonable); *Nestle USA-Beverage Division, Inc. v. Manasquan River Regional Sewerage Authority*, 330 N.J. Super. 510 (App. Div. 2000) (Sewerage authority has the authority to assess fees against its direct and indirect users pursuant to N.J.S.A. 40:14A-8; however, absent new or additional physical connections to any sewer system, the authority may not charge an additional connection fee based solely on increased water usage); *Bi-County Development of Clinton, Inc. v. Borough of High Bridge*, 174 N.J. 301, 805 A.2d 433 (2002) (holding that developer of residential and commercial units in township cannot force adjoining municipality to allow developer to connect to adjoining municipality's sewer system); *Airwick Industries v. Carlstadt Sewerage Auth.*, 57 N.J. 107

(1970); *In re Passaic County Utils. Auth.*, 164 N.J. 270, 293 (2000); *Meglino v. Twp. Comm. of Eagleswood*, 103 N.J. 144 (1986).

13. N.J.S.A. 40:14A-5.

14. N.J.S.A. 40:14B-1 et seq.

15. N.J.S.A. 40:14B-4.

16. N.J.S.A. 40:14B-20.

17. N.J.S.A. 40: 14 B-20(14).

18. N.J.S.A. 40:14B-22.

19. N.J.S.A. 40:14B-4.

20. N.J.S.A. 40:14B-4.

21. N.J.S.A. 40:14B-17.

22. N.J.S.A. 40:14A-15.

23. N.J.S.A. 40:14B-20.

24. N.J.S.A. 40A:5A-1 et seq.

25. N.J.S.A. 58:11B-1 et seq. and N.J.A.C. 7:22-10.1 et seq.

26. See also N.J.A.C. 7:22A for Sewage Infrastructure Improvement Act Grants relevant to the application for and award of planning and design grants to abate combined sewer overflows and to eliminate interconnections/cross-connections of sanitary and stormwater sewers and for rules for distribution of grants to implement requirements of the Sewage Infrastructure Improvement Act.

27. N.J.S.A. 40A:9-22.1 et seq.

28. N.J.S.A. 40A:11-1 et seq.

29. N.J.S.A. 10:4-6 et seq.

30. N.J.S.A. 47:1A-1 et seq.

31. As defined at N.J.S.A. 58:11-24(e).

32. N.J.S.A. 58:11-25.

33. N.J.S.A. 58:11-36.

34. N.J.S.A. 58:11-24.1.

35. N.J.S.A. 58:11-44.

36. N.J.S.A. 58:11-25b.

37. N.J.S.A. 58:11-25.1.

38. For TWA Permitting Information and forms, see: http://www.nj.gov/dep/dwq/forms_twa.htm.

39. N.J.A.C. 7:14A-22.5.

40. N.J.A.C. 7:14A-22.5(e).

41. N.J.A.C. 7:14A-22.5(e) 3.

42. N.J.A.C. 7:14A-22.8(a)3.

43. N.J.A.C. 7:14A-22.8(a)3v(1).

44. N.J.A.C. 7:14A-22.8(a)3v(3).

45. N.J.A.C. 7:14A-22.8(a)3v(4).

46. N.J.A.C. 7:14A-22.8(a)3v(5).

47. N.J.S.A. 40:55D-136.1 *et seq.*

48. N.J.A.C. 7:14-8.8 (a).

49. N.J.A.C. 7:14-8.8(b)(3).

50. N.J.A.C. 7:14A-22.16(e).

51. N.J.A.C. 7:14A-1.4. Examples include pellets, compost, alkaline materials, food processing by-products, and water treatment residuals.

52. N.J.A.C. 7:14C-1.1.

53. Beneficial use of residual as a fertilizer or soil conditioner is regulated under a NJP-DES permit issued by the Bureau of Pretreatment and Residuals and may require site specific approvals, depending upon the nature of the residual.

54. Incineration of residual is regulated under New Jersey's Air Pollution Control Program.

55. See New Jersey Division of Water Quality, http://www.nj.gov/dep/dwq/ and N.J.A.C. 7:14C - Sludge Quality Assurance Regulations, prescribing the method and frequency for reporting on the quantity, quality and management of residual generated by treatment works.

Chapter 9

Solid Waste Management

Melissa A. Clarke, Esq.

The Solid Waste Management Act (SWMA), N.J.S.A. 13:1E-1 et seq., was enacted to provide a comprehensive regulatory scheme for uniform regulation of solid waste in New Jersey. In enacting the SWMA, the State has substantially preempted the field of solid waste management.[1] The statute vests expansive regulatory and planning authority in the New Jersey Department of Environmental Protection (NJDEP or Department), including the ability to adopt administrative rules related to solid waste collection and disposal and to enforce those regulations.[2]

Solid waste is defined to include garbage, refuse, sludge, or any other waste material.[3] "Any other waste material" includes, but is not limited to, spent material, sludge by-product, discarded commercial chemical products, or scrap metal resulting from industrial, commercial, mining or agricultural operations, from community activities, or any other material which has served or can no longer serve its original intended use.[4] Source-separated food waste collected by livestock producers, recyclable materials, spent sulfuric acid, and dredged materials are specifically exempted from the definition of solid waste.[5]

A solid waste facility is "any system, site, equipment or building which is utilized for the storage, collection, processing, transfer, transportation, separation, recycling, recovering or disposal of solid waste."[6] It does not include a recycling center, a regulated medical waste collection facility authorized pursuant to N.J.A.C. 7:26-3A.39, or an intermodal container facility authorized pursuant to N.J.A.C. 7:26-3.6.

A number of regulatory requirements apply to solid waste activities and facilities. Apart from certain identified exceptions, parties seeking to engage in the collection, transport, or disposal of solid waste in New Jersey must be identified in the District Solid Waste Management Plan, file registration and disclosure statements, and obtain a Certificate of Public Convenience and Necessity.[7]

SOLID WASTE MANAGEMENT PLANS

District Plans

Each county and the Hackensack Meadowlands serve as a solid waste management district (district) and is required to develop a District Solid Waste Management Plan (District Plan), subject to NJDEP approval, for solid wastes generated within their respective borders.[8] Each district must also have an advisory solid waste council. For counties, this council is comprised of municipal mayors or their designees, persons engaged in the collection or disposal of solid waste, and environmentalists; for the Hackensack Meadowlands District, the Hackensack Meadowlands Municipal Committee serves as the advisory solid waste council.[9] The District Plan is to be accompanied by a report containing the following:

(1) An inventory of the sources, composition, and quantity of solid waste generated in the solid waste management district in the year in which the report is prepared;
(2) Projections of the amounts and composition of solid waste generated in the district in each of the ten years following the first report;
(3) An inventory and appraisal of all solid waste facilities within the district and the identity of every person engaging in solid waste collection or disposal within the district;
(4) An analysis of solid waste collection and transportation systems within the solid waste management district;

The District Plan shall include the following:

(1) Designation of a department or committee to supervise the implementation of the District Plan and report thereon as necessary;
(2) A statement of solid waste disposal strategy encompassing the maximum practicable use of resource recovery procedures and a plan for using terminated landfill disposal sites, if any, in the district;
(3) A site plan including existing solid waste facilities and additional available sites;
(4) A survey of proposed collection districts and transportation routes and costs;
(5) Procedures for coordinating collection and disposal, including agreements; and
(6) Methods of financing solid waste management.[10]

Upon the development and formulation of a District Plan, and after consultation with the relevant advisory solid waste council, the district must also prepare a map detailing its boundaries and the location of all existing and proposed solid waste facilities therein.[11]

Section 23 of the SWMA sets forth the procedure for adoption of the District Plan, including a public hearing, proper notice, adoption by resolution, and submission to NJDEP for study and review. The NJDEP Commissioner submits copies of the District Plan to the State Advisory Council on Solid Waste Management and any other NJDEP bureaus concerned with solid waste management.[12] A copy of the District Plan also goes to the Board of Public Utility Commissioners for review and recommendations on the economic aspect of the plan.[13] After consideration of any recommendations, the NJDEP Commissioner then approves, modifies, or rejects the District Plan and certifies its determination to the applicable board of chosen freeholders or Hackensack Commission.[14] If the Commissioner decides to modify or reject the District Plan, or any part thereof, the certification must be accompanied by a detailed statement indicating the reasons for the modification or rejection, outlining the action to be taken thereon, including whether to schedule additional public hearings.[15] If the Commissioner directs the holding of another public hearing, the hearing must be held within forty-five days.[16] If a public hearing is not required, the board of freeholders or Hackensack Commission must adopt the NJDEP's modifications within forty-five days.[17]

Matters not identified in a particular District Plan, such as proposals for new or modified solid waste facilities, require an amendment to the District Plan, which must comply with N.J.A.C. 7:26-6:10, as NJDEP is not statutorily authorized to issue a solid waste facility permit for a facility not included in the adopted and approved District Plan.

Statewide Plan

The role of NJDEP in the establishment of a statewide solid waste management plan (Statewide Plan) is set forth in N.J.S.A. 13:1E-2(b)(6). The SMWA requires NJDEP to develop, review, and update a Statewide Plan at least every two years to encourage the use of resource recovery procedures and establish the objectives, criteria, and standards for the evaluation of District Plans and assist in the development and formulation of these plans.[18] NJDEP has the authority to monitor the District Plans and to fill any gap caused by a district's inaction or noncompliance with the statewide scheme.[19]

SOLID WASTE FACILITY REGISTRATION

The SWMA directs NJDEP to "require the registration of all solid waste collection activities, solid waste facilities and solid waste disposal operations in this State."[20] As a result, anyone engaging in the collection or disposal of solid waste must first file an application for a registration statement or engineering design approval and then obtain approval from NJDEP.[21] A registration statement will not be approved by NJDEP unless the Department finds that the registrant exhibits sufficient reliability, expertise, and competency to operate a solid waste facility. Moreover, registration will not be approved if a person required to be listed in the disclosure statement (discussed below), or having a beneficial interest in the business, has been convicted of certain crimes under the laws of New Jersey or any other jurisdiction.[22]

The application procedures for a solid waste facility (SWF) permit are set forth at N.J.A.C. 7:26-2.4. Prior to preparing and submitting the application, the applicant may schedule a pre-application conference with the NJDEP to discuss requirements and review procedures.[23] Per N.J.A.C 7:26-2.4, a complete application for a SWF permit includes the following:

(1) All fees required by N.J.A.C. 7:26-4;
(2) Documentation establishing that the facility has been included in the applicable District Plan;
(3) The disclosure statement described in N.J.A.C. 7:26-16 (unless specifically exempted under N.J.A.C. 7:26-16.3(d));
(4) A registration statement meeting the requirements of N.J.A.C. 7:26-2.8;
(5) An Environmental and Health Impact Statement (EHIS) prepared in accordance with N.J.A.C. 7:26-2.9;
(6) An engineering design prepared in accordance with N.J.A.C. 7:26-2.10; and
(7) For sanitary landfills, a closure plan prepared and submitted in accordance with N.J.A.C. 7:26-2A.9.

Upon full compliance with the submission requirements, NJDEP may begin processing the application. After review and a determination that the application is complete, NJDEP provides notice of the application[24] and schedules a public hearing[25] at which the applicant is required to appear and answer all relevant questions concerning the project.[26] NJDEP may not, however, grant a SWF permit for a facility which is not included in the adopted and approved District Plan since a facility cannot be said to "conform to" (N.J.S.A. 13:1E-4b) or be "consistent with" (N.J.S.A. 13:1E-26) the District Plan if it is not provided for in the plan.[27] Moreover, NJDEP may deny a solid waste license for any crimes enumerated in N.J.S.A. 13:1E-133b, if the applicant has shown insufficient "integrity, reliability, expertise" or competence in collecting and transporting solid waste, or for a violation of any solid waste law.[28]

Additions or alterations to the facility, new data, and evolving NJDEP standards and/or case law may require modification of a registration statement, and failure to do so could result in revocation or termination of the registration.[29] Solid waste collection, transportation, and disposal facilities must also update the information contained in the registration statement annually and notify NJDEP in writing within thirty days of any changes; failure to update or pay the associated fees can result in revocation of the registration statement or a declaration of expiration.[30]

A SWF must also obtain all other relevant permits, including air permits or NJPDES groundwater discharge permits, as applicable.

DISCLOSURE STATEMENT

As a result of organized crime's history of involvement in the waste collection and disposal industry of this State, a disclosure statement is required for virtually all parties engaged in hazardous and solid waste activities.[31] All nonexempt[32] solid and hazardous waste facilities must file a disclosure statement which includes information on officers and "key" employees, their competency, reliability, and integrity, and requires that applicants list any notices of violation or prosecution, administrative orders or license revocations, whether pending or adjudicated and determined.[33] The State

Attorney General or NJDEP may also require other information relating to "the competency, reliability, honesty, integrity, or good character of the applicant, permittee or licensee."[34] Any person required to be listed in the disclosure statement, other than non-supervisory personnel, must be fingerprinted.[35] There is a continuing duty on the part of applicants to regularly update disclosure statements with any pertinent changes.[36]

CERTIFICATE OF PUBLIC CONVENIENCE AND NECESSITY

Solid waste collection or disposal also requires a Certificate of Public Convenience and Necessity from NJDEP.[37] NJDEP must first determine that the business or individual is qualified by experience, training, or education to engage in such business has provided sufficient evidence of financial responsibility, and has registered with and been approved by the Department. NJDEP may suspend or revoke a Certificate of Public Convenience and Necessity for violations of the Solid Waste Utility Control Act (Utility Act)[38] or any related rule, regulation, or administrative order, any pollution-related laws, or as a result of NJDEP's registration revocation.

COLLECTOR AND TRANSPORTER REQUIREMENTS

Solid waste regulations require that service route lengths be "consistent with the proper operation of solid waste vehicles and/or equipment in order that the area or route services can be completed during a normal operating day."[39] Barring an emergency, such as inclement weather or an equipment breakdown, storing waste in a vehicle for more than twenty-four hours is prohibited, and solid waste vehicles must not be improperly used or operated so as to cause solid waste materials to leak.[40] A vehicle transporting solid waste must display a solid waste decal and its NJDEP registration number, carry a registration certificate in its cab, and may utilize only those routes designated in the relevant District Plan.[41] Additional requirements apply to the collection and transportation of sewage sludge, fecal matter, radioactive materials, and asbestos-containing waste.[42]

GENERAL OPERATIONAL REQUIREMENTS

N.J.A.C. 7:26-2.11 identifies the general operational requirements for all solid waste facilities, including, but not limited to, cleaning, storage, maintenance, and control of dust, emissions, insects and pests.[43] Additional operational requirements for sanitary landfills are set forth at N.J.A.C. 7:26-2A.8; for thermal destruction facilities at N.J.A.C. 7:26-2B.8; and for transfer stations and materials recovery facilities at N.J.A.C. 7:26-2B.9.

A SWF permittee must maintain a daily record of wastes received.[44] The record must include identification of the SWF by name and facility identification number; identification of the transporter by NJDEP registration number and solid waste decal number; cubic yard, tonnage, or gallon capacity of the solid waste vehicle or solid waste container for solids, septage, and liquid sewage sludge, and bulk liquid and semiliquids; date and time of delivery to the facility; license plate number and State initials of the solid waste vehicle; and place of origin of the waste identified by municipality, county, and state, except where the waste is transported from a transfer station or materials recovery facility to a final disposal facility.[45] Sanitary landfills that accept asbestos and asbestos-containing waste materials must maintain a separate daily record of the asbestos and asbestos-containing waste received.[46]

Subchapter 2A of the Solid Waste regulations provides additional disposal regulations for sanitary landfills, including rules governing the design, construction, operation, maintenance, closure, and post-closure care of sanitary landfills. These requirements, which are in addition to the general engineering design submission requirements in N.J.A.C. 7:26-2.10 and the general operational requirements in N.J.A.C. 7:26-2.11, apply to all newly proposed sanitary landfills and all existing sanitary landfills proposing to expand their existing operations onto previously unfilled permitted areas and any existing sanitary landfills operating as an open dump or in an environmentally unsound manner which NJDEP determines needs to be environmentally upgraded.[47]

LANDFILL CLOSURE AND POST-CLOSURE

The Legislature established the Sanitary Landfill Facility Closure and Contingency Fund (Closure Fund) when it enacted the Sanitary Landfill Facility Closure and Contingency Fund Act, N.J.S.A. 13:1E-100 et seq. (Closure Act) in 1981. The Closure Act provides: "Every owner or operator of a sanitary landfill facility shall be jointly and severally liable for the proper operation and closure of the facility, as required by law, and for any damages, no matter by whom sustained, proximately resulting from the operations or closure."[48]

The Closure Act imposes a tax on owners and operators of sanitary landfills, and these tax revenues are placed in the Closure Fund.[49] The purpose of the Closure Fund is to provide compensation for damages resulting from the improper operation or closure of sanitary landfill facilities.[50] The Closure Fund is "strictly liable for all direct and indirect damages, no matter by whom sustained, proximately resulting from the operations or closure of any sanitary landfill."[51] Claims against the Closure Fund must be filed within one year of the date of discovery of damage and in the manner prescribed in the Landfill Claims Rules, N.J.A.C. 7:1I-1.1 et seq., which implement the purposes and objectives of the Closure Act, establish rules for administration of the Closure Fund, and protect and ensure that the taxes credited to the Fund are spent in a proper manner and for the intended purposes.

Because "the proper closure of sanitary landfills is essential to the public health, safety and welfare,"[52] all landfill facilities must have a Closure and Post-Closure plan ("Closure Plan")[53] and maintain an escrow account.[54] Among other requirements, the Closure Plan must provide for the design and implementation of the following:

1) A Soil Erosion and Sediment Control Plan certified by the local soil conservation district in accordance with the Soil Erosion and Sediment Control Act of 1975, N.J.S.A. 4:24-39 et seq.;

2) Final cover, final cover vegetation, and a program for the maintenance thereof;
3) A program for the maintenance of side slopes;
4) Institution of run-off control programs and a program for maintenance thereof;
5) Groundwater monitoring wells and a program for monitoring well maintenance;
6) A methane gas venting or evacuation system and a program for its maintenance;
7) A leachate collection and/or control system and a program for the operation and maintenance of such system;
8) A program for the installation of a facility access control system and maintenance thereof; and
9) Measures to conform the site to the surrounding area and a program for the maintenance of those measures.[55]

NJDEP may require additional closure and post-closure care measures or waive any of the above requirements, should specific health and/or environmental circumstances justify such action. Every owner and operator must notify NJDEP at least 180 days prior to the termination of operations at a facility.[56] The post-closure care period continues for thirty years unless it has been adequately demonstrated that a reduced period is sufficient to protect human health or the environment.[57]

The Closure Act prohibits the sale of land used as a sanitary landfill facility unless the contract of sale describes the use and period of use.[58] There is also a deed notice requirement. Upon closure of the sanitary landfill, a detailed description of the landfill, including types, locations, and depths of wastes on the site, depth and type of cover material, dates of landfill operation, and other information must be recorded with the deed at the county recording office.[59]

WASTE CONTROL ACT

The Waste Control Act, N.J.S.A. 13:1I-1 et seq., authorizes the NJDEP Commissioner to promulgate rules and regulations to control "the incineration or landfill of solid waste and the treatment or disposal of liquid wastes within the State which originated or were collected outside the territorial limits of the State."[60] The U.S. Supreme Court has held, however, that an absolute prohibition on the importation of out-of-state solid waste violates the Commerce Clause of the U.S. Constitution.[61] NJDEP has authority to institute an action for injunctive relief to prevent any violation of the Waste Control Act, and the court may proceed in a summary manner.[62]

THE COMPREHENSIVE REGULATED
MEDICAL WASTE MANAGEMENT ACT

During the summers of 1987 and 1988, medical waste refuse, including syringes and blood vials, washed ashore in New Jersey, devastating the economies of beach communities.[63] As a result, the Comprehensive Regulated Medical Waste Management Act (Medical Waste Act), N.J.S.A. 13:1E-48.1 et seq., was enacted to address the threat medical waste poses to public health and the environment.

The Medical Waste Act authorizes a system of manifesting, tracking, identification, packaging, storage, control, monitoring, handling, collection, and disposal of regulated medical waste, as set forth in the regulations for Regulated Medical Waste, N.J.A.C 7:26-3A.1 et seq.[64] Every shipment of regulated medical waste released by any generator to a transporter for delivery to a facility for disposal must be accompanied by a manifest as prescribed by the NJDEP and as required by federal law.[65] Any person that generates regulated medical waste in New Jersey must register with NJDEP and pay annual fees, in accordance with N.J.A.C. 7:26-3A.8.

THE TOXIC PACKAGING REDUCTION ACT

The Toxic Packaging Reduction Act[66] prohibits the sale of any package or packaging component which includes inks, dyes, pigments, adhesives, stabilizers, or any other additives containing lead, cadmium, mercury, or hexavalent chromium which has been intentionally introduced as a chemical element during manufacturing or distribution.[67] The Toxic Packaging Reduction Act's primary requirement is a written certification of compliance stating that a package or packaging component is in compliance with the law's requirements.[68]

RECYCLING

Statewide Recycling Programs and Funds

The Clean Communities Program Act, N.J.S.A. 13:1E-213 et seq., imposes a user fee upon the sales of persons engaged in business in New Jersey as a manufacturer, wholesaler, or distributor of "litter-generating products."[69] Those user fees are deposited in the Clean Communities Program Fund to be appropriated for litter pickup and enforcement of litter-related laws and ordinances.[70] In addition, 25 percent of the estimated annual balance of the Clean Communities Program Fund is appropriated to the State Recycling Fund, N.J.S.A. 13:1E-96, to be used by the NJDEP for direct recycling grants to counties and municipalities.[71] The State Recycling Fund is administered by NJDEP and credited with all revenue collected pursuant to a tax on solid waste accepted for disposal or transfer at solid waste facilities.[72]

The Mandatory Statewide Source Separation and Recycling Act (Recycling Act), N.J.S.A. 13:1E-99.11 et seq., mandates source separation of goods that can be recycled and "returned to the economic mainstream in the form of raw materials or products."[73] Under the Recycling Act, counties are responsible for the development of a District Recycling Plan which includes, among other things, the designation of a district recycling coordinator and a strategy for collection, marketing, and disposition of recycled materials.[74] The Recycling Act further requires State and local agencies to give preference to the use of recycled materials whenever possible, including, for example, using recycled and composited materials on all land maintenance activities which are to be paid for with public funds.[75]

Recycling Facilities

A "recycling center" is any facility designed and operated solely for receiving, storing, processing, or transferring source-separated recyclable materials but does not include a scrap processing facility.[76] Recycling centers are not required to obtain a registration statement, engineering design approval, or approval of an EHIS, but they cannot "receive, store, process or transfer any waste material other than source-separated non-putrescible or source-separated commingled non-putrescible metal, glass, paper, or plastic containers, and corrugated and other cardboard without the prior approval of the [D]epartment."[77]

The rules governing the operation of recycling centers and the conduct of recyclable materials generators and transporters are set forth at N.J.A.C. 7:26A-1.1 et seq. (Recycling Rules).[78] There are four classes of recyclable materials (Class A, Class B, Class C, and Class D).[79] The Recycling Rules generally require type B, C, or D recycling centers to obtain NJDEP's written approval prior to operation.[80] The applicant must publish a notice in a newspaper of general circulation within the municipality in which the recycling center will be operating, and file for inclusion in the applicable District Plan, prior to filing an application with the NJDEP for recycling center general approval.[81] The notice must be published two times, with the second publication no less than fifteen days prior to the public hearing, with a copy to NJDEP's Division of Solid and Hazardous Waste and to the municipality.[82] The application submitted by the owner or the operator of a Class B, C, or D recycling center must include all of the particulars set forth in N.J.A.C. 7:26A-3.2. If NJDEP determines that the performance standards pertaining to the receipt, storage, processing, and/or transfer of recyclable materials are not being followed, it may declare the recycling facility a SWF and require it to submit a registration statement, engineering design, and EHIS.

NOTES

1. See, for example, *So. Ocean Landfill v. Mayor & Council Twp. of Ocean*, 64 N.J. 190 (1974); *Rollins Envtl. Servs. of N.J., Inc. v. Logan Twp.*, 209 N.J. Super. 556 (App. Div. 1986). But see *Clyde v. Mansfield Twp.*, 263 N.J. Super. 140 (App. Div. 1993) (clarifying that SWMA does not preempt municipal ordinances restricting traffic routes that can be used by solid waste haulers).
2. See N.J.S.A. 13:1E-6 and -9.
3. N.J.A.C. 7:26-1.6.
4. *Ibid.*
5. Source-separated or commingled source-separated recyclable, recycled, or secondary nonhazardous materials for reintroduction into the economic mainstream as materials for further processing or as products for use are also specifically excluded from the rules governing solid waste. N.J.A.C. 7:26-1.1(a)1.
6. N.J.A.C. 7:26-1.4.
7. See N.J.S.A. 48:13A-6.
8. N.J.S.A. 13:1E-20.
9. N.J.S.A. 13:1E-20(b)(I).
10. N.J.S.A. 13:1E-21.
11. N.J.S.A. 13:1E-23(b).

12. N.J.S.A. 13:1E-24(a)(2).

13. N.J.S.A. 13:1E-24(a)(3).

14. N.J.S.A. 13:1E-24(b).

15. N.J.S.A. 13:1E-24(d)-(e).

16. N.J.S.A. 13:1E-24(e)(1).

17. N.J.S.A. 13:1E-24(e)(2).

18. N.J.S.A. 13: 1E-6(a)(3). See also *A. A. Mastrangelo, Inc. v. Comm'r of Dep't of Envtl. Prot.*, 90 N.J. 666 (1982)(finding NJDEP documents composed of guidelines for development and formulation of district plans, management manuals which discussed aspect of district planning, policy, and procedure for the review of district plans, and regulation concerning interdistrict solid waste flows sufficiently comprised "statewide plan" for solid waste management to satisfy statutory mandate).

19. See *Application of Combustion Equip. Associates, Inc.*, 169 N.J. Super. 305, 310 (App. Div. 1979).

20. N.J.S.A. 13:1E-4.

21. N.J.S.A. 13:1E-5.

22. These offenses include, for example, murder, kidnapping, theft, arson, burglary, gambling, deceit, forgery, fraud, racketeering, antitrust violations, and criminal usury. N.J.A.C. 7:26-16.8. Also included are violations of the Solid Waste Utility Control Act and a pattern of violations of the environmental protection statutes or regulations. N.J.A.C. 7:26-3.2.

23. N.J.A.C. 7:26-2.4(a).

24. N.J.A.C. 7:26-2.4(g)(6) and (7).

25. N.J.A.C. 7:26-2.4(g)(13).

26. N.J.A.C. 7:26-2.5.

27. See *Regional Recycling, Inc. v. State, Dep't of Envtl. Prot.*, 256 N.J. Super. 94, 102 (App. Div. 1991) *aff'd sub nom.* 127 N.J. 568 (1992).

28. See N.J.S.A. 13:1E-133a; N.J.S.A. 13:1E-134.

29. N.J.A.C. 7:26-2.6. Minor modifications can be made without public notice or hearing. N.J.A.C. 7:26-2.6(d).

30. N.J.A.C. 7:26-2.8(d); N.J.A.C. 7:26-3.2(e) and (f).

31. See, for example, *New Jersey Dep't of Envtl. Prot. v. Circle Carting, Inc.*, A-3907-03T1, 2005 WL 3465561 (N.J. Super. Ct. App. Div. December 20, 2005) (*citing Trade Waste Mgmt. Ass'n, Inc. v. Hughey*, 780 F.2d 221, 223 (3d Cir. 1985)).

32. There is an exception for facilities operated by government agencies and, under certain circumstances, persons handling their own solid waste.

33. N.J.S.A. 13:1E-127e(1)-(9); N.J.A.C. 7:26-16.4.

34. N.J.A.C. 7:26-16.4(a)(11).

35. N.J.A.C. 7:26-16.3(c).

36. N.J.S.A. 13:1E-128b.

37. N.J.S.A. 48:13A-6.

38. n.j.s.a. 48:13A-1 et seq. NJDEP, through the SWMA, and the Board of Public Utilities (BPU), through the Utility Act, exercise concurrent jurisdiction over solid waste collection and disposal. See N.J.S.A. 48:13A–6a; *State v. Moscato*, 253 N.J. Super. 253, 258-59 (App. Div. 1992).

39. N.J.A.C. 7:26-3.4.

40. Ibid.

41. N.J.A.C. 7:26-3.4(h).

42. See N.J.A.C. 7:26-3.5.

43. N.J.A.C. 7:26-2.11(b).

44. N.J.A.C. 7:26-2.13.

45. N.J.A.C. 7:26-2.13(a).

46. N.J.A.C. 7:26-2.13(a)(7).

47. Subchapter 2A does not apply to hazardous waste landfills. For hazardous waste regulation, see N.J.A.C. 7:26G.

48. N.J.S.A. 13:1E-103. See *New Jersey Dep't of Envtl. Prot. v. Gloucester Envtl. Mgmt. Servs., Inc.*, 800 F. Supp. 1210 (D.N.J. 1992) (finding individual will be considered an "operator" under "usual meanings" of term such that individual liability may be imposed where individual shows high degree of personal involvement in operation and decision-making process of business).

49. N.J.S.A. 13:1E-104. The tax is levied on all solid waste accepted for disposal.

50. See, for example, *Gloucester Envtl. Mgmt. Servs., Inc.*, 800 F. Supp. at 1217 ("The Closure Act was enacted to 'ensure proper closure of sanitary landfill facilities' and to provide compensation to persons adversely affected by 'improper operation or closure of any sanitary landfill.'").

51. N.J.S.A. 13:1E-106a. Historically, the Closure Fund has paid claims predominately to individual homeowners impacted by improperly operated and closed landfill facilities after the homeowners have exhausted all other reasonably available sources for compensation. Financial Management, available at http://www.nj.gov/dep/dshw/fm/slf-fund.html.

52. N.J.S.A. 13:1E-101.

53. N.J.A.C. 7:26-2A.9. A copy of the approved Closure and Post-Closure Plan must be kept on file at the sanitary landfill during the course of the sanitary landfill's operation and, after closure, filed with the municipal clerk. N.J.A.C. 7:26-2A.9(d)(10).

54. N.J.S.A. 13:1E-109; N.J.A.C. 7:26-2A.9(g).

55. N.j.a.c. 7:26-2A.9(e)(2).

56. N.J.A.C. 7:26-2A.9(c)(2).

57. N.j.a.c. 7:26-2A.9(c)(9).

58. N.J.A.C. 7:26-2A.9(c)(3).

59. N.J.S.A. 7:26-2A.9(c)(8). The deed must also provide notice that any future disruption of the closed landfill requires prior approval from the Department in accordance with N.J.A.C. 7:26-2A.8(j).

60. N.J.S.A. 13:1I-4.

61. *City of Philadelphia v. New Jersey*, 437 U.S. 617, 98 S. Ct. 2531, 2532, 57 L. Ed. 2d 475 (1978).

62. N.J.S.A. 13:1I-5. There is also a penalty provision.

63. See Diane E. Sugrue, *Protecting Our Surf from Syringes: The Comprehensive Regulated Medical Waste Management Act*, 15 SETON HALL LEGIS. J. 568 (1991).

64. N.J.A.C. 7:26-3A.1 et seq. establishes a program for regulated medical waste, which includes any solid waste, generated in the diagnosis, treatment (e.g., provision of medical services), or immunization of human beings or animals, in research pertaining thereto, or in the production or testing of biologicals, that is not excluded or exempted under N.J.A.C. 7:26-3A.6(b), and that is listed or meets any waste characteristic classification criteria described in a table set forth at N.J.A.C. 7:26-3A.6.

65. *Ibid.*

66. N.J.S.A. 13:1E-99.44 et seq. The Toxic Packaging Reduction Act was enacted in response to Legislative findings that discarded packaging constitutes the largest single category of solid waste within New Jersey's waste stream.

67. N.J.S.A. 13:1E-99.47.

68. N.J.S.A. 13:1E-99.51.

69. N.J.S.A. 13:1E-216. "Litter-generating products" are defined as specific goods which are produced, distributed, or purchased in disposable containers, packages, or wrappings; or which are not usually sold in packages, containers, or wrappings but which are commonly

discarded in public places; or which are of an unsightly or unsanitary nature, commonly thrown, dropped, discarded, placed, or deposited by a person on public property, or on private property not owned by that person. They include beer, wine, and distilled spirits; cigarettes; cleaning agents and toiletries; food for human or pet consumption; glass and metal containers; groceries; tires; newsprint and magazine paper stock; drugstore sundries (not including prescription or nonprescription drugs); paper products; and soft drinks and carbonated waters. N.J.S.A. 13:1E-215(e).

    70. N.J.S.A. 13:1E-217.

    71. N.J.S.A. 13:1E-217(f).

    72. N.J.S.A. 13:1E-96.5.

    73. Enacted in 1987, the Recycling Act was the State's solution to inadequate landfill space and was lauded as "the most comprehensive mandatory recycling program in the nation." Anthony T. Drollas, Jr., *The New Jersey Statewide Mandatory Source Separation and Recycling Act: The Nation's First Comprehensive Statewide Mandatory Recycling Program,* 12 SETON HALL LEGIS. J. 271, 272 (1989). The Recycling Act further requires that the State study future requirements for the recycling of plastic and bi-metallic containers, N.J.S.A. 13.1E-99.18 and .19, and automobile tires, N.J.S.A. 13.1E-99.20. It also establishes certain State purchase preferences. N.J.S.A. 13.1E-99.24 to .28.

    74. N.J.S.A. 13:1E-99.13.

    75. N.J.S.A. 13:1E-99.23.

    76. N.J.S.A. 13:1E-99.12.

    77. N.J.S.A.13:1E-99.34.

    78. This chapter of the Recycling Rules also includes the Department's electronic waste recycling program rules regarding the recycling of a used covered electronic device, pursuant to the Electronic Waste Management Act, N.J.S.A. 13:1E-99.94 et seq., but does not apply to hazardous waste, except for universal waste exempted from hazardous waste regulation as provided at N.J.A.C. 7:26A-7.

    79. N.J.A.C. 7:26A-1.3.

    80. N.J.A.C. 7:26A-3.1. The procedures for obtaining approval are set forth at N.J.A.C. 7:26A-3.2, 3.4, 3.5, 3.7, 3.8, 3.10, and 3.18 through 3.20.

    81. N.J.A.C. 7:26A-3.1(c).

    82. N.J.A.C. 7:26A-3.1(d).

Chapter 10

Hazardous Waste Management

Jeffrey W. Cappola, Esq., Yin Zhou, Esq.,
and Emily D. Vail, Esq. (8th Ed.)

The Resource Conservation and Recovery Act (RCRA) authorizes the U.S. Environmental Protection Agency (EPA) to delegate the implementation of the RCRA program to states whose hazardous waste management programs are at least as stringent as RCRA.[1] The New Jersey Department of Environmental Protection (NJDEP) implements the RCRA program in this state.[2] The New Jersey Solid Waste Management Act (NJSWMA) establishes the statutory framework for the management and coordination of New Jersey's Hazardous Waste Management Program, which authorizes the NJDEP to promulgate and administer regulations governing the identification and management of hazardous wastes.[3] In addition, NJDEP's hazardous waste prospectively incorporates all provisions of forty CFR Parts 124, 260-266, 268, and 270 by reference. As a result, New Jersey's hazardous waste rules are automatically updated to remain current with the federal rules.[4]

New Jersey's assumption of the federal RCRA Hazardous Waste Program included the authority to enforce RCRA, with two exceptions. The first exception is the RCRA Corrective Action Provisions, which are incorporated into New Jersey regulations but for which NJDEP did not seek delegated authority.[5] The second exception is the RCRA Loss of Interim Status Provisions because New Jersey regulations provide a right to a hearing before interim status is lost, while RCRA's Loss of Interim Status Provisions take effect immediately upon a triggering event.[6] New Jersey has been implementing the RCRA Hazardous Waste Program successfully for two decades.

WHAT IS HAZARDOUS WASTE?

RCRA regulates hazardous waste, which is defined as a solid waste with properties that are either harmful to human health or the environment or which has the potential to be harmful. In Section 1004(5) of RCRA, Congress defined hazardous waste as a

solid waste, or combination of solid wastes, which because of its quantity, concentration, or physical, chemical, or infectious characteristics may

(a) cause, or significantly contribute to, an increase in mortality or an increase in serious irreversible, or incapacitating reversible, illness; or

(b) pose a substantial present or potential hazard to human health or the environment when improperly treated, stored, transported, or disposed of, or otherwise managed.[7]

The definition was purposefully broad, and Congress instructed EPA to develop more specific criteria for defining solid and hazardous waste by using two different mechanisms: (1) identifying and listing certain specific wastes and (2) identifying characteristics that make the waste hazardous. Unfortunately, determining whether a waste is a regulated hazardous waste is still a complex process. Therefore, EPA developed a series of questions to determine whether a "waste" is hazardous: (1) Is the material a solid waste? (2) Is the material excluded from the definition of solid waste or hazardous waste? (3) Is the waste a listed or characteristic hazardous waste? and (4) Is the waste delisted?[8]

STEP-BY-STEP PROCESS TO DETERMINE IF THE MATERIAL IS HAZARDOUS WASTE

Is the Material a Solid Waste?

The EPA has complex rules for determining whether a material is "discarded" and therefore a solid waste.[9] A "discarded material" includes any material that is abandoned, recycled, or inherently waste-like, as well as certain military munitions.[10] There are additional rulings and advisory opinions on the difference between materials that are "abandoned," "recycled," or "inherently waste-like" and their status as solid waste.[11] This chapter will side-step the nuances of those terms for the sake of brevity and focus on whether a material or by-product that is reused or recycled is considered "discarded" and therefore a solid waste.[12] The manner in which a material is recycled will ultimately determine whether or not the material is a solid waste and how it is regulated. The determination that a material is being recycled and not "discarded" is highly fact-sensitive, and the generator has the burden of demonstrating to NJDEP that it is "recycling" the material rather than stockpiling hazardous waste.[13]

The simpler of the two categories of recycled materials involve those materials that do not have to be reclaimed prior to reuse. If a material is directly used as an ingredient in a production process without first being reclaimed then that material is not a solid waste.[14] If a material is directly used as an effective substitute for a commercial product without first being reclaimed, then that material is also not considered a solid waste.[15] Additionally, when a material is returned directly to the production process without first being reclaimed for use as a feedstock or raw material, that material is not a solid waste.[16]

If a material is reclaimed (e.g., processed to recover a usable product or distilled to remove contaminants), its regulatory status as being "discarded" depends on the type of material, and whether it can fall into one of the regulatory exclusions. Secondary materials that are reclaimed before use typically fall into five broad categories: (1) spent material, such as a solvent, that may be reclaimed and put back into the production process; (2) sludges generated from wastewater treatment plants, water supply treatment plants, or air pollution control devices; (3) by-products that can include residues like slag or distillation bottoms; (4) commercial chemical products, which include unused or off-specification chemicals; and (5) scrap metal.[17] Spent materials and scrap metal are typically considered solid waste when reclaimed. Sludges and by-products are also considered solid waste when reclaimed if they are listed wastes, as will be discussed in greater detail below. Sludges and by-products exhibiting hazardous characteristics, as well as commercial chemical products, are generally not considered solid wastes when reclaimed.[18] These exceptions for recycled and reclaimed material only apply so long as the materials are not used in a manner constituting disposal, burned for energy recovery, used to produce or are contained in fuels, accumulated speculatively or are dioxin-containing wastes.[19]

Is the Material Excluded from the Definition of Solid or Hazardous Waste?

The RCRA rules provide the following exclusions from the definition of solid waste: domestic sewage and mixtures of domestic sewage, point source industrial wastewater discharges, irrigation return flows, radioactive waste regulated by either the Nuclear Regulatory Commission or the U.S. Department of Energy (DOE) under the Atomic Energy Act (AEA),[20] in-situ mining waste, pulping liquors, spent sulfuric acid, reclaimed secondary materials,[21]; spent wood preservatives, coke by-product wastes, splash condenser dross residue, hazardous oil-bearing secondary materials and recovered oil from petroleum refining operations, certain excluded scrap metals, shredded circuit boards, condensates from kraft mill steam strippers, mineral processing spent materials, petrochemical recovered oil, spent caustic solutions from petroleum refining, hazardous secondary materials used to make zinc fertilizers, used cathode ray tubes, hazardous secondary material generated and legitimately reclaimed within the United States, hazardous secondary material generated and transported for the purpose of reclamation, hazardous secondary material exported from the United States and reclaimed in a foreign country, solvent-contaminated wipes sent for cleaning and reuse, and hazardous secondary material generated and transferred for the purpose of remanufacturing.[22] Of these exceptions, perhaps the two most significant are industrial wastewater that is discharged into a publicaly owned treatment works[23] and industrial wastewater that is discharged to surface water pursuant to a New Jersey Pollutant Discharge Elimination System (NJPDES) permit.[24]

The so-called transfer-based exclusion at 40 CFR § 261.4(a)(24) and (25) is also significant in connection with the off-site recycling of secondary materials. In 2015, EPA amended the definition of "solid waste" by replacing the then-existing transfer-based exclusion with what was known as the verified recycler exclusion to exempt off-site recycling of hazardous waste in certain situations. After the 2015 verified recycler rule was vacated in part by the U.S. Court of Appeals for the D.C. Circuit in 2017 and 2018,[25] EPA reinstated the transfer-based exclusion with modifications, as it currently appears in the rule.[26] EPA has also developed four "legitimacy" factors to determine whether the recycling of secondary hazardous materials is legitimate as opposed to sham recycling and thus exempt from RCRA regulation. As part of the 2015 rulemaking, DEP made the fourth factor—whether the product of the recycling process must be comparable to a legitimate final product or intermediate—a mandatory condition in order for recycling to be considered legitimate.[27] This was also vacated by the Court of Appeals. In addition to the above exclusions, the following solid wastes are excluded from the definition of hazardous waste: household hazardous waste; agricultural waste; mining overburden; fossil fuel combustion waste; oil, gas, and geothermal wastes; trivalent chromium wastes; mining and mineral processing wastes; cement kiln dust; arsenical-treated wood; petroleum-contaminated media and debris from underground storage tanks (USTs); spent chlorofluorocarbon refrigerants; used oil filters; used oil distillation bottoms; landfill leachate or gas condensate derived from certain listed wastes; and certain solvent-contaminated wipes.[28]

Hazardous wastes generated in raw material, product storage, or process (e.g., manufacturing) units are also exempt from certain hazardous waste regulations. These units include tanks, pipelines, vehicles, and vessels used either in the manufacturing process or for storing raw materials or products but specifically do not include surface impoundments. Once the waste is removed from the unit, or when a unit temporarily or permanently ceases operation for ninety days, the waste is considered generated and is subject to regulation.[29]

Is the Waste a Listed Hazardous Waste?

After it is determined that the material is a "waste," and it is not excluded from the definitions of solid or hazardous waste, one must consider whether the waste is a listed hazardous waste. The hazardous waste listings consist of four waste categories: the F list, the K list, the P list, and the U list. These waste categories are further broken down in the lists located at 40 C.F.R. Part 261, Subpart D.

Generally, listed wastes are classified as follows:

The F list includes wastes from common industrial and manufacturing processes, which are considered wastes from nonspecific sources. The F list is codified in 40 CFR §261.31.

- Spent solvent wastes (waste codes F001 through F005)
- Electroplating and other metal finishing wastes (F006 through F012 and F019)
- Dioxin-bearing wastes (F020 through F023 and F026 through F028)
- Chlorinated aliphatic hydrocarbons production wastes (F024 and F025)
- Wood preserving wastes (F032, F034, and F035)
- Petroleum refinery wastewater treatment sludges (F037 and F038)
- Multisource leachate (F039).

The K list includes wastes from specific industries that are considered source-specific wastes. The K list is found in 40 CFR §261.32.

- Wood preservation
- Organic chemicals manufacturing
- Pesticides manufacturing
- Petroleum refining
- Veterinary pharmaceuticals manufacturing
- Inorganic pigment manufacturing

- Inorganic chemicals manufacturing
- Explosives manufacturing
- Iron and steel production
- Primary aluminum production
- Secondary lead processing
- Ink formulation
- Coking (processing of coal to produce coke, a material used in iron and steel production).

The P list and the U list include pure or commercial grade formulations of specific unused chemicals. Chemicals are included on the P list if they are acutely toxic. The U list is generally comprised of chemicals that are toxic but also includes chemicals that display other characteristics, such as ignitability or reactivity. Both the P list and the U list are codified in 40 CFR §261.33. For a waste to qualify as P- or U-listed, the waste must meet the following three criteria:

- The waste must contain one of the chemicals listed on the P or U list,
- The chemical in the waste must be unused, and
- The chemical in the waste must be in the form of a commercial chemical product.

Delisting

The RCRA regulations stipulate a process whereby a waste handler can apply to NJDEP to demonstrate that even though the waste stream generated at its facility is a listed hazardous waste, there is no significant risk or sufficient hazard to the public welfare or the environment, and therefore, the waste should be "delisted." This is a site-specific determination for the applicant's waste and cannot be applied to other facilities without prior approval from the NJDEP. To "delist" a hazardous waste, the applicant must demonstrate that the waste does not (1) meet the criteria the agency cited when it designated the waste as a "listed waste," (2) exhibit any hazardous waste "characteristics," and (3) pose a threat to human health and the environment. Delistings can be a burdensome process and take years to accomplish.

Is the Waste a Characteristic Hazardous Waste?

If the material is a waste and is not a "listed waste" it still may be regulated by RCRA if it demonstrates a "characteristic" of hazardous waste. EPA established four hazardous waste characteristics:

1. Ignitability[30]
2. Corrosivity[31]
3. Reactivity[32]—A waste is reactive if it meets any of the following criteria:
   a. It can explode or violently react when exposed to water or under normal handling conditions;
   b. It can create toxic fumes or gases at hazardous levels when exposed to water or under normal waste handling conditions;

c. It can explode if heated under confinement or exposed to a strong igniting source, or it meets the criteria for classification as an explosive under DOT rules;
d. It generates toxic levels.
4. Toxicity[33]

The Mixture Rule, Derived-from Rule, Contained-in Policy and Other Policies

There are other ways in which a material may become regulated by RCRA. The "mixture rule" is employed when RCRA regulated waste mixes with other nonhazardous waste.[34] If any amount of a listed hazardous waste is mixed with any amount of nonhazardous waste then the entire amount is deemed to be a hazardous waste. Another rule is the "derived-from rule" where a solid waste that is derived from a listed waste is a hazardous waste.[35] Generally, a hazardous waste classified as such through the application of the "mixture rule" or the "derived-from rule" is only regulated by RCRA if the end product itself exhibits the characteristic.[36] Sometimes listed and characteristic wastes are spilled onto soil or contaminate equipment, buildings, or other structures. The mixture and derived-from rules do not apply to such contaminated soil and materials because these materials are not actually wasted. Soil is considered environmental media, while the equipment, buildings, and structures are considered debris.

In order to address such contaminated media and debris, EPA created the contained-in policy[37] to determine when contaminated media and debris[38] must be managed as hazardous wastes. Environmental media are not in and of themselves wastes but are regulated as hazardous waste when they contain (are contaminated by) a RCRA listed hazardous waste or exhibit a characteristic. In these cases, the media and debris must be managed as if they were hazardous waste. The EPA and NJDEP consider contaminated media or debris to no longer contain hazardous waste when they no longer exhibit a characteristic of hazardous waste. This applies when the hazardous waste contained within the media or debris is either a characteristic waste or a waste listed solely for a characteristic. Otherwise, when dealing with listed waste contamination, NJDEP can determine that media and debris no longer contain hazardous waste by determining that the media or debris no longer poses a sufficient health threat to deserve RCRA regulation. Once this contained-out determination is made, the media and debris are generally no longer regulated under RCRA Subtitle C. However, under certain circumstances, the RCRA Land Disposal Restrictions, discussed below, might continue to apply.

OBLIGATIONS OF GENERATORS AND TRANSPORTERS

A generator is "any person, by site, whose act or process produces hazardous waste . . . or whose act first causes a hazardous waste to become subject to regulation."[39] A generator has the responsibility to determine if it is subject to the requirements and to characterize the nature of its waste stream. Generators are required to apply for and obtain a RCRA permit to fully comply with the requirements of RCRA section 3005(e) and 40 C.F.R. § 270.10 for interim status in order to store hazardous waste at its facility. Generators that produce 1,000 kilograms or more of hazardous waste per month or more than 1 kilogram per month of acute hazardous waste are large quantity generators (LQG). Generators that produce more than 100 kilograms but less than 1,000 kilograms of hazardous waste in a calendar month are small quantity generators (SQG) and are exempted from certain requirements.[40] Generators that produce 100 kilograms or less per month of hazardous waste and no more than 1 kilogram of acutely hazardous waste are considered very small quantity generators (VSSQG) and are exempt from most requirements.[41] LGQs and SGQs are subject to the regulations contained in 40 C.F.R. Part 262 that generally relate to identifying and qualifying the waste, obtaining an EPA Identification Number, complying with the accumulation and storage requirements, preparing waste for transportation, tracking the shipment through the manifest system, and meeting the recordkeeping and reporting requirements.

Effective May 30, 2017, EPA significantly overhauled the regulations governing generators of hazardous waste.[42] Aside from a reorganization and consolidation of the existing rules applicable to generators at 40 CFR Part 262, EPA also expanded regulatory flexibility for generators in some circumstances.

First, EPA eliminated the category of "conditionally exempt small quantity generator" (CESQG) and replaced it with the VSGQ category. The thresholds for qualifying as a VSGQ remain the same as those for a CESQG.[43] As part of the increased flexibility intended by EPA, VSQGs are also now allowed to send hazardous wastes to a LQG that is under the control of the same person.[44] The recent changes also take into account episodic generation events that might otherwise cause a generator to fall under another generator category with more onerous regulatory requirements.[45] Previously, any non-routine, episodic event that resulted in exceedance of the applicable thresholds for the various generator categories would result in that generator being subject to more stringent generator requirements. Under the new rule, a generator can maintain its existing generator category during an episodic event. However, there are limits on the number of such events allowed per year, along with additional notification and record-keeping requirements.[46]

The Manifest

The hallmark of the RCRA cradle-to-grave management of hazardous waste is the manifest system. On March 4, 2005, EPA adopted the Uniform Hazardous Waste Manifest regulations and the manifest forms.[47] The manifest must include such information as (1) the generator's name, address, telephone number, and the EPA ID number; (2) the name and EPA ID number of all transporters; (3) the name, address, and EPA ID number of the designated and alternate Treatment, Storage and Disposal facilities; (4) the manifest document number; (5) the Department of Transportation name and handling code of the hazardous waste being shipped; (6) the quantity of the waste being shipped; and (7) a description of the type and number of containers.[48]

In accordance with the Hazardous Waste Electronic Manifest Act, EPA launched its Electronic Hazardous Waste Manifest (e-Manifest) system in June 2018. Currently, use of the e-Manifest system is strongly encouraged, but not required.

A transporter is a "person engaged in the offsite transportation of hazardous waste by air, rail, highway, or water."[49] A transporter of hazardous waste must comply with the regulations of 40 C.F.R. Part 263, including the requirement to obtain an EPA Identification Number. The regulations also incorporate portions of the U.S. Department of Transportation regulations, such as requirements for labeling and using proper containers. Most importantly, a transporter is prohibited from accepting hazardous waste that does not have a manifest.[50]

TREATMENT, STORAGE, AND DISPOSAL
OF HAZARDOUS WASTES

Treatment, Storage, and Disposal Facilities (TSDF) are the last component of the cradle-to-grave Hazardous Waste Management System governed by RCRA. The requirements for TSDFs are promulgated in 40 C.F.R. Parts 264 and 265; they include general facility operating standards, as well as standards for the various types of units in which hazardous wastes are managed, described in detail below.[51] Unless otherwise exempt, all facilities that treat, store, or dispose of hazardous wastes must obtain a permit from the NJDEP.[52] The general standards require that each TSDF obtain an identification number, obtain or conduct waste analysis, implement security measures, schedule regular inspections, and provide personnel training.[53] The TSDF must also take special precautions handling ignitable, reactive, and otherwise incompatible waste and may not locate facilities in floodplains or near seismic faults.[54] There are various recordkeeping requirements with which these facilities must comply, and TSDFs must implement pollution prevention measures to minimize non-sudden potential releases.[55] Groundwater monitoring programs must be implemented for land disposal units, which may vary depending on whether the facility is under interim status or permanent status.[56] Corrective action may be required if groundwater protection levels are exceeded.[57]

A TSDF facility is typically engaged in one or more of the following activities:

1. Treatment, which consists of any method, technique, or process designed to physically, chemically, or biologically change the nature of hazardous waste[58];
2. Storage, which is the holding of hazardous waste for a temporary period, after which the hazardous waste is treated, disposed of, or stored elsewhere[59]; and
3. Disposal, which is the discharge, deposit, injection, dumping, spilling, leaking, or placing of any solid or hazardous waste on or in the land or water. A disposal facility is any site where hazardous waste is intentionally placed and where the waste will remain after a TSDF ceases operation.[60]

Owners and operators TSDFs are also subject to RCRA's Closure and Post-Closure care and Financial Responsibility regulations in order to ensure that a TSDF does not pose a significant threat to human health and the environment when operations cease.[61] Each facility must have a written Closure Plan that identifies how each unit will be closed in conformance with EPA standards, including procedures for removing contaminated soil, cleaning equipment, and performing necessary sampling and analysis.[62] Post-Closure Care Plans are required for land disposal units where hazardous wastes are to be left in place after the facility's closure.[63] Groundwater monitoring and maintenance for any engineering control must be included in the Post-Closure Care Plans for a period of up to thirty years.[64]

The financial assurance regulations require that each TSDF demonstrate its financial ability to meet Closure and Post-Closure obligations, as well as third-party liability.[65] The rules allow TSDFs several means to demonstrate financial ability, including self-insurance, insurance policies, surety bonds, and parent company guarantees.[66] Most TSDF facilities use the self-insurance option to meet the financial assurance obligations under RCRA.

Permits and Interim Status

All facilities that treat, store, or dispose of hazardous wastes onsite are required to obtain a permit.[67] RCRA has standards for new TSDFs and for facilities that were already in operation at the time of RCRA's enactment in 1976. The RCRA permit provides for the standards and requirements applicable to the specific activities conducted at that facility, including both the general facility standards and the standards applicable to each type of unit at that facility.[68] These performance standards address all aspects of the citing, construction, operation, and monitoring of a TSDF to ensure the protection of human health and the environment. For example, a typical permit describes the construction requirements for the hazardous waste management units at the facility and requirements for testing the waste periodically. A RCRA permit holder must understand the complex requirements and conditions of a permit. The costs to obtain such a permit can be substantial.

EPA created a special category of regulations to allow facilities in existence prior to the enactment of RCRA in 1976 to gradually achieve compliance with the requisite standards. Such facilities are called interim status facilities.[69] The interim status facilities must comply with separate standards that are typically less stringent than the standards for permitted facilities.[70] RCRA provides for certain exemptions in order to promote certain beneficial activities or to avoid overlapping with requirements of other parts of RCRA or other environmental laws.[71]

With certain exceptions, compliance with a RCRA permit constitutes compliance with Subtitle C (the hazardous waste regulatory portion) of RCRA for purposes of enforcement.[72] If a TSDF complies with its permit, it will be considered to have a "permit shield." Although the permit shield protects against enforcement with respect to most new rules promulgated after an operating permit is issued, the permit shield does not afford protection for the following: (1) requirements effective by statute; (2) land disposal restrictions promulgated under 40 C.F.R. Part 268; (3) rules governing certain performance standards promulgated under 40 C.F.R. Part 264 for surface impoundments, waste piles, and landfills; and (4) rules limiting air emissions promulgated under 40 C.F.R. Part 265, Subparts AA, BB, and CC.[73] The RCRA permit shield makes it the duty of the permittee to report all instances of non-compliance at the TSDF facility.[74]

In determining whether or not a facility is required to obtain a RCRA permit, there are various aspects of the facility's operations that need to be analyzed, which include, but are not limited to, handling of regulated hazardous wastes; "treatment," "storage," or "disposal" at a facility, as defined in the regulations; and any potential exclusion in accordance with RCRA requirements.

Exemptions

RCRA exempts certain types of facilities or operations from the TSDF requirements in order to promote certain beneficial activities or to avoid overlapping with the requirements of other parts of RCRA or other environmental regulations.[75] First, if an operating TSDF has a permit for certain activities under another environmental law, that facility may qualify for a special form of a RCRA permit, known as a permit-by-rule.[76] There are various other exclusions from having to obtain a RCRA permit, including the following:

- Generators of hazardous waste that temporarily accumulate hazardous waste at their facilities in accordance with 40 C.F.R. § 262.34.[77]
- Farmers who dispose of pesticide waste from their farm provided they follow the disposal requirements set forth in 40 C.F.R. § 262.70.[78]
- Owners or operators of facilities who handle hazardous waste in small quantities under 40 C.F.R. §§ 261.4 and 261.5 (VSQG).[79]
- Owners or operators of a "totally enclosed treatment facility" as defined under 40 C.F.R. § 260.10.[80]
- One of the operators of "Elementary Neutralization Units" and "Wastewater Treatment Units" and defined under 40 C.F.R. § 260.10.[81]
- Transporters storing manifested shipments of hazardous waste in containers at a transfer facility for no more than ten days.[82]
- A person adding absorbent material to waste in a container, at the time the waste is first placed in the container.[83]
- Universal waste handlers and universal waste transporters managing a listed universal waste.[84]
- A New York State utility central collection facility consolidating waste in accordance with 40 C.F.R. § 262.90.
- A person undertaking an emergency spill response action.[85]

Facility Standards

If an exemption does not apply, then the TSDF must comply with the standards for fully regulated facilities. These regulations cover good management practices, including keeping track of the amount and type of hazardous wastes entering the facility, training employees on safety management aspects of operating a TSDF regarding hazardous waste, and preparing to avoid hazardous waste emergencies.[86] This section will outline part 264 and the general scope and applicability of the regulations in requiring hazardous waste facilities to comply with general facility standards.[87]

EPA provides TSDF owners and operators with identification numbers and is required to notify EPA of the types of hazardous waste they plan to treat, store, or dispose of by applying for said identification number.[88] EPA identification numbers are typically used when remediating contaminated properties for the disposal of contaminated soil that is considered to be hazardous waste. As such, before accepting a hazardous waste for treatment, storage, or disposal of the facility an owner or operator must obtain a detailed chemical and physical analysis of a representative sample of the waste.[89] Typically, the generator of the waste provides chemical analysis from a licensed laboratory. The TSDFs permit will list the types of hazardous waste that a facility is authorized to treat, store, or dispose of.[90] Hazardous waste facilities accepting off-site waste must inspect each hazardous waste shipment coming to that facility. EPA requires all TSDFs to prepare a waste analysis plan that outlines the procedures necessary to ensure proper treatment, storage, or disposal.[91] This analysis plan must describe the waste inspection and analysis procedures, including tests and sample methods, the parameters to be analyzed, and the corresponding rationale and frequency of review of the analysis.[92] The waste analysis must be repeated periodically to ensure that the information on a given waste is accurate and current.[93]

TSDFs must prepare and implement security provisions that are intended to prevent accidental or unauthorized entry into the facility, especially where hazardous waste is treated, stored, or disposed of. The facility must implement a twenty-four-hour surveillance system that continuously monitors and controls entry into the facility, or it may create an artificial or an actual barrier that completely surrounds the active portion of the facility and serves as a means to control entry to the facility at all times through gates.[94] In addition, the facility must post a sign that states "danger-unauthorized personnel keep out" at the entrance to the facility and must be written in English and any other language that is predominant in the area surrounding the facility.[95] The NJSWMA further provides for weekly inspection of major hazardous waste facilities by the NJDEP.[96] A major hazardous waste facility is defined in the act as[97]

> any commercial hazardous waste facility which has a total capacity to treat, store, or dispose of more than 250,000 gallons of hazardous waste, or the equivalent thereof, as determined by the Department, except that any facility which would otherwise be considered a major hazardous waste facility pursuant to this section solely as a result of the recycling or refining of any hazardous wastes which are or contain gold, silver, osmium, platinum, palladium, iridium, rhodium, ruthenium or copper shall not be considered a major hazardous waste facility for the purposes of this act.

The NJDEP may make an assessment against any hazardous waste facility to cover the costs of the inspections.[98] In addition, the local board of health or county health department may conduct a weekly inspection of major hazardous waste facilities.[99] The NJDEP, local board of health, or county health department has the right to enter any major hazardous waste facility or solid waste facility at any time in order to determine compliance with the registration statement, engineering design, and all applicable laws or regulations.[100]

The location standards for building new TSDFs include restrictions on sitting in floodplains or earthquake sensitive areas.[101] TSDFs must implement preparedness and prevention standards that are intended to minimize and prevent emergency situations, such as a fire, an explosion, or any unplanned release of hazardous waste constituents into the air, soil, groundwater, or surface water.[102] Owners and operators must prepare and maintain a written Contingency Plan at the facility, and all personnel must understand their duties with regard to carrying out the plan immediately in the event of a catastrophe.[103] There must also be an emergency coordinator at the facility at all times to assist with the situation and make decisions on how to respond to emergencies.[104]

TSDF owners and operators are required to keep records and submit reports to EPA to document and track hazardous waste activities at the facility. RCRA Part 262 requires that most generators must obtain an EPA identification number and comply with its packaging, labeling, marking, place carding, recordkeeping, and reporting requirements.[105] RCRA also requires generators that ship hazardous waste off-site for treatment, storage, or disposal to prepare hazardous waste manifests accompanying each shipment with the transporter.[106] When a waste shipment is received from off-site, the TSDF owner and operator must sign and date all copies of the manifest to verify that the waste has reached the appropriate designated facility.[107] Owners and operators of TSDFs must keep a written operating record regarding all wastes received, methods and dates of treatment, storage, and disposal in order to keep track of hazardous waste activity at the facility.

Standards for Hazardous Waste, Treatment, Storage, and Disposal Units

Hazardous waste at TSDFs may be treated, stored, or disposed of in several different types of units. In order to ensure that hazardous wastes are managed properly and in a safe manner, RCRA imposes design, construction, operation, maintenance, closure, and financial assurance requirements on hazardous waste management units.[108] An overview of the currently used disposal units follows.

Containers

Containers are generally used for storing rather than disposing of hazardous waste. Containers represent the most common and generally least expensive method of storing hazardous waste. A container is any portable device in which hazardous waste is stored, transported, treated, or otherwise handled.[109] Examples of hazardous waste containers include, but are not limited to fifty-five-gallon drums, large tanker trucks, railcars, small buckets, and test tubes.[110] TSDFs must use containers that are in good condition and not deteriorating in any way. Waste stored in defective containers must be transferred to containers in good condition or to another type of disposal unit.[111] The owner or operator must use a container made of or lined with material that will not react with the hazardous waste to be stored so that the ability of the container to contain waste is not impaired.[112]

Tank Systems

Tanks are stationary devices used to store or treat hazardous waste. They are widely used for storage or accumulation of hazardous waste because they can accommodate large volumes of material. In order to ensure that a tank system can hold hazardous waste for its intended lifetime, owners and operators must ensure that the tank is properly designed. All tank systems and components must be designed to provide adequate foundation, structural support, and protection from corrosion to avoid leaking.[113] An independent engineer must certify that the tank meets all the RCRA requirements prior to operation.[114] RCRA requires the owner or operator to inspect the tank at least once each operating day to ensure that the tank system is being operated according to its design.[115] All tanks must have secondary containment systems to prevent the release of hazardous waste to the environment.[116]

Surface Impoundments

A surface impoundment is a natural topographic depression, manmade excavation, or dyked area created primarily of earthen materials (although it must be lined with manmade materials) that is used to treat, store, or dispose of liquid hazardous waste. Examples include holding ponds, storage pits, and settling lagoons.[117] For new surface impoundment units on which construction began after January 29, 1992, the owner or operator must install two or more liners, a leachate collection and removal system between the liners, and a leak detection system.[118] A surface impoundment must also be designed to prevent the flow of liquids over the top of an impoundment.[119] Surface impoundment units must be inspected, including liners and leachate collection and removal systems, to make sure they are working properly.[120]

Waste Piles

A waste pile is an open pile used for treating or storing non-liquid hazardous waste. The standards for these units are very similar to those for landfills and surface impoundments, but the difference is that the Waste Piles are intended to be used for temporary storage and treatment only, not disposal. The owner or operator of this type of unit must minimize the potential for leachate from the waste pile. Accordingly, EPA's design standards include double liners, double leachate collection and removal systems, leachate detection systems, and construction quality assurance standards.[121]

Land Treatment Units

Land treatment units involve the placement of waste on the ground surface, or the incorporation of waste into the upper layers of the soil column, in order to degrade, transform, or immobilize hazardous constituents present in the hazardous waste.[122] The design and operating requirements for land treatment units are quite different from other waste management units because they utilize degradation as a method of hazardous waste treatment. These units also require a treatment demonstration prior to implementation to show that the hazardous constituents in the waste can be completely degraded or immobilized in the treatment zone.[123] The waste must be placed above the water table to let the soil microbes and sunlight degrade to hazardous waste.[124] With regard to design standards, the main considerations are stormwater runoff and wind dispersal, which must be prevented at all times.[125] The owner and operator must inspect the treatment area weekly and after storms to ensure that the unit is in compliance with the operating requirements.[126]

Landfills

A landfill is a disposal unit in which non-liquid hazardous waste is disposed of in place or on the land. Landfills are the final disposal site—the ultimate grave for a significant portion of hazardous waste that is generated in the United States.[127] The design standards for landfills include a double liner, and a double leachate collection and removal system above and between such liners that must be operated in accordance with § 264.301(c).[128] The owner or operator must also design, construct, operate, and maintain a run-on and run-off control system, the peak discharge, and water volume resulting from at least a twenty-five-year storm.[129]

All landfills must also develop a Response Action Plan that sets forth the actions to be taken in the event of a leak from the landfill.[130] In the event of a leak, the owner or operator must notify the EPA Regional Administrator and submit documentation regarding any responsive actions taken or planned.[131]

Closure Requirements

All TSDFs must be closed in accordance with RCRA requirements. After these facilities are closed, the owner and operator must either remove all waste that has accumulated in the units at the facility or leave the waste in place while maintaining the units in a way that ensure that they will not pose a future threat to human health in the environment.[132]

The closure and post-closure regulations are divided into two parts: the general standards applicable to all TSDFs and the technical standards for specific types of hazardous waste management units. Hazardous waste landfills typically have the most onerous post-closure requirements and long-term monitoring and maintenance obligations.[133] Each unit has its own specific closure requirements; however, several of the requirements are similar with regard to closing a treatment, storage, or disposal unit. The following discussion will provide general guidance with regard to the closure of these units.

To ensure that a TSDF is closed properly, the owner and operator must prepare a Closure Plan that details exactly how and when facility closure will take place. These plans must be submitted to the NJDEP for approval.[134] With regard to permitted facilities, a Closure Plan must be submitted to the appropriate regulatory agency at the time of permit application submission. The approved Closure Plan then becomes an enforceable component of the permit.[135] Interim status facilities must have a written Closure Plan six months after they become subject to RCRA.[136] In general, all Closure Plans must address the design of the closure elements when the closure will occur, an estimate of the maximum amount of hazardous waste kept on site over the life of the facility and a description of the closure methods with regard to either removing or managing waste and decontaminating the site for final closure.[137]

The RCRA rules contain timeframes for the completion of various closure activities in order to ensure closure is completed in a timely manner after the facility stops accepting hazardous waste.[138]

Post-Closure Requirements

Post-closure care is not required for all units; however, these requirements are required for land treatment units, landfills, and surface impoundments where hazardous waste has been permanently disposed of.[139] These types of units inherently have the potential for releases from the unit over a long period of time, and therefore owners and operators must conduct post-closure monitoring and maintenance activities.[140] Owners and operators must close land treatment units and surface impoundments as landfills and comply with the post-closure requirements for landfills.[141] The general landfill post-closure requirements typically include groundwater monitoring and maintaining the waste containment system, such as final covers, caps, and liners.[142] Stormwater run-off controls may need to be implemented as well. The post-Closure period normally lasts for thirty years after closure is complete.[143] To ensure that these units are operated and maintained properly for the thirty years post-closure period, a Post-Closure Plan must be submitted for approval, which should include a description of groundwater monitoring activities, maintenance activities, contact information for the facility manager, proposed maintenance timeframes for the cover, cap stability, gas system, and leachate collection system.[144]

Financial Assurance

The RCRA closure and post-closure financial assurance requirements are designed to protect human health and the environment from long-term threats of releases of hazardous waste and the permanent disposal of hazardous wastes by requiring owners and operators to demonstrate that sufficient resources are available to fund proper closure of the facility and to satisfy post-closure care requirements, which can be very costly.[145] Typically, the most costly closure and post-closure requirements pertain to RCRA landfills and surface impoundments.

After a TSDF owner and operator prepare the required Closure and Post-Closure Plans for its facility, they must prepare a cost estimate that reflects how much it would cost to close the facility, and an estimate of the annual cost of post-closure monitoring and maintenance.[146] These estimates provide the base figure for the amount of financial assurance required for a facility.[147] The cost estimate must reflect the cost of conducting all activities outlined in the Closure and Post-Closure Plans. The post-closure cost estimates are based on projected costs for an entire post-closure period, typically thirty years.[148] An owner and operator may demonstrate financial assurance through various mechanisms, including a trust fund, surety bond, letter of credit, insurance, financial tests, or a corporate guarantee.[149]

LAND DISPOSAL RESTRICTIONS

The permanent disposal of hazardous waste in land-based units, such as landfills and surface impoundments, has the potential to threaten human health and the environment through groundwater contamination.[150] As a result, the RCRA program contains extensive technical requirements to ensure that land-based units prevent hazardous leachate from entering the environment.[151] To complement the unit-specific design and operating standards, which alone do not fully protect human health and the environment from the potential risks of land-based hazardous waste management, RCRA also implements the land disposal restrictions (LDR) Program.[152] These regulations identify hazardous wastes that are restricted from land disposal and define those limited circumstances under which an otherwise prohibited waste may continue to be land disposed.[153] The LDR program consists of three restrictions, which will be discussed in detail below: (1) the disposal prohibition, (2) the dilution prohibition, and (3) the storage prohibition.

The LDR Program approaches groundwater protection differently from unit-specific technical standards. Rather than establishing physical design and operation standards, the program instead requires that hazardous wastes undergo treatment and establishes treatment standards so that the wastes pose less of a threat to the groundwater, surface water, and air when disposed.[154] The obvious advantage of such hazardous waste treatment is that it provides a longer lasting form of protection than containment, which may breakdown or fail over time.[155]

While the LDR Program generally applies to all material that meets the RCRA definition of hazardous waste, there are exclusions from the LDR requirements.[156] The following hazardous wastes are not subject to the LDR Program:

1. Waste generated by very SQGs;
2. Waste pesticides and container residues disposed of by farmers on their own land;
3. Newly identified or newly listed hazardous waste for which EPA has yet to promulgate treatment standards (discussed below); and
4. Certain waste releases that are mixed with a facility's wastewater and discharge pursuant to the Clean Water Act.[157]

For all other wastes identified as hazardous (whether listed, characteristic, or both), the waste is assigned a waste code.[158]

If EPA has established a treatment standard for that waste code, the waste becomes subject to the LDR treatment requirements. Otherwise, newly identified or newly listed wastes can continue to be disposed of without treatment.[159] The LDR requirements apply to hazardous waste at its point of generation and require that it must be treated in accordance with LDR requirements before being disposed of.[160] For purposes of the LDR Program, a generator of a listed hazardous waste must determine if a waste also exhibits any hazardous waste characteristics.[161] If it does, the waste must be treated to meet both the listed and the characteristic treatment standards before land disposal.[162]

LDR Prohibitions

The primary prohibition of the LDR Program is the disposal prohibition, which prohibits the land disposal of hazardous waste that has not been adequately treated. The disposal prohibition incorporates treatment standards, variances, alternative treatment standard, and notification requirements.[163] The criteria that hazardous waste must meet before being disposed of are known as treatment standards.[164] These treatment standards can be either concentration levels for hazardous constituents that the waste must meet all treatment technologies that must be performed on the waste before it can be land disposed.[165] Concentration-based treatment standards appear in the table located at 40 C.F.R. § 268.40 as numerical values.

Both listed and characteristic hazardous waste must meet the LDR treatment standards before they are eligible for land disposal.[166] The treatment standards for most characteristics hazardous wastes entail rendering the waste nonhazardous, which means decharacterizing the waste or removing the characteristic. However, some wastes have underlying hazardous constituents, which do not cause the waste to exhibit a hazardous characteristic but can still pose a hazard. The underlying hazardous constituents must be treated to meet contaminant-specific levels, which are referred to as the Universal Treatment Standards (UTS) and are listed in a table in the RCRA regulations at 40 C.F.R. § 268.48. Once the characteristic hazardous wastes have been decharacterized and treated for underlying constituents, they can be disposed of in a nonhazardous waste landfill.[167]

The second component of the LDR Program is the dilution prohibition.[168] When a waste treatment standard is expressed as a numeric concentration level, it is often easier and less expensive to dilute the waste in soil in order to reduce the concentration of the hazardous constituents.[169] However, this type of activity does not reduce the overall toxic load that would be released into the environment and is inconsistent with the goals of the LDR Program. This is why EPA has established the dilution prohibition to avoid and circumvent the proper treatment necessary to reduce the contaminant levels and hazardous waste.[170]

The third component of the LDR Program is the storage prohibition, which bans the indefinite storage of untreated hazardous waste for reasons other than accumulation necessary for effective treatment or disposal.[171] If waste storage exceeds one year, the facility has the burden of proving that such storage is being maintained in order to accumulate quantities necessary for effective treatment or disposal.[172]

CORRECTIVE ACTION

The operations at RCRA facilities over the years have resulted in discharges of hazardous waste and hazardous constituents into soil, groundwater, surface water, sediments and air.[173] RCRA mandates that owners and operators that have identified a release must investigate and cleanup or remediate these hazardous wastes at their facilities.[174] This program has been criticized by both stakeholders (i.e., owners and operators) and environmental groups for various reasons, such as being unworkable, too expensive, and too slow in cleaning up contaminated sites. The Corrective Action Program is a unique part of RCRA, as it is mostly implemented by EPA through guidance rather than comprehensive regulations.[175]

The Corrective Action Program was established under the authority of the Hazardous and Solid Waste Amendments of 1984 (HSWA).[176] Prior to the HSWA, EPA's statutory authority to require cleanup of hazardous releases was limited to situations where the contamination presented an "imminent and substantial endangerment to

health or the environment."[177] Regulatory authority was limited to releases identified during groundwater monitoring at RCRA-regulated land-based hazardous waste
units, such as landfills or surface impoundments.[178] RCRA Section 3013 authorized
the EPA to issue orders requiring testing and analysis of certain releases of hazardous wastes, and Section 7003 authorized EPA to either issue administrative orders or
seek court orders to abate imminent and substantial dangers posed by hazardous or
solid waste.[179] The EPA developed guidance and policy documents to assist facilities
conducting cleanups, including a set of targeted administrative reforms known as
the RCRA Cleanup Reforms, which represent a comprehensive effort to address key
impediments to cleanups, maximize program flexibility, and spur progress toward
a set of national cleanup goals.[180] Despite these provisions, RCRA was essentially
a prospective statute, addressing current waste management practices, until HSWA
added key corrective action provisions providing authority for corrective actions as
a consequence of both current and past waste handling activities at permitted facilities.[181] EPA commonly implements corrective action requirements by incorporating
corrective action during the facility permitting process or issuing administrative
orders.[182]

   Under current EPA policy, much of the focus of the RCRA Corrective Action
Program is on achieving environmental indicators—measures which indicate current
environmental conditions, including whether people are being exposed to environmental contamination at unacceptable levels and whether any existing plumes of
contaminated groundwater are getting larger or adversely affecting surface water
bodies.[183] In 2009, EPA established the 2020 RCRA Corrective Action Baseline, consisting of a list of over 3,700 facilities expected to require corrective action to satisfy
the environmental indicators.[184] If a facility is undergoing remediation pursuant to
RCRA and the Corrective Action Program, the facility may apply for a Remediation
in Progress Waiver under the Industrial Site Recovery Act if there is a "triggering"
event such as the cessation of the facility or the sale of the property.[185]

RCRA'S RELATIONSHIP WITH OTHER
ENVIRONMENTAL LAWS

Although RCRA interfaces with several other environmental laws such as the Clean
Water Act and the Clean Air Act, this chapter will focus on the relationship among the
RCRA, the Comprehensive Environmental Response, Compensation, and Liability
Act (CERCLA) and the Toxic Substances Control Act (TSCA).

TSCA

TSCA authorizes EPA to require reporting, recordkeeping, and testing requirements,
in addition to certain restrictions for specific chemical substances and/or mixtures.[186]
Thus, TSCA requires notification to EPA for new chemical substances prior to their
manufacture. RCRA, on the other hand, regulates the treatment and disposal of a
range of chemicals, typically addressing waste streams rather than individual chemical substances.

TSCA also has a particular focus on polychlorinated biphenyls (PCBs) and regulates the disposal of PCB materials depending on their physical form and concentration.[187] PCBs that are discarded are not generally considered RCRA hazardous wastes, although they may be regulated when they are found in other wastes that qualify as listed or characteristic wastes under RCRA. Those wastes are subject to all RCRA requirements, including manifesting. Certain PCB-containing wastes that may otherwise exhibit toxicity characteristics (e.g., dielectric fluid and associated electronic equipment) are also expressly exempt from RCRA requirements.

CERCLA

CERCLA, commonly known as Superfund, governs the cleanup of sites contaminated with hazardous substances and provides a liability scheme for persons responsible for releases of those hazardous substances.[188] Under CERCLA, hazardous substances are defined to include all RCRA hazardous waste. Thus, EPA has the authority to respond to releases of hazardous wastes and to clean up hazardous wastes at sites designated on the National Priorities List. RCRA, however, is focused on prevention, whereas CERCLA is responsive to threats to the environmental and public health, governing response actions typically at abandoned or unused hazardous waste sites. Both statutes, however, authorize cleanup actions that follow similar procedures under different nomenclature. In addition, CERCLA and RCRA enforcement authority may both apply under similar circumstances.

THE NEW JERSEY MAJOR HAZARDOUS WASTE FACILITY SITING ACT

New Jersey adopted the Major Hazardous Waste Facility Siting Act (MHWFSA) as a result of intense public criticism with regard to hazardous waste control and siting of hazardous waste facilities.[189] MHWFSA applies to a facility with a total capacity of more than 250,000 gallons generated at the facility or at locations off-site, provided the facility was constructed after September 10, 1981.[190] The act and related regulations have specifically designated certain areas in the State for new Major Hazardous Waste Facilities.[191] The regulations specifically provide that such facilities may not be within one-half mile of any structure which is routinely occupied by the same person or persons more than twelve hours per day or by the same person or persons under the age of eighteen for more than two hours per day.[192] The legislature created the New Jersey Hazardous Waste Siting Commission (Commission) to address siting Major Hazardous Waste Facilities in New Jersey. The Commission must approve all proposed new hazardous waste facilities. The NJDEP has the authority to approve the registration statement and engineering design of a proposed new major hazardous waste facility; however, it is not authorized to approve the siting of a proposed facility, as this authority remains solely with the Commission.[193]

In 1985 the Commission prepared and adopted the Major Hazardous Waste Facilities Plan (The Plan),[194] which is used in deciding where hazardous waste facilities should be sited in the State. The NJDEP has authority to approve new major hazardous

waste facilities with regard to the technical and engineering design, registration statement, engineering design, and EHIS prior to the facilities construction.[195] In addition,
the NJDEP must take into consideration several environmental aspects with regard
to citing such facilities, including avoiding flood hazard areas, wetlands, endangered
species and other natural resources of the State.[196]

LIABILITY AND ENFORCEMENT PROVISIONS

The NJSWMA provides that owners and operators are strictly, jointly, and severally
liable for cleanup and the removal of any discharges of hazardous substances and
for all damages whether direct or indirect caused by the operation or closure of the
facility.[197] As described above, owners and operators are liable for proper Closure
and Post-Closure at all facilities and must provide financial assurance to meet those
responsibilities.[198] The municipality in which a facility is located is entitled to be paid
a 5 percent gross receipt tax by owners and operators of such facilities to defray the
municipality's costs for police, fire, inspections, and other expenses related to the
facility.[199] NJSWMA's enforcement requirements are similar to RCRA's requirements to ensure that major hazardous waste facilities are in compliance with the
permits. NJSWMA also requires either the local board of health or the county health
department to conduct weekly inspections of the facility and authorizes inspections by
officials to conduct weekly inspections.[200] NJSWMA further provides NJDEP with the
authority to enforce the regulations and seek penalties for violations and provides for
criminal prosecutions related to operation and maintenance of the facility.[201]

NOTES

1. 42 U.S.C. § 6926.
2. On February 21, 1985, the State of New Jersey received final authorization under Section 3006 of RCRA to operate a hazardous waste program in lieu of the federal Hazardous Waste Program; however, New Jersey received only certain delegated authority. 50 Fed. Reg. 5260 (February 7, 1985). New Jersey incorporated the federal RCRA regulations by reference, with a few modifications.
3. N.J.S.A. 13:1E-1 et seq.
4. N.J.A.C. 7:26G-1.4(b).
5. 67 Fed. Reg. 76995, 76997 (December 16, 2002).
6. Ibid.
7. 42 U.S.C. § 6903(5).
8. U.S. Environmental Protection Agency, RCRA Orientation Manual, III-4 (2014).
9. 40 CFR Part 261, Subpart A.
10. 40 CFR § 261.2(a)(2).
11. Ibid.
12. *Id.* at § 261.2(a)(2)(i).
13. *Id.* at § 261.2(f).
14. *Id.* at § 261.2(e).
15. *Id.* at § 261.2(e).

16. *Id.* at § 261.2(e).
17. *Id.* at § 261.2(c)(3).
18. *Ibid.*
19. *Id.* at § 261.2.
20. If a radioactive waste is mixed with a hazardous waste, the resultant mixture is regulated by both AEA and RCRA as a mixed waste. RCRA ORIENTATION MANUAL, III-10.
21. Provided that only tank storage is involved, and the entire process, through reclamation, is closed to the air (i.e., enclosed). Further this exemption only applies if (1) reclamation does not involve controlled flame combustion, such as that which occurs in boilers, industrial furnaces, or incinerators; (2) waste materials are never accumulated in tanks for more than twelve months without being reclaimed; and (3) reclaimed materials are not used to produce a fuel, or used to produce products that are used in a manner constituting disposal. RCRA ORIENTATION MANUAL, III-10.
22. 40 C.F.R. § 261.4(a)(1) through (a)(27).
23. *Id.* at § 261.4(a)(1)(ii).
24. *Id.* at § 261.4(a)(2).
25. *American Petroleum Institute v. USEPA,* 862 F.3d 50 (D.C. Cir. 2017); *American Petroleum Institute v. USEPA,* 883 F.3d 918 (D.C. Cir. 2018).
26. 88 F.R. 24,664 (May 30, 2018)
27. The other three factors are whether the hazardous secondary material provides a useful contribution to the recycling process, whether the recycling process produces a valuable product or intermediate, and whether the persons controlling the secondary material manages it as a valuable commodity. 40 C.F.R. § 260.43.
28. 40 C.F.R. 261.4(b).
29. *Id.* at § 261.4(c).
30. *Id.* at § 261.21.
31. *Id.* at § 261.22.
32. *Id.* at § 261.23.
33. *Id.* at § 261.24.
34. 40 C.F.R. § 261.3(a)(2)(iv).
35. *Id.* at § 261.3(c)(2)(i).
36. 66 F.R. 27,266 (May 16, 2001). These rules have been the subject of significant litigation and enforcement actions, and there are numerous agency letters addressing the same on EPA's website.
37. 53 F.R. 17,578 (May 17, 1988).
38. 40 C.F.R. § 261.3(f).
39. 40 C.F.R. § 260.10.
40. *Id.* at § 262.13.
41. *Ibid.*
42. 81 F.R. 85808 (November 28, 2016).
43. *Ibid.*
44. *Ibid.*
45. *Ibid.*
46. *Ibid.*
47. 70 Fed. Reg. 10776 (March 4, 2005).
48. *Ibid.*
49. 40 C.F.R. § 260.10.
50. *Id.* at § 263.20(a)(1).
51. 40 CFR Parts 264 and 265.

52. 42 U.S.C. § 6925.
53. 40 C.F.R. § 265.11-16.
54. *Id.* at § 265.17-18.
55. *Id.* at § 264.70-77.
56. *Id.* at § 265.90-91.
57. *Id.* at § 264.100.
58. RCRA ORIENTATION MANUAL III-54.
59. *Ibid.*
60. *Ibid.*
61. 40 C.F.R. § 264.110-120.
62. *Id.* at § 264.112.
63. *Id.* at § 264.110(b).
64. *Id.* at § 264.117, 265.117.
65. *Id.* at §§ 264, 265, Subpart H.
66. 40 C.F.R. Part 265.
67. 42 U.S.C. § 6925.
68. 40 C.F.R. § 270.4.
69. 40 C.F.R. Part 265.
70. *Ibid.* While the standards for permitted facilities are often similar to those for interim status facilities, there are circumstances where the standards for new facilities would be impractical for existing facilities to implement immediately.
71. RCRA ORIENTATION MANUAL, III-54.
72. 40 C.F.R. § 270.4.
73. 40 C.F.R. § 270.4(a)(1).
74. *Id.* at § 270.30(h)(10).
75. *Id.* at § 270.1(c)(2)(3).
76. *Id.* at §270.60.
77. 40 C.F.R. § 270.1(c)(2)(i).
78. *Id.* at § 270.1(c)(2)(ii).
79. *Id.* at § 270.1(c)(2)(iii).
80. *Id.* at § 270.1(c)(2)(iv).
81. *Id.* at § 270.1(c)(2)(v).
82. *Id.* at § 270.1(c)(2)(vi).
83. *Id.* at § 270.1(c)(2)(vii).
84. *Id.* at § 270.1(c)(2)(viii).
85. *Id.* at § 270.1(c)(3).
86. 40 C.F.R. § 264.1.
87. *Ibid.*
88. *Id.* at § 264.11.
89. *Id.* at § 264.13(a)(1).
90. RCRA ORIENTATION MANUAL, III-57.
91. *Id.* at 57-58.
92. 40 C.F.R. § 264.13(b).
93. *Id.* at § 264.17.
94. *Id.* at § 264.14(c).
95. *Ibid.*
96. N.J.S.A. 13:1E-42.1.
97. *Ibid.*
98. N.J.S.A. 13:1E-42.2.

99. N.J.S.A. 13:1E-64.

100. N.J.S.A. 13:1E-9(a); N.J.S.A. 13:1E-65.

101. *Id.* at § 264.18(a).

102. *Id.* at § 264.31.

103. *Id.* at §§ 264.51(b), 264.52.

104. *Id.* at § 264.55.

105. *Id.* at §§ 262.12, 262.30-44.

106. *Id.* at § 262.20(a), 262.23(b).

107. *Id.* at § 262.20(c).

108. RCRA ORIENTATION MANUAL.

109. *Id.* at III-61.

110. *Ibid.*

111. 40 C.F.R. § 264.171

112. 40 C.F.R. Part 264.

113. *Id.* at § 264.192.

114. *Id.* at §§ 264.192, 193.

115. *Id.* at § 264.195.

116. *Id.* at § 264.193.

117. RCRA ORIENTATION MANUAL, III-67.

118. 40 C.F.R. § 264.221(c).

119. *Id.* at § 264.221(g).

120. *Id.* at § 264.226.

121. *Id.* at § 264.251.

122. RCRA ORIENTATION MANUAL, III-63.

123. 40 C.F.R. § 264.272.

124. RCRA ORIENTATION MANUAL, III-63.

125. *Ibid.* To prevent wind dispersal, owners and operators of Land Treatment Units must apply a wind dispersal control, such as a cover, to the unit.

126. RCRA ORIENTATION MANUAL, III-64.

127. *Id.* at III-64.

128. 40 C.F.R. § 264.301(c).

129. 40 C.F.R. § 264.301(g) and (h).

130. *Id.* at § 264.304.

131. *Ibid.*

132. RCRA ORIENTATION MANUAL, III-74.

133. See 40 C.F.R. § 264.310.

134. RCRA ORIENTATION MANUAL, III-74; 40 C.F.R. § 264.112(a).

135. 40 C.F.R. § 264.112(a).

136. 40 C.F.R. § 265.112(a).

137. RCRA ORIENTATION MANUAL, III-74.

138. 40 C.F.R. § 264.113.

139. 40 C.F.R. § 264.110.

140. RCRA ORIENTATION MANUAL, III-76.

141. *Ibid.*

142. 40 C.F.R. § 264.111.

143. RCRA ORIENTATION MANUAL, III-76.

144. 40 C.F.R. § 164.118.

145. RCRA ORIENTATION MANUAL, III-77.

146. 40 C.F.R. § 264.142,

147. *Id.* at §§ 264.142, 264.144.
148. *Id.* at § 264.144.
149. *Id.* at §§ 264.143, 264.145.
150. RCRA ORIENTATION MANUAL, III-87.
151. *Ibid.*
152. *Ibid.* See 40 C.F.R. Part 268.
153. 40 C.F.R. § 268.1(a).
154. RCRA ORIENTATION MANUAL, III-87.
155. *Ibid.*
156. *Ibid.*
157. 40 C.F.R. § 268.1(e).
158. RCRA ORIENTATION MANUAL, III-88.
159. *Ibid.*
160. *Ibid.*
161. *Ibid.*
162. *Ibid.*
163. 40 C.F.R. Part 268.
164. See 40 C.F.R. Part 268, Subpart D.
165. See *Ibid.*
166. *Id.* at § 268.9.
167. RCRA ORIENTATION MANUAL, III-89.
168. See 40 C.F.R. § 268.3.
169. RCRA ORIENTATION MANUAL, III-932011.
170. *Ibid.*
171. 40 C.F.R. § 268.50.
172. *Ibid.*
173. RCRA ORIENTATION MANUAL, III-119.
174. *Id.*
175. *Id.*
176. P.L. 98-616, November 7, 1984, 98 Stat 3221.
177. *Ibid;* see also, RCRA ORIENTATION MANUAL, III-119 .
178. RCRA ORIENTATION MANUAL, III-119.
179. *Ibid.*
180. *Id.* at III-120.
181. 42 U.S.C. § 6924 (u).
182. RCRA ORIENTATION MANUAL, III-120.
183. See *Id.* at III-122.
184. *Ibid.*
185. N.J.A.C. 7:76B-5.4(c)3.
186. See 15 U.S.C. § 2601 et seq.
187. 40 C.F.R. Part 761.
188. See 42 U.S.C. § 9601 et seq.
189. N.J.S.A. 13:1E-49 et seq.
190. N.J.S.A. 13:1E-51(1); N.J.A.C. 7:26G-14.6.
191. N.J.S.A. 13:1E-57; N.J.A.C. 7:26G-14.7(a).
192. N.J.A.C. 7:26G-14.7(a).
193. N.J.S.A. 13:1E-60; N.J.A.C. 7:26G-13.2(a).
194. N.J.S.A. 13:1E-58.
195. N.J.S.A. 13:1E-60(a), (b).

196. N.J.A.C. 7:26G-14.
197. N.J.S.A. 13:1E-62.
198. N.J.S.A. 13:1E-68.
199. N.J.S.A. 13:1E-80.
200. N.J.S.A. 13:1E-64, 65.
201. N.J.S.A. 13:1E-66, 67.

Chapter 11

Health and Safety, Prevention, and Right-to-Know Reporting

David A. Roth, Esq.

Multiple federal and state laws have been enacted to protect workers, public health, safety, and the environment. Common threads run through effective environmental, health, and safety (EHS) programs: the full support and participation of senior management; a knowledgeable and experienced EHS team; careful recordkeeping and reporting; and continual employee education and training. The program must be afforded top organizational priority status and be adequately funded, even when economic conditions are less than optimal. Compliance with legal requirements and company policies must be tracked, documented, and enforced.[1] Performance and compensation reviews should have an EHS component.

No program or facility is perfect. As issues arise, they must be promptly addressed by senior officials. EHS matters are often multifaceted, implicating various financial, legal, public relations, and other interests. The company's options should be carefully evaluated with the assistance of in-house professionals, consultants, experts, and legal counsel. Consideration should be given to any potentially applicable governmental notification requirements. Prompt and candid reporting of incidents and appropriate corrective actions will aid in establishing and maintaining beneficial relationships with employees and governmental authorities, and should reduce claims and pave the way for reduction or avoidance of penalties or the forbearance of enforcement actions.

The U.S. Environmental Protection Agency's (EPA) self-disclosure policies[2] provide penalty mitigation and other incentives for companies that self-police, disclose, correct, and prevent violations.[3] To receive the full benefit of the policies the organization asserting the policies must have an appropriate environmental management system. On December 9, 2015, the EPA announced the launch of an "eDisclosure" portal to modernize the implementation of EPA's self-policing incentive policies.[4] eDisclosure uses EPA's Central Data Exchange (CDX) to allow entities to promptly disclose violations and submit timely compliance certifications under EPA's Audit Policy[5] and Small Business Compliance Policy.[6]

On May 15, 2018, EPA announced a renewed emphasis on encouraging regulated entities to voluntarily discover, promptly disclose, expeditiously correct, and take steps to prevent recurrence of environmental violations. The agency outlined steps to enhance and promote (1) its online "eDisclosure" program, (2) additional flexibility for new owners who self-disclose violations, and (3) increased compliance through the use of existing self-disclosure policies or tailored audit programs.[7]

The EPA is in the process of developing a New Owner Clean Air Act Audit Program for the oil and natural gas sector. This program will provide environmentally protective efficiencies and certainty in the oil and natural gas sector based on the agency's analysis of the sector's unique operations. EPA views the program as an opportunity for timely and cost-effective Clean Air Act compliance.[8]

HEALTH AND SAFETY

Federal Occupational Safety and Health Act

The Occupational Safety and Health Act of 1970 (OSH Act)[9] mandates that employers provide their workers with a safe and healthful workplace and protection from hazardous conditions.[10] "Employer" is broadly defined as "a person engaged in a business affecting commerce who has employees."[11] The OSH Act covers most private sector employers and workers in all fifty states, the District of Columbia, and other U.S. jurisdictions either directly through the statute or through a state plan approved by the Occupational Safety and Health Administration (OSHA).[12] Workers at state and local government agencies are not directly covered by the OSH Act, but have protections afforded by the statute if they work in a state that has an OSHA-approved state program.[13] The OSH Act's protection applies to all federal agencies.[14] The self-employed, immediate family members of farm employers, and workplace hazards regulated by another federal agency (e.g., the Mine Safety and Health Administration, the Department of Energy, or the Coast Guard) are not covered under the OSH Act.[15]

The OSH Act authorizes the OSHA to promulgate worker health and safety standards.[16] "Occupational safety and health standard" is defined as "a standard which requires conditions, or the adoption or use of one or more practices, means, methods, operations, or processes, reasonably necessary or appropriate to provide safe or healthful employment and places of employment."[17] The OSHA's regulations include standards for General Industry,[18] Construction,[19] Maritime,[20] Agriculture,[21] and Recordkeeping.[22] The OSHA's General Industry standard regulates, among other things, electrical hazards,[23] fire protection,[24] personal protective equipment,[25] machinery and equipment hazards,[26] walking-working surfaces,[27] certain hazardous materials,[28] and certain toxic and hazardous substances (e.g., asbestos, lead, formaldehyde, ionizing radiation, and benzene).[29] Some General Industry standards apply to "special industries" (e.g., paper mills, textiles, telecommunications, and electric power).[30]

Employers must comply with the OSHA's regulatory standards as well as the OSH Act's "general duty clause."[31] The general duty clause provides that each employer must furnish each of its employees with employment and a place of employment free from "recognized hazards" that are causing or are likely to cause death or serious physical harm to the employees.[32]

Recently, the OSHA revised the requirements for the recording and reporting of occupational injuries and illnesses. On May 12, 2016, the OSHA published a final rule that requires employers in certain industries to electronically submit to the

OSHA injury and illness data that employers are required to keep under OSHA's regulations.[33] At the time it published the rule, the OSHA announced its intention to post the data from these submissions on a publicly accessible website.[34] The rule also amended requirements for how employers must inform employees to report work-related injuries and illnesses to their employer, requires employers to inform employees of their right to report work-related injuries and illnesses free from retaliation, confirmed that an employer's procedure for reporting work-related injuries and illnesses must be reasonable and not deter or discourage employees from reporting, and clarified the rights of employees and their representatives to access their injury and illness records.[35]

On January 25, 2019, the OSHA published a final rule to amend the recordkeeping regulation to remove the requirement to electronically submit to the OSHA information from OSHA Form 300 (Log of Work-Related Injuries and Illnesses) and OSHA Form 301 (Injury and Illness Incident Report) for establishments with 250 or more employees that are required to routinely keep injury and illness records.[36] The amendment is intended to better protect personally identifiable information or data that could be re-identified with a particular worker. Now, covered establishments need only electronically submit information from OSHA Form 300A (Summary of Work-Related Injuries and Illnesses). The amendments also require covered employers to electronically submit their Employer Identification Number with their information from Form 300A.[37] The final rule does not alter an employer's duty to keep and maintain OSHA Forms 300, 300A, and 301 for five years, and maintain OSHA Forms 300 and 301 on-site. The OSHA will continue to obtain these forms as needed through inspections and enforcement actions.

New Jersey

State and local government workers are not protected by the OSH Act's standards because the federal law's definition of "employer" excludes a "state or political subdivisions of a State."[38] Twenty-five states, including New Jersey, as well as Puerto Rico and the Virgin Islands operate "state programs" that have been approved by the OSHA.[39] The OSHA's approval of a state program is conditioned on the state's standards and enforcement of the standards being at least as effective in providing safe and healthful workplaces as the federal OSHA standards.[40]

New Jersey's program was established under the New Jersey Public Employees' Occupational Safety and Health Act (PEOSH Act).[41] The program only applies to New Jersey's state and municipal government employees and is administered by two departments.[42] The New Jersey Department of Labor and Workforce Development (NJDLWD) adopts applicable occupational health and safety standards, amendments or changes adopted or recognized by the federal OSHA, and investigates complaints regarding safety hazards in the workplace.[43] The New Jersey Department of Health (NJDOH) investigates complaints regarding health hazards in the workplaces of public employers and enforces the New Jersey Indoor Air Quality Standard.[44]

Private sector workers in New Jersey are covered by the federal OSH Act's standards and regulations. They are also covered by the New Jersey Worker Health and Safety Act (WHSA).[45] Given the comprehensive scope of OSHA's standards and jurisdiction, the WHSA has limited practical significance concerning health and safety standards or enforcement.

The NJDLWD, Division of Public Safety and Occupational Safety and Health, provides a free On-Site Consultation Service.[46] The service allows private employers to find out about potential hazards at their worksites, improve their occupational safety and health management systems, and arrange safety and health training.[47] The service is primarily targeted for smaller businesses (less than 250 employees) and, under the Small Business Focus (SBF) initiative, companies with fifty or fewer employees receive special priority in scheduling consultations.[48] The consultation program is completely separate from the OSHA inspection effort. In addition, no citations or penalties are issued or proposed.[49]

Employee participation is required in all site visits conducted by the consultation service.[50] At unionized sites, an employee representative must be afforded the opportunity to participate in the opening and closing conferences and to be present during the walkthrough.[51] Following the closing conference, the service provides the employer with a written report that contains their findings and confirms the abatement periods agreed upon with the employer. The employer must agree to post a "List of Hazards" identified by the service in a prominent place for three working days or until the hazards are corrected, whichever is later. If an employer fails to abate identified serious hazards or imminent danger in accordance with the agreed upon plan, the consultation service must refer the matter to a federal OSHA enforcement office.[52]

Enforcement

OSHA has the authority, upon presenting appropriate credentials, to enter a workplace without delay to inspect and investigate all pertinent conditions, structures, machines, apparatus, devices, equipment, and materials at the facility and to privately question any employer, owner, operator, agent, or employee.[53] A representative of the employer and a representative authorized by the employees must be provided with the opportunity to accompany the inspector to aid the inspection.[54] Providing advance notice of an inspection that is pending pursuant to the OSH Act is prohibited, except in limited situations.[55]

In most cases consent to an OSHA inspection is advisable. However, employers have the right, under the Fourth Amendment to the U.S. Constitution, to refuse an inspector entry to the workplace without a proper administrative inspection warrant.[56] Refusal of entry until a warrant is obtained may not be used to support probable cause for the warrant or to establish that a violation existed.[57] Probable cause for the issuance of an administrative inspection warrant may be established based upon specific evidence that supports a reasonable suspicion of an existing violation of the law,[58] including a general duty clause violation.[59] Probable cause also may be established by showing that neutral and reasonable legislative and administrative standards for conducting an inspection have been satisfied.[60] Examples of the latter justification include demonstrating that a specific business has been chosen for a safety inspection based on a general administrative plan for enforcement derived from neutral sources[61] or random selection based on a neural inspection plan.[62]

An employer may limit its consent to an inspection to specific plant areas or operations and may revoke its consent at any time during the inspection and require the inspector to obtain a warrant.[63] Warrants must contain enough specific information to apprise the employer of the nature and scope of the investigation and the basis for probable cause.[64] Overly broad warrants may render them defective.[65] A warrant limited to specific operations and areas in "plain view" where violations are observed may not be defective as overly broad.[66] The scope of an inspection conducted pursuant to a warrant must be reasonably related to the probable cause basis for issuing the warrant.[67]

OSHA is authorized to issue citations for alleged violations of any standard, rule, or order issued under the OSH Act,[68] as well as "general duty clause" violations for the alleged failure to eliminate "recognized hazards" in the workplace that are likely to cause death or serious physical injury to the employees.[69] A "recognized hazard" is a condition that is known to be hazardous to the industry in general, not necessarily by the specific employer, taking into account the standard of knowledge in the industry.[70] OSHA violations are classified as Other-than-serious, Serious, Willful, Repeat, and Failure-to-abate.[71] The penalty classification is a factor in determining the penalty amount.[72]

On June 18, 2010, OSHA instituted the Severe Violator Enforcement Program (SVEP) to more effectively focus enforcement efforts on recalcitrant employers who demonstrate indifference to the health and safety of their employees through willful, repeated, or failure-to-abate violations of the OSH Act.[73] The program replaced the Enhanced Enforcement Program (EEP), an earlier program that the Office of the Inspector General (OIG) found to be an inefficient and ineffective means of identifying and addressing the most severe violators.[74] According to the OSHA, the SVEP met key goals, including significant increases in follow-up inspections and enhanced settlement, and succeeded in guiding the OSHA enforcement efforts toward recalcitrant employers and high-emphasis hazards.[75] On August 16, 2012, OSHA issued a memorandum detailing criteria for being removed from SVEP.[76]

When OSHA issues a citation and notification of penalty to an employer, it usually offers the employer an opportunity for an informal conference with the OSHA Area Director to discuss the citations, the proposed penalties, abatement dates and any other information pertinent to the inspection. The citation may contain an informal settlement offer granting a reduction in penalties, usually 25 percent, if the OSHA's form of the informal settlement agreement is promptly returned with any required abatement plan. During settlement discussions, employers should explore, among other things, elimination or downgrading/reclassification of violations as a means of reducing penalties. If a settlement is reached, the agreement should contain exculpatory language and indicate that the OSHA proceedings may not be used for any purpose in any non-OSHA proceedings. The violations listed in the settlement will nevertheless be part of the employer's OSHA compliance record and may be considered in future enforcement actions, including for classification of the violation and the penalty amount.

If the matter is not settled the employer has the right to contest the violations and penalty assessment in a hearing before the Occupational Safety & Health Review Commission and, thereafter, seek judicial review.[77]

Worker Claims

The federal OSH Act does not create a private right of action on behalf of injured workers.[78] Furthermore, in exchange for granting employees automatic entitlement benefits, the New Jersey Worker's Compensation Act bars common law claims for work-related injuries or death, except for "intentional wrong."[79] The burden of proving the exception for intentional wrong is "formidable."[80] The exception is interpreted very narrowly "so that as many work-related disability claims as possible [can] be processed exclusively within the worker's compensation system."[81]

PREVENTION AND RIGHT-TO-KNOW REPORTING

Toxic Catastrophe Prevention Act

The goal of the New Jersey Toxic Catastrophe Prevention Act (TCPA),[82] which became effective in 1986, is to protect the public from catastrophic accidental releases of extraordinarily hazardous substances into the environment. The TCPA requires owners or operators of facilities that handle extraordinarily hazardous substances at certain threshold quantities to anticipate the circumstances that could result in accidental extraordinarily hazardous substances releases and to take precautionary or preemptive actions to prevent such releases. The impetus for the TCPA was the December 1984 accidental release of methyl isocyanate at a plant in Bhopal, India, that resulted in the deaths of 2,500 people.

The New Jersey Department of Environmental Protection's (NJDEP) TCPA program rules[83] incorporate by reference, with some amendments, the provisions of the U.S. EPA Accidental Release Prevention/Risk Management Plan (RMP) rules[84] that were developed under Section 112(r) of the Clean Air Act Amendments of 1990. These rules require facilities that use extraordinarily hazardous substances to develop an RMP which identifies the potential effects of a chemical accident and identifies steps the facility is taking to prevent an accident and spells out emergency response procedures should an accident occur.[85] RMPs provide valuable information to local fire, police, and emergency response personnel that assists them in preparing for and responding to chemical emergencies in their community.

Covered facilities in New Jersey must be cognizant of any differences in reporting requirements under the state and federal programs, particularly any reporting thresholds that may be lower than those under the federal rules.

Incorporating the federal RMP rules into the state rules enabled the NJDEP to obtain federal authorization to implement the TCPA program in New Jersey in 2001 in lieu of the federal program. The NJDEP program reviews RMPs; reviews inherently safer technology reports; audits risk management programs; inspects regulated facilities; and administers enforcement actions.[86] The state TCPA rules automatically incorporate future amendments to the federal RMP rules into the state TCPA rules unless the federal rules conflict with, and are less stringent than, the state rules. The state TCPA rules were readopted with technical changes on February 1, 2016,[87] with a new expiration date of January 8, 2023.

As of February 1, 2016, the NJDEP changed its reporting method for RMP submissions under the TCPA program. The new web-based reporting format "eNJRMP" can be accessed from an NJDEP online portal at www.njdeponline.com. The new eNJRMP system replaced the previous RMP*Submit 2004 which was outdated and required submission of a disc containing the RMP data.

On December 3, 2018, EPA published a final rule that incorporated the federal 2017 RMP Amendments into the code of federal regulations: Final Rule: Accidental Release Prevention Requirements: Risk Management Programs Under the Clean Air Act.[88] The effective date of the amendments was delayed due to challenges in federal court.[89] The NJDEP issued a table intended to assist regulated TCPA facilities in understanding how they are impacted by the 2017 amendments to EPA's RMP Rule.[90] The table includes the effective dates of the federal RMP rule amendments; lists the amendments that are incorporated into the state TCPA program; and notes the actions required by TCPA registrants, and the time frame to complete those actions.

Pollution Prevention Act

The New Jersey Pollution Prevention Act (PPA)[91] was enacted in August 1991. The central goal of the PPA is to identify and implement procedures for the reduction in use and the generation of hazardous substances at covered industrial facilities (P2 Planning).[92] The P2 Planning process involves the collection of data and the development of goals at the "facility level" and the "process level."[93]

"Facility-level" information requirements may be satisfied with the state's Release and Pollution Prevention Reports (RPPRs) if they are included or referenced in the facility plan annually.[94] Facility-level information is intended to determine the facility's mass balance of chemical "inputs" versus "outputs."[95] Information is collected on chemical throughput data (materials accounting) and "Non-product Output"—environmental release, on-site management, and off-site transfer data.[96]

"Process-level" information is gathered to assist in evaluating a facility's pollution prevention techniques and progress during a given year. Pollution prevention data and pollution prevention progress data are collected.[97] According to NJDEP's Office of Pollution Prevention and Community Right-to-Know, "pollution prevention" means techniques such as input substitution, product reformulation, production process modification, in-process recycling and improved operations; it does not include treatment systems, control systems, using one hazardous substance in place of another or shifting risks from one media to another.[98]

Any "employer"[99] or any "priority industrial facility"[100] that must file a Toxic Release Inventory (TRI) Form R or a form for any chemical substance pursuant to Section 113 of the federal Emergency Planning and Community Right-to-Know Act (EPCRA)[101] must comply with P2 Planning requirements.[102] Generally, these are facilities in specific industrial sectors, determined by North American Industry Classification System (NAICS) code, with ten or more full-time employees that exceed an activity threshold (manufacturing, processing, or otherwise) of 25,000 pounds or 10,000 pounds of a listed chemical per year.[103]

The EPCRA Section 313 chemical list contains over 600 chemicals and chemical categories.[104] Essentially the same chemicals that are subject to EPCRA Section 313 reporting are subject to P2 Planning.[105] The list of chemicals subject to reporting can change and should be checked every year. A change to the federal toxic chemical list invokes an identical change to the state RPPR and P2 planning list of substances and compound categories.

Importantly, reporting requirements established by the PPA have set a reporting threshold of 10,000 pounds for every listed substance manufactured, processed, or otherwise used (unless the substance is a Persistent, Bioaccumulative and Toxic (PBT) with a lower threshold).[106] Therefore, a facility must consider listed substances that are manufactured or processed below the federal TRI threshold of 25,000 pounds, yet at or above the New Jersey threshold of 10,000 pounds.[107]

Reports/documents required for P2 Planning include a Pollution Prevention Plan, a Pollution Prevention Plan Summary, and Pollution Prevention Plan Progress Reports.[108] Facilities are required to develop Pollution Prevention Plans to identify pollution prevention opportunities and maintain them at the facility. Pollution Prevention Plan Summaries and Progress Reports must be periodically updated and submitted to the NJDEP.[109]

Worker and Community Right-to-Know Act Reporting

The New Jersey Worker and Community Right-to-Know Act[110] and the federal Emergency Planning and Community Right-to-Know Act (EPCRA)[111] have similar reporting requirements. New Jersey's reporting documents are the Community Right-to-Know (CRTK) Survey and the Release and Pollution Prevention Report (RPPR).

CRTK Survey. The CRTK Survey is an annual inventory of hazardous substances that are produced, stored, or used at a place where business is conducted at a facility in the State of New Jersey.[112] The information collected is available to the public and to emergency responders such as police and fire departments.[113] It is used to supplement other regulatory programs within the state, provide important information to residents about hazardous substances in their community, and to facilitate proper planning for a response to an emergency at a facility, which may threaten the surrounding community or environment.[114]

The CRTK Survey must be filed by New Jersey employers with businesses covered by a North American Industry Classification System (NAICS) code listed in the New Jersey Worker and Community Right-to-Know regulations.[115] A list of NAICS codes is available on the NJDEP Office of Pollution Prevention and Right-to-Know P2RTK website.[116] The surveys must list the environmental hazardous substances[117] present at each of the employer's facilities in quantities that exceed 500 pounds unless the environmental hazardous substances is on the federal EPCRA Section 302 list of extremely hazardous substances[118] with a lower reporting threshold.[119]

New Jersey businesses whose NAICS codes do not appear in the list of covered codes may still be required to complete the survey under Section 312 of EPCRA.[120] If the facility owner/operator is required to maintain Material Safety Data Sheets (MSDSs) for hazardous substances in accordance with OSHA's Hazard Communication Standard, and quantities of these substances at the facility were at or above 10,000 pounds at any one time during the reporting year, the facility must complete the survey for these substances, unless federal exemptions apply.[121]

The completion of the CRTK Survey replaces the federal forms (Tier I or II) required by Section 312 of EPCRA.[122] The survey must be completed and submitted to the NJDEP and the required agencies each year by March 1.[123] CRTK surveys are submitted at: https://www.state.nj.us/dep/online//.

RPPR. The New Jersey reporting requirements for the RPPR are closely linked to the requirements for the federal Toxic Chemicals Release Inventory (TRI) pursuant to EPCRA Section 313.[124] An RPPR must be submitted by every "employer," as defined in the New Jersey Worker and Community Right-to-Know regulations,[125] that is, subject to the reporting requirements of Section 313 of the federal EPCRA.[126] All substances subject to reporting under the TRI, whether reported on Form R or Form A, must be reported on the RPPR.[127] A complete list of reportable substances may be found on the Office of Pollution Prevention and Right-to-Know website.[128]

The NJDEP uses the RPPR to collect data for the NJDEP Community Right-to-Know and Pollution Prevention programs on toxic chemical throughput, multimedia environmental releases, on-site waste management, and off-site transfers, collectively known as materials accounting.[129] Most of the covered facilities are also subject to Pollution Prevention Planning requirements and, therefore, required to report pollution prevention progress information on the RPPR.[130]

The completed report is due to the NJDEP by July 1 of the year following the Report Year.[131] Electronic submission of an RPPR has been mandatory since the reporting year 2004.[132] RPPR preparation and submission is accomplished on the NJDEP's electronic reporting website.[133] The annual pollution prevention progress reporting requirements for all facilities that have prepared a Pollution Prevention (P2) Plan and have submitted a P2 Plan Summary to the NJDEP are satisfied by using the Pollution Prevention Process-Level Data Worksheet (P2-115), or alternatively, the RPPR Sections C and D, as incorporated into the RPPR.[134]

NOTES

1. A number of software programs are available to assist with these functions. Many programs provide notification of new or changing legal requirements.

2. See, for example, EPA's "Incentives for Self-Policing: Discovery, Disclosure, Correction and Prevention of Violations," 65 Fed. Reg. 19618 (April 11, 2000); EPA's "Interim Approach to Applying the Audit Policy to New Owners," 73 Fed. Reg. 44991 (August 1, 2008); EPA's "Small Business Compliance Policy," 65 Fed. Reg. 19630 (April 11, 2000).

3. Id.

4. "Notice of eDisclosure Portal Launch: Modernizing Implementation of EPA's Self-Policing Incentive Policies," 80 Fed. Reg. 76476 (December 9, 2015).

5. EPA's "Incentives for Self-Policing: Discovery, Disclosure, Correction and Prevention of Violations," 65 Fed. Reg. 19618 (April 11, 2000).

6. EPA's "Small Business Compliance Policy," 65 Fed. Reg. 19630 (April 11, 2000).

7. https://www.epa.gov/sites/production/files/2018-05/documents/refreshannouncement fordisclosures.pdf.

8. https://www.epa.gov/enforcement/new-owner-clean-air-act-audit-program-oil-and-natural-gas-exploration-and-production.

9. 29 U.S.C. §§ 651 et seq.

10. 29 U.S.C. § 651.

11. 29 U.S.C. § 652(5).

12. "All About OSHA," Occupational Safety and Health Administration, U.S. Department of Labor, https://www.osha.gov/Publications/all_about_OSHA.pdf, pgs. 5-8; OSHA is part of the U.S. Department of Labor and the administrator for OSHA is the Assistant Secretary of Labor for Occupational Safety and Health, All About OSHA, supra.

13. *Id.*, pgs. 5-8.

14. *Id.*

15. *Id.*

16. 29 U.S.C. § 655.

17. 29 U.S.C. § 652(8).

18. 29 CFR Part 1910.

19. 29 CFR Part 1926.

20. 29 CFR Part 1915, Part 1917 and Part1918.

21. 29 CFR Part 1928.

22. 29 CFR Part 1904. There is a partial exemption to recordkeeping requirements for employers with ten or fewer employees. 29 CFR §1904.1.

23. 29 CFR Part 1910, Subpart S.

24. 29 CFR Part 1910, Subpart L.

25. 29 CFR Part 1910, Subpart I.

26. 29 CFR Part 1910, Subpart N (Materials Handling and Storage), Subpart O (Machinery and Machine Guarding), Subpart P (Hand and Portable Powered Tools and Other Handheld Equipment), and Subpart Q (Welding, Cutting, and Brazing).

27. 29 CFR Part 1910, Subpart D.

28. 29 CFR Part 1910, Subpart H.

29. 29 CFR Part 1910, Subpart Z.

30. 29 CFR Part 1910, Subpart R.

31. 29 U.S.C. § 654(a)(1).

32. *Id.*

33. 81 Fed. Reg. 29624 (May 12, 2016); 40 CFR 1904.41.

34. *Id.*

35. *Id.*

36. 84 Fed. Reg. 380 (January 25, 2019); 29 CFR 1904.41.

37. *Id.*

38. 29 U.S.C. § 652(5).

39. "OSHA At-A-Glance," Occupational Safety and Health Administration, U.S. Department of Labor, https://www.osha.gov/Publications/3439at-a-glance.pdf, p. 3; 29 U.S.C. § 667.

40. 29 U.S.C.A. § 667(c)(2); 29 CFR Part 1952; All About OSHA, supra.

41. N.J.S.A. §§34:6A-25 to 50; N.J.S.A. §34:6A-29.

42. N.J.S.A. §34:6A-26; N.J.S.A. §34:6A-27c and d.

43. N.J.S.A. §34:6A-30a; https://www.nj.gov/labor/lsse/employer/Public_Employees_OSH.html.

44. *Id.*; N.J.A.C. 12:100-13.

45. N.J.S.A. §§34:6A-1 to 50.

46. https://nj.gov/labor/lsse/employer/Occupational_Safety_and_Health_Onsite_Consultation_Program.html.

47. *Id.*

48. *Id.*

49. *Id.*

50. *Id.*

51. *Id.*

52. *Id.*

53. 29 U.S.C. § 657(a).

54. 29 U.S.C. § 657(e).

55. 29 CFR §1903.6(a). Any person who gives an employer advance notice of any inspection to be conducted pursuant to the Act, without OSHA's authorization, is subject to fine or imprisonment. 29 U.S.C. § 666(f).

56. See, for example, *Marshal v. Barlow's, Inc.* 436 U.S. 307 (1978), *Matter of Establishment Inspection of Kelly-Springfield Tire Co.*, 808 F.Supp. 657 (N.D. Ill. 1992), affirmed 13 F.3d 1160 (1994). *Burkart Randall Division of Textron, Inc. v. Marshall.*, 625 F.2d 1313 (7th Cir. 1980); *Matter of Establishment Inspection of Asarco, Inc.*, 508 F.Supp. 350 (N.D. Tex. 1981).

57. *Marshall v. Horn Seed Co., Inc.*, 509 F.Supp. 1 (W.D. Okla. 1979) affirmed 647 F.2d 96 (1979).

58. *Marshal v. Barlow's, Inc.*, supra.; *Matter of Establishment Inspection of Kelly-Springfield Tire Co.*, supra.

59. *Matter of Establishment Inspection of Kelly-Springfield Tire Co.*, supra.

60. *Marshal v. Barlow's, Inc.*, supra., *Matter of Establishment Inspection of Kelly-Springfield Tire Co.*, supra.; *Martin v. International Matex Tank Terminal-Bayonne*, 928 F.2d 614 (3rd Cir. 1991).

61. *National Engineering and Contracting Co. v. Occupational Safety & Health Review Comm'n,* 45 F.3d 476 (C.A.D.C. 1995).

62. *Donovan v. Trinity Industries, Inc.*, 824 F.2d 634 (8th Cir. 1987); *Donovan v. Hackney, Inc.* 769 F.2d 650 (10th Cir. 1985) cert. denied 475 U.S. 1081 (1985); *Donovan v. Enterprise Foundry, Inc.*, 751 F.2d 30 (1st Cir. 1984).

63. 29 CFR §1903.4(a).

64. *Marshall v. Pool Offshore Co.*, 467 F.Supp. 978 (W.D. La. 1979).

65. *Id.*

66. *Rockford Drop Forge Co. v. Donovan*, 672 F.2d 626 (7th Cir. 1982).

67. *Trinity Industries, Inc. v. Occupational Safety & Health Review Comm'n,* 16 F.3d 1455 (6th Cir. 1994).

68. 29 U.S.C. § 658 (a).

69. 29 U.S.C. § 654(a)(1); *Brennan v. Occupational Health and Safety Commission,* 501 F.2d 1196 (7th Cir. 1974); *U.S. v. B&L Supply Co.*, 486 F.Supp. 26 (N.D. Tex. 1980).

70. *Id.*

71. 29 U.S.C. §§ 666(a)-(e).

72. *Id.*

73. https://www.osha.gov/enforcement/directives/cpl-02-00-149.

74. Severe Violator Enforcement Program, White Paper, January 2013, https://www.osha.gov/dep/enforcement/svep_white_paper.pdf, p. 1.

75. *Id.*

76. https://www.osha.gov/dep/enforcement/memo_SVEP_removal_criteria_082012.html.

77. 29 U.S.C. §§ 658 – 661.

78. *Douglass v. United Auto Workers, Local 31*, 368 F.Supp. 2d 1234, affirmed 188 Fed. Appx, 2006 WL 1459009, cert. denied 549 U.S. 1080.

79. N.J.S.A. 34:15-8.

80. *Van Dunk v. Reckson Associates Realty Corp.*, 210 N.J. 449,451 (2012).

81. *Mabee v. Borden, Inc.*, 316 N.J. Super.218, 226-227 (App. Div. 1998) (citing *Millison v. E.I. Du Pont de Nemours & Co.*, 101 N.J. 161,177 (1985).

82. *N.J.S.A.* 13:1K-19 et seq.

83. *N.J.A.C.* 7:31.

84. 40 CFR Part 68.

85. *Id.*

86. https://www.nj.gov/dep/enforcement/tcpa.html.

87. 48 N.J.R. 206(a).

88. 83 Fed. Reg. 62268, December 3, 2018.

89. On August 17, 2018, the U.S. Court of Appeals for the District of Columbia Circuit issued a decision vacating an EPA regulation (82 FR 27133, June 14, 2017) that delayed the effective date of the final RMP Amendments rule. *Air Alliance Houston, et al., v. Environmental Protection Agency, et al.*, 96 F.3d 1049 (D.C. Cir. 2017).

90. https://www.nj.gov/dep/enforcement/tcpa/downloads/EPA_Rule_Amendments_1-13-17_crosswalk5.pdf.

91. *N.J.S.A.* 13:1D-35 et seq.

92. https://www.nj.gov/dep/enforcement/opppc/p2plan.html.

93. NJDEP May 8, 2013 Webinar "Pollution Prevention Planning Process," http://www.nj.gov/dep/opppc/rppr%20workshop%202012/2012%20P2%20Plan.pdf.

94. *Id.*

95. *Id.*

96. http://www.nj.gov/dep/opppc/rppr%20workshop%202012/RPPR%202012%20Basics%20Update.pdf, NJDEP May 8, 2013 Webinar, "RPPR Basics."

97. *Id.*

98. *Id.*

99. *N.J.A.C.* 7:1G-1.2.

100. *N.J.A.C.* 7:1K-1.5.

101. 42 U.S.C. §§ 11001 - 11050.

102. NJDEP May 9, 2013, Webinar "Pollution Prevention Planning Process," http://www.nj.gov/dep/opppc/rppr%20workshop%202012/2012%20P2%20Plan.pdf.

103. EPA TRI Program website, https://www.epa.gov/toxics-release-inventory-tri-program/basics-tri-reporting.

104. *Id.*, https://www.epa.gov/toxics-release-inventory-tri-program/tri-listed-chemicals.

105. *Id.*

106. NJDEP May 8, 2013 Webinar, "RPPR Basics," http://www.nj.gov/dep/opppc/rppr%20workshop%202012/RPPR%202012%20Basics%20Update.pdf.

107. *Id.*

108. *Id.*

109. *Id.*

110. *N.J.S.A.* 34:5A-1 et seq.

111. 42 U.S.C. §§ 11001 - 11050.

112. NJDEP Community Right-to-Know Guidance Document, https://www.nj.gov/dep/enforcement/opppc/crtk/crtkguidance.pdf.

113. *Id.*

114. *Id.*

115. *N.J.A.C.* 7:1G-1.2

116. https://www.nj.gov/dep/enforcement/opppc/crtk/rtknaics.pdf.

117. https://www.nj.gov/dep/enforcement/opppc/crtk/ehscasno.pdf.

118. https://www.epa.gov/toxics-release-inventory-tri-program/tri-listed-chemicals.

119. NJDEP Office of Pollution Prevention and Right-to-Know website, https://www.nj.gov/dep/enforcement/rtk.html.

120. NJDEP Community Right-to-Know Guidance Document, supra.

121. *Id.*

122. *Id.*

123. *Id.*

124. NJDEP Office of Pollution Prevention and Right-to-Know website, supra.

125. *N.J.A.C.* 7:1G-1.2.

126. NJDEP Release and Pollution Prevention Report, Reporting Instructions, https://www.nj.gov/dep/enforcement/opppc/forms/rpprinstruc08.pdf.

127. *Id.*

128. NJDEP Office of Pollution Prevention and Right-to-Know website, supra.

129. *Id.*

130. *Id.*

131. *Id.*

132. *Id.*

133. See NJDEP Release and Pollution Prevention Report, Reporting Instructions, supra.

134. *Id.*

Chapter 12

Wildlife Protection

Doris Lin, Esq.

With a few exceptions, wildlife in New Jersey is managed by the New Jersey Division of Fish and Wildlife (NJDFW), within the New Jersey Department of Environmental Protection (NJDEP).[1] The exceptions include those species governed by federal law, including the Endangered Species Act,[2] Marine Mammal Protection Act,[3] and the Migratory Bird Treaty Act.[4] Wildlife is managed as public trust property, for all citizens.[5] Statutes addressing a variety of wildlife issues fall under Titles 13 and 23, but the two main issues of concern to the public are hunting and endangered species.

HUNTING

Within the NJDFW, the Fish and Game Council (Council) is charged with formulating comprehensive policies for the protection and propagation of fish, birds, and game animals, subject to the approval of the Commissioner of NJDEP.[6] The Council is comprised of eleven members, appointed by the governor to four-year terms, with the advice and consent of the Senate. State law[7] requires that three members are farmers, six are sportsmen recommended by the New Jersey State Federation of Sportsmen's Clubs, one is the chair of the Endangered and Nongame Species Committee, and one is a person knowledgeable in land use management and soil conservation.[8] The law also requires geographic diversity among the farmer and sportsmen members.[9] The director of the NJDFW is appointed by the Council, subject to the approval of the governor, and is a person with special training and experience in wildlife management.[10]

In addition to formulating comprehensive policies, the Council is also charged with promulgating regulations for a system of protection, propagation, increase, control and conservation of fish, birds, game animals and fur-bearing animals, for their use and development for public recreation and food supply. The Council determines when, where, in what amounts, and by what means the animals may be taken.[11] These regulations are the State Fish and Game Code ("Game Code"), which is regularly updated and can be found at N.J.A.C. 7:25-5 et seq. The Council may adopt the Game Code only "after first having determined the need for such action on the basis of scientific investigation and research."[12]

411

Violations of fish and game laws are civil, not criminal or quasi-criminal.[13] Violators are subject to "penalties," not imprisonment or fines, and the state's burden of proof is a preponderance of the evidence.[14] Double jeopardy does not apply, so if a defendant is found not guilty of a fish or game law violation, the state may appeal.[15]

One of the most contentious wildlife issues in New Jersey has been the black bear hunt. After the species was hunted to near-extinction in the state, the Council closed the bear season in 1971. In 2000, the Council began proposing new bear hunts and has battled lawsuits with every new bear hunt proposal, leading to a string of decisions clarifying the authority and duties of the Council and the Commissioner.

After the 2003 bear hunt revealed that the bear population was actually half of what the Council had believed it to be, NJDEP Commissioner Bradley Campbell requested that the Council forgo the 2004 bear hunt. The Commissioner wrote: "The Council's defiance is due in part to the composition of the Council, which by law has only one seat designated for a person with scientific training, and in part to the absence of any check on the council's seemingly absolute authority over the game code."[16] As the scheduled hunt approached, the Commissioner withheld bear hunt permits and ordered all state-controlled lands closed to bear hunting. Two hunting organizations appealed the Commissioner's decision to close the state lands, and the Appellate Division found that, like any other public or private property owner, the Commissioner has the authority to determine how state lands are used, and that the closure was not arbitrary or capricious.[17]

The 2004 conflict culminated in a lawsuit filed by sportsmen's clubs and individual hunters, challenging the Commissioner's authority to withhold bear hunt permits after the Council approved the hunt.[18] Days before the 2004 bear hunt was scheduled to begin, the NJ Supreme Court effectively canceled the hunt and held that the Council could not approve a bear hunt without a comprehensive bear management policy approved by the Commissioner, pursuant to N.J.S.A. 13:1B-28. The Commissioner does not have veto power over the day-to-day operations of the Council, and once the Commissioner approves a policy, he/she cannot veto a bear hunt.

When the Council and Commissioner come together to approve a comprehensive black bear management policy for 2005, including a bear hunt in 2005, animal advocates appealed the adoption of the policy and moved for emergent relief to stay the 2005 bear hunt. While appellants lost their motion for emergent relief and were not able to stop the hunt, the Appellate Division eventually ruled in 2007 that the 2005 black bear policy and 2005 black bear hunt were both invalid because the policy had not been adopted in substantial compliance with the Administrative Procedure Act, N.J.S.A. 52:14B-4 (APA).[19]

In 2006, Commissioner Lisa Jackson withdrew approval of the comprehensive black bear management policy that her predecessor, Bradley Campbell, had approved, and effectively canceled the 2006 bear hunt. Hunting clubs appealed the decision, arguing that the withdrawal of the policy did not comply with the APA. Appellants' emergent motion to compel the state to conduct the bear hunt in 2006 failed, and in the same decision that found that the 2005 bear policy was invalid, the Appellate Division found that there was no need for the Commissioner to follow APA procedures to withdraw the policy because there had never been a valid policy from the start.[20]

The other species that tends to garner wildlife lawsuits in New Jersey is white-tailed deer. In a 2002 case, animal advocates challenged the Council's authority to issue permits for local authorities to capture or kill deer under community-based deer management plans (CBDMP). Activists argued that the CBDMPs were invalid because they had not been adopted in accordance with the APA, but during the course of the litigation, the legislature passed N.J.S.A.23:4-42.3, which cured the defect in the adoption and rendered the issue moot.[21] Appellants also argued that the CBDMPs lacked scientific research and investigation as required by N.J.S.A. 13:1B-30, but the court rejected that argument, finding that the Division and the Council have the discretion to evaluate the data and determine which theories and approaches to adopt.[22]

Other cases have tested the authority of the Council and the Division over municipal authority to regulate hunting and firearms within their own borders. In *Chester v. Panicucci*, the defendant argued that a municipal firearms ordinance could not be enforced against him while he was hunting on state-owned public hunting grounds because the state had preempted the field.[23] The State Supreme Court disagreed, finding that the legislature did not clearly intend to occupy the field and that state preemption of the field would mean that no municipality could adopt more stringent regulations to protect its citizens.[24] N.J.S.A. 23:4-16 prohibited possessing a loaded gun "for the purpose of hunting, taking or killing any bird or animal" within 300 feet of an occupied dwelling. The municipal ordinance prohibited the same but omitted the quoted language regarding the purpose of the gun possession. Because of the broader language, the ordinance was more restrictive than the state statute. Municipalities are explicitly granted the power to regulate the use and sale of firearms and fireworks under N.J.S.A. 40:48-1(18). The *Panicucci* Court briefly discussed *Township of Hopewell v. Gruchowski*, in which the Court invalidated a municipal ordinance prohibiting hunters from trespassing because the State had already prohibited hunter trespass under N.J.S.A. 23:7-1 and had never extended that authority to municipalities.[25] The *Panicucci* Court also discussed *State v. Pinkos*[26] and *State v. Hackney*,[27] two cases that invalidated municipal ordinances prohibiting hunting in the entire municipality. The court refrained from commenting on the correctness of these three decisions but noted that in *Gruchowski*, *Pinkos*, and *Hackney*, there was a stronger indication of state legislative intent to preempt the field.

ENDANGERED SPECIES

In 1973, the same year that the federal Endangered Species Act[28] was signed into law, New Jersey enacted the Endangered and Nongame Species Conservation Act (Act), N.J.S.A. 23:2A-l et seq. The statute protects "any species or subspecies of wildlife whose prospects of survival or recruitment are in jeopardy or are likely within the foreseeable future," including animals listed on any federal list of endangered species. By including species whose survival are in jeopardy "within the foreseeable future," the legislature empowered the NJDEP and the Commissioner to protect threatened species, in addition to endangered species.[29] While the federal Endangered Species Act protects plants as well as animals, only animals are protected under the state law. International trade in endangered and threatened species is also restricted under the Convention on International Trade in Endangered Species of Fauna and Flora (CITES), which had 178 member countries as of 2013, including the United States.[30]

The Act prohibits taking, possessing, transporting, or selling protected wildlife, except with a permit. Permit regulations are published in the administrative code at N.J.A.C. 7:25-4.6 et seq. Possession permits are issued if the applicant can demonstrate that the animal will be properly fed, housed, and cared for.[31] Categories of permits include individual hobby, scientific holding, zoological holding, pet shops, animal dealers, animal exhibitors, animal theatrical agencies, depredation control, rehabilitation, and bird breeder.[32] To qualify for a permit, an applicant must have a sponsoring organization, such as a scientific institution or zoological society, and a designated professional who will monitor and guide the applicant.[33]

"Take" is defined in the Act as "to harass, hunt, capture, kill, or attempt to harass, hunt, capture, or kill, wildlife" but the Act does not define "harass." In *State v. Cullen*, the court looked to the federal Endangered Species Act for guidance and held that harassment under the Act is "an intentional or negligent act which creates the likelihood of injury to an endangered species by annoying the species to such an extent as to significantly disrupt its normal behavioral patterns."[34]

The administrative code also establishes the Endangered and Nongame Species Advisory Committee (Committee) at N.J.A.C. 7:25-4.18. The Committee is comprised of eleven members with special knowledge, expertise, and/or interest in endangered and nongame species, appointed by the Commissioner in consultation with the Committee. The eleven members include four from the academic/research communities, one affiliated with public health/veterinary medicine, three from qualified nonprofit organizations with a strong interest in promoting the nonconsumptive use of wildlife, and three from the public at large. Unlike the Fish and Game Council, the Endangered and Nongame Species Advisory Committee does not promulgate regulations directly. Instead, the Committee advises and assists the Commissioner, who is charged with promulgating and amending the list of endangered species, published at N.J.A.C. 7:25-4.13. The Commissioner is also charged with establishing programs, including the acquisition of land or aquatic habitats, which are necessary for the conservation of endangered and nongame species of wildlife.[35]

Violators may be subject to an order to comply, civil administrative penalties, or civil penalties. The Commissioner is also authorized to recover costs of investigation, inspection, sampling, and monitoring, as well as costs incurred by the state in removing, correcting, or terminating the adverse effects of the violation.[36] The Commissioner may also petition the Attorney General to bring a criminal action, and any person convicted of purposely, knowingly, or recklessly violating the Act is guilty of a crime of the third degree.[37]

ADDITIONAL STATUTES

In addition to hunting and endangered species, New Jersey has wildlife protection laws that address numerous issues, including the intentional feeding of black bears, marine fisheries, commercial fisheries, shellfish, fur-bearing animals, sale and purchase of wildlife and wildlife parts, community-based deer management plans and wild birds.

Fish and Game Council N.J.S.A.13:1B-24 et seq.

State Fish and Game Code N.J.S.A. 13:1B-29 et seq.

Fish, Game, Wild Birds and Animals Statutes, N.J.S.A. 23:1-1 et seq.

Powers and Duties of Division of Fish and Wildlife N.J.S.A. 23:2-2

The Endangered and Nongame Species Conservation Act, N.J.S.A. 23:2A-1 et seq.

Black Bear Feeding Ban N.J.S.A. 23:2A-14

Marine Fisheries Management and Commercial Fisheries Act, N.J.S.A. 23:2B-1 et seq.

Ban on steel-jaw leghold traps N.J.S.A. 23:4-22.1

Unlawful sale, purchase of wildlife N.J.S.A. 23:4-27

Protection of fur-bearing animals N.J.S.A. 23:4-37

Application for special deer management area designation (community-based deer management plans) N.J.S.A.23:4-42.3 et seq.

Wild birds other than game birds N.J.S.A. 23:4-50

Wild pigeons protected N.J.S.A. 23:4-53

Possession, release of certain animals N.J.S.A. 23:4-63.3 et seq.

Open season for certain fish N.J.S.A. 23:5-1.

Prevention of lawful taking of wildlife prohibited N.J.S.A. 23:7A-1 et seq.

Striped Bass Act N.J.S.A. 23:5-43 et seq.

Game fish N.J.S.A. 23:9-5 et seq.

Shellfish Statutes, N.J.S .A. 50: 1-5 et seq.

NOTES

1. N.J.S.A. 23:2B-15.

2. 16 U.S.C. §1531 et seq.

3. 16 U.S.C. §1361 et seq.

4. 16 U.S.C. §703 et seq.

5. See, generally, *Humane Society of the US v. NJ Fish & Game Council*, 129 N.J. Super. 239 (Ch.Div. 1974), overturned on other grounds, *Humane Society of the US v. NJ Fish & Game Council*, 70 N.J. 565 (N.J. 1976); *Arnold v. Mundy*, 6 N.J.L. 1, 71 (1821).

6. N.J.S.A. 13:1B-28.

7. N.J.S.A. 13:1B-24

8. While the statute requires only six of the eleven members of the Council be sportsmen, the other five members have often been hunters in addition to their other roles, resulting in a Council where every member, or nearly every member, is a hunter. Without a voice on the Council, environmental and animal protection advocates have been critical of the Fish and Game Council's management of wildlife, and even hunters have sued the Commissioner over hunting decisions. Such controversies and lawsuits have concerned the composition of the Council, the extent to which municipalities can regulate hunting within their borders, and the authority of the Council and the Commissioner.

9. N.J.S.A.13:1B-24.

10. N.J.S.A. 13: 1B-27.

11. N.J.S.A. 13: 1B-30.

12. N.J.S.A. 13:1B-30.

13. *Dept. of Cons. and Eco. Dev. v. Scipio*, 88 N.J. Super. 315, 320 (App. Div. 1965), *certif. den.* 45 N.J. 598 (1965).

14. *Id.*

15. *Id.*.

16. Bradley M. Campbell, Commissioner's Message, *New Jersey Fish & Wildlife Digest* Vol. 18 No. 1 Aug. 2004 at 7. http://www.nj.gov/dep/fgw/pdf/2004/dighnt2-8.pdf (last visited February 22, 2019).

17. *Safari Club v. NJDEP*, 373 N.J. Super. 515 (App. Div. 2004).

18. *U.S. Sportsmen's Alliance Found. v. NJDEP*, 182 N.J. 461 (2005).

19. *NJ Animal Rights Alliance v. NJDEP*, 396 N.J. Super. 358, 371 (App. Div. 2007).

20. *NJ Animal Rights Alliance v. NJDEP*, 396 N.J. Super. 358, 372 (App. Div. 2007).

21. *Mercer County Deer Alliance v. NJDEP*, 349 N.J. Super. 440, 444 (App. Div. 2002).

22. *Id.* at 449.

23. *Chester v. Panicucci*, 62 N.J. 94 (1973).

24. Id. at 101.

25. *Township of Hopewell v. Gruchowski*, 29 N.J. Super. 605 (Co. Ct. 1954).

26. *State v. Pinkos*, 117 N.J. Super. 104 (App. Div. 1971), *certif. den.* 60 N.J. 195 (1972).

27. *State v. Hackney*, 83 N.J. Super. 400 (Co. Ct. 1964).

28. 16 U.S.C. §1531 et seq.

29. *Zrb, LLC v. NJDEP*, 403 N.J. Super. 531, 554 (App. Div. 2008).

30. http://www.cites.org/ (last visited February 22, 2019).

31. N.J.A.C. 7:25-4.7.

32. N.J.A.C. 7:25-4.6.

33. N.J.A.C. 7:25-4.14.

34. *State v. Cullen*, 424 N.J. Super. 566, 582 (App. Div. 2012).

35. N.J.S.A. 23:2A-7.

36. N.J.S.A. 23:2A-10a and b.

37. N.J.S.A. 23:2A-10f.

Chapter 13

Chemical Manufacturing, Storage, and Transportation

Steven Barnett, Esq.

FEDERAL

Toxic Substances Control Act (TSCA), 15 USC 2601 et seq.

TSCA was enacted in 1976 to invent and regulate chemicals, both man-made and natural, to prevent unreasonable risks of injury to health or the environment associated with their manufacture, processing, distribution, use, or disposal. TSCA regulates pre-manufacture, manufacture, and intended uses of chemicals, whereas most other environmental laws apply to chemical waste streams, byproducts, and unintended uses and effects. The current TSCA inventory contains about 85,000 chemicals. Any chemical not on the inventory cannot be manufactured or imported without notifying EPA at least ninety days prior. Anyone using chemicals should be aware of TSCA requirements, but particularly manufacturers and importers because they are primarily responsible for ensuring compliance and notifying downstream users of TSCA-imposed use limitations and TSCA labeling, warning, recordkeeping, reporting, and other requirements. State and local requirements may be pre-empted by TSCA.

PCBs

TSCA Section 6 authorizes EPA to promulgate regulations controlling the manufacture, processing, use, and the disposal of substances deemed a threat to human health or the environment. Pursuant to this, EPA regulations governing the manufacture, processing, distribution, and the use of PCB's are at 40 CFR Part 761. These include the "PCB Ban" which prohibits manufacturing, processing, distribution, or use unless totally enclosed, authorized by rule, or exempted from rules; and regulations governing the cleanup of PCB's which have been leaked or spilled.

Asbestos, Asbestos Hazard Emergency Response Act (AHERA) (TSCA Title II), 15 USC §§2641-2656

AHERA was enacted in 1986 as Title II of TSCA. It directed EPA to promulgate rules requiring school districts to inspect for asbestos and describing what schools should

417

do when they find it, including developing an asbestos management plan. Those rules are found at 40 CFR Part 763.

Radon, 15 USC §§2661-2671

TSCA Title III was added in 1988 to address radon. It established that indoor radon levels should not exceed ambient outdoor levels and required EPA to develop guidance and technical programs to assist states in studying and mitigation radon risks. They are not regulations due to being guidance and technical programs.

Lead, 15 USC §§2681-2692

In 1992, the Residential Lead-Based Paint Hazard Reduction Act of 1992 was passed as Title X of the Housing and Community Development Act of 1992. This amended TSCA to add a new Title IV called Lead Exposure Reduction, which in turn directed EPA to consult with the federal USDHHS and USDOL to promulgate rules for the training and certification of those who assess and abate lead-based hazards. Existing state and local certification programs were required to be used. EPA's rules are at 40 CFR Part 765, Lead-Based Paint Poisoning Prevention in Certain Residential Structures.

TSCA Amendments, June 22, 2016, the Frank R. Lautenberg
Chemical Safety for the 21st Century Act (LCSA)

TSCA was amended in June 2016 due to perceptions that EPA was not assessing chemicals quickly or completely enough and that therefore (a) risks were going unaddressed or (b) state and local authorities were imposing disparate and inconsistent requirements making manufacture, distribution, and use across jurisdictions difficult or impossible. The basic structure of TSCA was not changed, that is, a chemical inventory and various regulatory means to prohibit or limit manufacture, distribution and use based on risks. LCSA provided different and in some cases more specific guidance, timelines, and deadlines for EPA to inventory and assess chemicals. Thus the same holds true as for the original TSCA, that all chemical users should be familiar with TSCA, but especially manufacturers and importers since they are primarily responsible for compliance and advising downstream users.

FIFRA. Federal Insecticide, Fungicide and Rodenticide Act, 7 U.S.C. §136 et seq., 40 CFR §§150-189.

FIFRA was originally enacted in 1947 and was in essence rewritten by the Federal Environmental Pesticide Control Act (FEPCA) of October 1972. Before a pesticide can be manufactured, distributed, or imported it must be approved by EPA. Registration can take years and millions of dollars of testing, and then years for EPA to approve. A pesticide is any substance intended for preventing, destroying, repelling, or mitigating any pest and includes insecticides, fungicides, and rodenticides as subsets. Importantly, a substance that does not have claims, labels, or advertisements calling it a pesticide is not a pesticide under FIFRA, even though it may be an effective pesticide. EPA FIFRA regulations are at 40 CFR Subpart E (40 CFR Part 150 et seq.).

U.S. Department of Transportation Hazardous Materials Regulations, 49 CFR §§100-185 (HMR)

Enforcement is by DOT Pipeline and Hazardous Materials Safety Administration (PHMSA), the Federal Aviation Administration (FAA), and the Federal Railroad Administration (FRA). Shippers and transporters must file an annual registration and pay a fee. Requirements include labeling, packaging, shipping papers, driver supplies, incident reporting, marking, placarding, emergency response information, loading/unloading and segregation, and training and security. USDOT Special Permits are needed for loads not addressed in the HMR. Carriers transporting certain types and amounts of hazardous materials must obtain a Hazardous Materials Safety Permit (HMSP) by submitting Form MCS-150B. A 2011 final rule on commercial driver's license testing changed the definition of tank vehicle to require drivers carrying Intermediate Bulk Containers (IBCs) with an individual capacity greater than 119 gallons and an aggregate capacity of 1,000 gallons or more to have a tank endorsement. Companies with commercial vehicles, including those required to be placarded for hazardous materials, must comply with Federal Motor Carrier Safety Regulations (FMCSR) enforced by Federal Motor Carrier Safety Administration (FMCSA) including driver hours of service limitations, training, recordkeeping, drug and alcohol testing, placarding, vehicle inspections, and cargo securement.

Chemical Facility Anti-Terrorism Standards (CFATS), 6 CFR 27 et seq.

All facilities possessing specified quantities of specified chemicals are required to submit an assessment to the Department of Homeland Security (DHS). DHS may notify the facility it must complete a Security Vulnerability Assessment and a Site Security Plan (SSP) or an Alternate Security Program (ASP). DHS conducts Compliance Inspections to ensure that facilities have implemented their SSPs/ASPs.

Rail Transportation Security Rule, 49 CR 1580

This rule, enforced by the Transportation Security Administration (TSA), imposes requirements on those involved in rail transportation of security sensitive hazardous materials, such as toxic inhalation hazards (TIH). These include securing the chain of custody, designate a rail security coordinator (RSC), report security concerns, and track locations. These requirements are ongoing and subject to inspection at any time.

Controlled Substances Act, 21 USC §801 et seq., U.S. Department of Justice Drug Enforcement Administration (DEA) regulations, 21 CFR 1300 et seq.

Regulations establish guidelines for distributing, importing, and exporting controlled substances and List I and II chemicals. DEA Office of Diversion Control administers and enforces the regulations. Any company that distributes List I Chemicals must register with the DEA, implement diversion control measures to include container security, personnel surety, and know-your-customer procedures, keep records, and report suspicious orders to the DEA. Import/export reporting requires importers and exporters to obtain a DEA transaction identification number before proceeding.

Food and Drug Administration (FDA) Regulations

Public Health Security and Bioterrorism Preparedness and Response Act (PHSBPRA, "Bio-Terrorism Act"), Public Law 107-188, 116 Stat. 594.

Requires facilities handling food/food additives to register with the FDA, update the registration if the registrant's data/ownership/functioning changes in any significant way, or ceases, and notify U.S. Customs and Border Protection or FDA if the entity is importing a food/food additive prior to the imported product arriving to the Port. What constitutes a food or food additive is broadly construed and can include substances and materials that come into contact with food, such as packaging and substances used to make packaging.

Food Safety Modernization Act (FSMA), 2011 Public Law 111-353

Facilities that manufacture, process, pack, or hold food for human or animal consumption must register with the FDA. These requirements extend to facilities that handle food grade chemicals or chemicals that will be used in food packaging. Additional information must be submitted to FDA, including the email address for the contact person of the facility and an assurance that FDA will be permitted to inspect the facility at the times and in the manner permitted by the Federal Food, Drug, and Cosmetics Act. Regulated companies will also be required to adopt several written plans under which hazards must be identified and interventions identified to prevent, reduce, or control those hazards, including the following:

1. Sanitary transportation of food regulations. Training and recordkeeping for certain types of food such as food ingredients or food additives.
2. Mitigation to protect food against intentional adulteration. Develop a written "food defense plan" to protect against vulnerabilities to the intentional adulteration of food.
3. Preventive controls for human and animal food. Create a written food safety plan setting forth hazard analysis, preventive controls, monitoring, verification, and a recall plan.
4. Accreditation of third-party certification bodies to conduct food safety audits and to issue certification. Framework for third-party certification bodies seeking accreditation by FDA as well as requirements for accreditation bodies that seek recognition to perform certifications. Third-party certification bodies must perform unannounced facility audits and inform the FDA upon discovering a condition that could cause or contribute to a serious risk to public health.

Alcohol and Tobacco Regulations

The Alcohol and Tobacco Tax and Trade Bureau (TTB) of the U.S. Department of the Treasury regulate both Specially Denatured Alcohol (SDA) and Completely Denatured Alcohol (CDA)

Companies that produce, withdraw, sell, transport, or use SDA or CDA are required to obtain a permit. 27 CFR Part 20 regulates the distribution and use of denatured alcohol and rum. 27 CFR Part 21 regulates formulas for denatured alcohol and rum, formulation of completely denatured alcohol, specially denatured alcohol, and specially denatured rum, specifications for denaturants and uses of denatured spirits.

Export Control Regulations

Companies that ship chemicals, expertise related to making certain items, specialized shipping containers, and certain chemical handling equipment outside of the United States are subject to export control regulations. The Bureau of Industry and Security (BIS) of the U.S. Commerce Department implements and enforces the Export Administration Regulations (EAR). These regulations generally apply to the export of all items, including many common chemicals. The EAR requires a license before a product can be shipped to many destinations if the item is on the Commerce Control List (CCL), the end-user is on one of the U.S. government's prohibited lists, or the end-use is prohibited. The EAR also includes recordkeeping requirements for covered shipments. Penalties for even one shipment of a covered item without a required license can be severe—$250,000 per shipment or twice the value of the shipment, whichever is higher. Criminal penalties are also possible in certain situations.

International Traffic in Arms Regulations

U.S. chemical companies that make certain listed chemicals or that design or modify chemicals or related products, equipment, or technical data for military, intelligence, or space applications are generally subject to the International Traffic in Arms Regulations (ITAR), administered by the U.S. State Department Directorate of Defense Trade Controls (DDTC). If the material is on the ITAR U.S. Munitions List (USML) they must register with the DDTC and pay an annual fee. Recordkeeping and other paperwork requirements apply such as invoicing and bills of lading. Penalties for violations of the ITAR can include criminal and civil charges and penalties of up to $1 million per violation. Violations of export control provisions (EAR or ITAR) can lead to the loss of the ability to export anything from the U.S. and/or sell to the U.S. government.

The Chemical Weapons Convention

The United States is a party to the Chemical Weapons Convention (CWC), which prohibits member states from developing, producing, stockpiling, or using chemical weapons. The CWC imposes a number of export obligations on its members, which in the United States are primarily implemented through the EAR and the ITAR. The Convention also considers imports, and in the United States these considerations are reflected in both the CWC Regulations and the Alcohol, Tobacco, Firearms, and Explosives Regulations. Finally, the CWC Regulations impose several unique requirements on producers of certain chemical products, including making annual declarations regarding certain production activities and undergoing initial and routine inspections of declared facilities. Those required to make declarations and undergo inspections must also maintain related records in specified ways.

NEW JERSEY

Medical Waste. The Comprehensive Regulated Medical Waste Management Act, NJSA 13:1E-48.1 et seq.

The law was passed in 1989 and the DEP rules at N.J.A.C. 7:26-3A.1 et seq. implementing the law was effective from August 25, 1989. All generators, transporters, handlers, owners, and operators of destruction facilities of regulated medical waste must register with NJDEP as solid waste transporters, pay an annual fee, obtain a Certificate of Public Convenience, and notify USEPA. Regulations direct segregation, packaging, storage, decontamination, labeling, marking and manifesting of packages.

Toxic Packaging Reduction. The Toxic Packaging Reduction Act, N.J.S.A. 13:1E-99.44 et seq.

Since January 1, 1993, it has been prohibited to sell or offer packaging or packaging components such as inks, dyes, pigments, adhesives, stabilizers, or any other additives which contain prohibited levels of lead, cadmium, mercury, or hexavalent chromium. A written certificate must be furnished by packaging manufacturers that they are in compliance. NJDEP may issue an order for return or removal of any non-compliant packaging and civil penalties may be assessed.

Dry Cell Battery Management Act, NJSA 13:1E-99.59 et seq.

Manufacturers of mercuric oxide batteries, nickel-cadmium batteries, and sealed lead rechargeable batteries absorb the cost of removing them from the waste stream, redesign their products to facilitate metals reclamation, and are responsible for collection, transportation, and recycling or proper disposal. Certain alkaline manganese batteries and mercuric oxide batteries are prohibited from sale.

Mercury Switch Removal Act, N.J.S.A. 13:1E-99.82 et seq.

Since 2005, vehicle recyclers and scrap recycling facilities must remove mercury switches before recycling steel and other automobile parts. Mercury switches are usually found in anti-lock braking systems and hood and door lights. Vehicle manufacturers must develop plans that identify the number and location of switches and provide methods for their removal, and they must pay for transport and disposal.

The Radon Act, N.J.S.A. 26:2D-70 et seq.

In 1986, New Jersey enacted legislation to require certification of those employed for radon testing and mitigation. The Radon Hazard Subcode of the New Jersey Uniform Construction Code specifies radon resistant and mitigation construction techniques in certain areas of the State. Radon laboratories are also required to be certified.

Asbestos. The New Jersey Asbestos Control and Licensing Act, N.J.S.A. 34:5A-32 et seq.

USEPA regulates asbestos under a number of federal statutes, including the Clean Air Act, Clean Water Act, Safe Drinking Water Act, Resource Conservation and Recovery Act, Toxic Substances Control Act, and the Asbestos Hazard Emergency Response Act. New Jersey's Asbestos Control and Licensing Act and its regulations at N.J.A.C. 8:60 et seq. and N.J.A.C. 12:120 et seq. become effective in 1985. They require most asbestos abatement in New Jersey to be done by licensed employers using trained employees using specified work methods including personal protective equipment and engineering controls and proper disposal of remove materials. Separate training and permits are required for supervisors and workers. And the training course must be certified as well. Notice to the New Jersey Department of Labor and Workforce Development and the New Jersey Department of Health and Senior Services is required to be provided ten days in advance of any work. The Asbestos Hazard Abatement Subcode of the New Jersey Uniform Construction Code applies to schools, public buildings, day care centers, nurseries, building exteriors among others. Where applicable, notice must be given to the Department of Community Affairs within three business days of issuance of a construction permit.

Lead-Based Paint, N.J.A.C. 8:62-62 et seq.

USEPA regulates lead under a number of federal laws including Clean Air Act, Clean Water Act, Safe Drinking Water Act, Resource Conservation and Recovery Act, and other laws. New Jersey regulations providing standards for certification of employees working with lead were promulgated in 1995. Lead workers and supervisors must be certified, and the training agencies must be certified. Certification by the Department of Community Affairs is required for any individual or business conducting lead evaluation or lead abatement. New Jersey's lead hazard evaluation and abatement subcode applies to the abatement of lead-based paint hazards and certification of lead-based paint hazard evaluation or abatement contractors. The removal, repair, encapsulation, or enclosure of lead-based paint or lead-contaminated soil requires a construction permit in accordance with the New Jersey Uniform Construction Code.

Mold

New Jersey has not enacted laws governing mold investigation or remediation. Regulations of the New Jersey Department of Labor and Workforce Development at N.J.A.C. 12:100 Subchapter 13 Indoor Air Quality Standard apply to buildings occupied by public employees and require control of microbial impacts such as repair of water leaks and other actions. A person must be designated to ensure compliance and there must be a preventive maintenance schedule to check HVAC systems, air filters, belts, lubrication, equipment parts, motors, and repair or replacement of damaged or inoperable components. Certified Industrial Hygienists (CIHs), certified by the American Board of Industrial Hygiene, are often retained to investigate and remediate mold. Other certification bodies and certifications or mold, newer than CIH's and the ABIH, have come into existence as well. There are no binding federal or New Jersey remediation standards for mold in terms of measurements or quantitative levels. The American Society for the Testing of Materials (ASTM), American National Standards Institute (ANSI), American Society for Heating, Refrigeration and Air Conditioning Engineers (ASHRAE), American Industrial Hygiene Association (AIHA), American Conference of Governmental Industrial Hygienists (ACGIH), and the Institute for Inspection of Cleaning and Restoration Certification (IICRC) all have recommended standards, guidelines, and procedures for mold investigation and remediation.

Noise. The Noise Control Act of 1971, N.J.S.A. 13:1G-1 et seq.

NJDEP noise regulations are at N.J.A.C. 7:29-1.1 et seq. Under the Act, if NJDEP fails to regulate noise-producing activity, a local board of health can take action provided that the noise constitutes a nuisance.

Radiation

The Radiation Protection Act, N.J.S.A. 26:2D-1 et seq. This law created the Commission on Radiation Protection within the NJDEP. New Jersey's Radiation Protection Programs become effective in 2000 and the regulations are at N.J.A.C. 7:28-1.1 et seq.

The Radiologic Technologist Act, N.J.S.A. 26:2D-24 et seq. This law created the Radiologic Technology Board of Examiners to license and regulate radiologic technicians.

The Radiation Accident Response Act, N.J.S.A. 26:2D-37 et seq. This law requires NJDEP in consultation with other State agencies to adopt a State Radiation Emergency Response Plan to respond to a radiation accident or threatened accident.

The Fissionable Source Material Act, N.J.S.A. 13:1J-1 et seq. This law prohibits extracting, milling, or processing in New Jersey of any mineral intended for use as fuel for nuclear reactors or weapons, subject to certain exceptions.

Pesticide Control Act of 1971, N.J.S.A. 13:1F-1 et seq.

This law authorizes NJDEP to promulgate rules governing the sale, purchase, transportation, labeling use, and application of pesticides. It establishes the Pesticide Control Council to advise NJDEP on control and regulation of pesticides. Subject to requirements of the federal FIFRA law including exceptions to pre-emption, NJDEP is authorized to register pesticides. Also, registrations are required for pesticide dealers, operators, applicators, and businesses. NJDEP regulations are at N.J.A.C 7:30-1.1 et seq. Separate from this law and related to pests and pesticides, N.J.S.A. 4:7-15 et seq. allows the Department of Agriculture to direct growers and dealers of plants to abate nuisances caused by injurious insects. N.J.S.A. 4:7-36 et seq. declares the gypsy moth to be a public nuisance and the Department of Agriculture is authorized to enter the property and take action to abate the gypsy moth. N.J.S.A. 26:9-1 et seq. established the State Mosquito Control Commission within NJDEP and county mosquito extermination commissions. NJDEP and county commissions can require private property owners to abate mosquito breeding grounds and can enter the property to abate if the owner does not.

Chapter 14

Energy and the Environment

Michael K. Plumb, Esq.

New Jersey recently amplified its long-standing policy of promoting renewable energy. The 2019 Energy Master Plan includes an ambitious "comprehensive blue-print for the total conversion of the State's energy production profile to 100% clean energy sources on or before January 1, 2050."[1] The policy is intended to mitigate global warming impacts by curtailing carbon dioxide emissions, increase reliability of the electricity distribution grid, and create jobs.

A combination of new and proven mechanisms will be used in an effort to reach the 100 percent clean energy goal, including renewable energy portfolio standards, revisions to existing solar programs, development of offshore wind, energy efficiency initiatives, a new community solar energy program, and promotion of energy storage. In addition, the Zero Emission Certificate program promotes continued use of carbon-free nuclear power, and participation in the Regional Greenhouse Gas Initiative provides additional incentives toward adopting renewable energy and raises funds for renewable energy projects. This chapter sets forth a brief introduction to New Jersey's established and incipient renewable energy and carbon-free-related programs and, where applicable, addresses the traditional environmental law issues associated with each.

RENEWABLE ENERGY PORTFOLIO STANDARDS

The electric power industry in New Jersey was restructured in 1999, pursuant to the Electric Discount and Energy Competition Act ("EDECA").[2] Among the many changes associated with the restructuring, EDECA permitted electric power utilities to petition the Board of Public Utilities ("BPU") for cost recovery of investments in renewable energy programs.[3] In addition, EDECA directed the BPU to adopt Renewable Energy Portfolio Standards ("RPS"), which require that electric power suppliers sell a certain percentage of electric energy from renewable energy sources.

The RPS requirements were revised over time[4] and increased substantially with passage of the Clean Energy Act on May 23, 2018.[5] For Class I renewable energy, the

RPS now requires sourcing of 21 percent renewable energy in 2020, 35 percent by 2025, and 50 percent by 2030. Energy is considered "Class I renewable energy" if it is produced from solar technologies, photovoltaic technologies, wind energy, fuel cells powered by renewable fuels, geothermal technologies, wave or tidal action, small-scale hydropower facilities, and sustainably harvested methane gas from landfills or a biomass facility.[6] In addition, 2.5 percent of energy sales must be sourced from Class II renewable energy, which is produced by either hydroelectric or resource recovery facilities.[7] Solar and wind are the primary areas of activity among RPS requirements and are discussed in more detail below.

Solar

Most renewable energy produced in New Jersey today is solar. As of November 2018, over 100,000 solar projects had been installed throughout the state,[8] representing approximately 2,701 megawatts (MW) of installed capacity.[9] Essentially all of New Jersey's installed solar capacity has been constructed since 2000, with half of that installed since 2014. Of that capacity, approximately 2,113 MW is behind the meter, that is, the electricity generated is used for a specific purpose such as providing power to a school, municipal building, or farm. The remaining capacity was built for grid supply.[10]

The current RPS requires that solar energy makes up 5.1 percent of energy sales by 2021. The Solar Renewable Energy Certificate ("SREC") is the primary mechanism by which electric power suppliers satisfied that requirements.[11] Applicants apply to the BPUs to have proposed solar installations entered into the SREC Registration Program. Accepted proposals must meet stringent construction and interconnection timelines.[12] Once connected to the grid, the registrant earns one SREC for every 1,000 kilowatt-hours (kWh) of electricity generated by the project. Electric power suppliers then purchase the SRECs from the registrant to satisfy their RPS requirements.

Registered solar projects only produce SRECs for a limited time. Pursuant to the terms of the Clean Energy Act, solar projects registered on or before October 29, 2018, produce SRECs for fifteen years. Projects registered after that date produce SRECs for ten years. The Clean Energy Act also requires the BPU to close the SREC program to new registrants by no later than June 1, 2021. As current SRECs expire, the percentage required to be held by electric energy suppliers will decrease to 1.1 percent of sales by 2033.[13] However, by May 2020, the BPU is required to complete a study to evaluate how to modify or replace the SREC program to continue development of solar projects throughout the State.[14]

The Clean Energy Act requires that the BPU establish a Community Solar Pilot Program in 2019, and, three years later, a permanent program.[15] A community solar program will permit customers of a public utility to participate in a solar energy project that is remotely located from their properties but within their public utility service territory. Participants will have their utility bill credited for an amount equal to the electricity generated by the solar project and attributable to the customer's participation in the project.[16]

Individual community solar projects will be limited to 5 MW each, and may be restricted to brownfields, landfills, areas designated in need of redevelopment, underserved communities, or commercial rooftops.[17] The Pilot Program Rules have an annual capacity limit of 75 MW the first year and at least 75 MW for the last two pilot years. Forty percent of pilot program projects are reserved for low and moderate income projects.[18] The permanent community solar program will have a goal for the development of at least 50 MW of solar energy projects per year.[19]

The development of solar projects requires compliance with land use and other environmental laws and regulations. Unless inconsistent with state law,[20] local zoning ordinances may restrict where solar energy facilities may be located and otherwise impose construction requirements.[21] Challenges to solar facilities often demonstrate the inherent environmental tradeoffs associated with building out solar infrastructure. For example, the Appellate Division upheld a decision to permit the construction of a solar facility within the Pinelands Regional Growth Area of the Pinelands National Reserve on land protected by both a recorded conservation easement and the New Jersey Green Acres Land Acquisition and Recreation Opportunities Act, *N.J.S.A.* 13:8A-35 – 55. In approving the diversion of protected lands for construction of a solar installation, the DEP determined that the construction of the solar project would yield a significant public benefit in the form of renewable energy.[22]

Wind

Wind projects in New Jersey are scarce. Despite consistent legislative and administrative efforts to facilitate construction of wind energy systems, only a handful of land-based wind energy projects are operational in New Jersey[23] and no offshore projects have been constructed.

Regulations relating to the permitting of wind turbines are primarily set forth in the Coastal Zone Management Rules, which establish a tiered system of regulation intended to streamline review of coastal permit applications for wind facilities.[24] The smallest wind facilities connected to an existing building are not regulated under CAFRA.[25] Construction of one to three wind turbines less than 200 feet in height and with a rotor swept area of less than 2,000 square feet may be eligible for a permit-by-rule, which does not require written approval from the NJDEP prior to undertaking the regulated activity.[26] Construction of one to three turbines less than 200 feet in height and with a rotor swept area of less than 4,000 square feet may be eligible for a general permit.[27] General permits require NJDEP approval but are approved if the general permit criteria are satisfied. Construction of one to three turbines less than 250 feet in height and with a rotor swept area of less than 20,000 square feet may be also be eligible for a general permit if the turbines are located outside of specific mapped areas that pose an unacceptable risk to birds and bats.[28] Regulated turbines that are not eligible for a permit-by-rule or general permit require an individual permit.[29]

In an effort to further facilitate construction of wind projects, the Legislature enacted *N.J.S.A.* 40:55D-66.11-15, which makes wind facilities a permitted use on parcels of twenty or more acres within industrial districts, limits municipal regulation of the installation of small wind systems, and required DEP to issue a technical bulletin with a model municipal ordinance for the construction of small wind energy systems.[30] Accordingly, municipalities may not prohibit small wind energy systems, restrict tower height through application of generic ordinances, require setbacks greater than 150 percent of the system height, set noise limits lower than 55 decibels at the property line, or require design that exceeds the State Uniform Construction Code. While the intention of the statute was to "stave off parochial aversion to small wind energy systems using zoning ordinances," municipalities are still permitted to "reasonably regulate within the enumerated limits of the statute."[31]

Offshore Wind Economic Development Act

In 2010, EDECA was amended to include the Offshore Wind Economic Development Act ("OWEDA"), *N.J.S.A.* 48:3-81.1 – 87.2. OWEDA directs the BPU to establish an offshore wind renewable energy certificate ("OREC") program. The price of ORECs for a project would be established by the BPU on a case-by-case basis.[32] An OREC represents one megawatt hour of electricity generated by a qualified offshore wind project. As originally enacted, OWEDA required a program to support 1,100 MW of generation from qualified offshore wind projects.[33] Rather than adding to the RPS requirements, the offshore wind requirements would reduce the corresponding Class I renewable energy requirements.[34]

OWEDA was ahead of its time. In 2010, there were not any commercial offshore wind farm projects operational in the United States. As of this writing, the 30 MW Block Island Wind Farm in Rhode Island is still the only commercial offshore wind farm in the United States. However, the United Kingdom and Germany, among other countries, have robust offshore wind infrastructure. Accordingly, OWEDA requires that project applicants provide the global history of proposed turbines and other equipment to BPU so that project feasibility can be evaluated.[35]

In 2011, when the BPU first solicited applications for offshore wind energy projects, only one application was filed, the Fisherman's Atlantic City Windfarm.[36] After years of review, the BPU denied the application in 2014 because the project costs were too high and the project involved unproven technology.[37]

Fisherman's submitted a renewed application in 2018, which was challenged by environmental organizations,[38] alleging that the project failed to demonstrate environmental benefits.[39] Specifically, the challengers alleged that the applicant had failed to identify potential impacts to endangered right whales during construction and failed to identify the likely impacts to migratory birds during operations. A proposed project should assess both the net reduction in air emissions and impacts on avian and marine life and the seabed.[40] In denying the application, the BPU noted that it was not presented with enough information to determine whether the project satisfied the environmental requirements of OWEDA and therefore did not reach any conclusion regarding potential impacts on avian and marine mammal populations.

Despite not having approved construction of any offshore wind since the OWEDA amendments in 2010, the Clean Energy Act of 2018 increased the 2030 OREC goal from 1,100 MW to 3,500 MW. Significant changes since the BPU's first solicitation for offshore wind projects in 2011 have improved the likelihood of successful offshore wind development. In 2014, the National Renewable Energy Laboratory completed an assessment of offshore wind energy leasing areas off New Jersey.[41] In 2015, the Federal Bureau of Ocean Energy Management awarded two leases for wind power on the outer continental shelf off the shore of New Jersey. The leaseholds are approximately

160,000 and 180,000 acres. Together the leases extend east-west from 7 to 23 miles offshore and north-south from Avalon to Barnegat Light.[42] In addition, ORECs now reflect the complete cost of a project, that is, the total capital and operating cost for an offshore wind project. In return for the sale of ORECs, qualified projects must return to New Jersey all revenue received from all sales, including sales of energy, capacity, and ancillary services.[43]

In 2018, the BPU solicited applications for up to 1,100 MW of offshore wind energy projects.[44] Three firms submitted applications to build projects. The BPU awarded the project to Ocean Wind, a developer backed by a memorandum of understanding between Ørsted and PSEG Renewable Generation. The first year OREC price will be $98.10 per MWh, with a levelized cost (actual cost after revenues are refunded to ratepayers) of $46.46 per MWh.[45]

Two additional solicitations, for 1,200 MW each, are expected in 2020 and 2022.[46]

ENERGY EFFICIENCY AND ENERGY STORAGE

Several BPU programs incentivize the reduction of carbon dioxide emissions through energy efficiency and energy storage. Various incentives promote or directly pay for portions of projects that install energy efficient systems at existing facilities.[47] These incentives are intended to reduce energy demand, which serves all of the objectives of the clean energy goal.

Energy storage is a rapidly advancing field useful for a variety of grid stability and resiliency reasons.[48] Regarding renewable energy, energy storage can level the intermittent supply sometimes associated with wind and solar power production. In addition, because renewable energy is generated in response to natural processes rather than electricity demand, energy storage can be used to shift the timing of delivering the renewable supply to the grid. Current State policy calls for the rapid expansion of energy storage from essentially none in 2019 to 600 MW by 2021 and 2,000 MW by 2030.[49]

In 2015, grants to incentivize energy storage in New Jersey were largely unsuccessful.[50] Since then storage systems have been deployed throughout the country, increasing the likelihood of future success. The first large-scale energy storage project in New Jersey is a 1 MW storage system associated with the Atlantic City Utilities Authority wastewater treatment plant, installed in 2018 with the assistance of a $300,000 grant from the BPU. Grants for additional projects have been approved by the BPU.[51]

ZERO EMISSION CERTIFICATES (ZECS)

Three nuclear power plants, Hope Creek 1, Salem 1, and Salem 2, have a combined 3,500 MW capacity and produce approximately 40 percent of the electricity generated in New Jersey. Those nuclear power plants do not emit carbon dioxide or substantial amounts of the criteria air pollutants associated with natural gas or coal fired electricity generation.

Other forms of energy generation, including natural gas combustion at current gas prices, can be more profitable than nuclear power generation. As a result, several nuclear power plants throughout the country have closed for economic reasons, despite obtaining license extensions.[52]

ZECs are intended to recognize and compensate nuclear energy generators in a manner similar to other non-emitting energy generation resources to the extent required to prevent the premature retirement of nuclear power plants for economic reasons.[53] While New Jersey's ZEC program has not been litigated, federal courts have rejected federal preemption challenges to similar programs in New York and Illinois.[54]

Nuclear power plants must apply to the BPU to be certified for ZEC eligibility. To be certified, a nuclear power plant must (1) be licensed to operate through 2030 or later, (2) demonstrate that retirement would negatively impact New Jersey's ability to comply with State air emissions reduction requirements, (3) demonstrate through the submission of confidential financial information that the plant is projected to not fully cover its costs and risks, or not cover its costs including its risk-adjusted cost of capital, and will cease operations in three years absent a material financial change, and (4) certify annually that it does not receive other payments that would allow it to stay open.[55] The BPU will rank eligible nuclear power plants based on their ability to satisfy the statutory criteria for eligibility, and other relevant factors such as sustainability and long-term commitment to nuclear energy production.[56] Plants to receive ZECs will be the highest ranked nuclear power plant down to the plant that, combined with those ranked above it, represents 40 percent of the electricity distributed by electric public utilities.[57]

Electric public utilities are required to pay for ZECs in proportion to the electricity they sell. Each utility is therefore authorized to charge retail customers $0.004 per kilowatt hour for ZECs. The collected fees are then paid to the ZEC eligible nuclear power plants in proportion to their energy generation.[58]

On April 18, 2019, the BPU awarded ZECs to the three operating nuclear power plants in New Jersey—Salem 1, Salem 2, and Hope Creek.[59] Each of the three facilities is expected to receive approximately $100 million per year in ZEC payments for each of the next three years.[60]

REGIONAL GREENHOUSE GAS INITIATIVE (RGGI)

The RGGI is the northeast's carbon cap and trade program. State participation in RGGI is voluntary. Participating states include Connecticut, Delaware, Maine, Maryland, Massachusetts, New Hampshire, New York, Rhode Island, and Vermont. New Jersey and Virginia are in the process of joining RGGI with New Jersey scheduled to re-enter in 2020.[61]

RGGI requires natural gas, coal, and oil-fired power plants with electricity generation capacities greater than 25 MW to obtain an allowance for each ton of carbon dioxide emitted annually. Approximately 100 power plants in New Jersey will be required to purchase RGGI allowances. The power plants purchase allowances at quarterly auctions conducted by RGGI, Inc. Each year, the number of allowances decreases, with the intention of creating an incentive for the power plants to decrease emissions. Proceeds from allowance sales are distributed to the participating states, which invest in programs intended to further reduce carbon dioxide emissions. New

Jersey will have a RGGI cap of eighteen million tons of carbon dioxide in 2020. The cap will decline 3 percent annually through 2030.

The proposed RGGI rules include some compliance flexibility. Emissions from the combustion of eligible biomass are deducted from compliance obligation.[62] Offset allowances can be used to meet up to 3.3 percent of compliance obligations. Three categories of projects are eligible for offset allowances: (1) landfill methane capture and destruction; (2) sequestration of carbon due to reforestation, improved forest management, or avoided conversion; and (3) avoided methane emissions from agricultural manure management operations.[63] Combined heat and power (cogeneration) units may deduct from their emissions compliance obligation the carbon dioxide emissions resulting from the thermal energy and electricity supplied directly to the co-located facility.[64] In addition, power plants can bank carbon dioxide allowances for use in meeting future compliance obligations.[65]

RGGI Proceeds

NJDEP expects to collect approximately $84 million from the sale of carbon emission credits in 2020. The value of the credits is expected to increase as the budget allowance cap decreases from 2020 to 2030.[66] Three state agencies will receive the RGGI funds: the Economic Development Agency (which will receive 60 percent of RGGI funds), the BPUs (20 percent), and the Department of Environmental Protection (20 percent). The agencies will collaborate to develop a strategic funding plan every three years, identifying which projects should be funded.

A ranking system will be used to determine which projects will be included in the strategic funding plan and funded with RGGI proceeds. Pursuant to *N.J.S.A.* 26:2C-52.b., the ranking system must include consideration of the following: (1) a net reduction in greenhouse gas emissions or a net sequestration of carbon; (2) significant reductions in greenhouse gas emissions, reduction of impacts on ratepayers, and a significant contribution to the achievement of the State's 2050 Global Warming Response Act limit, relative to the cost of the project or program; (3) reductions in energy use; (4) responsiveness to the recommendations submitted by the Department to the Legislature pursuant to the Global Warming Response Act; and (5) the provision of co-benefits. In addition to these required standards, ranking will also include guidelines set forth in Executive Order Number 7 to (6) ensure that RGGI funds will serve communities that are disproportionally impacted by the effects of environmental degradation and climate change.[67]

Agency discretion regarding how to distribute RGGI funds is limited by statute.[68] The EDA must use its funds to support energy efficiency projects, new efficient energy generation including "state of the art" and combined heat and power, carbon abatement technology, and the development of offshore wind. The BPU must use its funds to reduce electricity demand and reduce costs to electricity customers, particularly in urban areas subject to heat island effects. The DEP will split its funds. Half must be dedicated to greenhouse gas emission reductions relating to efficiency, renewables, distributed energy, and land use planning. The other half of DEP's funds will be spent on efforts to enhance carbon sequestration in state forests and tidal marshes.

CONCLUSION

New Jersey has the potential to reach its 2050 goal of carbon-free electricity production if the programs set forth above are successfully implemented and maintained.
Keeping existing nuclear plants open and developing some of the world's largest
offshore wind projects are the two key components to achieving that goal and will
account for the vast majority of carbon-free electricity.

While the clean energy goals are intended to create jobs, increase grid reliability
and mitigate global warming through emission reductions, they also raise conflicts
with competing concerns. For example, SRECs, ORECs, ZECs, and RGGI are all
directly funded through increases in the cost of electricity which are passed on to
residential and commercial consumers. Development of solar and wind generation
and distribution infrastructure can also conflict with land preservation and habitat protection objectives. These conflicts will be addressed on a case-by-case basis as New
Jersey proceeds toward the conversion of the State's energy production profile to 100
percent clean energy sources by 2050.

NOTES

1. See Draft 2019 New Jersey Energy Master Plan: Policy Vision to 2050 (June 10, 2019)
(setting forth seven main strategies to reach 100 percent clean energy and 80 percent emission
reduction from 2006 by 2050); see also E.O. 28 Par. 3 (May 23, 2018).

2. *N.J.S.A.* 48:3-49 to 98.5.

3. *N.J.S.A.* 48:3-98.1.

4. The Electric Discount and Energy Competition Act established RPS standards of 4
percent for Class I and 2.5 percent for Class I or Class II resources by 2012. In 2004, the BPU
moved the 2012 deadline to 2008. In 2006, the BPU again adjusted the standards, requiring
22.5 percent renewable by 2021. The BPU Solar Transition Order of 2007 directed changes
to the details of the RPS to improve program efficiency, which between 2001 and 2007 had
spent $170 million in rebates for the construction of 40 MW of solar capacity. *In re Renewable
Energy Portfolio Standards*, Decision and Order, Docket No. EO06100744 (September 12,
2007). In 2012, new rules were promulgated to codify changes to the RPS. *N.J.A.C.* 14:8.

5. A3723/S2314 (May 23, 2018).

6. *N.J.A.C.* 14:8-1.2. Small-scale hydropower facilities are those with capacities of 3
megawatts or less and put into service after July 23, 2012.

7. See *N.J.A.C.* 14:8-2.6. Eligible hydroelectric facilities have a design capacity of more
than 3 megawatts and no more than 30 megawatts. Eligible resource recovery facilities (incinerators) are those within New Jersey and operating in compliance with all New Jersey environmental laws, or those outside New Jersey in a state with retail competition for energy sales and
has been determined by NJDEP to meet or exceed all NJDEP operating requirements.

8. BPU Press Release, New Jersey Surpasses 100,000 Solar Installations as the Garden
State Looks to a Clean Energy Future, November 23, 2018, available at https://www.state.nj.us/
bpu/ newsroom/2018/approved/20181123.html.

9. New Jersey Clean Energy Program, Solar Installation Report (December 31, 2018),
available at http://njcleanenergy.com/renewable-energy/project-activity-reports/project-activ
ity-reports.

10. *Id.*

11. The BPU initiated the SREC Registration Program by order dated January 19, 2007, *In re Renewable Portfolio Standards*, Docket No. EO06100744.

12. See *In re Implementation of L. 2012, C.24, The Solar Act of 2012 . . . Brickyard, LLC*, Docket No. A-4666-15T3, 2017 WL 4700553 (App. Div. 2017) (addressing the deadlines relating to subsection q of the Solar Act). Grid supply projects eligible for SRECs were developed pursuant to subsections q, s, and t of the Solar Act (*N.J.S.A.* 48:3-87(q), (s), and (t)). Subsection (q) provides a process for approving grid supply facilities not exceeding 10 MW. Subsection (s) provides a process for approving grid supply facilities constructed on farmland. Subsection (t) provides a process for approving facilities constructed on brownfields, historic fill, or properly closed sanitary landfill facilities.

13. *Id.*

14. *N.J.S.A.* 48:3-87.38.d.(3).

15. The Pilot Program Rules were adopted by the BPU on January 17, 2019. See NJBPU Approves State's First Community Solar Pilot Program Rules, BPU Press Release (January 17, 2019) (available at https://nj.gov/bpu/newsroom/2019/20190117.html); see also N.J.A.C 14:8-9 (adopted rules).

16. *N.J.S.A.* 48:3-87.11.a, f.

17. N.J.S.A. 48:3-87.11.b(1), d.

18. Low- and moderate-income provisions are set forth at N.J.A.C. 14:8-9.8.

19. *N.J.S.A.* 48:3-87.11.f(2).

20. See *N.J.S.A.* 40:55D-66.16 (solar energy facility is a permitted use on the site of any landfill or closed resource extraction operation within every municipality).

21. *Dalessio v. Township of Upper Deerfield*, 2011 WL 6260662 (App. Div. 2011), citing *N.J. Shore Builders Ass'n v. Twp. Of Jackson*, 199 N.J. 38, 55 (2009).

22. *In re Certificate of the Department of Environmental Protection Granting Partial Release of Conservation Restrictions*, Docket No. A-2316-10T2, 2017 WL 3225723 (App. Div. 2017).

23. As of January 2019, New Jersey had two utility scale wind projects. The Jersey-Atlantic Wind Farm in Atlantic City, commissioned in 2006, is a 7.5 MW facility located at the Atlantic County Utilities Authority Wastewater Treatment Plant. Since 2012, the Bayonne Municipal Utilities Authority has operated a single turbine which it uses to power a sewage pumping station.

24. See 41 N.J.R. 3168 (proposing "a new permit-by-rule and two new coastal general permits for the construction of wind turbines on land; a new permit-by-rule for the construction of solar panels; and describing the situations in which construction of a wind turbine or solar panel does not require a costal permit"). While the Coastal Zone Management Rules only apply to the coastal zone, the coastal zone coincides with areas where wind development is most likely.

25. *N.J.A.C.* 7:7-2.4(d)4. Exempt turbines are on or attached to legally existing buildings, less than 200 feet in height, have a rotor swept area of 2,000 square feet or less, and any portion above 100 feet is attached to a freestanding monopole.

26. A rotor swept area of less than 2,000 square feet applies to most 50kW and smaller turbines that are typically used at single family homes and small businesses. See 41 N.J.R. 3173. Siting requirements also apply to eligibility for the permit-by-rule regarding mapped threatened and endangered species, floodways, dunes, beaches, and wetlands, among others. See *N.J.A.C.* 7:13-7.29.

27. *N.J.A.C.* 7:7-6.25 (N.J. Coastal Zone Management General Permit 25). Additional siting criteria apply as set forth in the cited regulation.

28. *N.J.A.C.* 7:7-6.26 (N.J. Coastal Zone Management General Permit 26). Additional siting criteria apply as set forth in the cited regulation.

29. See *N.J.A.C.* 7:7-15.4(r)1(vi) (must not detract from scenic or recreational values) (vii) (minimize effects on birds and bats onshore) (viii) (minimize effects on birds and bats offshore); (r)3 (large-scale wind turbine siting map); N.J.A.C. 7:7-23.6 (permit requirements include pre- and post-construction monitoring and proposed monitoring and proposed monitoring methodology to establish the flight patterns and distribution of birds and bats and the impacts of the operation on birds and bats).

30. A "small wind energy system" is a wind turbine, tower, and associated control or conversion electronics, and which will be used primarily for onsite consumption. *N.J.S.A.* 40:55D-66.12.d.

31. *Bayshore Regional Sewerage Authority v. Borough of Union Beach*, A-2086-12T1, 2014 WL 2971460, *5 (App. Div. 2014), cert. denied, 219 N.J. 630 (2014) (local ordinance may not be used to unreasonably restrict siting of small wind energy project).

32. *N.J.S.A.* 48:3-87.1.c. ("An order issued by the board pursuant to this subsection shall specify the value of the OREC and the term of the order.")

33. A qualified offshore wind energy projects is "a wind turbine electricity generation facility in the Atlantic Ocean and connected to the electric transmission system in this State, and includes the associated transmission-related interconnection facilities and equipment, and approved by the board." *N.J.S.A.* 48:3-51.

34. *N.J.S.A.* 48:3-87.c.(4)

35. *N.J.S.A.* 48:3-81.1(a)(1).

36. The application was submitted pursuant to *N.J.S.A.* 48:3-87.2 which allows for a small wind project of less than 25 MW to be sited near Atlantic City, provided that it meets the same standards as any other offshore wind project. The application window was only open for one month. See *In re Offshore Wind Economic Development Act Application Window Designation for State Water Proposals in the Atlantic Ocean*, Dkt. No. E011050290V, 2011 WL 2525533 (N.J. Bd. Reg. Com. May 16, 2011).

37. See *In re Fishermen's Atlantic City Windfarm*, A-3932-13T3, 2015 WL 3454540, (App. Div. 2015), cert. denied, 223 N.J. 281 (2015), (affirming BPU order denying application).

38. The Board again rejected a 25 MW wind farm off Atlantic City proposed by Nautilus Offshore Wind, LLC, a wholly owned subsidiary of Fisherman's Atlantic City Windfarm, LLC, in December 2018. In that Order, the BPU found the project failed the net benefits test, which requires a demonstration of positive economic and environmental net benefits to the State. The petitioner had provided insufficient data to demonstrate that ratepayers and the State will realize purported benefits sufficient to justify a guaranteed twenty-year OREC price that is "four to five times the value of the energy revenues generated by the Project and returned to ratepayers." See *In re Consideration of the State Water Wind Project and Offshore Wind Renewable Energy Certificate*, Dkt. No. QO18080843, 2018 WL 6812640 (N.J. Bd. Reg. Com. Order December 18, 2008).

39. See *N.J.S.A.* 48:3-87.1.a.(10)(c) ("an application . . . shall include . . . a cost benefit analysis for the project including at a minimum . . . an analysis of the anticipated environmental benefits and environmental impacts of the project").

40. See *In re The Opening of Offshore Wind Renewable Energy Certificate (OREC) Application Window for 1,100 Megawatts of Offshore Wind Capacity in Furtherance of Executive Order No. 8*, Dkt. No. QO18080851, 2018 WL 4538471 (N.J. Bd. Reg. Com. September 17, 2018).

41. Available at https://www.boem.gov/NREL/.

42. See Proposed Sale Notice, 79 FR 42361 (July 21, 2014); Call for Information and Nominations, 76 FR 22130 (April 20, 2011).

43. *N.J.A.C.* 14:8-6.5(a)12.vii.

44. By way of comparison, the largest offshore wind farm in the world, The Walney Extension operating off northern England, has a generating capacity of 659 MW. Adam Vaughn, World's largest offshore wind farm opens off Cumbrian Coast, The Guardian (September 6, 2018) (available at https://www.theguardian.com/environment/2018/sep/06/worlds-largest-offshore-windfarm-opens-cumbrian-coast-walney-extension-brexit).

45. New Jersey Board of Public Utilities Awards Historic 1,100 MW Offshore Wind Solicitation to Ørsted's Ocean Wind Project, BPU Press Release (June 21, 2019) (available at https://www.bpu.state.nj.us/bpu/newsroom/2019/approved/20190621.html).

46. New Jersey Board of Public Utilities Takes Crucial Steps Toward 3,500 MW Offshore Wind Goals, BPU Press Release (December 18, 2018), available at https://www.bpu.state.nj.us/bpu/newsroom /2018/20181218.html; New Jersey Board of Public Utilities Receives Applications for 1,100 MW Solicitation, BPU Press Release (Dec. 31, 2018) (available at https://www.nj.gov/bpu/newsroom/2018 /approved/20181231.html)

47. The various programs are fully described at www.njcleanenergy.com.

48. See U.S. Battery Storage Market Trends, U.S. Energy Information Administration (May 2018) (available at www.eia.gov/analysis/studies/electricity/batterygystorage/pdf/battery_storage.pdf).

49. By way of comparison, the U.S. large-scale battery storage power capacity in 2017 was 708 MW. *Id.* at 4.

50. Compare BPU Press Release, Christie Administration Approves First-Of-Its-Kind Energy Storage Solicitation Awards (March 20, 2015) (stating that the BPU had approved $2.908 million for thirteen proposed projects to install energy storage systems integrated with renewable energy generating facilities), with the BPU's Renewable Electric Storage Project Report (January 7, 2019) (listing fifteen canceled electric storage projects, two projects with the project pipeline, and one project installed).

51. New Jersey Clean Energy Program website, Renewable Electric Storage Project Report (January 7, 2019)

52. See "The Nuclear Power Dilemma: Declining Profits, Plant Closures, and the Threat of Rising Carbon Emissions," S. Clemmer et al., Union of Concerned Scientists (November 2018).

53. 2018 NJ S.B. 2313, Sec. 1.b(5).

54. *Coalition for Competitive Electricity, Dynergy Inc. v. Zibelman*, 906 F. 3d 41 (2nd Cir. 2018) (New York's zero emissions credit (ZEC) program was not preempted by Federal Power Act.); *Electric Power Supply Association v. Star*, 904 F. 3d 518 (7th Cir. 2018) (Illinois statute establishing ZEC program for nuclear electricity producers was not preempted by Federal Power Act.).

55. 2018 NJ S.B. 2313, Sec. 3.e.

56. 2018 NJ S.B. 2313, Sec. 3.g.

57. *Id.*

58. 2018 NJ S.B. 2313, Sec. 3.j. As of this writing, the BPU had not yet determined the eligibility of or ranked the applicant nuclear power plants.

59. See In re Matter of the Implementation of L. 2018, c. 16 Regarding the Establishment of a Zero Emission Certificate Program for Eligible Nuclear Power Plants, Order Determining the Eligibility of Hope Creek, Salem 1, and Salem 2 Nuclear Generators to Receive ZECs (April 18, 2019), BPU Docket Nos. EO18080899, EO18121338, EO18121339 & EO 18121337.

60. BPU Press Release, Citing Urgency of Climate Change, New Jersey Board of Public Utilities Awards ZECs to Preserve Salem One and Two and Hope Creek (April 18, 2019).

61. The Global Warming Solutions Fund Act of 2007 authorized New Jersey to join RGGI. New Jersey withdrew from RGGI in 2012.

62. *N.J.A.C.* 7:27C-1.2 (defining eligible biomass as sustainably harvested woody and herbaceous fuel sources available on a renewable or recurring basis, dedicated energy crops and trees, agricultural food residues and feed crop residues, aquatic plants, wood and wood residues, animal waste, other clean organic wastes not mixed with solid wastes, biogas, and other neat liquid biofuels derived from such fuel sources); *N.J.A.C.* 7:27C-6.9, 8.7 (permitting deduction of emissions from eligible biomass).

63. *N.J.A.C.* 7:27C-10.3.
64. *N.J.A.C.* 7:27C-5.3.
65. *N.J.A.C.* 7:27C-6.10.
66. 2018 N.J.R. 511825.
67. E.O. 7, Par. 4 (January 29, 2018).
68. *N.J.S.A.* 26:2C-51.7(b).

Index

NJSWMA. *See* New Jersey Solid Waste
Management Act
NOAA. *See* National Oceanic and
Atmospheric Administration
No Further Action (NFA), 5; in remediation,
32–33
NOI. *See* net operating income
Noise Control Act, 424
nonagricultural structures, 274
nonattainment, 301
non-condemnation redevelopment, 122
nongovernmental entities: borrowing process
for, 54; public financing and, 53–54
North American Industry Classification
System (NAICS), 403–4
Notice of Violation (NOV), 316
Novak Group, 133
NOx. *See* nitrogen oxides
N-propyl bromide, 312
NRD. *See* natural resource damages
NSR. *See* New Source Review
nuisance, air pollutant regulatory programs
for, 313–14

OAL. *See* Office of Administrative Law
occupancy certificates, NJSEA, 262
occupational injuries, 398–99
Occupational Safety and Health Act
(OSHA): Area Directors, 401; definitions
under, 398; enforcement of, 400–401;
Form 300, 399; Form 300A, 399; Form
301, 399; general duty clause of, 398;
informal settlement agreements, 401;
violations of, 401; worker claims under,
402
Occupational Safety and Health Review
Commission, 401
occurrence definition, 113
Office of Administrative Law (OAL), 161,
164, 264
Office of Dispute Resolution, NJDEP,
223n52
Office of Inspector General (OIG), 401
Offshore Wind Economic Development Act
(OWEDA), 430
off-site disposal, 84
Ohio v. Kovacs, 134
OIG. *See* Office of Inspector General
O&M. *See* Operating and Maintenance
O'Neill v. State Highway Department, 238

On-Site Consultation Service, 400
Open Fields doctrine, 181
Open Public Meetings Act, 347
Open Public Records Act, 167, 347
open waters, development adjacent to,
258–60
Operating and Maintenance (O&M), 63
operating certificates, air quality permitting
programs and, 303–5
operating permits, air quality permitting
programs and, 305–7
options, 60
ordinance requirements, for historic
preservation, 293–94
Orient Way Corp v. Lyndhurst, 154
OSHA. *See* Occupational Safety and Health
Act
OSP. *See* Highlands Open Space Partnership
Funding Program
OWEDA. *See* Offshore Wind Economic
Development Act
Owens-Illinois, Inc. v. United Ins. Co.,
114–15
owned property exclusion, environmental
liabilities and, 110–11

PA. *See* Preliminary Assessment
*Pan Chemical Corp v. Borough of
Hawthorne*, 154
parallel proceedings issues, 181–82
parking lots, 286
particulate matter, air pollutant regulatory
programs for, 314
Passaic River, 134, 138n26
Passaic Valley Sewerage District, 331
PBR. *See* Permit-By-Rule
PBT. *See* Persistent, Bioaccumulative and
Toxic
PCBs, 417
Penick Court, 189
Pennsylvania Coal Co. v. Mahon, 296
Penn Terra Ltd. v. Dept. of Envtl. Resources,
130
PEOSH Act. *See* Public Employees
Occupational Safety and Health Act
Periodic Monitoring Procedures (PMPs), 305
Permit-By-Rule (PBR), 26, 328
Permit Extension Act, 349
permit review function, HPC, 295
permits-by-rule, FHACA, 230–31

Quincy Mut. Fire Ins. Co. v. Borough of Bellmawr, 113

RACT. *See* Reasonably Available Control Technology
Radiation Accident Response Act, 424
Radiation Protection Act, 424
radioactive waste, 391n20
Radiologic Technologist Act, 424
radium, 93
RADIUS. *See* Remote AIMS Data User System
radon, 418
Radon Act, 422
rail security coordinators (RSC), 419
Rail Transportation Security Rule, 419
RAO. *See* Response Action Outcome
Rapanos v. U.S., 258
RAPs. *See* Remedial Action Permits
RATE. *See* Resiliency, Air Toxics and Exemptions
RAWP. *See* Remedial Action Workplans
RCRA. *See* Resource Conservation Recovery Act
RDSO. *See* residential dwelling site opportunity
real estate development: construction risks in, 63–64; control of property in, 60; debt financing in, 69–71; entitlement risk in, 61–62; environmental risk in, 62–63; equity financing in, 68–69; equity investor in, 67–71; financial risk underwriting in, 66–67; joint ventures in, 73–74; major risks in, 60–61; market risk in, 64–65; Mezzanine financing in, 69; yield measurement in, 71–73
real estate investing, 59
real estate transactions, points of view in, 6–7
real property tax appeals: *Inmar Associates v. Borough of Carlstadt* and, 151–53; recent decisions in, 154–57
realty improvement, 343n60
Realty Improvement Sewerage and Facilities Act, 331, 347–48
reasonable use doctrine, 323, 341n11
Reasonably Available Control Technology (RACT), 304
reclaimed materials, 372–73
recognized hazards, 401

Recreation Open Space Inventory (ROSI), 285
recycling, 391n27; facilities, 367; funds, 366; programs, 366; of solid waste, 372
Recycling Act, 370n73, 370n78
redevelopment, 123; agreement, 125; description of, 125; implementation of, 124–25; NJSEA on, 260–61; non-condemnation, 122; Planning Board in, 121; process, 121–22; purchase/sale agreement and, 13; remediation and, 13; schedule of, 125; steps in, 120; studies on, 120–21
Redevelopment Area Ordinance, 61
Regional Greenhouse Gas Initiative (RGGI), 315, 432; proceeds, 433
regulated activities: in channels, 232; defining, 217; in flood fringe, 233; in floodways, 232; permit requirements for, 233; in riparian zone, 232; Wetlands Act of 1970 on, 217
regulated areas, FHACA, 227–29
regulated development, 204–7; permitting procedures and, 211; substantive standards and, 211; under WFD, 209–10
Regulated Medical Waste Act, 178
regulated waters, 229t
regulatory agencies, 180
regulatory programs, for mitigation of civil penalties, 164–68
rehabilitation, 122–23
release, in purchase/sale agreement, 14
Release and Pollution Prevention Reports (RPPRs), 403, 405
Remedial Action Permits (RAPs), 10
Remedial Action Workplans (RAWP): defenses and, 5; implementation of, 62–63
remedial fines, 44–45
remediation: of building materials, 31–32; capitalization and, 41–43; deductibility and, 41–43; Deed Notice in, 23; excavation in, 23; ex-situ treatment in, 24; groundwater, 27–31; of indoor air, 31; in-situ treatment in, 23; ISRA on, 110; life cycle, 7; of media, 21–22; NFA in, 32–33; post-closing, 10–14; pre-closing, 9–10; primary measures of, 22; RAO in, 32–33; redevelopment and, 13; responsibilities, 126; of sediment, 32;

About the Editor and Contributors

ABOUT THE EDITOR

Albert I. Telsey, Esq., is a partner at Meyner and Landis LLP, Newark, New Jersey. Mr. Telsey has practiced environmental law for more than thirty-five years. He focuses on environmental compliance, counseling, and litigation as it relates to the purchase, sale, lease, mortgage, foreclosure, condemnation, redevelopment, and cleanup of contaminated property in New Jersey. He has been named a *Super Lawyer* in environmental law by *New Jersey Monthly* magazine. He is also the author and editor of the *ABCs of Environmental Regulations* (2016, 3rd ed.) published by Bernan Press. Mr. Telsey has been an adjunct professor on environmental topics at NJIT and an instructor for Rutgers University and the New Jersey Redevelopment Authority. He teaches his own popular seminar entitled, "10 Clever Ways to Buy/Sell Contaminated Property in NJ," which is approved for 2.4 CLE credits. He has also been an expert witness in NJ litigation matters involving contaminated property. He provides his environmental expertise to many attorneys throughout the state. He is a master with the New Jersey Environmental Inns of Court and is a member of the New Jersey State Bar Association, the Newark Regional Business Partnership, and the New Jersey Commerce and Industry Association. Mr. Telsey began his environmental career in the 1980s as an environmental prosecutor with the New Jersey Attorney General's Office. Mr. Telsey is an avid runner.

ABOUT THE CONTRIBUTORS

A. Vincent Agovino, PhD, P.W.S., L.S.R.P., is an environmental professional with more than thirty years of diversified experience in environmental science, ecological science, public, environmental, and occupational health. His areas of technical expertise include soils, wetlands, sewage disposal, contamination assessment, site remediation, environmental health program administration, project management, regulatory enforcement, and technical training. Dr. Agovino has conducted soil evaluations, wetland evaluations, and habitat assessments throughout New Jersey, New York, Pennsylvania, Maine, Massachusetts, and Maryland utilizing currently accepted methodologies.

Diane Alexander, Esq., is a partner at Maraziti Falcon LLP in Short Hills, New Jersey. She practices in the areas of environmental compliance and permitting for the public and private sectors including wastewater discharge issues, compliance and permitting, industrial wastewater pretreatment, discharges to groundwater, surface water allocation and water supply issues and permitting, disposal of contaminated media, and conveyance of property subject to environmental regulations.

Christopher D. Ball, Esq., is in solo practice in Newtown, Pennsylvania, and was formerly a partner at Manko, Gold, Katcher & Fox LLP in its Bala Cynwyd, Pennsylvania, office. He focuses his practice on environmental litigation and regulatory compliance. Chris's litigation experience includes complex federal Clean Air Act citizen suit actions, state solid waste enforcement cases, and administrative challenges to EPA rulemaking.

Steven Barnett, Esq., is a partner with Connell Foley in Roseland, New Jersey. For more than twenty years, Steve Barnett has represented clients concerned with health, safety, and environment, in transactions, court proceedings, and regulatory permitting and compliance matters. Prior to his legal career, Steve practiced as a licensed professional engineer and certified industrial hygienist and obtained a master of science in public health, industrial hygiene emphasis. He also proudly served as Captain, U.S. Air Force Bioenvironmental Engineer.

Jeffrey I. Baron, Esq., is a principal in the firm of Baron & Brennan, P.A. in Voorhees, New Jersey. Mr. Baron has practiced for forty years with special emphasis in the areas of zoning and planning, real estate, appellate representation, and representation before administrative agencies (including The New Jersey Pinelands Commission). He assists clients in resolving issues arising under land use, zoning and related areas.

Robert Beinfeld, Esq., is a partner with Hawkins Delafield & Wood LLP in Newark, New Jersey, where he specializes in public finance matters of New Jersey counties, municipalities, school districts and state and local agencies and authorities. His work with such issuers involves all phases of the authorization, sale and issuance of general obligation and project revenue bonds including attention to securitization, federal tax, and disclosure-related matters.

William J. Beneduce, Esq., is an attorney in the law firm of Norris McLaughlin & Marcus, PA, in Bridgewater, New Jersey, and New York and practices in the Environmental Law Department. Bill represents and counsels manufacturers, commercial, and industrial landlords, and highly regulated service businesses in all aspects of environmental law and litigation. He has written several articles published on a wide range of environmental law topics including land use and development, brownfields, and various issues involving site remediation. Since 2003, he has given several presentations relating to environmental law and the environment.

Franklin W. Boenning, Esq., has been practicing environmental law for eighteen years and has handled a wide variety of matters, including corporate transactions, litigation, regulatory compliance and permitting, administrative appeals, and regularly oversees complex environmental remediation projects. Mr. Boenning's previous experience as a chemical engineer, environmental consultant, and environmental, health, safety, and regulatory affairs manager in the chemical industry provides a deep understanding of the scientific and practical issues involved in his clients' cases. His global workload has provided experience in a multicultural environment and the ability to interact with plant and corporate personnel and regulatory agencies on local, state, and federal levels. Mr. Boenning regularly assists clients managing real estate with environmental issues, including buying and selling contaminated properties and managing the risks and cleanup responsibilities associated with managing these properties. In addition, he routinely assists solid and hazardous waste collection and disposal companies with a wide variety of permitting, licensing, regulatory, transaction, and enforcement matters. Mr. Boenning also assists policy holders recover environmental remediation costs from insurance companies issuing comprehensive general liability policies as well as newer pollution liability policies.

Edward R. Bonanno, Esq., is Of Counsel to the Law Firm Pringle Quinn Anzano, Belmar, New Jersey, where he chairs the firm's Environmental Practice Group and is a member of the Insurance, Healthcare, and Financial Fraud Litigation Practice Group. Mr. Bonanno served as a prosecutor in the New Jersey Division of Criminal Justice for twenty-five years from 1985 to 2010. During that time, he was the Supervising Deputy Attorney General and Bureau Chief for Environmental Crimes in the New Jersey Attorney General's Office Division of Criminal Justice and a deputy attorney general in the Appellate Bureau. Mr. Bonanno handled and supervised the investigation and prosecution of numerous complex criminal cases involving environmental crimes, including oil spills, chemical fires and explosions, illegal dumping as well as racketeering, major fraud, and corruption cases. The New Jersey Environmental Crimes Bureau was one of the first units of its kind in the nation and was a pioneer in the investigation and prosecution of all types of environmental crimes. Mr. Bonanno has represented public entities and corporations before the federal, state, local, and interstate agencies and boards for environmental and renewable energy issues and has represented citizen groups in environmental litigation. He is a recipient of the NY/NJ Baykeeper's Outstanding Service Award and the Hackensack Riverkeeper's Lifetime Achievement Award. Mr. Bonanno previously served as chair of the New Jersey State Bar Association's Criminal Law Section and holds a bachelor's degree from Hamilton College, Magna Cum Laude-Phi Beta Kappa and a Juris doctorate degree from Fordham Law School. He is a member of the New Jersey and District of Columbia Bars.

Henry R. Booth is president of R. M. Fields LP of West Chester, Pennsylvania. With more than twenty-nine years in the insurance archaeology field his career has focused on reconstructing the historical insurance programs of entities facing the potentially catastrophic threat posed by latent injury claims. His clients run the gamut from Fortune 500 companies to small business concerns. In addition to insurance archaeology services, he provides expert consulting and testimony on a variety of lost policy issues.

Aileen Brennan, Esq., is a senior associate at Maraziti Falcon LLP where she concentrates her practice in redevelopment and eminent domain. On behalf of municipalities and other public entities, she negotiates and drafts redevelopment agreements and documents for the designation of redevelopment areas. With significant experience in Green Acres, she helps municipalities draft legislation to accept and implement grant funding for the remediation and development of open space and parklands. Ms. Brennan drafts enabling legislation for zoning and land use ordinances, and negotiates and drafts multiple agreements for the redevelopment of property to provide both affordable and market rate housing as well as increased retail and recreational activities. Ms. Brennan has also counseled businesses and communities related to aviation and airports regarding compliance with federal and state environmental regulations, including the development of OSHA-required coursework for airport employees. Before she was an attorney, Ms. Brennan was a duty manager for a major airline. Ms. Brennan founded the Land Use and Redevelopment Committee and is chair of the Essex County Bar Association.

Andrew Brewer, Esq., is a partner at Maraziti Falcon LLP in Short Hills, New Jersey. He has represented both public and private sector clients in redevelopment, transactional, land use, and litigation matters. He currently serves as counsel to the Pompton Lakes Redevelopment Agency, the South Amboy Planning Board, and Pompton Lakes Planning Board. He represented the Palmyra Board during the designation of approximately 200 acres as an area in need of redevelopment, and has represented the Borough in negotiations with potential redevelopers. Mr. Brewer has also represented the Perth Amboy Redevelopment Agency in the negotiation of several redevelopment agreements, and has represented numerous municipalities in litigation upholding redevelopment designations and plans. He represents developers in connection with applications before both Planning and Zoning Boards and he represents municipalities and public sector clients in litigated matters, including bench and jury trials, in matters involving eminent domain, redevelopment, tax appeals, construction contracts, and land use applications.

Glenn P. Brukardt, P.E., is the managing member of Eikon Planning and Design, LLC in Hackettstown, New Jersey. Mr. Brukardt has focused his consulting practice on environmental issues associated with real estate transactions, property valuations/set-offs, Brownfield redevelopment, insurance claim support, third-party peer reviews, and litigation support projects. Mr. Brukardt has represented buyers, sellers, tenants, insurance companies, financial institutions, and the law firms representing said entities.

Jeffrey W. Cappola, Esq., is a shareholder at Wilentz, Goldman & Spitzer, P.A. Mr. Cappola concentrates on brownfield and landfill redevelopment and regulatory compliance. He provides counsel to businesses and developers by developing strategies for obtaining environmental and land use permits at the local, state, and federal levels. He has extensive experience with all aspects of real estate development, which includes due diligence, financing, acquisition, permitting, liability protection, environmental insurance and drafting purchase agreements, and redevelopment agreements.

Another expertise is prosecuting/defending administrative, enforcement, cost recovery, contribution, and insurance actions.

Brent Carney, Esq., is a partner at Maraziti Falcon LLP in Short Hills, New Jersey. Mr. Carney advises and represents public sector clients in the areas of municipal law; municipal and county utilities authorities law; sewerage authorities law; energy procurement; local public contracts law; land use; construction contracts, claims and defenses; eminent domain; affordable housing and redevelopment. Mr. Carney is also a litigator representing the firm's clients in administrative agencies and at the trial and appellate levels in Federal and State courts.

Melissa A. Clarke, Esq., is an associate at Saul Ewing Arnstein & Lehr LLP in Princeton, New Jersey. Melissa Clarke assists clients with civil litigation, especially matters involving state and federal environmental laws and CERCLA/Superfund actions. She also handles complex title and foreclosure litigation. In addition to her litigation work, Melissa advises corporate and real estate clients on environmental compliance and land use matters. Her experience includes drafting and negotiating environmental provisions in commercial real estate and corporate agreements, and providing best practice recommendations. Following law school, Melissa served as a clerk to the Honorable Thomas W. Cavanagh of the New Jersey Superior Court (Monmouth Vicinage, Chancery Division, General Equity Part).

Michael W. Cole, EA, Esq., is the manager in Charge of Taxation for Ironstate Holdings, LLC, located in Hoboken, New Jersey. Mr. Cole has a concentration in taxation with special emphasis on flow-through and transactional taxes. Mr. Cole conducts planning for federal and state tax compliance matters.

Stefanie Colella-Walsh, Esq., is an associate in the Civil Litigation Department at Stark & Stark, P.C., in Lawrenceville, New Jersey. Ms. Colella-Walsh has a concentration in mass tort/class action, intellectual property and general commercial litigation, with special emphasis on mass tort environmental contamination and products liability actions. She has experience litigating on the trial level of the federal and state courts of New Jersey, and is also licensed to practice law in Pennsylvania and New York.

Matthew R. Conley, Esq., is a partner at Archer in Haddonfield, New Jersey, in the firm's litigation and environmental law departments. Matt concentrates his practice on complex environmental, toxic tort, and products liability litigation in state and federal courts. He has considerable experience prosecuting and defending claims relating to environmental contamination, including cost recovery, contribution, and property diminution. Matt has particular expertise in the area of natural resource damages (NRD) and is a frequent speaker and commentator on NRD issues. Matt also currently represents Fortune 100 companies and multinational companies at large Superfund sediment sites and in response to claims relating to per- and polyfluorinated alkyl substances (PFAS). Matt has conducted and managed all phases of discovery in complex litigation and has significant experience with ESI discovery. Matt also has extensive experience advising clients on environmental regulatory matters in New Jersey, Pennsylvania, and other jurisdictions, with particular experience relating to the Site Remediation Reform Act, the Licensed Site Remediation Professional program, and the Industrial Site Recovery Act in New Jersey, RCRA corrective action, as well as the Act 2 process in Pennsylvania. Matt also has significant experience advising clients on the sale and development of commercial properties, particularly properties undergoing active remediation. Prior to joining Archer, Matt worked for the New Jersey Department of Environmental Protection as a Case Manager in the ISRA department.

James Cosgrove, P.E., is vice president and principal of Kleinfelder, an architectural, engineering, and science consulting firm. He is a registered professional engineer in New Jersey with twenty-five years of experience in water resources management, with specific expertise in water quality modeling, storm water management, and environmental impact assessment. He is often retained to obtain challenging land use permits, especially when critical water resources are present (e.g., Category One streams), and speaks regularly on NJDEP permitting issues.

Vanessa Day, Esq., is an attorney with the New Jersey Department of Environmental Protection. She provides counsel on all aspects of environmental justice and is a frequent lecturer on the topic. She is a graduate of Seton Hall University Law School.

Michele R. Donato, Esq., is a sole practitioner in Lavallette, New Jersey. She specializes in land use, historic preservation, and environmental protection. She represents individuals, developers, public entities, and environmental organizations. She is general counsel to New Jersey Planning Officials and a trustee of the Institute of Local Government Attorneys.

Amanda Dumville, Esq., is an associate at McCarter & English, LLP where she assists clients with environmental and energy law litigation and transactional needs. Amanda represents companies in environmental and environmental insurance litigation, including cost recovery actions involving Superfund sites, landfills, groundwater and soil contamination, and underground storage tanks. She counsels clients on the complexities of the New Jersey Spill Act and on federal and state natural resource damages (NRD) law. When clients are negotiating business, brownfields, and renewable energy transactions, Amanda advises them on how to comply with federal and state environmental laws and regulations, including the New Jersey Industrial Site Recovery Act, the Toxic Substances Control Act (TSCA), and the Emergency Planning and Community Right-to-Know Act (EPCRA). She is a *cum laude* graduate of Vermont Law School, which has a nationally renowned environmental and energy law program. While in law school, she was an extern in the highly selective externship program with the U.S. Department of Justice, Environment and Natural Resources Division, Environmental Enforcement Section. She was also a law clerk for the U.S. Department of the Interior, Office of the Solicitor, supporting the Bureau of Land Management and the Bureau of Reclamation, and for the New Jersey Office of the Attorney General, Environmental Enforcement Division. Committed to pro bono efforts and community service, she is helping a Jamaican woman seek asylum in the United States.

Gordon C. Duus, Esq., is a partner and chairman of the environmental law department at Mandelbaum Salsburg in West Orange, New Jersey. Gordon has more than thirty years of environmental law experience and has represented clients, from Fortune 100 companies to family partnerships, in the environmental aspects of commercial and real estate transactions, including the sale, purchase, leasing, and financing of contaminated real estate. He has assisted clients with the purchase of environmental insurance for over 200 properties.

Brian Friedlich, P.E., is a licensed professional engineer with nearly a decade of experience in the fields of environmental engineering, water resources, stormwater management, and environmental permitting. At Kleinfelder, Brian has provided consulting services to public and private sector clients for projects that involve design of innovative stormwater management facilities, wetlands and flood hazard area permitting support, watershed restoration planning and design, and wastewater treatment plant planning and design. He has presented on his projects and work at numerous conferences and seminars.

Steven R. Gray, Esq., is an executive partner at Waters, McPherson, McNeill, P.C. He heads the firm's environmental practice, and represents developers, institutional and small business clients on a range of matters including transactions involving contaminated properties (including bankruptcies), permitting of projects involving wetlands/open water impacts, site remediation and compliance, environmental insurance and cleanup contribution claims, renewable energy projects, and development projects on former landfilled sites. Prior to joining his present firm, he was a deputy attorney general representing the New Jersey Meadowlands Commission and the NJDEP for almost ten years. He also worked as counsel to the NJ Legislature Environmental Committees.

Susan Gruel, P.P., and **Fred Heyer, P.P., A.I.C.P.**, are New Jersey licensed professional planners and partners in the planning consulting firm of Heyer, Gruel & Associates in Red Bank. With a combined fifty plus years of planning experience between them, Mr. Heyer and Ms. Gruel are recognized experts in the field of planning and redevelopment. They represent municipal and regional entities on a broad range of planning issues including redevelopment, strategic planning, multi-jurisdictional coordination, affordable housing, and urban design. They have participated on redevelopment panels and teach continuing education courses in land use planning. They also serve as instructors at the Bloustein Graduate School of Planning and Public Policy at Rutgers University where they teach comprehensive planning and planning studios.

Daniel E. Horgan, Esq., is a member of Waters, McPherson, McNeill, P.C. in Secaucus, New Jersey. For more than thirty-five years, he has handled riparian claims in diverse circumstances, from large tracts in the Hackensack Meadows to lands under

Atlantic City casinos, large riverfront redevelopments, marinas, piers, public parks, and grants for properties insured by title companies. He also reviews riparian issues for corporate acquisition and commercial lending due diligence. This area is but one part of a large and diverse real estate practice that includes, permits, development, taxation, litigation, and more at Waters, McPherson, McNeill, P.C.

William L. Horner, Esq., practices law with his father, William C. Horner, at the Salem, New Jersey, firm of Horner & Horner, L.L.C. For the last eighteen years, Mr. Horner has represented municipal planning and zoning boards as well as private land purchasers, sellers, and developers, including many farmers. He currently serves as solicitor for the Pittsgrove Township Planning Board and the Township of Mannington, and also as associate counsel to the New Jersey Planning Officials organization, and a trustee of the New Jersey Institute of Local Government Attorneys.

Marty M. Judge, Esq., is a shareholder in Flaster/Greenberg PC's Environmental Law Department. He focuses on all facets of environmental litigation, in addition to environmental compliance and counseling work. Mr. Judge has widespread experience in environmental matters concerning CERCLA (Superfund), RCRA and New Jersey Spill Act actions; Natural Resource Damage (NRD) claims; ISRA applicability and compliance matters; underground storage tank issues; and indemnity and contribution actions among jointly responsible parties. His experience also includes water discharge and water allocation/resource law, brownfields and redevelopment, the environmental permitting components of land use, wastewater planning and federal/state wetlands jurisdiction matters, solid waste permitting and compliance, air pollution permitting and compliance, pesticide compliance and enforcement, administrative agency litigation and appellate jurisprudence, environmental insurance coverage claims and toxic tort litigation (including class action defense).

Kim Ball Kaiser, Esq., is senior counsel for the New Jersey Highlands Council in Chester, New Jersey, experienced in environmental and land use law. Prior to joining the Highlands Council staff, Kim was the Highlands Project Director for the Association of New Jersey Environmental Commissions where she worked with municipal officials to promote public interest in long-term natural resource protection. In that role, she was a Work Group member of the USDA Forest Service NY-NJ Highlands Regional Study: 2002 Update.

Lanny S. Kurzweil, Esq., is a partner at McCarter & English, LLP where he helps clients address complex environmental litigation, navigate regulatory matters, and assists them with environmental issues involved in business transactions. He represents oil, chemical, financial services and manufacturing companies, as well as real estate and solar developers, in environmental matters, while continuing to counsel a range of domestic and foreign companies on general commercial and product liability matters. He is serving as a custodial receiver for the Superior Court of New Jersey for a large environmentally impacted site. An experienced trial attorney in federal and state courts, Lanny handles environmental cases involving Superfund and New Jersey Spill Act sites, landfills, groundwater, river systems and sediments, soil contamination and underground storage tanks, and cost recovery actions at sites of various size and environmental significance. He advises clients on the intricacies of the New Jersey Spill Act and on natural resource damages (NRD) issues under federal and state law. He also maintains an active general practice focusing on commercial matters, products liability, toxic torts, contracts and reinsurance issues. Lanny has successfully mediated and arbitrated several cost recovery actions in New Jersey and New York, resulting in very substantial awards in favor of the firm's clients. He also negotiated the transfer of responsibility for many sites. Additionally, he co-moderates the bimonthly round table of the Environmental Business Council (EBC) of the Commerce and Industry Association of New Jersey (CIANJ), which routinely draws about 100 professionals. He is also an active member of the EBC steering committee and a member of the CIANJ Executive Council. He has received the EBC Service Award and the CIANJ Chairman's Outstanding Volunteer Award and Outstanding Leadership Award.

Christine A. LaRocca, Esq., is chief council for the New Jersey Highlands Council. She is an experienced attorney specializing in environmental, land use, and real estate law. Prior to joining the Highlands Council, Christine spent more than a decade working with a large consumer products company. She provided counsel on all aspects of environmental and safety compliance and managed numerous complex site remediation and Superfund projects throughout the United States. In her most recent role with the company, Christine had overall responsibility for administering safety programs across North America and also managed the internal corporate safety, health and environmental compliance audit program. Christine's experience also includes a number of years in private practice, most recently at Riker Danzig Scherer Hyland & Perretti, LLP in Morristown as a member of the Environmental Practice Group. Prior to becoming a lawyer, she spent many years as an environmental professional at Bergen County Utilities Authority.

Alexander D. Lehrer, Esq., is an associate at McManimon, Scotland & Baumann, LLC in Newark, New Jersey. His primary practice areas include environmental and land use law. Prior to joining the firm, Alexander focused his practice on CERCLA litigation, other environmental law issues and representation of both municipal planning and zoning boards and representation of developers before planning and zoning boards. Alexander served as a law clerk in the Superior Court of New Jersey, Union Vicinage.

Doris Lin, Esq., is an animal rights attorney, the director of legal affairs for the Animal Protection League of New Jersey, and a former chair of the New Jersey State Bar Association's Animal Law Committee. She is also the expert on animal rights for About.com.

Keith E. Lynott, Esq., is a partner in the Environment & Energy Practice Group of McCarter & English, LLP. He concentrates his practice in environmental law. In addition to representing clients in connection with environmental litigation, environmental insurance coverage and regulatory matters, he has represented clients in connection with a variety of business, brownfields, and renewable energy transactions involving audits, due diligence, preparation, and negotiation of acquisition and financing agreements, and compliance with federal and state environmental laws and regulations as they relate to transactions, including the New Jersey Industrial Site Recovery Act (ISRA).

David J. Mairo, Esq., is a member of the Environmental Group at Chiesa Shahinian & Giatomasi located in West Orange, New Jersey. Mr. Mairo's practice focuses on Environmental Law and Brownfield Redevelopment. He counsels clients on issues of compliance, applicability, and adequacy of remediation concerning the Site Remediation Reform Act, Spill Compensation and Control Act and Industrial Site Recovery Act, as well as a variety of other state and federal environmental regulatory, enforcement and permitting matters. Mr. Mairo represents both public and private entities in the redevelopment of environmentally impaired properties. He works closely with the NJDEP and provides counsel to clients on issues related to Natural Resource Damages, environmental due diligence and liabilities associated with the purchase and sale of real estate.

Mark L. Manewitz, Esq., is of counsel with Spolsino Smith Buss & Jacobs LLP. Mr. Manewitz has clients in energy, manufacturing real estate, and high tech. Mark is a nationally recognized expert in environmental law. His practice includes the environmental aspects of business transactions and environmental litigation, and the various aspects of the development of contaminated property for commercial and residential use, or Brownfield Development. He has advised clients on the development of alternative energy projects, including geothermal and solar energy projects. He has negotiated recently a ground-breaking Administrative Consent Order for Solar Development of a Superfund Landfill site in New Jersey. He has more than thirty years of experience in energy and environmental law and during that time has represented his clients in a wide variety of matters, including state and federal enforcement actions in New York, New Jersey, and many other jurisdictions. Mark obtains favorable results before administrative agencies and in litigation, and enables clients to reach favorable agreements in complex environmental issues with private parties and State and Federal agencies. Mark helps clients obtain permits and settle claims with State and Federal as well as local governmental Agencies.

Manko, Gold, Katcher & Fox LLP, is an environmental law firm with offices in Pennsylvania and New Jersey that provides significant expertise in air issues. The attorneys practicing in this area, Bart Cassidy, Carol McCabe, Todd Kantorczyk, Kate Vaccaro, Bryan Franey, Diana Silva, and Michael Dillon, provide a complete range of expertise in the areas of air permitting, compliance counseling, auditing, reporting/ risk management planning, enforcement, and regulatory updates. The firm also has a full-time, in-house technical consultant, Michael Nines. Michael is a licensed professional engineer and is degreed as a civil/environmental engineer.

Joseph Maraziti Jr., Esq., is a partner at Maraziti Falcon LLP in Short Hills. Mr. Maraziti represents both public and private sector clients in regulatory, transactional, and litigation matters having local and national significance involving environmental and redevelopment issues. He has many years of experience representing public sector clients throughout New Jersey in redevelopment projects, condemnation, land use, real estate transactions and litigation in federal and state courts. He is well-versed in redevelopment law. With decades of experience in legal issues related to infrastructure and the environment, Mr. Maraziti is an active leader and driving force in the redevelopment arena. He served as Chairman of the New Jersey State Planning Commission, which adopted the State Development and Redevelopment Plan in 2001. In that role, he worked with the Governor's cabinet, counties, local communities and the private sector to ensure that development and redevelopment in New Jersey enhance the quality of life for all citizens. Mr. Maraziti has been frequently recognized as a leader in his field and for his many contributions. He is a member of the Counselors of Real Estate (CRE), a membership organization of high-profile property professionals. New Jersey Future awarded him with the Cary Edwards Leadership Award. In 2017 he was honored by New Jersey Planning Officials with the President's Award. Mr. Maraziti has been continuously identified since 2007 as a New Jersey Super Lawyer in environmental law by *New Jersey Monthly*.

Thomas J. O'Connor, Esq., is an executive partner at Waters McPherson, McNeill, P.C. in Secaucus, New Jersey. His primary area of expertise is land use and real estate development, representing developers and business owners requiring federal, state, and local governmental approvals for a wide range of commercial, industrial and residential projects, often involving very large and complex development applications. He has been actively involved for many years in the expanding areas of urban redevelopment, brownfields, transit villages, and affordable housing. In addition to appearing before planning and zoning boards throughout North Jersey, Mr. O'Connor has been very active in representing clients in matters before the New Jersey Meadowlands Commission. He has served on various advisory committees to the New Jersey Meadowlands Commission for proposed regulatory amendments and special projects.

Thomas M. Olson, Esq., is a partner in the firm of McKirdy & Riskin, P.A. in Morristown, New Jersey. His litigation practice concentrates on valuation litigation, including real property assessment and eminent domain litigation. He has also served as special tax counsel for numerous municipalities including the Town of Hackettstown and the Borough of Morris Plains. He has lectured nationally and internationally on eminent domain and taxation matters and has written articles in these areas which have been published by the New Jersey Law Journal and the American Bar Association.

Susan Peticolas, Esq., is a director in the Real Property and Environmental Department at Gibbons, PC, in Newark, New Jersey. Ms. Peticolas represents clients in Superfund and Spill Act cases, as well as in companion personal injury and property damage matters. She represents a number of companies in the massive Lower Passaic River Study, as well as in the state litigation filed by the State of New Jersey for past costs incurred in connection with the Newark Bay Complex. She counsels clients on general regulatory compliance questions, including issues relating to RCRA, TSCA, OSHA, and the New Jersey Site Remediation Reform Act.

Michael K. Plumb, Esq. is an associate at Chiesa Shahinian & Giantomasi, PC. He represents clients in environmental litigation claims, regulatory and compliance counseling, and enforcement. He also represents clients building and permitting new and existing energy infrastructure. Michael's litigation experience covers all aspects of environmental law, representing a diverse array of clients in litigation related to environmental permitting and enforcement, and responsibility for discharges of hazardous substances, through all stages of litigation, including mediation, arbitration, trial and appeal. He routinely defends property owners and other responsible parties against NJDEP enforcement actions. He also regularly advises clients in environmental due diligence related to the purchase and sale of commercial property. If necessary, he works closely with environmental consultants and LSRPs to efficiently resolve environmental issues that arise during due diligence. Within the energy sector, Michael helps clients navigate through the permitting and siting processes of such infrastructure projects as natural gas transmission pipelines, electricity transmission lines, combined cycle natural gas EGUs, and solar facilities. Michael teaches the "Legal Environment of Business" to graduate students as an adjunct professor at Seton Hall University's Stillman School of Business. He is also a member of the Board of Directors and an officer of the Environmental Law Section of the New Jersey State Bar Association. Additionally, he is an active member of the Justice Stewart G. Pollock Environmental Inn of Court. Prior to attending law school, Michael worked as an environmental engineer specializing in environmental due diligence and regulatory compliance.

David A. Roth, Esq., is a partner in the Environmental Department at Greenbaum Rowe Smith & Davis LLP in Woodbridge, New Jersey. Mr. Roth has a concentration in real estate, environmental, and health and safety law with special emphasis on compliance counseling and environmental aspects of real estate and business transactions. He assists clients in resolving issues arising under solid and hazardous waste laws, the federal Clean Water Act, the New Jersey Industrial Site Recovery Act (ISRA), the Toxic Substances Control Act, right-to-know programs, the Occupational Safety and Health Act and emerging product safety laws.

Alan Rubin, Esq., is a member of the Corporate and Business Transactions Department and the Tax, Trust and Estates Department at Cole Schotz in Hackensack, New Jersey. His professional focus includes mergers and acquisitions, joint venture planning, secured financings, shareholder and partner governance, and acquisition and disposition of distressed debt. His practice is national in scope, and he has extensive experience in implementing tax, business, and estate planning strategies for closely held businesses and venture capital. Alan is a certified public accountant and is admitted to the bars of New Jersey, New York, Pennsylvania, the District of Columbia, and the United States Tax Court.

Martin P. Schrama, Esq., is a partner in the Civil Litigation Department at Stark & Stark, P.C., in Lawrenceville, New Jersey. Mr. Schrama has a concentration in mass tort/class action, intellectual property and general commercial litigation, with special emphasis on mass tort environmental contamination and products liability actions. He has extensive experience litigating on both the trial and the appellate levels of the federal and state courts of New Jersey and New York, as well as numerous other jurisdictions and alternate dispute resolution forums throughout the nation.

Katherine E. Suell, Esq., is an associate with McCusker Anselmi Rosen Carvelli in Florham Park, New Jersey. Ms. Riopel concentrates her practice on general business/ commercial litigation as well as environmental regulatory, litigation, and transactional matters. Ms. Riopel has extensive experience representing clients in all manner of complex commercial matters and has experience representing clients in administrative and judicial proceedings before state and federal courts, as well as agencies such as the New Jersey Department of Environmental Protection. She has counseled clients across a wide range of industries including pharmaceutical, real estate, cosmetics, asphalt and cement production, commercial chemical manufacturing, glass manufacturing, and petroleum distribution. Ms. Riopel also negotiates stipulations, consent orders and decrees, and prepares all types of environmental agreements, including purchase/sale, cost allocation, environmental investigation, indemnification, and access agreements for the purpose of environmental investigations. She also has substantial experience representing clients' interests as members of potentially responsible party (PRP) groups at complex remediation sites. Kate guides clients through site remediation and redevelopment projects throughout the country.

H. Matthew Taylor, Esq., is senior counsel in the Philadelphia office of Gordon & Rees, concentrating his practice on complex commercial and civil litigation with a focus on employment law and products liability matters. Mr. Taylor counsels clients in cases pending across the country, and regularly handles all aspects of litigation in both Pennsylvania and New Jersey. Mr. Taylor represents employers in state and federal court, as well as before administrative agencies, in a broad spectrum of employment-related matters including claims involving Title VII of the Civil Rights Act of 1964, the Americans with Disabilities Act, the Age Discrimination in Employment Act, the Family and Medical Leave Act, the Fair Labor Standards Act, the Pennsylvania Human Relations Act, the New Jersey Law Against Discrimination, as well as many other federal and state employment discrimination laws. He also counsels clients on a broad range of employment and labor law matters helping them to comply with federal, state and local laws. Additionally, Mr. Taylor has prosecuted and defended numerous trade secret and restrictive covenant actions in state and federal court. These cases concern covenants not to compete, non-solicitation agreements, unfair competition, and other related torts.

David B. Thompson is CEO of Phoenix Advisors, LLC, a New Jersey–based independent financial advisory firm that works with governmental entities of all sizes and types concerning the issuance of debt and other fiscal matters. He is a veteran of nearly forty years in the municipal bond and public finance fields. Dave is knowledgeable in all aspects of municipal securities, including their authorization and issuance, underwriting, sales and trading practices, and regulatory and compliance requirements.

Eric E. Tomaszewski, Esq., is a partner McManimon Scotland & Baumann in Newark, New Jersey. He concentrates in all aspects of environmental law including transactional matters, redevelopment projects, site remediations, regulatory compliance counseling, permitting, solid waste and recyclables, wastewater, cost recovery litigation, and insurance coverage litigation. His clients include manufacturers, gasoline retailers, real estate developers, municipalities and public entities. Eric has practiced environmental law in New Jersey since 2005 and has worked on many notable projects involving the redevelopment of contaminated property, including several warehouse and trucking facility projects in the City of Newark. He has also been involved in the defense and trial of several high-profile environmental cases including litigation related to the Passaic River Restoration Initiative undertaken by the U.S. EPA, and the trial of a former energy company against $160 million environmental and construction claims related to the development of waterfront property in Miami. Eric has extensive experience in remediations related to underground storage tanks, whether in the commercial, industrial, or residential context, including the regulatory framework for conducting those remediations and obtaining insurance coverage to pay the costs related to them.

Emily D. Vail, Esq., is an associate with Ackerly Brown located in Bantam, Connecticut. Her practice focuses on environmental law, regulatory compliance, and transactional work. Her experience includes representing private, municipal, and corporate clients in regulatory enforcement proceedings, claims under state and environmental statutes, commercial disputes, and state statutory and common law. Ms. Vail is particularly experienced in regulatory compliance, permitting, and administrative law, as well as counseling clients on energy issues and environmental quality review issues. Her transactional experience includes drafting and negotiating service contracts and access agreements, as well as conducting due diligence for real estate closings

George T. Vallone is the cofounder and president of the Hoboken Brownstone Company in Hoboken, New Jersey. For more than thirty-three years, George has been developing real estate along New Jersey's Hudson River "Gold Coast." His firm focuses on the redevelopment of large-scale mixed use urban brownfields, including the successful redevelopment of 1.8 MSF of mixed-uses at the Maxwell House Coffee property on the Hoboken waterfront. George is actively involved in numerous trade groups, community, and educational development activities.

John (Jack) Van Dalen, Esq., is a partner at Van Dalen Brower LLC in Trenton, New Jersey. His practice focuses on land use permitting, penalty defense, tidelands ownership matters, eminent domain and takings cases, general administrative law matters, appellate cases, real estate title disputes, and state government contracting. He previously served as chief counsel to the New Jersey Meadowlands Commission from 2001 to 2002, and as a senior deputy attorney general with the New Jersey Attorney General's Office from 1972 to 1999.

Joanne Vos, Esq., is a partner at Maraziti Falcon LLP in Short Hills, New Jersey. She focuses her practice in environmental law, including compliance, regulatory, and transactional matters as well as environmental litigation. She routinely counsels clients regarding environmental liability in connection with Real Estate Purchase and Sale Agreements, Lease Agreements, Asset Purchase Agreements and Access Agreements. She also counsels clients on various contamination and remediation issues including Federal and State due diligence requirements as well as ISRA compliance. She has successfully litigated numerous complex environmental matters involving both private and public entities. She previously served the Township of North Brunswick as Special Environmental Counsel.

Allan C. Zhang, Esq., is an associate at McKirdy and Riskin, P.A. focused on eminent domain and property tax appeal matters. Prior to joining the firm, he served as law clerk to the Honorable Charles W. Dortch Jr., Presiding Judge of the Superior Court, Family Part, in Camden, New Jersey. Mr. Zhang received his B.S. and M.S.W. from New York University. He received his J.D. from Rutgers Law School in 2017. In law school, he served as a staff editor on the *Rutgers Journal of Law and Religion* and as student director of the Planning Estates *Pro Bono* Project for two years. As a certified legal intern, he represented clients in the Civil Practice Clinic and served as student director of the Domestic Violence Project. In 2016, Mr. Zhang was awarded the prestigious Mary Philbrook Public Interest Award for public service. In 2017, Mr. Zhang received the Dean's *Pro Bono Publico* Award for Exceptional Service to the Community, Family Law Certificate, and Dean's Award for Service to Rutgers Law School.

Yin Zhou, Esq., is chair of the Environmental Law Department at Parker McCay in Mount Laurel, New Jersey. She concentrates her practice in environmental law, and utilizes her engineering background and extensive knowledge of environmental laws and regulations to navigate technical and regulatory complexities on behalf of her clients. She counsels clients through complex compliance and liability issues, including site remediation, the Industrial Site Recovery Act, solid and hazardous waste, and surface water and stormwater permitting. She also helps clients secure environmental permits and approvals for development, such as CAFRA and other land use authorizations. Yin has successfully counseled clients on due diligence and transfer of environmental risks in multimillion dollar corporate and real estate transactions, and advises on environmental insurance recovery. She also delivers solutions to clients in complex matters related to contaminants of emerging concern, such as the PFAS family of chemicals. Yin started her legal career as a Deputy Attorney General in the NJ Office of the Attorney General representing the Department of Environmental Protection (DEP). As a Deputy Attorney General, she was DEP's lead counsel on solar matters, advising the State on solar projects located on brownfields, landfills, and historic fill. Her practice includes counseling clients on renewable energy projects. Yin's passion for environmental work began as an environmental engineering student, with projects that ranged from sustainable energy to vertical farming.